TEA, WAR & CROCODILES

Tales from an extraordinary life

Ferdinand J Brockhall

Tea, War and Crocodiles
Tales from an extraordinary life

First published in Australia by Ferdinand J Brockhall 2022
www.ferdinandbrockhall.com

Copyright © Ferdinand J Brockhall 2022
All Rights Reserved

A catalogue record for this
book is available from the
National Library of Australia

ISBN: 978-0-6453812-2-1 (pbk)
ISBN: 978-0-6453812-0-7 (hbk)
ISBN: 978-0-6453812-1-4 (ebk)

Typesetting and design by Publicious Book Publishing
Published in collaboration with Publicious Book Publishing
www.publicious.com.au

No part of this book may be reproduced in any form, by photocopying or by any electronic or mechanical means, including information storage or retrieval systems, without permission in writing from both the copyright owner and the publisher of this book.

Disclaimer: This work is based on the memory of events that happened nearly a century ago. While great care has been taken to recall and confirm the names of places and people, and the timelines of events, it likely that there are incongruities. The names of some people have been changed for their privacy.

CONTENTS

FOREWORD i

INTRODUCTION v

PART 1: DAYS OF INNOCENCE

    Chapter 1: A Childhood Camelot 1

    Chapter 2: Terra Australis Incognito 29

PART 2: CHILDHOOD LOST

    Chapter 3: Second World War 77

    Chapter 4: The Interregnum 85

    Chapter 5: The Japanese Occupation
    Administration and its Reign 99

    Chapter 6: The Concentration Camp Years 107

    Chapter 7: The End of the War 151

    Chapter 8: A Time of Repair 167

    Chapter 9: Return to Java 185

PART 3: HOLLAND

    Chapter 10: Going Dutch 199

    Chapter 11: Shaping a Future 205

    Chapter 12: A Change in Direction 213

PART 4: AUSTRALIA

    Chapter 13: The New Australians 219

    Chapter 14: Life in Naracoorte 259

    Chapter 15: Life in Millicent 273

    Chapter 16: Millicent to New Guinea 289

PART 5: NEW GUINEA – TIMES OF GREAT ADVENTURES
    Chapter 17: A World Away 297
    Chapter 18: Bainyik 331
    Chapter 19: Port Moresby 373
    Chapter 20: Daru 383
    Chapter 21: First Patrol 405
    Chapter 22: Adventures up the Fly River 443
    Chapter 23: A Time for Consolidation 471
    Chapter 24: The Times They are a Changing 505

PART 6: IN RETROSPECT
    Chapter 25: Starting Over 517
    Chapter 26: Finis 527

AUTHOR'S NOTE AND ACKNOWLEDGEMENTS 529
ENDNOTES 531
BIBLIOGRAPHY 535

FOREWORD

by Rachael Giblett (granddaughter)

I cherish my grandfather. He is an extraordinary person with a story to match; a tale so full of adventure it would seem more plausible were it spread across five lifetimes rather than one. Traces of his life are imprinted in his broad, lined, farmer's hands and in the creases around his eyes. His dapper country-gentleman style hints at a bygone era when formality was the norm and, on entering his home, the easy mixture of European and Asian décor speak of his multicultural identity. As a child, I was very fond of my grandpa and loved this kindly, laughing old farmer in his gumboots and scratchy woollen jumper. As an adult, that affection has deepened with a growing respect for what he has experienced over the course of his life. Even now, I marvel at his soft heart.

Covering three continents and almost a century, this memoir takes the reader on an epic journey across vastly different settings: from the jade-green tea fields of central northern Java, to the soul-less dust bowl of Tjimahi prison camp; through the bone-cold winter of the Netherlands – with equally cold disposition toward its repatriated countrymen – to the far flung land of hope and hardship in Australia; from the mysterious jungles of Papua and New Guinea, panting with life – and danger – to the carefully demarcated boundaries of a Gippsland cattle farm, as meticulously tended as the tea plantations of Java.

This is a strange riches-to-rags-to-riches tale. A story of finding one's place in the world after profound loss and displacement. Of starting from scratch again… and again. Of the identity and healing that come from working the earth. Many wonderful and improbable turns of events punctuate this true story of a young boy journeying into manhood, and later fatherhood.

We are privy to the 'virtual Camelot' of colonial Dutch-Indonesian life, and the jarring shift to brutal wartime rule. We witness the twin miracles of survival and reunification of an entire family against the chaotic backdrop of Japan's surrender to Allied forces. We journey with the family through the therapy of refugee life under the warm embrace of Thailand, before being cast back into an Indonesia lit by the candent coals of burgeoning national independence. Along with the family, we embark on a journey into the social wilderness of the Netherlands – the motherland that struggled to welcome home her estranged colonial children. We experience the unique vulnerability of newlywed migrants landing in post-war Australia, and the mixture of desperation and opportunity that leads a young family into the wild frontier of what was then the Australian Territory of Papua and New Guinea. Finally, we pack our bags with Ferdinand and his beloved Wilhelmina to return to a more tolerant, though far from perfect Australia.

As significant as the journey is how it is told. Born with a thirst for understanding, my grandfather began his education with a slate board and pencil in a classroom of two. Although his schooling was interrupted by war, he later studied tropical agriculture, social anthropology, Melanesian history, and education. Much later, at age eighty-one, he completed a doctorate in trans-migration. His reflections reveal a profound insight into the human condition, underscored by references to philosophers, poets and novelists. Even as a boy, my grandfather was deeply moved by the likes of Rudyard Kipling and John Donne, finding in their words the strength he needed to survive the dark years as a prisoner of war. As difficult as it must have been to relive these experiences through the pages of this book, I am deeply grateful that Grandpa has made his story known.

On behalf of my family, it is our pleasure to share with you this at times light-hearted, at others sobering account of recent history. Grandpa's memoirs were written as a legacy to his family, particularly his grandchildren, that we might know the path before us more clearly for having understood the one behind. It is my hope that this is true for every reader. I give you my grandfather, Ferdinand J Brockhall.

Terry as he is known today by his grandchildren:
a warmly affectionate country gentleman, full of quiet wisdom.

INTRODUCTION

by Graham Truscott (son-in-law)

Regional history[i]

Indonesia is the largest and most densely populated country in Southeast Asia, scattered across the seas between the Indian and Pacific oceans in an area reaching 5470 kilometres from east to west and some 1600 kilometres north to south. Eighty-five per cent of the landmass is within its six largest islands – Kalimantan (Indonesian Borneo), Sumatra, Irian Jaya (also known as Papua Barat or West Papua), Sulawesi (Celebes), Java and Madura.

From earliest times the islands maintained a unique identity. Small, agriculturally wealthy and self-sufficient communities were scattered around the shores of the major islands. There was little inter-island warfare, as no group was large enough to dominate its neighbours. Of these major islands, Java developed some of the highest levels of cultural sophistication.

A very active spice trade began with Africa and Arabia in the first century AD, with overland trade-routes developing through to Europe via the gateway of Constantinople (now Istanbul). During the fifth century China joined the trade. Rich trading saw Indonesia exporting camphor, resins and food preserving spices. Through this trade, various parts of the islands embraced Hinduism in the fifth and sixth centuries, Buddhism in the seventh century; and Islam (now practiced by 90 per cent of the archipelago's population) in the thirteenth century, fostering the establishment of warring kingdoms.

The overland trade was forever changed in 1511, when one of Portugal's greatest adventurers, Alfonso de Albuquerque, rounded the Horn of Africa and ventured across the Indian Ocean and into the Straits of Malacca. There he established the great Portuguese fort that served as the keystone to Portuguese holdings. During the entire sixteenth century, this small, Catholic, seafaring nation transported untold wealth from the region, rendering the Muslim control of Constantinople irrelevant. Profit was now made not from the tedious overland camel routes through the Levant but from seaborne traffic.

With the arrival of the Dutch East India Company (Vereenigde Oosindische Compagnie or 'Jan Company', established in 1602), regional Indonesian warfare was quashed and a strong colonial rule established, specifically for the advancement of Dutch business interests. Capturing the Portuguese fort at Malacca in 1641, the Dutch wrested control of the Straits leading to spice-rich Java and the Dutch headquarters in Batavia (now Jakarta). While the Dutch maintained major colonial control, at no time did they control all of what is now modern Indonesia. The British, French and Portuguese all maintained their own spheres of influence in the islands – Britain through its own East India Company (known as 'John Company').

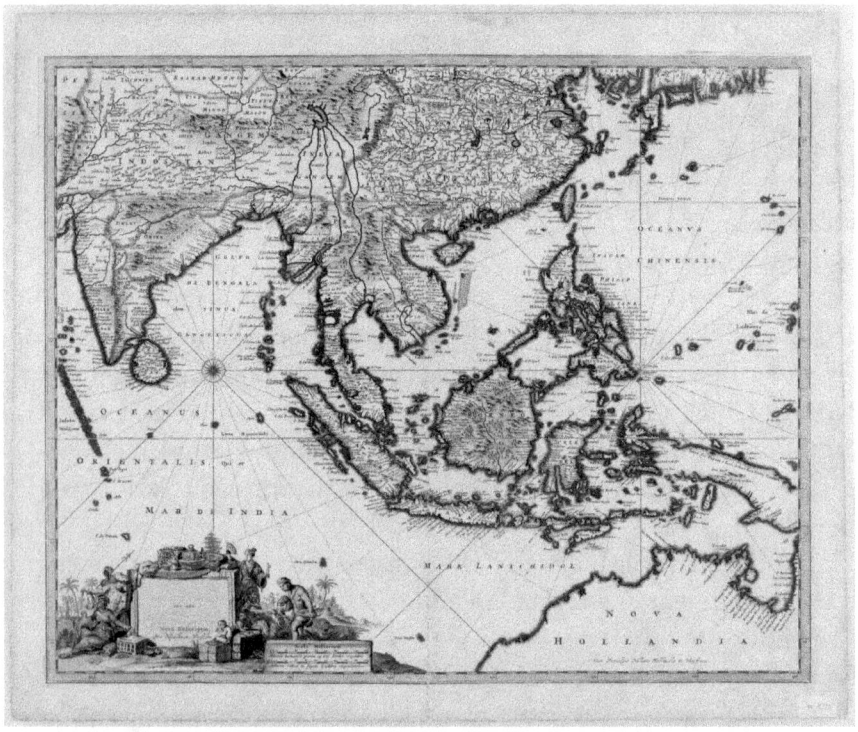

Seventeenth century map of Indiae Orientalis (the Dutch East Indies) by Nicolaes Visscher II (Image is from the collections of the State Library of New South Wales, file number FL3680663).

Introduction

Indonesian nationalism began to emerge between 1908 and 1912, and by 1927 a young Dr Soekarno had formed the Partai Nasional Indonesia (PNI). Although the Dutch and British attempted to resist the independence movement, its progress was unstoppable. Japanese imperialist advancement under the guise of 'The Greater East Asia Co-Prosperity Sphere' was propagated to the Asian populations occupied by the Empire of Japan from 1931 to 1945. The Japanese occupation of Indonesia from 1942 to 1945 further fuelled Indonesian nationalism and the drive for independence. After 350 years of Dutch colonial rule, Indonesia declared its independence in 1945, followed by a local revolution from 1945 to 1947, with the Dutch finally ceding power to Soekarno in 1949.

During this 1900-year trading history, Indonesia has been known variously throughout Europe as the 'East Indies', the 'Spice Islands' and 'the Dutch East Indies', providing the spice bin of Europe and the Levant. However, much of the well-known part of Indonesian history took place on Java. It was the centre of powerful Hindu-Buddhist empires, the Islamic sultanates, and the core of the colonial Dutch East Indies. Java was also the centre of the Indonesian struggle for independence.

Family background[ii]

In the earliest days of Dutch colonialism, Holland sent considerable numbers of young, single men to the dependency to occupy administrative, military and other posts. These men were proscribed within ten years to return to Holland, or to get married. With very few Holland-born women in Java, not surprisingly, many of the Dutch expatriates established relationships with Indonesian women. While frowned on at the time, such relationships and marriages produced local communities of mixed ancestry families.

It was into the emerging but as yet unknown twilight years of the Dutch East Indies that Jacobus Johannes Antonius (JJA) Broekhals (paternal grandfather of Ferdinand J Broekhals Jnr) arrived in Batavia in the late 1800s. Already a prominent merchant banker in Holland, he established the colony's first branch of the Nederlandsche Handelsbank (Netherlands Merchant Bank). After his arrival, JJA Broekhals married into the Angenent family. His wife's father (Ferdinand Jnr's great-grandfather Angenent) had arrived in Batavia from Holland in the mid 1800s by sailing ship. Recruited overseas as a private in the Koninklijke Nederlandsch

Indische Leger ('KNIL' or Royal Dutch East Indian Army) he fought in the North Sumatran Aceh wars where, on grounds of conspicuous bravery, he received a field promotion to Lieutenant, eventually retiring with the rank of Major.

Although the Angenent family never spoke of this, Ferdinand Jnr is quite convinced that his 'Oud Opa' (great-grandfather) Angenent married a Timorese woman. Thereafter, to deflect community criticism, the family always referred to her as being of Spanish extraction.

As a young man, Ferdinand Jnr's father, also named Ferdinand Jacobus Broekhals, was encouraged to enter the Batavian banking industry and was even sent to Holland to study banking practices. However, banking was never to his liking. On his return to Batavia, after various plantation jobs, he took up the position of manager of the Djolotigo Plantation, in the hinterland of the town of Pekalongan in Central Java, growing tea, rubber and cinchona[iii].

Ferdinand Jnr's maternal grandfather, Anton de Bruyn, was born in Holland and also came out to the Java colony in the late 1800s. He later became Managing Director of a large plantation and refinery in the then very prestigious sugar industry. Like so many in the colonial sugar trade of the times, he was fabulously rich, socially prominent and highly respected. His wife, Matilda (Ferdinand Jnr's maternal grandmother), was from Pemalang – the daughter of a rich, highly respected Indonesian Dutch family also engaged in the sugar plantation industry. Their third of eight children, Anna Theodora (Theo), became a primary school teacher and in 1927 married Ferdinand Jnr's father and moved to the Djolotigo Plantation.

Tea, War & Crocodiles contains the memoirs of Ferdinand Jacobus Broekhals Jnr (Broekhals was later Anglicised to 'Brockhall' and Ferdinand was changed to 'Terry'). His story begins at the Djolotigo Plantation.

PART 1:

Days of Innocence

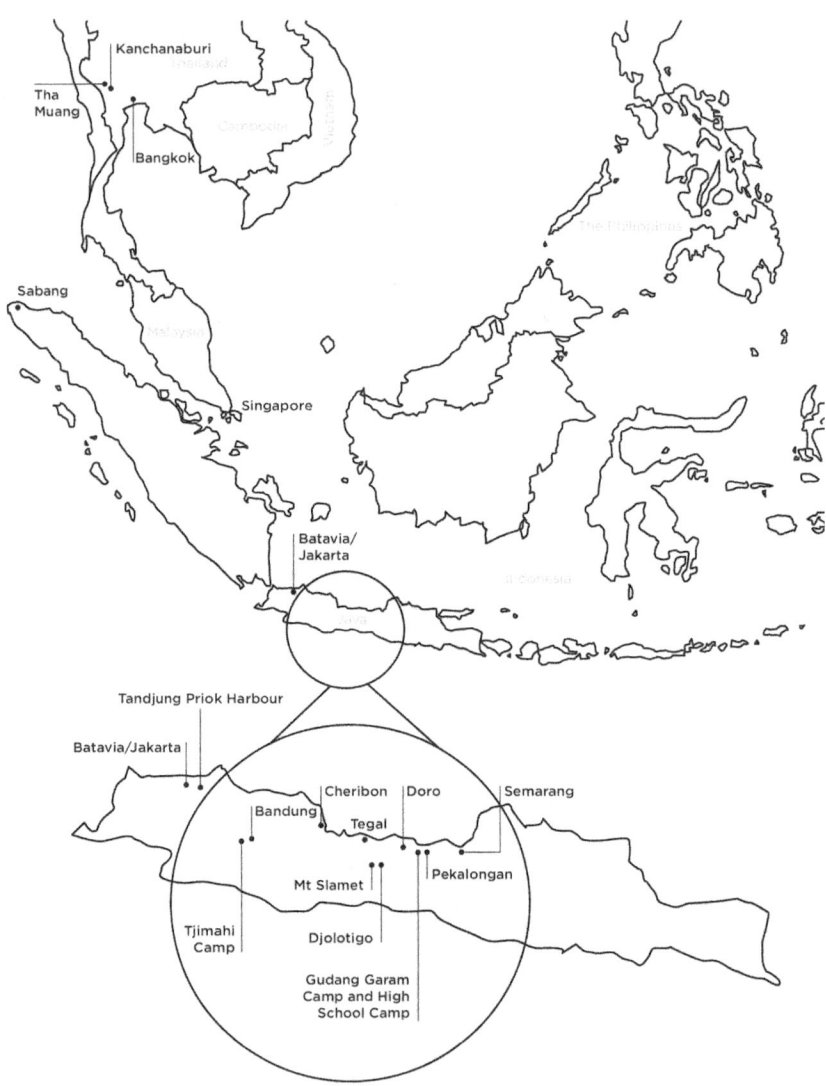

CHAPTER 1

A Childhood Camelot

Happiness is no laughing matter
Richard Whately, *Apophthegms* (1854)

I was born in paradise – the Dutch East Indies of 1928. My parents were 'tea planters', the designation given to those engaged in the manufacture of that universally sought-after beverage. On our isolated plantation in the high country of the dormant Mount Slamet volcano, the early years of my life were exceptionally happy, even idyllic.

At the time, the only suitable medical establishment for the expatriate Dutch community of our small provincial town in central Java was the Amalgamated Sugar Refinery Companies' Hospital, where my mother gave birth to me and my younger sister, Conny.

Unselfconsciously privileged, in the early twentieth century my family and others in our Dutch East Indies community were perhaps the last to recognise the coming end of the Dutch Empire. With the arrogance that marks colonialism, any suggestion of the Empire's demise would have been swiftly decried as arrant nonsense – if not treasonable lunacy. In the Dutch East Indies of the early to mid-twentieth century, the colony dwelt in a dream-like Camelot, taking for granted the glorious, seemingly unending fields of jade-green tea plants adorning the mountaintops of central-northern Java.

Ferdinand with his sister Conny
at Djolotigo Plantation, 1932.

Ferdinand with his mother (Anna Theodora)
and Conny at Djolotigo, 1938.

Ferdinand's father, Ferdinand Jacobus Broekhals Snr,
in the tea fields of Djolotigo, 1937.

The jungle surrounds

Among memories of life on the Djolotigo plantation, I recall the majesty of the tropical rainforest that surrounded us, supporting urgent life in a myriad of forms, from largest to smaller, yet smaller, and to tiny life shapes which managed to exist in mysterious, unknown ways. Huge trees standing singly where nature had permitted them to out-compete rivals provided nutrient and shade for dense undergrowth, saplings, lianas, mosses, fungi and uncounted bushland flora and fauna. Inside the forest, sound is muffled, and the air is not-unpleasantly dank with decaying matter. At the time, I was too young to comprehend that the circle of life begets new life, which breaks down and in turn creates new living that arises from death itself; for even the tiniest organism and the largest living being fulfil the 'Law of the Jungle'.

Of the larger forms of animal life, the jungle which bounded the plantation fields held many species, including panthers. Exactly how many of these denizens of the forest lived there, not even the Javanese knew. Shy as these nocturnal creatures are, from time to time we would find evidence of their presence when we happened upon where they had feasted on a kill, often a deer or a feral pig. One night, a bold or perhaps desperately hungry panther came to our house, raising a terrified howl from our six dogs when, enacting the Law of the Jungle, it snatched one of our pets to disappear with it into the forest. Looking for our dog the next day, my father found its remains – no more than a scatter of bones.

Other forest dwellers were small colonies of rusa deer that roamed the bush and the bushland meadows. These nervous creatures seemed to constantly anticipate falling prey to man or beast. Sometimes when we were on a walk, our dogs would pick up scent and give baying chase to the deer, which would dart away in a flash of long, beautifully executed leaps. The dogs never once succeeded in bringing down the prey, and giving up the pursuit, in a while they would return, panting, slobbering and spent:

> Lolling, Lapping, Limpid Tongues,
> Ugggh, Ugggh, Ugggh…
> Slobbering, Spitting, Slurping Air,
> Filling Bursting Lungs,
> Their Prey Escaped in Gracious,
> Practiced, Fluid Bounds; and the
> Contest was over 'Tween Rampant
> Deer and Routed Hounds.
>
> FJB

The forest was also home to quite large numbers of feral pigs. These cunning beasts were much loathed by the people in nearby *kampongs* for the damage that they would inflict on their garden crops, no matter how well fenced. In an effort to help the villagers as much as it was an excuse for my father to mount a hunt, he used volunteers from the kampongs to drive the pigs out of their hiding to a clearing in the bush where he stood ready to shoot. So numerous was their unwelcome presence in the forest that a hunt sometimes resulted in bagging half a dozen swine at a time. As their meat was unacceptable to us – due to the risk of it being infected with internal parasites dangerous to humans – my father never took any of the kill home. Equally unacceptable to the Javanese for the parasite and for religious reasons, the slain pests remained where they had fallen. In time, the brood they had produced would eventually return from the forest to again raid gardens.

Bands of agile, coal-black, long-armed and long-tailed lutung monkeys frequently came so close to our house that these splendid wild animals were almost like pets until, as if by command, the entire troop suddenly swung off and we could trace their path back into the deep forest by their fading cries. Beside the lutung that came to visit were their cousin gibbon monkeys, in Java called *Wau Wau* after their far-reaching, whooping cries. We would know when these long-armed, soot-black, tailless tree dwellers had arrived in a nearby clump of the forest by the noise they made. Unlike their gregarious cousins the Rhesus Macaque monkeys, almost a feral pest that lives and sometimes terrorises human communities throughout Asia, the gibbons would never be too closely approached. When we came to look at them they would not flee, but remained purposely aloof in their treetop position. In their own time, prompted by their own reason and purpose, the gibbon troop would retreat back into the forest, swinging from branch to branch to the next tree, one confident handhold after another in long-armed flight. In gracious, faultlessly sure motion, the visitors would melt back into the green-blackness of their home territory, their whooping calls growing more and more faint.

My memory of the magnificence of the surroundings of our home on the high slopes of Gunung Slamet (Mount Slamet) volcano brings to mind its bird life, particularly that of the *rangkok* (hornbill) that lived in the jungle. In these black-feathered birds the size of a small turkey, the distinguishing features were its large, hooked, yellow beak and the vividly coloured red, and sometimes blue, skin around the eyes. Taking wing from out of the forest where they nested, we would become aware of them by the peculiar 'sawing' sound that they emanate in flight; somewhat like loud, rhythmic snoring and audible long before they became visible. At the time not a rare sight, it is sad to know that indiscriminate habitat destruction and illegal hunting have brought these superb birds ever closer to extinction – surely a loss for those who treasure the grandeur of unspoilt Nature.

Another truly splendid rainforest bird was a family of eagles, *geleek* to the Indonesians after their hunting cry high up in the sky: '*Ge-leeeek, ge-leeeek*'. The eagles often circled overhead our house, sailing from current to current, soaring on magnificent wingspan of 2 metres until they were no more than a speck in the firmament. The majesty of these mountain eagles and how they were at one with everyday life on the plantation is imprinted in my mind. It was in this world surrounded by Nature in all its magnificence that our family lived, worked and played in a jade-green Camelot.

A world surrounded by Nature. Ferdinand and his father swimming in the river at Djolotigo, 1938.

The plantation

My earliest childhood coincided with the Great Depression that in much of the Western world became so disastrous. I do not remember if the economic calamity of the 1920s and early 1930s touched us on the plantation. There, we lived an existence that was unapologetically privileged, wonderful and fulfilling. Dutch colonial pride and chauvinism reigned. Our home in Central Java was nestled in a fold of the Gunung Slamet foothills, at an elevation of some 3000 metres above sea level. The house stood on a huge terrace, cut more than 50 metres deep into the sheer mountainside by labourers who used only picks and shovels. An equally grand second terrace lay some 10 metres downhill, with the two plains connected by a splendid 3-metre-wide cement stairway. Sixteen steps led down from the house block, with another stairway of nine steps from the second terrace to the plantation service road that ran past the home grounds. This second plain sported a tennis court and croquet lawn, both infrequently used. In hindsight, 'Who's for tennis?', was a signature line for colonial opulence, part of the self-indulgent contemporaneous tea planter's lifestyle.

When people remark upon a tea plantation, they almost invariably describe the plants as emerald in colour. However, I remember the expanse of tea plants around my home as a less assertive imperial Chinese jade-green. The perfume they emanated, a spicy scent, held the promise of the aromatic beverage it would soon produce.

A Childhood Camelot

Djolotigo's terraced tea gardens clothed the steep sides of the dormant Mount Slamet volcano.

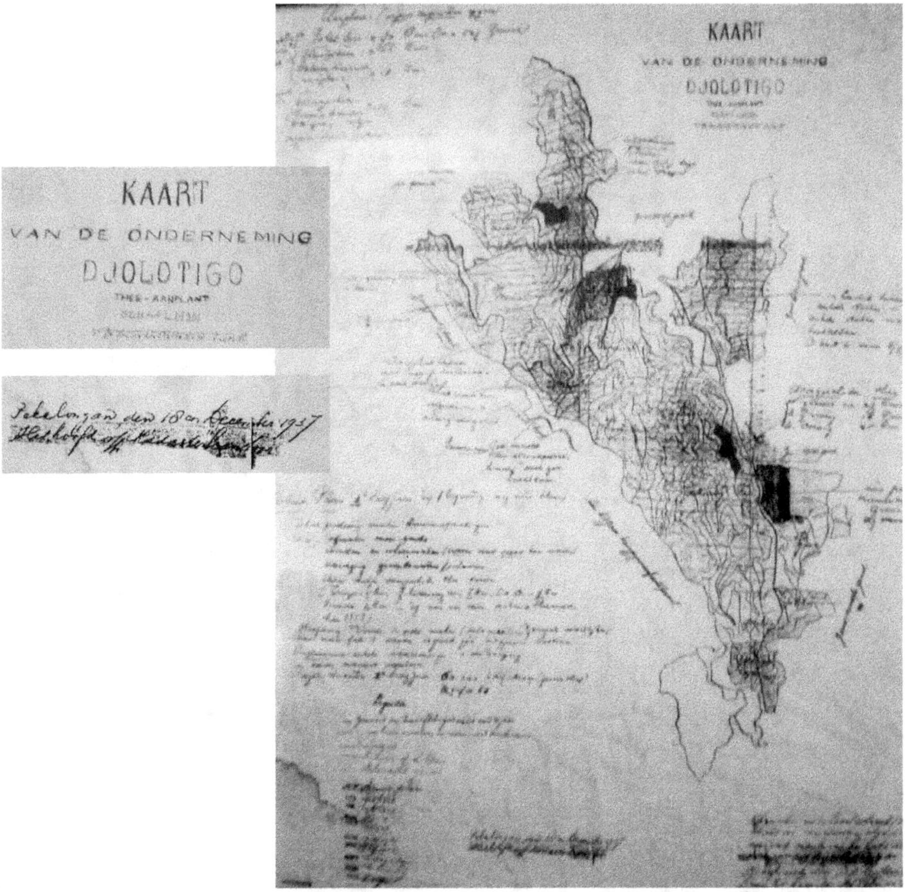

The original Dutch map of the Djolotigo Plantation, Central Java, 1937.

The rolling expanse of tea gardens that painted green clothing on the hillsides was but an extension of the lawns around the house, and the remnants of tropical rainforest at the edge of the plantation was but part of our backyard. On the front lawn, my parents had erected a large pergola, its umbrella-shaped frame covered in a luxuriously flowering purple vine. A sturdy teakwood table with chairs and benches provided comfortable seating, and there, weather permitting, we would take afternoon tea. We would gaze out over the tea bushes covering the terraced plantation fields that clung to the contours of the terrain.

The family taking tea under the pergola at Djolotigo, 1933.

Viewed from our highland vantage point, the northern coastal lowlands that lay between mountain and sea unfolded in a spectacular panorama. Some 300 kilometres of Java's shoreline stretched across our view, from near the seaside city of Cheribon in the west, to that of Semarang in the east. We often sat under the pergola in the fading light of evening, watching as the enveloping dark reached ever higher up the mountains towards our home until, with a last fiery shaft of light, the sun disappeared into the sea. With darkness came the need to escape mosquitoes, and we would beat a hasty retreat to the homestead.

My father's passion was growing the species of tea that originated in Assam, India. In his spare time he also loved to experiment with growing indigenous and imported species of flowers and vegetables. In my mind's eye I behold how the profusely blooming flowers, on shrub and vine, created a rainbow of colours around the house, startling between the green of the tea bushes.

The plantation was not merely our very own playground, but our world. Ferdinand and Conny in front of their cubby house, 1938.

Every morning my mother would wander out into the garden to gather all sorts of flowers that she then arranged in vases placed throughout the house. She never overlooked my father's desk, on which stood a photograph of his youngest brother, who had lost his life in America. In later years, when the Second World War had broken out and my father had become a prisoner of war, my mother replaced the photograph of her brother-in-law with one of her husband, and each day she would cut him fresh roses, his favourite flower, and place them in a vase beside his portrait.

When I look back upon my early years on the plantation, though I had no one else but my sister for company, I never felt lonely. Dependent on each other, my sister and I would act out fantasies such as building castles from sticks that we found lying under the shade trees in the tea field. With these building materials we manufactured a frame that we covered with grasses and weeds pulled out of the surrounding grounds. Mother would sometimes let us take some rags that became our carpet, on which we would sit to partake of biscuits, bread, favourite cordial or fizzy soft drink.

For my sister and me, the plantation was a private kingdom where we reigned and roamed at will. On some days we played at cowboys and Indians when, and nowadays somewhat to my shame, I managed to always be the winner, with my sister never protesting that she always lost. Other times we made a small fire over which we roasted corncobs in the hull. We even experimented smoking my father's pipe filled with the dried hair of a corn cob. At our tender age a clandestine activity, but because of the burning mess's pungent smell and evil taste it luckily involved just a few symbolic puffs. These and other children's games made the plantation not merely our very own playground, but our world.

Language and 'manners'
The complex interactions within Javanese society during my youth were influenced by the meeting of Javanese and Dutch cultures. While I did not witness overt conflict between the two, it was clear that social mores and public interactions were regulated by the authority of class. Language is often a site of conflicting convention, and colonial Java was no different – language choices reinforced rank, status and social categories. On the plantation, from the most menial labourer to the *Hoofd Mandur* (Chief Overseer), the only term of address used for my father was *Kandjeng*, which in the Javanese language is an expression of great respect and fealty. Our people addressed my mother as *Njonja Besar*, Grand Lady, a title which she utterly unselfconsciously wore and enacted all of her life. My sister and I the Indonesians called respectively *Nonni* and *Sinjo*, Indonesian derivatives from the Portuguese *Señora* and *Señor*, meaning 'Miss' and 'Mister'.

The reflection of cultural codes in language did not only apply to the colonial situation in Java. The works of Rudyard Kipling[iv] and other writers of the period include examples of the idea of Western racial superiority. This concept, taken for granted at the time, was underpinned by, for example, Herbert Spencer[v] and Friedrich Nietzsche's[vi] socially adjusted interpretations of Charles Darwin's theories of biological evolution. This lent authority to the concept of racial superiority and gave weight to the colonial powers' claim of pre-eminence over the subject races that they ruled.

A point of order in our household, strict attention was paid to 'manners' – respect for the beliefs, customs and traditions of others. An enlightened man for the era that became the closing decades of the Dutch empire, Father explained that manners, custom and tradition are interconnected concepts in human interaction. Thus, long before the Second World War when a bow became a detested 'must' for Japanese Prisoners of War and civilian internees, when shopping in our coastal town, Father reciprocated the greeting bow of the Japanese shopkeeper Arai-san with a counter incline of his body. 'This,' he explained, 'is custom and courtesy in Japan. It is polite that we reciprocate.' I believe that in teaching us 'manners', Father gave recognition to the notion that all people have traditions and ways by which they identify themselves, and the way that they are is satisfactory, self-respecting and sacred to them.

Transport

Until my parents were married, my bachelor father's only access from the plantation to the small village at the base of the mountain was on foot, on horseback, or (and it was much preferred) on his treasured Harley Davidson motorcycle. I believe that this magnificent machine played a part in my parents' days of courtship – what better chance for my father to show off his driving skills when his Harley took the young romantics up over rain-slicked clay mountain paths? And what better chance had my mother to find excuse to cling tightly to her daring suitor for protection? I cannot of course vouch for this guesswork, but a touch of conjecture may not be misplaced.

After I was born, my parents became proud owners of a second-hand Essex motor car. However, as the road from our town terminated at the foot of the mountain, the vehicle was garaged with the cheerful Chinese storeowner in the small lowland hamlet of Doro. My parents could still only descend from the plantation on the Harley, on horseback, or on foot, so the motorcycle continued to play an important role in transporting them around the plantation and when commuting to the shopping town.

On the plantation time hesitantly marched on, and modernity was slow to bring about change. In the early to mid-1930s, my father decided that he wanted to build a roadway down the mountain to link the plantation with the public road in the lowland. I was too young to remember this, but recall the stories told. His plan caused great excitement among our workforce and in the nearby villages. Not formally qualified in engineering or road building, the enormity of the task that my father had undertaken was illustrated in photographs – now lost in the war but still remembered. I recall snapshots of him standing hunched over a theodolite, measuring gradients, and others of bare brown backs bent over the ubiquitous *patjoel,* the Javanese hoe with which the men dug out the sides of the mountain into the gradients of a winding road. Travelling back and forth like a stream of ants, other workers filled the waste materials into bamboo baskets that they carried away to dump. Some parties went down to the nearby river to collect granite rock, which they carried back to the road. Men, women and even older children, using bamboo tongs to hold the stones, would crush the granite into gravel with a steel mallet. In this manner they created a 6-metre-wide carriageway over a distance of 15 kilometres, the whole length being covered with no less than 10 centimetres of hand-crushed gravel. In time, when the roadway from our home down the mountain was completed, my father's initiative and the sweat of the labour force had transformed a bush track into a road; a pathway to modern times.

On the plantation two other forms of transportation served us. One of these was a *tandu,* a sedan chair. This is how my mother and sister would occasionally be carried, but was something that I did not like, instead preferring to walk. Resembling an oversize armchair covered by an overhead wicker roof, the contraption had two long bamboo poles attached either side. Needing four porters, one at each end of the poles with two extras to spell, the carriers hoisted their ends of the tandu poles onto a shoulder. Setting off with its human cargo, the contraption softly creaking to the hauliers' rhythmic, slogging gait, at a grunted signal between them every now and then the porters briefly halted to transfer the chair's weight onto the other shoulder. Nowadays an incongruous and even inappropriate mode of transportation, a tandu was unremarkable at the time, and it earned the porters ten cents extra in their day's wages.

The other form of transportation on the plantation was our horses. Of a stable of six, a magnificent dappled Arabian gelding was my father's favourite. In spite of its majesty and for reasons that are unclear to me, this splendid animal went by the surely somewhat low-class Dutch name,

Piet (pronounced Pêêt). Next was my mother's horse, the name and gender of which escape me. Because of its brown colour, I shall give it the Indonesian name Sawo[vii]. The three other horses I think were used by the Hoofd Mandur, and by two other overseers in line of their authority. Finally, there was the pony that my parents bought especially for my sister and me. Each of the steeds has a story of its own to tell.

My father was an excellent horseman. Stabled at the nearby tea factory, I remember when Piet was brought to us by our horse handler. I watched fascinated as my father personally saddled his horse and, when my mother went riding, her animal Sawo also. First came the neatly draped saddle blanket. In my mind I can still hear the small, muffled sound that it made as it was laid over the horse's back. Next was the saddle, its attached stirrups landing on the horse with a clinking of metal. Finally, the creak of leather belts when my father tightened the girth straps neither too tightly nor too loosely, but safe for the rider to mount.

Anecdote has it, but I believe practice confirms, that horses instinctively know the nature of their rider. Somewhat unusual for a normally high-spirited Arabian horse, my father's steed, Piet, had a placid disposition and was an obedient and well-behaved animal. However, on one occasion his reputation was almost undone when my parents had gone on a pleasure ride towards a nearby village in the local highlands. The track was sometimes steep and treacherous with loose stones, but they made good progress. The countryside was beautiful, the high-altitude air refreshing, the day rather romantic… and then, totally out of character, placid Piet whinnied, reared violently and bolted. Heading back downhill on the steep path, my father clung on for dear life, knowing that one misstep on the rough track could cause the animal to fall, spelling disaster for man and beast. Eventually the angry and frightened horse calmed down and my father was able to return to where my mother sat helplessly on Sawo, who – perhaps just as well – had refused to go either forward or back. Piet's uncharacteristic scarper was later found to be caused by the poor animal having been stung by a bee or a wasp. Needless to say, a romantic horseback outing that day had been quite ruined.

If it is a fact that animals are capable of either liking or disliking a person, that premise apparently applied to my mother and Sawo. One could never be sure if or when she and her horse would quarrel with each other, which they too often did. It cannot be known if Sawo instinctively knew that my mother secretly feared and even somewhat hated her mount, or whether she simply did not ride well and that she should not be on a horse in the first place. Whatever the reason, my mother and Sawo literally and figuratively never saw eye-to-eye, and it was only when my father rode with them that Sawo reluctantly performed its duty as a horse.

For the sake of our and my mother's safety, my parents decided that it was best that she ride alone, and as small children my sister and I would double up with my father on his steed. Looking down from my high perch in the saddle I watched the small things on the ground – lizards, squirrels and sometimes an odd snake – scamper or slither out of the horse's path. At times we would come past a party of women from our kampong picking tea leaves off the bushes. Carried in a *slendang*, a cloth knotted over a shoulder, the loads on their backs made them look like hunchbacks. And as we passed them, they tilted their faces up at us, appearing beneath their conical hats like pixies among the lush green tea bushes. Following polite Indonesian custom, the women would crouch down low as we passed, their hats making them appear like so many large mushrooms. For us, times were uncomplicated, the conventions unquestioned, and life was comfortable.

At times we would come past a party of women
from our kampong picking tea leaves off the bushes.

A Childhood Camelot

The top three tea leaves were always the best quality pick.

The last of the horses was a pony that my sister and I jointly used, from when I was seven or eight years old. At the time, we were greatly influenced by children's literature situated in the American Wild West. In these writings the heroes performed great adventures in which their horses played prominent parts, and in keeping with that romantic spirit we named our pony *Vuurpeil* (Burning Arrow). My sister, in particular, found that Vuurpeil quite lived up to its moniker.

Father and mother with Ferdinand and Conny on their pony, Vuurpeil.

Like many girls of her age, Conny was very keen on horse riding, but she and our pony were simply not partial to each other. Vuurpeil would tolerate Conny only as long as it took her to settle down in the saddle, when it would buck and toss her off before she could tighten the reins and control her steed. To her very great credit my courageous sibling would immediately climb back on the horse and try again, but too often with the same result. Vuurpeil and I must have reached some kind of understanding, but although it never threw me off, I did not enjoy riding it. In the end my parents decided that the pony had to go; it simply had a bad temperament and could not be trusted. Of the horses, in time only Piet remained. Retired and dignified, old Piet never again had to bear anyone on his back. My sister and I often visited him at the stables to feed him bananas. These we placed on outstretched hand so as to prevent the horse unintentionally biting us, which at his advanced age, without teeth, Piet could not have done much damage anyway.

Plantation staff

The tea plantation counted some 200 permanent Javanese employees. When at certain times the need arose in the production cycle, further casual labourers were recruited from surrounding hamlets and the labour force could grow up to 1000 hired hands. With my father the principal, directly responsible to him was the Hoofd Mandur, the Javanese Chief Overseer in charge of the plantation workforce. I remember the highly respected Pak Wardjo (Mr Wardjo) as a charismatic, quietly mannered, dignified Indonesian gentleman. However, as my father sometimes put it, 'If necessary, Wardjo can be quite insistent on his authority among the labour force.' Pak Wardjo's connection with my family would become a crucial part of our life early in the Second World War.

We employed three *kebon* (gardeners) to maintain the cultivations that sprang from my father's hobby of growing flowers and planting vegetable gardens. As well as weeding, scarifying, composting and watering the plants, I remember how as part of their maintenance work the kebon used to mow the vast lawns with only a hand-held, sickle-shaped instrument called *arit*. I now cherish the memory of these

Javanese and the landscape they helped to shape. They worked hard in the shadow of my ancestral home, amidst the terraces of jade-green tea bushes that serrated the mountainside.

When I think back on my youth on the tea plantation, I especially remember our three Indonesian home helpers. In order of seniority, they were: *Jongos* (manservant) Pak Kasim, *Kokki* (cook) Bu Mienem[viii] (Mrs Mienem), and *Babu tjutji* (washerwoman) Bu Sitjas[ix]. While both cook Mienem and washerwoman Sitjas were called by their given names, not one of us ever addressed Kasim other than by his title, Jongos. Among his many tasks, Jongos would ensure that my mother was informed when it became necessary to replenish household necessities. As the plantation's water-turbine-powered electricity supply was never a certainty, a major item Kasim had to keep an eye on was fuel. Kerosene was used in the kitchen stoves and in the pressure lamps that were lit when the electric lights unpredictably went out. It was also used in the small wicker lamps, *lampu templok*, that were lit and hung on hooks on the bedroom wall at 10 pm, providing a small light in the pitch darkness when the electricity from the tea factory ceased.

To me, the approximately twenty-five-year-old Jongos was like an uncle. I often relied on him to teach me the skills that Javanese parents passed on to their sons. Thus it was he, Jongos, who taught me how to cut down the bamboo that grew in clumps amongst the tea bushes. If my hands became covered with the stinging bamboo hairs, it was he who showed me how to get rid of them by rubbing the affected area through my hair; and it always worked. I remember when, on a few occasions, when the season was right and Jongos had time, we used the bamboo to make a kite. After we had cut down a green stalk of the bamboo, I would watch Jongos as he cut it into about half meter lengths. He whittled them into slender round spikes that he assembled into a diamond framework. After pasting Chinese rice paper over the frame, we tied the kite to a cotton reel which I 'borrowed' from my mother's sewing box for the purpose; but I am sure that she would have known this. When all was ready, a dozen or so metres away Jongos held the kite up for me, ready to release it to handy gusts of wind. It was a thrill to see our kite climb upwards into the sky; up, up, up, higher and higher, diving and twisting and soaring until it was only a speck in the firmament. Jongos was more than merely one of our servants; he was a companion, a tutor, and to me, like an uncle.

Our cook, Bu Mienem, was a striking woman, somewhat younger than my mother. Her crowning glory was the long, raven-black hair that she wore in a generous *kondé* (chignon). When Mienem sometimes let her tresses flow freely, they reached to just above her knees. Every day after breakfast, Mienem would wait for my mother at the pantry where foodstuff was stored: flour, rice, salt, sugar, cooking oil and other staples and ingredients for cooking and baking. Carried on a silver clasp, Mother always had the one and only key to anywhere in the house, with which she ceremoniously opened the pantry door. I imagine that with this daily ritual, Mother consciously acted out the role of Njonja Besar, Grand Lady, chatelaine, queen of her castle.

Mother and Mienem had a special relationship, a mutual liking and respect. Before planning the day's menu, with mother seated on a low chair and Mienem sitting on the ground Javanese style, legs folded under her, the women would engage in *omong kossong* (local gossip). When they had satisfied their pastime, they began planning the menu. Breakfast never varied, a frugal meal of porridge, toast, cheese, peanut butter, homemade jam or other spreads and fruit in season. In the East Indies, lunch was customarily the main meal of the day, receiving careful consideration and discussion. When I remember the few cents Mienem asked for with which to buy various ingredients – coriander, half a cent; cumin, 1 cent; small brown onions, 1.5 cents, and so on – I marvel at how she produced the delicious meals that she prepared for us at such little cost.

There is another, sadder side to the relationship between my mother and her cook. Mienem had a shy personality and an inward-looking disposition that hinted at something tragic in her life. Only as a grown-up did I learn how Mienem had been in an out-of-wedlock relationship with a young Dutch planter on a nearby estate. This had resulted in the birth of two sons, but when the children were still very young the planter had broken off the liaison. Not only had he sent the mother of his illegitimate children back to her village but, indeed, she was cruelly forbidden to associate with her sons. I recall Mother telling me, as an adult, what happened when the planter and his sons, aged around ten and twelve, arrived uninvited on our plantation. Mienem must have been terribly distressed to be so close to her children but unable to approach them. To their credit, my parents refused to host the unwanted guest and asked him to leave immediately. There was nothing they could do for Mienem or for her two sons. With two children of her own, Mother had a deep sympathy for our cook's heartache. This unvoiced bond between them underscored their camaraderie.

Also part of our household was babu tjutji (washerwoman) Bu Sitjas. Almost a teenager still, Sitjas was given to flirting with Jongos, frequently bursting into the giggles and skittishness that often mark the behaviours of those craving attention and recognition. But no one could fault our will-of-the-wisp Sitjas at her work. Every day she would strip the family's beds of sheets and pillowslips, putting them into the washing cauldron, a 44-gallon (220 litre) petrol drum cut in half and filled with boiling water. I often watched as, armed with a stout stick, petite Sitjas hauled the heavy, water-soaked spreads out from the tub one at a time, to thoroughly scrub and pound them by hand on the ribbed washboard. Something that always fascinated me was to see Sitjas ironing sheets, pillow slips and clothes using a heavy, cast-iron device stoked with *arang arang* (charcoal). With the lid held down by a small clip in the form of a rooster, Sitjas used the iron to meticulously flatten out the washing that she had pulled down from the line. A treasured member of our household, Sitjas had the meanest workload, but it was one that she cheerfully performed.

Until the mid-1930s, when my father had built the private road from the tea factory to the lowlands, another person who worked for us was an Indonesian man whom we knew only by his title, *Pesuratan* (Postie). Except for Sundays, Pesuratan daily walked some 15 kilometres down the mountain to the government road and back with the mail and anything else that had been left for collection at the small trade store operated by its Chinese owner. In an era when few if any people possessed a refrigerator, Pesuratan also carried two blocks of ice – each measuring about 30 centimetres wide by 60 centimetres long and 25 centimetres thick – back up the mountain for our icebox. Each block was wrapped in a gunny bag and bedded in rice hulls to prevent it melting. Upon its delivery at our home, Jongos would wash the hulls off the ice, chop the bricks into cubes, and fill a number of thermos flasks with ice blocks that cooled my father's daily glass of beer and the rest of the family's treat of a glass of rose-flavoured cordial. When the plantation road was built and a brand-new truck began collecting our mail and ice, Pesuratan's service was unfortunately made redundant.

Daily routine

Our family usually arose at 6 am. Unless it rained, we would climb the steep hill behind our house to the large reservoir that stored water for the hydroelectric turbines that supplied electricity for our home and the plantation kampong. The reservoir doubled as our swimming pool. After our morning swim we had breakfast, consisting of porridge, tea and toast. My father donned khaki shorts, a khaki safari-type jacket, hobnailed boots (to prevent a fall on the slippery dirt paths) and ankle-to-knee puttees (to prevent scratches and being attacked by leeches) then went about his work inspecting the factory and tea gardens.

My mother liked to be prettily dressed – she had a good figure, and I believe she liked to show it off! The local dress of white *kebaya* blouse and sarongs of traditional browns and black she considered rough, preferring colourful Western dresses. My sister and I ran all over the plantation in shorts and short-sleeved shirts, but never seemed to be troubled by the leeches. We rarely wore shoes, and when we were made to, they hurt our feet. We much preferred being barefoot.

Our daily diet was heavily influenced by the Javanese cuisine. Thus, even the 'porridge' for breakfast was usually made from mung bean – *katjang hidjau*. When Mother occasionally thought it necessary to make us eat Dutch oatmeal porridge, we ate the food only because she made us do so. The main meal of the day, served at around 1 pm, was always rice with a few side dishes to accompany it. At the time, meat was difficult to obtain and we seldom had beef on the menu, other than perhaps as a minor ingredient in a side dish. More often we had chicken prepared in a number of Javanese ways. Other than for special occasions, we never had 'afters'; instead, we enjoyed a choice of Java's many varieties of delicious seasonal tropical fruits. While our meals were certainly more lavish than those of the general Javanese community, in the colonial society of the day the provisions in our home were by no means extravagant or of the decadent indulgence otherwise enjoyed by the very privileged.

Early education

When I reached school age, my mother – a qualified primary school teacher – supervised my sister's and my correspondence education at home. Unlike some children, who also lived too far away from a formal school or whose parent was not a trained teacher, my sister and I did not have to be boarded out in town; something too terrible for us to imagine. We were lucky indeed.

The first lesson in my educational career was my mother teaching me the 'art' of sharpening slate pencils with which to write on a slate tablet, instead of entering notes and other writings in a paper notebook with the nowadays ubiquitous biro. She took me outside to where a concrete wall stood and watched over me as I rubbed the slate pencil on the rough surface, whittling it to a point. I then undertook the very basis of all formal learning: from a large demonstration board I laboriously copied the twenty-six letters of the alphabet and formed them into words – apple, boat, cat... Time has surely moved on to where, in this digital age, new generations learn to employ mouse and computer instead of stylus and slate. I am very glad that, on a last visit to the Netherlands, before my mother passed away, I was able to thank her for the passion that she kindled in me for the pursuit of knowledge and learning that has continued to inspire me throughout my life.

Being taught at home allowed for a flexible schooling regime that enabled my family to take days off, sometimes even a couple of weeks, when we went on motoring trips around Java. These excursions enabled me to glimpse some of the history and substance of the Javanese civilisation beyond the school curriculum. To provide Conny and me with extra-curricular learning, our parents took us to see the Hindu *Prambanan* temple complex, the Buddhist *Borobudur* pagoda, the ruins of temples on the Dieng Plateau, and to visit various musea and many other places with historical background, the knowledge of which has stayed with me. I particularly recall that although the Javanese material culture represented a world outlook other than ours, I was taught to owe it as much respect and regard as is due to our Western civilisation.

An appreciation of Javanese culture is wanting if it does not recognise the fact that Javanese people deeply believe in spiritual matters. During my childhood, many engaged in activities that related to the supernatural and 'the other world'. *Selametan* food offerings at certain celebrations and events, advice steeped in spiritualism sought from a local *dukun* (mystic), the magical potency of *pusaka* that is ascribed to certain weapons such as the *kris* (traditional dagger) – these are but some examples of *Adat* (custom) that formed the distinctive warp and woof of the fabric of Javanese society; a system of beliefs and traditions that were deeply embedded in the soul of Java.

My parents were aware of the ingrained influences of the Javanese world view, and although many colonial Dutch also believed in the supernatural, they forbade our involvement with the paranormal. However, my 'almost-uncle' Jongos Kasim could not help but 'enlighten' me about out-of-this-world-things with myths and even ghost stories. I recall the myth of *Loro Kidul*, the goddess of the seas to the south of Java who dislikes the colour green. The fable warned that, at risk of being snatched by this vengeful goddess and drowned for their indiscretion, a person should not wear this colour of dress on the sea or the seashore. More frightful was mention of *Loro Jongrang*, a spirit more malevolent even than Loro Kidul. The Loro Jongrang spectre acted much like the Pied Piper who, in Western myth, lured away children never to be seen again. Another, truly evil supernatural being, whose name I cannot remember, appeared as a beautiful maiden. The long black hair that reached to below her knees hid that she had no back. The evil being punished and killed those who fell for her deceptive charms, men and male youths in particular. As a child, when I heard about this abominable being, I looked with suspicion upon poor Kokki Mienem, whose glorious, long, black hair reached to her knees – but who in fact was a sweet woman, certainly never a ghostly spirit. In learning about what influenced and defined the way that the people of Java lived their lives, I gained a small measure of insight into the complexity of the Javanese culture. With the cross-cultural traditions that have influenced my life, and the romance of living in a virtual Camelot, as in Voltaire's satire *Candide*, I have lived in 'The best of all possible worlds.'[x]

Celebrations
Other than on highpoints of the calendar such as Christmas and New Year, the midday lunch and evening dinner were informal occasions for which no one 'dressed'. However, for the former two special events our family would put on festive gear, and Jongos would change from his work shorts and shirt into long white cotton trousers and a white

jas tutup – a buttoned-up jacket with stiff grandfather collar. On these high occasions Jongos's 'uniform' would be complemented by a beautiful batik sarong folded around the waist over the jas tutup in the way of a cummerbund.

Growing up in our small plantation community there were occasions of great expectation and joy, particularly in respect of our birthdays. There is one very special occasion that I remember. Probably in order to 'make a man of the boy', on my sixth birthday I was presented with an 8mm Flobert rifle that could fire either a bullet or a cartridge loaded with birdshot. Much later, in my adulthood, my mother confessed that this gift to me had been against her better judgement and feelings. She had eventually given in to my father's reasoning that, 'From an early age our boy should learn to handle weapons safely.' Indeed, it must be said that Father drilled me very thoroughly in the practices and care of firearms and other weaponry. Closely supervised by him, I was allowed to practice shooting at the squirrel-like coconut rat that gnaws holes in, and feeds on, coconuts growing on the tree, spoiling them for human use. Since I felt that I was doing the farmer a service I felt no qualms about hunting the feral pest, and as my marksmanship improved, many literally 'bit the dust'.

For a child who was given much freedom from cloying or even close parental control, the tea fields and the forest around our home was an adventure land beyond compare. One of the first incidents with my rifle that comes to mind is that of a late afternoon when I shot my first quarry, an indigenous bush fowl. As usual, after lunch the family had retired for their siesta till about 3:30 pm, when we would all rise and have afternoon tea. It may have been that I had slept for some time but, with half an ear apparently still wakeful, I heard the unmistakable crowing of a nearby wild fowl calling its 'name' – 'çekèkèr --- çekèkèr'. On the spur of the moment, and without waking my parents, I grabbed my rifle and one or two cartridges and sneaked out of the house. Guided by the fowl's cries I estimated where it should be found in the tea plantation on the hill above the house. Inexperienced hunter that I was, what followed was a blur. Suddenly I found the bird in a small clearing among the tea bushes. Clad in its glorious orange, red, black and off-white plumage, the fowl reared its startled head high when it saw me. No less shocked, I shouldered, aimed and fired my loaded rifle. When the bird fell, flopped and then died, I remember that I honestly had not expected this to happen. Slowly, reality dawned on me that I was responsible for the death of this splendid creature of the wild; consternation registered in my mind and regret set in for a deed that could not be undone. Dead bird in one hand, rifle clasped in the other, I ran back home down the hill with tears streaming down my face, crying with a sense of overflowing excitement – but also with bitter grief for the poor, lifeless creature that burdened my hand nearly as much as it did my conscience.

My father was a kindly man, but he knew when to teach his children respect, decency and morality in matters of high principle. After my startled parents had consoled my grief over what I had done, Father instructed me to take the bird to Kokki Mienem: 'We will have it for our midday meal tomorrow.' When I dared question this verdict my father explained, 'Except for exterminating vermin, one eats what one shoots. To do otherwise is murder and disrespect for Nature, which affords us its bounty.' The next day at lunch, I was made to eat my portion of the game that I had shot, the image of the live bush fowl featuring rather too largely in my mind. Little doubt due to my troubled conscience, the meat tasted disagreeable, and this was not improved by the fact that I had to spit out the occasional lead pellet left in the flesh. For all time after, I have disliked the savour of game, whether it be exotic farmed gourmet fare or taken out of the wild for sport.

Birthdays were celebrated with joy. After the excitement of unwrapping our presents, we would often walk to a favourite spot on the plantation, taking with us a small picnic basket with snacks prepared by Mienem. Much-loved fare for the occasion was *lemper* – sticky rice sausage filled with curried mincemeat and wrapped in banana leaf. At the chosen spot, my father would make a small fire and we would place the sausages on the hot coals, roasting them till the outer banana leaves turned black and the filling inside was hot and deliciously tasty. Lunch for such a feast day was also special when Mienem made us *sate* and other delicacies which she did not often serve. But the eagerly anticipated highpoint of the birthday was the evening dinner, finishing with home-made ice cream.

In the days when no or very few households on Java – and arguably in the world – possessed a refrigerator, making ice cream on the plantation required an amazing exercise in logistics. Wrapped in a hessian bag filled with rice husks as insulation, several more slabs of ice than usual had to be carried up the mountain to our home. On their arrival, Jongos washed the slabs and hacked them into ice cubes, filling them into a wooden tub roughly the size of a 10-litre bucket, around a stainless-steel tub held down by a clamp with an inbuilt wormed wheel that functioned as the cylinder's lid. The cylinder was filled with a vanilla egg custard. In Java, home-made ice cream was called *es puter,* literally meaning 'rotated', or perhaps better expressed, 'churned' ice cream. Churning the basic ingredient required that the cubes of ice in the wooden bucket were liberally sprinkled with coarse salt to lower the temperature. Vigorously turning a handle built into the clamp set the wormed wheels in motion, churning the cylinder's contents. After a long, hard physical exercise the custard set and became the only-too-rare after-dinner treat of home-made birthday ice cream.

A fixture on the annual festive calendar that the Dutch people looked forward to even more than Christmas, was the reputed birthday on 5 December of the Spanish Saint Nicholas, *Sinterklaas* in Dutch. Families would gather where the 'saint' appeared seated on a horse and accompanied by his servant *Zwarte Piet* (Black Peter). The latter was supposedly charged with chastising naughty children and rewarding good ones with gifts of lollies and scatterings of *pepernoten,* small balls of gingerbread, which children would chase after.

Although Christmas was not as well observed by the Dutch as it is in English-speaking countries, we celebrated with a pine tree decorated with candles, tinsel and baubles, the singing of carols, and a few small presents. Close on the heels of Christmas came *Oud en Nieuw* – New Year's Eve and New Year. In the East Indies both Dutch and Javanese were wont to detonate great quantities of fireworks in celebration of the year's end, and even days after the event the air was heavy with the smell of cordite. At home, at precisely midnight, my father would light a long string of firecrackers hung from a large rubber tree on the road just down from the house. The deafening noise of the exploding fireworks underlined the passing of time, and heralded in a new beginning.

The recollection of these major holidays on the Western nation's calendar would not be complete without mention of *Lebaran,* the Indonesian New Year. Lebaran was the one day in the year when all

Javanese on the plantation, including our servants, had the entire day off from work. Apart from the significance of the Indonesian festive calendar day, I looked forward to the occasion as something special and exciting. 'Substituting' our servants, my sister and I would set out the breakfast table with the usual bread and spreads. After our customary swim in the reservoir, Mother – who had stayed in the kitchen at home – would have the porridge ready and either my sister or I would be allowed to carry it to the table. After breakfast we would tidy away the breakfast things. My father usually found something 'urgent' to which he had to attend, so my mother, sister and I would wash the dishes and kitchen implements. By about ten in the morning a delegation of the senior Javanese plantation overseers – *Mandurs* – outfitted in impeccably starched and ironed sarong and jas tutup would call on our family to bring Lebaran greetings. And all day long the Indonesians on the plantation would follow rounds of celebrations that included *selametan* culinary feasts, *wayang* shadow puppet shows and other special treats and appointments of the day. When I look back on these joyful times, they represent a period of innocence and peaceful co-existence of our two races, Javanese and Dutch. The memory of this blending of cultures is as alive with me today as it was then.

In the shadows of my mind, not unlike the puppets in the Javanese wayang folklore plays, the people of my early childhood have surrounded me. In a dreamlike sense they have retold to me stories of an almost forgotten life in which the figures of Jongos Kasim, Mienem, and Sitjas have again become animated. I have relived my easy and caring relationship with almost-uncle Pak Kasim; I have tasted again the lovely food that Bu Mienem prepared for us with such skill and for so little money; I recall the clothes and the linen that Bu Sitjas ironed with such care. Stored in my mind I hear echoes of the laughter of small Javanese children on the plantation; I can almost see again the inky-black storm clouds of the wet season gather and whip up gusts of howling wind over the mountain ridges above our home; I slightly flinch with the memory of the sound of rain released over the countryside and the violent thunderclaps that followed one after another with each sizzling lightning strike. I look into history, and of all the images that I have brought back into living memory, I most recall the peace and security that once was my home amongst the jade-green tea bushes on the hills of Mount Slamet on Java. This was my childhood.

A Childhood Camelot

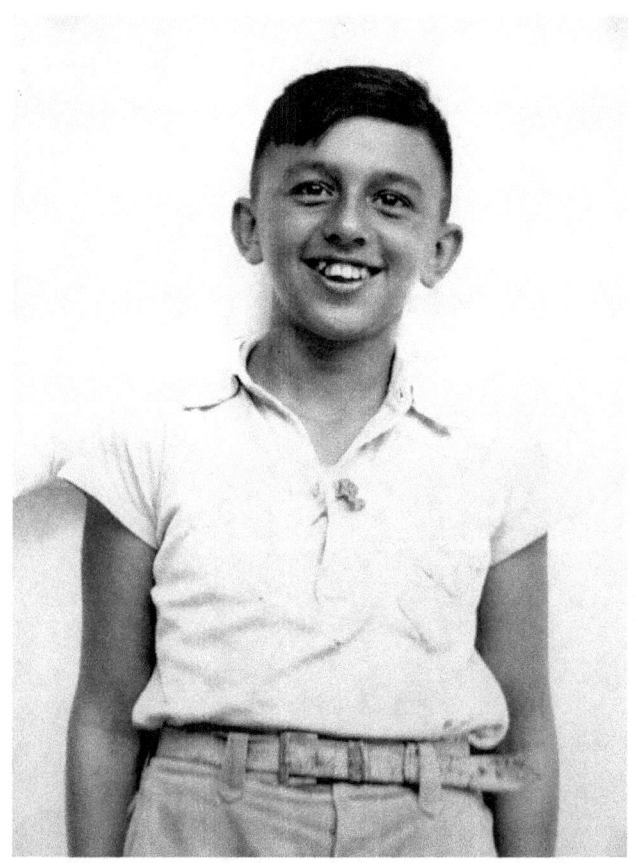

This was my childhood. Ferdinand aged ten years, 1938.

CHAPTER 2

Terra Australis Incognito

It takes all sorts of people to make a world
Douglas William Jerrold, *Story of a Feather* **ch 28**

In 1939, when I was eleven years old, my parents took my sister and I on a six-month-long holiday. My father's dislike of Holland and its citizens became apparent when, instead of going to Holland, as was then generally expected of those going on leave, their chosen destination was the little-known land of *Australia*, down under from Java.

Why Australia?

Australia was an anonymous other world to me, and in my mind's eye I began imagining what the country would be like. Not even my parents or their friends knew other than that Australia was a land of romantic cowboys, sheep, rabbits and a strange animal called 'kangaroo'. My parents had travelled to Holland together once, but never anywhere else. They simply had no idea of how different Australia would be. When the family pored over maps of the Australian continent, the amazingly sparse distribution of towns and cities made us wonder at how vast Australia appeared to be compared with our homeland of Java. Even the archipelago of the East Indies itself did not measure up with the giant continent 'next door'. What a discovery! What an adventure! But when their holiday plans became public, many family and friends reacted, 'Holidaying in *Australia? Why?!*'

Australia

An issue that had first concerned my parents was Australia's historical connection with Britain. Even in the twentieth century this was not a spurious qualm, as in Britain *and* in Holland memories still lingered of when the two nations had been fierce rivals for the lucrative trade in pepper, nutmeg and other exotic commodities from the Spice Islands[xi]. Recollections were also still alive on both sides about maritime encounters, even a naval war between Holland and England during which the Dutch defeated England's fleet at sea. In the British East Indian and Malayan colonies, resentment further rankled about competition to their industries from the colonial Dutch tea and rubber planters. Given these real or imagined impediments to their holiday plans, when my parents finally decided to proceed with their intentions it was a leap of faith and no small matter.

The lead-up to our holidays involved the usual round of parties, family visits, shopping trips for clothes, and of course buying new suitcases in which to pack these. My parents may perhaps have enjoyed these hectic social rounds, but my sister and I loathed them as they upset comfortable routines that few children like to see disturbed. We also disliked the oppressive heat and humidity of the lowlands where most of these parties were held, and we were always pleased when we were back in the cool highlands. 'All good things come to an end, but also do "bad" ones' and the parties finally stopped. It was late February 1939, and the family stood at the beginning of our great Australian discovery.

Selamat Jalan

On the day of our departure my father had put his motorcar in storage at home, and we left for the regional coastal city of Semarang in our plantation truck, Mother and Father sitting up front with the Indonesian driver and we children in the back on the open tray. At Semarang we would embark on a ten-day journey on board a Blue Funnel Line coastal merchant vessel plying between Singapore and Perth in Western Australia. After a long, hot drive we reached the port city of Semarang where our ship, MV *Charon*, lay at anchor out to sea. All along Java's northern coastline, a problem for shipping taking on cargo and/or passengers is that the waters are shallow. Only at Batavia – now Jakarta – and at Surabaya, are ships able to dock at a wharf. Everywhere else, 'lighters' (flat-bottomed craft) ferry cargo and passengers between the shore and the ships out to sea. We boarded one such lighter, and as it moved off, our servants and gardeners farewelled us with prolonged toots of the truck's horn and calls of '*Selamat Jalan*' (propitious journey). We were embarked on the first leg of a holiday of undreamed-of experiences.

From on land, in the glare of the noonday sun the sea had seemed flat and shiny, with hardly a wave rippling the surface. But when wharf labourers untied our lighter and it began to make its way towards the waiting ship, that smooth appearance of the seawaters proved entirely deceptive. We were a mere few hundred metres away from land when the pontoon began to noticeably dip and sway. The set of my father's jaw bore out his previous declaration: 'I am not a good sailor.'

On reaching the waiting *Charon*, the ship was rising and falling on the waves, towering high above our flat-bottomed lighter. As we wallowed alongside the vessel someone from the crew came down the gangplank that hung down the ship's hull. Jumping down into our boat, he addressed my father in English. My parent translated the conversation in Dutch: 'The man says that he wants us to climb aboard the ship.' My father's school-book English suffered practice; using his hands to indicate the distance between ship and lighter, and pointing at the intimidating action of the waves between us, my father complained, 'I want, but I not know how.' It took the ship's officer quite some trouble to persuade first my mother, then we children, and finally my father, to climb onto *Charon*'s rising and falling gangplank. Shaken by the experience but blessedly safely on board, we made our way to our reserved cabins below decks. These were small, with four beds arranged in two bunks. After we had deposited our suitcases, we returned to the deck to watch the loading of cargo until the last lighter returned to its base on land. It was a strangely elating feeling when the engines in *Charon*'s belly thumped into life, the ship hauled anchor, the captain turned a course away from land, and Java began to recede farther and farther into the distance. The adventure had begun: we were on our way to somewhere called Fremantle.

Aboard the *Charon*

Besides *Charon* of the Blue Funnel Line there were another three or four sister ships, whose names I cannot now recall, that plied a general cargo route between Fremantle on Australia's west coast, and Singapore Island at the extreme end of the Malay Peninsula. Mainly cargo vessels, these ships carried sugar and bananas to Australia, and returned with live sheep. They had limited passenger accommodation, sleeping only a couple of dozen travellers – usually students and businesspeople travelling from Australia to Singapore or vice versa, and sometimes tourists like us. The irony escaped us – and perhaps not even the crew or the Australian passengers realised – that sailing us to 'Down Under' Australia, our vessel *Charon* took its name from the mythological Greek boatman Keiron, who ferries the souls of the dead across the river Styx to Hades!

MV *Charon* of the Blue Funnel Line (image courtesy of Fremantle City Library History Centre [LH002970]).

Being aboard *Charon* was to enter a different world. For the first time in our lives my parents, my sister and I met with 'another' society. Although living with the culture of indigenous Indonesia, even after three hundred years of colonisation the Dutch ruled their East Indies colony as an extension of the motherland – little notice was taken of the cultural differences between the colonialists and their Indonesian subjects. Even my for-the-times enlightened family, born and bred in the Indies, simply accepted as a fact that the culture of a few hundred thousand Dutch mattered and that the majority Indonesian culture counted for little. It was not until we mixed with our Australian fellow passengers that we became aware that we had become the foreigners, and we were treated as such by our culturally different Anglo-Saxon hosts.

The immediate and most pressing problem on the Australian vessel was our lack of fluency in the English language. In Holland and in the

Dutch East Indies, instruction in foreign languages began at primary school; French and German was taught in Grades 4–6, but English was not introduced until secondary school. My parents had received high school educations and had acquired a basic knowledge of 'schoolbook English'. However, as became apparent on board, their ability in conversational English was limited. Our parents had taught my sister and me a few words – Yes, No, '*Sankyoo*' – and this was somewhat the extent of our English vocabulary.

On board *Charon* we discovered certain curious Australian customs that were never part of our Dutch way of life, and that stood us apart from the other passengers. One of these instances was when we saw fellow passengers taking a brisk morning's stroll several times around the ship's deck. In Indonesia, the Dutch only walked if this became unavoidable; it was not quite *de rigueur* for 'we Europeans' to be seen on foot in the streets. Instead, we used the motor car, rode on horseback, took the horse-drawn *dokkar* cart or were portaged in the tandu sedan chair. In short, in the colony 'we' walked only as a last resort. So when met with the well-meaning 'Come along' of fellow passengers inviting us to join them on their rounds of the deck, we politely declined, 'No, sankyoo.' This strange Australian habit made us feel out of place and foreign. From being 'we' Dutch colonialists, superior to 'them' native Indonesians, on an Australian ship we learned a lesson in humility, this time 'we' became 'the others', and not like 'us Australians'. Yet another curious observation was of the tables in the ship's dining room, decorated with vases holding a green plant material that we could not identify. To our astonishment, at mealtimes we saw Australians help themselves to some of the 'bouquet' and consume it with their repast. It was only later that we learned that the 'flower arrangements' were celery and spring onions, at the time unknown in Indonesia. We had no idea that in Australia they were a kind of condiment enjoyed with meals!

Still on the subject of unusual fare, being underage, and as was the custom at the time, my sister and I attended meals before the adult dining times. When one day the dish of tripe and onions appeared on the ship's menu, my sister and I were unable to stomach the food. At home our parents always insisted that we should eat everything that was served on our plate, but when our mother fortunately decided to sample the tripe and onions herself, she excused us from having to finish eating this rather too foreign fare. My sister and I were mercifully spared the admonition, 'The poor children who go hungry in China would be thankful for the food' – a routinely delivered object lesson in gratitude that my mother always voiced when difficulties arose with our eating at home.

If life on board *Charon* held many surprises for us, there still remained a reassuring familiarity with home. Plying the coast of northern Java, ships of the Blue Funnel Line made a number of routine stops at ports to load cargo for Australia. At one, as *Charon* lay waiting at anchor to take on cargo, my sister and I looked on as some of the Chinese crew engaged in fishing from the ship's decks. Hailing from Singapore and speaking a lingua franca close to that which we used in the Indies, we easily conversed with the men. When we came to know them better, some of them lent us a line and my sister and I spent hours fishing beside our new friends. Giving our catch to the Chinese sailors, they gutted, cleaned and pickled the fish in coarse salt to finally hang them out in the sun, producing the salted dried fish that was a staple Asian food supplement. To our delight, when we told them about missing the rice and accompaniments that our kokki cooked for us at home, some of the fresh fish went to the crew's kitchen where the Chinese chef fried it and gave it to us with rice: fare that we much preferred over the potatoes, vegetables, meat and gravy, and especially the dreaded tripe and onions, in the dining room.

At the last port of call on the south-eastern coast of Java, after the ship took on a huge cargo of bananas, *Charon* pulled up anchor, and this time headed across the open sea, bound for Australia. About the seven days of sailing that followed, I most clearly remember the deck games that we played – quoits, deck tennis and shuttle board – and also the noon-day treat of a serve of beef tea. I looked forward to the latter, and these days when I sometimes treat myself to it, memory resurfaces of our family holiday to Australia travelling on *Charon*.

As my father had predicted, he indeed was not a good sailor and when the ship ploughed the open sea of the Indian Ocean to Australia, for the first two or three days he was laid low with *mal de mar*, the dreaded seasickness. Among *Charon*'s crew, a nurse – most probably a nurse's aid – looked after any babies, young children and unwell passengers. On this trip, it was only my father who fell into the latter category, and from time to time 'Nurse', a stout and rather formidable woman, would undertake her duty to check on him in his cabin. 'Can I do anything for you, sir?'; 'Would you like something to eat?'; 'Why don't you go up on deck? The fresh air will do you good.' To all these well-meaning questions and suggestions, some of which he found difficult to understand in the Australian-accented English, my suffering parent answered in the negative, 'No, sankyoo.' And to us he would complain in Dutch, 'I wish the darn woman would leave me alone!' After a night of sailing on somewhat rough seas, when my mother and we children were at breakfast one morning, Nurse called on my decidedly squeamish father. After admonishing him for staying in bed instead of being on deck and active, when my father complained about being too nauseous to do so, she suggested, 'Well, perhaps I shall get you some boiled eggs today?' To this my parent angrily replied, 'No, I not want play on deck today.' Nurse equally tersely replied, 'I didn't suggest anything of the sort - - - *Sir*.' We later deduced that there had been a language problem when my father had mistaken the rapidly spoken, Australian-accented 'boiled', and 'egg', to be one word '*boildeck*', and had taken this to be yet another attempt by Nurse to encourage him to participate in one of the interminable sports Australians indulged in, even in the middle of an ocean.

Arriving in Australia

On the tenth day from when we had boarded *Charon*, we were to make landfall at the port of Fremantle on the west coast of Australia. In the late afternoon the distant outline of the Western Australian mainland drew nearer with each revolution of the ship's screw. As we stood on board watching the vessel's progress, we became aware that the tang of the air was less salty, it was fresher and began smelling of good earth again. As we docked at the wharf I stood fascinated, watching the activity of the wharf labourers who caught the long lines tied to the ship's cables stern and aft, which they drew in and tightened against the bollards until all the slack had been taken up and *Charon* lay fast. Next the gang plank went down, and a number of immigration and other officials climbed aboard. By the time the passengers were cleared to disembark, the early evening had set in and we gingerly negotiated the quay, through parked heavy equipment, boxes and other unidentifiable gear. After ten days of the ship's rolling and pitching on the ocean, we made our way with an involuntary 'sailor's swagger' to where taxis were waiting to take passengers into Fremantle town or to the capital city of Perth. I do not remember much of the trip to the Perth hotel where my parents had reserved accommodation, except for the sight of shop windows advertising their facilities with blinking neon signs. Never before seen on Java, surely this modern technical advancement left us lacking in *Indië*.

We arrived in Australia halfway into the month of March. Coming from the tropical East Indies to Australia's temperate climate zone on the cusp of autumn, the temperature in Perth felt almost painfully cold to us. The air was sharp to breathe, much like the high altitudes of Java's mountains. Tired and somewhat confused after the day's excitements, our family retired early – using every available blanket to protect us from the unfamiliar chill. Tomorrow was another day, and six months of adventures in the Great South Land lay ahead.

First impressions of Perth

By custom – by the accepted, commonplace way that things are done by people in their society – every country, every city, has a distinctive character. At home on Java, familiar sounds on the streets and byways included the distinctive cry of vendors of all sorts of wares. The rattle of stick on saucepan announced the tin smith looking for customers, or in the early evening the long drawn call of the satay vendor, '*Satay, sááátaaaay... ayàm*', brought out the nature of public life and itinerant business. In the days following our arrival in Perth, we learned that Australia had its own typical sounds. Among these I most remember the cry of the paperboy on street corners echoing down the chilly street, '*PÁÁÁIPER!! PÁÁÁIPER!! Read all ab-OUT it! Ostráilian Test Team saiiling for Eng--lan--d! Austráália to play the Poms at Lo-or-d's! READ ALL ABOU-OUT IT!!*' When we took a stroll and found the youth serving a passer-by, we saw the exchange of copper pennies and heard the tinkle of money as it changed hands. 'Thank you, Sir,' the boy said. And when he again took up his '*PÁÁÁIPER, PÁÁÁIPER*' that rang out afar, bouncing off buildings, I admired and even somewhat envied the child entrepreneur for his prowess.

For the first few days in Perth we felt complete strangers, foreigners out of our depth and almost overwhelmed by nearly everything that we saw, heard and smelt. It seemed to me that the wafts of thin, cold air in Perth were permeated by the sweet aroma of exotic fruits – plums, apricots, pears, grapes – stacked in small heaps on barrows that were parked at the street curbs. It was a pleasantly gentle odour so different from the pungent smell of durian, mangoes, jackfruit and like wares in the kampong (village) markets at home. Our parents bought us some of these fruits; the delicate, sweet astringency of the pear, tartness of the crunchy Granny Smith apple and honeyed sweetness of grapes as they cracked open in one's mouth are never-forgotten memories of the first time we enjoyed the flavours of Australia.

During our first few days in Australia, we were still clad in our tropical clothes. On top of shivering in what to us was an almost unpleasantly cool temperature, we noticed how differently the men, women, and children in Australia were dressed. Unlike my parents in their tropical gear, most men wore hats and many women were outfitted in stylish autumn dress, hatted and gloved. For me, dressed in my khaki shorts and shirt, I personally felt envious of the distinctive school uniform worn by youngsters of my age. Given these differences that set us apart from the Australian general public, high on the list of my parents' priorities was to buy us suitable Australian wear. In the next day or two, now 'properly' dressed, much of my sense of self-assurance returned. My father refused to wear a hat because it made him feel ridiculous, but I, now wearing a cap such as those of Australian schoolboys, no longer felt quite as conspicuous on the streets as before.

Embedded in memories of our introduction to Australian society is the oddity that we found with the habits and customs of the Australian public in general. One of my recollections is that of the differences between shopping in Dutch stores and those in Perth. We had never been in a department store, and I can no longer recall the name of the main Perth emporium at the time, but the behaviour of shop assistants in it and in other stores was quite peculiar to us. Accustomed to being served by staff that fawned over their customers, the casual manner in which Australian salespeople treated shoppers seemed extraordinary to us. In our recent expedition of buying clothes, my parents were startled when an assistant – whom we had to *find* rather than have someone rush out to serve us – addressed my mother with a cheery, 'G'day Love, what c'n I do fer ya?' Also, instead of carefully and neatly parcelling up the articles in special paper like at home, our local purchase in Perth was wrapped in some brown paper and tied up with string. Worse, instead of ceremoniously handing the item to the customer, the salesperson in the Perth store slapped it in front of us on the counter, 'There y'are, Love'. *Curiouser and curiouser*, as Alice would have said[xii]. My parents were taken aback by the abrupt service in Australian shops, and they didn't think it quite appropriate for my mother to be addressed 'Love' by a complete stranger, especially a socially subordinate shop assistant.

Among other first impressions of Australia, we were amazed to notice the haste, the *pace* at which people moved, almost ran, up and down the streets of Perth. In the East Indies we seldom walked, and if we must do so it was never very far and always without unseemly haste, nothing like the pounding of hurrying feet on Australian pavements. Where did these people come from, where did they go to, what drove them so hastily and why?

One day, our family was taking a stroll and we were stopped by a man who identified himself as a school inspector. 'I say, Sir and Madam, why are the children not attending school today?' The situation was of course quickly explained to the inspector when, with my parents' reply in imperfect English, it was made clear that we were tourists and that the Australian law had not been broken by its citizens. Under today's social conditions truancy appears to no longer be met with such official interest and diligence, making a comparison with 'the good old days' a matter for reflection.

Gracefully draped alongside the spectacular Swan River, Perth became our favourite Australian city. On the first few days we did little more than explore its central business district on foot. Wandering farther out we explored beautiful Kings Park overlooking the city and river below, where we picnicked on freshly baked bread, crisp lettuce, tomatoes, and lovely seasonal fruit: plums, apricots and bunches of blue-black or green grapes. One late afternoon when we walked along the bank of the Swan River, we watched a party of local men trawling for prawns in the shallows. Their wives and children watched over a small fire on the sandy shore, over which water boiled in a converted 4-gallon kerosene can. When the men returned with the catch, the family cooked it on the spot and enjoyed a good picnic meal of freshly caught prawns. These and many other impressions made our stay in Perth feel somewhat like window-shopping – observing on the outside of, but not quite entering into, Australian society. Little by little our excursions gave us insight into the lives of Australians whose customs and habits were in many ways very different from how we lived in the Dutch East Indies. Perth introduced us to Australia, but we still had much more of the country and the nation to discover.

Before we embarked on our holiday, my parents had entertained a vague idea that we should travel around Australia, though other than visiting the nation's major cities they had made no firm plans. After a week or so in Perth, the novelty was beginning to wear off and staying in the hotel was beginning to pall. My parents discussed this with a casual hotel acquaintance, seeking the person's advice on what to do and where to go, and a few days later a taxi took us to the seaside village of Scarborough. Here, the informant had told my parents, many city people spent holidays or weekends sunbaking on golden beaches or fishing and swimming in the waters of the Indian Ocean. Our stay in the then humble village of Scarborough would become one of our most treasured memories of Australia.

Scarborough

The taxi that took us to Scarborough drove through outer suburbs of Perth that we had not explored on foot. Beyond the city outskirts stretched a sandy, semi-desert countryside. The vegetation mainly consisted of tough, tall, green-black herbage, which our driver called kangaroo grass, that reminded us of notorious *ilang ilang* sward back home, an indicator of badly leached soils. Scattered through the landscape we also saw clumps of eucalyptus trees, native to and ubiquitous in Australia. In Indonesian called *kajuputih* – literally 'white timber' – we knew it as growing in the chain of islands from Ambon to Timor. The leaves of the tree produce oils well-known as a disinfectant and mosquito repellent, explaining the faint medicinal odour we had detected in the Australian air. Here and there we also spotted what looked like large tufts of grass growing on blackened stems, about two metres tall. 'Them's blackboys,' the driver told us, 'Sometimes they're called grass trees'.

The road through the arid savannah to Scarborough unfolded in a flat, narrow, black band. Presently we reached undulating terrain covered with dense, shrubby growth in a landscape devoid of human habitation. The taxi driver called the bushes *ti-tree*. By and by, the rolling country turned into the coastal dunes of Scarborough.

Lying at almost the farthest end of the immense Australian continent, in 1939 Scarborough was inconsequential, a mere pinprick on the map. When we reached the small township nestled in a corridor of dunes, we saw that Scarborough village had only a single main fare. From this, the unimaginatively named and respectively numbered First, Second, Third, Fourth, Fifth (and so on) Streets branched out left and right at right angles. The taxi driver turned into one of them and cheerfully announced, 'This is where you get out!' We had reached the small cottage my parents had rented. 'Boot's open mate, help yerself,' the driver called out from behind the wheel of his vehicle. In Java my father would not have entertained the thought of unloading our luggage – that was the work of a servant. However, realising that this must be yet another unfamiliar Australian custom, my parent began to collect our suitcases from out of the car boot, carrying them to the small veranda of our cottage. The job completed, when he paid the taxi driver and added a tip, the man cheerfully declined, 'She'll be right mate, you don't owe me any more than the fare.' This was yet another experience in assimilating Australian culture and customs. I remember that my father concluded, and that he impressed on us, 'When in Rome, do as the Romans. In Australia we must try to adapt.'

In 1939, Scarborough's permanent population numbered perhaps no more than two or three hundred residents. Looking around us when we drove in from Perth, we noticed that due to the salt-laden air many of the weatherboard-clad houses suffered peeling paintwork and brown patches where rusting iron nails showed through. No different from many other local dwellings, the outside of our rented cottage looked a little scruffy and in need of a fresh coat of paint. Elevated on stumps about 3 feet above ground level, a practice common in Australia for the purpose of ventilation and protection from insects and white ants, our bungalow matched the general architecture of houses of the period. The cottage featured an open-sided veranda covered by a corrugated iron bull-nose roof. Protected from the weather, the veranda made an outdoor living area in which the owners had provided furniture considered 'good enough still for at the beach' – a couple of dilapidated armchairs, a battered sofa and a wobbly former kitchen table. Having taken stock of the outside, when we entered the interior of the house through a door creaking on dry hinges, we found the room unimpressive, to say the least. Reminding ourselves that 'in Australia we must adapt,' we simply would have to make do with 'good enough'.

Exploring the interior, behind an island bench in the kitchen area stood a Kookaburra-brand fuel stove, a facility which was totally unknown in the Indies and a somewhat wondrous contraption to us. In the remaining part of the room the owners had again provided 'good enough for at the beach' cast-off furniture: an old table, several non-matching dining chairs, two or three worn armchairs and an overused sofa with springs threatening to poke through the fabric cover. Opposite the front door, an arched doorway in the kitchen/sitting room opened into a narrow passage that ran the length of the building, giving access to a bedroom on either side. At the very end of the corridor passage we found a small bathroom, but failed to find a toilet. Eventually, exercising some imagination aided by a sensitive nose, in the backyard we located an old-fashioned 'dunny', the notorious Australian outdoor toilet. Soothing my mother's consternation at finding such a primitive facility that surely would not do, my father reassured us – and likely himself: 'When in Rome, we have to do as the Romans.'

In the 1930s, Scarborough's major attraction was doubtlessly its fabulous golden beaches stretching for miles along the coastline. In our cottage, within walking distance from the beach, we could hear the constant growl of surf where the Indian Ocean came rolling into shore. On some days, early autumn winds blew hard, whipping up thundering seas. At other times, when barely a zephyr stirred a glassy sea, with a *SSHSSS-ssshuhshus-sshuss*, half-hearted wavelets made their almost inaudible way to shore before being sucked back out to the ocean. In our rented cottage far from our mountain home on Java, the drumbeat of the Indian Ocean's surf, the wind singing through overhead power lines, and the slithering sound of the sea creeping inshore and then retreating over the sand at Scarborough, became the living sounds of the Australian beach.

On the draughty streets of Perth and in our unheated hotel room, we had felt chilly and sometimes even decidedly cold. After several weeks in Australia, at Scarborough we were perhaps becoming less sensitive to the cold and were beginning to acclimatise to such an extent that we almost daily swam in the sea, or, lightly clad in shorts and shirt, went for long beach walks. My sister and I became avid amateur beachcombers, collecting spectacular multi-coloured shells that lay washed up on the sand in countless thousands. To these collections we sometimes added bizarrely twisted, bone-white, sea-sun-and-salt-bleached branches that had washed up on shore. Other times on our beach excursions my sister and I hunted little sand crabs, catching them for sport before they disappeared too far down into burrows, but soon releasing them. One day we caught a helpless little crab that we tied to the tail of a small dog that had followed us on the beach. The poor pet went wild, chasing its own tail and trying to rid itself of the unwanted encumbrance. My mother admonished us, '*CHILDREN!!*' But she could not quite hide a smile.

During the week when most residents were at work, we had Scarborough village and the beach practically to ourselves. At low tide, when the retreating sea left shallow pools, my sister and I could walk from one puddle to the next, and we would sometimes fish with our hands for small fry trapped by the retreating sea. Like the tea gardens of our Camelot on the plantation, the dunes and beaches of Scarborough became another special, happy playground.

Among the many new impressions that were crowding in on us, I remember fascinating insights into life in a small Australian village of the time. Everyone, especially the older residents, kept a lawn and small flower and vegetable gardens growing on their premises. At home, Java's fertile soils made growing plants, shrubs and lawns seem effortless. In seaside Scarborough, it was touching to observe the effort with which people tended their plots of essentially pure sand with a minimum of topsoil in which to grow the plants. On top of this, there was the usually dry Australian weather to contend with; unlike back home on our mountain, sometimes no rain fell for weeks on end. In a valiant but not necessarily altogether successful substitute for rain, Scarborough gardeners employed sprinklers – unknown and unnecessary on Java. Circling a parsimonious, stingy curtain of water over the thirsty surface of peoples' gardens, the sprinklers did not do much to sustain the vegetation that wilted, suffered, and almost audibly asked for, 'More, please?'[xiii]

Apart from the weather conditions, the salt-laden air and the poor soils, Scarborough's gardeners faced another natural hazard. We had not long been in our cottage when neighbours told us that very early in the morning one sometimes caught a glimpse of horses roaming free on the street – wild animals that the Australians called 'brumbies'. We were told that these lived in the savannah country behind the sand dunes. During the night or in the early morning they often came out of the bush to maraud the town's gardens for easy pickings, eating everything from grass to the flowers and the vegetables that took people such efforts to grow. In my youthful imagination, however, the brumbies were more like the romantic mustangs on the American prairies and nothing like the nuisances and feral pests that Australian gardeners made them out to be. I remember an early morning when the muted clip-clop of un-shod hooves on the bitumen road signalled that brumbies were about. When I rushed outside, there they were – steeds of the Australian bush, wild like the panthers back home, creatures of the natural world and magnificent in real life.

The longer we stayed at Scarborough the more we discovered of the local way of life. On weekends, the lazy pace of the seaside town's working week changed when people from Perth came by car or on the regular bus service to swim, play, and especially to fish. The sleepy village then bustled with visitors patronising the butcher's, the baker's and the greengrocer's shops, which did a brisk trade catering for barbecues and picnics. Without a doubt, however, Scarborough's milk bar, the Kool Korner Kafé on the grandly named Esplanade became the town's social hub. It attracted the largest crowds and was the place where everyone met everyone else. Despite its modest shopfront, its commanding position only a few steps distant from the beach made it impossible to overlook. On one of its windows, written in red copperplate script on a golden background, a large sign proudly read, 'WA – The Glorious Golden West'. On another window a second advertisement boasted, 'Peters Ice Cream, Health Food of the Nation'. None of the other public buildings in Scarborough displayed such promotions and thus the Kool Korner Kafé's prominent position and status in the community stayed assured and unchallenged.

Inside the café on Saturdays and Sundays there was always a queue of customers waiting to be served a snack or a drink; something with which to still a hunger pang or to wash down the thirst of sun-baked sand and salty surf. Covered by large, oval, gauze covers – to keep off flies – small and large cakes, scones and trays of sandwiches were displayed. In cases with sliding glass panels were mouth-watering red, green and yellow jellies, chocolate mousse, and fruit salads generously topped with thick whipped cream. Special glass jars held barley sugars, the multi-coloured boiled lollies curiously named 'gob stoppers', and similar sweet delights. Particularly enticing to my sister and me was the ubiquitous malted milkshake, and ice creams with choices of single, double and even triple cones – to us a rare delight. We had also discovered a fizzy drink curiously called a 'spider'. I always enjoyed watching the preparation of milkshakes in a tall aluminium beaker, or scoops of ice creams being deftly placed in their cones by one of the proprietors. 'There y'are love, is that all fer t'day? That'll be eight 'n sixpence thanks.' The money handed over, the clang of a bell, the cash register drawer opening, the change taken out, 'Thank you darlin'. Ta ta. Next one, please?'

The Kool Korner Kafé had a particular charm, an atmosphere of its own. Half of the room was reserved to seat patrons around tables covered with chequered cloths, and the other half was left open to accommodate those who came in for their ice creams, milkshakes, sandwiches and other take-away trade. Large and small posters advertising a variety of well-known products decorated the walls, and here and there prints also hung. I remember one was of an English hunting scene, the other of famous Australian diva Dame Nellie Melba. The café was unpretentious and perhaps even somewhat pedestrian in presentation, but its ambience, its closeness to spectacular Scarborough beach, and its absence of pomposity produced an impression of unaffected, genuine old-fashioned welcome and service.

On Saturday and Sunday evenings, garish neon lights above the entrance of the Kool Korner Kafé spelt its name in flickering letters, drawing the crowd like moths to a flame. On Sunday when in the darkening early evening the last visitors straggled home, the sign was turned off and the village took a deep breath... until the next weekend when Scarborough's sleepy peace would again be disturbed. Our family, especially my sister and I, were always glad when the roar of surf was no longer contaminated with the squealing of children and the yapping of dogs, and when the stale smell of used barbecue grills had been cleansed by the healthy sea air. We were relieved when Scarborough again became our private playground, cleared from the din of weekend humanity.

When the 'normal' way of life at Scarborough had returned, the locals resumed their leisurely pursuit of apparently nothing much to do, and proprietors in their shops took time out to again engage in long conversations with customers, usually about the weather or sport. We quickly learned that these were topics that *mattered*; particularly sport, *any* sport. Even if they did not actually play it themselves, the Australians almost religiously followed a sport's progress. The Dutch did not really support any code other than football (soccer), which in Australia was considered 'sissy' and not quite a 'proper' game. Hence my parents often found it difficult to engage in 'polite' conversation about sport in general, and in particular about the game of cricket, which apparently particularly fascinated Australians, or Australian Rules football. 'Football?' my father would say. 'The ball held in a player's hands and only now and then actually kicked with a foot?' Although my father tried to at least comply with custom, he could not for long hide his deficient knowledge.

Although intended to be a brief visit, the family enjoyed life at Scarborough so much that my parents decided to extend our stay there. One consideration was that, while the rented cottage had proved reasonably acceptable for a short time, my mother in particular was now eager to move to more desirable accommodation. While shopping at the greengrocer's or the butcher's, my parents discovered that the gossip in Scarborough's small business community proved invaluable. One of our contacts, the town's only butcher and likely its 'town crier' – Mr Lesley Melon ('Call me Les, mate.') – apparently knew all those living in, and everything about, Scarborough. When Les heard about us wanting to move to new quarters, he told my father, 'I reckon Mrs Forster's Penteila flats just up the road from here will suit you, mate.' Les arranged for us to meet with proprietor Mrs Violet Forster and, having inspected one of her vacant flats, my parents agreed to move from our present quarters to her establishment. Les even offered to move us and our luggage in his truck. 'No worries,' the butcher replied when my parents thanked him.

During our stay at Scarborough, Les Melon and Mrs Forster became our good friends. Widowed and of indeterminate age, Violet Forster was a friendly person who had obviously decided to take 'the foreigners' under her motherly wing. Helping us settle in at one of her five (hence 'Penteila') flats, she noticed that my father had trouble lighting a fire in the open hearth on the chilly evenings, something he had never done before. Violet took over, saying, 'You first have to get some newspaper.' She then showed my father how to lay kindling on top of it. 'Next you put some larger pieces of wood on top of the kindling, and then you light the newspaper underneath. When the kindling is alight, the bigger pieces of firewood will catch on and you'll have your fire; too easy!' On another occasion she noticed my mother washing up dishes in cold water and without soap. When Mrs Forster remarked on it in a friendly way, my mother explained – not boastfully but as a simple matter of fact – that in the Indies everyone had servants to do this kind of work. Violet reacted, 'My, my, but have you truly never washed up dishes, then? Well,' the good lady decided, 'in that case we'll just have ta teach ya.' With my mother watching, Mrs Forster reached under the sink for the little soap sudser that was then a standard appliance in Australian kitchens; until now we had not known its purpose. She placed a cake of Sunlight soap in it and then filled the kitchen sink with hot water in which she vigorously shook the wire cage with soap in it into a foaming wash. 'See, that's how it's done!' Handing my sister and me a tea towel each, she continued, not unkindly, 'Yous youngsters c'n do the dry'n up like all kids in Australia do for their parents.' It was another lesson of life in everyday Australian society to which 'we must try to adapt'.

Although the new flat did not resolve the unfortunate matter of the outdoor dunny, in a decided improvement on the earlier rented cottage – and to my mother's considerable delight – our new accommodation boasted a water heater over the bath. In the previous cottage this had been lacking and we had to shower with cold water, which – especially given it was mid-autumn – was beginning to be rather too spartan for us from the tropics of Java. The chip heater in the bathroom was an ingenious Australian invention operated by lighting a small fire of newspaper and wood chips under a cylinder holding about ten gallons of water. Once heated, the vacuum created inside the cylinder made hot water run into the shower or bath through copper pipes. Cheap, effective, and exclusively Australian, it seems a pity that the chip heater has disappeared, its existence probably remembered by only a few of my generation.

Regardless of the weather, be it summer or winter, Mrs Violet Forster of the Penteila Flats always wore hat, gloves, and a full-length coat on the street. 'Wouldn't be seen without, love. It wouldn't be ladylike, see,' she declared when my mother commented on it. We gained another insight into contemporary Australian custom when Mrs Forster came to visit us and matter-of-factly made for the spare bedroom, where she neatly laid out her hat, folded coat and gloves on one of the beds. 'If yous had an umbrella and hat stand I'd hang me coat 'n hat on the hooks, but ye don't have one here – that's why a person has ta put their things away on the bed', Mrs Forster explained. Her visit at an end, before venturing back onto the street, Mrs Forster would collect her gear from the bedroom, firmly put hat on head, slip on white cotton gloves and shrug into her coat. 'Ta ta, I'm off,' she would say before disappearing down the street.

'It is how things are done in Australia,' my father explained, but he did not seem altogether certain why.

Apart from Lesley Melon and Violet Forster, among other memorable characters was the baker. Every day of the week except Sunday, we waited for the baker to arrive at the Penteila Flats selling freshly baked breads. At around eight in the morning, with money in hand, we listened for the clip-clop of his horse-drawn cart turning into our street. When they pulled up, the animal immediately put its head down into some grass that was growing on the verge, grazing and ruminating as the baker priced his wares for us. 'Eight pence for the white, nine pence for a Vienna loaf. Tank loaves are a shillin' and the scones a ha'penny each.' At home there was nowhere the choice of breads that we found in Australia, and some of those mentioned by the baker we had never heard of. 'What is scone? How you eat small bread like this?' my mother enquired. The baker replied patiently, 'Scones are for morning or afternoon tea, lady, and you eat them with cream and jam; best with *red* jam, but.' A legacy from those early times, we never ate scones other than with cream, and of course red jam. Further tuition in the etiquette of scone consumption came from Mrs Forster who demonstrated, 'You never cut a scone with a knife, but you twist them open like this, see.' When my mother asked why, Mrs Forster explained, 'Cutting open a freshly baked scone would make the cook think them tough, not fluffy as they should be.' Thus we learned another way that things were done in Australia.

Another favourite local identity was the 'Bottle-oh'. Dishevelled in appearance and sometimes smelling suspiciously of probably very cheap liquor, the Bottle-oh announced his sporadic rounds of the village streets with '*BOTTLE-OH, bottle-o-o-oh.*' On our expeditions around Scarborough or on the beach, my sister and I pounced on empty bottles, littered by careless people – especially weekend visitors. By the time Bottle-oh came around to the Penteila Flats we were eagerly awaiting his arrival, when we could cash in the small hoard that we had collected. Our Bottle-oh was a wily trader; 'Nah, that one's no good, son,' he rejected a specimen; for another he offered, 'This one's a bit dirty, kid. Needs wash'n, but I'll give ya a ha'penny for it, all right?' Business completed, with a 'See yez next time, kids,' the old vagabond trudged off with clinking bag slung over a shoulder. Announcing business, his cry rang out anew to all who would like to know, '*BOTTLE-OHH...!*'

Of the shops at Scarborough the one that we called at most often was Les Melon's butchery, at the corner of the intersection of the main road and the Esplanade. Like most buildings in the village, his shop would have benefited from a fresh coat of paint, and Les should perhaps also have oiled the hinges of the creaking flywire door. The rest of the door wasn't in much better repair, its gauze – corroded by the salt-laden air – doing little to deter the flies and other insects that were about. Indeed, shopping for cuts of meat at the butchery we had noticed that when someone entered, dozens of persistent little black bush flies stuck to the back of shirt or frock – but neither the butcher nor his clients seemed to worry about the pests. Les made an exception for the fat blowflies, 'blowies', that he hunted until he had killed every one of them. Asked why he took notice of the blowies and not of the little bush flies, Les wordlessly disappeared to the back of his shop. He returned with a piece of meat crawling with maggots. '*That's* why,' he laconically explained.

Seeing Les Melon at work was a treat. I admired the deft way that his shiny, razor-sharp cleaver never missed its target, reducing a side of lamb into neat loin, chump and forequarter chops on his huge wooden chopping block. Fascinating, too, was to see the butcher open his meat safe – in those days not yet a freezer – where carcasses of lamb, beef and pork hung on hooks. On one occasion, when Les asked what he could sell us today, my father replied, 'I want a piece of the pig, please.' Les laughed out loud, 'Can't do that, mate, the squeals would be terrible!' Seeing that my father did not comprehend, the butcher explained, 'The word "pig" stands for the live animal; when it is dead and butchered, the meat is called "pork", see?' With that, we foreigners learned something new of the complexity of the English language.

Les Melon and my father became good friends, or 'mates', as Les called it. An avid fisherman, after closing time the Australian liked to go down to the beach where he introduced my father to the art and skills of surf fishing – not with an expensive surf rod, but a much cheaper hand line, at the end of which was attached a lead sinker. Fishing in this way required one to wait for the sea to retreat, swing the hooked and baited line with its sinker above the head, and, before the next wave came rushing in to shore, run after the receding water as far as one dared. Under tutelage from Les – and having once or twice been overtaken by the sea – my father quickly learned the technique. Much to his delight, he sometimes came home with snapper or salmon, and once a gummy shark. Fishing off Scarborough Beach with his friend Les Melon became a holiday passion, and back home on Java it became the source of many tall tales of 'the one that got away'.

Les and my father often celebrated their friendship when the butcher went to the Perth abattoirs in his truck for supplies, taking my father along for the ride. After business, the friends would often call in at a pub for a drink or two, and it was in the bars of hotels that my father gained some further understandings of Australian society. To my father – a romantic by nature – Les Melon, with his working-class background, typified the ideal Australian. Using the Australian idiom 'Jack is as good as his master', which my father had somewhere picked up in conversation, he admired the egalitarian spirit, fierce independence and self-assurance of the Australian people. In his eagerness to find merit in the Aussie notion of social equality, my father never considered the irony that at home on the plantation we lived anything *but* a life of equality. He never discovered this contradiction in respective outlooks, and until the day he died he loved Australia and idolised Australians as 'salt of the Earth'.

The Overlander: Perth–Kalgoorlie

As autumn began to turn into early winter, my parents decided that it was time to leave Scarborough, where we could no longer swim in the increasingly cold waters of the sea. On our walks of the wind-swept beach the late-autumnal chill had become unpleasant, and not even the small fire that they lit could keep my father and Les warm when they went fishing. New adventures in the eastern states were beckoning us.

Seen off by Les Melon and Mrs Violet Forster, one chilly day we left Scarborough by taxi for Perth's Central Station, where we were to board the then called Overland Express to the eastern states. As a long-distance train, in many respects the 'Overlander' was very different to the kind of transport that ran the relatively short-haul routes on Java. The overnight west-to-east express connecting Batavia with Surabaya consisted of a medium-sized locomotive pulling perhaps three coaches offering sleeping berths, several second-class carriages with seating only, and half a dozen third-class carriages followed by a small number of freight wagons. On the station at Perth, the huge coal-fired locomotive of the Overlander impressed us; however, it was not until the train was in motion, and we looked back when it rounded a curve, that we noticed the seemingly endless procession of carriages and freight wagons that followed behind.

Another difference between the Overlander and the Batavia to Surabaya express train was the standard of accommodation. In the daytime, in our first-class Overlander compartment, we were seated on leather benches, one facing forward, the other back. Above the seats a beautiful wrought-iron luggage rack stored our suitcases, and between us and the neighbouring compartment we shared the luxury of a toilet, shower, and a recessed washbasin made of shiny red copper. The cabins and the passageway of carriages were lit by elegant wrought-iron lamps with brass fittings. However, the Overland Express lacked both heating and air-conditioning, then still world-wide unknowns. This meant that in the early daytime when we boarded in Perth, our first-class compartment was cold and clammy inside, and to ventilate it required opening the picture window. However, as we later discovered, when a steam train is in motion, showers of hot cinders from the locomotive's stack come raining in, burning skin, eyes, and clothes. After we left Perth, we had to therefore keep the window closed, and later in the day this caused our compartment to turn from cold to unpleasantly hot. Impossible to relieve the condition, like everyone on board we simply endured what was an unavoidable state in contemporary Australian train travel.

We left Perth in full daylight, and once we had cleared the city and the suburbs we found ourselves journeying through an increasingly arid, almost barren, landscape. It was covered with wiry khaki-coloured grass, the ever-present bottlebrush and low-growing shrubs, and was sparsely studded with gumtrees. This semi-wilderness comprises the Australian nation's marginally habitable land, where farm properties are measured in thousands – sometimes hundreds of thousands – of square miles. As the train moved farther and farther inland, away from the arable coastal margin, the enormity of the virtually untouched Australian continent was breathtaking when compared with densely populated and heavily cultivated Java. In the open landscape of the Australian Outback a lonely homestead or small hamlet created the impression of distances that extended into sheer vastness. The immensity of the Australian land is expressed in the pithy phrase 'the Never-Never' – an apt description of the Outback's ever-receding horizons.

From our coach, the enormity of the Outback was scored by uncountable miles of barbed wire fences that cut the farm country into enormous portions. One could only wonder about the industry and fortitude of those who had dug holes in the desiccated, rock-hard soil to hold innumerable posts, between which the fence wires sometimes strung taut and shiny but often – due to neglect or the effects of time and the elements – hung in dispirited rusty loops.

On our travel through the countryside we could not help but wonder about the flocks of sheep that in their hundreds foraged the areas of red-raw soil, with its miserly covering of tough grasses and stunted shrubs. What did these animals feed on and where did they drink? And if these matters seemed enough of a struggle for their existence, then how could they possibly share their apparent little sustenance with competing mobs of kangaroos and high-legged, long-necked emus?

Sitting at the picture window of our compartment, I watched how, startled by the din of the train's wheels on their iron path, the sheep and wildlife grazing nearer to the tracks scattered in all directions. The sheep seldom ran very far before they regrouped and continued their feeding, but the kangaroos often bounded away in desperately long leaps until they judged it a safe distance to stop and stand upright, their alert little faces turned in the direction of the unwelcome intruder. Reassured when the menace was judged outdistanced, sitting on long hind legs and supporting their body weight on their powerful tails, eventually the kangaroos would tilt their heads back towards the earth to resume their peaceful feeding.

As the train continued its traverse of the Outback, it was evident that in Nature all did not always go well for the wildlife. Every now and again I was saddened to notice where a kangaroo had misjudged its great leaps for safety, or to perhaps move to a new feeding ground, and when it had become inextricably entangled in the fence wires. Paying for a fatal mistake in judgement, here and there hung a dead kangaroo, dangling head down by a leg caught in cruelly twisted wire. I would sometimes spot an unfortunate one, still half alive, hopelessly struggling against its fate. The dead and dying victims on a farmer's fence served as reminders of how transient the natural world's beauty is, and how perilous it can be for the unwary individual. In Nature the lessons of survival can be cruel to any who would disregard its caveats and dictates.

When we grew tired of looking out from the train we read, talked, and sometimes dozed off a little. The day was punctuated by morning and afternoon teas, served in the compartment by our steward, and by lunch and dinner, which we would take in the dining car. In the early evening when we returned from our meal, we would find that the steward had converted our daytime seats into four single sleeping bunks by turning up and securing the hinged backrest of the benches. On the first evening, as darkness fell over the land, weary with the emotions of our departure from Perth and the many impressions that had crowded in since, my family retired early. While the non-air-conditioned carriage had been baking hot in the daytime, during the night – despite the covering of several blankets – we suffered the surprisingly low desert temperature of the Nullarbor Plains.

On the second day of our train journey, soon after we had taken breakfast, the Overlander pulled up at a lonely siding, huffing and puffing in the vast desert, so it could take on a fresh supply of water and coal for the locomotive. Beside the track we noticed a group of men standing, their coal-black skin and tightly crinkled black hair crusted with desert dust. In the biting cold of the early morning, most wore only a loincloth, and only one or two had singlets pulled over their chest. We had not yet encountered Australia's Indigenous inhabitants – nor the colonialists' attitude towards them. We were somewhat taken aback when a fellow passenger noticed us looking at the group and volunteered, 'Don't pay them any attention or they'll be all over ya for handouts!' As he spoke, several individuals left the group beside the track and, with arms stretched out, walked from one carriage to the next, calling, 'Backie, backie!' – to which none of our fellow passengers responded. When they reached our carriage, thinking that their outstretched arms were extended in greeting, we – much to the horror of the Australians – shook hands with one of the men. He withdrew, almost recoiled, from the touch, but soon half dozen or so Aboriginal men had joined him, crying 'Backie, backie', with renewed vigour. The passenger who had spoken earlier now explained that the men were begging for tobacco. He cautioned that we must not give it to them or the whole tribe would surely come to clamour for it. With clear disapproval that we had shaken hands with an Aboriginal man, the passenger added, 'Ya mustn't let blackfellas touch ya, or shake hands with 'em. They'll only get cheekier and soon they'll be sitting next to yous in the train.' My family were shocked by this reaction; this would never happen on the plantation. Of course, it may not have been the case in all of Java, but within my family we had great respect for the local people and would never denigrate them. When we observed this situation in Australia – a sad representation of widespread attitudes – we felt we could not actually react to it; it wasn't our place. Feeling somewhat chastised about our apparent lack in understanding of what was and was not considered appropriate in these relations, we ignored any further attempts from the group outside the train to engage us. Finding that we did not respond to their entreaties, the desert dwellers moved on to try their luck at the next carriage, and the next… but always without success. In time the replenished locomotive sounded several long blasts of its whistle, its engine huffed in a series of quick exhaust shots of steam, the train slowly picked up momentum, and we were off again. Time and distance quickly swallowed up the lonely siding and the Aboriginal men who frequented it. Apart from our brief encounter with these representatives of an ancient past, the rest of our second day of train travel much resembled that of the previous one, with the arid desert of the Nullarbor Plain continuing to unfold mile upon mile upon mile of Australian countryside.

Kalgoorlie and the Overlander to Adelaide

On the third day at around noon we reached the famous mining town of Kalgoorlie, where my parents had decided to break the journey for a few days. The hotel where we stayed, the name of which I cannot recall, stood near a small monument of the olden-time prospector Paddy Hannan, famed for discovering the goldfield that would become known as 'the Golden Mile'. Soon after we had installed ourselves in our room, a fellow train passenger and Kalgoorlie local came to take us on a promised visit of his town. He had boasted that, apart from the gold mines, Kalgoorlie's beer brewery was the town's major tourist attraction: 'Our brew is the best in Australia. Until you have tasted it you haven't lived!'

The Overlander at Kalgoorlie (image courtesy Museums Victoria; Creator: Chung; https://collections.museumsvictoria.com.au/items/766532).

As we followed our guide through the streets of the town, then home to fewer than 5000 residents, he warned us that the beer factory would close at sharply five in the afternoon, and we should waste no time or we would miss out on sampling the local brew, Kalgoorlie's singularly *excellent* beverage. At the brewery he quickly guided us around huge, musty smelling steel vats that held fermenting yeast and grain and water. His guided tour of the factory did not last very long; our host soon turned to what he considered the real purpose of the visit: sampling the product. My sister and I were treated to a glass of lemonade, and were amazed when even our mother – who normally drank little alcohol but *never* beer – partook of the local brew. What was more, she did not refuse the next glass, nor the next... Thus, again and again confirmed over glasses of the local ale, in increasingly good fellowship my parents proclaimed Kalgoorlie's beer unsurpassed.

At five o'clock sharp, when the brewery's siren announced closing time, our host and both our parents were in high humour. We departed from our genial companion at the factory's front gate, where our parents earnestly assured him that Kalgoorlie's brew easily excelled any that they had ever drank. Furthermore, that we had been privileged to have met a person of obviously excellent taste and who was decidedly a gentleman. Our new friend reciprocated the compliments with similar courtesies, and after cheerful goodbyes and many a 'Sankyoo', our family set out to return to our hotel. My sister and I followed our animated parents at as discreet a distance as we dared, trying to make ourselves as inconspicuous as possible and avoiding the amused glances of passers-by to whom the reason for the demeanour of our merry parents was only too obvious.

Down the street on our way back to the hotel, my mother suddenly remembered the freezing night temperatures that we had endured on the train, and her resolve to buy extra blankets for the next leg of our journey to Adelaide and Melbourne. Unaware that in Australia blankets are usually sold in department stores, we wandered up and down one street and the next, looking for them in vain. Eventually we spotted several rugs displayed in the window of a small shop – it did not really occur to us that it was rather strange for them to be found together with hats, boots, saddles, stock whips and other equestrian gear. Still merry from the brewery visit, my parents declared that like so much else, in Australia things were different from at home, and that 'We must simply allow for it.' At least partly due to the intake of more beer than they were used to, my parents failed to explain to the young salesperson what they wished to purchase from the shop. Like many Australians did then – and still do when they have difficulty understanding halting English – the assistant reacted by raising his voice and emphasising each word: 'WHAT... CAN... I... DO... FOR... YOU... SIR, MADAM? WHAT... ARE... YOU... LOOKING... FOR?' In turn, our parents began to then also speak more loudly, which confused everyone even further, until in desperation my mother pointed to the items in the shop window, 'DAT WUN, I want DAT WUN!' The assistant's eyes lit up in understanding and he almost literally jumped to the task of taking down whole stacks of drab, grey 'blankets' from shelves along a shop wall. After a quick glance and a feel of the materials, however, my mother rejected the samples he showed her, 'No, I want not.' Pointing to an overhead shelf, she indicated a collection of gaily-coloured fabrics and declared, *'DAT I want.'* Stacked too high for the now perspiring assistant to reach them, with a brief 'I won't be a sec,' the young man rushed to the back of the shop. Returning with a ladder, he climbed up the steps, reached out, and pulled hard. The stack wobbled, and to everyone's consternation he and the bedding came tumbling down the stepladder. By now my parents were so tired of the whole business – and so sorry for the trouble and embarrassment that we had caused the hapless chap – that my mother indiscriminately picked out four of the 'blankets' from the heap, saying 'I buy diss.' The salesman wrapped up the goods, and my father paid. 'Thank you, Sir', said the clerk, to which my father replied, 'Sankyoo.' And with that we left the bewildered youth to restock the shelves in his shop and recover from tending to foreigners.

Back at the hotel, exhausted, we retired early, leaving the new purchases wrapped up for the next morning. When we awoke the next day and undid the parcel, even to our inexperienced eyes, in the full daylight the multi-coloured coverings looked strangely unlike any blanket that we had ever seen. Stating the rather obvious, my mother commented, 'They are colourful,' and few would have contradicted her. Perhaps what we had purchased was not exactly what we had thought, but, '*In Australia...*'

Due to board the Overlander again at midday, we had left packing our cases until after breakfast. We soon discovered that the new 'blankets' could not fit inside our ports, but my father solved the problem by strapping one each to the lid of a valise. When we vacated our room and placed our luggage in the hotel foyer, I noticed the receptionist and other guests glancing at them with amusement. The reason for it escaped me until someone remarked, 'Going to the races today?' I was very young and vulnerable, an impressionable child, and although my command of the English language was not great, I understood the stranger's comment only too well. I almost died in agony of embarrassment as it dawned on me that the 'blankets' must really be Australian *horse rugs*, more colourful than the drab grey ones on our horses at home. Being strapped to our suitcases and discomfortingly on public display, from that time on I hated the detestable, gaudy, 'blanket'. The mirth I imagined they would elicit from those we came past on our travels made me feel an oddity, an object and cause of ridicule. A small mercy, admittedly, thanks to the otherwise objectionable horse rug, on the next legs of our train travel we no longer suffered the night-time's freezing temperatures.

The next day the Overlander again halted at a small railway siding. It was here that we discovered that Australian states operated their train services on different railway gauges. As a result, at the siding travellers had to disembark and transfer to a new train bound for Adelaide. In the complete absence of a porter service, passengers had to transport their own baggage between the trains. 'When in Australia we simply have to adapt,' my resigned father again declared. Small consolation was that an enterprising local resident sold travellers cups of hot tea liberally laced with sweetened condensed milk, which helped thaw out freezing cold bodies and mend ruffled moods.

I do not recall much of the rest of the journey to Adelaide. With the great emptiness of the Nullarbor Plains behind us, we began to pass smaller and larger settlements and increasingly also large towns as we neared Adelaide. We were all looking forward to the end of our Overland journey.

Kangaroo Island

It is both a platitude and a debatable fact that all cities are much the same. In a sense, what we found in Adelaide when compared with Perth *was* much of the same. On street corners here stood the paper boy, whose cries echoed up and down the road and nearby lanes. And here, too, we explored the city on foot, shopped, visited a museum and the Botanic Gardens, or went on family picnics – this time beside Adelaide's River Torrens. Much to my sister's delight, and mine, we sometimes hired a dinghy that we children were allowed to row, and in which the family explored Adelaide from on the water. However, all cities being much alike, after a week and a bit our family tired of this sightseeing. On advice from the local travel bureau, we took a small ferry to Kingscote, on the intriguingly named Kangaroo Island off the South Australian mainland.

I do not recall much about the sea crossing to the island, except that reasonably calm weather conditions prevailed – fortunate for my seasickness-prone father. The ferry took some three or four hours to reach the island's wharf, where we boarded a bus to the town of Kingscote. From there we would travel on to the small coastal village of American River, renowned for its sport fishing (of special interest to my father), where we had booked guesthouse accommodation.

At Kingscote we were met by a representative of the village. I clearly remember that neither the waiting motorcar nor its chauffeur inspired much confidence, and that these impressions were not altogether unreasonable. The venerable Chevrolet vehicle's dented body and flaking paint aroused suspicion about its mechanical condition under the bonnet. Our chauffeur introduced himself with, 'Name's Colin.' Being barely adolescent, although he was pleasantly spoken and generally helpful to us, his tender age did not improve our confidence in his ability to handle a motorcar. But under the circumstances, and with no alternative, we simply had to trust that the tired old car and its youthful driver could deliver us to our destination. Colin strapped our luggage to the old-fashioned luggage rack at the back of the vehicle, and we settled ourselves on worn seats. A sluggish motor under the car's bonnet sputtered into life and, after a rather alarming clanging and grating of gears, we were off!

We had only travelled a mere few hundred yards outside the town when the asphalt ended and the road became a dirt track, slick with mud churned up by earlier traffic. As the vehicle lurched through a pothole, our driver cheerily understated the obvious: 'It'll be a bit slippery, you'd better hang on.' Pointing to the grey sky above, he explained, 'Its winter, see, and we get a lot of rain this time of the year. Doesn't do the road much good.' All around a fine drizzle fell. On inadequately treaded – almost bald – tires, the Chevrolet kept slipping and sliding from one side of the dicey road to the other. While our young friend seemed unperturbed, this was certainly not the case with his passengers. It did not help that, steering with one hand and gesticulating in the air with the other, Colin had evidently decided that he would point out the island's tourist sights to us. This he did with an almost unbroken stream of words – 'See, that's where...'; 'There you have...'; 'Look, that is...' – punctuated by gestures. We were left wishing that our enthusiastic, self-appointed tour guide should rather concentrate on his driving. If there is truth in the saying that all bad things will pass, then it is fortunately also true that good things will surely follow, and after a nail-biting trip we eventually reached the American River township – thankfully safe and sound.

Our impression of American River was that – like many small Australian settlements of the time – it looked in need of material care. A lot of its dwellings were wanting more than licks of paint and the sea air had badly rusted many corrugated iron roofs. On the day we arrived, only a few people could be seen on the street – winter's cold grip evidently discouraged inhabitants from being unnecessarily exposed to the elements, and even the village dogs seemed resigned to let us pass unchallenged, staying curled up somewhere warm.

However, the impression of unwelcoming bleakness that enveloped American River changed a few hundred metres out from the village where appeared a sign bearing the name The Haven. We turned into a short driveway and Colin announced, 'This is it!' With our limited command of the English language, we misread the name of our hostel as 'The Heaven' – in a most encouraging way, it belied our doubts about what to expect at American River. Situated on a large block of land, the guesthouse was a typical example of Australian period architecture. Like many of the country's contemporary homes it was built up on stumps, clad in weatherboard and topped with a bull-nose corrugated-iron roof. A set of stairs led up to a large, open veranda outfitted with chairs and tables. These were currently vacated, but under more clement conditions provided a spot where guests could enjoy views of a neatly kept lawn and cheerful flower beds and shrubs, which even at this time of the year provided colour. The guesthouse exuded a feeling of genuine warmth and cheer, and the welcome we received from amiable hosts Mr and Mrs Larsen encouraged us further. 'Danish, you know, a couple of generations back', they cheerfully informed us. 'Here, let us help you.' Chatting gaily all the while, the Larsens even lent a hand with carrying some of our luggage to our rooms. 'Make yourselves comfortable, afternoon tea will be in half an hour – come and join us,' our hosts said, leaving us to settle in to our accommodation.

On closer inspection, our rooms were spotless and adequately furnished with cupboards, shelves and a stand with ceramic wash bowls and water jugs. On the beds the white linen sheets and pillow slips were stiffly starched, and with enough blankets provided – we did not have to make use of our horse rug 'blankets', which at least to me came as a relief. It did not take us long to unpack our suitcases, and when this had been completed we joined our hosts for the promised afternoon tea in the kitchen – in pre-central heating times the warmest place in Australian homes, hotels and similar establishments alike.

Later, in the common room that Mrs Larsen referred to as 'the parlour', our hosts kept up an amiable conversation. 'You *have* to meet our Mr and Mrs Darcy. They live in the village, but they've been overseas, you know, to England. That's close to Holland, where you people are from, isn't that right?' My parents tried to make the Larsens see that on Java we were nowhere near England, nor for that matter close to Holland but, 'Oh, yeah?' Mrs Larsen's reply was not very convincing – although the warmth and sincerity of their hospitality was and remained real and generous.

A major attraction of our stay at American River was to almost daily join Mr Larsen in his 46-foot trawler. A fisherman by trade, but now retired, weather permitting Mr Larsen often took his guests on trips around the island and to reefs teeming with marine life. With many years of experience at sea, Mr Larsen always managed to find the best spots to begin the day's sport, and judging that we had reached the right location, would call 'ST-A-A-ND CLEAR!' With a great rattling of the chain as it unwound off the drum, he dropped the anchor. Next, he would cheerfully announce, 'Let's FISH!' And with baited lines hitting the water, the entertainment began.

Wherever our skipper took us out to sea, the fish proved plentiful, and no sooner did a multi-baited line splash into the water then the hungry creatures took the feed on one, two, sometimes three hooks at a time. Colin, the youth who had chauffeured us, now doubled as a deck hand on Mr Larsen's boat. He assisted the more squeamish guests with baiting their hooks with live shrimp, and with unhooking the catch when they had caught a fish. The small fry were tossed back into the sea, and fish of good size ended up in a large wooden drum filled with seawater, where they swam around 'for later', as Mr Larsen replied laconically when someone asked what he intended to do with them.

The skipper's cryptic reply, 'for later', became clear as lunchtime approached. The multi-talented youth, Colin, had now turned ship's cook. While the passengers continued fishing, from on deck we could see Colin busy himself preparing the meal in the open galley. First he dipped a net into the drum, bringing it up full of thrashing live fish that he emptied out into the kitchen sink. One at a time, with quick strokes of flashing knife, he deftly produced perfect, fresh, succulent fillets ready for the pan. It all happened so fast that, head, bones and tail intact and still convulsively alive, when the dismembered beast was thrown overboard it swam away, only to be cannibalised by its fellows lurking somewhere in the deep. One severed fish after another thus being returned to the sea, when lunch was later served there were several among the more fastidious passengers who passed up the beautifully golden, pan-fried fish fillets that attested to the cook's skill.

In the early evening, after dinner, The Haven's proprietors called for a 'singalong' around the pianola in the parlour. Selecting a music roll from their generous collection, Mrs Larsen loaded the pianola, and, feet pumping the paddles of the instrument, her husband produced the music to which everyone who knew the words sang along. Some reminders of a past gentle period, for our singalongs I remember learning popular tunes, folk classics of the times, such as *Gypsy Melody, Goodbye Melbourne Town, The Road to Gundagai*, and others, which, I daresay, have probably been forgotten by many people not of my generation. In our modern times these jolly melodies have been drowned out by the cacophonies of today's 'music' – which to many people of my generation are almost offensively discordant.

Our stay on Kangaroo Island came to an unexpected end. On a rainy day when Mr Larsen decided against fishing, we and two other guests decided to visit a particular tourist spot. Our host offered, 'The young fella'll take you to see the seals,' and we crammed into the Chevrolet, to be driven by Colin. Our driver again had mostly one hand on the steering wheel, waving the other one in the air and describing the sights. Rain had made the dirt road extremely slippery, but in spite of the adverse conditions our chauffeur again drove quite fast. This began to only worry not only us, but another of the Australian passengers, who directed Colin to 'Slow down a bit mate, will ya?' But to little avail. A fairly predictable result eventuated – Colin was unable to correct a bad skid and the old Chevrolet went into an unstoppable slide, careering off the road and into the bushes. The crash happened in a flash, and when the vehicle came to a bumpy stop, badly shaken, everyone got out of the fortunately still upright vehicle. At first it seemed that we had survived the mishap with little worse damage to ourselves than some scratches and bruises – until we noticed my father, who was bleeding profusely from a broken nose. He had been sitting on the side of the car where it had hit a small tree, and had struck his face on one of the old-fashioned wooden hoops that held up the vehicle's canvas roof. Efforts to staunch the bleeding were unsuccessful, and one of our fellow passengers declared, 'There's nothing for it mate, I'll have to set your nose.' Before anyone had time to object, the 'bush doctor' gave my parent's badly skewed organ a quick twist, and my father uttered an involuntary yelp. My mother exclaimed, 'My goodness, my goodness,' and my sister and I cried tears of terror. Surveying his handiwork, the Good Samaritan congratulated my father and himself, 'Job well done, mate.' With typical, sardonic Australian humour, he added, 'Big improvement from how you looked before. You're now so handsome that your own mother wouldn't recognise you – and I daresay the Missus won't object either!'

On getting back to The Haven, my parents decided to return to Adelaide to have the repaired facial injury checked by a qualified medical doctor. If all should be found well, we would then continue our visit of the eastern states, taking the train to Melbourne. Thus decided, the next morning we departed, warmly farewelled by Mr and Mrs Larsen and fellow guests at The Haven. The hospitality and camaraderie that we had enjoyed at American River, the evening's singalongs around the pianola, the cook's unforgettable filleting of fish, even the car crash, remain treasured memories of our visit to Kangaroo Island.

Tasmania

Back in Adelaide, we stayed at the Grosvenor Hotel, where we had stayed previously. The bellboy, who remembered us, looked my father up and down and cheekily asked, 'How's the other man, Sir?' Not understanding the question, when my father asked him what he meant, the young chap quipped, 'Looks like you copped one on the nose, Sir, but I bet you taught the other bloke a lesson.' Together with our bush doctor's wisecrack at the site of the car crash, I added this one from the bellboy to a growing repertoire of Australian humour.

A doctor's visit in Adelaide confirmed that there was no lasting damage to my father's injured nose, and a day or two later we travelled on to Melbourne; this time not on the Overlander but by an interstate train. After several days of sightseeing in and around that city, on advice from a travel bureau we boarded the ferry to Tasmania. It now being winter, we hoped to see snow on Mount Wellington, near Hobart. The overnight ferry terminating at Devonport, we travelled to Hobart by bus and then by taxi to the appropriately named Halfway Hotel on the slopes of Mount Wellington. With Tasmania experiencing unseasonably warm weather for the time of year, the Hobart taxi driver informed us that the snow that had earlier covered the higher parts of the mountain had melted. 'Don't worry, it'll soon snow again,' he promised when he noticed my sister's and my disappointment.

Situated part way up Mount Wellington, our stay at the Halfway Hotel on a small rural holding became another memorable experience of our Australian holiday. Waiting for the taxi driver's promise that it would snow again to come true, my sister and I took solace in being allowed to hand-feed apples to a tame old Jersey cow, of course named Daisy. First thing in the morning we awoke to find that there was still no snow on the mountain. However, all around us the water in hollows had turned into crusts of ice and white frost made the grass in the paddock stiff underfoot, crackling as we walked to feed the old Jersey cow. We took great delight in breaking up the ice in the puddles, but all the time we waited for the mountain to turn white with the magic of snow that we knew only from Christmas cards.

For several days after arriving in Tasmania, it stayed quite warm and clear. With no change anticipated in the weather, one morning our family decided to hike to the summit of Mount Wellington. When we left the hotel, the sun shone and the day was balmy, and although we were wearing only light clothing, the exercise of walking up the mountain on a steep footpath made us perspire. After about an hour and a half on the track, we had just reached the summit of Mount Wellington when we were taken completely by surprise by a fierce, icy Antarctic wind. Blowing in from the Southern Ocean, it unleashed a raging snowstorm over the mountain and us. Heavy snow was now falling, and the blizzard wind chilled us to the marrow of our bones. With nowhere to shelter and our clothes damp with perspiration from the steep climb, the only thing for us to do was to keep moving. As quickly as possible, we needed to get back to the hotel for a change of clothes and a thorough warming near the open fire in the lounge. 'Keep walking, keep going,' our parents urged my sister and me, who otherwise would have sat down, tired from the exertion.

On the vehicular road on the lee side of the mountain, although the snow kept falling heavily, walking was easier and the temperature was comparatively milder than on the summit. We finally made it back safely and, warm in our hotel room, when we looked out of the window we found what we had come for – as far as the eye could see, the countryside had changed into a world of dazzling white; grass, trees and shrubs feet-deep in magical snow.

The next few days in Tasmania, we continued to explore the bushland in the near vicinity of the Halfway Hotel, following a network of walking trails that ran all over the mountainside. Having learned our lesson, we made sure that we were adequately dressed, or that we at least carried warm clothing with us in case it should suddenly turn cold. On one of these expeditions we chanced upon a scene that could have come straight from a children's illustrated fairytale book. We had been walking on one of the bush tracks when we suddenly came upon a small hut in the forest. Its walls were entirely constructed from neatly placed granite rocks, local material that lay strewn all over the mountainside. Above its shingle roof – from the stack of a magnificent, tall chimney of the same granite material – curled a lazy column of white smoke. A single door of hand-hewn planks, kept closed to keep out the cold, gave access to the interior of the hut. When we discovered the dwelling, part of its roof was covered with patches of snow, and icicles hung down in clusters from the eaves. The weak sunlight that shone on them made them sparkle like purest crystal. We had stumbled upon a virtual Christmas card scene.

As we stood on the track that ran past the little house, a voice called, 'Hello!' and the hut's occupant, who had obviously noticed us, appeared in the door. Tall and sparse but strong and sinewy of build, judging by his snow-white hair the man was probably in his sixties. His untroubled bright blue eyes were youthful, and as he looked us up and down, they danced with a merry sparkle. In courtly fashion, the stranger inquired, 'Whom do I have the pleasure of meeting, then?' Upon which we introduced ourselves, adding that we were guests at the Halfway Hotel and that we had come to see the snow and the forest on Mount Wellington. The man responded, 'Well, you've come to the right place at the right time, then.' He continued, 'My name is Daniel Frances Xavier… Surname is Griffiths, but you may call me Dan.' He paused, then, 'When I was born, as is the custom in all proper Irish Catholic baptisms, my parents gave me ten good Christian names, but except for Daniel Frances Xavier, I sometimes forget a few.' I remember that it greatly impressed me for a person to have been bestowed with so many given names, but I had not yet learned to distinguish probable truth from good-natured humour. But... maybe... did 'Mr Dan' actually boast ten Christian names?

With a friendly, 'Come inside, it's cold out in the open,' Dan Griffiths invited us into his cottage. We followed the local forest ranger – as he described his occupation – inside. When we had become used to the somewhat dark interior of the one-roomed dwelling, we saw it contained a large, handmade, timber table, and several straight-back wooden chairs. Also hand crafted, in one corner stood a neatly made bed. In the base of the grand chimney a large, open fireplace provided both heating and cooking facilities. Near it, Dan had cleverly fashioned a number of timber planks into shelves, on which he stored supplies of tea, sugar, flour, tins of milk, canned vegetables and meats – sufficient to last him between occasional visits to Hobart. Offering to make us a cup of tea, our host stoked the embers in the hearth into flames. These began to heat up water in the soot-blackened, cast-iron pot that hung permanently from a chain above the fire. Soon the water began to sing, and when it reached a roiling boil, Dan dipped a tin on a long handle into it for water to make our tea. 'Hot and strong, plenty of sugar and lots of sweetened condensed milk,' said the ranger as he dealt us each a mug of the steaming brew.

After our 'cuppa' and some more talk, when we left to return to the hotel, we had gone only a short distance along the track when Mr Dan surprised us, raising his voice in a beautifully clear farewelling yodel. The haunting notes of this sound followed us a long way up the mountain footpath, bouncing off the tall gum trees and reverberating among the rocks. It almost made the icicles hanging down from twigs and branches tinkle in accompaniment. Snow began to fall in fat white flecks, this time not a blizzard but a gentle albescence, softly spreading a blanket of white over the mountain wonderland.

We visited Dan Griffiths several more times during our stay on Mount Wellington, and we became quite friendly with him. A recluse by choice, as he described his way of life, Dan still cared for the chance company of people. He was a kindly man, and he treated my sister and me without the condescending and patronising tolerance that adults sometimes adopt when they interact with children. He also had a magic touch with the animals of the bush, some of which came to his hut when he called or whistled for them. Dan was an entertaining host, and his knowledge of the fauna and flora of his beloved Australian bush was fascinating. He was also a good listener when my father told stories of life on the tea plantation in the mountains of Java.

The day before we left Tasmania to return to the mainland, we paid 'Old Dan' a last visit. The time came for us to leave and we began to say farewells but, holding up a warning hand, Dan stopped us, 'One should never say goodbye,' said he, 'rather, "Till we meet again."' On the path back to the hotel, long after we lost sight of him and his magic hut, Dan's beautiful farewell yodel reverberated through the forest on Mount Wellington, melting into the sounds of white silence.

Carefree times come to an end

After our return to Melbourne, where we spent a few days sightseeing, my parents decided that instead of travelling to Sydney, we had seen enough of the eastern states. Time had slipped by all too fast; it was already the middle of August and we had to return home in September. They wanted to spend the rest of their holidays with Les Melon and Mrs Violet Forster at Scarborough. On a freezing cold winter's morning, we boarded the Overland Express in Melbourne; this time we did not break our journey at Kalgoorlie but stayed on the train all the way back to Perth. We then went by taxi to Scarborough, where we stayed for the remainder of our Australian holiday. We had barely settled back in at the Penteila Flats when, on 3 September 1939 in a radio broadcast to the Australian nation, Prime Minister Robert Menzies announced the shocking news that Britain had declared war on Germany, and that Australia was now also at war.

The start of armed hostilities in Europe would soon become an international event, but did not yet directly involve our Dutch motherland and her colonies. The effect that the war had on our Australian holiday, however, was to place our return to Java in sudden jeopardy. Upon the declaration of hostilities, the Australian Government had immediately commandeered all Australian ships, including vessels of the Blue Funnel Line, into war service. The mobilisation of shipping meant that we might not be able to return to Java by sea; and in those early days of the aviation industry, nor could we hope to travel home by air. As a result, my parents feared that we should have to stay much longer in Australia than they had planned, in the worst case until the end of war, or perhaps even for an indefinite time. We now faced the possibility that, at almost the end of a free-spending holiday, my parents' funds would run out. How then would we manage to live in Australia? Furthermore, if we did not return to the plantation, what would be the consequences? These and other worrying questions kept my parents awake many a night, while my sister and I slept the sleep of innocents.

Hoping for official representation to help us in our predicament, my father immediately took up contact with the Dutch consulate in Perth. Although the officials confirmed that the Australian Government had mobilised Australian shipping for war and that it would be difficult for private passengers to book passage to Java on a Blue Funnel ship, a glimmer of hope remained. Although the Dutch consulate was very tentative about being able to assist us, it appeared that two of the Blue Funnel Line vessels had been excluded from the general mobilisation order to maintain a freight and passenger service between Australia and Singapore. One day – after months of waiting, and to my worried parents' great relief – the consulate informed us that by sheer luck it had succeeded in booking ship's passage for us back to Java. To our amazement it was none other than our fondly remembered MV *Charon* of the Blue Funnel Line that was to return us again to the real world of Java to resume our former lives. If we had known what fate held in store for our future, it may have been better for us if we had stayed Down Under.

A dramatic departure

The day we sailed for Java, Les Melon drove us to Fremantle in his truck, and the suitably hatted and gloved Mrs Forster also came with us to the wharf where our ship lay moored. After unloading our luggage, my father and Les decided that there was plenty of time for them to visit a nearby hotel for what they called 'a last roundup'. Laughing off the women's protests, they assured my anxious mother and equally uncomfortable Mrs Forster, 'We'll soon be back.' Waiting for the men to return, time went slowly, but the longer they stayed away, the faster the minutes seemed to tick over. An hour passed, but my father and Les had not rejoined us. On the wharf and aboard ship, preparations for departure were well underway, and then the ship's siren sounded its first call for passengers to embark. A quarter of an hour later came the second warning, and by now my mother's face clearly showed anxiety. Mrs Forster paced up and down as if walking on hot coals, and we children were crying freely. It did not help us either when *Charon*'s purser came down the gangplank to urge us to come aboard, 'Now, please.' One hour after the ship's siren had first sounded came its third and last call for passengers to board, but there was still no sign of my father and Les Melon. Alongside the bollards, foreshore men began to cast off the cables with which the ship was tied, and now without any other option, we said a tearful farewell to an upset Mrs Forster. My mother, sister and I were halfway up the gangplank when a long way down the wharf Les Melon's truck came racing towards the ship. Precariously perched on a front mudguard, waving a half-empty glass of beer in his hand, sat my very merry father. Les Melon was behind the steering wheel, also with beer in hand, driving the old truck as fast as he could in and out among the cargoes and the wharfies. The truck screeched to a stop and my father dismounted. He handed his now empty beer glass to Les, and the friends vigorously shook hands. As they had promised, the men had returned – but the ship was beginning to move away from its moorings, and several feet of water now lay between ship and wharf. How should my errant parent manage to join us on board? On the ship and on land everyone held a collective breath.

A quick look at the widening gap between land and ship seemed to finally strike a note of warning in my father's beer-befuddled brain; he suddenly raced to the edge of the wharf and with a mighty leap he launched himself into the air. Whether by athletic ability, fear-induced adrenalin, or sheer good luck, he managed to land on the gangplank that still hung down *Charon*'s side. Receiving hearty applause from the public on the wharf and from passengers on board, my father climbed the gangway onto the deck where, in perhaps cheeky response to the encouragement he had received or by alcohol-fuelled bravado, he suddenly began to recite a ballad that he had picked up on one or another of his and Les Melon's visits to

Fremantle. The words, which I can now only vaguely remember, sang the praises of what were supposedly national beverages, and they went something like this:

> The Englishmen drink their warm beer
> because it gives them good cheer;
> A Scotsman's treat,
> he drinks his whisky neat;
> The Irishman drinks his toddy hot,
> to hit just the right spot;
> The French drink their red wine,
> That suits them just fine; ...
> (and so on, to reach the punchline)
> But the Aussie has no national drink,
> So he drinks the bloody lot!

This final piece of bravado earned my father another round of applause from his audience. However, it caused *Charon*'s skipper to send his purser to 'invite' my father to see him in his cabin 'For a little talk.' From the captain's cabin, my now sober parent emerged a chastised man.

After his interview with the captain, my usually ebullient father remained quiet and withdrawn. The skipper's reprimand, however, did not compare with my mother's rebuke. In the privacy of our cabin, my mother gave my father her unchecked opinion of his recklessness and lack of consideration for his family. Warming to her subject, she added what she thought of Les Melon's abetting him in the foolishness of their 'last roundup' escapade, and finished with the scolding conclusion that her husband's daring acrobatics could have resulted in injury or worse! As the possible consequences of his tomfoolery sank in, my mother's justified wrath affected Father deeply, and his remorse lasted days.

Journey back to Java
Charon sailed much closer to the coast than normal, staying well within sight of land as we headed north for Geraldton. At the outbreak of the war several German ships in Australian ports had escaped before the government could impound them. The authorities believed that some of these ostensibly cargo-carrying vessels were heavily armed, and it was feared that they could pose a threat to Allied shipping in

the Indian and Pacific oceans. A further reason for *Charon* to sail a different course was the risk, not unlikely, that enemy submarines now prowled the oceans. To avoid a chance meeting with a German raider or becoming a target for a lurking submarine, our ship took to sailing a random zigzag course. On board, as a further wartime safety measure, the *Charon* observed a complete blackout. The ship had been repainted black, including the portholes, and at night all outside lights were extinguished. After dark, we had to keep doors and portholes closed, uncomfortably raising temperatures inside the ship.

The first day at sea out from Fremantle, *Charon*'s captain made it known among the passengers that he intended to defend his ship in case of an enemy attack. When he called upon male passengers to volunteer for weapons training and other preparations for possible combat, every able-bodied male passenger – including my father – stepped forward. As The Netherlands and her colonies were neutral countries, the captain regretfully declined my father's offer to join the Australian volunteers on board. However, when he found out that my father was a hunter and a crack shot, in a compromise the captain gratefully accepted him as an adviser, teaching others the art of weapons handling and firing. Clearly, if the folly of his earlier behaviour at Fremantle had put him offside with the skipper, my father's unreserved offer to help in the defence of the ship now redeemed him in the captain's eyes.

The plan to defend the ship, though gallant in its intentions, was rather less than practical in application. For 'exercises in discipline', as the skipper called it, every morning the volunteers assembled on the fo'c'sle deck for instruction that consisted mainly of close column drill marching. '*LEFT, RIGHT, LEFT,*' the men went diligently back and forth upon the deck, and no one on board asked what purpose it could feasibly serve to fend off German pirates. When it came my father's turn to demonstrate loading and unloading ammunition, and how to shoulder and aim a rifle, again no one remarked that the ship's armoury consisted of one .303 rifle and two clips of ammunition each containing five bullets. For understandable reasons not a single shot was fired in practice shooting. The captain's intention behind this training was touching, but in reality it served little better purpose than boosting morale. It was fortunate that the occasion did not arise when *Charon* should have to defend itself against an enemy.

In spite of the nervousness on board, we reached the Western Australian port of Geraldton without trouble and without seeing any suspicious enemy shipping. Staying at Geraldton only long enough to take on some general cargo for Singapore, two more days of sailing took us to the small township of Broome – our northern-most and final port of call in Australia. Our ship reached Broome well after we had retired to our cabin for the night, and we lay awake for some time listening to what seemed like more activity than was usual for the ship to make fast to the wharf. The reason for the unusual noises became clear first thing in the morning when we awoke and, opening the porthole, saw to our amazement that the ship lay on nothing but dry land. As far as the eye could see, not a drop of water remained in which a vessel could float. This phenomenon was the result of neap tides after the moon's first and third quarters, when sometimes twenty feet or more difference could occur between ebb and flood levels. After breakfast, taking advantage of the novelty, we walked all around the ship until, first in little ripples, then in small waves, the incoming tide brought back immeasurable tons of sea water to refill Broome harbour and fully float *Charon* again.

All that morning our ship took on a cargo of live sheep destined for the Singapore markets. On the wharf below us, stockmen and members of our crew were busy herding the terrified stock into the holds. We stood at the railing on deck, witnessing the sights and sounds of rural Australia: stockmen whistled piercingly, dogs barked excitedly, and – as they went into the ship's holds – a pushing, shoving stream of sheep bleated pitifully. When there was not a woolly beast left on the wharf, the stockmen stopped their whistling. Wherever they could find shade and relief from the blazing sun, the dogs lay panting with lolling, dripping tongues. On the cusp of high tide, wharf labourers unmoored the ship and *Charon* cautiously turned away from the wharf. We were finally heading back to Java, Australia vanishing behind in the ship's wake. In the future, my wife and I would return. My mother and sister would visit us, but my father – who had given the country his heart – would never again see his beloved Australia.

Travelling with live sheep in the holds became a very unpleasant experience for passengers and crew on board *Charon*. Although the sailors had erected huge canvas funnels that hung down from the ship's riggings to blow in fresh air and reduce the temperature below decks, the breathtaking stench of ordure from thousands of penned animals penetrated every part of the vessel. Hard to bear even with open doors in the daytime, when sailing under nightly blackouts, the tainted air could not escape through windows and portholes, and conditions below deck became dreadful for everyone on board.

When we left Broome, again deviating from its normal course, *Charon* sailed an unusual northern direction that within a day or two took the ship past countless small and larger islands. These were the so-called *Buitengewesten* or 'Outer Regions' – far reaches of the archipelago that I only knew from the maps in my geography books at home. In spite of persisting fears of a surprise attack by German raider ships or submarines, nothing untoward happened, and although the trip took several days longer than normal, we arrived safely at Semarang on Java – from where, a half-year earlier, we had started our magnificent Australian adventure.

The owners of our plantation had arranged that one of them would come and 'babysit' the property while we were away, while the Indonesian overseers kept the place running; everything was in very good shape when we returned. Back at home, family and acquaintances eagerly questioned us about our holiday in what was then considered an exotic, almost unknown part of the world. My father in particular took every opportunity to relate to them our experiences in the land Down Under, describing its people as 'salt of the earth'. In the dying days of 1939, the routines of everyday life and increasing concerns over the European war soon pushed the memories of our happy holiday into the background. The war in the Northern Hemisphere would only too soon spill across the world, reaching even the as yet peaceful Dutch East Indies.

PART 2:

Childhood Lost

CHAPTER 3

Second World War

War has no fury like a non-combatant
Charles Edward Montague, *Disenchantment*

In late 1939, with faith in Holland's past neutrality in the Great War, many expatriate Dutch in Java felt at a comfortable distance from the strife in Europe. We were as yet quite safe, but in the early days of the Second World War Germany's apparent military superiority began to raise concerns. People read in the newspapers of events in Europe, and heard news broadcasts on the radio. As European nations fell one after another under an apparently unstoppable German onslaught, people wondered and worried about the eventual outcome. In the East Indies we quaked, fearing the eventual invasion of France, which had heavily fortified its Maginot Line defences in anticipation of a German attack. People began to speculate whether Holland would be next on the list of German targets, and whether – in a reverse of scorched-earth tactics – the Dutch nation would carry out plans to deliberately breach its famous system of dykes, inundating the country along its borders with Germany. When the day came that Germany launched its '*Blitzkrieg*', simultaneously attacking a number of neighbouring countries, the French and Dutch defensive strategies failed miserably. In May of 1940, the Germans invaded and conquered the Low Countries, including the Netherlands, then moved on to France. In spite of evidence to the contrary, Dutch East Indies armchair strategists continued to reason that the occupation of the motherland could only last briefly. In the East

Indies colony, many believed that the war in faraway Europe could not and would not reach us. Among those who thought differently was my mother. On one of our shopping trips into the town, she prophetically warned, 'I do not know what is happening in Holland, but I do not like hearing about events in Japan. There is a witches' brew bubbling in the cauldron. Heaven forbid that it spills over and reaches us in Indië.'

In the late months of 1940, there came signs of Japan's increasing appetite for expansion, following its invasions of Manchuria and China. Even so, few in the East Indies considered it feasible that Japan's conquests in northern Asia could spill over into the Southeast Asian countries. In my childhood anything labelled 'Made in Japan' was considered shoddy and poor quality. Similarly, a 'Made in Japan' warlike move towards the Dutch in Java was commonly considered an unthinkable fantasy.

Early hints of approaching conflict

A year after Britain's declaration of war, in 1940 Japan joined forces with Germany. The Dutch East Indies community reacted with disdain to what it regarded as preposterous military opportunism. The sanguine comfort we took in being a culturally and materially superior white race made us believe that we had little to fear from the nuisance of a meddling Asian upstart. Even so, although the Dutch colonial government and the public at large basked in their self-assurance and disdain for the Japanese, our authorities instigated a large-scale propaganda campaign aimed at reassuring the population. Throughout the archipelago, caricatured posters appeared depicting the Japanese with narrow-eyed, bespectacled faces wearing stupid grins, and showing ape-like Japanese soldiers armed with broken or bizarre weaponry. In retrospect the irony became clear that this campaign intimated we *did* have a potential enemy to fear.

While the practicality of the poster campaign was questionable, it did serve to create suspicions about the presence and purpose of expatriate Japanese persons living in the Dutch East Indies. This sentiment affected a Japanese business family in our town, Mr and Mrs Mikimori. Ugly rumours would have it that they were *agents provocateurs* sent to the Dutch East Indies to organise a fifth column of traitors and Japanese

This anti-Japanese war poster shows the growing threat of Japan, with Holland encouraging the Dutch East Indies people to work for victory ('Indie moet vrij! [Indie must be free!]' by Pat Keely, 1944. Image courtesy of the Australian War Memorial [ARTV10465]).

sympathisers. People even began to shun and sometimes abuse our previously well-regarded Japanese shopkeeper, Mr R Arai, whom it was presumed was a spy with the rank of colonel in the Japanese army. Clumsy and childish though it was, the poster campaign did influence public thinking, and throughout the Dutch East Indies grew anti-Japanese sentiment and disdain for 'the yellow monkeys'. At least some of the Dutch commented on how awful the propaganda was, but very little was spoken about with other people; there was some avoidance of speaking in public about the Japanese. My family knew very little about Japan or its culture or people, but we felt sorry for the Japanese people we knew.

In the earlier months of the 1940s, radio bulletins and newspaper reports of the situation in the Northern Hemisphere had turned ugly.

As my mother had forecast, our elders worried that it looked as if the 'witches brew' in Japan *was* threatening to spill over. Despite the sinister portents of coming change, life in the Dutch colony continued much as it had done for nearly four centuries. For me, having completed the Dutch Primary Grade 6 curriculum, in early August 1940, I successfully passed the prescribed examinations to progress to First Year at High School. Due to commence in September 1941, my parents decided that I would begin my secondary education in our regional city of Semarang, which had superior educational facilities than those in our nearby shopping town of Pekalongan. The prospect of boarding in the city thrilled me, and with a child's unintentional thoughtlessness I looked forward to leaving the parental home.

Although my sister had one more year of primary education to complete, it was decided that she, too, would attend school in the city. If any of this hurt my mother's professional pride and motherly feelings, she did not allow herself to let us know it. Her capacity to hide her deepest sentiments was evidence of a grit that no one suspected; this strength of spirit would be of inestimable value to us in the not-so-distant future.

Three months after I had commenced high school at Semarang, after a weekend visit home in November, my parents decided not to let my sister and me return to the city. Increasing tensions between the United States of America and Japan had become worrying. At almost year's end, few Dutch in the East Indies yet realised the catastrophe which lay mere days ahead.

War in the Pacific

On the morning of 7 December 1941, when my father tuned in to the radio, news came of a surprise Japanese air attack on Hawaii, destroying most of the American Pacific Fleet in Pearl Harbour. With it, war in the Southern Hemisphere had begun. Neither Dutch East Indian officialdom nor the general public foresaw the consequences of the Pacific War on the Dutch Empire and its citizens.

Two days after the calamity of Pearl Harbour, on 9 December 1941, my father joined his Army Reserves Unit on active military duty in the city of Cheribon. At the time, much was made of the assumed inferiority of Japan's fighting forces, and of the inverse superiority of the

Royal Dutch East Indian Army; the latter, it was asserted, being ready to meet any improbable attack on home soil. In the early days of war in the Pacific – not just in the East Indies, but also further abroad – the public seemed not to realise that the virtually invincible Japanese army was on an unrelenting march towards Singapore, ultimately posing a threat to the Dutch East Indies. The ostrich's head-in-the-sand attitude of the Dutch in the East Indies would soon be punished by raw reality.

Soldiers during the Dutch East Indies Athletics Union march, Surabaya, 1937. The distinctive uniform is what Ferdinand's father wore when he reported for duty (Image courtesy of Tropenmuseum, part of the National Museum of World Cultures, CC BY-SA 3.0 <https://creativecommons.org/licenses/by-sa/3.0>, via Wikimedia Commons).

The Japanese onslaught continued, with Thailand the first to fall. Next, with fierce fighting on the Malay Peninsula, the British Army desperately tried to halt the Japanese war machine invading its territory. Attempting to justify what were obvious Japanese military conquests, Allied propaganda euphemistically portrayed defeat after defeat not as retreats and territorial losses, but as a tactic of 'regrouping our forces at predetermined strongholds'. Inexplicably, and in spite of much evidence to the contrary, in the Dutch East Indies the official and public belief persisted that Japanese soldiers were ineffectual, poorly equipped and not well-trained fighters, and that their 'slant-eyed' pilots were of little consequence in air battles with our aviators. When next Malaya fell, the

Allied propaganda campaign turned to convince the public that the tide of war would surely turn at 'invincible' fortress Singapore. But when, against all faith and hope, Japan invaded Singapore Island on 8 February 1942, nothing stood between Japan's Imperial Army and the Dutch East Indies. Against all logic the Dutch view persisted, 'We will beat the Japs!'

In the aftermath of the fall of Singapore, unending columns of Allied military vehicles evacuating British and Allied soldiers from Singapore to Australia, began to choke the roads leading from Java's west to its eastern seaports. Without really knowing what we were afraid of, we held grave fears for my father. And still the Dutch community in the Indies persisted with its ostrich-like denial, refusing to admit that war had now arrived and the Japanese Army was on our doorstep. On 3 March 1942, in a radio broadcast from his palace in Batavia, the Governor General of the Dutch East Indies announced that the country was under attack from Japan. On that fateful day, reality had to be confronted; the long-denied actuality of war had reached us.

In the mid-morning after the Governor General's radio broadcast, my mother, sister and I were taking morning tea under the pergola on the terrace. With an almost unimpeded 180 degrees of vision, from our vantage point high on the mountain we overlooked the Java Sea for hundreds of kilometres to the east and to the west, as far even as the city of Cheribon where my father presently served with his army unit. In good weather the northern coastline was normally clearly visible from the plantation, but that morning a thick fog prevented us from seeing much of the lowlands bordering the Java Sea. In the distance out to sea we could hear a continuous, deep rumbling noise, somewhat like – but different from – the thunder that follows lightning. After the Governor General's radio broadcast, too dejected to listen to any further and possibly worse news, my mother had turned off the radio. It was not until later, when word of mouth from our coastal connections reached us, that we learned that the 'thunder' we had heard had been a naval battle between ships of our small fleet and an attacking Japanese armada.

The Japanese had annihilated our valiant though utterly outnumbered Royal Dutch Navy. However, even with this latest defeat, there were many Dutch who believed that although we had lost at sea, 'Our army will beat the Japs on land.' A few days later Japanese storm troops invaded Java on the northern coast of the island near Cheribon. After a few days of ineffectual resistance, the once proud Royal Dutch East Indies Army capitulated to the victorious Imperial Japanese Army. It would be many years before we heard that the fighting on land had been near where my father's army unit was stationed, and discovered what had become of him.

Japanese occupation

After our army surrendered to the Japanese, the enemy's occupation spread throughout the archipelago. Before the invasion there had been much talk of Japanese atrocities perpetrated on the civilian populations of Manchuria and China, and, it was rumoured, in Burma, Malaya and on Singapore Island. There was great fear, especially among the women, about what could happen at the hands of the Japanese, but my sister and I remained blissfully ignorant. We didn't know what it meant to be invaded – there was no precedent and we were too young to fully understand. While the truth of certain atrocities was later confirmed, our own experience of the Japanese storm troops that captured Java was that they were strictly disciplined by their High Command. I recall that the Imperial Japanese Army Command maintained a tight military discipline and control over its invasion forces, and that it issued *written advice* to the general public that any misdemeanour perpetrated by any Imperial soldier would be harshly punished. In the early stages of their conquest of the East Indies, although the Japanese were contemptuous of the expatriate Dutch, their officers and troops generally conducted themselves commendably.

Spreading rapidly from Batavia, in short time the Japanese succeeded in occupying the entire chain of islands that now constitutes the Indonesian archipelago. When eventually an army occupation unit reached our town of Pekalongan, a sizeable crowd of Javanese had gathered and – to the shock of many whites – they met our enemy soldiers with cheers and applause. It was naive, even arrogant, that in these early days of the occupation the Dutch dismissed signs of local nationalist sentiment as the work of 'a few malcontents and traitors'. Many Dutch believed that most of 'our natives' remained loyal to us: 'They love us and they are thankful for what we have done for them.' Few questioned if, after 350 years of colonial rule, the 'natives' may have had a different opinion, asking not what we Dutch had done *for* them, but, rather, what we had done *to* them.

The Japanese conquerors initially did little more than introduce a few petty and sometimes irritating changes to former ways of life and business in the East Indies. One of these, a rather silly measure, was to replace local time with Japanese time, resulting throughout the country in noon *today* becoming 4 am *yesterday*. A more important step was the Japanese replacement of Dutch East Indies currency with Japanese occupation money; no more than mere promissory paper currency that looked, felt, and even smelt 'Made in Japan' – at the time synonymous with cheap rubbish. Dutch and Javanese alike distrusted this occupation lucre, and although prohibited by the Japanese, silver Dutch coinage remained the preferred tender. Somewhat like a drowning person clamping onto anything that offered hope, some argued that this proved 'our natives' remained loyal to the Dutch Empire and rejected the Japanese.

The conquest of the Dutch East Indies in 1942 drew the East Indies into Japan's expansionist dream of the Greater Asia Co-prosperity Sphere. Presented with the slogan 'Asia for the Asians', some of Indonesia's aspiring leaders discovered that the Japanese 'liberators' merely replaced the former Dutch colonial administration with arguably a more ferocious military rule. Although elements of the local population appeared to have welcomed the Japanese, for a long time the greater part of their countrymen remained undecided as to who they should support; the devil we know, or the one we don't? Not surprisingly, in case the 'Asia for the Asians' slogan should fail, many Javanese decided to put off committing themselves to one side or the other.

At the start of war in the Pacific, many if not most Dutch believed that the conflict could only last weeks, a few months at most. They were staunchly convinced that 'the Japs can never stand up for long against the British and their allies.' Few if any of our people would admit that the Imperial Japanese Army had proved every 'armchair expert' and every commentator wrong with their relentless military conquests. And this formidable enemy was now on Australia's doorstep.

CHAPTER 4

The Interregnum

*I carry all my possessions with me
(Omnia mea porto mecum)*
Cicero, *Paradoxa Stoicorum*

Having conquered the strategic land mass to the north of Australia, before embarking on an attack on this last goal, the Japanese war machine allowed its hard-pressed troops a rest. Their military and later occupation administrations had a direct effect on my family and on our plantation on Java. The Japanese foresaw at least a temporary need for Dutch and Chinese business and technical expertise to keep the country functioning as normally as possible. The seeming benevolence of the resulting 'interregnum' lulled many expatriates into a false sense of security and, as we would soon enough find out, an unwarranted complacency about the reality of life under Japanese occupation.

Keeping the plantation running

In the early stages of the war, the Japanese occupation policy required that our tea, rubber and cinchona plantation remained operating – in particular for the purpose of producing raw rubber, an essential wartime supply. In the absence of my father – of whom we had heard nothing; we did not know if he was alive or had been killed in action – the Japanese policy presented my mother with a considerable problem. Born and raised in the immediate post-Victorian era with still hidebound ideas of the right and proper roles of men and women, in order to comply with the Japanese demands she would have to run the plantation business herself. While our Indonesian Hoofd Mandur (Chief Overseer) had so far managed the plantation's routine maintenance work, he lacked commercial and financial business expertise. With no option but to submit to the pressure of Japanese demands to keep the plantation production going, my mother made unprecedented changes in Dutch colonial and Indonesian social custom. This was a courageous initiative, and not an easy one. Decades later an acquaintance remarked that though my mother physically resembled an exquisite porcelain Dresden doll, the core of her inner being was pure steel.

In any culture, language reflects the warp and woof of social fabric – but arguably nowhere more so than in Javanese society. In that light, the business and management strategy that my mother devised was a masterful mix of pragmatism and canny insight. She knew that the Javanese on the plantation valued *alus* (politeness) in behaviour and speech, and abhorred *kasar* (rudeness and crude directness), a lack of polite manners. After some time, the plantation staff – from Hoofd Mandur to humble labourer – changed the form of address they used towards my mother. Previously *Ndoro Njonja* (Grand Lady), with the title *Kandjeng Ndoro Njonja* (Excellency, Grand Lady) – by implication 'Boss' – my mother knew that the plantation community had accorded her the respect that had previously been reserved for my father.

My mother knew that, as far as the daily cycle of plantation activities was concerned, all eyes on the plantation would be judging her every move. She was astute enough to realise that she knew little about the cycle of pruning and harvesting, the maintenance in the tea gardens, or the tapping and processing of sap from the rubber trees. Where my mother wisely left these tasks to our Hoofd Mandur, Pak (Mr) Wardjo, the real stroke of genius in her strategy was that she treated him not merely as an employee, but as a valued senior advisor in the plantation's business. She collaborated closely with Pak Wardjo, avoiding any tension by sharing the decision making. In the end, they made a very good combination.

An uncommon friendship – Soekarno

The new social climate allowed me to establish a friendship with a Javanese boy of my age, Soekarno, son of Pak Wardjo – something that would not have been possible in colonial pre-war times. It is a matter of historical truth that until the Second World War, people of different races in the Dutch East Indies rarely, if ever, mixed socially. To be sure, I think that this was based less on racial prejudice, and more a matter of mutually valued customs and traditions. This meant that, before the war, although hundreds of Indonesian children lived in the kampongs (villages) surrounding us, my sister and I had no one but each other with whom to associate and play. My chief playmate, besides my sister, was my beloved dog, Mickey. We had a real bond, and he would accompany me on my plantation wanderings. One contributing factor to the pre-war division between white and brown children was the matter of their respective education. Other than the Indonesian overseers and more senior technical staff, most plantation workers and their children were illiterate. Contrary to the 'education' that many Indonesian boys received at Islamic schools – where they learned little more than to read and quote from the Qur'an – Pak Wardjo had insisted that Soekarno follow the same Dutch correspondence education that my sister and I received. Through its expedient contrivance, Soekarno and I were equals; our camaraderie easily ignored and straddled the racial gap. When I befriended Soekarno, both he and I broke with long-established tradition, and – at the time unbeknown to us – our friendship would have far-reaching consequences for my family.

My chief playmate, besides my sister, was my beloved dog, Mickey.

When Soekarno came into my life, we must have been about eleven or twelve years old. I don't remember what started our association or why we became friends; what comes to mind are the many adventures we shared. I remember that Soekarno and I had a unique way of calling each other when we wanted to meet. At that time the plantation had but one single telephone to connect us with the outside world. It was long before the nowadays ubiquitous mobile phone – no one in the world even dreamed of such a means of communication. I called Soekarno by imitating the yodelling call of Johnny Weismuller in the *Tarzan* film series – a heroic figure, he would swing from tree to tree on a daring mission to rescue man or beast from the jungle.

During the week we would both attend our respective primary schools. If I planned to meet with Soekarno for the weekend, I would climb the hill to our swimming pool, directly above where Soekarno and his family lived in the small plantation kampong. I would stand on the large pipeline, which transported water down to the turbines driving the machinery in the factory, and supplying electricity to our homes and the plantation kampong. At the very edge of the escarpment I would copy Tarzan's unique call. Although it sounded magnificent in the picture theatre and set one's heart racing with admiration for the champion of the African jungle, it was debatable that *my* Tarzan's call sounded quite as stirring; but it *could* be heard a very long distance.

The Japanese occupation of the Indies interrupted our Dutch education for the entire length of the war, but I am uncertain if or how the war affected Soekarno's schooling. It is probably safe to assume that he would have furthered his learning in the sovereign Indonesian Republic's education system. At the time of the occupation, however, since all formal teaching had ceased and my mother had no means of continuing her instruction of me, I did not have to attend school. This meant that my friend and I had ample time to pursue things of interest.

When I taught Soekarno to use my 8 mm Flobert rifle to hunt small game, my friend in return showed me the art of setting snares to catch birds, or if we were lucky a bush fowl. Some days we went for long adventure walks on the steep and slippery bush tracks around the plantation, and at other times we fished for trout in a swift mountain stream. On these hunting expeditions we would leave Mickey at home, fearing that he would, in his excitement, chase off our quarry. Despite this, probably lacking skill or the right equipment, we never shot, snared nor caught any of the prey. When we grew tired of this unfruitful pastime, we swam amongst huge granite boulders in the fast-flowing river; the current had gouged out deep natural pools, the waters swirling in a roaring rush on its urgent way to the faraway sea. On a few occasions, carrying a small tent, gear and provisions, Soekarno and I went camping in the bush. In the evening we cooked our meal of rice, a few vegetables and the Javanese staple of salted fish, which we roasted over the embers of a smoky but picturesque campfire.

Soekarno and I continued hunting small game the whole time we were friends. If we were successful, for admittedly rather more selfish reasons than out of generosity, I always gave our kill to my friend to take to his home – because then I did not have to give it to Kokki to cook, whereupon I would have had to eat it. Even if he had known my reasons, I do not think that Soekarno would have minded, and he always graciously accepted the offer: '*Baik. Terima kassih, bung.*' ('Fine. Thank you, my friend.')

Through my friendship with Soekarno I received yet another glimpse into the culture of people in the land of my birth. Walking around in the tea plantations, but especially when we entered the brooding forest, we were always on guard in case we encountered deer, dangerous wild pigs and other smaller game. However, much more frightening was the possibility of meeting certain real or imagined creatures, which local wisdom, legend or myth suggested might inhabit the deepest interior of the jungle.

Not just Soekarno but other Indonesian people, even some family members and certain of my parents' social contacts in our shopping town, spoke about what they claimed were 'true' encounters with spirits, ghosts and other apparitions – stories that made the hair on my neck stand up and gooseflesh rise on my arms. Whether truth or myth, in the forest where we hunted neither Soekarno nor I ever saw any *memreng* or *bawong* – supposedly otherworldly beings, mythical centaurs and Minotaurs. Admittedly this did not prevent me from being excited – and also frightened – by wondering 'What if...?'

Much more believable were the peacocks that Soekarno mentioned. He said that old people in the villages on and around the plantation believed the birds lived in the jungle, but we never personally saw one. *Actually* true was the existence of *adjag*, the 'wolves' or more correctly wild dogs that lived in the deep forest. People had in fact seen these creatures, particularly in the Diengs, a chain of high mountain country in Central Java. My friend and I fortunately never had to encounter either the fabled beings or the wild dogs of living legend. Neither did we run into wild pigs or a panther, which we knew really *did* exist. Had we done so, what good would have been my small rifle and Soekarno's snares?

It is often in retrospect that the meaning behind an incident can fall into place, sometimes many decades after it occurred. One day in 1940, before the outbreak of war in the Pacific, I had met up with my friend Soekarno. We had swum in the reservoir that was our swimming pool, and we were lazing around in the sun when Soekarno offered, 'I will teach you my new song.' He then sang me a tune, and attempted to teach me the words of it. Later, Soekarno warned me, 'You must not sing this song when adults can hear you.' When, puzzled, I asked him why not, Soekarno replied, 'Because your *Orang Belanda* won't like it.' At the time I did not understand his explanation, but I remember being somewhat dismayed at the way in which he uttered the phrase 'Orang Belanda' – Indonesian for 'Dutch'. It was only later, during the war, that I realised Soekarno's song was what became the Indonesian national anthem: *Indonesia Raya*.

I believe my friend Soekarno teaching me his song proved two highly emotional points. Firstly, by obviously and unmistakably taking me into his confidence, Soekarno demonstrated true friendship, trust, and a liking of me. I have never, even in dark despair, forgotten his affection – what is called, in the Australian idiom, 'mateship'. Secondly, I still remember that he referred to my family as 'Orang Belanda' when he had never before used this word for the Dutch race in connection with us. When he pronounced that phrase in a certain tone of voice, I sensed – though I could not yet truly comprehend – the active dislike, if not enmity, that Soekarno and his people held towards my race. Looking back down the line of time, I now know that my friend in that moment had driven the beginning of a wedge between us, which only the passage of time and mutual goodwill would eventually repair.

The Interregnum

The Harley

After the occupation of Java, we no longer received mail on the plantation and, as my mother could not drive our motorcar, we could no longer travel to town to do the shopping. Typically for her, my mother solved the problem. One day she said to me, 'I want you to learn to ride your father's Harley Davidson so that if we need help we have some way in which to contact people in town.' For a thirteen-year-old boy, this was like a dream come true – except that neither she nor I had any idea how I should learn to handle the large, heavy and very powerful 750cc motorcycle. When I told Soekarno of the dilemma he reassured me, 'I will speak with my father. He will know what to do.'

True to Soekarno's promise, the next morning Pak Wardjo and our tea factory mechanic, Pak Kasmo, came to the rescue. Soekarno's father confessed that neither he nor Pak Kasmo had ever ridden a motorcycle. However, he assured me, Pak Kasmo knew how to kick start the motorbike and also, at least in principle, how one should operate its gearshift and clutch. Besides, Pak Wardjo continued, riding a motorcycle should be essentially no different from riding a bicycle.

Pak Kasmo took over from Pak Wardjo, delivering a few hefty kicks on the starter pedal, with a 'This is how it is started.' To everyone's delight, the machine burst into life with the characteristic deep-throated growl of a Harley. But when I asked my advisors what I should do next, they replied, 'We don't know for certain, but you probably need to put it into gear and operate the clutch.' My heart was in my throat and I could hardly breathe for excitement when I straddled the bike and planted my feet firmly on the ground. When I slowly turned the accelerator and the Harley responded with increased roar and vibration, I could feel its power course up my arms. Pak Kasmo, standing beside me, shouted, 'Too fast, too fast!' Heeding his advice, I slowly let out the clutch until, to my delight, the Harley began to move over the ground. I made several trial rounds with Wardjo and Kasmo running alongside, and slowly gained confidence. Then, waving them good-bye, I mustered the courage to drive off. The exhilaration of that first ride was overwhelming; I can still almost smell the petrol and the oil, and hear the crunch of road gravel under the Harley's wheels. The wind through my hair and tearing at my shirt gave me a magnificent sensation of freedom. A boy's dream! I rode home to show my mother that I had accomplished her bidding on what was now *my* motorcycle.

All too soon home loomed ahead of me, and I realised that my tutors had forgotten a vital lesson – how to stop. A moment later, fortunately at only moderate speed, I hit the far wall of the open garage where I came to an undignified halt and the engine stopped. Youthful pride kept me from revealing this to my mother, and whether or not she knew of my near mishap, she thankfully did not mention it. I have ever suspected that my mother had a great capacity to conveniently disregard what was 'not quite right'. Her, 'There you are, you are able to ride your father's motorcycle,' was a compliment to me, as much as it was an expression of her serene confidence in having made a decision which quite suited her purposes.

Colonel Ota

The Japanese occupation administration encouraged, indeed it compelled, many of the region's major industries to continue operating. Of perhaps greater interest to the Japanese than any of the tropical agricultural produce were the archipelago's rubber plantations. These produced the raw material for car and truck tyres and other essential war material, as well as products readily sold on the local market for processing and manufacture into bicycle tyres and other rubber-based products. It was no surprise, and to an extent it was a relief, when my mother received written orders from the Japanese commander of the occupation troops in Pekalongan to continue production – especially of rubber. The order gave her some assurance that we would be allowed to remain living on the plantation, and that the Japanese would hopefully pay us for the product that would keep our business operating.

Several weeks after the Japanese invasion of Java, our telephone service to the town was disconnected by the military. When one day a party of Japanese soldiers arrived at the plantation in a car and a truck, we were taken completely by surprise. The officer was immaculately dressed in a dark, khaki-coloured jacket with shoulder badges of rank, and his stiffly ironed white shirt carefully folded over the collar and lapels of the jacket. On his closely cropped head he wore a small, dark-green cap and around his waist a broad leather belt and a holstered revolver. Completing his uniform were khaki jodhpurs neatly tucked into highly polished, knee-length leather boots.

The uniforms of the non-ranking soldiers were less elaborate; a rather shabby-looking light khaki cap from which hung flaps of material to protect neck and face against the sun, khaki shirt without jacket, khaki trousers, and instead of knee-length leather boots, linen puttees which covered the soldiers' legs from ankle to knee. An interesting addition to their outfit was a length of khaki fishnet material in which they carried a few days' emergency battle rations – so different from the heavy backpacks that our solders carried, which made them all the less mobile under battle conditions. Another curious part of the Japanese uniform was their canvas boots, split at the front, holding four toes and encasing the big toe separately. These afforded the wearer a better grip on the ground when walking and fighting in muddy jungle terrain. Jungle and battle-hardened men, these enemy troops surely put a lie to Allied propaganda that they were an inferior fighting force.

As we stood taking in the situation, the officer emerged from his car. He made us a stiff Japanese bow and, though not discourteously, he brusquely addressed my mother in somewhat broken and heavily accented Dutch, 'I am Colonel Ota, Imperial Japanese Army. I come to inspect tea factory. Madame will please show me.' In spite of the colonel's courtesies, war had reached our peaceful plantation home.

The factory inspection lasted an hour or two, in which time Colonel Ota wrote copiously in a pocket notebook. Sometimes he would utter an order or instruction to his men, whereupon the soldiers would uncover or remove a section from a particular machinery part that had attracted their officer's interest. When he had apparently completed his mission, Colonel Ota bowed to my mother, 'No more work today. I now return to town.' With another stiff bow, and 'Goodbye, Madame,' our first contact with the Japanese Imperial Army ended. It had been without incident, but also without a word of explanation as to its purpose.

A few weeks later, Colonel Ota returned – this time accompanied by dozens of soldiers on a small fleet of army trucks. On his first visit the colonel had paid particular attention to the power generators, the plantation truck, our private motorcar stored in the factory workshop, and the Harley Davidson motorcycle at home. The news that he now delivered dismayed us. 'I have orders from Imperial Japanese Army High Command. We must confiscate everything: tea factory machinery, plantation truck, also motorcar and motorcycle. High Command order me to tell you that tea plantation close down, all finish now. So sorry,' Colonel Ota declared. Issuing orders to his men, the soldiers sprang into action, dismantling machinery in the factory and loading the various parts onto the waiting trucks. To his credit, throughout the procedure Colonel Ota seemed ill at ease. As his men worked, he avoided looking at us or at Pak Wardjo, Pak Kasmo, or the many of our plantation labourers who watched the proceedings with bewilderment and a dismay that matched ours.

The colonel's work completed, he demanded, 'Please Madame, sign this paper. I date today, declare Colonel Ota, Imperial Japanese Army, confiscate factory machinery and truck, also private car and motorcycle. Best to keep signed paper as proof; by and by Imperial Japanese Government pay compensation money.' My mother knew that it was doubtful that the Japanese would honour them, but under the circumstances all she could do was to sign the documents. History proved her right: not only the Japanese but indeed the Netherlands government failed to compensate the war damage to our business and personal effects. Although not unexpected from the Japanese, the Dutch government's failure to compensate us for our losses was disappointing, to say the least.

After having supervised the dismantling of our factory, Colonel Ota returned several times on private visits to the plantation. I recall that he behaved as a gentleman and *Bushido*, a man of martial honour. On his occasional visits the colonel would ask for no more than a cup of tea served to him under the pergola on our front lawn. Appreciatively sipping the freshly brewed beverage, Colonel Ota would drink in the amazing, peaceful panorama that unfolded before his gaze. On one such visit, having apparently noticed how there were always fresh flowers beside my father's portrait, the colonel remarked to my mother, 'My wife in Japan, she too places not flowers but tea and food beside my portrait. That way she honours me, like you honour your husband.'

On another visit, as Colonel Ota sipped his tea under the vine-covered pergola, the setting sun cast long shadows over the tea gardens, and the chill of the approaching early evening made itself felt.

When taking his leave the colonel said, 'I say good-bye. I will not come back. My regiment leave town, to fight in the South Pacific.' Before he entered his car, he added in Japanese, '*Arigato gozaimasu*', repeating this in English, 'Thank you.'

Feeling the pinch

> Poverty is no disgrace to a man,
> but it is confoundedly inconvenient
>
> Sydney Smith *Wit and Wisdom of the Rev. Sydney Smith*

Despite closing down the tea plantation, the Japanese occupation policy of maintaining rubber production saved us from also having the rubber factory closed down. Nevertheless, the loss of the tea factory left us with a critically reduced cash flow. With sufficient funds to only keep employing a small labour force of rubber tappers, we had no choice but to dismiss all our workers on the tea and cinchona plantations. Even then, with a desperately small cash reserve, my mother had to tell our servants that we could no longer afford to employ even them. Touchingly, Jongos Kasim, kokki Mienem and babu Sitjas refused to leave us – an act of loyalty that went beyond mere servant and employer relationship. They asked only to be allowed to move into the now vacant garage and abandoned stables.

Without an income, we had to drastically economise our spending – even on food. Instead of purchasing supplies from our shopping town, we now sent our servants to the local market where, for much less money, they bought rice, flour, coconut oil, salted dried fish and other basic household necessities. In our garden, Kasim and I had also started a vegetable plot. Tilling the soil with the swan-necked Indonesian hoe – patjoel – we planted corn, beans, some leaf vegetables and a variety of spices used in Javanese cooking. In this way I imagined that I assisted my mother to help stretch our dwindling finances, and with the innocence of youth, I rather looked on the situation as an adventure. We were not aware that the ever-tightening Japanese grip on our occupied country would soon have a devastating effect.

In spite of all efforts, our precarious financial situation rapidly deteriorated to a point where drastic action became inevitable. One morning my mother began to empty out cupboards and drawers, setting aside bed linen, towels, damask tablecloths, napkins and some of our silverware, saying, 'We must start selling some of these things. We have almost no money left.' All that morning she sorted goods into different piles on the floor. From a shelf of her bureau my mother took down a small metal box in which she kept her jewellery, my father's gold shaving kit and a beautiful gold fob watch on a heavy gold chain, inherited from my paternal grandfather. She took these latter valuables out slowly and looked at them for minutes. When she put them back, my mother paused, and I clearly heard her whisper, 'I can't bear to sell them... not yet.'[xiv]

After she had sorted out everything that she considered disposable and saleable, my mother said to me, 'We will sell these things to rich Chinese merchants in the town. Without even our motorcycle for transport I can't go myself, but from time to time we will make up parcels that I want you to take to possible buyers.' When I asked her how, since we no longer had the Harley Davidson, I should be able to get to town, my pragmatic mother stated as a simple matter of fact: 'On your bicycle, of course.' Mum once again confirmed the steely resolve that underlay her character and that belied her physically delicate figure.

A young peddler
The distance between the plantation and town was about 35 kilometres. This didn't seem great when travelling by motorised transport, but the mountainous terrain – and the heat and humidity of the tropical climate – made pedalling a pushbike a considerable effort. Riding a bicycle over the shifting gravel surface and steep gradients of the plantation road made it difficult not to slip and fall – even if the road from home into town let me coast downhill, I could not do so at speed.

Before I departed, my mother would suggest names of potential buyers to me – usually wealthy Chinese people. I had no experience selling things, or even bartering at the market; I just had to do the best I could. The jewellery and silverware my mother gave me spoke for themselves; it got more difficult when we got down to selling linen and such, because the people buying already had plenty of their own. I would speak to both the man and lady of the house, but the lady would usually make the decision. I stuck it out as long as I could to get a reasonable price. I don't know if they respected me, but they saw me as someone who had something to sell, and it was up to me to say yes, no or maybe.

When returning home, I had to pedal my bicycle up an increasingly steep, unmade road until I reached the foothills where the plantation road began. From there, I often had to get off my cycle, pushing it up the mountain, which took hours of exhausting effort in the tropical heat. My mother never told me, then or in later life, whether she had worried about the effects these expeditions had on me. Nor, for that matter, did she outwardly question if it were wise for me to carry goods of considerable value through kampongs that even pre-war had not been very safe places. But under the circumstances what choice did we have?

On my expeditions to town, as a somewhat feeble precaution, I used to leave home very early in the morning, hoping to avoid unwelcome attention from people in the villages through which I had to travel. At this early hour I was able to peddle through the hamlets mostly unobserved, but returning home in full daylight I could not pass unseen. After two or three such trips, when the locals began to take notice of me, small children began to call me names and older ones laughed, pointed and sneered at me. At first merely annoying, on subsequent passages the catcalls became more hostile and worrying to me. Realising how vulnerable I was on my pushbike I hoped and prayed that I would not suffer a punctured tyre in the middle of a kampong.

The derision and hostility of the local population towards me was unprecedented at the time, and not easily explained. Javanese attach great importance to courtesy, and the reason for such overtly rude behaviour as yet escaped us. The villagers' taunting calls of *assu londoh* (Dutch dog) should have signalled the increasing antagonism towards the country's former overlords. It heralded the beginning of the end of the Dutch colonial empire, but even my mother did not take the hostility of the kampong youths seriously. 'They're just a few silly kids; the Japanese have put ideas into their heads. After the war all will be well again,' she promised me. Unlike her pre-war premonition that the witches brew in Japan was ready to spill over, history would this time prove my mother disastrously wrong.

If people showed me hostility in the kampongs, the Javanese on the plantation continued to show my family nothing but courtesy and respect. My friend Soekarno and I continued to hunt, swim and hike together, and I never mentioned to him that his countrymen in the villages now called me names and treated me unpleasantly. Neither my friend nor I could then have believed that we would be on opposite sides of a bitter struggle that was to develop between his people and mine. In later years I learned that my good friend Soekarno *had* been among his country's freedom fighters, those that would ultimately dispossess me of the shared land of our births.

CHAPTER 5

The Japanese Occupation Administration and its Reign

The greater the power, the more dangerous the abuse
Edmund Burke, *Speech* (1771)

Colonel Ota's departure from our town marked a new and ominous phase in the Japanese occupation of Java. The Imperial Japanese Army had initially installed a temporary military authority to maintain civil order in the recently occupied territory. However, once it had established security and stability in our town, Colonel Ota's regiment again became an active fighting unit to be moved on to the next military theatre. The new head of the Japanese Occupation Administration in our region, Captain Nakamura, was not a member of a combat unit; his function was to institute wartime governance. Under his command was the dreaded Kempei Tai – the Japanese military's Secret Police.

Captain Nakamura and the Kempei Tai

Differences between Captain Nakamura and Colonel Ota soon became evident, and while some of the changes were of minimal importance, others would turn out to be of particular consequence for we Dutch. If in the early days the Japanese military had turned out to be much less brutal than the general public had expected, the new Japanese Occupation Administration rekindled dark fears when it imposed and enforced often harsh rules and restrictions on the community. The Japanese 'witches brew' would soon leave a bitter taste in the experience of my family and other Dutch in the East Indies.

I speculate that differences between Colonel Ota of the Imperial Japanese Army and his successor Captain Nakamura of the Kempei Tai lay in their respective career backgrounds. While both men were officers in the Imperial Army, Colonel Ota was a Bushido warrior, a fighting soldier in the Japanese martial tradition. Whereas, as a member of the Secret Police and strictly speaking therefore not a fighting man, Captain Nakamura lacked the stature and prestige of the true warrior. Supremely confident of his heroic status, Colonel Ota looked upon civilians, and indeed on drafted soldiers such as Nakamura, with a measure of disdain. There was no doubt that Captain Nakamura was bitterly resentful of his position, and all too soon our town of Pekalongan in general – but my family personally – came to experience his chagrin. By his actions, we discovered the dread in which Japan's Secret Police, the Kempei Tai, was held.

Not long after Nakamura succeeded Colonel Ota, people began whispering about what went on inside the walls of the local Secret Police headquarters. Under orders not to fraternise with the enemy, during the command of Colonel Ota, soldiers had mixed little with the public, and the community had been generally unaffected by their presence. Under Captain Nakamura's new and harsh regime, word spread that the Kempei Tai had begun picking people up from their homes or simply off the street, seemingly at random. No one really knew what happened to those who disappeared into Secret Police headquarters, but the raids instilled terror in the region. One day, for the most bizarre and unlucky of reasons, Captain Nakamura and the Kempei Tai affected us personally.

In the earlier days of the occupation, my mother's twenty-one-year-old youngest sister, Frieda, had asked if she could join us on the plantation. She had been living in the regional city of Semarang, and was married only months before the outbreak of the Pacific War. Before the war her husband had worked in Semarang, but – a military reservist like my father – on the cusp of a feared Japanese invasion he had been called up for active duty. Like my mother, my aunt did not know if her husband had been killed in battle or, hopefully, if he may at least have become a prisoner of war. My mother took pity on her sister, and thus my aunt came to live with us in our home.

The Japanese Occupation Administration and its Reign

After Colonel Ota's departure, no Japanese had visited us on the plantation, but one fateful day a Japanese officer and half a dozen soldiers arrived at our home. The soldiers approached, rifles pointing at us, and our hearts sank when, glaring at us, the officer barked, 'I am Captain Nakamura, Kempei Tai. You are Dutch spy, very bad enemy for Dai Nippon!' Nakamura's reputation had preceded him, and as he continued to harangue us we cowered under his abuse. Bitter experience would later teach me to spot the danger signs of this type of Japanese officer's rage that always began with words and violent gesticulating, and usually led to an uncontrolled fury of kicking, slapping and beating a victim senseless. On the day of his visit to the plantation, Nakamura's wrath was undeniable, but the cause of his rage was a mystery to us: what did he mean when he used the word *spy*?

The torrent of Japanese words directed at us went on for some time until Nakamura snapped a command upon which his men began to ransack the house. After some time, they returned – without having found whatever they had apparently expected to find. This time Nakamura directed his fury at his men, shouting at them, even slapping one or two of the soldiers. My mind registered that when Nakamura physically punished a man, the victim of his rage came stiffly to attention shouting, '*Arigato gozaimasu*' ('Thank you very much'). When Nakamura stopped haranguing his men he again turned to us. 'You,' he shouted at my mother, 'You will tell me where you hide weapons, revolver and rifle. And radio transmitter, and signal code you use to spy on Dai Nippon. You are very, very BAD people. I, Captain Nakamura, will punish!' When my mother protested that we had done nothing wrong, Captain Nakamura whipped out a piece of cardboard the size of a postcard from a tunic pocket, exclaiming 'Look! This is proof you send spy message to enemy America!!' The card he produced depicted a seventeenth-century Dutch sailing ship ploughing through ocean waves. From the vessel's topmast, streaming magnificently in the wind, flew our national Dutch red, white and blue tricolour flag. We recognised the offending item to be a hand-drawn birthday card from my aunt to a friend in Semarang, which the Kempei Tai had obviously intercepted and taken to be the work of an enemy spy.

Nakamura's fury did not abate. Waving the 'coded message to the American enemy' in our faces, the situation became ever more threatening as his fury increased and he yelled abuse and accusations in Japanese and imperfect English. He continued to demand that we tell him who was responsible for the 'spy message'. In the end, my aunt could not deny that she had drawn the illustration, insisting that it was not a secret code but only a simple birthday card for a friend in town. Nakamura took no notice of her explanations or of my mother's pleas. He shouted directions to his men and they marched Frieda to the vehicles, leaving my mother in tears at the thought of a terror that my sister and I could only dimly comprehend.

The day after the Kempei Tai took my aunt into custody, we walked to the small village at the foot of the mountain where we hired a dokkar, a horse drawn cart, to take us to town. We stayed with acquaintances, and every day my mother called at the Kempei Tai headquarters to inquire about my aunt – but to no avail. After ten days Frieda was released and she returned home with us. We children learned little of what ordeals she had undergone; all that my mother would tell us was that she had suffered 'the worst, the very worst, that could happen to her.' At our age, my sister and I could not imagine what this meant, but the tone of my mother's voice sent a chill through us. Many years later, as adults, we learned that for the sake of a silly but innocent act our aunt had been interrogated, tortured and raped by none other than Captain Nakamura of the Kempei Tai.

Increasing unrest
In late 1942, throughout the East Indies, the Japanese Occupation Administration had begun to replace any remaining Dutch officialdom with native Indonesian functionaries. Though the Japanese kept a tight hold on power, the takeover of many government functions by Indonesians bolstered nationalist ambitions. The dismantling of the former Dutch colonial administration that heralded the beginnings of future Indonesian national independence caused considerable unforeseen problems. Soon after the invasion of Java, the Japanese closed down many foreign-owned businesses and government services, and vital infrastructures began to collapse. This caused widespread unemployment, and workers sacked from businesses or previously on government payrolls had no choice but to return to their kampongs,

falling back on traditional means of livelihood. Many, however, remained in the urban areas – and numbers of them turned to minor and sometimes major crimes. For unclear reasons, and adding to social unrest, the Japanese further released many hardened criminals from the country's gaols – murderers, rapists and common bandits alike. Some of these organised themselves into bands of roving opportunists called *rampok*, which sometimes committed serious crimes, particularly targeting the comparatively affluent Dutch and Chinese in the area. It remains unanswered whether the Japanese and Indonesian authorities were unable or perhaps even disinclined to curb this criminal activity, or whether it may have been a forerunner of, and an excuse for, the later internment of civilians in Japanese concentration camps.

Rampok at the plantation

One day, rampok trouble literally came to our doorstep when a plantation worker arrived at our home, greeting my mother, 'Kandjeng Ndoro Njonja [Greetings, dear lady], I bring a message from Pak Wardjo. Armed rampoks have arrived in our kampong. Pak Wardjo is negotiating with them, but he begs that Kandjeng and her children come now to the factory. If you should remain in your home, he fears that harm might come to you.' My mother acted quickly and decisively, turning to us and saying, 'Quick, there is trouble and we must leave the house.' We took nothing with us but, naively thinking that I could defend us against the bandits, I grabbed my 8 mm Flobert and a pocketful of bullets. Possibly for the sake of moral encouragement my mother did not make me desist. Although with merely a pea rifle I would obviously have stood no chance against the armed men, my good intentions luckily remained untested.

'Please, my lady,' the messenger urged as we followed him, 'Pak Wardjo suggests that we do not come by the main road. It may be that another rampok band is lurking in our area. It is better that we use the small plantation tracks, as the strangers will not know their way through the tea gardens.' We followed our guide over well-known plantation tracks until we reached our reservoir swimming pool, from where we were able to survey the factory and the nearby plantation kampong complex. The messenger excused himself, saying he would scout ahead to see if the bandits were still around. Returning sometime later, the man brought the good news that Pak Wardjo was still talking with the rampoks and that these had not turned to violence and looting. Taking good care for us to remain unseen, he led us to the tea factory where we took refuge in one of the storerooms. Unable from there to see or hear anything, the time passed very slowly. We knew that we were in a very dangerous situation – if Pak Wardjo should fail in his talks with the rampok, we would be facing more harm than merely losing property. Time seemed to stand still, we waited and we hoped, and all we could do was to trust in Pak Wardjo.

Late that afternoon, when our Hoofd Mandur joined us in the factory he seemed visibly moved, even triumphant. Indonesians consider public displays of emotion to be kasar – uncivilised – so Wardjo's uncharacteristic mood belied customary formality. His good manners, however, did not leave him when with bland understatement he said, 'Kandjeng Ndoro Njonja, her family and the plantation are safe.' When my mother asked him how he had fended off the bandits, his cryptic reply was brief, lacking even a hint of a boast: 'Kandjeng Ndoro Njonja, it was negotiated.' My mother knew polite Indonesian manners well enough not to press him for elaboration, and with an understatement of her own she replied, '*Aku matur kesuwun sanget, Pak Wardjo* (My great thanks, Mr Wardjo).' Indonesian courtesy further demanded that Pak Wardjo acknowledge this with 'I thank my lady in return,' but we were well aware that if not for Pak Wardjo's mediation we could have lost everything, perhaps even our lives.

We never learned exactly what accord had been struck with the rampoks by Pak Wardjo. Overhearing snippets of our servants' conversations – or it could perhaps have been that they casually dropped us information – we gathered that our Chief Overseer had told the bandits that he himself was the local rampok head, and that for the greater good of Indonesia he had requisitioned the Orang Belanda plantation. Acknowledging that just and proper goodwill demanded from him that his fellow rampok friends should not leave empty-handed, he presented the 'visitors' with gifts of goods, food and a little money, in return extracting their promise that the strangers leave the area and tell others of Wardjo's sovereignty over this plantation and everything on it.

After my mother had thanked Pak Wardjo she turned to my sister and me. 'You must also thank Pak,' she said. When he replied, Wardjo looked me directly in the eye as he gravely said, 'My son, Soekarno, would have been very sad if harm had come to your family.'

I have sometimes wondered about Pak Wardjo's true reason for saving us. How fanciful was it that he declared himself a rampok and Indonesian patriot? Was the real reason for his intervention an act of insurance in case the Dutch regained power after the war? Was his mention of my relationship with his son a cryptic message that but for this friendship our fate may well have been very different? If so, I suspect that I owe a debt of deep gratitude to Soekarno, the companion of my youth. It is truly an ironic twist of fate that another Soekarno, the father of Indonesian independence, would dispossess me of my Dutch Indonesian heritage and the country of my birth.

As a lone Dutch family living among many thousands of Indonesians whose continued goodwill towards us was becoming uncertain, it took the rampok incident to alert us that we lived on borrowed time. Taking afternoon tea under the pergola one day, my mother said, 'I don't know how much longer we can stay on the plantation.' Low down in the afternoon sky, about to sink into the Java Sea, the sun painted a spectacular blaze of colours on the horizon. In a distant tea garden a bush fowl crowed, heralding the approaching night. The cool of early evening was already noticeable, but my mother's words added a different kind of chill as we considered that we may have to abandon our home, and our virtual paradise would then perhaps be lost for ever.

Another increasingly pressing reason for my mother to seriously consider leaving our home was our now acute financial situation. We had lived very frugally off the small proceeds from selling household goods, silverware and some of my mother's jewellery, but there was not much left of anything that could be turned into money. But if we were to leave home, where would we live in town? Conveniently overlooking that we are not of the Roman Catholic faith – which in those years acutely discriminated against and separated communities on grounds of their religious beliefs – my mother's steely pragmatism approached at least the problem of accommodation when she said, 'We shall ask the nuns to take us in.'

As fate would have it, we would indeed leave our plantation home. But we would not be petitioning the nuns for help.

CHAPTER 6

The Concentration Camp Years

Whom they fear, they hate
(Quem mettuunt, oderunt)
Cicero, *De Officiis* ii, 23

In the first quarter of 1942 the Japanese Occupation Army's Kempei Tai began 'inviting' civilian Dutch males to attend what Captain Nakamura euphemistically called 're-education centres'. As groups of our men were sent off to these 'schools', few of us doubted that they were in reality being dispatched to a concentration camp. When this happened to our men, many began to ask if, and when, women and children would also be sent for 're-education'. The answer to that question would be given only too soon.

Christmas 1942 and New Year 1943 hardly proved joyous occasions for our expatriate community. By then, except for our doctor and two Catholic priests, every Dutch male above the age of fourteen years was now ensconced with the men in the concentration camp. When the Japanese began large-scale building renovations on a disused warehouse on the fringe of town, the so-called *Gudang Garam* (salt warehouse), rumours sprang that they were preparing a camp for the Dutch women and their dependants.

People's guess as to the purpose of the restored warehouse was confirmed when, in the middle of 1943, the long anticipated 'invitation' came for expatriate Dutch women and children to present at the Gudang Garam for the purpose of being 're-educated'. Curiously, I remember that it came as almost a relief when we received the letter. We had reached the point when within weeks we should be left without a livelihood and would have to call on the Roman Catholic nuns for charity. Desperate and without knowing how we should survive for much longer, the prospect of escaping these concerns in a Japanese camp seemed an almost acceptable end to our financial woes, not to mention the rapidly deteriorating social conditions that made public safety a matter of increasing concern. Naively, we had no idea of the reality of life in a Japanese concentration camp.

Fond farewells

The first thing my mother and I did when the summons reached us was to put her engagement and wedding rings and her remaining few items of jewellery in a glass jar, which we sealed with wax. Confident that we could retrieve it after the war, at night when no one could see us we buried the jar in a location near the house that we thought we would be able to identify in the future. The rifle my father had given me, I wrapped and hid in a small cave on the plantation, which I then covered over to bury it.

When the men had been rounded up, they were allowed to take only what they could pack in a small suitcase. When the Japanese summons to women came, it made no mention of how much luggage we could bring. My mother packed as much of our personal effects as she could into one large cabin trunk and a suitcase for each of us. Anything that we could not carry or that she thought that we would not need, she gave to the servants. Never doubting that we would return to reclaim them after the war, my mother asked our trusted home help to mind for us some items that were too large or not of practical value. Despite their undoubted help and goodwill, we never retrieved any of these goods.

The evening before we left, my mother called Kasim, Mienem and Sitjas to join us in the sitting room. In a small speech my mother addressed them, 'Tomorrow my children and I must leave for the Gudang Garam in the town. The Japanese have prepared these gudang to keep Orang Belanda women and children in them as prisoners.' Neither Dutch nor Indonesian people are very demonstrative, but our staff cried, and we cried. There was a great feeling of closeness – of family – between us, but we had to say goodbye. Mother continued, 'We thank you for your loyalty. I have not been able to pay you the wages that you should have received from me, but I now want you to take what you need from the things that we leave behind. When we return, I shall be able to pay you all that I owe you.' In her last remarks my mother made a promise, 'After the war, we Dutch shall be back.'

Although we really believed that war would soon be finished, that we would be reunited and be able to go back to the old ways, my parents and sister never returned to the plantation. Half a century later, my wife and I, now elderly, visited Indonesia as tourists. Taking a taxi in the town where I was born, we drove into the mountains where I showed my wife what should have been our home on the tea plantation. When we came to almost the end of the road, marked by two giant rubber trees that had survived the years, I knew exactly the place where our house had stood. The home of my boyhood paradise was gone; every trace, even its foundations, had disappeared. So too had the once magnificent terraces, the tennis court and croquet lawn, the grand concrete stairway and the pergola under which we had so often overlooked the spectacular scenery of the northern Java lowlands. Amidst my sadness, I found consolation in the brilliant jade-green foliage of tea bushes, which gently covered the site that war had disfigured. That day I faced the cruelty of war, and the knowledge that no clock could turn back to bygone times.

Leaving the plantation
The morning that we left for the concentration camp has remained deeply etched in my memory. During the night it had rained very softly, as if the heavens were shedding secret tears. When daylight broke, four hired men shouldered our luggage, which was strapped to bamboo carrying poles. In the typical rhythmic slog of Indonesian bearers carrying a heavy load, they set off ahead of us to the small village at the foot of the mountain. Our servants had assembled on the lawn, and there we tearfully embraced as we said our goodbyes. My mother did not once look back. When I did, it was with pain in my heart that I saw my loyal dog being held by his collar so that he would not follow me. Jongos Kassim had promised me he would look after Mickey... until I returned.

I cannot think of leaving my ancestral home without remembering the pine tree that my parents had planted on the day that I was born. In fourteen years it had grown to at least 30 feet high. Swinging on ropes from one to another of its stout branches, my sister and I had enacted *Tarzan of the Apes* fantasies. Many Indonesians and Indonesian Dutch are given to superstition, and soon after the Japanese invasion we noticed that the tip of the now huge fir had begun to die. To see its magnificence thus threatened, I could perhaps have been forgiven for taking it as an omen. But I have always known that the fir tree's wilting death and having to leave behind my dog constituted violations of my childhood by a war that had only just begun its devastation.

In the village at the foot of the mountains, my mother hired two horse-drawn carriages at the marketplace. While she negotiated the fare, we keenly felt that hundreds of Indonesian eyes were watching our every gesture and move. In Indonesia news travels fast and we knew that few market goers would be unaware of what was about to befall the Orang Belanda in Pekalongan. All around us the crowd surged and ebbed; from somewhere came the now familiar taunt, '*Assu! Assu londoh*! (Dogs! Dutch dogs!)'

Looking back to the rising heights of Gunung Slamet where the plantation lay, the veil of mists from the overnight rains had cleared. Silhouetted against a blue sky, the crags and valleys that marked the sides of the mountain seemed like outstretched arms wanting to pull us back. When our dokkar with us in it took off, we could only hope that we should one day find our way back to a paradise lost.

The Gudang Garam women's camp

> Abstract liberty, like other mere abstractions, is not to be found
> Edmund Burke, *Speech* (22 March 1775)

When our dokkar drew up at the Gudang Garam there was not a Japanese officer or soldier in sight. People in a crowd who are under duress act like sheep, milling around until a bellwether begins to lead the mob. That day, individuals and groups of women and children stood or walked around indecisively until someone suggested we elect persons to organise the chaotic situation. A 'camp leader' and several assistants – including my mother – were elected, and women and children began to trickle through the gates until all were inside. As we entered the Gudang Garam concentration camp, the lean and mean years of life under the Japanese occupation of my homeland had begun.

It is a truism that there will be individuals in a community who choose to ignore the principle of democratic election and who, for mischievous reasons, will work against appointed authority. In the Gudang Garam camp this soon became clear when arguments flared about mainly petty matters. The large warehouse building had been partitioned by flimsy plywood and woven bamboo screens into 3 metre by 2 metre 'rooms', each of which accommodated up to ten people. Disputes erupted over who would occupy these, and with whom. In effect, this created 'them-and-us' situations, distinguishing between people who formed themselves into discrete groups. People perceived these dramas as great problems – we had no idea of what still lay ahead for us.

By the end of the first day, the women and children had eventually settled in and people began to take stock of the new surroundings and its facilities. Spread over approximately 2 or 3 acres of grounds, the Gudang Garam camp provided dormitory accommodation for 500-odd people, communal ablution facilities, and one of the converted warehouse buildings functioned as the camp's communal kitchen. Wood-fuelled ovens provided cooking facilities for large numbers of people. The kitchen was further equipped with cauldrons, ladles the size of small oars, and instead of jugs, buckets in which to store water and liquids of one sort or other. Large 44 gallon drums – the tops of which had been cut off and made into lids – served as food containers and canisters, and other basic utensils were equally oversized. However, on this first day in the concentration camp, no matter how we searched for it, the Japanese had not stocked the pantry with food.

With the discovery that there was no food supplied, it was fortunate that many people had privately brought considerable quantities with them. These ranged from biscuits, chocolates, cakes and pastries to large bags of rice, flour, salt, sugar, tins of cooking oil and other basic household items. When camp leaders appealed for donations the response was largely positive and that evening the kitchen was able to feed everyone. Sadly however, instead of donating to the common good a few individuals had decided not to give, but to sell some of their hoard. We learned that some may be willing to profit from the want of others, but we also came to discover that this is fortunately not inherent in all people.

My family soon settled in reasonably well. With our financial worries somewhat relieved, and in the company of so many others, we imagined that we were protected from the adversities that the war had created. And given in these early days the Japanese rule of the concentration camp was not harsh, we naively believed that our imprisonment was the price we had to pay to 'sit out' a war that certainly would not take too long to conclude in our country's favour.

For many, and especially the young people in the Gudang Garam camp, the first few weeks seemed almost an adventure. Although Japanese soldiers now guarded the front gate, they left us much to our own devices inside the camp. After the bad start when no food had been provided, plentiful commodities of quite fair quality had since been organised. To enable the purchase of provisions from the local market, the camp organisers established a communal fund, to which everyone contributed what they were able. Being poor as church mice, my family was limited to the basic fare, but others were able to buy themselves more and better foods. Basic survival having been apparently ensured, the community turned to creating the necessary structures of organisation for social life in a concentration camp. We began making friends and forming friendship groups, who we would eat with. There was no furniture supplied, but there were lots of broken things and old furniture that we made into benches. We didn't have enough to make tables, just something to sit on, and to this day I don't like eating off my lap.

Without any help from servants or tradesmen, all the work in the camp still had to be done. Women and older children were arranged into work parties called *corvée* and allocated tasks in the communal kitchen, laundry, ablution facilities, storeroom and other places of general purpose in the camp. The town's female chemist and a small number of nurses from the hospital set up a first aid centre that treated minor ailments and accidents. In addition, the Japanese allowed the town's only doctor – now held in the nearby men's camp – to once a week visit us and treat the more serious medical conditions. With limited resources of books, paper and writing needs, teachers – including my mother – started basic education classes for the young of school age. Everyone pulling together overcame the chaotic situation that had marred the first few days in the camp. Sharing a common lot had made most of the detainees begin to feel members of a close-knit community; many still thought that the war would soon be over and that our short time in a Japanese concentration camp should then rate a minor entry in the history books. It was only weeks later when our idea of life in the camp was shattered by a bizarre incident.

After work and school, many of the younger generation turned to play football – soccer – on a vacant block of land that we had levelled and cleared of rubbish as best we could. One afternoon when a group of us were playing the game, among the onlookers was a Japanese officer whom I did not recognise. For some time our play went back and forth when, without warning, the 'visitor' burst onto the field, screaming, ranting and chasing after us in a state of almost surreal rage. Darting among and around us like a dog rounding up sheep, he herded us into a semblance of a line-up. Then he pounced on a stack of rubbish that a clean-up corvée had dumped nearby. Snatching a couple of broken chair legs from the discarded furniture, he returned to where we stood lined up, bewildered and uncomprehending. Wielding a leg in each hand, screaming with maniacal agitation, the officer hit the first one of us in the line-up, and the next, and the next. I stood farther down the line, and when he reached me I registered one, two, three blows to my body and several more to the head. Before I passed out, I recognised our 'visitor' as Captain Nakamura of the Kempei Tai.

When I awoke on a stretcher in our improvised sick bay, I found my mother and sister sitting beside me as our chemist, the camp medico, staunched copious bleeding where a blow with the chair leg had sliced a small section off my ear. After she had cleaned me up, the chemist found that, apart from the wounded ear, I had no serious injuries. I suffered a terrible headache and my ear hurt badly, and for the next few days my body was covered in large purple bruises. But, young and fit, I soon recovered from my injuries.

I later found out that the incident had been Nakamura's punishment for us not having halted our game to make the prescribed Japanese courtesy bow to him. A lesson learned the hard way, in other concentration camps I attempted to always stand as near as possible to the head of a line-up, so as to hopefully receive the least possible punishment. Strangely enough, no matter how enraged, before a soldier or a guard began to beat up someone wearing glasses he would order him in the Indonesian lingua franca, '*Buka katja mata* (Take off your glasses).' I cannot find an explanation for this concern that a victim must not be left without sight.

Post the war, stories have been told in books and in films about the 'heroics' of prisoners of war and civilian internees who, at terrible cost to themselves, stubbornly refused to perform the ritual Japanese bow. Such defiance is often portrayed as an act of pride and courage, however I suggest that it pointlessly ignored matters of custom: the Japanese bow to each other, Polynesians rub noses, Northern Europeans commonly shake hands with everyone in a room, and 'Old' Australians used not to extend their hands but politely salute with, 'How do you do.' In my case, I knew that disregarding the customary Japanese bow to officers and guards resulted in very unpleasant repercussions, and I felt no qualms in performing the salutation that their culture demanded. I may not have been heroic, but self-preservation and common sense taught me that bowing to the Japanese concept of civil courtesy saved me from unnecessary beatings.

We had been in the Gudang Garam camp four months when Captain Nakamura announced that, in two days, boys from upwards of thirteen years would be transferred to the nearby men's camp. Aged almost fifteen, I was included in the group of around two-dozen youths affected by Nakamura's decree – but we had little time to grieve. My mother and sister helped me select things to take with me to my new camp. Two pairs of shorts, shirts, underwear, socks, handkerchiefs, a small mirror, scissors, an enamel plate and mug, fork, knife and spoon, all packed into a small suitcase – my worldly goods appeared almost ludicrously inadequate. My mosquito net and the Australian horse rug that I had once so detested completed the outfit. Before I closed the suitcase, my mother rummaged among her possessions and handed me a tin of Dutch speculaas biscuits. 'I want you to have these,' she said. I knew that my mother had wanted to save the biscuits for when we celebrated our 'soon to be expected' liberation, but when I protested she was adamant, 'We are poor and I have nothing else to give you.' She took a deep breath and added, 'I also want you to have these.' Into my hand she pressed two shiny silver *rijksdaalders*, coins of two-and-a-half Dutch guilders each. I knew this was practically all the money we had left, but when I again attempted to refuse the gift my mother insisted. 'Your sister and I have each other on whom to rely,' she said. 'If ever you should need help, all I can do is hope that, little as it is, this money may buy you someone's assistance. From tomorrow you will be alone; while the money may help you a little, we must now trust in God to look after you.'

The now not-so-shiny silver *rijksdaalder*, which was pressed into Ferdinand's hand by his mother on leaving for the men's POW camp.

The next day, the women and children in the camp lined the street to the front gate. As we marched past them, I was proud that not a mother, sister or single person in the group shed a tear, and nor did we boys. All that had needed saying had been said the evening before, and we denied Nakamura the satisfaction of knowing the sorrow that we carried in our hearts. I had not yet turned fifteen years old, but when the day arrived that the Japanese came to take me and our small party away from our families, my childhood ended.

The men's high school camp

Unto everyone that hath shall be given, and he shall have abundance: but from him that hath not shall be taken away even that which he hath.
Matthew 30:29

As the crow flies, the men's camp in the local high school was only a short distance from the Gudang Garam camp. On the road we passed many Indonesians but – as armed Japanese soldiers accompanied us – they refrained from hurling the usual insults. Before the guards allowed us inside the new camp, they predictably lined us up for the usual head count and to search the baggage for 'contraband'. I remembered the lesson from Nakamura, and moved myself as near as possible to the head of the line. As I had hoped, our new camp guards frisked me only perfunctorily. Although they confiscated my knife and mirror, they did not find the speculaas biscuits wrapped in the mosquito net, or the two rijksdaalders that my mother had sewn inside the lining of my shoes. The Nakamura lesson paid off for me – farther down the line, the search became rougher and more thorough. Before they marched us into our new camp, the guards stripped the last person down to his shoes, confiscating many of his things. The lean and mean years of the Japanese occupation had truly begun.

The difference between the high school and Gudang Garam camps was startling. The men had been interned for months longer than we in the women's camp, and they looked wan and undernourished. Stoop shouldered, they shuffled rather than walked, and the hollow eyes in their heads lacked animation. Silence hung in the camp. We new arrivals were apprehensive; being left totally on our own made us a bit scared. We had no idea what to expect, really. But the men didn't really take much notice of us; they were apathetic, lifeless.

Within the camp, former classrooms had been converted into dormitory accommodation for about twenty people. With no beds or even raised platforms on which to live off the ground, people slept on the concrete floor on mattresses or mats that they rolled up in daytime. The most basic living facilities were woefully inadequate, and in the former sports hall almost 500 internees shared six toilets and showers. For no apparent reason the partitions had been removed from every cubicle, affording no privacy for even the most intimate ablutions.

The Concentration Camp Years

The camp's water supply came on for only one hour in the morning and for the same short while in the evening, so that we had to ensure we had enough drinking water saved to last the day. Not quite fifteen years of age, separated from my family and quite alone, from then on my life in the concentration camps became visited by the unholy three-headed monster of hunger, fear, and a crippling sense of utter helplessness.

In today's affluent Western society perhaps only few truly understand the difference between 'appetite' and 'hunger', where the former is nothing more than an edge of want, but the latter a relentless, devastating physical deprivation. Decades after the Second World War, a television documentary on famine-ravaged Ethiopia showed the suffering of an anonymous, terribly emaciated village woman. On a mat on the ground before her lay all she had left to eat – a handful, ten, no more than fifteen dried broad beans. Most of the woman's fellow villagers had died or they had fled the area to find food and better conditions somewhere, anywhere. One day, a girl from a deserted village had come to the starving woman's house. Orphaned by the famine she had wandered the country in search for survival. The older Ethiopian took pity on her, and though she was desperate for food herself and with no prospect of relief, she did not hesitate to share her last few beans with the orphaned girl, a complete stranger. The camera showed them eating a pitiful meal of these last few raw beans, and I could hardly bear to continue looking on at such misery. Some days later, when the television crew returned to the village to find that the woman had died, I could almost physically feel her suffering, which Death had perhaps mercifully ended. The orphan girl with whom she had shared that last meal had wandered off to who knew where. The humanity, the sheer selflessness of the Ethiopian woman humbled and deeply touched me because I remembered the Japanese concentration camps where, so much worse than a teasing touch of appetite, I too had experienced the horror of famine.

On my first day in the men's camp a murmur rang throughout in the late afternoon: 'The truck has arrived.' There followed a rush of bare feet on the concrete paths, and a throng of my fellow inmates lined up towards where several Indonesians in prison clothing stood on the back of a truck, dealing out food from drums. Following suit, I also lined up, but before I reached the distribution point the Indonesians called out, '*Habis* (Nothing left).' That afternoon, having gone without a midday meal, I thought that I was starving – but I was yet to find out how petty these first small pangs of an unsatisfied want were, and what it was truly like to feel real hunger.

Apart from the very poor quality of the food – which was prepared in the local jail by Indonesian criminals – there was never enough of it. The morning dish was a ball of cassava starch, like a big dumpling. If you were very lucky you would find a little blob of brown sugar inside. The evening meal, if it can be called that, was rice – not much, it would have filled two matchboxes – and a little bit of watery vegetable soup. Nearly every day came the shout from the meal truck, 'Habis, habis.' The shortages and the atrocious quality of food in this and other concentration camps, I have come to ascribe to a deliberate Japanese policy aimed at starving out enemy prisoners of war and civilian internees. I also have little doubt that the guards stole from the maintenance funds, with which they lined their pockets. This was possible because, while a superior officer was in charge, the daily business was delegated to badly trained, junior, mostly non-commissioned soldiers – ill-suited and ill-disposed towards a job that held no Bushido honour for them.

Soon after I was transferred to the high school camp, like many of my fellow prisoners I began getting up early in the morning to look for snails that had crawled into the camp during the night. But whereas they had once been in abundance and a pest, even snails were 'habis' when other prisoners had beaten me to finding them. I also attempted to set snares for small birds, in the way Soekarno had taught me on our carefree adventures. However, having nothing to temp the creatures, my efforts once again were fruitless.

Not long after I entered the men's camp, late one evening I gave in to temptation. Tucked under my mosquito net, I opened and ate the whole tin of speculaas biscuits my mother had given me. Making as little noise as possible so as not to let my neighbours know what I was doing, I tried not to crunch the mouthfuls too loudly – I even feared that the very smell of the spiced biscuits would give me away. At the time I thought that I was famished, and that gave me the excuse to succumb to what I later realised was little better than gluttony; a hankering after relief from the discomfort of an unsatisfied appetite. I was still to learn the difference between appetite and real want.

The saying that hunger sharpens the appetite came true one day when, near the food truck, I noticed a cabbage stalk on the ground, apparently overlooked by others. Before anyone beat me to it, I quickly picked it up. In better times, even in the women's camp across the road from us, I would not have given thought to the six inches of bare cabbage stem without a leaf on it – but on that day I ate the entire raw stalk and I still remember how good it tasted.

In the Japanese concentration camps food was an inexhaustible topic of conversation. People recalled banquets or parties they had attended, or they swapped notes of certain favourite recipes, even recalling and commenting upon the smell of a dish or meal. With forbidden pencil on contraband scraps of paper, some of the gourmands recorded and collected recipes that they had discussed with their friends. Years later, well after the war, I had an Indonesian recipe book written by a former internee from a Japanese concentration camp. I have sometimes wondered if he may have been one of those collectors of recipes in my camp, who took notes when favourite foods were discussed. Those conversations were pointless to me, and only added to my discomfort. I have never been able to forget the physical pain, the torture of desperate starvation; even today I cannot abide wasting food. In post-war, affluent, Western society, there is a great and seemingly unlimited cornucopia of everything. I sometimes fear that this leads people to a lack of respect for the blessing of such abundance. More than half a century later, I consider wanton waste of food disrespectful, in memory of those in POW and concentration camps who suffered, and all too often died, in their desperate destitution.

Christmas 1943 was only days away when Captain Nakamura himself came to the camp. In a long speech to us Nakamura announced that 'very soon' he would send us to another, undisclosed destination. 'The Imperial Nippon Army,' he declared, 'has decided that the re-education you have so far received in this camp will be continued elsewhere.' He then went on to warn us that we should continue to diligently reform our past bad behaviour so that, 'One day you too may benefit from Nippon's Greater East-Asia Co-Prosperity Sphere.' Nakamura's ranting struck fear into the hearts of many, but as people sometimes cling to the illogical belief that 'the devil you know is better than the one you don't,' some would have stayed in our camp rather than take a chance on conditions in the next one. Without choice in the matter and with the threat of the unknown hanging over us, Christmas 1943 was not a time of rejoicing.

Following Nakamura's announcement that we would 'soon' leave the high school camp, only hours later orders came for our departure the next day. Many, including me, despaired at having to leave loved ones behind in the women's camp across the road. On the other hand, our hopes were raised for better conditions in the next camp. *Any* change, many hoped, would surely be better than our present, increasingly sorry state of affairs.

That evening, at a point nearest our camp, we heard women in the Gudang Garam camp singing Christmas carols, and we knew that our mothers and sisters had learned of our impending departure. Our camp fell still; we gathered to listen to our loved ones' farewell. With great sadness I mentally took leave of my mother and sister.

Very early the next morning the Japanese guards lined us up, counted us, searched our luggage and dismissed us. Within a short time, we were lined up again for another counting, searching and then dismissal. For the rest of the day, as morning passed into afternoon, and early evening into night, for no apparent reason they repeated the process many more times. The camp had almost come to the conclusion that all this nonsensical business must surely be yet another of Nakamura's schemes, when, very early in the morning at around two o'clock, we heard heavy vehicles approaching the front gate. At the sound, the guards sprang into action, prodding us into line with fists and rifle butts and yelling in Indonesian, '*Lekas, lekas* (Quickly, quickly),' as they herded us through the gates. Outside we found a party of armed Japanese soldiers waiting to assist our guards, who again stood us in a line-up to count and search us. Although the Japanese searched and frisked me more thoroughly than they had done so far, they found nothing on me or in my luggage, and to my relief my mother's rijksdaalder coins remained hidden in the lining of my shoes. Finally the order came, and flanked by the soldiers we marched away to an unknown destination. I took one last look in the direction of the

Gudang Garam camp where my mother and sister stayed behind, and silently bade them, 'Till we meet again.'

In transit
Along the far-eastern horizon the night sky had begun to lighten and the stars were losing their brilliance, but even at that early hour of the morning our departure did not go unnoticed by Indonesians in their kampongs. As we made our way down the road anonymous voices hurled the familiar insult, Assu Londoh (Dutch dogs), along with a new taunt, 'Matti, assu Londoh, matti (Die, Dutch dogs, die).' When we turned a corner, I realised that we were on our way to the railway station, and beyond the town, in the dawning morning I caught sight of the distant ranges of my mountain home. At the time I did not suspect we would never return to live in my childhood haven – a virtual paradise forever lost to us.

At the station the soldiers herded us to a waiting train that stood shunted on a siding. They pushed us inside what soon became badly overcrowded carriages, then tightly shuttered all windows and barred the doors. It was still early in the day and conditions inside were hot but not yet unbearably stifling. All we could hope for was that we should leave before the sun's heat began to mercilessly beat down on the metal skin of the wagons, but after the previous frenzied activity the train did not move. A claustrophobic fear began to take hold of me – I was gripped by a new sensation of utter helplessness, of being absolutely unable to control even the slightest aspect of life in captivity. With this feeling came the knowledge that I could do nothing but endure.

To everyone's great relief, when daylight broke we heard a huffing and puffing steam locomotive arrive and felt it bump into the line of wagons. There was a clanking of couplings and safety chains being applied. Then, with a few listless whistle blasts, the train finally began to move. Underway to who knew where, I was happy to escape the high school camp – which in my memory has remained as merely an introduction to the miseries of life in a Japanese concentration camp. As each turn of the train's wheels took me farther away from my family, I was sad – but carried also a hope that the conditions in a new concentration camp should surely be better than in the one we had just left. I was on my own, and as my mother had put it, I was in God's care.

Even before the war, the Dutch East Indies railway service was not known for reliability or for comfortable and speedy travel. Our train was no different, struggling ahead even more slowly and erratically than was usual, often stopping to let apparently priority traffic pass us when we stood shunted onto a siding. These stops sometimes lasted only minutes, but occasionally we would wait for hours. Later in the day conditions inside the tightly shut carriage became terrible with heat and stifling humidity. So tightly packed together were we that anyone wanting a drink of water from a vessel in one corner of the carriage could only manage it if others moved his cup forth and back – which people did. Another problem was that anyone needing to relieve himself had to literally crawl over others to reach the toilet. As it got increasingly uncomfortable inside, people began to complain and bicker, and as the day wore on, nerves that were already frayed began to unravel, leading to jostling and abuse, 'Damn it, stay where you are! *Must* you move?' Normally reasonable individuals became irascible mobsters.

In this halting, unnervingly uncertain manner, the train stopped and started throughout the night and the next day. When we weren't stationary, shunted onto a siding for hours, the train travelled so slowly that its movement hardly stirred up air to somewhat cool the heat inside the carriage. Where people had at first been irritable and often unreasonable, on the second day most of us suffered the cramped conditions and the sun's fierce heat with dull, animal-like resignation. Farther and farther away from the town of my birth, at almost a snail's pace, I had no idea to where we were travelling.

On the second day, although I could not see outside, I could feel that we were on a winding and ever-ascending track that seemed to be taking us into mountain country. Inside the carriage, the stifling heat that we had so far endured began to ever so slightly abate, becoming even cooler as the early afternoon passed and night fell. Then came yet another stop to let a priority train pass. Unexpectedly, this time came footsteps and voices, and then the carriage doors opened. 'Lekas, lekas (Quickly, quickly),' Japanese soldiers herded us outside onto a station platform. We had arrived at a still unknown destination.

Tjimahi camp

After two days in the half darkness of the railway carriage, the early evening's light dazzled my eyes. Having been crammed in an uncomfortable posture for such a long time, with only one small serve of plain rice since leaving the high school camp, I was unsteady on my feet as the soldiers prodded and pushed. However, I felt a great relief at standing on firm ground and breathing cool, fresh air. I had no idea where we now were, but some of our fellows recognised the village and spread the news that we had come to a small provincial town in West Java. 'Tjimahi, this is Tjimahi!'[xv] came the cry. My spirits lifted and hopes soared – this was not my highland plantation home, but I was back again in mountain country.

The first few days in the new Tjimahi concentration camp are a blur in my memory. After they herded everyone out of the railway carriages, Japanese soldiers marched us down a narrow road through what seemed to be the outskirts of the town. In a short while we came to a walled compound where soldiers guarded the entrance gate. A sign chiselled into the stone archway over the front gate read, '*4/9 Battaljon Koninklijke Nederlandsch Indische Leger* (4/9 Battalion of the Royal Dutch East Indies Army)'.

Current front gate to the previous Tjimahi prison camp
(4/9 Battalion of the Royal Dutch East Indies Army barracks).

Entering through the large main gate of the former military barracks, we were led past a large grassy quadrangle that had been a former parade ground. Bordering it were barn-like buildings – some with light showing through their windows, indicating that they were occupied. When we came to what seemed a large assembly hall, the Japanese threw open the doors and we were bullied until all 500-odd of us were inside, packed tight as sardines in a tin. I had just enough room to put down my suitcase, on which I sat. Totally exhausted and with my spirits dashed, I felt utterly despondent.

Slumped on my suitcase, inside the tightly locked and barred building it was stifling hot. I had had nothing to drink for hours, but there was no tap in sight. There was not even a toilet in the building. But the hall was so crammed with people that even if there had been one or the other, I could not have reached it. Without sufficient room to lie down and sleep, I remained perched on my suitcase, dozing off in catnaps of exhaustion. After a night of acute discomfort, when daylight came the doors finally opened and the guards hustled us outside. The fresh chill of the early morning mountain air felt like a balm and my battered spirits lifted a notch. At the routine assembly that morning, each of us received a wooden badge with a camp identification number that we had to always wear. If my memory does not fail me, mine was number 2875. I was one of the earlier arrivals at Tjimahi camp, but would soon be one of more than 10,000 fellow civilian prisoners.

After the Japanese left us, a small group of men, earlier arrivals in the camp – whose light I had noticed the evening we arrived – showed us the way to the central kitchen, where we received the first meal since we had left our old camp. I was heartened to see that fellow internees had prepared the food – not Indonesian criminals, as in my old camp. And whereas we had previously suffered miserably inadequate and unpalatable food, when the cooks here filled my plate, I could barely believe my luck. I received a goodly portion of the Indonesian staples of rice, some steamed vegetables, a small portion of salted dried fish and even some sweet potato. Hope lives eternal, and on that first day in the new concentration camp I fancied that the previous lean period of my internment had ended.

The Concentration Camp Years

How wrong sanguine hope can sometimes turn out to be. The next two years at Tjimahi would teach me the reality of the mean and lean way the Japanese treated their prisoners.

The Tjimahi concentration camp occupied an area of around 10 acres near the major city of Bandung on West Java, and was the pre-war home to the 4/9 Battalion of the Royal Dutch East Indies Army. It contained a complex of barracks (each intended to house fifty non-ranking, single Dutch East Indies soldiers), a central kitchen, a small infirmary, and a parade ground. At the entrance to the camp was an office and guardroom. Pre-war, in each battalion the barracks had accommodated around 500 men, but after the capitulation of the Dutch government to the Japanese, it had held thousands more Dutch military prisoners of war. When the latter were moved on, the concrete walls between the cubicles in each wing had been demolished, converting the buildings into dormitory accommodation. Pre-war, fifty single military men had lived in a barrack; now, two hundred of us civilian internees were crammed together into the space. We were each allocated living space – 4 feet wide by 6 feet long – on the wooden platforms that ran along the walls on either side, with a narrow aisle between. Until the end of the war, this was my home.

Before our arrival, Tjimahi had apparently been very recently occupied by Dutch military prisoners of war, who had been transferred to an unknown destination. We found evidence of their presence all around us, indicating the Dutch POWs must have been forced to hastily vacate the premises. Strewn about was an amazing collection of Dutch Army uniforms, a variety of tools, utensils, books, magazines and writing paper. I collected some items: a set of Dutch army-issue clothing, a pair of aluminium ramekins that I took to replace my chipped enamel plate and mug, and a small aluminium box that formerly had held a gun-cleaning outfit. On the lid, an unknown artist had engraved by hand the words 'Tjimahi 1943', and a line drawing showing a prisoner with pick in hand, and ball and chain around his ankle. As I had begun smoking – everybody did, it kept the hunger cravings at bay – it became my tobacco tin, eventually becoming a souvenir that I have kept as a reminder of my two years in the Tjimahi concentration camp.

The gun-cleaning box found amongst the discarded Dutch army equipment and used as a tobacco tin.

But my most treasured find I dug out from among a heap of discarded paper and office supplies. The volume of Rudyard Kipling's collected poems became a true treasure. In the bad times that lay ahead, one ballad, 'If'[xvi], became more than just any poem in just any book for me:

> If you can keep your head when all about you
> Are losing theirs and blaming it on you,
> If you can trust yourself when all men doubt you,
> But make allowance for their doubting too;
> If you can wait and not be tired by waiting,
> Or being lied about, don't deal in lies,
> Or being hated, don't give way to hating,
> And yet don't look too good, nor talk too wise:
>
> If you can dream – and not make dreams your master;
> If you can think – and not make thoughts your aim;
> If you can meet with Triumph and Disaster
> And treat those two impostors just the same;
> If you can bear to hear the truth you've spoken
> Twisted by knaves to make a trap for fools,
> Or watch the things you gave your life to, broken,
> And stoop and build 'em up with worn-out tools:

> If you can make one heap of all your winnings
> And risk it on one turn of pitch-and-toss,
> And lose, and start again at your beginnings
> And never breathe a word about your loss;
> If you can force your heart and nerve and sinew
> To serve your turn long after they are gone,
> And so hold on when there is nothing in you
> Except the Will which says to them: 'Hold on!'
>
> If you can talk with crowds and keep your virtue,
> Or walk with Kings – nor lose the common touch,
> If neither foes nor loving friends can hurt you,
> If all men count with you, but none too much;
> If you can fill the unforgiving minute
> With sixty seconds worth of distance run,
> Yours is the Earth and everything that's in it,
> And – which is more – you'll be a Man, my son!

The last stanza took on very special meaning, giving me the courage to endure and the wish to survive.

Korean guards

The history of the brutality towards and maltreatment of POWs, civilian internees and possibly the so-called *romusha* (mixed-ancestry Indonesian Dutch forced labourers), has generally – and apparently unquestioningly – been blamed on the Japanese. The Japanese soldiers were certainly not to be discounted for what they could do, and often did, to their captives – bashings, deprivation of liberty in a cell, and in the very worst case tying a victim's hands behind his back and suspending him with both feet off the ground. But it must be said that the Japanese generally acted only in such instances when, in their opinion, a serious crime had been committed. However, it is either not known, or it has been overlooked, that throughout the occupied Dutch East Indies, the soldiers that guarded the internment camps were mostly *Korean* non-commissioned officers and privates under the command of ranking Japanese officers. The Japanese generally despised the Koreans, who were seen by them as barbarians and barely acceptable as conscripted men in the Imperial Japanese Army. The Japanese military treated the Korean soldiers very harshly, and many of them suffered abuse – including physical maltreatment – from their

Japanese superiors. Smarting over their low status and the disdain in which they were held by the Japanese, the Koreans took their frustrations and humiliation out on us defenceless internees with a brutality that often exceeded what they themselves had received. Under Japanese internment, fear was all pervading and omnipresent. I feared the Japanese, but even more so the Korean guards. Among our guards I particularly remember Korean Sergeant Wadda. Like many of his countrymen, he was a tall and very powerfully built man, prone to unpredictable and violent temper tantrums. We feared Sergeant Wadda more than we did the Japanese guards. Few dared get noted by him, for anything that could set Wadda off into a rage would inevitably finish by someone being brutally bashed by him. Popular wisdom in the concentration camp held that Koreans performed the dirty work of terrorising and maltreating the internees while their Japanese superior stood by, smiling.

Corvées

The morning *Tenko* (assembly) was usually conducted by junior officers and soldiers, but one day the Japanese commandant himself attended the rollcall. By then our numbers had reached close to 10,000. Apart from what were now routine camp maintenance work parties, people had nothing to do but while away the hours with card games, half-hearted physical exercises or other fairly pointless pursuits. On the former army parade ground the Japanese officer began a long speech in which he essentially said that every prisoner would contribute with his labour to the camp's services, specifically the daily supply of food. Whereas the benevolent Imperial Japanese Government had until now fully provided for our upkeep, without exception everyone must now work for the benefit of everyone else. 'One man work help other men eat,' he said. The Japanese camp administration would pay a paper entry-wage of 10 cents per person, strictly only to those who presented for work. On any given day the exact number enrolled for duty would determine the quantity of the camp's food supply. 'Not everyone work, not everyone eat.'

The injustice and cruelty of the new policy was obvious; through serious illness, temporary or permanent invalidity or other excusable contingency, absences were unavoidable in such a large community. It was clearly impossible for every person to turn up for work every day, and that directly affected us all. But in the first few months, when most people were still relatively fit, reasonable numbers of people turned up for duty. While the situation was not good, it was bearable. However, when absences inevitably increased through sickness, acute malnutrition and other factors beyond a person's control, our living conditions became truly desperate, and I shall not ever forget the experience of prolonged, devastating starvation.

Inhumane as it was, the commandant's work policy had a positive effect on camp morale – surely not intended by the Japanese. Knowing that it would adversely affect the common welfare if one did not somehow contribute his labour, unless a person quite literally lay dying, not one of us *ever* shirked doing their share of work. Only the most severely ill or incapacitated prisoner, perforce and excusably, did not – could not – contribute to the common cause. Patients in the camp hospital washed and rewound bandages or they performed light but necessary cleaning and maintenance work. The stronger and fitter of us, each to the extent of their capacity, contributed to the more strenuous camp duties or site work on Japanese projects outside the camp. These were hard times, and forged in my conscience the conviction that it is a person's moral obligation not to take society's benefits for granted, but to add their share to the common good. After the war there were occasions when my work colleagues went on a strike, but I could never compromise what I had learned at Tjimahi, namely that no one should have the right to withhold his labour, which he should contribute for the good of all. Having learned these lessons in prison camp survival, this personal 'philosophy' remains chiselled in my mind, and in civilian life I have come to detest not necessarily individuals, but the greed and the power of labour unionism and the imposition of compulsory unionism in particular. Borrowing from past American president John F Kennedy, who in his inaugural address to the nation said, 'Ask not what your country can do for you, ask what you can do for your country,' I wonder: should this rhetorical question not also apply to Australians and Australia?

In spite of exhausting daily hard labour, after working hours, back in their barracks many internees kept up an active social life. In the early evenings, men congregated in small friendship groups to talk or to follow common interests or pursuits. The most popular pastime was the game of bridge, often played with such passion that the participants almost became combatants. When a game was in progress, players watched their hand of cards with hypnotic concentration, and the atmosphere of silent communication between partners was intense. When a card game was over, it was nearly always followed by lengthy and often heated replays, '*You should have known that when I called...*', or similar comments and often recriminations. In spite of the acrimony that the card games sometimes evoked, they did have a positive value, substituting for otherwise possible open conflict. An outlet for repressed aggression that would have endangered our only weapon against the Japanese, the card games served to cement the cohesion of our people; our '*we*' pitted against their '*them*'.

The camp population

Among the 10,000 prisoners in the Tjimahi camp, the majority were Dutch nationals. But there were also quite a number of ethnic Chinese, Indians, a few Armenians, even Indonesians. For a few weeks there were several wounded Australian and British nationals who, in the chaos of army and civilian retreat from Singapore through Java, had been unable to keep up with their fellows trying to escape to Australia. The Japanese held the latter prisoners of war in a separate section of the camp, but some of us managed to visit and speak to them through the barbed wire fence. One of these men was an Australian pilot, Bill Howard, who was shot down in an air battle over Singapore. With both his legs broken and in splints, he was unable to keep up with retreating Allied Forces on Java. He had been captured by the Japanese Army and sent to join the small number of POWs temporarily held at Tjimahi. My English was not very good, but when Bill found out that I had visited Australia with my parents before the war, he became quite friendly. We talked about his home state of Western Australia – he, too, had spent weekends or holidays swimming and surfing in the sea at Scarborough. He remembered the Kool Korner Kafé and the brumbies that sometimes came out of the bush to steal the grass and flowers from people's gardens. Our brief acquaintance ceased when the Kempei Tai came and took away all the POWs. I never saw Bill Howard again, nor heard of him or his fate, but I hope that this young and good man made it safely back to his beloved Perth.

Among the internees there was also a group of mixed ancestry Indonesian Dutch. They did not associate with the rest of the camp, but had established a community of their own. In Dutch, they had been dubbed the derogatory nickname '*Ballen Jongens* (Ball Boys)' – so named for the large red dot on their camp badges, symbolising Japan's national emblem of the Rising Sun. It was rumoured that they were collaborators who the Japanese had put in the camp to spy on us, although this seems unlikely given their badge made them so easily identifiable. Still, the rest of the camp shunned the Ballen Jongens on suspicion that they were at least enemy sympathisers. It was thought that they were only temporarily interned until they proved themselves worthy of the Japanese cause. It was certainly true that they received markedly better treatment than the rest of us in the camp; we envied the Ballen Jongens, who were excused from the Japanese commandant's work rule and who received extra rations and privileges. When the Kempei Tai came for them it was generally taken for granted that these enemy sympathisers had been released. After the war, the world learned of the horrors and the ordeals of Allied prisoners of war on the notorious Burma to Thailand railway line, and of their brutal treatment by the Japanese. Much less is known of the Indonesian romusha, who were volunteered by president-to-be Soekarno – Father of the Indonesian Republic – as labour for the Japanese war effort. Whether or not Soekarno knew what would become of them is debatable, but the Japanese considered the romusha not as Indonesian patriots, but dispensable slave labour. They were sent to construction sites on Borneo and Sumatra, and even as far abroad as Burma and Thailand. With little historically recorded about them, word of mouth alleges that the Japanese treated the romusha even worse than they did the Allied prisoners of war, and that their death toll exceeded that of the POWs. As many of us in the camp suspected, perhaps it was true that the Ballen Jongens were Japanese sympathisers. However, if the Kempei Tai included them in romusha slave labour units, then no one would wish that they suffered what would have been a terrible fate. For many of these unfortunates, death was probably preferable to the truly inhumane treatment that they were said to have received at the hands of the Japanese – who they once idolised as liberators from the Dutch colonists.

At Tjimahi, new contingents of internees from all over Java arrived daily. As the camp population continued to swell, living conditions that had so far been reasonable began to deteriorate. Thus began the leanest and meanest years of the Japanese occupation for me and my fellow inmates.

Camp fathers

> No man is an Iland, intire of its selfee
> John Donne, *For Whom the Bell Tolls*

An enduring social value that ameliorated the brutality of life in a Japanese concentration camp was the care of the older generation for the young. Not uncommonly, some adults in the camp, men with children of their own who had remained with their mother, extended a kind of father and son relationship by becoming 'camp fathers' to an adopted 'camp son'. Hailing from far and wide on Java, the camp population consisted of mainly adult males and youths from upwards of fourteen years of age – such as me. At a later stage it also included several groups of very young boys, no older than ten to thirteen years. For unknown reasons, the Japanese had taken these children from their mothers and had interned them in what we called, *'Jongens kampen* (Boy camps)'. When they joined us at Tjimahi, these youngsters were physically little better off than in their previous camp, but they at least gained the concern of adults who extended them the protection of a nurturing relationship. How these boys had managed their incarceration all alone in the Jongens kampen, I cannot understand. Their story has never been given attention: an inexplicable act of war cruelty perpetrated on mere children has passed unremarked by history.

In my own case, I owe a debt of great gratitude to my 'camp fathers' – *Mijnheer* Piso and *Mijnheer* Frankel. Mr Piso was a man of about thirty years old. He was married and had two children, a boy and a girl. He and his friend Mr Frankel were my near 'neighbours' on the platform in our barracks. Colleagues on one of the large sugar refineries on Java, Mr Piso was a scientist who had been classed exempt for military duty, and slightly humpbacked Mr Frankel had been declared medically unfit for active war service. Apart from often playing bridge in the evenings, my neighbours and a small group of their acquaintances sometimes discussed a wide range of topics that interested me. The men encouraged me to participate in these talks, which included snippets of academic subjects. To an extent these discussions substituted my formal education, which had been interrupted by the war and was strictly forbidden by the Japanese. Mr Piso in particular took time to further explore and explain topics that had interested me, and my friendship with him and Mr Frankel gradually grew. When I felt down at heart Mr Piso would offer encouragement; when I was sometimes ill he looked after me like a kind and considerate father, supporting me when the occasion or the need arose. At one time, I suffered a very bad tropical ulcer on my leg and also a large boil in my groin. They were so bad that I could not walk, so Mr Piso carried me on his back to and from the camp clinic until the sores healed. In my turn, I would try to look after him. I made sure that if he was still at work when I returned to the barracks, I collected his share of a meal, keeping it for him until he was back 'at home'. It was in that context and in terms of mutual consideration that Mijnheer Piso and I were 'camp father-and-son' in the 4/9 Battalion at Tjimahi.

In my youth people did not talk freely about sex and sexuality, so that I will never know if – in spite of the harsh conditions of work and near starvation – these matters remained part of adult life in the camp. The question arises if in some instances homosexuality may have underlain some 'camp father-and-son' relationships. Within the small community of the barracks that I shared with adult men I did not see any signs of paedophilia; to my knowledge, no camp father violated the *in loco parentis* connection with his adopted camp son. We perhaps lived in an era of a more honourable, caring and moral world than that of today, but probably my youthful innocence prevented me from being aware of the possibility that a violation of substitute parental care could have occurred.

Mr Miles
In many respects the population in the 4/9 Battalion camp resembled that of the outside world of before the war. In a wide cross section of the camp society, we had the timid and the brave, the movers and the shakers, the downcast and upbeat, the successful and the no-hopers; there were givers and takers, do-gooders and parasites, scallywags and virtuous. Irrespectively, every internee recognised that there was 'us' and that there was 'them' – we and the Japanese enemy. The former outside world was also fully represented in occupational terms that counted the trades, the business world,

academics, musicians, artists, doctors, scientists, priests and clergymen... in short, a range of those who had made up the pre-war society.

Among all these, my camp father Mr Piso was my significant other. For quite different reasons, another man also became important to me. After the defeat of Singapore, Mr Miles – an engineer in the merchant navy – had sailed for Java trying to escape to Australia, but the vessel was bombed and had been so badly damaged that it barely managed to limp into the harbour at Batavia. He and his ship's crew were caught by the Japanese and he was initially held in an Indonesian prison, before joining us in the Tjimahi concentration camp. A small, wizened, rather dark brown-skinned man, Mr Miles had the intensity of eye, the darting hands and the nervous quickness of a monkey – but of course I never told him that. He spoke with a lilt in his speech that I knew was different from Bill Howard's nasal Australian accent, but when I asked if he was an Englishman, Mr Miles quickly responded, 'Oh, goodness, no. No, my goodness, not English, no, no, I am Brrrittishh.' Only years later I came to realise that Mr Miles was not an Englishman, but, rather, of British and Indian origin.

Mr Miles and I had met when we were both working in a corvée work party, and although he lived in another barrack we had become quite friendly. He often asked me to tell him more about my family holiday in Australia, a subject that I had once mentioned to him and that he found endlessly fascinating. 'Goodness but it is a most remarkable country indeed, doesn't it!' he exclaimed as I told him about the 'Glorious Golden West', the Swan River at Perth, and the brumbies at beloved Scarborough. About our Australian friends in that country, Mr Miles remarked, 'Oh goodness, but it seems you tell me how different the Australians are. They not at all hoity-toity like the bahadur Sahib Englishmen in Hhindja, doesn't it.' My school education of the English language having been interrupted by the war, I was uncertain of how to pronounce English words and for a long time I copied how Mr Miles pronounced the name of his country, India: 'Hhindja'.

There were times in the camp when I was overcome by the gnawing despair of what I can only describe as helpless loneliness. In order to somewhat understand this condition, recall the fact that I had been just fourteen years old when I was separated from my mother and sister, and I still didn't know if my father had survived fighting against a Japanese enemy – if he lived, where was he? With a poem by the sixteenth century metaphysical poet John Donne, my mentor, gentle Mr Miles, provided me some solace. 'You are *not* alone, my young friend,' said he, quoting:

> No man is an Iland, intire of itselfe;
> ...
> any man's death diminishes me,
> because I am involved in Mankinde;
> And therefore never send to know for whom
> the bell tolls; It tolls for thee.[xvii]

Donne's words, 'No man is an Iland, intire of itselfe', somewhat assuaged my fear of dying a lonely death. As Mr Miles assured me, I was *not* left entirely alone and abandoned at Tjimahi. Although I survived in the long run, for too many unfortunates 'for whom the bell toll(ed)', they did not outlive their captivity.

Before I met Mr Miles, I had begun to read the book of Kipling's verses that I found discarded at the camp. But it was only when my humble acquaintance began to tutor me in its contents that I began to gain a feeling for the beauty and power of language, an insight that has remained with me for life. 'In a work of prose or poetry,' said Mr Miles, 'a writer "paints" pictures, mental images, with language his medium.' Emphasising the point with curiously fluttering raised hands and small sideways movements of his head, he continued, 'By carefully selecting the words in his verses, Rudyard Kipling captures the real, living Hhindja.' He picked up Kipling's book, and turning to the ballad 'A Tale of Two Cities' he intoned:

> Where the sober-coloured cultivator smiles
> On his byles[xviii];
> Where the cholera, the cyclone, and the crow
> Come and go;
> Where the merchant deals in indigo and tea,
> Hides and ghee...[xix]

Mr Miles stopped, and he thought carefully before he continued, 'Here you can see what I mean when I say that by carefully selecting and using words, Kipling "painted" a picture of his subject with them, isn't it? With the words "the sober-coloured cultivator" Kipling conjures up an impoverished Hindjan peasant who knows joy when he, "smiles on his byles". And, "Where the cholera, the cyclone, and the crow come and go", this captures the fatalism of poor, helpless people beset by misfortunes and many kinds of disasters over which they have no control. But as Kipling points out, these woes will come, and in time they also go. Kipling has captured real life in my homeland, where people endure because they have no alternative but to endure, though where life is still not devoid of some joy.' He added, 'In this camp we endure, but sometimes we still know joy.'

One day when I felt very downhearted, I confessed to Mr Miles my thought that the war may perhaps never end and that we may die here. He wagged a wrinkled brown finger at me, 'No, but indeed you must never give up hope and courage. It is your duty to your family as also to Mankind.' He scanned my book of verses and, bending closely over the poem 'If', in his lilting tongue he recited its resounding, sage words:

> If you can keep your head when all about you
> Are losing theirs and blaming it on you…

I have never forgotten that language can give intimate meaning and beauty to life, and that it can also impart courage when it is necessary to have a firm heart. This is the wisdom that humble Mr Miles showed me.

On one occasion, I asked Mr Miles how *he* had come to discover the beauty and the value of words. He did not immediately reply, but looked at me silently for a while, and then thoughtfully said, 'It is a good and a fair question, oh, yes, by golly.' He then continued, 'Now I shall tell you something that I have not wished to think about for a long time, isn't it. My daddy was an Englishman from the Old Blighty, from England you know, and my mother a Hhindjan woman. When I was a boy of about your age, he left my mother and his children in Hhindja to return to the "auld sod" as he sometimes called it. I do hope that he was sad to leave me, but even if he did promise one day to come back for me, I was sadder still, as I knew that I would not see him again. Before my daddy left us, he gave me all his books, oh goodness, many beautiful books with coloured covers, don't you know. I began to read them, but at first without insight. Like you, I did not see beneath the surface of the written words. To me they were only two-dimensional lines of writings, letters without the depth of feeling that is woven into poetic language and prose. At home next to us lived an old, old lady who had once been a grand *memsahib* from England, don't you know it. Her British Army husband and she used to go on tiger hunts sitting on top of a marvellously big elephant, and they had many servants. The husband died, not fighting the Pathan at the frontier, no, but from the cholera; probably because the lazy servant put unboiled water with his whisky, oh my goodness, so very sad. The lady's husband had no money left when he died, and she had to live like we, poor people. She could no longer meet important gentlemen and ladies from the Blighty, so very bad and sad isn't it? In time she forgot to live like a pukka memsahib English woman. She ate cheap Hhindjan curry food instead of superior Brrittishh potato and gravy, and it turned her skin nearly as dark as ours. We all forgot what an important person she had once been. It was only when she saw me struggling to read my father's books that she remembered her grand English upbringing – and she began to teach me such as I am now trying to pass this knowledge on to you, isn't it.'

When the Kempei Tai came for Mr Miles I never saw or heard from him again. I hope that my gentle teacher – who taught me to appreciate the joy and the beauty, but also the power of language – made it safely back to his beloved Hhindja.

Conditions deteriorate

> It is misery enough to once have been happy
> Francis Bacon, *Essays of an empire*

During the two years of my internment in Tjimahi, conditions turned from bad to worse. Protests to the Japanese administration by our own camp leaders made no difference to our increasingly harsh conditions. A possible reason was that the Japanese did not extend the articles of the Geneva Convention to civilians in their concentration camps. A possible further explanation may be related to the Japanese notion of martial honour. This underscored the disdain in which the Japanese held civilians who did not fit the warrior code and who, therefore, did not deserve even a defeated soldier's treatment. As living conditions in our camp changed for the worse, ever greater demands were made on us for hard physical labour. Despite the 'One man work help other men eat' policy, not only the quantity but also the quality of our rations failed to improve. The evening meal had initially been a reasonable portion of rice, a small piece of salted fish and cooked or steamed vegetables. New conditions changed this to a jealously measured, meagre 75 grams – five spoonfuls – of cooked rice per person, accompanied by nothing more than a watery vegetable soup. We never again received salted fish, let alone meat. Even worse fare was the breakfast meal that consisted of a vile 'porridge' made of cassava flour and water – which was, in fact, the common household starch used to stiffen clothing. Without milk, sugar or even salt, the taste of this concoction was so bad that, although I became desperately hungry, I could barely swallow the stuff. I knew that I had no choice but to eat it. *Willing* myself not to gag and throw up as I forced the evil, reeking, gooey starch down, I used to sit with the bowl of 'porridge' in my lap, my eyes so tightly closed that tears often ran down my cheeks. To not eat the slop was unthinkable.

Risks and consequences

The rhythm of camp life never varied greatly, and as one day was almost a copy of the previous one, time was of little consequence. Until the end of the war, the Japanese strictly enforced an embargo on contact with the outside world, and the concentration camp was a closed institution – absolutely devoid of any kind of communication by radio or newspaper, let alone by personal contact with anyone outside its walls. However, in spite of the known risks – and also in spite of the hideous punishment that followed when the guards caught an internee in a clandestine act – there were some men who were willing to chance extreme danger. Sometimes their motivation was selfish, for personal advantage, and a man would barter valuables with the Japanese or other persons on the outside, especially offering highly prized wrist watches. However, there were some who bargained for certain items that had a high value in the camp – foodstuff of all sorts and kinds, but especially medicines for our hospital.

The Japanese supplied very little for the needs of the camp's hospital. Doctors and nursing staff did not even have conventional bandages – they used linen bed sheets torn into strips to cover wounds and sores. Even this makeshift material was in such short supply that the bandages were washed and dried again and again, until the material disintegrated. Prescription medicines were either not at all available or so scarce that only the most direly ill of patients received any. Instead, the doctors often turned to using alternative medications from certain plants, bark and leaves thought to have curative properties. Nothing useful was ever wasted. In our barracks, even people's urine had to be deposited into specially placed 44-gallon drums. The basic ingredient from which yeast was produced, it was collected daily and taken to a makeshift laboratory, where it was used to cultivate the single unrestrictedly available 'medication' that the doctors were able to dispense. A most unconventional source, we had nothing else. But due to the ingenuity of our scientists in the hospital laboratory, the yeast no doubt saved countless lives.

We always knew when someone had been caught trading. Instead of being marched off to work, the guards lined up as many of us abreast as the internal roads allowed. Herded in a long, snaking line to the front gate, we were made to march past the gruesome sight of the punishment that the Japanese had meted out on the unfortunate member of our community. Brutally beaten into bloody, almost caricatures of human beings, the trader and any civilian with whom he had dealt were a sight that sent chills of fear throughout the camp. As we filed past the wretches, their grotesquely swollen faces – sometimes with ears or lips torn and dangling by a shred of skin and flesh, and the entire body covered in weals and blue-black bruises – attested to a degree of barbarism that one could not comprehend from even the Japanese. The ultimate horror was to see someone hanging with arms bound behind the back, toes tantalisingly touching the ground but not supporting the pain-racked body. Sometimes the Japanese kept a man suspended like this for a few hours, sometimes for a whole day. Sometimes when they cut him down, the person was dead. These terrible warnings had the intended effect upon most people in the camp – few were prepared to tempt fate by buying or bartering vitally needed items. For the truly brave men who continued to take such dreadful risks, their selfless motivation was nothing less than an act of pure humanitarianism. Had it not been for these men, perhaps many more people in the concentration camp would not have survived the war.

Pinching

As the days, weeks and months crept by, hunger passed into famine, and more and more people succumbed to starvation. By mid-1944, only months after we first arrived at Tjimahi, the population of internees had fallen from 10,000 to around 8000 prisoners – a number that decreased by the day. I, too, starved, but probably due to having enjoyed a healthy and active lifestyle at home in the mountains, I was in better physical condition than many of my fellow internees who had lived in the energy-sapping lowland heat and humidity. Also, whenever possible I chose to work in a corvée outside the camp, which gave me the opportunity to scrounge anything that was edible. An unpopular task was to work at the railway station emptying carriages loaded with bags of cement, building materials or other cumbersome and heavy cargo. However, at times the wagons were loaded with 100-lb bags of rice, sugar, flour and other consumable produce. Either at loading or unloading it was inevitable that some of these goods were damaged and their contents spilled. Where it concerned edibles such as sugar, flour or raw rice grains, it gave me the opportunity to collect spillage off the floor and swallow some of it to bolster dwindling energy. It was also possible to 'accidentally' tear a hole in the bag I carried, or to let it slip and burst open. I did not mind having to sweep up and re-bag the stuff, nor even did I mind when I received kicks or slaps from our guard for my 'carelessness'. It was a small price to pay for a chance to scrounge a precious few mouthfuls of sustenance.

I was also keen to work in the large fields planted with vegetables for the Japanese kitchens. Weeding and tilling the soil gave me the opportunity to surreptitiously eat raw beans or tomatoes off the vines, or to dig up a sweet potato tuber that I had to eat unwashed – but who cared?! It was good food that filled the stomach. While the scrounging of edible cargo at the railway station or 'pinching' from the harvest in the vegetable fields was inherently dangerous, the ultimate in risk-taking was to 'steal' food from the Japanese kitchen, something I sometimes chanced. On one memorable occasion, I was working alone in a small vegetable plot behind the Japanese kitchens when the door opened. There stood the Japanese cook, no more than a couple of centimetres taller than me, but he wore boots while I went barefoot. The cook's feared command, '*Tobang, koko ni!* (Prisoner, come here!),' was usually followed by slaps, kicks or beatings. I expected the worst.

However, a surprise was in store – he raised his arms, not threatening, but rather in a kind of invitation, beckoning me, 'Koko ni, koko ni,' into the kitchen.

Inside, the cook pointed to a table on which stood a small hand-operated meat mincer and under it an enamel bowl. Next, he pointed to two buckets – one filled with roasted peanuts, one with sugar – and a small container of salt. I couldn't believe the sight of these delicacies from an almost forgotten past. Noticing my confusion, the cook made winding movements in the air, indicating the mincer. Dropping peanuts into it and continuing his winding movements over the mincer, he mimed adding sugar and salt to the nuts. In a flash of clarity, it came to me – I was to make peanut butter!

Left alone, I began making the raw ingredients into paste by loading the mincer, turning the handle and watching a crumbly substance tumble from the spout. Judging it rather too coarse, I stuffed it back into the machine for another go. After a third round, I judged it to be a reasonable imitation of the pre-war, store-bought variety. Even though the process of making this wartime peanut butter was laborious, I did not mind. It was certainly easier than digging ditches or performing the other heavy labour I was used to. And in truth, the situation was ripe for an opportunistic exploitation! Every time I had to reload the small mincer with partly ground paste, taking care that the cook could not see me, I stuffed a portion of the delicacy into my mouth. I cannot describe the sensation of the taste of it at the time, or the surge of energy that coursed through my entire body, other than to say that it was overwhelming.

For the rest of the war the Japanese cook kept me working in his kitchen. Cleaning and dishwashing, he allowed me to scrape caked-on food residue from his pots and pans and eat it: at last I could hope to survive. The deprivations we were made to suffer in the concentration camp justified me remembering an old Australian saying: Pinching and stealing are two different things. Stealing is when you take something that you want but do not really need. Pinching is when you need something and there is no other way to get it.

At Tjimahi there *was* no other way.

Rumours and beliefs

For many people, the longer the war lasted, the more life seemed unreal – even surreal. Time lost meaning: days seemed like weeks, months crept by as if they were years, but nothing ever changed. Increasing famine, desperation and death marked the reality of concentration camp life. An absolute blackout on any news from the outside world gave cause to wild rumours that were sometimes circulated in the camp. Inmates claimed their 'information' about military events and progress in the war were real and true, as they came from 'an impeccable source'. On one occasion, someone said he had come across an Indonesian lady who held a chilli in her hands. She dropped the chilli to the ground, which was taken as an irrefutable sign that the island of Lombok (Indonesian for chilli) had fallen to the Allies and we would soon be liberated. It was an 'absolute truth' that the woman knew about the island. But of course nothing happened. Unhappily, these rumours were always proved wrong. Such wishful thinking, rumour mongering and humbug led to bitter disappointment, which had an extremely negative effect on already despondent people. For some it meant that they gave up hope, and – perhaps mercifully – died.

In such times of great uncertainty, people who do not actively practise a religion sometimes turn to the church for solace and the sense of security that they crave. Arguably, some of those persons in our camps who claimed to have 'rediscovered' religion were really opportunists whose devotions were little better than putting on a show of religiosity *in case* that religion and prayer actually 'worked'. For days and weeks and months and years that felt devoid of time – that may just as well have been counted in ages – the committed and the opportunistically religious ones in our camp prayed for a desperately longed-for return to peace. Their prayers, however, seemed not to have been heard or granted.

Opposite to logic, belief is a force to which people cling more strongly and dearly than to reason. In times of severe misfortune, if religion does not 'work', some people turn to superstition and the supernatural. In the evenings and on Sundays many people attended church services, prohibited by the Japanese. There were also those who gathered at soothsayings and séances, calling on some agency in the forces of nature to assuage their loss of spirit with hope. One such *deus ex machina* power purporting to predict the future, so some 'believers' thought, was to be found in the writings of Nostradamus[xx] whose prophecies in vague language describe events from the mid-1500s up to the end of the world, predicted to happen in AD 3797. It is known that some people in general society have interpreted these prophecies by connecting them with events that have taken place since Nostradamus's times[xxi]. There were most certainly those in our prison camp who, in the absence of certainty, avidly discussed and even hotly debated their probability, seeking for any sign or omen that seemed to promise a desired outcome. Sadly for those who put faith in the conventional wisdom of their church and for those who turned to the supernatural, neither saw their entreaties fulfilled. Leading to great disappointment, the bitter reality of life in a Japanese concentration camp went on unabated, seemingly forever.

It is written that in every society exist myths, legends and prophecies that attempt to explain whence people came and whither they shall go. In the Christian Bible from Genesis to Revelation, propositions of humanity's origin and future are advanced. Counterpart explanations of different beliefs and myths are found in other cultures. In Indonesia, an ancient Javanese text the *Jojobojo*, presages the unknown future. Greatly debated in our camp, a subversion of a particular Jojobojo myth related an epic fight between a white and a black buffalo for the possession of a rice paddy. It purported that the black buffalo defeated its white adversary, enabling the victor to reclaim its home ground. In an apparently self-serving explanation of the Jojobojo, some in our community argued that buffaloes are not actually black, but grey, and therefore symbolise the Indonesian Dutch, whilst the white buffalo 'obviously' represented the ivory-coloured Japanese. This wishful thinking 'proved' to its believers that we would soon reclaim 'our *sawah*' – the rice field that was our birthright – from the Asian intruder. But by the end of 1944, nothing indicated that the war and our misery in captivity would ever end.

Increasing Indonesian nationalism
Even though the Japanese maintained a strict embargo on our contact with the outside world, by 1944 we began to notice a change taking place in Indonesian society. Whereas in the earlier years of the

Japanese occupation of the Dutch East Indies most Indonesians had maintained an ambivalent attitude towards their 'liberation' from the Dutch, their attitude had more recently markedly changed into the stirrings of Indonesian nationalism. As a corvée passed through a kampong, in the village square we noticed loudspeakers on poles, blaring forth propaganda that ranged from the Indonesian anthem to harangues on Indonesia's future as a partner in Japan's Greater East Asia Co-Prosperity Sphere. An even clearer sign of the rise of Indonesian nationalism came when we passed platoons of *Pemuda* – a paramilitary national force of Indonesian youths in training by the Japanese military. Sometimes called *Perlopor* – derived from the Dutch word *voorlopers* (forerunners) – these young men in superb physical condition were the pick of fanatically nationalistic young Indonesians. In the future they would form the core of recruits in the National Army of Indonesia. When I came across such a platoon, I sometimes wondered if any of these Pemuda may have been village youths from my home province – even including my boyhood friend Soekarno – who had cursed me and my people, 'Assu londoh (Dutch dogs)'. Though the Pemuda totally ignored us, whenever we encountered the grim-faced youths, they intimidated me just as much as the Japanese soldiers. Their hatred of the despised Dutch was almost palpable, and as we passed their platoon on the march I felt almost protected by our Korean or Japanese guards. The signs were there that the former Dutch East Indies was rapidly changing into what would soon be the sovereign Indonesian Nation. In the isolation of the captive world of our prison, we still did not see this coming.

A visit from the Red Cross
As Christmas 1944 approached, hope suddenly surged when the Japanese commandant announced that representatives of the International Red Cross were due to inspect our camp. Eagerly anticipating the visit, people argued that the Red Cross delegation would surely notice our dreadful state of affairs in Japanese captivity. Hopes sprang that, being such a prestigious and influential organisation, the International Red Cross would surely convince the Japanese to grant us the same protection as was applicable to prisoners of war under the Geneva Convention. Like my fellow internees, I was elated. How could I not but trust that the

International Red Cross had come if not to set us free then at least to relieve us from our present dire want?

In a clear attempt to cover up any evidence of bad management or abuse in the camp, the Japanese commandant and his guards made a considerable effort to clean up the premises and the grounds. They made us transform the punishment cells at the front gate into storage rooms stocked with office supplies. The badly neglected 'hospital' received a coat of fresh paint and even a supply of medicines and cheap but adequate cots that replaced stretchers or straw mats that had been the only bedding on which patients could lie. Special corvée removed rubbish, mowed grass, and raked and swept paths until we hardly recognised the premises. When the Japanese even increased the quantity and quality of our rations, it was seen as a sure sign that things were changing for the better. Perhaps no more than a handful of realists saw the improvements as cynical Japanese window dressing; very few of us did not believe that the International Red Cross would end the Japanese commandant's notorious work edict and ensure that the present changes would become permanent.

When the day of the Red Cross delegation visit came, the guards confined anyone with obvious and visible disabilities to the barracks, forbidding them to show themselves. After days of scrubbing, our living quarters gleamed clean and fresh and the guards made sure that we wore our 'best' clothes. On the parade ground, able-bodied people were made to play soccer or other forms of sport, while residents indoors were ordered to show themselves playing cards or engaging in some other recreational activity on their platforms. Not a single corvée went outside the gates that day, and other than staff in the kitchen and hospital, no one worked; it was my first 'holiday' in a long time.

When the Red Cross delegates on whom the entire camp had pinned such high hopes came, the event proved to be an anticlimax, a bitter disappointment. To be fair, we had no way of knowing if or what preconditions the Japanese had imposed on the Red Cross before they agreed to their visit. Apparently to make certain that they saw only what he wanted them to see, the Japanese commandant accompanied the visitors everywhere they went. There could be little doubt that the delegation's 'inspection' amounted to little more than a sightseeing tour. When they walked straight past us without exchanging a word, the tired adage that we must have looked to them like animals in a zoo seemed not altogether inappropriate.

From my mat on the platform, I saw the Red Cross representatives only from a distance; not one of the delegates that passed through the barracks tried to establish eye contact, let alone speak with any of us. I watched for signs of emotion from them who surely could not overlook our miserably crammed living conditions or notice that the majority of us were undernourished and in uncertain health. The expression on the visitors' faces did not reach out to us, but focused on something in the distance. To me it was as if they wished not to see what they could and indeed should have seen on their inspection. As they came and went, in their wake trailed an unfamiliar perfume of soap and shaving cream that only served to make us realise how well these fortunate, sleek, well-groomed and well-fed men of the Red Cross were; they would have recently bathed, put on clean clothes and eaten well, while we wallowed in neglect and starvation. I envied them, and when they passed and then left without a sign of possible interest in us, I also resented them. The feeling of bitter betrayal by these apparently professional 'do-gooders', has left in me a lifelong antipathy towards the International Red Cross. In my detestation of them I include welfare agencies in general; organisations that may be brilliant in fundraising to pay for the salaries and good soap, shaving cream and clean clothes for their executives, but who lack heart, and in whose veins runs cold, blue writing ink, not red blood.

The Red Cross delegation's 'inspection' of the camp made not the slightest difference to previous conditions, and when they left we returned to the Japanese commandant's 'normal' work ethic – slave labour and starvation continued unabated. The apparent failure of the Red Cross delegates to negotiate concessions from the Japanese left people so disheartened and robbed of hope that many simply gave up and died. I will never know if I, too, may have reached that point of utter despair, if not for my camp father. It may have made the difference, when he said to me, 'Remember from Kipling's Book of Verses that Mr Miles taught you the meaning of: *hold on when there is nothing in you / Except the Will which says to them: Hold on!*'

By Christmas 1944, but unlikely as a result of the Red Cross visit, the Japanese commandant gave us permission to write a single letter only, to a nearest relative. By then it had been nearly two years since I had been taken away from my mother and sister, and much longer than that since I had seen or heard from my father. I was issued with something like an airmail form that came with a sheet of prepared phrases, this allowed a choice of no more than six sentences. I wrote my mother something along the lines of, 'The Japanese authorities are very kind to me and they look after me well,' and, 'We are in excellent health with plenty to eat and much spare time to play games or enjoy other amusements,' and similar lines of flagrant untruths. But I thought that the letter, addressed to her last known address at the Gudang Garam camp, would at least serve to show my mother that I was still alive. In a way I was glad that the prepared text gave me no chance to tell her about the real situation in my camp. Thanks to the kindness of an acquaintance that had no one to contact, I also sent a letter to my father. As I had no idea where to send it, I addressed it with only his identification number and Army brigade name. After the war I found out that our camp administration had not forwarded any of these letters, and nor did any of us ever receive mail from our loved ones in other camps until almost the end of the war. The 'privilege' of this writing to one's relatives remains yet another example of inexplicable Japanese thought and conduct, yet another act of abject cruelty.

Changing conditions

The early months of 1945 slipped slowly past. In about May, for unknown reasons, we began to see small but significant improvements in our living conditions. First we noticed that the breakfast 'porridge' of revolting cassava starch – that I could still only swallow with great difficulty – was replaced with a much more nutritious and better tasting cornmeal gruel. Next, in about June, we were delighted but puzzled when, entirely unprecedented, we received Red Cross food parcels. I later found out that the Japanese had kept these from us for many months. The reason for the release of the precious articles to us was yet another unknown.

When with thumping heart I unpacked my carton, I found such incredible things as a tin of Spam meat, a block of chocolate, a packet of Camel brand cigarettes, a toothbrush and toothpaste and a cake of soap. I could not decide which one of these I should begin to enjoy first, or even if at all. Perhaps I should allow myself just one square from the bar of chocolate, or one *real*, tailor-made Camel cigarette? I had not for years brushed my teeth with anything but a moistened finger dipped in salt, nor bathed myself with soap. Should I therefore use the soap or toothpaste now, or keep them until the end of the war when I rejoined my family? Each in our own way, my fellow inmates and I solved these 'problems', but something that no one waited to enjoy was their packet of tailor-made cigarettes. For the next few days the camp smelt luxuriously of this manufactured tobacco, so much better than the acrid smell of the coarse native tobacco and palm leaf 'paper' from which we rolled our Indonesian peasant cigarettes. After ablutions, the perfume of real soap smelt almost foppish, and when I brushed my teeth with paste and toothbrush, the taste in my mouth felt unreal. When I ceased struggling against temptation and opened the tin of Spam, I ate that delicious treat with my rice and vegetable soup in one sitting. After years of meat-less fare the taste was unbelievable.

If we prisoners wondered at the reasons for these improvements, an explanation of sorts came from as unlikely a source as the Korean bully, Sergeant Wadda. In escorting us to our work of late, on a number of occasions Wadda had released snippets about the progress and fighting in the war. As the Japanese had always clamped a strict prohibition on information about the outside world, fearsome Sergeant Wadda's disregard of the taboo was unprecedented and inexplicable. With ample evidence of Wadda's previous unpredictable nature, his recent strange conduct raised suspicions of it being yet another example of a twisted mind. However, when the Korean confided to a *honcho* (corvée leader), 'Nippon soldier number one, fight *baka* (stupid) America soldier Iwo Jima,' it was the first time in years that news about the war – with specific reference even to a combat zone – came from a *truly* identifiable source rather than from an anonymous 'informant', from whence much proven-to-be-false information had caused so much damage to the camp's morale. Few of us knew that Iwo Jima, annexed by Japan in 1891, was the largest of the Volcano Islands in the western Pacific Ocean. Regardless, Wadda's mention of American and Japanese fighting was without precedent. Not long after, he again divulged fresh information, 'Nippon *kamikaze* (suicide pilot) boom boom *takusan* (many) America ship Okinawa.' Again, few people knew what the word kamikaze meant, but Wadda's seemingly casual gossip importantly inferred that it had something to do with Allied ships fighting the Japanese navy, somewhere called 'Okinawa'. Whatever the veracity of Wadda's ramblings, the fact remained that whereas until recently he had made it a virtual sport and his pleasure to terrorise us, nowadays he was suspiciously meek and almost pacific. This change of heart from a previous bully, together with improved conditions in our camp, was enough to kindle a flicker of hope in long disheartened minds. However, lest it all should turn out to be no more than yet another devilish Japanese tactic to demoralise us, having known so many disappointments in the past few years, who dared place too much hope on what seemed signs of better times?

In spite of our fears, the camp's improved diet remained in place and the work parties became less onerous. The Japanese improved these conditions even more when, in July 1945, fully loaded trucks dumped virtual mountains of sweet potato near the kitchens. The cooks were miraculously allowed to distribute as much of this delicious and nutritious food as we could eat, supplementing the now more palatable diet of cornmeal porridge, rice and vegetable soup. It was with oversensitive trepidation that even the most sceptical and cautious among us began to speculate what these changes in our living conditions might mean.

After two years without another almost-forgotten luxury, another small miracle took place when we were issued a generous portion of cane sugar. The first time I received mine, I could not restrain myself from wolfing it down to the last grain in one sitting. That July, every day seemed to bring a new surprise, such as trucks bringing in a huge load of second-hand but good quality clothing to which we could help ourselves. I had only one shirt left and a worn but clean pair of khaki army shorts, my 'best clothes' that I had carefully kept for at the end of the war, when I should return home to my family. Like many in the camp, I wore only an upper body covering made from a flour bag with holes cut out for my arms, and a pair of shorts made from another flour bag with holes to let my legs through. Making me feel as if I had received a birthday present, I helped myself to underwear, shirts and shorts that looked almost elegant on my skinny body.

One day, my hands shook and I became dizzy with excitement when I received a letter from my mother; the same kind of 'letter' with pre-prepared sentences that I had sent her many months ago. Nevertheless, with my mother's letter in my hands, I now had something tangible to connect me with my family – proof that when she wrote it she and my sister were both alive.

Then, one morning at Tenko, with characteristic abruptness of speech, the commandant himself announced the end to his notorious work policy, 'No more one man work help other men eat. Is all finish. Now everyone in camp *yasumi* (rest).' With this new twist, the often onerous and sometimes dangerous corvée work parties ceased. Inside the camp, maintenance work parties of course continued, but other than this necessary work the camp now enjoyed a state of unaccustomed rest.

Until Sergeant Wadda had recently begun to drop hints about military action between Japanese and Allied Forces we had known nothing of world events. We were unaware that on 1 April 1945, General Douglas MacArthur's forces invaded the island of Okinawa, marking a critical turning point in the Pacific war. Although we speculated that there must be a compelling reason for the living conditions in the camp improving so noticeably, we had no way of knowing that the fall of Okinawa to the Americans on 14 June 1945 must have signalled to overseas Japanese soldiers that their nation had lost the war. Still, so great was our fear of previous Japanese deceit, and even of our own pitiful delusions, that although life in the camp had become more bearable, few dared hope that these might be signs of an end to the war.

CHAPTER 7

The End of the War

At about noon on 27 August 1945, I happened to be standing beside one of the towering mountains of sweet potato near the kitchens when I heard the sound of an approaching aeroplane. At first I paid scant attention to what I thought was a Japanese aircraft on a routine exercise from the nearby military airstrip. When the plane came closer and was almost overhead, as people seem to instinctively do, I looked up. The aeroplane was coming straight towards where I stood beside the sweet potato mountain. Although it was flying at an unusually low altitude, I did not recognise the type of aircraft, but I noticed that it had three distinctive tail panels – a feature that I later learned is unique to the American-built Liberator bombers. When it was directly overhead, to my utter amazement a shower of papers suddenly came bursting out from an open hatch in the fuselage, tumbling towards earth, dancing and twirling in the air, raining down over the camp. The aircraft disappeared into the distance, but I saw it turn around over the nearby village and re-approach the camp, the noise from its engine growing louder as it again came towards where I stood transfixed. This time I thought that I could see a pair of hands in the plane's open bomb bay, releasing another shower of papers. By then many people had rushed out of their barracks and we all stood gazing up in the air, unable to make sense of what was happening until a cry went up from somewhere in the crowd, '*English!! It is an English aeroplane!*' Many hands went up in the air, pointing to where we could clearly make out a red, blue, and white insignia on the aircraft's fuselage and wings, and a chorus of voices exclaimed, 'Yes, yes, it is an English plane! It's English, it's English!!!' As yet no one dared say aloud, 'The war is over.' None of us could believe that a miracle had finally happened. I can still vividly remember that I climbed the sweet potato mountain as high as possible to catch a copy of the tumbling pamphlets that came down from the sky. I do not recall the exact wording of the message, but I do recollect that the black and white print I read off the sheet in my hand told me that on 15 August 1945 Japan had unconditionally surrendered and that Allied Forces would soon set us free. I wish that I had kept a copy of this remarkable document that fell from the sky on 27 August 1945, released over the 4/9 Battalion concentration camp by unknown English hands from the bomb bay of an aptly named Liberator aircraft. Rumours and deceptions had finally been put to rest; the pamphlet was incontrovertible proof that the war was over. We had survived the concentration camp – we were free!

In limbo

All that afternoon and long into the night people talked about and re-read the message on the pamphlets that told us of the end of the war – and therefore our suffering. But we still sometimes feared whether all this was true. Was the war *truly* over? Confirmation that the pamphlets had told the truth – that it was not a devilish trick by the Japanese – came the next day. On the morning of 28 August 1945, in full dress uniform including medal ribbons and with ceremonial samurai sword at his side, the Japanese camp commandant faced the assembly on the parade ground. Standing stiffly at attention and saluting, he issued a command in Japanese whereupon two guards beside the flagpole lowered the flag, Japan's national emblem, and then hoisted the Dutch red, white and blue tricolour flag aloft. Thereupon the commandant issued a statement partly in English and partly in Indonesian, announcing that Japan had surrendered and that the Second World War was over. Every year on 15 August, people now commemorate VJ Day – 'Victory over Japan Day'. *My* liberation came on 28 August 1945, when the Japanese commandant confirmed that the shower of pamphlets from the Liberator bomber had told the truth and that I was free. On 28 August every year, I remember and I pay honour to friends and fellow inmates who did not live to see the end of our misery in the Tjimahi concentration camp.

Although the war had ended and the Japanese could no longer intimidate and harm us, so great was the residue of our fear of them that no one dared walk through the now wide-open front gates. These were still manned by Japanese soldiers, who continued to prevent us from leaving the camp, '*Tidak bisa. Sajang sekali* (We can't let you [go]. Such a pity. Sorry!)' How meek the previous bullies had become!

When Japan surrendered, the Allied Forces were thinly spread throughout the southern Pacific region. On Java a single Scottish Seaforth Highland regiment and a British Indian Gurkha regiment, both stationed in Batavia, were impossibly meant to maintain peace and security on the entire island. Allied High Command therefore decreed that the defeated Imperial Japanese Army would be responsible for the safety and welfare of former prisoners of war and civilian internees in the liberated camps. This was not well received by many in our former prison community. While people remembered the bands of Indonesian nationalist youths, surely if these Pemuda or Perlopor recalcitrants caused trouble, we Dutch would soon put them back in their subservient place? Whether through ignorance or colonial arrogance, it was difficult to accept that while we were free, we were not free to leave our former camp: '*Tidak bisa jalan; ah sayang* (You may not leave, so sorry).'

As days went by, people became increasingly impatient to leave the camp. The Dutch leadership, who had taken over from the Japanese, confirmed that the army must continue to guard us from increased Indonesian militancy against the Dutch. Not until Allied Forces reached us could there be safety. Out of touch with the political and social situation in Indonesia, every one of us still thought of the country as 'Our Indië', and many did not understand why they should remain locked up inside the camp. In spite of the as yet latent menace of the Pemuda youths, very few realised how urgent the drive of Indonesian nationalism had become. Beyond the walls of the former concentration camp, the dying stage of Dutch colonialism had begun.

The capitulation of the Japanese Army left a vacuum in civil authority. This led to increasing unrest throughout Indonesia, and anyone with their eyes and ears open could not have failed to recognise that resentment against a return of colonial Dutch rule was growing in the former colony. The Japanese had long encouraged Indonesia to move towards their Asia Co-Prosperity ideal, knowing it would eventually translate into independent nationhood. Massive propaganda campaigns during the four years of war in the Pacific had emboldened Indonesian public sentiment against the Dutch, but most threatening to the Dutch cause had been Japan's military training of ultra-patriotic Indonesian youths, who would become a national army for Indonesia.

Whether or not it was done with Japanese collusion, following Japan's surrender, groups of Pemuda swiftly moved to take over certain strategic infrastructure and local services on Java. The railway station at Tjimahi was now in their hands, as were the local power station, the radio broadcasting station and other facilities.

A letter, and a decision

The takeover of the local railway station by Pemuda would become a particular problem for me. After some time waiting in the camp, free but unable to leave, I received a letter. Written on thin, poor quality paper, this time it was a *real* letter from my mother. In her own words, not the previous Japanese pro forma message, my mother wrote that she and my sister had been moved from the Gudang Garam camp to several other locations on Java, and that they were now in a women's camp called Tjideng[xxii], in Batavia.

> We have learned from the Red Cross that, thank God, you have survived and that you are in a camp at Tjimahi… Sadly, we have so far been unable to find any trace of your father's whereabouts and I am very worried about him.

Ironically, after being so bitterly disillusioned by the Red Cross, I could now thank it for putting me in touch with my family.

My mother's letter presented me with a dilemma. I now knew where to find her and my sister, and I felt that I could not delay being reunited with them. I knew that if I were caught outside the camp, the Japanese would return me there, though nowadays of course without punishment. I also realised full well that the most serious risk was to fall into the hands of the Pemuda, who would certainly treat me even more harshly than the Japanese had. 'We must not get impatient,' Mijnheer Piso cautioned me when I complained that I wanted to leave the camp. 'You and I have survived the war and it would be foolish to now risk being killed by Pemuda. Let us wait just a little longer until our troops come to free us. Let us not do anything rash and dangerous.' Such was the imprudence and ingratitude of my impulsive youth that a few days later I disregarded my camp father's wise advice.

One evening I was speaking with three other young men who, for reasons of their own, also wanted to travel to Batavia. Somehow we made the quick decision to escape. We had no real plan, but we knew that it was critically important that we should have identification and travel papers, particularly in case we were challenged by Pemuda. One of my acquaintances had a Chinese family friend in Bandung who, he assured us, could help us with forged documentation for travel to Batavia by train. That night we waited until just before dawn, when most people in the camp would be in deepest sleep and when the Japanese soldiers at the gate were hopefully least alert. When the stars began to dim, the eastern sky was beginning to colour and roosters were noisily welcoming a new day, we scaled the no longer patrolled barbed wire fence of the 4/9 Battalion camp. On 7 September 1945, after two long and terrible years, I finally escaped the concentration camp without a backward glance, elated that we had survived the war. My only regret was that I had been unable to say goodbye to my camp father, Mijnheer Piso, who I was never to see again.

We scaled the no longer patrolled barbed wire fence of the 4/9 Battalion camp on 7 September 1945 – free at last.

A quick trip to Bandung

So as not to arouse suspicion, we waited till daylight before joining other people, Indonesians on their daily business. It was a strange, even a scary sensation to be on our own among civilians as we made our way on foot along the main road to Bandung. Though we had planned to walk the 11 kilometres from Tjimahi to Bandung, we decided that we would be less conspicuous if we travelled by dokkar, horse-drawn carriage. Other than the two rijksdaalder coins my mother had given me, I had no money. But my companions would not hear my objections when they kindly paid my share of the coach fare. Of course, by hailing a dokkar we had to take a chance that the Indonesian coachman would not betray and hand us over to the Japanese – or worse, to the Pemuda. Perhaps the cabby decided that we were not Orang Belanda from the nearby camp, or perhaps he did not wish to forgo the lucrative fare to Bandung. Whatever his reasons, not a word or glance betrayed his thoughts as he cracked the whip over his long-suffering horse and began driving. Our risk had paid off – we were on our way to meet the man whose counterfeit paperwork would hopefully get me to my family in Batavia.

On reaching Bandung, the man made us very welcome and – what was more – he assured us that he could provide us with the identity papers. However, when he learned that we planned to take a train to Batavia, he warned us against boarding it at Bandung, 'The Pemuda are especially vigilant at the railway station in Bandung. They will be looking for anyone without genuine identification,' he warned. 'The papers that I will give you are good, but it would be unwise to take unnecessary risks.' We took the advice to heart. After he had made out the promised documents, instead of boarding a train locally, we again took a dokkar back to Tjimahi where we hoped that the much smaller station would make it safer for us to catch a train to Batavia.

Our return journey was again uneventful. Back at Tjimahi we decided that it would be foolish for us to climb the fence back into the camp, as we would have to make a second escape. Instead we hid overnight in a nearby clump of bushland.

Journey to Batavia

The next day, soon after sunrise, we walked to the village railway station to wait for a train to Batavia. Afraid that a zealous official might catch us and hand us over to Pemuda, we did not buy train tickets. Sneaking undetected onto the railway platform, we mingled with a crowd of travellers, hoping that when the train came, in the push and shove of the mob we could squeeze into a carriage without having to show tickets. Our plan fortunately succeeded, and once on board we had little fear that a conductor could reach us in the densely packed carriage. The journey reminded me of when, two years earlier, the Japanese had transferred me from the high school camp to Tjimahi. Both times I suffered the discomfort of being squeezed inside a baking hot railway carriage, but at least I now travelled of my own will, and was on my way to be reunited with my family.

It was late in the afternoon when we reached Indonesia's capital city, and though we kept a close lookout for Japanese soldiers and Pemuda, we disembarked without problems. Leaving the railway station, we followed one of our friends to the home of his parents' acquaintances, an Amboinese Indonesian family who – like most Amboinese Christians – had remained loyal to the Dutch cause and who he trusted would help us.

After a long, hot walk, asking many times for directions, we arrived at the home of Dr and Mrs Tupemahu. As we had hoped, they welcomed us most hospitably, allowing us to stay with them until we could make other arrangements. Later, when I told my hosts that I planned to call at the women's concentration camp to look for my mother and sister, they shook their heads, 'The Japanese guards at Tjideng still keep the gates closed and turn away all visitors. Yesterday we ourselves unsuccessfully tried to reach friends in the camp.' Having come so far and with such difficulty I was not prepared to give in to defeat, 'If necessary, if I can't get in through the gates, like at Tjimahi I will have to scale the wall.' My worried hosts did not try to talk me out of the plan, but that night I slept fitfully, troubled and not at all certain how to make good my promise.

A reunion

The next day I thanked Dr and Mrs Tupemahu for their hospitality and, following their directions, left on foot for the camp in one of the city's suburbs. I was wearing shoes for the first time in two years, and it did not take long for large blisters to form. I gave up, took off the unaccustomed shoes and continued much more comfortably on my bare feet.

It was an hour before noon when I reached my destination. As my hosts had warned me, the gates there were securely closed and guarded by Japanese soldiers. There have been occasions in my life when I have been inexplicably saved from harm or assisted to overcome a predicament. I am not speculating on either blind chance or otherworldly intercession, but strange things have happened to me from time to time that I cannot explain. On that day, at almost the instant I reached the front entrance of the camp, the guards swung open the gates. '*Boleh jalan*,' said they, 'You may pass.' At 11 o'clock in the morning of 9 September 1945, I was literally the first post-war visitor to enter the former Tjideng women's concentration camp in Batavia.

Before the Japanese requisitioned the entire suburb as a concentration camp for the Dutch, Tjideng was a pre-war housing development mainly occupied by minor Indonesian public servants, clerks and shop assistants. I did not know either the name of the street or the house number where my mother and sister lived. Able only to give my family name, the best I could do was ask directions. I was the first young Dutch man that the women and children in the camp had seen for more than two years, and everywhere I went people stopped and stared at me – I felt almost like a celebrity. Conversely, I had trouble keeping from staring at the women in the camp. In the time of my youth women were always dressed demurely, but to my consternation this was certainly not the case in Tjideng. Many ladies and young women wore nothing more than a brazier or a knotted cloth over the upper body, and tight-fitting shorts or skirts covering the lower body. I did try not to stare, but I confess that I was not always successful in keeping my eyes on the road before me.

After many turns and false trails, I asked at yet another small hut if my mother and sister lived in this street. Staring, silently frozen for a moment, she suddenly called out my mother's name and burst out,

'Your son! Your son! Come quickly, your son is here!' Two years after Captain Nakamura had separated us, on 9 September 1945 my mother, sister and I were reunited.

The feeling of that moment is too great to put into words.

Batavia

Although we had found each other and were able to spend most of that day together, my mother pointed out that it was impossible for me to stay in the women's camp as it was so overcrowded. But she worried about where I would live. As I had nowhere else in Batavia, I said that I would ask Dr and Mrs Tupemahu if I could stay with them until I had found accommodation and work to pay for board and lodging. Late that afternoon back with the Amboinese family, I explained the situation and asked them for temporary lodging. They immediately agreed, 'Of course you can stay with us!' I remembered the silver rijksdaalders that I had kept all this time and which I now pried from under the lining of my shoes. But when I offered to pay her until I hopefully found work and lodging, Mrs Tupemahu indignantly refused. 'It is not necessary,' she insisted. 'No, no, these are lucky, very special, very propitious coins that you must only spend on making a selametan, a thank-you offering to Heaven for finding your mother and sister.' I knew and respected Indonesian custom, and I did not insist on paying my kind hosts with these particular coins. I agreed, 'Yes, a selametan would indeed be proper.' Adding, 'When I find work tomorrow you must allow me to then pay you.' After more polite refusals my hostess gave in to me, 'Yes, that will be an acceptable thing to do.'

The next morning at the Red Cross head office in Batavia I started my search for work and somewhere to live, but was met with, 'Sorry young man, we cannot help you.' I went to leave and was almost outside the building when a man overtook me. 'Perhaps I can help?' he offered. Explaining that he had contacts with the military in the Scottish Seaforth Highland regiment stationed in Batavia, he suggested I try them for employment. 'When you speak with the colonel in charge you may mention my name, and perhaps he can put you to work in the mess or the office. There is no guarantee that you will be successful, but I thought that you may at least try your luck with them.' I thanked the stranger for his help, and I felt that there was at least one person in the International Red Cross who had not cold ink, but warm blood running through his veins.

At their regimental headquarters, in my best English, I told an officer my business. He asked me many questions: how old I was; the names of members of my family and where they now were; my father's Dutch army unit; where on Java had he served and his present whereabouts; and other personal details. When I mentioned how I had escaped from the former 4/9 Battalion concentration camp at Tjimahi and how I had travelled to Batavia by train, he asked to see my fake identity papers and explain how I had obtained them. I despaired that, as had happened at the Red Cross, I would be sent away, but looking up from his notes the officer said, 'Stay here young fellow, while I talk with my superior.' I waited, but without much hope.

After what seemed ages, the officer returned quite jovial. 'My superior, the colonel of the regiment, has agreed that we can employ you and that you may board with us in the barracks here.' More than my heartfelt, 'Thank you, Sir,' the expression on my face must have shown the officer how relieved I felt, and he smiled as he replied, 'That's fine, old boy.' He then became businesslike again. 'You told me that you speak the Indonesian lingua franca and also the Javanese language. The colonel feels that we can employ you as an interpreter, particularly to help us at the wharves at Tandjung Priok. Men from the Ghurka regiment run regular convoys of trucks to the harbour where they collect material and supplies for our troops. As none of us speak Indonesian, this is often a problem for them. We will of course pay you a small wage, but I must warn you that even though you are a civilian aide, you will sometimes work in situations that are not without danger for yourself.' I agreed and the officer added, 'I must point out that to and from the harbour, Indonesian snipers have sometimes shot at our trucks and have attempted to drop grenades on our convoys. You must therefore understand that there is always a danger that we will run into a combat situation and that we cannot guarantee your safety'. Without hesitation I assured the officer that I understood the warning and we shook hands: 'Done.'

Selametan

A non-commissioned officer from the regiment showed me a vacant spot in the barracks where I put up my mosquito net and lay the old horse rug, my 'bed', on the floor. I then walked the long way back to the house of Dr and Mrs Tupemahu to collect the few personal belongings that I had left with them. They were glad to hear that I now had paid work and accommodation. 'If you should ever need us, you must let us know,' said kindly Mrs Tupemahu, and as it was late in the afternoon, she insisted that I stay one more night. She had not forgotten the thanksgiving feast for my mother and sister, and she suggested that the next morning I use my lucky silver coins at the *passar* (market) to buy ingredients. 'I shall help you to make sure that the vendors give you many times more value for the silver than for Japanese occupation currency,' my savvy host said. The following day we bought two live chickens, a dozen eggs, a bottle each of coconut cream and peanut oil, and vegetables and spices. 'Your mother will know how to prepare a great feast,' said Mrs Tupemahu. She admonished me, 'At your selametan, be mindful to thank God and praise Him for having spared you and your mother and sister. You can trust that He will also return your father to the family.' With my few personal belongings and the chickens and ingredients for the thanksgiving feast under my arms, I bid Dr and Mrs Tupemahu farewell. I have never forgotten what these Indonesian nationals showed me: regardless of race, there is kindness and humanity and inherent decency in people of any society.

There was nobody around to butcher the chickens in Tjideng, so I had to do the deed myself. And my mother had no equipment to fry them, so they had to be boiled. But in all, it tasted well. My mother reminded me that when I was taken away from the first camp she had said 'This is all I can do for you, now you're in God's hands.' With selametan we said, 'Thank you, God.'

Scottish Seaforth Highlanders

My work with the Scottish Seaforth Highlanders started the next day. Every morning a jeep took me from the Scottish Seaforth Highland regiment's barracks to the Ghurka regimental compound in another part of the city. I was then allocated a seat in the convoy of trucks that plied back and forth to Tandjung Priok harbour on the northern side of Batavia. In the back of each truck a machine gunner covered the tail end. Standing on the passenger side, with his upper body through a manhole in the roof of the vehicle, another soldier kept a lookout ahead for possible hostile action from hamlets along the road or an ambush from clumps of vegetation. I gladly volunteered to also act as a lookout in the truck in which I rode. It gave me at least an illusion of watching out for myself, keeping an eye out for Indonesian 'insurgents'. I had no idea of the risk I was taking; I was blissfully ignorant and never gave it a thought. All the other trucks had soldiers with their head out, and I thought I'd better do the same. At the time it did not occur to me that, with the trucks normally travelling slowly at about thirty feet distance apart, my head above the manhole probably made an excellent sniper's target. I shall never know if I tempted fate that way – the trips were usually uneventful and boring. On a few occasions adrenaline flowed when the convoy ran into an Indonesian attack or when the lookouts spotted suspicious action in a kampong ahead, but these were quite mild. There were just a couple of shots fired from the village or in the paddies and that was it. It didn't feel dangerous at all at the time – and we mostly did not encounter mischief.

On the wharf at Tandjung Priok I was kept busy translating between the Ghurka soldiers and Indonesian stevedores and labourers unloading the ship. My association with the Scottish Seaforth Highlanders and the Gurkhas was brief, but I developed a regard for both. The Scots treated me very considerately, although I could barely understand a word most of them said in their thick Scottish brogue, and I gained great respect for the fearless but likeable Gurkha warriors.

A brief return to Tjimahi, and a fateful choice
Following the Japanese surrender in the Pacific, even in Batavia – the safest city on Java – security was becoming a problem. In the surrounding countryside, rampok bandits operated virtually unchecked, looting, raiding homes and businesses and sometimes killing anyone who put up resistance. The Pemuda youth gangs, well trained and disciplined by the Japanese were also increasing their paramilitary

action. This unrest had so far not reached the Tjideng camp, but by October 1945 the security situation in Indonesia had deteriorated to the point that Batavia was under virtual siege. Despite the clear evidence of social unrest and danger, I decided to take a day or two off from my work to return to Tjimahi, where as well as retrieving the belongings I had left behind, I especially wanted to thank and say goodbye to my camp father, Mijnheer Piso. In retrospect, it was a foolish decision.

The train trip back to Tjimahi was uneventful. When I disembarked, I was still wary of Pemuda, so I again mingled with a throng of Indonesian fellow travellers leaving the station. To my relief, the Japanese who still guarded the front entrance to my old camp let me enter unchallenged. Inside I noticed that there were now decidedly fewer people living in the camp and that some of the barracks were even deserted. In my old barracks I found no sign of Mijnheer Piso. When I asked some people if they knew where I could perhaps find him, they said that he, too, had left to be rejoined with his family. I realised that I had left it too late to thank him. On 28 August when I annually remember the day of my liberation, I also remember my camp father, and in my thoughts I thank him: Dank U, Mijnheer Piso. My conscience has never been fully unburdened, and I regret that he will never know that I shall forever be indebted to him for his kindness and his care of me.

The next day, the train back to Batavia stopped as usual at every station, making frustratingly slow progress. Impatient to get back to my family, at the village of Tasikmalaya – where the regional service joins with Indonesia's major rail line between Batavia in the west and Surabaya in the east – I opted to transfer to the express train, paying the extra fare to Batavia. It was a decision that saved my life.

Between Tasikmalaya and Batavia, the overnight express from Surabaya did not stop anywhere and we reached the city in good time. In good spirits I immediately made my way to my family in their camp. However, when I walked into the house my mother and sister looked at me as if they were seeing a ghost. With tears streaming down their faces they exclaimed, 'You are alive!' I had no idea why my family was in such distress until my mother told me that after Tasikmalaya a band of Pemuda had stopped and ransacked the train in which I had travelled, killing every white person on board. The news of the massacre had reached British Army Headquarters, and some people who knew of my trip to Tjimahi had come to check with my family if I could have been on that particular train. It was a sobering thought – but for the sake of the extra fare my distraught family could indeed have been mourning for me.

Indonesian nationalism

After my almost ill-fated trip to my old camp, security on Java rapidly deteriorated further. Preparing for repatriation to their homeland, the Japanese Army had begun to largely withdraw most of their troops to major centres – leaving much of the rest of the Indonesian archipelago without substantial military or civic control. As time went by, what had been little more than opportunistic Indonesian rampok activity began to turn into insurgencies by freedom fighting Indonesian nationalists. On Java in particular, occasional fierce fighting broke out between the revolutionaries and British Forces. At the major cities of Surabaya and Batavia the presence of Allied troops was able to at least curtail the uprisings, but by November 1945 guerrilla war had broken out and much of what was still officially the Dutch East Indies was now under virtual siege. Indonesia had declared its independence when Japan surrendered to the Allies, but it would take another four years for Holland to recognise Indonesian sovereignty.

As the volatile military situation increasingly moved towards anarchy, the undermanned Allied Army practically abandoned much of the countryside to the Indonesian freedom fighters. The situation may have been part of an Allied strategy that placed greater emphasis on bolstering their occupation forces in the Japanese homeland rather than supporting the Dutch colonial powers to regain their pre-war territories. In Dutch circles it was suspected that the British agricultural fraternity in Malaya had much to gain from supporting Indonesian nationalism. Preventing or hindering a rebuilding of the Dutch plantation industry would see the competition from the Dutch East Indies tropical plantation industry neutralised. Another aspect of the immediate post-war period was that no Dutch Armed Forces were sent – or, debatably, politics prevented them from being sent – to curb and control social unrest in the East Indies colony. This would be left to returning Dutch military POWs. In the yet early days of Indonesia's fight for freedom, the outcome of the conflict was nowhere near a foregone conclusion. Few in Holland and the Dutch East Indies doubted that we would soon reclaim the ways of life such as they had been before the war.

Some good news

In spite of Mrs Tupemahu's optimism that God would soon reunite us with my father, by the end of 1945 the Red Cross had failed to find him in former POW camps in Indonesia and even as far away as Singapore and Malaya. All attempts to locate him had so far been unsuccessful. My mother never gave up hope; she almost beleaguered the Red Cross to keep looking for him. Not long before Christmas 1945, we finally learned that my father had been found in a POW camp at the village of Kanchanaburi on the Burmese border with Thailand. The relief we felt was immense – it was the first we'd heard of my father in four years. All that time we had no idea where he was or if he had survived. And now we knew.

It has often intrigued me that my mother, rather than considering the practical feasibility of a plan, at times made decisions that to her must have been foregone conclusions. Having finally located her husband, without a moment's hesitation she declared, 'We will leave for Thailand to be reunited with your father.' Even though she had no idea how we should find a way to travel across the sea to faraway Thailand, my mother never questioned but that we *would* rejoin him.

CHAPTER 8

A Time of Repair

Wherever the storm carries me, I go a willing guest
Horace, *Epistles* **bk 1, epis I**

By the end of November and into mid-December 1945, the political and social climate in Indonesia was so bad that Allied authorities began to re-locate civilians from regions to more protected major centres. In response to the deteriorating safety, the Dutch government in Europe finally decided to recall any able-bodied soldiers in overseas camps for active military duty in the Dutch colony. In addition, it began to evacuate groups of dependants of ex-POWs to Thailand, to be reunited with their loved ones. By the end of 1945, family reunifications in Thailand had already begun.

Not long after my mother's declaration that we must somehow be reunited with my father, I was on one of my trips with the Ghurkas to Tandjung Priok harbour. I noticed a British troop ship that had sailed from Thailand to Java, returning the first contingent of former Dutch POWs to Java for active military duty. When I told my mother that the vessel was due to return to Bangkok, she contacted authorities in Batavia to arrange passage on the ship. On 20 December 1945 we joined several hundred women and children to sail for Thailand.

The day we left Batavia, our trip to Tandjung Priok in a convoy of British Army trucks was uneventful, and we did not run into Indonesian insurgent activity. Our embarkation took little time, and the British troop carrier – with an Indian crew under the command of English officers – soon sailed. Equipped for troop transport, its facilities were rather spartan – dormitory accommodation with row upon row of hammocks suspended from the bulkheads; a common dining area with trestle tables and benches; and common ablution facilities that provided no privacy. Being a troop-carrying ship on which the soldiers shared in shipboard work, no provision had been made to change these arrangements and we were expected to do our share of routine duties. After years in the Japanese camps we were used to working in corvée, and we young people soon formed work parties to carry out general maintenance, clean the dormitories and ablution facilities, scrub the decks and assist the cooks in the kitchens. As we sailed out of Batavia's harbour bound for Thailand, behind the ship's wake disappeared the final era of our colonial history. So too ended the lean and mean years of the Japanese occupation of my country of birth, the Dutch East Indies.

Bangkok
Out of Tandjung Priok harbour, the ship sailed a northerly direction from Java towards Bangkok. The sensation of the ship ploughing steadily through the ocean, the sight of sea birds serenely drifting overhead, the smell of salt-laden wind over an endlessly lonely sea – these were exhilarating experiences of safety and normalcy, an escape from the turmoil that had enveloped our country. Though our corvée duties kept us busy, there was still plenty of spare time for the young on board to relax and enjoy ourselves. For me it was sensational to sometimes just stand at the railing and watch the foam curling away from the ship's hull, tracing long ribbons of white bubbles in its wake as the bow lifted in the air and then sank again into the 'vasty deep' of the Indian Ocean. Other times I might join others to talk, or to listen to someone in our group playing music on his piano accordion. With the joy of simple pleasures, and relief from living with apprehension and anxiety, I rediscovered some of what had been the carefree years of my youth before the war with Japan.

After four days of sailing, on Christmas Eve 1945, we reached Bangkok in Thailand. On disembarking the ship, Dutch ex-POWs welcomed us. They supervised gangs of Japanese prisoners of war, who unloaded our luggage onto a convoy of army trucks that were to take groups of the evacuees to reserved accommodation in several hotels in the city. My family was assigned a room in the famed Oriental Hotel, located on the banks of the Chao Phraya, Thailand's major river. At the time we knew nothing of the hotel's illustrious history and its name meant little to us, nor did we know that it counted many famous and wealthy people among its patrons, past and present. Inside the hotel, however, we discovered opulence from a virtually bygone era of splendour when we were taken to a room of truly grand proportions. Situated in an older wing of the building, the floors, furniture and fittings were of solid teak timber. On the mattresses the bone-white linen sheets and pillowslips were stiffly starched, and the huge beds were covered over with tent-like mosquito nets that billowed down from the high ceiling. Even the bathroom was extraordinary – instead of modern plumbing, one still showered in the Oriental way by dipping a small bucket into water stored in large, terracotta Ali Baba-type jars, 5 feet tall and 3 feet wide.

Although the war had not spared Thailand, the Oriental Hotel had retained much of its past grandeur. Under the circumstances it was surely incongruous for refugees to join and mingle with the wealthy visitors at this privileged address. This became no more obvious than when we joined the guests for Christmas Eve dinner. In the grand dining room, the tables were set with starched and immaculately ironed linen, gleaming silver tableware and sparkling crystal glasses. For the festive season the room was gaily decorated with bells, tinsels and an impressively adorned Christmas tree. At their tables, the hotel's patrons were elegantly dressed, but even though we had donned our 'best' clothes, my poor mother and sister's pre-war frocks were painfully unfashionable and inappropriate for the occasion. And while they were washed and clean, my cut-down army shorts and Dutch army shirt – found years ago in the abandoned barracks at Tjimahi – were ill fitting and had never been pressed, simply because we did not own an iron. The contrast between our fellow hotel guests and us could not have been more dramatic, but to their great credit not one among the elegant diners on that remarkable evening make us feel uncomfortable or ashamed of our appearance and plight.

After the concentration camps, the opulence of our surroundings and the service that we received at the Oriental Hotel was unaccustomed and almost overwhelming. On the evening's menu the choice between a fabulous Asian banquet and a traditional Western Christmas dinner – with all the trimmings from turkey and ham to plum pudding dessert – was almost too difficult for us to decide. As we feasted on the surfeit of almost-forgotten delicacies that came to our table, I recalled how only too recently, starving people in the camps had fantasised about recipes and aromas and flavours; about the pleasure of a good meal. I felt almost guilty that with a nod of my head to an attentive waiter I could now commandeer an almost reprehensible excess in eating and drinking. At the end of the feast, I only just in time prevented my sister from scraping the gravy and every last morsel of food off her plate with a finger; a habit that good table manners forbid, but that we had all acquired in the lean and mean years in the concentration camps.

My mother spent the next few days at the offices of the Dutch Military Command to confirm my father's whereabouts and to make travel arrangements to rejoin him at his camp at Kanchanaburi, about 200 kilometres northwest of Bankok. As we discovered, reunification with my father proved difficult, partly because – due to the rapidly deteriorating safety situation in the East Indies – the mass evacuation to Thailand had been so sudden that it caught the authorities not fully prepared. In considerable part also, transport by either road or train to Kanchanaburi proved equally problematic. During the war, Allied bombing of Japanese targets in inland Thailand had destroyed many strategic roads and particularly bridges over rivers. The destruction of these bridges meant that passengers had to disembark the train to be ferried across the river and board a waiting train to take them farther until the process had to be repeated at yet another destroyed bridge or tangled mass of broken railway lines.

Three or four days after arriving in Bangkok we received news that the next morning we would leave for the small village of Tha Muang, where the local Dutch military had constructed a reunification camp for ex-POW dependants. It was unknown when we would be reunited with my father who, suffering malaria and severe malnutrition, was in the military hospital at Kanchanaburi.

On the day of our departure a party of Japanese POWs came to the hotel to load our luggage onto trucks that took us to the central railway station. With the memory of the concentration camps still fresh in our minds, it was a curious sensation to now see these Japanese working in a corvée for *us*, and to notice how greatly changed these once-feared bullies had become. Stripped of insignia, they had become meek men, humble labourers in their now crumpled and untidy uniforms. Reduced to the humiliation of portaging for us, the one-time frightful but now toothless tiger had ridiculously bitten its own tail. It seemed to me that the old enemy had received their just deserts, in which I perhaps uncharitably took a degree of satisfaction.

Journey to Kanchanaburi

Most of Thailand's rolling stock had been commandeered by the Japanese wartime military, and much of it had been lost or destroyed in Allied air raids. At Bangkok's railway station we discovered that, as passenger carriages were in critically short supply, we would have to travel on open tray-top freight wagons. Though lacking shade, the wagons had been equipped with benches for us to sit on, and each had a large cistern of drinking water supplied. We were told that, as we would have to frequently stop at bombed-out bridges or destroyed sections of the railway line, there would be suitable facilities for us to use before joining a waiting train on the other side. While it would prove to be a somewhat arduous way to travel, war and the Japanese camps had taught us that one made do with what was available. Eager to journey for Kanchanaburi, no one complained.

It was still quite early in the morning when our train left Bangkok, following a roughly north-westerly direction through a countryside that reminded me of my homeland on Java. Small Thai settlements – like the kampongs of home – sat amidst village plots of fruits and vegetables, banana groves and clumps of coconut trees, and – such as in Indonesia – small boys herded grazing buffalo on fallow land. The peasant men generally wore only shorts and singlets and the women sarong and bodice. While most female villagers commonly wore black sarong and white blouse, their national dress differed in that it often used the beautiful and very colourful Thai silk. From our carriage we caught glimpses of the traffic on foot, on pushbikes, and – as common as in Indonesia – bullock carts loaded with all kinds of cargoes. Now and again antiquated passenger buses appeared. These did not run on petrol or diesel, but on gas manufactured by burning firewood in a contraption attached to the rear of the vehicle. Possibly because of the densely populated land, we saw little of ground-dwelling wildlife, but in the air or on the ground we occasionally saw vultures, not found in Indonesia. These efficient disposers of carrion, with their gawky frame, sombre black plumage, and ugly head with great hooked beak and fierce eyes, had a sinister appearance – perhaps in keeping with the unappealing nature of their funereal but useful function in the circle of life and death.

Before we left Bangkok, as we had been warned, we came across many bombed-out locations. At a demolished bridge we had to exhaustingly disembark to be ferried across the river by pontoon to a waiting train at its side of the bombed-out railway track. Having to wait for Japanese POWs to transfer our baggage from one train to the other took time and our progress was consequently tardy. A consolation of sorts, the slow pace of travel afforded us an excellent opportunity to view the Thai countryside.

A hundred kilometres out from Bangkok the dry and dusty savannah changed to rich alluvial soils, as we entered the fertile region referred to as Thailand's rice bowl, cultivated with rice paddies. Peasants, their heads covered with large bamboo-weave hats, waded through the inundated fields behind patient buffalo, pulling a plough and turning the paddy soil with a simple shear. In some of the flooded fields, women were at work planting bundles of sprouted rice shoots grown in village nursery beds. Old men and women watched over babies and toddlers while the parents toiled, and young boys engaged in a game of soccer as their sisters sat patiently beside their elders under the shade of some newly cut palm fronds stuck into the soil. These ageless routines, be they ever so humble, produce the staple food crop of rice, which literally feeds billions, and gives a peasant existence substance and meaning in Indonesia and Thailand.

On the open carriage, the sun beat down on us all day. The train travelled only slowly over the problematic railway track, so its passage hardly stirred up a breeze to cool us. With nothing better to do and with no alternative but to simply endure, we sat and we sweated. Where we had to disembark our train and wait to board a new one, we ate our lunch, drank water from the cistern and occasionally snatched some sleep. The sun was already far down on the western horizon when we pulled up at a modest whistle stop, no more than a concrete platform in the Thai landscape. With a hiss from the steam engine that almost matched the sigh of relief from passengers, the accompanying Dutch army officer announced that we had reached our goal – the Tha Muang village siding.

After disembarking, we were to join a convoy of trucks in which to be driven the 5 kilometres to the reunification camp near Tha Muang village. Some of the passengers were immediately reunited with family when they discovered an ex-POW relative waiting with the trucks. These were the lucky few, but for others there was consolation in the knowledge that we, too, would soon be reunited and when we were, the lean and mean years of war would have truly ended.

The trip to our camp is something that I shall never forget. When our convoy left the siding, darkness was gathering and an amazing sight unfolded before our eyes. The entire distance of the 5-kilometre road to our camp was ranked with man after man, each holding up a small candlewick oil lamp that lit up his face. Hundreds of Dutch former prisoners of war had come from Kanchanaburi in the hope of finding relatives among the newly arrived women and children. Holding the lamp high so that we could see his face, person after person called out his name, '*I am* ──── *Is* ──── [wife, mother, sister, brother, sweetheart] *among you?*' Luck rewarded some, and a waiting man would jump onto the truck to be jubilantly received by a loved one on board. However, for many of us there was no response; for my family, no call came from my father. The memory of that ride, of those 5 kilometres, the road faintly lit by small oil lamps held aloft with such hope, remains cemented in my mind.

Tha Muang camp

The trucks took us a little further than the small village of Tha Muang, to a large clearing in the land. It was a moonless night and the countryside was already pitch dark. With the thump of electricity generators hard at work sounding us a welcome, the illuminated reunification camp stood out like a beacon. It was little better than a bush camp, but for evacuees like us it was a haven of peace. The two dozen 100-feet-long barrack-like buildings were entirely constructed of local materials; sawn timbers and planks, walls of bamboo-weave sheets and roofs clad with palm-leaf thatch. The barracks were raised about 3 feet above the ground to provide air circulation and prevent inundation with rainwater, which was unleashed in frequently occurring tropical storms. On 6-foot-wide verandas, single doors gave access to windowless rooms of about 15 square feet. These were really only partitioned cubicles, divided by walls of single sheet, pleated bamboo that provided occupants modesty but little privacy. Each room was furnished with four single beds, a rack on the wall to store and hang clothes, a small wooden table and four folding canvas chairs. A single electric light bulb hung from the ceiling, giving uncertain illumination to the cubicle, and a small oil lamp on the table was meant as emergency lighting when the generators were turned off at 10 pm each night. A kitchen and common dining area in the centre of the quadrangle of barracks, and a large communal entertainment facility completed the Tha Muang family reunification camp – a small Dutch enclave in the Thai host nation.

The morning after we arrived at Tha Muang my mother called at the administration building to ask for transport to Kanchanaburi, to seek my father in the hospital. But the Dutch army officer who administered our camp claimed that he was unable to help as he had no transport to take us there. When she returned from her fruitless mission, my mother decided that we would simply have to walk the ten or so kilometres to Kanchanaburi. We had barely left our barracks and we had not reached the camp's main entrance when my mother exclaimed, 'My God, here comes your father!'

Staggering towards us on the internal road, barely able to keep upright, I saw a gaunt figure. A far too loose Dutch army uniform hung on his thin-as-a-rake frame. The man was so foreign in appearance that I truthfully did not recognise him as my father. In the four years that we had been separated, I had remembered him as he had been before the war – a powerfully built man with a vibrant zest for life. That man was nothing like the poor wretch before me. His dull eyes under knitted eyebrows evidenced a pain and suffering that, to my horror, reminded me of people in the Tjimahi concentration camp who stood on the very threshold of death – at that point, a fate often kinder than living. As I watched, I despaired for my father.

For the next several weeks we cared for my father in the small room of our quarters. He had refused to return to the hospital at Kanchanaburi and we simply could not deny my poor father his wish to remain with us. Before lapsing into semi-comas with racking bouts of malarial fever, in periods of lucidity my father told us that he had seen our names in a bulletin of evacuees from Java. Against medical orders, he had simply got out of his hospital bed and hitchhiked on a local bus from Kanchanaburi to Tha Muang village. From there he had walked, or rather staggered, the few hundred yards to our camp. Once we had been reunited, he refused to be parted from us. So my mother, sister and I began to gradually nurse him back to health. With the help of the then modern anti-malarial drug of Atebrin, my father was surprisingly more easily cured of the malaria than of the malnutrition that was affecting him badly, even dangerously. A side effect of the malaria tablets, his skin began to look a strangely yellow colour, but the medication began to cure the fevers until in time the condition was under control. However, typical of acute malnutrition, he seriously lacked an appetite and we had great trouble getting him to eat. The 'treatment' that we used to build up his emaciated body was to make him drink whole cans of undiluted Carnation evaporated milk. Tears of determination wet his cheeks, and he gagged on every mouthful of the 'medicine', which he forced down. I remembered well doing the same in my camp, when I tried to stomach the horrible starch porridge, and I felt guilty at inflicting yet more suffering on my father, no matter how necessary and well meant. After anxious weeks of anti-malarial medication and almost force-feeding my father with strengthening food and fluids, his health slowly improved to where we no longer feared for his survival. By February 1946 our family was beginning to be whole again.

Our immediate post-war life in Thailand was nothing less than idyllic, a gentle process of physical and psychological recovery. In modern times, trauma counselling has sparked a lucrative industry, and cynics might conclude that every mishap is nowadays smothered with psychotherapy 'repair works'. After the Second World War, when professional counselling had not yet come in vogue, one simply got on with life. Without access to today's professional psychological tinkering, it was the time spent in genial Thailand that brought us back to a measure of normality.

Our reunification camp on the outskirts of Tha Muang town was an enclave of Dutch culture and customs. While we were aware of Thailand's modes and customs, a vestige of the Dutch colonial mindset had not yet been shaken off by many of our countrymen. Although there was no doubting that we were guests of the sovereign Thai nation, for some of the ex-POW and civilian refugees, their relationship with our Thai hosts reflected the pre-war relationship with Indonesians – who were regarded as being subservient to the needs and wants of their Dutch masters. When this attitude was displayed, the locals at Tha Muang responded in two ways: the peasant farmers generally remained aloof from the foreigners, whilst the small business entrepreneurs of Tha Muang did not hesitate to exploit the lucrative presence of the *falang* (foreigners). Everywhere in the erstwhile sleepy village their markets, small restaurants, shops and bars sprang into life. Thus flourished a symbiotic relationship between the Tha Muang society and its foreign guests in the Dutch refugee camp.

Tha Muang commerce

Before the war, Tha Muang village in southwestern Thailand was a rural service centre for the region's rice growing industry. In these immediate post-war times, the presence of large numbers of foreigners in the nearby reception camp meant that business was booming – new entrepreneurs hastened to set up a wide range of commercial enterprises. Portable food stalls selling Thai curries and rice and noodle dishes made their way into our camp. Small restaurants prospered, where people indulged in every imaginable exotic Thai cuisine and sweetmeat. At risk of contracting a stomach complaint, or even cholera, at these establishments, many refugee families drank the freshly squeezed *nam manao* (Thai lemonade), or tea and hot or iced coffees on offer. Some of the establishments even provided beer and alcoholic liquor. In other shops especially catering for the foreigners, one could buy distinctive Thai silverware, gold jewellery and, reputedly but perhaps doubtfully, genuine gems of many kinds. Almost inevitably responding to the law of supply and demand, some less reputable Thai entrepreneurs set up massage parlours, likely fronts for bordellos. Whatever were the true sentiments in the Thai population about the falang, as sleepy rural Tha Muang sprung into profitable commercial life, the locals treated their visitors with a courtesy and tolerance that, despite lingering colonialist sentiments, most foreigners generally reciprocated.

A Time of Repair

My father's health gradually improved, and together we began to explore the nearby village and the satellite settlement that had sprung up around our reception camp. His army pay reinstated and civilian evacuees receiving a small monthly allowance from the Dutch government, we had money to spend at the trade stores, or we sometimes took a bus to nearby Thai villages. One of the more picturesque of these was the medium-sized town of Nakorn Pathom, with its distinctive Buddhist pagoda that featured in many picture postcards of Thailand. In this way we familiarised ourselves with the countryside and the villages and hamlets around our base at Tha Muang, and we re-learned a peaceful way of life which had been lacking for so long.

After the evening meal in the common canteen, our family would often sit on the veranda talking or just listening to the sounds of the tropical night. Inside the room the single electric light bulb only faintly relieved the darkness, and on our table on the veranda we would light the small oil wick lamp, which burnt with a sooty splutter. Sometimes, like a faraway flash of lightning, it erupted into a quick burst of gasses that exploded brightly, briefly illuminating the nearby bush.

Apparently unperturbed by our presence, nearly every evening a sloth came to visit. This large-eyed, slow moving, nocturnal mammal with curved, long-clawed feet arrived to claim the treat we had put out for it – a banana. The animal climbed down from an overhanging tree onto the roof of our barracks, then noiselessly glided down a veranda post. Having eaten its fill, it sinuously climbed back the way it had come, disappearing into the void of the night. This almost banal experience, and other peaceful cameos of life in Thailand, served to repair our family and social life.

Tales of Burma

The same as most people, our family dwelt little on our experiences during the war. My father made only brief mentions of his experiences when separated from us. He had been involved in fighting a Japanese incursion near where his regiment was stationed on Java. When the Dutch East Indies Army capitulated to the Japanese, he and his fellow POWs had been sent overseas to the notorious Changi prison in Singapore. Sometime later, their contingent was sent to the Burmese border to work on the Burma to Thailand railway construction.

Although he did tell us some lighter incidents of his time as a POW, he left out much detail of his life in the slave labour camps in the jungles of Burma and Thailand. Whatever my father related always had a 'funny' touch. One of his stories was about when the Japanese guards caught him stealing a dried salted fish from their kitchen. His punishment was to keep his face tilted into the sun with the large, heavily salted fish in his mouth, standing to attention until he passed out. 'But,' my father laughed, 'the bloody Japanese wouldn't eat the fish, soggy with my spit and caked with the mud I had fallen into when I fainted. When they released me, I smuggled the fish back to my hut and for once enjoyed a grand meal!'

The most harrowing deprivation that he had suffered, however, was the torture of a burning, desperate, unquenchable thirst. It was a cruel irony that although the POWs often stood waist-deep in creek or river water all day long, for fear of contracting cholera, everyone knew they must not drink the water unboiled. Under inhuman conditions, labouring a long distance away from their base in the searing heat of the sun, their supplies of drinking water from the camp often ran out. With the Japanese flogging them on to unceasing '*Speedo, Speedo*' toil, the prisoners were not allowed to take time out to boil a new supply of water. Nor did they have the means to do so, even if they had been allowed. When they could no longer resist the desperate need to quench their unbearable thirst, some men gambled with their lives and drank from the water in which they stood. 'And,' my father said sadly, 'many, too many, of them died.' Making light of his own ordeal, he laughed that he sometimes had visions of great pots of steaming, freshly made plantation tea, or huge glasses of icy-cold ice cream soda. Rather than succumb to the terrible temptation to slake his thirst, he steeled himself to not give in – drinking the unboiled water could kill him, meaning he would never again see his family. Until he died, my father always kept a bucketful of drinking water close at hand in the house. We never questioned him about this left-over response to wartime trauma. It was enough to know he would never again have to suffer the thirst and utter desperation brought on by the lack of a draught of common water.

In another story of Burma my father recalled, 'Our Dutch army unit worked somewhere close to where there was an Australian POW party laying a section of railway line. In one of their huts, I found a man suffering badly with malaria.' The man was shivering, with nothing other than his tattered pants to cover himself against the chills of his illness. 'The next day,' my father said matter-of-factly, 'I cut my blanket in two and gave him half.' A few days later, the Japanese moved the Australians to somewhere else on the line. Unable to check on the sick man, my father did not know if he had survived or died, or if he would ever see the Australian again. 'Some months later,' he continued, 'I was lying very ill with malaria. I was only half conscious on my bench in the barrack when I heard someone calling out, "Where's the bloody Dutchman who gave me half his blanket? Where's the bloody Dutchman who gave me half his blanket…?"' The voice belonged to the man with whom my father had shared his blanket. This time it was the Australian who took care of his friend's illness. He returned the next day and presented my father with a full bottle of precious quinine tablets. Asked how he got them, the Australian only laughed, 'Courtesy of the Jap hospital, no worries mate,' and he would not elaborate. When my father told him that he must keep the priceless medicine for himself he replied, 'Mind your own business. Just don't let the bloody Japs catch you with the stuff.' Like ships that pass in the night, they met briefly in the jungles of Burma and never saw each other again. My father survived the horrors of the Thai-Burma POW slave labour camps, and he wished that the Australian, whose name he had forgotten, had likewise lived to see freedom.

In today's world of plenty for most, of affluence for some and even of extravagance for a few, people may not think it very remarkable that a 'bloody Dutchman' gave half his precious blanket to a stranger. And nor perhaps would many people realise how extraordinary it was that a nameless Australian repaid a foreigner, but a mate, for his kindness with a bottle of quinine tablets. Neither man had any doubt that if the Japanese had caught the Australian stealing medicine from their aid post, he would have died horribly. These are but two examples of great decency and human empathy. The world is fortunate to have people who are capable of extraordinary compassion towards fellow human beings in need. For the lack of these anonymous heroes our societies would be so much the worse.

Peaceful days at Tha Muang

In the Tha Muang reunification camp, my sister Conny and I took an important step towards repairing our education, interrupted as it had been by the war. A number of qualified civilian and ex-POW teachers from Kanchanaburi were seconded by the Dutch military to start teaching primary and secondary school classes in our camp. Having lived four years without attending school, to be truthful I did not very much like resuming my formal education. In part I secretly feared that I should never be able to repair my badly neglected secondary education. Of course, the choice was no longer mine – my mother insisted we go – and when I recommenced education under fairly primitive conditions it was the first step in reclaiming a pathway towards the future. We were also encouraged to join the Scouts – a step towards learning to be part of a group of young people again. The academic element of our learning was fairly basic, but the re-socialising aspect was very important for us. In later years I came to realise that in the bush school at Tha Muang I began to revive my lifelong quest for the treasure of knowledge. As wizened, gentle Mr Miles in the Tjimahi concentration camp had put it, cognisance – to which language is the key – unveils everything that can be known.

For the young in the bush camp at Tha Muang there was ample time to participate in sporting activities, attend entertainment activities in the communal recreation hall, or dance to recorded gramophone music and sometimes even a live band of POW and refugee musicians. Another very favoured pastime for young and old was to walk a short distance through the paddy fields to a swimming hole in the nearby river. On our way to the river, we had to pass through a Thai hamlet with the huts of a dozen or so peasants who tilled their crops in the surrounding rice cultivations. Before leaving the camp we always took some hard-boiled eggs from the kitchen with us, to feed to a one-eyed village dog we had appropriately named Nelson. Our friendship with Nelson also served to maintain good relations with the Thai farmers who amiably let us cavort in the shallows of their river.

Only about 20 kilometres from the infamous River Kwai Bridge, the river at Tha Muang is a wide, fast-flowing waterway that follows a twisted course through lowland rice fields. Though constantly shifting sand banks made navigation problematic, a network of deep-water channels enabled experienced skippers to take their river barges far inland over this water highway that linked the Thai coast with the hinterland. Swimming in the shallows close to the river's bank we often saw a steady stream of barges making their way upstream, their noisily chugging engines emitting foul black clouds of diesel fumes. Loaded with cargoes and passengers for destinations up or down the river, the barges provided an inter-rural taxi service for local people – preferable to the uncertain services of the nation's bus networks. When we heard the 'chug-chug' of a barge engine downstream, before the vessel rounded the river's bend we would swim out into the channel to wait for it. Indulgently watched by the boat's crew and passengers, when it came alongside we would grab hold of the small tethered dinghy that trailed a safe distance away from the propellers and let the barge pull us upriver. When we had gone some distance, with a wave to those on board, we let go and allowed the current to leisurely take us back to our swimming hole.

Often, right beside us in the water, young mahouts bathed their elephants. The familiarity with which they treated the enormous beasts, and the command they had over them, reminded us of our homeland where small boys, *katjonges*, herded their buffalo on the sawahs of Java. The pastoral serenity of the country was beguiling, and as we began to recuperate from the preceding years, we almost forgot how lucky we were to have escaped the rising tensions in the Dutch East Indies.

Politics in the South Pacific

By the middle of 1946, news was arriving in peaceful Thailand of seriously deteriorating conditions in the East Indies, and especially on the island of Java. Referred to as 'rebel action' and later rephrased 'Indonesian Pemuda insurgency', the tension had escalated into frequent, often major, military confrontations with the Allied Forces. Most recently, rumours circulated at Tha Muang that in Batavia – and particularly Surabaya – heavy fighting had erupted between Indonesian paramilitary units and the British Army. The news frustrated the younger and more militant Dutch ex-POWs, who were eager to assist the sorely pressed British Army to reclaim our homeland. So far only a few token units of the liberated Dutch Army in Thailand – the so-called Gadjah Merah (Red Elephant) Brigade – had been allowed back to the Indonesian archipelago; something that the Dutch would later ascribe to naked political advantage by certain countries, including Australia.

At the end of the Second World War, suspicion arose in Dutch circles that Great Britain had opportunistically watched Indonesian freedom fighting escalate in the Dutch colony. But perhaps only a very few at the highest levels of the Netherlands Government knew of Australia's surprising interest in seeing the end of Dutch colonialism, and the role that it played in the unparalleled change the region was undergoing. Until the Second World War, Australia had traditionally relied on Britain as its 'great and powerful friend'. Never just a British lapdog, many of Australia's interests nonetheless coincided with those of the Empire. Its attachment to Britain, however, did not prevent Australia from making capital from its support to the motherland in military adventures, from the Boer War to the Great War of 1914–1918 and the Second World War 1940–1945. In an aggressive domestic strategy of nation building, particularly at the end of the Second World War, Australia quite adroitly turned loyalty to empire to its own advantage.

At the conclusion of the Second World War, Australia emerged more confident and assertive than before. It increasingly departed from relying on British influence and protection, and with a changed outlook on its own destiny it developed a new sense of identity and its place in the world. Playing an important and even defining role in this, the Australian Labor Government began to champion the notion of self-determination for other nations in the region. Embracing the Indonesian cause, prime minister of the day Ben Chifley offered Australia's constructive support for Indonesia, its nearest neighbour, to gain independence from the Dutch. Perhaps more than any other reason, the combination of British and Australian political and economic opportunism eventually contributed to the emergence of the sovereign Indonesian state. Whether cynical British self-interest or Australian idealism, the outcome came at the cost of the once proud Dutch East Indies colonialists when we became wartime 'Displaced Persons'– denied of our birthright and homeland.

My father adored Australia, and he treasured the memory of our visit there. He idolised 'Aussies', men with larrikin spirits such as his Australian friend in the Burma jungle. Though that spirit is no more evident than in the doughty nature of the 'ordinary' Australian's generosity towards a deserving cause, none of it takes away from the fact that Australia's fledgling geopolitics in respect of Indonesia denied the Dutch the right to deal with their own affairs in the East Indies.

In Thailand, we were too far away from and too ill-informed of the developing situation in our homeland to be aware of what some (but not my family) saw as a betrayal by the Aussies.

A nagging question remains in the minds of many of my displaced fellow Indonesian Dutch compatriots: if Australia's politicians supported the Indonesian freedom cause, why did they not also turn against the British colonialists in Singapore, Malaysia and Burma? When contemporary Australian politics was actively promoting Indonesian sovereignty in the archipelago, why did the politicians not also expect the Portuguese to surrender their colony in East Timor to the Indonesian state? These questions will of course never be publicly answered because no fair-minded justification can conceivably be found. Our family preferred to believe that if 'ordinary Aussies' had realised the implications of their Labor government's geopolitical adventurism, then they may have thought it not quite fair to single out the Dutch in the East Indies, while not applying the same pressure on Britain, France, and Portugal.

Presumably also because of international diplomacy, apart from a token few hundred ex-POW Dutch military that had returned early to active duty in Indonesia, our army had remained quarantined in Thailand. It was only after the British Forces very nearly lost a major battle in Java's second largest city, Surabaya, that this international policy changed. In about July 1946, Dutch Army Command in Thailand began to despatch most of its bachelor soldiers back to the colony. Not long after, married men from the former POW camps also received orders to transfer to Bangkok, where they were required to stand by for a return to active duty. When at Tha Muang the order came for us to move, it was the end of the Thai idyll.

There was such excitement about our imminent return to the Dutch East Indies that I do not remember much of leaving hospitable Tha Muang. Waiting for the day of departure, we would not of course have forgotten to have a last swim in the river, nor to feed the now fat dog Nelson some last few eggs. On the evening before leaving our camp, we once more sat on the veranda to watch our sloth climb out of the inky darkness and eat its fill of banana. Before turning in to sleep, for the last time we pinched out the flame in our oil wick lamp. I still have that humble little lamp at home to remind me of what made our time at Tha Muang and in Thailand a specially treasured experience.

The humble little lamp from the Tha Muang Dutch refugee camp in Thailand.

CHAPTER 9

Return to Java

'The Time has Come,' the Walrus said,
'To talk of Many Things ...'
Lewis Carroll, *Through the Looking Glass*

Due to a shortage of shipping, we remained longer in Bangkok than had been anticipated. Staying in chartered Thai Army barracks not far from the notorious prison known as the 'Bangkok Hilton', the Dutch Army in Bangkok did not have facilities to train or otherwise gainfully engage its troops. This left my father a great deal of time to explore the city's many attractions with us. We often visited one of the large markets where a great choice of all sorts of merchandise tempted us. We bought some quite unique Thai silver, brassware and porcelains that are still in my possession. This welcome interlude ended in September 1946, when we finally received the order to depart. The ship would take us to Java, where my father's regiment was sent to the city of Surabaya, in East Java, to relieve the British Army.

When our ship sailed from Bangkok, we left behind a time of personal healing from the war that had greatly touched our lives. Standing at the railing as we sailed out into the Gulf of Thailand on our way to Java, every turn of the ship's screws took me farther away from the idyllic river where elephants bathed right beside us, and from the barges that pulled us up the river to drift back to our swimming hole. In my mind I still hear echoes of young Thai villagers singing their traditional songs

Thai silver, brassware and porcelains purchased while staying in the Thai Army Barracks in Bangkok.

as they gaily danced around a kerosene pressure lamp in the Tha Muang village square. I was sad to think that we could no longer spoil the poor one-eyed dog Nelson with eggs from the camp kitchen, and how he would soon enough become a painfully thin, rough-coated village cur again. The memories of our Thai sojourn remained brilliant highlights in my family's lives.

Although some married soldiers and especially many women had misgivings about our soldiers returning to possible combat conditions, others were eagerly looking forward to getting back to the Dutch East Indies. Few among even the more pessimistic of our people doubted that we would return to life as it had been before the war. With the exception of only the most cautious, there was a brimming faith that if any 'troubles' should arise with the Indonesians, then our soldiers would soon enough get rid of the 'misguided natives' and teach them to be 'our servants' again. The more sober-minded Dutch, however, remembered the fanatical Indonesian Pemuda youths, not mere troublemakers, but paramilitary freedom fighters that we would soon face. On our way back home to Java we thought we were returning to old ways of life. But when we landed at Surabaya, we discovered the reality of Indonesia's progress towards sovereignty.

Return to Surabaya

After four days sailing, our ship berthed at Tandjung Perak harbour where we disembarked into Surabaya. Only a very few weeks ago there had been ferocious encounters between paramilitary Indonesians and the British Army, with Surabaya showing noticeable evidence of the recent fighting. Pivotal in the Indonesian fight for freedom, casualties on either side of the battle for Surabaya have never been accurately revealed, but anecdotal information contends that they were high, maybe even very high. An astounding aspect of the combat was that ill-equipped units of Pemuda, followed by bands of undisciplined but fanatic peasants, effectively fought a well-trained, modern Allied army. So fanatical were the irregulars that when a Pemuda fell, a camp follower took up his weapon and, although untrained, ferociously fought until he too died in battle. Other peasants behind him took his place in turn, and they too fought until killed, and the supply of these volunteers did not dry up. The impact of their undoubted heroics incalculably furthered Indonesian nationalistic aims, but when the Dutch soldiers in my father's army unit arrived in Surabaya, the second main city on Java had become a ruin in the war for Indonesian independence.

The men, having returned to active duty, were transported to army barracks in Surabaya. No longer able to stay with them, we families were taken in a convoy of army trucks to a disused school on the city outskirts. On the drive from the wharves to Surabaya city we noticed that the walls of houses were pockmarked with bullet holes, and many buildings were practically destroyed. This bore evidence of the recent heavy fighting between the British and the Indonesians. In our new camp there were also unmistakable indications that combat had taken place in the grounds and inside the classrooms of the former school. Our homecoming to Java was less than we had expected, and rather more daunting than some of us had feared.

The Surabaya camp

Inexplicably, given such recent fighting in Surabaya, once at the camp we civilians were left almost totally unprotected by our army. The camp was run by a Dutch lieutenant in charge of a dozen or so unranked soldiers, but if hostile Indonesians should have attacked us, they could not have defended the camp. The detachment of my father's army unit was half an hour's drive away and we were not even connected by telephone. Had our camp been attacked by freedom fighters or opportunistic rampok bandits, it did not require a great deal of imagination to understand what could have happened to the defenceless women and children.

A more immediate problem was our discovery of certain lethal – and sometimes gruesome – reminders of the recent battles in Surabaya. The day we arrived, the lieutenant in charge of the camp warned everyone not to wander over the school grounds as live ammunition, grenades and even land mines lay strewn around. While the lieutenant's warning about this dangerous, uncleared war matériel was sound and reasonable, it seemed inexplicable that the authorities allowed civilians – and especially children – to be so exposed to this legacy from military combat.

In spite of the danger, and against the lieutenant's advice, many of the young – myself included – could not resist the temptation to explore the area. We found a considerable variety of abandoned army gear, including rifles, bayonets and ammunition that we were fortunately wise enough not to touch. We did not find landmines – a much worse hazard than other war matériel if we had discovered them. We came across other evidence of the fighting that had taken place right here in the form of several evidently hastily dug graves: those without Christian crosses on them must have been Indonesian combat casualties. Sad as were these reminders of the loss of human life, we found other, truly gruesome evidence of recent combat and death.

In Indonesia, in private backyards or on public premises, wells were often dug for the maintenance of premises and gardens, supplementing the reticulated water supply. In the former school grounds, we came across several wells from which now emanated the smell of death. Decaying corpses drifting in the water testified to the price these freedom fighters had paid for their ideals.

The sub-standard and even dangerous conditions in our camp gave us little reassurance that the Dutch authorities had prepared the city of Surabaya for the reception of civilians. Besides the apparent lack of safety in the camp, we discovered that though sufficient in quantity, the food that we received from the kitchen was of poor quality. When our first meal consisted of nothing more than boiled rice accompanied by a small tin of sardines that we even had to open ourselves with an issued small tin opener, we put this down to teething troubles in the kitchen. On subsequent days when we continued to receive the same frugal fare, people began to protest. Asked to explain the poor catering, the lieutenant merely replied that his budget did not allow him to supply us with better quality food, and day after day we continued to eat boiled rice and sardines for the main meal, and army-issue dry biscuits and Spam meat for breakfast and lunch. Some wags suggested that of course one could vary this by having the Spam with one's main meal, and the sardines for breakfast and lunch. But jokes aside, without a telephone connection to Army Head Office it was difficult to refer the uncertain safety of our location and the poor standard of food to higher authority. Our lieutenant commandant remained stubbornly unresponsive to any complaints made to him, and perhaps because of the army's concerns about a possible return to combat conditions, headquarters in Surabaya paid scant attention to the dependants of their married soldiers.

School, and a new friend

Despite the unpromising conditions in which we lived, parents were still keen to resume their children's interrupted schooling. My mother was adamant that I should continue the work started at Tha Muang at a school that had been set up elsewhere in the city. 'It is important that you continue your education,' she urged. I did recommence attending classes, but at some risk. I had to ride a considerable distance through little better than no-man's land on a rusty old bicycle that we had found in abandoned rubbish on the camp grounds. Although my mother was keen that I should resume *my* education, she would not let my sister attend school, saying, 'The city is too dangerous for girls.' Our mother must have clearly known that it was risky for *me* to be moving around in the city but, trusting in Fate and in God, she believed that I would exercise 'common-sense to stay out of trouble.'

I recall that I was initially less than enthusiastic about going back to school. However, this reluctance changed when I came to notice a girl named Magdalena. Fourteen years old and starting her first year at high school, Magda's long, light brown hair reached down to her shoulders, framing a fine-featured face in which hazel eyes looked contemplatively out on the world. Slightly built for her age and, like me, apparently preferring her own company, she was shy in the presence of others. In my formative years in the camps, I had known only male fellowship and I was diffident in dealing with members of the opposite sex. But during mid-morning and lunch breaks I joined Magda where she used to sit alone on a bench in the corridor. As she and her family had also been evacuated to Thailand, we talked about our experiences; Magda about Nakorn Pathom and I about Tha Muang. I told her about watching young Thais in the village square singing and dancing around a kerosene pressure lamp; of how I often went to bathe in the river, where next to us little mahouts scrubbed down elephants whose enormous bulk we could almost touch; and of the delight in being towed up the river by barge. When I mentioned the one-eyed dog Nelson and how he waited for us to bring him eggs, Magda laughed, but like me she worried that I could now no longer feed him. On her part, Magda described Nakorn Pathom and how she and her family had visited temples and the markets, and had sat in small restaurants eating Thai cuisine and drinking nam manao. As we sat and talked, we formed an association that over time developed into a little more than friendship. Thus budded a gentle, unselfconscious intimacy between shy little Magda and me. While we became more than friends, neither she nor I yet knew how to convert that into a boyfriend-and-girlfriend relationship.

As we began to gain confidence in each other, we looked for opportunities to spend more time together. Before returning home after school, I began to take Magda on my bike some way down the street to where she and her family lived in converted army barracks. As the bicycle had no carrier, Magda sat perched in front of me. Gripping the handlebars of the bike, I felt protective of her when my arms framed her slight figure. We never put into words what special quality we found in the other's company, but in an innocent prelude to adulthood, I believe that we both felt we had discovered something to cherish in our friendship.

There was no immediate recurrence of major hostilities in Surabaya, but elsewhere on Java and in the archipelago outbreaks of violence were becoming commonplace. In the Dutch community, increasing mention was made of the self-proclaimed Indonesian president Soekarno and the

Soekarno-appointed vice-president Mohammad Hatta, and their role in the recent conflicts. As the tide of nationalism swelled in Indonesia, many of our Dutch people stubbornly refused to concede that a virtual state of war now existed between the Dutch and the Indonesians, and that the once proud Dutch East Indies Empire was inexorably disintegrating, being replaced by the sovereign Republic of Indonesia.

Mismanagement at the camp

For us women and dependent children, more pertinent than political and military concerns about the future was the continuing mismanagement of our camp by the Dutch lieutenant. True, the contaminated wells had been emptied and the dead bodies in them had been removed. But the former school grounds were still littered with abandoned armoury, and as Army headquarters sorely lacked sappers to clear away this dangerous war matériel, it remained a constant hazard to our safety. To us the most vexing matter was that the quality of the food had not improved. We still largely subsisted on rice and tinned fish, sometimes varied with tinned meats. With practically no vegetables or fruit supplied, we suffered a poor and monotonous diet. This unsatisfactory situation may well have continued if some women had not begun to involve themselves in the camp's business, challenging the lieutenant's competence and, incidentally, his honesty. From our concentration camp experiences we had learned of the greed and dishonesty of our Japanese captors, but our own Dutch commandant?

After some time, the election of a representative body of camp residents was approved by the lieutenant, who apparently expected that the group would rubber stamp his administration. Contrary to what he had anticipated, the delegates – including my mother – refused to whitewash his management. Indeed, no one was more persistent than she in campaigning for better conditions. When the committee continued to receive excuses from the lieutenant – who blamed military headquarters for a lack of funding – my mother began to secretly scrutinise the commandant's financial administration and to record evidence of the camp's unsatisfactory state of affairs. While she hoped this information would help support our complaints to Military headquarters, she did not foresee how vitally important it would become.

News of the sub-standard conditions in our camp had of course spread among the soldiers in their army compound. In an attempt to improve our conditions some of the husbands – including my father, who took a leading role in this – began collecting surplus food from their kitchens with which to supplement our rations. This initiative incurred the lieutenant's ire, and he had the deliveries from the soldiers' kitchens stopped. He also took a particular dislike to my father, who would not be talked out of continuing to deliver extra food to our camp, and their disagreement turned into open confrontation.

Meanwhile, in the course of my mother's investigations into the lieutenant's management practices, little by little the pieces of a puzzle began to fall into place. My mother kept the details of this strictly to herself. She was gradually able to record incontrovertible evidence of how the commandant embezzled funds and misappropriated much of the camp's stores and supplies that, aided and abetted by his staff, he sold on the black market. With parallels to the Japanese concentration camps, when the opportunity presented itself, certain of our own countrymen could not resist the temptation to profit from people in a vulnerable position. In time, my mother's knowledge of this criminal activity would save my father from a military court martial.

Since our arrival in Surabaya in early September 1946, my father's health had deteriorated to the point where the army approved his early demobilisation on medical grounds. When the news of it came, he and my mother faced a difficult decision: remain on Java hoping that in time we could return to our home on the plantation, or accept the Dutch government's offer to repatriate the family to Holland. After much soul searching and mental anguish, my parents eventually choose the latter. They knew full well that this meant the end of our family history in the Dutch East Indies, and that they were terminating our birthright and future in a rapidly changing Indonesia. Contrary to the popular wisdom of many fellow Dutch in Indonesia, who continued to believe that the empire would soon be restored, my father predicted, 'We will never see our home on the plantation again, and for our future we must first look to Holland and next to Australia.' His premonition sadly came true – my parents never returned to the land of their birth and never again saw the plantation that had been their life's purpose and work.

Another dramatic departure

Preparations for our departure quickly got underway, and every passing day brought us closer to the time when we would leave for Holland. Our belongings were packed and ready and we even knew the name of the ship on which we would soon sail. But, as in the adage about 'the best laid plans of mice and men,' with fewer than the five fingers on one hand to count down to the day of our departure, catastrophe struck – the simmering hostility between my father and the lieutenant erupted into physical blows.

The commandant was hosting a party for army officer acquaintances. At some stage, and apparently under the influence of alcohol, it seems that he made an improper advance towards my mother who, as head of the camp residents' committee, had been invited to attend the function. When my father became aware of the indiscretion, he furiously confronted the lieutenant. After a heated argument, and unfortunately in public view, my father knocked the lieutenant to the ground. Blinded by anger at the slight to my mother's reputation, my father had given in to an impulse that in better judgement he should have avoided; the altercation now threatened to jeopardise the future of his family. Even if my father had acted under provocation, Army Command could not overlook that the fight involved soldiers on active duty and, as he had struck the first blow, the Military Police had no choice but to apprehend my father pending a probable court martial. When my mother visited my father in the prison, he entreated her that we should sail to Holland, leaving him to await the outcome of his court martial.

The day before we left for Holland saw a small personal heartache for me when I had to say goodbye to my friend Magda. I had secretly hoped that her family would also choose repatriation to Holland and that we would sail together, but her parents had elected for resettlement in Dutch New Guinea, and for the time being Magda and her family remained at Surabaya. On our last day together, I as usual rode Magda to her home on my old bicycle. Before we parted I gave her a present by which I hoped she would remember me. At the local market I had bought a small wooden statue of a Balinese girl executing a traditional Indonesian dancing step. With slender arms gracefully stretched above her head, I thought that it resembled how Magda sometimes held out hers in our discussions, when she tried to dramatise a story or emphasise a point. Above all, I had chosen that particular small carving because of the gentle facial expression that an unknown woodcarver had bestowed upon his work, which seemed to me to match Magda's contemplative eyes. We had known each other only a matter of a few months and we had never overtly demonstrated the budding of our mutually special feeling. When I said goodbye to Magda, I knew that there would not be a 'Till we meet again,' and when we parted that day it was with sadness in my heart. Not yet my girlfriend, but the first girl who was a special friend, I hope that, like me, gentle Magda has had a good and happy life.

When the day of our departure dawned with my father still in military detention, my mother acted in her usual decisive way to undo the considerable harm to our impending repatriation. I have never been wholly privy to the particulars of how my mother achieved what she did, but this is what I have pieced together. When her pleading for clemency with Military headquarters fell on deaf ears, my mother had apparently gone to the lieutenant with a complete record of her investigations into the camp management, demonstrating conclusive proof that he had embezzled finances and supplies from our camp maintenance. In return for her promise that she would not supply evidence of his criminal action to Army headquarters, in a sworn deposition the lieutenant took full blame for having provoked the fight with my father, volunteering to face a military tribunal for his indiscretion. My father was absolved from all charges, immediately released and driven to the wharf by jeep. Recalling his late arrival when we departed Australia years earlier, literally minutes before our ship sailed for Holland, he rejoined my mother, sister and me. My mother had once again demonstrated her remarkable inner strength, averting what nearly turned out to be a catastrophe. Her capability for decisive and even ruthless action belied her deceptively fragile 'porcelain Dresden doll' image.

The prospect of soon going to live in Holland was both daunting and exhilarating. Standing at the railing of our ship as we left Surabaya harbour, as the country of my birth disappeared from sight, I remember how sad my parents were. They, too, stood watching the outline of land grow dim, until it disappeared leaving only the endless horizons of the sea around us. With the unintentional callousness and lack of insight of youth, in the grip of my excitement about sailing for an unknown destination I am sure that I did not fully appreciate the depth of my parents' grief, and I did not quite share their anguish. *They* were leaving lifetimes of family background behind, in the knowledge that, against all hope, they could never retrieve the past. It must have wrung their hearts. For my sister and me, the voyage to Holland was the beginning of a new life, but for my parents it was an end to the history of their yesteryear. When they decided on repatriating to Holland, my parents never mentioned to us that it was to give Conny and me a better chance in life than what they could foresee for us in Indonesia. In retrospect I can only imagine the heartache that my mother and father suffered by cutting the bonds with everything they held dear; their personal home and life on the plantation, and their social status in the community. Ultimately, they were putting the future of their children on the scales of blind chance in the essentially alien Dutch motherland.

A last goodbye

The port town of Sabang, on the tip of the island of Sumatra in the Açeh Province, is Indonesia's northern-most outpost. Strategically situated on a major South Asian shipping route, Sabang boasts a spectacular natural harbour and a very beautiful hinterland. With the country virtually at war and the region having a long history of truculence against the Dutch from the Muslim population, none of us passengers ventured farther than the wharf. Our ship berthed only long enough to replenish supplies before the long voyage to our next stop – the port of Aqaba in Jordan.

The day when our ship pulled away from the wharf, all contact with the land of our birth was severed. Soon, on the far horizon only a hazy smudge remained of the land where, in the Jojobojo myth, the black buffalo fought the white buffalo even unto death. On the sawahs of the Indonesian archipelago, the outcome of their struggle would result in the birth of the Indonesian Republic, with sovereignty over the land and its people. For the Indonesian Dutch, the past was dead, the future unknowable.

> Pure and complete sorrow is as impossible
> as pure and complete joy
> Leo Tolstoy, *War and Peace* bk xv, ch 1

PART 3:

Holland

CHAPTER 10

Going Dutch

Charity, colder than a bank manager's heart
An old Australian adage (FJB)

Early one morning in November 1946, we arrived in the Jordanian seaport of Aqaba, at the head of the Gulf of Aqaba, an arm of the Red Sea. In the times of British adventurer, soldier and author TE Lawrence – of *Lawrence of Arabia* fame – Aqaba had been part of Britain's pivotal strongholds in the Arabian region. With Holland heading into its usual cold winter and Britain and Europe still suffering major post-war shortages of every commodity, many items – including warm clothing – were procurable only on a very restricted coupons system. As a result, the International Red Cross maintained a large warehouse at Aqaba where evacuees from the British colonies of Singapore, Malaya and Burma, and the Dutch of Indonesia were issued with mostly second-hand clothes to meet the demand for the coming winter. We were given half a day in Aqaba, as the ship had to navigate the Suez Canal, which could only be done by day. The warehouse was full of clothing, and with no limit to the number of items we could take. With no real organisation, the experience of finding clothes was somewhat stressful. People would pounce on whatever they thought they needed – but we all needed the same things. Winter clothes, in particular, people would grab for. But in the end it was quite fun, and we found some outfits of warm clothing that were useable, though not very fashionable; but, as the old saying goes, 'Beggars can't be choosers.'

The rest of the voyage was uneventful, but the closer we came to the motherland the more anxious my parents became. Uppermost in their minds was the question of where we should settle in Holland. My father finally selected Amsterdam where, as a young man, he had studied at a business college and where we still had extended family and acquaintances. At last we arrived at Holland's harbour city, Rotterdam. Newly from the tropics, most on board our ship keenly felt the low temperature and chill of the late autumn winds, and were grateful for our stop at Aqaba. Having reached the end of our long sea voyage, a fleet of buses took us refugees to various destinations in the Netherlands. In our bus I sat with eyes glued on the foreign panorama of Holland, the almost mythical country that we had known only from photographs, illustrated books, Christmas cards and geography lessons at school.

In metropolitan Rotterdam – and in town after town that we passed through – I noticed the multi-storied houses that stood side by side with mere handbreadths between them, contrasting with the bungalow-type houses in the East Indies that were set in ample plots of land. As we drove through villages and towns the mostly blond-haired and blue-eyed Dutch, with cheeks ruddy from exposure to the chilly wind, contrasted with most of us – dark haired and sunburnt brown. With winter coming, at this time of year the brilliantly green Dutch meadows did not have animals in them, and looked nothing like Indonesia's dun coloured sawahs on which water buffalo grazed. The mother country had a charm of its own, but we would discover that it did not altogether reflect the sentiments of many of the people we would meet.

A rough introduction to Amsterdam

In Amsterdam we were allocated temporary accommodation in a privately owned and operated hostel chartered by the Dutch Government. One of our first impressions of our hosts was the offhand, almost contemptuous manner in which we were treated, by manager and staff alike. We would learn that this was not an exclusive experience, with other 'Holland Dutch' or 'burgher' countrymen receiving us in the same way. Suffice to say that for us newly designated 'beggar colonialists', life in the motherland was, and for long remained, unwelcoming.

My parents had previous experience of a holiday spent in Holland, and they had almost anticipated the attitude of the operators and their staff in the Amsterdam hostel. Perhaps reflecting the sentiments of many stolid Holland burghers in the Dutch society, we refugees from the East Indies colony were scorned, even resented. Apparently forgotten was that the East Indies colony had made the Netherlands a proud seafaring nation, and had made many Dutch rich – sometimes immensely so. Now that the fabled Spice Islands had been overtaken by war and that an apparently unstoppable Indonesian nationalism could lose Holland incalculable wealth and international prestige, the coldly dismissive residents of the motherland looked upon their East Indies cousins with disfavour, if not open dislike.

One of our disappointments with the Dutch in Holland, even with relatives and friends, was encountering the complete lack of interest in our wartime experiences. If someone asked where in Indonesia we were during the war, and what we did, it only served as an excuse for *them* to tell *us* their wartime tales of 'horror'. We were endlessly told of the 'terrible deprivation' that the Dutch in Holland had suffered – 'We had to eat tulip bulbs, you know.' History records that some months before the liberation of Holland from the Germans, critical food shortages arose in the major cities of Amsterdam, Rotterdam and several other heavily populated centres, and many people indeed starved to death. But terrible as the deprivations had been for the people of mainly western Holland, when we began to tell *our* story – not of months but of years of starvation in the Japanese concentration camps – our listeners would become impatiently dismissive. 'Well, yes, that must have been terrible,' they said. 'But can you imagine how *we* suffered.' We came to call the self-indulgent yarns of the Holland Dutch experience 'the tulip bulb stories' – and we heard them often repeated.

There were times in Holland when people in the street, mostly the younger generation, openly demonstrated their animosity towards us. In a deja vu of the 'assu londoh' taunting by Indonesian youths, Dutch youngsters in Holland would accost us, '*Vuile opvreters, ga terug naar je apenland* (Rotten parasites, go back to your monkey land).' Of course, not all Dutch people were antagonistic towards the people from the East Indies, but there were many who considered us *opvreters* (parasites) – competitors for the country's scarce resources. In the light of changing worldviews and politics, the refugees from Indonesia had perhaps become a political embarrassment, and we also presented the national government with an uncomfortable question: what to do with yet more unwanted souls in the already overpopulated Netherlands?

Settling in

Some months after we arrived in Holland, my parents were able to rent rooms in a private home so that we could leave the unhappy hostel. Living a lifestyle so different from what we had once been accustomed to, we often walked miles for our entertainment and to familiarise ourselves with what was to us a foreign country. We roamed the beautiful historical city of Amsterdam on foot – window shopping, exploring the neighbourhoods and discovering its old-world aesthetics and charm. The centre of Amsterdam was, and remains, a showcase of its mercantile seafaring past. With its very heart intersected by a network of canals, in olden days flat-bottomed barges ferried merchandise from sailing ships to city warehouses. In the late 1940s, barges only seldom appeared in the waterways, usually plying the canals to deliver winter stoking coal to local fuel merchants. However, the city waterscape remains quite exceptional. Here and there quite lovely arched bridges connect the cobbled streets on either side of the canals, along which – row upon row, cheek by jowl – stand quaint old-world Dutch houses. Their typical architectural style has been carefully preserved and many remain tenanted to the present day. At that time, with very few cars but uncountable bicycles on the road, Amsterdam had a feeling of uncluttered order, not diminished by the cheap and efficient tram network that connected the suburbs.

Because of our meagre finances – we had only my father's small army pay to rely on – we lived a frugal lifestyle. On our expeditions we sometimes returned home with yesterday's priced-down breads, less popular varieties of fish, or cheap cuts of meat that we purchased from markets or wayside stalls. So different to how we had grown up, in the warp and woof of a new life we discovered an alien society and an essentially foreign people whose goodwill towards us was not unconditional.

An unexpected silence

As we gradually assimilated into life in Holland, we seldom mentioned our past in Indonesia. This subject opened wounds of the soul that, especially where it concerned my father, never fully healed. Whilst we concentrated on adapting to the present life, we began to speculate on my father's dream that the future would take us to Australia.

After the war – in Thailand, later in Indonesia and again in Holland – my father had written many letters to try and re-establish contact with our friends at Scarborough in Western Australia, and even with people whom my parents had only briefly met on their holidays. To his great disappointment, my father never received acknowledgement of his letters, except that a well-to-do Perth businessman friend began to send us gifts of food parcels, without one word written. In immediately post-war Holland the packets of Kraft cheese, tins of steak and kidney pie, plum pudding, jam, tinned fruits and a variety of other delicacies were sheer luxuries, and these consignments caused us much excitement. The parcels continued to arrive at quite regular intervals, but my father was puzzled at not having his 'Thank you' letters to our charitable giver answered. Although disheartened, he never varied his favourite saying. 'Aussies, salt of the earth,' remained sacrosanct. After two years the parcels stopped coming, breaking even this tenuous contact with Australia.

My family has never been able to fully comprehend the reason for the silence from former friends. In retrospect I have come to think that their lack of communication perhaps reflected how the Australian nation had embarked upon new directions in political and commercial realities, and that this may have influenced even our former friends' attitude towards us 'colonialists'. Perhaps there is as much truth as there is untruth in thinking that when we visited Australia in 1939, many people considered us rich and privileged, which may have influenced their regard for us. Now war had dispossessed us and we had no money or even a country to call home – perhaps the idea of being associated with penniless displaced persons may have alarmed some of our Australian friends. Perhaps they remained silent in case we should ask them for help that they were not prepared to offer. We will never know the full truth of it, but my father never faltered in his love for 'the Aussies'.

Back to school
For my family, life in Holland had to go on, and when my father's many attempts to forge new beginnings in Australia failed, an alternative had to be considered. For hard-pressed people logic is often a first casualty, and despite evidence to the contrary we began to believe that we must remake the past; we must turn our sights back to Indonesia and wrest from it a new future. My parents decided that the way to achieve this goal was through

education; in particular, by equipping me with a diploma in tropical agriculture. This would serve to return me to the plantation industry that had been the heart of our previous life, which the war had taken from us.

During the Japanese occupation of the Dutch East Indies, I had been four years without formal schooling. I had somewhat tenuously restarted this lost education in Thailand and again in Surabaya, but through no fault of my own, my educational background was less than sound. Attempts to catch up on it in Holland were perhaps of dubious quality. The Dutch Education Department had made special provision for young refugees from Indonesia in what the authorities termed 'one year pressure cooker courses'. These were intended to yield us the high school Intermediate Certificate. Whether or not the government's strategy was academically sound may well be debatable. Regardless, it was the only way that I could claim to have completed my Intermediate Certificate, which I attained in 1947. This opened the door for me to further my education.

At the end of the 1947 academic year, I had to decide whether to go forward with advanced studies or to try my luck at obtaining paid employment. Although there was merit in continuing my studies, a major problem was money. Although my father still received his Army pay, his final discharge from the Armed Forces was imminent and his income would cease in the near future. My parents had lost all of their assets in the war, and would be without a salary or any chance of receiving compensation for the loss of their investments in Indonesia. Unless my father found work – any work that brought in a wage – we faced the ugly spectre of inevitable destitution. My father eventually obtained work as a warehouse storeman, for which he was grateful. But it was a menial job of a casual nature and he received only meagre pay with no employment security.

My parents were unable to afford my further education, so with nothing to lose and despite my questionable high school education, I applied for a National Government Study Grant, which would enable me to enrol in advanced studies. Although I held out little hope of success, in September 1947 I was granted a study subsidy from the Dutch Government. In the knowledge that I was financially independent and that I would not inflict an unbearable burden on my parents, I enrolled in the Diploma course of studies at the College for Tropical Agriculture in the provincial city of Deventer. A new phase in life had opened up for me.

CHAPTER 11

Shaping a Future

*The greatest thing in the world is for a man
to know that he is his own
(La plus grande chose du monde c,est de savoir être à soi)*
Montaigne, *Essais I*, **xxxix**

In autumn 1947, having become a student at the College for Tropical Agriculture, I found private lodgings with a family in the provincial city of Deventer in eastern Holland. A smallish city of perhaps few more than 100,000 citizens, Deventer had retained much of its rural past. Thus, only several houses from where I boarded, an operating farmhouse remained. Early every morning the farmer trotted off by horse and cart to wherever his business took him in the fields, and in the late afternoon he returned with a cart full of cabbages, potatoes or hay for his horses.

Deventer's inner-city architecture was quaintly old-fashioned; its narrow cobblestone-paved streets were lined with shops, small cafés, two or three hotels, and apartment dwellings. Near the city square stood what in olden times used to be the city wall. And where the main bridge spanned the IJssel – one of Holland's major waterways – ecumenically clustered together stood several churches of different denominations. This was the heart of Deventer, symbolising the 'Us' of the city's permanent citizens. The financial benefit to the local economy of the 'Them' of Deventer's temporary but welcomed population – including students like me – was not denigrated by the canny, bean counting Dutch burghers, including my landlady and her husband.

College of Tropical Agriculture

The College for Tropical Agriculture that I attended was located directly opposite where I boarded. At a time when national hopes of a return to the East Indies colony were still high, the college – an impressive, rambling, two-storey building set in several acres of carefully maintained grounds – boasted a population in excess of 500 students. A highly prized industrial asset, and the city's major revenue raiser, the college was understandably held in high esteem by Deventer City Hall and by most citizens. Its reputation was a source of pride for the body of students, but occasionally the regard in which the college was held by the community suffered somewhat when the students' behaviour was perhaps more boisterous than it should be. However, most of Deventer's populace tolerated this juvenile bumptiousness fairly amiably. The majority of those attending the college belonged to its Student Union, but I could not afford the membership fees and therefore was unable to participate in its social activities. I sometimes regretted that I could not also involve myself in the student life that my cohort enjoyed, but it at least helped me academically since I knew few distractions in my studies. At the end of the academic year – in spite of my less-than-solid secondary education – I passed the college's First Year examinations. I was now well on my way to shaping a new future.

Money troubles

Although the government study grant I received covered my boarding and college attendance fees, it left me with little to cover basic daily maintenance items such as toiletries, paper, pens and other school supplies, and similar small needs. I also had very little cash to spare on social activities which, to be truthful, hindered my hope that I might chance to meet up with some of the city's young female residents. On the few occasions that I had gone out to socialise, when a young lady discovered that I could not suitably entertain her, her interest in me only too predictably ceased. Such is life.

At the end of the 1948 academic year, I spent the long August holidays with my parents in Amsterdam. I continued to receive my Study Grant and, although my parents protested that I did not need to do so, I could afford to pay them for my board and lodging so that I would not be a burden on them. I did not, then, reflect on how it had taken so few years to so utterly change our lives, or that in truth I was on state welfare.

To solve the problems raised by my acute lack of finances, I found casual employment as a farm labourer in the cut flower industry of the famous village of Aalsmeer. I had to rise at five o'clock in the morning to ride my bicycle about 13 kilometres to Aalsmeer, where I started work at six. At five in the afternoon, I travelled back the same way. Young and fit, I was glad of this casual work, which gave me the chance to put some modest spending money in my pockets for the next year's studies at the college.

Making friends

When I entered my second year of diploma studies at Deventer, the money I had earned at the Aalsmeer flower nursery meant that I could now begin to modestly participate in the city's social life. However, while the state of my disposable finances had improved, I was aware that I was still entirely dependent on extensions of the study grant – which was judged on academic merit. Social activities, which featured in the life of most of my colleagues, were for me still somewhat restricted. The exceptions were on Saturday evenings, when I began to attend dances held at a social club – a favourite meeting place for the city's youth. It was there where young people met to dance, and where in truth I hoped to kindle a young lady's interest in me.

In time, I struck up an acquaintance with two girls. Wilhelmina was named after the reigning Dutch monarch; her friend went by the rather staid Dutch name Jacoba, but called herself Cobie. High hopes to the contrary and somewhat to my disappointment, mercurial Cobie showed little interest in me – which perhaps had much to do with my less than capital financial status. In the course of an evening, when the somewhat flibbertigibbet Cobie found herself a free-spending partner, Wilhelmina and I were often left to spend the evening together. Shy and reserved, of solid middle-class and very traditional Dutch burgher family background, Wilhelmina – Willy, to me – and I began to share a budding friendship. I did not as yet dare to let her know that I hoped our acquaintance might deepen. For the time being, while the two of us found enjoyment in each other's company, my young lady friend did not seem to encourage me to hold out much hope for more than a casual relationship.

Throughout my second year at college, my friendship with the girls continued and we often met each other for dances, picnics by the IJssel river, or other social outings. Good-hearted and vivacious, but footloose and fancy free – and a little scatterbrained – Cobie's friendship with anyone who succumbed to her wiles lasted only as long as the good times rolled. When money stopped being freely spent on her, like a butterfly that only lightly and briefly touches anything with which it comes in contact, Cobie moved on to the next gallant victim of her charms. I did not figure in her calculations and we remained just friends.

Willy

As time went on, I established an easy and dependable friendship with Willy. She was shy to begin with, but once we got to know each other, we had good conversations. We would do adventurous things like exploring the area. Like me, she was fairly stoic; she faced situations as they were. She was a very sensible, practical, and matter-of-fact person – she wasn't very cheeky or playful, but we had a very nice time together.

A turning point for us came towards the end of my third and final year at college. I had taken to often cycling with Willy in the countryside, and in summer we went swimming in the always icy-cold waters of a nearby lake. After she finished work at a local business establishment, Willy would come cycling past my boarding house, ringing her bicycle bell to let me know that she had arrived. Having been waiting for her, as I was not permitted to entertain friends in the boarding house, I would join her on the street for a chat and to make plans for our next meeting. When the final year examinations loomed large in my mind, I had confided to Willy the kind of self-doubts that many students experience when a crucially important time approaches. Willy knew how much I depended on achieving the diploma, which should set me on the road to my future and which, to some degree, would hopefully restore my family's pride and their fallen fortunes. This knowledge was reason for my friend to almost daily come past my boarding house to talk with and encourage me – something that buoyed my spirits and made me appreciate her friendship even more. In the summer of 1950, when I passed the final examinations and was granted my diploma, Willy was first to congratulate me. By now, though we were still only friends, we had become a little more than *just* friends. The evening after my graduation we went out together to celebrate at a small hotel where, both of us strapped for cash, we nursed our single order of drinks. Eventually, with suggestive swipes over our table with his serviette, the stern, tail-coated headwaiter intimated that we should leave. At the end of the evening I lacked the courage to ask for a goodnight kiss. But at the door of her home, when we parted with our usual handshake, Willy further responded with a fleeting peck of lips on my cheek. This set my heart thumping in my chest, raising hopes that I had found more than a friend – though I did not yet dare think a girlfriend.

Although I had completed the basic course in diploma studies at the College for Tropical Agriculture, I applied for and was granted a one-year extension of the government subsidy, which enabled me to undertake a specialised post-graduate course in industrial chemistry. Willy and Cobie planned to spend some of their annual long vacation with family friends in Amsterdam. Before I left Deventer to return home to Amsterdam, I suggested to Willy that she might like to look me up and meet my parents. This innocent invitation was the beginning of our partnership and our lifelong journey together.

Falling in love
Before Willy came to Amsterdam on holidays, we had corresponded but had not arranged a day or time to meet. When she called at my parents' home, I was away working at the Aalsmeer flower nursery. When I returned that evening and my parents informed me of my friend's visit, my father – who otherwise held grave reservations about 'Holland Dutch' – commented, 'Willy is a *nice* girl, I like her.' High praise from him, these few encouraging words tipped the scales for my relationship with Willy.

I arranged time off from my work in the flower nursery for the week that Willy was in Amsterdam. We went sightseeing around the city on foot or by tram, or we packed a picnic lunch and cycled out along the banks of the Amstel River, riding through picturesque Dutch polder lands crisscrossed by canals and small waterways. When we got tired, we found a bench or a log to sit on, to rest and eat our lunch. On another day we explored the markets in the inner city, and when lunchtime came we bought a cheap bowl of steaming soup and Dutch rookwurst sausage with a thick slice of farm-loaf bread – a grand treat. When I delivered Willy back to where she was staying and returned to my parents' home, I felt divided, as if part of me was missing. On saying goodnight to my friend Willy, I increasingly came to wish that I could call her my girlfriend.

For one of the last days of Willy's vacation we had arranged to go sightseeing at the tourist village of Volendam, which sits on a small island in what used to be the *Zuiderzee* (Southern Sea). After the Zuiderzee was dammed, and therefore no longer a sea, it became known as *IJsselmeer* – Lake IJssel. The fishing village of Volendam is world renowned for its people, who still wear traditional Dutch costume including wooden clogs. In Amsterdam at the time, Volendam fishmongers in traditional dress sold smoked eel and fresh herring from barrows in the city streets. If today the streetscape has changed, more is the pity.

The ferry to Volendam departed from near the Amsterdam Central Station and took about half an hour to cross the lake. Willy had never travelled by boat, so the trip over what had once been open sea was a novel experience for her. On disembarking at the village, we visited the usual tourist attractions: watching people producing different handcrafts; inspecting some of Volendam's 'open house' residences; and, at a fishmonger's barrow, sampling smoked eel for which Volendam is renowned and which is considered a delicacy in Europe. The day went all too fast and the time came to catch the ferry back to the mainland.

On board we found that the fickle Dutch summer weather had changed and an icy wind was blowing across the IJsselmeer waters. It had been quite warm when we left Amsterdam that morning, and Willy was wearing only a summer frock. She was visibly uncomfortable – I noticed that my friend was shivering in the biting wind that tore at her on the open ferry deck. I was wearing a windcheater over my summer gear, and I offered that we should share it. Willy gladly accepted my offer and, standing close together at the stern of the ferry, the kiss that I received from Willy this time was more than a 'thank you' peck. This small but precious incident began our commitment to each other that will outlast time. On a summer's day in the stern of a ferryboat, across the chilly, windswept waters of IJsselmeer from romantic, olden time Volendam to Amsterdam, I had found my future wife. Soulmates, we have shared in all that we have experienced and achieved together. When, after her holiday in Amsterdam, Willy returned to her home in Deventer, we both knew that we had become partners, but the direction and the implications of our future together lay yet to be discovered.

Postscript

At the commencement of my three-year course of studies at the College for Tropical Agriculture I had still hoped that I would return to my homeland in the mountains of Java. However, after two forceful military campaigns by the Netherlands had been unable to regain effective control of the Dutch East Indies, our hopes began to fade. Under the considerable pressures of world opinion and macro politics, in 1949 the Netherlands were compelled to formally recognise Indonesia's independence. In Indonesia, where social order had not improved, the Indonesian state had 'nationalised' – or rather it had confiscated – my parents' plantation. Indonesian resentment, even hate, of the Dutch remained strong. It had become clear that I could not hope to return to Java and that I should seek a future elsewhere.

When we had arrived in the Netherlands in 1964, my father was only forty-two years old but his slave labour on the Burma to Thailand railway had broken his health. Following Indonesia's independence, he never again mentioned our plantation and he very seldom admitted his abiding love of Australia. However, in spite of the hardships and the heartbreak of his post-war life with the 'Holland Dutch', my father did not turn bitter. Rather, he urged my sister and me to achieve goals in a new life. 'Life,' my father said, 'is like our plantation nursery where the tea seeds germinate and produce the seedlings, which you then plant out in the gardens. If you have done your work well, you shall harvest a good crop.'

Two decades later, when – at the relatively young age of sixty-six – my father died in coldly indifferent Holland, my mother had no money to buy him a gravestone. She asked Willy and me – who in 1952 had migrated to Australia – to buy her a small slab of locally quarried stone to place on his grave. Hand hewn by us, we sent her a tile of 6 inches by 9 inches of Australian slate, which my mother placed for a headstone where my father lies interred. He now rests eternally near this token from Australia, the only country other than Indië to which he had given his heart.

It took the Dutch Government more than fifty years to acknowledge, on behalf of the native Dutch people, how it had ignored the plight of the refugees from the Dutch East Indies. In the year 2000, the government enacted a Bill called *Het Gebaar* (The Gesture). Besides a public apology, the Bill entitled surviving repatriates to a small sum of compensation money. Pre-deceased by our parents, in 2002 my sister and I each received 3000 Dutch guilders of this conscience money. The money in itself meant nothing to us; however, the citation with which the Dutch Government officially announced its 'gesture' provided some restitution for the pain that my parents had suffered – and from which, at least in part, my father had died. The Dutch Government's document reads *inter alia*:

> In enacting into Law 'Het Gebaar', a monetary reparation to evacuees from its former Dutch East Indies colony repatriated to the motherland in the aftermath of the Second World War, the Dutch Parliament acknowledges that it, and the Dutch Public in general, received the Indonesian Dutch cousins in a chilly and often a less-than-welcoming way. (Translation FJB)

My mother and sister never returned to Indië, spending the remainder of their years in Holland. Many years later, in our older age, I took Willy to visit Indonesia. We went to where my family home had once stood, but not a stone of it remained standing. The past was truly dead, but I had since wrested from it a new future in Australia.

In Honour of my Parents

> I have eaten your bread and salt.
> I have drunk your water and wine.
> The deaths ye died I have watched beside,
> And the lives ye led were mine…
>
> Rudyard Kipling[xxiii]

CHAPTER 12

A Change in Direction

In 1950s Holland, jobs were scarce and the future seemed bleak. With this in mind, during my final year of post-diploma studies I began to make enquiries for immigration to Canada, the United States of America, Brazil, Argentina, and of course Australia. Willy and I were now officially engaged to be married, and she encouraged me in our quest for new opportunities.

I submitted countless official applications and wrote numerous letters to prospective employers in Holland and abroad, but – in much the same way that my parents' attempts to emigrate had been thwarted – these remained unacknowledged. Having completed my fourth and final year at the college, I no longer received the government study subsidy and I had to find a way to support myself financially. I was lucky to find temporary employment as a clerk in the National Government Social Services Department in Amsterdam. Despite her parents' disquiet, my fiancée followed me to the big city where she, too, was fortunate to find a secretarial position in the offices of a publishing company. Now we could do no more than wait for hopefully favourable advice from the countries to which we had applied to immigrate.

Willy had never been beyond Holland's borders and her family, not unreasonably, was less than enthusiastic about the prospect of seeing her leave them, perhaps forever, to an alien country. Born into a staid Dutch household, barely turned twenty years old and the third of four children in her family, Willy had a very traditional, solidly middle-class upbringing. When she announced that, before we emigrated, she intended to get married ahead of her older siblings, she broke with custom and tradition – and caused quite a stir. Her family considered it unthinkable that she would leave her close circle of kin and acquaintances for somewhere in the world that, in Holland, one barely even knew the name. Willy's support for our immigration plans was an act of courage, an unquestioning commitment to our future life together.

For six long months we lived in hope, but in vain. We were becoming disheartened with the lack of progress in our plans for the future, including our wish to soon get married. Then, just before Christmas 1951, I received a large envelope embossed with the Australian coat of arms. The sheaf of weighty documents that it held fulfilled a family dream when we read that Australia had accepted Willy and me for immigration.

Preparing for a new life

The Australian papers that made it possible for us to emigrate were one thing, but we discovered that actually making it happen involved a great deal of unanticipated problems. We had applied for immigration as a married couple, so Australia's acceptance of us required that we should get married as soon as possible. In conservative, hidebound Dutch society, the urgency with which we intended to be wed inevitably caused some people to raise eyebrows, and wonder 'Could it be… Was it because…?' Undeterred by this gossip, on a mild winter's day, 25 February 1952, Willy and I became husband and wife. We had a small wedding, because we couldn't afford much. We attended the registry first, then the church, followed by a family meal hosted by Willy's parents. The die was cast and, except for one vital problem, the Rubicon was almost crossed.

The single but most critical obstacle that threatened to prevent our immigration was our acute lack of finances. We couldn't afford our ship's passage to Australia. Since I had received a study grant for four years, the Dutch government turned down our application for emigration sponsorship. Although the Australian government was prepared to

A Change in Direction

On a mild winter's day, Willy and I became husband and wife; 25 February 1952.

financially assist the immigration of people of British and European origins, as their Dutch counterpart did not finance us, Australia also declined to financially support our immigration.

In the immediate post-war, government-subsidised economy, second- and third-class travel to Australia was strictly reserved for government-assisted migrants. Since Willy and I did not meet the conditions for government assistance, we had to privately arrange our own *first class* ship's passage. In addition, on our arrival in Australia we must have a mandatory cash sum of 50 pounds sterling of so-called landing money. The required finance was utterly beyond our means, and my parents – themselves financially stressed – could not assist us. Understandably my wife's parents, whose wish it was that their daughter should not emigrate, were disinclined to help us. Our plans for immigration to Australia appeared doomed.

Not knowing where else to turn, I approached my great-uncle in Amsterdam, a well-to-do retired businessman, to ask him for a loan of 5000 Dutch guilders to cover our fares and the mandatory landing money. In those days, that was a substantial sum of money, and it would be no surprise if even the most magnanimous person found it difficult to trust that two young, jobless migrants in a faraway country could ever repay it.

A salutary exception to the fair-weather friends in Holland, my father's uncle was one of few in our family and circle of acquaintances who had stood by us. A stern but kindly man, I had always enjoyed a very good relationship with him, and he had followed my academic career at the College for Tropical Agriculture with interest. When I later introduced Willy to him as my intended bride, like my father, he took a liking to her. 'Congratulations, my boy,' he said, adding what he had deduced about Willy's character: 'Loyalty is priceless; it cannot be bought. You are a fortunate man.'

With nowhere else to turn, one of the major watersheds in our life was my great-uncle agreeing to lend us the 5000 Dutch guilders, making it possible for us to immigrate to Australia. We could offer him no better surety for this loan than our word of honour that we were absolutely determined to repay our debt to him. My great-uncle essentially relied on that promise as a sufficient guarantee. Two years later, Willy and I had repaid every cent of our debt to my great uncle in Amsterdam, but we could never repay him for his trust.

PART 4:

Australia

CHAPTER 13

The New Australians

It is difficult to understand the unconscious assumptions of one's culture. Many values are lodged deeply within us before we even begin to open our eyes to the moral surroundings ... As Friedrich Nietzsche might have said, 'It is hard work to become what one is.'
Martin Leet, 'Nietzsche for beginners'
***Australian Financial Review* (27 May 2005)**

On a chilly spring day in May 1952, accompanied by my parents and sister, Willy and I took the train from Amsterdam to the seaport of Hoek van Holland, where we would board the overnight ferry to London's Tilbury docks. When the time for departure came we said our last farewells. At the time air travel was not commonplace, and for migrants leaving their homeland by ship, distance and cost meant that farewells to kith and kin were probably a goodbye forever. As the ferry sailed for the English Channel, Willy and I stood at the railing and watched until my family's outlines and their waving handkerchiefs, held up high, faded into the misty Dutch skyline. A young married couple, we literally and figuratively turned our backs on the past, full of hope for a new beginning and a future in a faraway land. In a farewell telegram that we received the next day, my father rather poetically expressed the beginning of our lifetime journey, '*Met forse breede vleugelslag* (Soaring powerfully on broad wingspan).'

The overnight ferry crossing to Tilbury was uneventful, and after disembarking, a bus took us to board MV *Strathaird* of the

Peninsular & Oriental line, on which we had booked passage from England to Sydney. Second or third class passage would have reflected our true financial status, but having been forced by circumstance to travel first class, we enjoyed the superior service for which the old-fashioned P&O liners were renowned. We could not have dreamed of a more romantic honeymoon.

Strathaird (Allan C Green, from the collection of the State Library of Victoria H91.325/532).

When we boarded the ship, an attentive steward showed us to our cabin on a lower deck. We unpacked some of our clothes and personal items and, when long blasts of the ship's siren signalled our departure, we joined the crowd that waved goodbye to relatives and friends on the wharf. As *Strathaird*'s bow turned to the south, we had begun the journey of ten thousand miles towards our new homeland, faraway Australia.

Voyage to Australia

Our introduction to life on board the *Strathaird* was uneventful. Other than the cabin steward who had taken us to our first-class quarters we had not met with anyone on the ship. On the first evening at dinner, in the lavishly furnished and appointed first-class dining room, we shared a table with a middle-aged English gentleman who travelled unaccompanied. After mutual introductions, when Willy and I attempted to exchange pleasantries with him, our fellow diner was courteous but aloof. Our attempts to involve the gentleman in discussion failed, for which we blamed our not very well-developed English vocabulary. As the conversation petered out, we ate our meal in silence, not even conversing with each other in Dutch in case it should further provoke the Englishman's wordless but unmistakable disapproval of us. When the Head Steward stopped at our table to inquire if all was well with the service and the meal, our fellow diner had a brief *sotto voce* conversation with the *maître de'* that pointedly did not include us. We will never know the nature of their conversation, but at the next mealtime the English gentleman no longer sat at our table. From that day on we shared it with three other migrants, German ladies who, like us, had out of necessity booked first class passage. A small salve on our wounded egos, my wife and I decided that their command of the English language was worse than ours, and that the ladies had probably experienced similar difficulty when conversing with English-speaking fellow travellers with whom they had shared a table.

If our speech and pronunciation of English set us apart from our fellow travellers, the way we dressed further made us stand out on board ship. In much of war-ravaged Europe the material and cut of practically all clothing was of questionable quality, and clothing was only available through the coupon system that applied to merchandise of most kinds. Before our departure for Australia, Willy and I had shopped for clothing that we thought would be suitable to wear on our travels, but both the price range and the availability of ladies and menswear in Holland limited our choice. On board *Strathaird* we soon discovered that our attire did not match that of our fellow travellers; the men generally favoured tweed or woollen tartan sports jackets and trousers, and the ladies mostly wore woollen twin sets and skirts for day wear. The disparity in dress between the British travellers and us was even more noticeable at the dinner table. On the first evening people had not 'dressed' for dinner; however, the next evening gentlemen wore their dinner jackets complete with cummerbund and black bowtie, and ladies appeared in elegant, long evening dresses. Willy's 'evening wear' consisted of a long skirt with several interchangeable tops, and we had only been able to afford a second-hand tuxedo for me. None of this would have escaped British eyes that could not but find us socially, 'Well, not quite… you know.'

It was just as well that Willy and I, in our newly married state, were so absorbed in each other that we were largely unconscious of how awkwardly we fitted into the community of our luxury liner. Other than fleetingly, we did not stop to wonder why the English gentleman had sat with us only for that first dinner. When we occasionally mixed with British travellers, although they were invariably courteous, we never thought greatly about why they seemed reserved and remained generally aloof from us. It did not occur to us that, when we conversed with British and Australian travellers, they adopted a peculiar way of speaking with us – slowly and carefully enunciating their words. And nor, when we thought that they complimented us with, 'I say, your English is awfully good, where did you learn to speak it,' did we detect a touch of well-meant paternalism towards 'the young foreigners'.

Not only the passengers, but indeed the ship's crew singled us out as 'Well, not quite… you know.' Although the cabin steward had at first seemed a jolly and helpful chap, after the first day we seldom saw him again. On embarkation our bunks had been immaculately made up with starched linen sheets and pillowcases, and crisp clean towels hung on the towel racks beside the washbasin. After the first day at sea, when the steward failed to make up our beds we thought little of it. As I had done on board the ships that had taken me to and from Thailand and later to Holland, I attended to this small chore myself. In later years it became clear to us that, more snobbish than their British 'betters', the cabin steward and the table waiters had not failed to notice our lack of *savoir-faire*, and that the ship's crew, even the *maître de*', treated us with a haughty disdain of which – at the time – Willy and I were innocently unaware.

Despite having to deal with foreign people whose different ways and manners often puzzled us, and other small irritations that cropped up during the month-long voyage from Europe to Australia, for Willy and me it was a honeymoon that many would have envied. After a few days we became used to the ship's fall and rise on the ocean waves and no longer felt queasy, and we began to enjoy the excellent conditions on board. Some two weeks out of England, when we reached our first port of call at Port Said in Egypt, we watched boys in small canoes alongside the ship dive for coins that people threw overboard.

Later in the day we went sightseeing on shore, where vendors offering all kinds of wares and services swarmed over the passengers, 'Hey, Mister MacGregor, buy from me, very good, very cheap!' Others, proclaiming themselves 'guides', and other riffraff and beggars who were after the tourist shilling, did their irritating best to attract attention, with persistent, 'Hey, Mister MacGregor!' The refrain of 'Mister MacGregor' we found was repeated at other ports of call as *Strathaird* carried us ever closer to our new homeland.

In Holland, when our immigration papers had required us to nominate an address of residence in Australia, we had vaguely intended to disembark in Sydney where we nominated a casual Dutch acquaintance of ours. However, the person had made it no secret that he could neither accommodate us, nor assist us to find work, and that allowing us to quote his address in the official documents was for the sake of helping us fulfil a formality. As each day took us nearer to Australia, without having either work or accommodation lined up, we began to worry where we should find employment and housing upon our arrival. Although we had no idea of conditions in Australian society, we knew full well that our emergency funds of 50 pounds sterling landing money would not suffice for very long. It was a relief when, at the second last of *Strathaird*'s ports of call before Australia, Aden in Yemen, we received a letter from another Dutch friend, Hans van Leuven, who had immigrated a year earlier. Before we left Holland I had written to ask him if he could help us with settling in Australia, and the positive information that we received in his letter took a load off my shoulders.

Hans had sent the welcome news that he had found both accommodation and work for us as a married couple on a sheep property some 60 miles outside the rural township where he lived – Naracoorte in South Australia. Although we did not understand what the term 'married couple' meant, we were delighted to learn that we would have somewhere to live and employment on a farm – which I naively believed very much suited my agricultural diploma qualifications. Fortune, we thought, had smiled on us; the prospects in the new country seemed brilliant, and hope soared – we had *made* it! In *Strathaird*'s office we arranged with the purser to now disembark in

South Australia's capital city, Adelaide, where my friend would be waiting to take us on the train to Naracoorte… wherever that was.

When our ship reached the Australian continent, our first port of call was Fremantle in Western Australia. Our ship remained only long enough to allow passengers to disembark. This having been accomplished in short time, *Strathaird* proceeded through the Great Australian Bight towards its next destination, where Willy and I would terminate our voyage. Three days later we reached the capital city of South Australia, packed and ready to disembark. We said farewells to the German ladies with whom we had shared our table in the dining room, and to a few other fellow travellers with whom we had become somewhat acquainted. When we were allowed to disembark we went below decks to collect our suitcases, and waiting there for us was the cabin steward. Although he had been elusive throughout the voyage and we had only occasionally seen him, we were not surprised that he was now waiting for us, and had anticipated his purpose. On nearing the Australian mainland we had discussed the custom of tipping with some in our small circle of acquaintances. Neither the immigrant German ladies nor a few others who travelled under similar circumstances knew what counted for good service or a reasonable amount of money to tip one's table waiter and cabin steward. Although Willy and I had not been well looked after by our cabin attendant, I handed the man a 1 pound sterling note – a not inconsiderable sum to part with, given our meagre landing money. The steward gingerly turned the banknote around several times. After he had studied it on both sides, when he nonchalantly slipped my tip into a shirt pocket, his, 'Thank you, *Sir*,' was pure mockery.

Arriving
On 22 June 1952, we walked down *Strathaird*'s gangplank and into the bitingly cold autumn air. Mud and decaying seaweed lay exposed by the low tide and the wind that blew at us from across the sea made the water smell brackish. After completing the routine of passport formalities, the immigration officer who had interviewed us extended his hand in a friendly gesture, 'Welcome to Australia, young people, and good luck.' It was encouraging to find a considerate person in our new homeland.

Ferdinand and Willy farewelling the *Strathaird* in Adelaide, 1952.

In the immigration reception hall we were glad to see that – true to his promise – Hans was waiting for us. After exchanging the usual pleasantries, we made our way to a nearby platform where a diesel train with a single carriage stood waiting to take us to the city. On our way to the train I had spotted a swarthy man with a brown paper bag, the neck of an open bottle poking through it. 'That's an Aboriginal,' Hans said in a disapproving tone of voice. As we passed the man, he barely glanced up from the kerb of the road where he sat. In contrast with the enthusiasm with which Willy and I keenly took in the country of the Southern Cross, our new homeland, the Indigenous Australian's face was vacant. 'Let's get to Adelaide,' Hans urged as he looked askance at the man on the side of the road, 'Don't pay attention to him, he'll only beg us for money.' This puzzled us, but Hans had been in Australia for a year already, so we thought he must know better than us.

The half-hour train trip from Port Adelaide terminated at Central Station. When we emerged from the station, I recognised across the road the Grosvenor Hotel, in which I had stayed with my parents in 1939. Hans, however, had wisely booked us cheaper accommodation in a modest guesthouse in a nearby working-class suburb. With he and I carrying a suitcase each, we walked the short distance to our lodgings, where our other baggage would be delivered by truck the next day.

After the long sea voyage it felt good to be on firm land again. After unpacking a few items we had time to spare, so Willy and I decided to stretch our sea legs in order to get our bearings in our new country.

A job interview

Many of the older dwellings in the suburb were of weatherboard construction, but the newer ones, Hans had said, used the modern asbestos-cement sheet building material. Throughout the suburb, homeowners had painted their houses a rainbow of colours – whites, greens, blues, yellows, even a garish pink. Most of these Australian homes boasted a usually well-kept lawn and shrubs or annual flowers in beds in the front garden. Not infrequently, Hans had told us, many residents grew tomatoes, climbing beans, potatoes and green vegetables in the backyard, and some kept half a dozen or so fowls in a pen.

When a bird called from a tree on the road in a high-pitched rolling cackle, I said to Willy, 'Listen! That was a kookaburra.' And where a large tree emanated the cleansing smell of eucalyptus, 'A gum tree,' I said. As we wandered farther into the suburb, we found the usual range of shops in its business district – a greengrocer, baker, butcher, chemist, a few clothing stores, the characteristically Australian milk bar and hotels, without which life in contemporary Australia would be unthinkable. Different from all that we had known in the past, everything we saw, heard and smelt was exciting and new. Back at the guesthouse, we talked with Hans about his experiences since he had left Holland a year ago and made chit chat about our families, our newly married life, the trip aboard *Strathaird*, but mostly about our hopes for our future in Australia.

On our second day in Adelaide, Hans had arranged that Willy and I would meet with the farmers from Naracoorte who happened to be in the city on business. The morning passed and it was well after noon when a car drew up in front of the guesthouse, 'There they are. Your prospective employers,' Hans announced. After introductions, we sat and talked. Mr and Mrs Armstrong seemed amiable, albeit as reserved as many passengers on board *Strathaird* had been. Mr Armstrong was the typical Australian farmer: tall, beefy, broad shouldered, ponderous in movement; red faced and with skin around his eyes permanently crinkled from scanning the vastness of the Australian landscape and squinting against the piercing southern sunlight. Mrs Armstrong was her husband's opposite: slightly built, with darting movements and seething with an intense, potentially volatile nervous energy.

Mr Armstrong did not mince words when he stated, rather than asked, 'You people are from Holland. Have you ever worked on a farm?' I answered in the affirmative, handing him my brand new agricultural diploma. To my disappointment Mr Armstrong only glanced at it, saying, 'Humph. What kind of farm?' When I said that I had been fortunate in Holland to have done my work experience on a 45-hectare, mixed crop and twenty-cow dairy farm, the taciturn Australian's face cracked with a slight smile. *His* property, he dryly replied, measured 10,000 acres and was stocked with 5000-odd sheep. As I was unable yet to convert hectares into acres all I could think of to say in reply was, '*Oh*.' Sensing that the comparison between the Dutch and Australian properties had not been flattering, I began to despair that I may have spoilt our chances of being employed on the Australian farm.

Mr Armstrong's next question made matters even worse, 'Can you kill and dress a sheep?' I was desperate that this time I should not let him find me wanting and I replied that I could probably kill a sheep. However, I confessed, even in winter, Dutch farmers did not dress animals but penned them in a barn – but I would certainly want to learn how to dress sheep in this country. The Australians startled themselves with the quick bark of a laugh that my answer elicited from Mr Armstrong. He explained that after slaughtering an animal, to 'dress' it meant taking its skin off the carcass. I had just learned that in Australia to 'dress' a sheep really meant to *undress* a dead one, and I added a local idiom to my deficient repertoire of Australian English.

After I answered several more questions from Mr Armstrong, his wife turned her attention to Willy, asking, 'Can you cook, dear?' When my wife confessed that she did not really have a great deal of experience in the kitchen, Mrs Armstrong reacted with a sigh, '*Oh, well.*' Next she asked hopefully, 'But you can iron, can't you, dear?' Willy had to again admit that she was not well trained in the art of laundering. Mrs Armstrong's tight face, thinly drawn lips and nervously darting eyes betrayed a growing sense of impatience. 'What *can* you do, then?' the farmer's wife snapped. When Willy replied that she had worked in an office in Holland, this elicited a sniff, and, 'Oh, well, we'll just have to work together and I shall have to show you the ropes, dear.' Her 'dear' was delivered with barely disguised exasperation. 'I will truly try very hard to work in your house,' Willy promised. Afraid to further damage our chances with the Australians and run the risk that they might not employ us, neither Willy nor I were game to ask what the possible connection could be between learning the tasks of cooking and ironing, and the 'ropes' of which Mrs Armstrong had spoken. For the time being, this remained a mystery to us.

After the Australians had asked us a few more questions, to our relief Mr Armstrong concluded the interview with, 'Well, it seems that you will both have to learn a lot about farm work, but Mrs Armstrong and I agree to employ you. As a married couple we will pay you each 2 pounds 10 shillings per week and you will have free board and lodging. As you have no use for money on the farm we will keep your wages in trust for you, and you can draw on the balance when we occasionally take you to town for shopping, haircuts and similar business. Understood?' Although we had no idea if '2 pounds 10 shillings per week each' constituted a fair wage, we had little option but to agree and we accepted the proposition, 'Thank you, Mr Armstrong.' With these words we took a first step towards earning our place in this new society and gaining acceptance by Australians.

When our employers rose and made for the door of the boarding house lounge room, I also got up to see the visitors off. But when I extended my hand in farewell, neither Mr nor Mrs Armstrong reciprocated, making their exit with a quick nod and a curt, 'Goodbye.'

Watching them walk to where their Jaguar car stood parked on the street I noticed Mr Armstrong's peculiarly stiff gait, often associated with hard, awkward labour. Mrs Armstrong's ramrod-stiff back, however, signalled something else – a no-nonsense quality and a sign that she, perhaps more so than her husband, was a person not easily crossed or denied. Whatever our impressions of our Australian employers, 'Beggars can't be choosers,' and we were thankful that we had found desperately needed employment and accommodation in our new homeland.

A day or two later, on our last day in Adelaide, Willy and I went shopping for suitable work clothes. At the time, Australian labourers customarily wore grey twill trousers and a blue or grey flannel shirt, but – possibly influenced by cowboy movies – Willy and I bought several pairs of blue jeans, which were then not very commonly worn. Shopping for suitable headgear, the price of the felt Akubra hat favoured by country people was too steep for our limited finances and we settled for a much cheaper cotton item – nowadays known as a bush hat. With still some money left, we made our final purchase of a .22 rifle. Costing 11 Australian pounds, with a packet of 100 bullets at 7 shillings 6 pence, this was somewhat extravagant given our meagre finances. Our buying spree had stripped our finances almost bare but, we rationalised, 'We'll soon be earning money from our wages.'

To Naracoorte

The next day, together with Hans, Willy and I took the train from Adelaide to Naracoorte in south-eastern South Australia. We had arranged for Mr Armstrong to collect us on his usual Friday shopping trip to town, which meant that we would have several days to wait for him at Naracoorte. The timing was of some concern to us, as the two train fares to the city, several days' accommodation in the Adelaide guesthouse, and our recently purchased provisions had made worrying inroads in our reserves of landing money.

The daylight express train to Naracoorte wound steadily through the Adelaide Hills until the track flattened out over Australia's seemingly endless rural land. Childhood memories of taking the Overland Express with my parents came crowding back to me. On either side of the railway line barbed wire fences still ran into an inconceivable distance, containing farm animals and marking out the paddocks that were grazed mainly by sheep and some cattle. 'Look!' I exclaimed, pointing out to Willy where rabbits sat on bare patches of red-raw earth, sunning themselves in front of their burrows. On our Adelaide shopping spree Willy had wisely been a little loath to spend so much money on a firearm that she thought we did not really need. But now I promised her, 'On the farm I'll teach you to handle and shoot a rifle, and we'll go hunting rabbits.'

In some paddocks a windmill stood outlined against an incredibly blue sky. The iron sails, spinning in the wind, operated a pump that filled precious water into drinking troughs for the sheep and cattle. As we later learned, on the driest continent in the world, one of Australia's critically scarce resources is rain. On many farms, artesian or bore water was pumped up by windmills and collected and stored in huge corrugated iron tanks and overflow dams. From there it would be reticulated to troughs, bringing life to a country where rain might not fall for a year. In the vastness of the largely tenantless landscape, our train now and then rushed past a settlement or township; the untidy jumble of dwellings beside the rail tracks punctuated the loneliness that is so greatly the hallmark of rural Australia – not *terra nullius*, but a vast land, much of it devoid of humans.

We reached Naracoorte in the late afternoon, and after we collected our few pieces of hand luggage Hans took us to one of the town's guesthouses – a bed and breakfast establishment where we would stay until our employers came to collect us to take us to their farm. Before she let us sign the guest register, the proprietor looked us over carefully and somewhat suspiciously, but she relaxed when my friend explained to her that in a few days time our employers would collect us at Naracoorte. 'That's all right then,' the woman agreed, 'at least yous have a job to go to, I gather.' As an afterthought she added, 'Mind you, this is a respectable establishment and we want no trouble.' Hans again reassured her, 'These are nice people, missus, they won't give you any trouble.' Accompanying us to the room, he somewhat apologetically explained to us that 'nowadays' many foreigners and itinerants came to Naracoorte to find work. 'Some are rough characters, troublemakers, and many have no money or job. Sometimes a guest sneaks off without paying for his stay, so you can't blame the landlady for being a bit cautious.' We said that we understood this and that we would of course behave. After bidding him goodbye, for the first time Willy and I were on our own in an unknown land.

It was winter, and as we settled in our room it soon became obvious that, with no heating provided, the chill would soon become unpleasant. After a while we were both shivering with cold, when I suddenly had a great idea. 'Let's take a stroll through the town,' I suggested. 'We'll find somewhere to have our evening meal, and before we return to our room I will buy a bottle of sherry in one of the hotels. A small drink will warm us before we go to bed.'

On our walk to the business centre of Naracoorte we noticed that our guesthouse stood in a public housing estate in a clearly less affluent area of the town. The same as the suburb where we had stayed in Adelaide, in this area of Naracoorte most houses were painted a spectrum of rainbow colours – green, pink, and blue apparently the most popular tints. In contrast, the central business district seemed to reflect the town's importance as a major service centre for the surrounding wool and sheep-meat producing rural industry. Certainly the architecture and the quality of Naracoorte's inner town buildings were markedly superior to what we had so far seen, even in Adelaide. Naracoorte's two main streets were lined with a variety of shops – pharmacies, doctors' surgeries, several banks and three hotels. Such as in many Australian country towns, foremost among Naracoorte's major establishments were its banks, either built in the symmetrical simplicity of the Georgian style, or the baroque elegance of Victorian architecture. Dating to more recent times, the hotels in particular were fine examples of Federation architecture, their façades and balustrades decorated with exquisite iron lace-work typical for the era. Modern-day shops and – in the more affluent areas of town – many private homes were constructed of slabs of Mount Gambier limestone, named after the nearby town where this local building material was quarried. Everything taken into account, one foot in the past the other firmly planted in the present, Naracoorte was both partly unattractive and partly beautiful – a typical rural Australian township with an aesthetically pleasing but also a businesslike and utilitarian character.

After taking in some of Naracoorte's sights, Willy and I began to look for somewhere to have our evening meal. Our meagre finances precluded that we should dine in one of the hotels, but in a side street we found a small café in which at this early hour only a few customers were waiting for their meal. As was then common in this kind of unpretentious eating establishment, it had laminex tables and chrome chairs with seats of the same material. None of the tables were covered with a cloth, and each was adorned with cutlery, glasses, pepper and salt shakers, and a tomato-shaped plastic container filled with tomato sauce – the condiment without which no Australian meal seemed complete. When the proprietor, a person of Greek origin, came to our table, he announced that we could have a choice of, 'Stike 'n eggs, stike 'n t'matoes, stike 'n onjons, stike 'n sausages, stike 'n eggs 'n t'matoes 'n onjons, stike 'n eggs 'n t'matoes 'n onjons 'n sausages – whaddaya want, mite?' Choosing steak and sausages, when the proprietor cum cook returned to his kitchen, we watched him slap a huge piece of 'stike' onto the cast-iron top of the wood-fired stove. He let it sizzle for a while then, judging one side done, with a quick twist of his fork he turned it over to sear the other side. In the meantime, in a large black frypan our sausages cooked, and in a large aluminium saucepan handfuls of potato chips spluttered until crisp and golden. Returning to serve us with two plates heaped high with food, our meal looked and smelt delicious. As our host plonked the fare down on the table he demanded, 'Fifteen bob, mite, ya c'n pie me now.' Noticing the puzzled look on my face and correctly deducing that we were newcomers to Australia, the Greek chef explained, 'In Owstrilia "bob" same as "shillin'". You pie me fifteen shillin', understand?' I had found a new idiom to enter in my list of Australianisms.

Replete after our meal at what the locals referred to as 'The Greasy Greek's café', we were ready to return to our guesthouse. As I had promised, on our way back we briefly stopped at one of the hotels where I bought a bottle of sherry – a nightcap with which to warm ourselves before going to bed in our chilly room. I carried the bottle, wrapped in a brown paper bag, back to the guesthouse in a pocket of my raincoat, and, tired after the long trip from Adelaide and our walk around Naracoorte, we went straight to our room. Before we turned in, we enjoyed some of the sherry – drinking it from a thick glass tumbler we had found on the washbasin. Whether because of the liquor, the large meal or the exhaustion of train travel, we slept well that night.

The next morning we awoke in good spirits and when we joined fellow guests for breakfast in the somewhat grandly called 'parlour' we were looking forward to seeing more of the town that day. However, we were no sooner seated than the landlady came over to our table with a face like a black thundercloud. 'After brekkie ya can pack yer gear 'n get out,' she snapped, bristling with indignation. Her English was too rapid for us to yet understand, so we asked if she indeed meant that after breakfast we must leave? '*Yes,*' the woman confirmed emphatically. I asked her why, since we had booked to stay till our employers came to collect us. Still in a fury she blurted out, 'Never ya mind that. After breakfast I want yous outta here.' Leaving us dumbstruck, the landlady turned on her heels, the rigid posture of her retreating body and determined stomp of her feet emphasising her wrath – the cause of which was beyond our understanding.

Under the circumstances the only thing I could do was to quickly find Hans, to ask him what could have caused our landlady to throw us out of the guesthouse – had he perhaps made a wrong booking? If we could no longer stay in the guesthouse while we waited for the Armstrongs to collect us, where else could we find accommodation? As it was early in the morning, I fortunately found my friend where he worked as an electrician. With his employer's permission to take some time off, we returned to the guesthouse where, in better English than mine, my friend conferred with the landlady. To my relief, after a while I noticed the woman's initial indignant expression gradually soften until, incredibly, a thin smile curled her lips and her face brightened. Beckoning me over to join them, my friend explained what had caused her displeasure. 'In *Australia*', he said, emphasising the word, 'alcohol is not allowed in a guesthouse. When the landlady saw you return last evening with a bottle showing from a pocket in your raincoat she concluded that you were trying to sneak in liquor, to drink and cause trouble. I explained to her that you do not yet know Australian custom and that you made an honest mistake.' My friend continued, 'I have guaranteed the lady that you are respectable people and she has accepted this, but she wants you to give her the bottle to mind until you leave, then you can have it back.' While we were talking, the proprietor confirmed every point with vigorous nods of her head, and when Hans finished she added, 'Yeah, well, yous New Australians are only new here, so I s'pose yah couldn't know about no grog in yer room.' With the suggestion of a smile on her face she warned, 'Mind yah, but no more drinkin' on my premises, understand?' An important Australian custom learned the hard way, we readily agreed, 'No, we won't do it again, thank you.'

The small crisis on our first day in Naracoorte now resolved, that morning we continued to familiarise ourselves with the town. Naracoorte was clearly benefiting from then very favourable conditions in the rural industry, especially in the wool business. In the two main streets of the town centre, the variety of expensive goods in shops ranged from imported foodstuff to luxury household items and appliances, clearly evidencing prosperous times. In the town's industrial park a steady stream of large trucks drove in and out to make deliveries of fertilisers, seeds, animal feed, hardware and other farm supplies to agricultural properties in the countryside. In machinery yards, expensive farm equipment – tractors, harrows, fertiliser spreaders and ploughs and all kinds of tilling and harvesting implements – stood waiting for buyers. Elsewhere in the industrial part of the town, leaning over the rails at the local sale yard, country people – distinguishable by their wide-brimmed Akubra hats – stood waiting for auctioneers to begin selling sheep and cattle in the pens. As someone said, *Anno Domini* 1952 was 'A bumper year for farmers, make no mistake.'

At Naracoorte we soon learnt that the public, shopkeepers, merchants, operators of the rural service industries and even the then highly respected bank managers and their staff accorded the agricultural fraternity – the man on the land who was doing so well – privileged status and a measure of deference. In the 1950s, in a nominally classless society, the Australian farmer – reaping huge financial benefits from 'riding on the sheep's back' – lived an enviable upper-class existence, and they acted accordingly.

The Armstrongs' farm

The day that Mr Armstrong came to collect us at Naracoorte we were packed and ready to leave after breakfast. As had been the case when he came to interview us in Adelaide, the morning went, and by late afternoon we were still waiting for him. Although the delay was tedious, more worrisome was our concern that the Armstrongs had changed their mind and decided against employing us. With almost all of our landing money spent, unless we started working we would soon not have a penny left. Without recourse to government financial assistance, accommodation or employment, our jobs on the farm were critically important to us. It was a relief when, late that afternoon, a noticeably liquor-flushed Mr Armstrong drew up in his utility. 'Get your gear on board, I want to leave for home,' our employer curtly urged from behind the steering wheel. Although we attempted to put our luggage in the back of the utility, I did not know how to undo the tarpaulin cover. Noticing my unsuccessful efforts, with a grunt of disapproval Mr Armstrong got out of the car. 'Here,' he said, 'That's how the tarp comes off, get it?' He watched us put our suitcases and cabin trunk into the utility, then ordered us to 'Hop in.' No sooner were we barely settled inside then our employer took off. He drove in such a hurry that Willy and I had to cling to each other as we raced around the town's streets. Out of town we turned off the bitumen onto an unsurfaced country road; with the vehicle's progress marked by a cloud of trailing dust, Naracoorte disappeared and the wide-open spaces of rural Australia unfolded.

It was almost dark when we arrived at the farm. The trip had seemed like entering another world – bushland of eucalyptus and native shrubs, grassed paddocks on which grazing, moving, continuously shifting sheep looked like multiples of the white handkerchiefs in my family's hands, waving us off at Hoek van Holland. I noticed a few huge gum trees that had been left to provide shade, standing tall and proud, almost as if posing for someone to paint them into quintessential Australian landscapes. Apart from these, the vegetation on the paddocks had been clear felled. At the late hour of the day, from behind the winter's cloud cover the setting sun sometimes sent a startlingly bright ray of light through this rural scenery of bushland and meadows. In the dying embers of its fiery descent, before it disappeared below the horizon, it briefly tinted the greyish khaki blue-green of Australian forest a mellow orange, yellow and pink glow. Mr Armstrong seemed oblivious to the raw beauty around us, and when we remarked on it he dismissed our attempt at conversation, 'Humph.'

At the entrance to his farm, 'Hop out and open the gate,' our employer instructed me. While 'hopping out' was easy enough, opening the gate to let the car through proved unexpectedly difficult. Try as I might, in the gathering dusk I could find neither a hasp, lock nor bolt to release. For a little while Mr Armstrong watched my fruitless efforts, then he impatiently wound down the car window. 'What's holding you up this time?' he growled, to which I shamefacedly replied, 'I cannot find the lock on your gate, Sir.' Our employer responded gruffly, 'You can drop the "Sir" – I am Mr Armstrong,' he said. 'You're on the wrong side. Go to the other end and let your hand drop halfway down the gate – there's a toggle that you have to lift up – then pull the gate towards you. Stop pushing against the gate or you'll never get it undone.' More by good fortune than by these only half-understood instructions I managed to open the recalcitrant contrivance, and, as he passed through, Mr Armstrong warned, 'Shut the gate, we don't want our sheep out on the road.'

Giving an idea of the size of this property, it took about ten minutes drive from the front gate to where the homestead – a large barn-like house – and several sheds stood surrounded by a clump of pine trees. With the vehicle's engine now switched off, in paddocks around us we heard sheep bleating a husky, '*Bàààh,*' to which lambs added their little voices in thin piercing cries, '*Mèèèh.*' The flock's chorus accentuated the otherwise enveloping quiet of the country, unpolluted by manmade noise. These romantic thoughts did not last long; Mr Armstrong sharply pulled us back to reality with a curt, 'You can get your gear out of the ute.' Waving his hand towards the long barn with bull-nose iron overhang that covered the bare earth front veranda, he said, 'Your quarters are over there.' He indicated two doors nearest to where we stood. 'You have the first two rooms,' he said. Pointing at another two entrances farthest from us he added, 'Those are reserved for the contractor and the wool classer when the shearers come.' Although the terms 'contractor' and 'wool classer' were unintelligible to us, we deduced that we would apparently share the barn with two other people. A far cry from what we had thought would be a quaint little house set in a country garden bursting with flowers, it dismayed us that our accommodation was nothing more than a section of a shared barn. There was nothing cottage-like about the rust-stained corrugated iron walls, the earthen floor of the veranda and the weather-stained doors from which the paint had peeled off in strips. 'Mrs Armstrong will soon want to see Willy,' Mr Armstrong said and, leaving us standing beside the car, our employer disappeared inside the homestead. With no choice but to unload our luggage from the vehicle, we carried it across the rain-soaked grass under cover of the bare earth veranda. Opening one of the creaking doors we entered not the quaint cottage we had hoped for, but the farm's meagre servants' quarters.

The internal walls of the rooms in our section of the barn were constructed of thin sheets of plaster board, reminding me somewhat of the flimsy bamboo partitions in the Gudang Garam concentration camp. The inside was furnished with a range of evidently surplus items considered suitable for the servants. In these times of financial liquidity in the Australian rural industry, 'good enough for the cottage' was quite good indeed. Before us stood a beautiful old rosewood sideboard and an elegant rosewood table with six balloon-back dining chairs – replaced in the homestead by 'modern' steel and glass furniture. In contrast, two tired lounge chairs – with some of their springs sticking up through the fabric – did nothing to complement the handsome appearance of the antique rosewood furniture. An inside door gave access to our bedroom, in the middle of which stood an ancient double bed. It was piled high with quilts and blankets that gave off the musty smell of badly aired bedclothes. Against a second wall, propped on three-and-a-half legs, stood a chest of drawers, and a little farther along a rickety old wardrobe completed the furnishings of what was now our *quarters* – as distinct from the *cottage* that we thought we had been promised. Not usually given to emotional outbursts, when Willy had finished surveying our 'home' she sat down in one of the dilapidated chairs and cried. When I looked back at our suitcases, standing in the room waiting for us to unpack them, for a fleeting moment the thought struck me that if we picked them up now we could leave and carry them back to civilisation. Of course, the reality was that we had neither transport nor money to make good such an escape, and all I could do was try to console my poor, unhappy wife.

After a while Willy stopped crying, and with the optimism of youth returning, we busied ourselves emptying the suitcases and storing our clothes in the chest of drawers and the wardrobe. Among the covers on the mattress we found old but clean linen with which we made up our double bed, and when we had finished this we returned to our living room. Trying to cheer Willy up, I pointed out a small vase full of flowers with a strong, sweet scent in the middle of the rosewood dining table, and to a cosy fire in the open fireplace. 'Someone has taken the trouble to welcome us,' I said.

A kitchen crisis averted

We were still busy installing ourselves in our 'quarters' when, without a knock, the door opened and Mr Armstrong walked in. 'Mrs Armstrong wants to see Willy now,' he said. I watched my young wife follow our employer until they reached the homestead, where a hastily closed door quickly extinguished a beam of light that briefly escaped from inside. When sometime later Willy returned from the big house, I again noticed tears in her eyes.

'What's the matter?' I asked. In a small, choked voice, hiccupping with sobs my wife replied, 'Mrs Armstrong wants me to cook tonight's dinner.' Trying to cheer her up I said, 'Oh well, I am sure that you and Mrs Armstrong can manage together. Remember that she promised to teach you the housework?' 'No, no, you don't understand,' Willy wailed, 'I have to do the cooking myself.'

Regardless of her promise that, 'We'll just have to work together then, dear,' for this evening at least Mrs Armstrong evidently did not intend to keep her pledge.

Tonight's dinner was to be mashed potato, beans, crumbed cutlets and gravy. Willy and I could manage to cook the potatoes and beans, but neither of us knew how to prepare crumbed cutlets – what were *they*? – or gravy – what was *it*? When I offered to help, Willy brought further bad news, 'The Armstrongs say that you are not allowed inside the homestead.'

I had no option but to defy our employers, and in spite of their ban I followed my wife into the kitchen where we topped and tailed beans and peeled potatoes. Pans with these vegetables placed on top of the stove, we next turned to the problem of preparing crumbed cutlets. These, we discovered, were a kind of meat. Reasoning that they must be covered with breadcrumbs, we located a packet in the pantry and – with some difficulty – translated the instructions on the box from English into Dutch. We dragged the chops through lightly beaten egg before coating them with the crumbs. That problem now solved, we set to working out how to cook them. I remembered how our steak in the Greasy Greek café at Naracoorte had been prepared, and suggested to Willy that we put the cutlets on top of the stove until done. And as for what was meant by gravy, we decided that – as with our 'stike' at the Greasy Greek's – it surely meant tomato sauce in a bottle?

The potatoes and beans were boiling and we were about to turn to cooking the meat when the kitchen door opened and a young woman entered. Willy introduced us, 'This is Miss Shadbolt, but Mr and Mrs Armstrong want us to always call her Nurse.' The young woman, a person in her mid-twenties replied, 'When we are alone I should like you to call me Elizabeth. But, as Mr and Mrs Armstrong want this, in the company of others you should call me Nurse.'

Elizabeth 'Nurse' Shadbolt – nanny to the Armstrongs' youngest child, a baby boy – was a fairly short and stocky person with a kind, open, face and a friendly manner. Before she came to work on the farm, Elizabeth had worked for the New South Wales Railway Department accompanying groups of children from the Far West, the state's desert hinterland, on school excursions or holidays to the seaboard. She loved working with children, she said, and she enjoyed meeting with people in general. Following my intuition, I asked Nurse if it had been she who had lit the fire in our quarters and put flowers on the table for us. 'I did,' she replied. 'I just wanted to make your arrival a bit more cheerful as the room looked so cold and uninviting.'

While we were talking, we had drained and prepared the vegetables, which now sat waiting to be served. I was about to put the crumbed chops on the top of the stove when Elizabeth exclaimed, 'What *are* you doing with the meat?' When we explained how we had seen the chef in the Naracoorte cafe prepare our steak, she burst into a merry laugh, 'Oh, my gosh no, you don't grill crumbed chops!' Putting two or three spoonfuls of dripping into in a large frying pan on the stove she kindly said, 'That's how you cook cutlets.' Thanks to Nurse Shadbolt, a small disaster was averted that evening. But, as time would tell, there were to be other such incidents in the Armstrong household, when Elizabeth would again become my wife's saviour.

After dinner when the empty plates came back to the kitchen to be washed up and dried, there had been no complaints from 'inside', and we had weathered the first unexpected challenge in our new jobs. Just before I fell asleep that night, however, memory of Mrs Armstrong's intense eyes, her tight face and lips and ramrod-straight back that warned, 'Beware!' appeared, and plagued me all night in my dreams.

Learning the ropes
The next day, just on daylight at around 6 am, Mr Armstrong called me out from the cottage into the cold winter's morning. 'First thing every morning I want you to chop wood for the three fireplaces inside, and refill the wood boxes built into the walls of the house.'

He paused, and then he added, 'Every day except Sunday. I reckon that job will take you till breakfast at seven, and when you're done with it you and your wife can have your meal in the servant annexe to the kitchen.' I was relieved that Mr Armstrong made no mention of my having helped Willy last evening in the kitchen, part of the homestead that I had been forbidden to enter.

At that time of the year it was wet and cold outside. After breakfast that morning and again after lunch, for the rest of the day until just before dark at around 6 pm, my employer and I worked on repair and maintenance jobs in the well-equipped workshop. I had never seen or even heard of many of the implements that it carried – stocks and dies, pipe cutters, a tool that Mr Armstrong called 'a pair of footprints', and many other tools that I had no idea of their names. At one stage pointing to several large files and asking me to hand him one, my employer startled me a little when he called it a bastard file. With my uncertain command of English, I did not know if he was swearing at me, or if for some reason he simply did not like that particular tool. When I mentioned this to the farmer, his stern face cracked into a sort of a smile as he commented, 'Yeah, well, that's what it's called,' leaving his 'explanation' at that.

That evening after I returned from the paddocks, I again ignored the ban on my being inside the homestead. I helped Willy in the kitchen with preparations for dinner, and later with washing and drying the dishes – a routine that except on Sundays did not vary the whole time that we worked on the Armstrong property.

During the week our working day usually ended at around 8.30 or 9 pm, when we were 'free' to retire to our quarters across the homestead lawn. Before we went to sleep, we had possibly an hour together in private, until at 5.30 am the next morning the alarm clock announced a new day. We routinely started working at 6 am, Willy began preparing breakfast, while I chopped firewood for the homestead's open fireplaces. After breakfast Mr Armstrong and I tended the animals, maintained fences, and worked on other farming chores. Although my boss was not easily approachable, he was not a hard man to work for, nor an unreasonable employer. In my inexperience when I made a mistake with something at hand, he might give a snort, and his, 'That's not how you do it!' was a statement of fact that bore me no ill will; he then showed me how to do a job correctly. Inside the homestead, an altogether different situation prevailed. Although Mrs Armstrong had assured Willy in Adelaide that she would teach her the housework, my wife was seldom taught anything. Left alone to do the family's washing, cleaning, cooking and housekeeping, not because of a lack of application but simply because she did not *know* better, Willy realised that she sometimes did not do very well. For this my poor wife often incurred Mrs Armstrong's displeasure and sharp tongue, 'You stupid girl, useless New Australian, can't you get anything right?' Over time, Mrs Armstrong's scoldings became increasingly more vehement, 'You stupid, useless, bloody New Australian!'

Where it concerned me, Mr Armstrong's question in Adelaide, 'Can you kill and dress a sheep?' one day took on meaning when my employer demonstrated to me how to select and slaughter a sheep for the farm's meat safe. Rounded up in a paddock, the small flock of animals milled around in a corner against the fence. Taking care to not frighten them, the farmer purposefully strode into the midst of the mob where seemingly at random he grabbed a beast by one leg, bringing it down to the ground. While we dragged the poor victim to a nearby tree, the rest of the flock scattered, weaving, running and some jumping with their four feet high up in the air in their panic. With a quick twist of its head between his hands, as my boss broke the sheep's neck he said, 'This is how you have to kill the animal so that it doesn't suffer.' Next he slit the skin between the hamstrings on each back leg, inserting a butcher's hook through the gaps. Attached to a block and tackle hanging from a stout branch we pulled the dead sheep clear from the ground and with deft punches to the still warm body Mr Armstrong demonstrated how to peel off the skin. 'You have to work fast before the body temperature is lost; when you have to flay the carcass with a knife, you could ruin the premium selling quality of the skin if you cut holes in it.' When the hide had come off, a knife stroke down the full length of its belly spilled the animal's warm guts out onto the grass with a 'whoosh'. From a reeking mass of steaming entrails my boss harvested only the liver 'For the table,' and some other organs 'For the dogs.' Wiping bloody knife and hands on the grass, 'The foxes'll finish off the rest,' Mr Armstrong concluded matter-of-factly, adding, 'Now that I've shown you the ropes, next time you'll know how to do the job yourself.' With these words I discovered the meaning of the expression 'the ropes', and in my mind I filed yet another Australian idiom in my growing lexicon.

When we had finished our job, the farmer and I carried the carcass to the small, fly-wired shed, the farm's meat safe, under a large tree in the backyard of the homestead. There my employer showed me how to saw the carcass into sides that had to be left hanging for a few days to cure. Mr Armstrong's instructions to me were business-like, fair and reasonable, and delivered with patience.

Willy's introduction to farm butchery came a few days after we had slaughtered the sheep when Mrs Armstrong called, 'Come along, we'll grab some chops from the meat safe for tonight's dinner.' For once it seemed the farmer's wife was going to make good her promise to teach Willy. Taking down a side of the meat from where it hung on a hook in the safe, the farmer's wife flung it onto the butcher's block and attacked the carcass – *chop, chop, chop*. Her rapid, practiced strokes with the meat cleaver's flashing blade miraculously produced neatly butchered cuts. 'These are loin, these are chump, and those are shoulder chops. This is how you make cutlets, these are flaps for the dogs, and the leg is for a roast,' Mrs Armstrong completed the lesson in butchering. Like her husband had done when he instructed me in killing and dressing a sheep, 'Next time you'll know how to do it yourself,' the lady of the house told Willy.

In Australia at the time, and certainly on an Australian farm, mutton or lamb featured prominently on people's menus. So, soon enough, Mrs Armstrong's, 'Go and grab chops for dinner tonight,' came for Willy and she was sent on her own to the meat safe. But when she got there, my poor wife soon discovered that she did *not* know how to butcher a sheep's carcass. Realising that there was no way out for her, Willy grabbed the side of lamb, and like Mrs Armstrong had done she flung it on the chopping block. In imitation of Mrs Armstrong's deft *chop, chop, chop*, Willy attacked the side of lamb with the cleaver. However, being unpractised, instead of cutting through the carcass with a single stroke, it took Willy repeated attempts to sever meat and bone, and the cuts that appeared behind the flashing blade bore little resemblance to those produced by her employer. Fearful of Mrs Armstrong's uncertain temper and biting words of disapproval when something displeased her, Willy decided that she would keep quiet about her poor efforts at butchering and she took the chops back to the kitchen the way they were. That evening when we were washing dishes in the kitchen, in strode a furious Mrs Armstrong with a plate full of small, sharp slivers of bone that had been found in the evening meal. If her displeasure was perhaps understandable, the choice of words by which she made her feelings known to us could not have been less intolerant: 'LOOK at THIS, you stu...pid bl...oo...dy New Austra...lians!' screamed the lady of the house.

Around the farm

On Sundays the work schedule was a little more relaxed, and having cleaned up after breakfast, Willy and I had the day off till the early evening. Then, instead of the usual cooked or baked evening meal, a collation of cold meats, salads, and bread – High Tea – was served in the homestead. On our day off we often went on long walks through the paddocks where, as I had promised, I began to teach Willy to hunt rabbits with the rifle we had bought in Adelaide. On these expeditions we learned to look out for the places that rabbits prefer – open, sunny spots, close to the cover of thickets or rock where the animals made their burrows. On warm afternoons it was not difficult to sneak up close enough to take a shot at families of rabbits dozing in the sunshine. *Crack* for a bullet that had gone astray, or the different sound *thwack* of a direct hit. Willy learned to shoot quickly and well, and she began to enjoy the sport as much as I did. The first time we went on a hunt, we made the mistake of taking the rabbits we had shot back to the homestead. When Mr Armstrong asked, 'What do you want to bring them home for?' we replied that rabbit meat was considered a delicacy in Holland. He reacted, 'Well if that's so, there's no point in wasting what to you is good food. From now on you can shoot as many rabbits as you like on my property and you will eat it instead of lamb.' From then until we left our employment some months later, we ate little other meat on the farm but the kill of our now obligatory Sunday hunt. It caused Willy and me to forever after swear rabbit off our menu.

I began to teach Willy to hunt rabbits with the rifle we had bought in Adelaide.

Other than Willy and I and Nurse Elizabeth, the Armstrongs employed a casual farmhand named Ross, referred to by them as 'the man'. Ross and his wife operated a small dairy on a leased portion of the Armstrong land, and every morning after milking his two-dozen cows – possibly as a condition of the lease – Ross would ride to the homestead on his horse, bringing a large billycan full of lovely, creamy milk. If there was any farm work for him to do that day, Ross would stay; otherwise he would return to look after his animals and tend his paddocks. Considering his tenuous position being neither a member of the 'landed aristocracy' nor a true working-class man – by dint of owning cows – perhaps unsurprisingly Ross was a bit of a man of straw, a fence sitter. His relations with the homestead were reflected in how he never addressed the farmer or his wife other than Mr or Mrs Armstrong. Also, when he delivered his daily contribution of milk, Ross only came as far as the door of the kitchen. Ross and his wife were neither friendly nor antagonistic towards Willy and me, but kept us at arm's length, remaining aloof and apparently careful that they should not displease the farm's owners.

One week followed another and Willy and I began to gradually ease into the routines of life on the farm, but this did not mean that the relationship with our employers changed much for the better. Although

I got on reasonably well with Mr Armstrong, Mrs Armstrong remained relentless in her disparagement and humiliation of Willy, calling her a 'stupid New Australian', or worse. While my work on the farm ceased at sundown, even if I continued to help Willy with the after dinner chores in the homestead, we often worked till after 8 pm. If we finished early enough, we might write letters to parents, relatives or friends in Holland, or we would just relax in front of our fireplace where the hiss of burning wood and the glowing red embers made the poor little room a cosy and homely place of refuge for us. However, when we awoke the next morning the cottage had turned cold – not just due to the winter's temperature – and another long day had begun.

Shearing

Towards the middle of July – although it was still winter, cold, and rainy – we began to make preparations for the annual sheep shearing in August. Weather permitting, every day Mr Armstrong, Ross and I herded a mob of sheep to the shearing shed to be 'dagged and toe-ed'. Shearers would refuse to handle a dirty animal, which in turn would slow down shearing. Each sheep needed to be 'dagged' by clipping the hardened lumps of dung and soiled fleece from its backside using a pair of hand shears. This was undertaken by Mr Armstrong and Ross. Having finished with their sheep, they passed it on to me to do the 'toeing', a job that my employer had demonstrated to me. I had to hold down the panicked, struggling sheep and inspect its hooves for footrot. If necessary, I would treat its horny nail on affected feet by paring it with secateurs down to bleeding healthy flesh, then chase the poor beast through a dip of bluestone disinfectant. These backbreaking, arduous and sometimes unavoidably quite brutal tasks were necessary work on a sheep farm before the shearers came. Day after day as Mr Armstrong, Ross and I bent over struggling animals, our muscles ached, and irrespective of the wintery cold, sweat poured down our faces. It was here that I learned that, rather than what urban dwellers might like to imagine is idyllic country living, for man and beast alike a farm is not always a happy pastoral valley.

With the arrival of the shearing gang rapidly approaching, dagging and toeing of sheep had priority. On rainy days when the animals were too wet to handle, we cleaned the inside of the shearing shed and repaired pens, floorboards and fixtures. In the shearers' quarters, a barnlike building similar to our 'cottage', we began to also clean out and prepare the men's quarters, particularly the kitchen. 'Bloody shearers go on strike at the drop of a hat,' Mr Armstrong growled, and gloomily predicted, 'The first thing they'll complain about is the kitchen and the quality of the food. We'll have to make sure that everything is up to scratch before they arrive, or the bastards'll be off in a cloud of dust.' The attention that beefy, imperious Mr Armstrong spent on preparing for the shearers' arrival seemed to suggest that he felt intimidated by these men – he clearly knew that his entire year's income depended on their critically important work. On the land, where the shearers' reputation for truculence is legendary, at peril of the cry of 'Down tools!' announcing a disastrous shearers' strike, these itinerant workers would reign like kings during their stay on the Armstrong farm.

In rural Australia, mid to late August is the start of the spring shearing season. In preparation, we had checked and oiled the swinging doors of the pens, in which the sheep were kept in the shed. In the holding yards outside we similarly checked the races and the access ramps into the building. Making certain that nothing had been overlooked, after we cleaned and oiled the diesel engine that provided power to the shed, Mr Armstrong started it up, and he and Ross tested the belts and pulleys that drove the shearing gear. A few days before the shearers were due, we had put up the sorting table in the shed, on which the wool classer, the so-called 'Expert', would sort the fleece. The 'Roustabout', a kind of apprentice, would pick up the shorn wool from the shed floor, and after it had been classed, load it in the baler. On the Armstrong farm, this was still a hand-operated hydraulic press that compressed the fibres into a tight, heavy, very valuable bale of Australian wool. The nervous anticipatory tension on the farm also had Mr Armstrong keeping a watchful eye on the unpredictable weather of the season, almost visibly trying to will away any rain or drizzle that might cause the shearers to refuse to handle the wet animals. A sheep farmer's greatest fear was if too many days were lost to wet weather, the men would abandon the farm, moving to somewhere else where it was dry. 'No wonder the boss is toey,' Ross remarked wryly when I commented on how short-tempered Mr Armstrong was. When the shearers arrived, to everyone's relief the weather held. Work could begin, and for the duration of the shearing, the Armstrong sheep farm became another kind of world.

In any shearing gang, the Expert and the 'Contractor' – the man who organises a particular group of shearers – are principal figures. Owners and shearers alike recognise the status of these men. As Mr Armstrong had told Willy and me when we first arrived on the farm, whereas the shearers shared a dormitory, the Contractor and the Expert each had their own room in the 'cottage' – the two doors next to ours. For the shearers' cooks – who in this particular gang were a husband-and-wife team – we had put up two beds in the huge pantry next to the kitchen. When, in spite of Mr Armstrong's misgivings about shearers, the gang settled in well with no complaints, all on the farm relaxed. The exception was Mr Armstrong who, with his 'henny-penny' approach of 'the sky is falling, the sky is falling', seemed to almost be inviting disaster to befall the farm.

Having arrived too late in the day to start work, after the shearers had settled in their quarters they came out and sat on the steps, opening bottles of beer and, such as only shearers can do, they began to drink. Well into the evening we heard the sound of 'empties' shattering in the rubbish bins – disused 44 gallon fuel drums that had been strategically placed within tossing distance of the shearers' quarters. 'A good sign,' I overheard my employer mutter under his breath. 'The bastards are happy.'

Early the next day, by 5.30 am, the husband-and-wife cooks began to prepare the huge breakfast, without which no shearers in the land would start work – sausages, eggs, slabs of steak, bread and pots of tea. At 6 am, the Contractor came to inspect the food to ensure that it was suitable in quantity and quality for his men, and at 6.30 the shearers sat down to eat. At precisely 7 am the Contractor struck a hammer on a length of steel suspended from a rafter in the shearing shed, announcing the beginning of the working day, and as the clear sound of this bell carried far into the distance, the men trooped inside. Mr Armstrong started the diesel engine, and the pulleys on the drive shaft began to revolve the belts that set the long-armed, jointed shearing gear in motion. The four shearers came off the platform to each grab their first sheep from out of the pen, and bending their backs over the animal, shears biting into the fleece, the first day's shearing had begun. With practiced strokes of the handpiece, the wool came clear off the animal and one by one a naked sheep came sliding down the chute onto the ground in the holding yard. The Contractor kept tally of each of his men's scores with a chalk mark on a blackboard. When a shearer had finished with an animal, Ross and I helped the Roustabout pick up bits of wool that had dropped off the sorting table, and we helped sweep the boards between and around the pens and the shearing stands to keep these clean of dung or dust that would have contaminated the wool. All the while Mr Armstrong stood watching proceedings intently but not speaking a word or in any way interfering with the work. A tradition in the country, when shearers are at work in a shed they barely tolerate the owner who, if he should cause them real or imagined offence, risks the gang going on strike, causing him financial hardship and the possibility that the brotherhood of shearers should blacklist his property. Mr Armstrong was the farm's owner, but for as long as the shearing lasted he was unquestionably not the boss.

After washing up and cleaning breakfast away, equally hard at work in their kitchen, cooks Wally and Pearl began preparations for 'smoko' – morning tea. On the kitchen bench lay a jumble of dough for scones to be baked for the morning's break, mountains of sandwiches, iced cakes, biscuits and patty cakes, and on the side of the stove, kettles full of water stood ready for heating and brewing large pots of tea. At 10.15 sharp when the Contractor rang the 'smoko' bell, everyone in the shed dropped tools and the men streamed out to the mess. Barely washing their hands, they fell to, and after demolishing the mountains of food and drink they sat, smoked and stretched their aching limbs. At 10.30 sharp the Contractor rang the bell and the shearing started again. At noon there was an hour's break for 'dinner', the midday main meal, and at 2.45 pm another quarter hour for 'smoko'. The working day finished at 5 in the afternoon. The men showered, changed into fresh clothes, and were ready for the evening meal, 'tea', at 6. Afterwards they again took up their favourite pastime of drinking beer and one after another tossing, often shattering, the 'empties' in the bins.

Wally and Pearl

In an unexpected way, when the shearers came to the Armstrong property it propitiously changed our future in Australia. Part of conditions being that the farm owners supplied meat for the shearers, one day

Mr Armstrong instructed me to help the cook, Pearl, carry to her kitchen a sheep that he had slaughtered. When we reached the meat safe, from inside the homestead came the raised voice of Mrs Armstrong, screaming and ranting. Pearl asked me what was going on and I explained that Mrs Armstrong not infrequently yelled at my wife, to which Pearl protested, 'Go on, you people shouldn't put up with such abuse!' When I replied that we had no money, that we had nowhere to go in Australia and that we had no choice but to put up with Mrs Armstrong's treatment, the shearers' cook made no further comment and we carried the sides of meat to her kitchen in silence. Before she let me leave, Pearl turned to me, 'This evening after work why don't you and your wife have a cup of tea and supper with us?' These few simple words were the start of new beginnings for Willy and me in Australia.

Pearl's invitation was the first time since coming to the farm that we had mixed socially with other people. Although Nurse Shadbolt sometimes sneaked into our quarters for a chat, we all three were conscious that this would displease the Armstrongs – who had made it no secret that they disapproved of fraternisation between any of the homestead household and us servants.

In the days of early mass immigration, when Australians and foreigners met for the first time, the former almost invariably began their conversation with two near-ritual questions, 'Where do you come from?' and 'And how do you like Australia?' To these twin questions many 'New Australians' equally ritually replied from which country they had come, then assured the inquirer that of course 'We love Australia, such a nice country, the people so friendly, yes, we love Australia.' When Pearl and Wally predictably also put these routine questions to us, we told them that we came from Holland and, 'We love Australia, such a nice country, the people so friendly.' It didn't occur to any of us that – given our treatment on the farm, especially by Mrs Armstrong – our statement was nothing less than disingenuous.

In conversation when we mentioned our combined weekly wage, our hosts reacted with surprise. 'How much did you say?!' Wally exclaimed, '5 pounds each?'

Thinking that he thought us overpaid we hastened to correct him, 'No, 5 pounds per week together.' To this Wally responded, 'You can't be serious.' When we confirmed, 'Yes, 5 pounds a week for us both,' he and Pearl shook their heads and I caught them exchanging glances. When next we told them that of course we had not actually *received* our wages and that Mr and Mrs Armstrong were keeping the money in trust for us, our hosts made no further comment, but their faces showed disapproval. Later in the evening, at supper, Pearl returned to the subject of our working conditions, asking, 'Have you thought of changing jobs?'

Pearl's query came as a thunderclap out of a clear blue sky. Noticing the look of consternation on my face she quickly chipped in, 'Something that came to my mind when you talked of your working conditions here may perhaps be of interest to you.' She told us that before she and Wally had turned shearers' cooks, she had been employed in a grocery store at Naracoorte. In fact, Pearl said, her employer had tried to recruit her and Wally to manage a Post Office store that he was building at a small village not far from Naracoorte. As cooking for a gang of shearers was quite a bit more lucrative for them, they had declined the grocer's offer. When Pearl proposed, 'Do you think that you two might like the job?' Willy and I replied in unison, 'Yes!' Before we returned to our rooms that evening, Pearl made a promise, 'After shearing when Wally and I get back to Naracoorte I'll mention you to the grocer. I'm sure he'll consider you for the job when I recommend you to him.' This chance meeting with the shearers' cooks and our social evening with them was the start of a new life and future for Willy and me. In spite of the late hour when we got to bed that night, sleep long evaded us.

First car

Pearl represented my father's memories of the intrinsic nature of Australians – salt of the earth – and their empathy with the underdog, while Wally showed us the other, larrikin, side of the Australian character. Over supper I had happened to mention that without our own transport we were dependent on our employers occasionally taking us to Naracoorte, and that we felt quite isolated on the farm. Wally sat up in his chair in a flash, 'I can help to get you a car,' he exclaimed, 'I'll sell you my buckboard.' Although I had no idea what the term 'buckboard' meant, I gathered that it was some sort of a vehicle. But Pearl's, 'Oh, Wally, you can't do that to these people,' and his reply, 'Shut up, woman, they're old enough to look after themselves,' should have warned me to treat Wally's offer with caution. Instead, 'How much do you want for it?' I asked eagerly. Wally responded, 'Well, I gather that you haven't got much money so I'll sell you the buckboard cheaply, how about 20 pounds?' His answer seemed to me to confirm Australians' innate decency and humane, generous public spirit. When I quickly looked over at Willy and saw no disagreement, I agreed, 'All right, 20 pounds.' Pearl's sigh of resignation did not register with me. The deal confirmed with a handshake, Wally promised, 'After the shearing I'll get the car from Naracoorte where it is stored, fair enough?' A few days later the shearing on the Armstrong farm ended and the gang left to start work in another shed. As he had promised, Wally drove to Naracoorte and he returned towing our 'buckboard', steered by an unhappy looking Pearl.

The 1927 Silver Anniversary Buick motorcar that we had purchased from the shearers' cook had been modified from its original design as a passenger vehicle by having the back seats and part of the roof removed. The now exposed rear structure of the car was fitted with the 'buckboard', a timber floored tray, making it a poor cousin of the later ubiquitous Australian utility. Thrilled to own transport of our own, the buckboard appeared a means to greater independence for Willy and me. When I asked Mr Armstrong for 20 pounds to pay for the car, he looked at me with a curious expression on his face, 'Are you sure you know what you're doing?' When I replied that I did, he said, 'Oh, well,' as he handed me the money. I paid Wally the agreed upon amount and we never saw he nor Pearl again.

Later that day when we took our lovely purchase out on the road for a test drive, I learned a valuable lesson. In my eagerness I had failed to heed Pearl's, 'Oh, Wally…' and my employer's, 'Are you sure you know what you are doing?', and Willy and I soon enough discovered the price that we had paid for our youthful inexperience and impetuousness. As soon as we had some time to spare, we started our precious motor vehicle and drove off for a test run down the farm road. The engine performed beautifully, and although I had never before driven a motorcar, I had no trouble negotiating the deserted track that led to the front gate. We had gone no farther than about a mile when the engine spluttered and died and the vehicle came to a halt. When no amount of inexperienced tinkering under the bonnet would start the engine, we had no choice but to walk back to the farm, leaving our car standing on the side of the road. Back at the homestead when we told Ross about what we thought would be a minor engine problem, he replied that 'everyone' knew that this particular model 1927 Buick had a vacuum tank located at the front that drew petrol from the fuel tank at the back – a vital but no longer obtainable device. 'Everyone' also knew, said Ross, that the buckboard Wally had sold us had a damaged and unserviceable vacuum tank, the reason why the shearer's cook had sold us the car so cheaply. The day Wally delivered it and there had seemed nothing wrong with it, Ross explained, the shearers' cook had manually filled the vacuum tank upfront with one pint of petrol, allowing him to demonstrate its 'reliability' to us. When we later took it for a 'spin', the vacuum tank inevitably ran out of fuel. When Ross' explanation sank in and we realised that our beautiful car was useless, that our dream of independence was lost and that we had wasted 20 pounds of very hard-earned money, we discovered another side of the Australian character – its larrikin spirit, with a degree of self-interest that blurred the distinction between right and wrong. When Wally the shearer's cook sold us his buckboard, his 'they're old enough to look after themselves,' overcame the scruples of mateship – which, in any case, did not seem to need to include *New* Australians.

Although we did not meet with the shearers' cooks again, not long after they left we received a letter from Pearl. Remembering our conversation on the evening that we had visited them for supper, she had spoken to her old employer, the grocer Mr Frank Drouin, in Naracoorte. As predicted, having recommended us to him, he had agreed to interview us for the job of managing his new store. Pearl had also explained to him that, having no transport of our own, we must rely on our employers to take us to Naracoorte. As we could not make a prior appointment with him, Mr Drouin had assured Pearl that when we came to town, we could call on him in his store at any time. Pearl's letter concluded, 'Good luck, and God bless you.' In spite of the disappointment that we had suffered with Wally, we knew that Pearl's sentiments were sincere, and her efforts on our behalf at Naracoorte were a kindness that gave us renewed heart and hope.

A day trip

After the excitement of having the shearers on the property, life on the farm returned to normal. Thanks however to Pearl and the news in her recent letter, we lived in hope of a more promising future. After two or three weeks, in early October Mrs Armstrong decided to take us to Naracoorte for, as she said, a haircut and personal shopping. She added, 'At the Council Offices in town I shall also have you registered as immigrants, foreigners working on our property.' To our probably oversensitive ears, the farmer's wife delivered her bald statement in rather the same dispassionate way as when having a dog registered.

Before she dismissed Willy from her work in the kitchen that morning Mrs Armstrong said curtly, 'Be ready in half an hour and mind that you are properly dressed; hat and gloves of course, as you will be meeting with the mayor.' When my wife replied that she owned neither, Mrs Armstrong sighed impatiently, 'Can people like you ever do anything properly?' She grudgingly added, 'Ask Nurse Shadbolt for a loan of hers, as I do not want the mayor to think that we employ riffraff.'

Half an hour later we were 'properly dressed' as instructed and waiting in the garage. When Mrs Armstrong arrived she slid behind the wheel of her Jaguar car, telling Willy and me to sit on the back seat. 'Servants do not travel next to their employer,' she had curtly rebuffed me when I made a gesture to open the front door on the passenger side.

We drove all the way into Naracoorte in silence. Mrs Armstrong pulled up at the Council Chambers where, apparently by appointment, the mayor was waiting to interview Willy and me. When Mrs Armstrong introduced us to him, the official cursorily acknowledged us. Unconcernedly acting as if we were out of earshot, he and Mrs Armstrong engaged in lively conversation, much of it about us. When the topic turned to our foreign ways and manners, Mrs Armstrong simpered, 'I had to tell the girl to get properly dressed to meet you today; hat and gloves of course.' And the mayor laughed appreciatively. His interview of us was of course preceded by, 'Where have you come from, and how do you like Australia?'. He carefully recorded the names and addresses of relatives in Holland and other personal details. After he had apparently finished with establishing our *bona fides*, the mayor concluded, 'Well, that will be all my business with you people.' As he accompanied us to the door he pulled up briefly and said to Willy and me, 'You two can count yourselves very lucky to be working for Mr and Mrs Armstrong, such good and admirable Australian citizens. We have you on the Council record now, so mind that you behave well, and that you appreciate your employers and repay them for their kindness. Or,' the mayor laughed, but without merriment showing in his eyes, 'I shall know how to deal with you.' To Mrs Armstrong he said, 'Dear lady, I am sure that you and your husband will know how to make good New Australians of these two little Dutch people, what?' Thus concluded our first acquaintance with contemporary Australian officialdom and its ways and means of keeping track of foreigners in the land.

Outside the Council Chambers, before she let us go out on our own, Mrs Armstrong handed us a 5-pound note, saying, 'Money for your haircut and shopping. Mind that you keep an eye on the time. I will meet you outside the Rose Café and Tearooms at 5 pm sharp.' Turning on her high heels, our employer walked away – her retreating, ramrod-stiff back almost visibly radiating righteousness. Wanting to take up the grocer's invitation to come to his shop at any time when we were in town, Willy and I completed haircuts and other small business as quickly as possible. With our hearts in our throats our hopes were high that, if he accepted us for the vacancy, Mr Drouin would give us a new start, a life that held a future for us away from the farm.

When we located the shop, as Pearl had promised the owner immediately agreed to speak with us. When Mr Drouin said, 'For some time now I have been looking for a young couple like you as managers for my new Post Office store,' it seemed that we were being seriously considered for the position to manage his business in a nearby village. In his mid-forties, Mr Drouin dressed conservatively in grey trousers and tweed jacket, making him appear more the banker that he had been before he went into private enterprise than the owner of a country grocery store. Softly spoken and – due to a war injury from service in New Guinea – slightly hesitant on his feet, he seemed a kindly man, and our hearts lifted as he outlined his soon-to-be completed building project at the village. Mr Drouin explained that due to major agricultural development projects in the region of South Australia known as the Ninety Mile Desert, his store would soon become a thriving service centre for the surrounding rural community. In further discussion with us, Willy's business experience in Holland and the favourable references from her previous employers apparently impressed Mr Drouin, and he was of the opinion that my agricultural background and training would be well recognised by the local farming community. When the grocer asked if Pearl had correctly informed him that we wished to change our present job on the farm, we emphatically confirmed, 'Yes, thank you, Mr Drouin.' After some further questions the grocer concluded, 'I am satisfied that I shall want to employ you and I shall offer you 20 pounds per week, plus free accommodation and grocery supplies at staff discount. If this is agreeable to you the position is yours.' It took my Willy and me no more than a second to agree, 'Yes, Sir, thank you. This is agreeable to us.' Mr Drouin smiled as he said, 'Fine, that's settled then – but call me Frank.' The interview ended, we took our leave, scarcely believing that our luck had changed.

Outside the grocery shop, on our way to the Rose Café and Tearooms to meet up with Mrs Armstrong, our heads swam with excitement – *20* pounds per week, free accommodation and groceries at discount rates; riches of which we had not even dared dream! 'Aren't we so very lucky,' we congratulated each other.

When we reached the Rose Café and Tearooms, Mrs Armstrong was waiting for us, 'You are late,' she snapped, and if it had not been for the presence of others we would not have been startled if she had added, 'Stupid New Australians!' The return trip to the farm was as silent as it had been on the way in to Naracoorte, but the slight that Mrs Armstrong had delivered that morning, 'Servants do not sit next to their employers,' had lost its sting now that we would soon no longer be her 'married couple', but business people in a Post Office store. However, the short temper and acid tongue of Mrs Armstrong made us fearful of how she and her husband would react to the notice that we would have to deliver them of wanting to terminate our employment on the farm.

Leaving the farm

The morning after our visit to Naracoorte, I was doing a job with Mr Armstrong in the workshop. My heart was beating fast with excitement, but also with undeniable fear that I had to face my employer with the news that we wanted to leave the farm. Trembling with anxiety I said, 'Excuse me Mr Armstrong, I have something to say.' To this he grunted, 'Humph, what is it?' I blurted out, 'Willy and I have found work elsewhere and… and we wish to give you a fortnight's notice from today, thank you.' When I finished speaking a deadly silence reigned for agonising seconds, and for a moment I thought that he had not understood me. Then Mr Armstrong almost literally spat out an incredulous, '*WHAT – DID – YOU – SAY*?!' His face had turned bright red and veins on his neck stood out as a violent rage gripped him. When I repeated that Willy and I were giving him notice of our intention to terminate our employment on the farm a fortnight from today, adding, 'We are sorry, Mr Armstrong,' his reaction was vicious and unexpected. '*RIGHT THEN,*' he bellowed, 'You can pack your gear right now! It's too late for the train to Naracoorte, but first thing tomorrow you're *off* my farm!' As he stormed outside to the homestead where he would doubtless tell Mrs Armstrong the news, in a towering rage Mr Armstrong shouted, 'You… *ungrateful*… BLOODY… NEW… AUSTRALIANS!'

I did not see my employer again that day, and soon after he burst into his house Willy emerged shaken. 'Mrs Armstrong told me to get out, this minute,' she said. It did not take us long to pack our few personal items in the cabin trunk and two suitcases with which we had arrived in Australia. In the two rooms of the 'cottage' in which we had lived in these past few months we cleaned and polished the floors and furniture, and with that done, we could do no more than wait for tomorrow. It took Willy and me quite some time to recover from the Armstrongs' reaction to our resignation, but now that the step had been taken it felt as if an oppressive fog had lifted. We promised ourselves that no one would ever again call us stupid New Australians and worse.

The next morning Mr Armstrong drove us to the small railway station at the hamlet of Frances to catch the train to Naracoorte. Very early that day Nurse Elizabeth Shadbolt had furtively crept over from the homestead to wish us well, but Ross the sharefarmer did not say goodbye to us. When we closed the door of our cottage for the last time, the homestead across the lawn seemed to glower at us and the very atmosphere of the dawn felt coldly hostile and disapproving. Before we left in his utility, his face still hard-set with anger, Mr Armstrong handed me several bank notes, saying, 'These are your wages that I have been keeping in trust for you.' The previous evening Willy and I had calculated that – allowing for occasional small sums of cash for shopping and the 20 pound outlay on our ill-advised purchase of Wally's buckboard – the wages owed to us should amount to no less than 60 pounds. However, Mr Armstrong handed me only 40 pounds. When I asked him for an explanation, the farmer replied roughly, 'I have deducted money from your wages to cover breakages of crockery in the kitchen, for "fair wear and tear" in the use of our cottage, and for furniture, bedding and linens. In any case, your work and that of your wife has been below standard and you can count yourselves lucky that I pay you any money at all.' Sensing that we were going to object to an unfair deduction from our wages Mr Armstrong threatened, 'Take it, or you can bloody well *walk* to Frances. Anyway, I should be charging you taxi fares, so don't press your luck.' Realising that this was not an idle threat, we kept quiet, and an oppressive silence reigned on our way to the railway station. Our now ex-employer dropped us off, barely staying long enough for us to get our luggage off the utility. When he left, the shower of gravel from the ute's fast-spinning wheels and the thick plume of dust that his speeding vehicle left trailing behind spoke louder than any harsh words the farmer might have liked to use.

Reflections on the Armstrongs

Poor Willy was never able to forget our introduction to Australia. Working on the Armstrong sheep farm for our first few months in the country was an experience that she could see in no other light than a time of humiliating endurance for us. I initially shared her opinion, but the very nature of the Australian environment that we found, and the at times trying conditions that affect people on the land, perhaps explains at least some of the Armstrongs' attitude towards us newcomers. From the earliest times of European settlement, the Australian continent has been subject to 'the tyranny of distance' – a cliché, but one that bears undeniable truth. The early settlers relied on wit, self-reliance and courage in the never-ending battle to survive the harsh elements. Even in modern times, Australia's agriculturalists resemble their forebears in many respects – and they are different people even from their city cousins. Beset by drought, floods, bushfires, plagues of locusts and mice, and marauding packs of wild dogs or feral pigs, the 'man on the land' is almost a sub-species of Australian. He is a tenacious and tough-minded individualist, who his fellow Australian city dwellers, let alone immigrants from foreign lands, have sometimes found difficult to understand. The dourness of the Australian farmer, which others sometimes see as arrogance, is really a defence against the disappointments that an Australian 'tiller of soils' fears he will suffer – if not this year then perhaps the next? New to Australia, Willy and I had been ignorant of the mindset of many Australian farmers in general. And until we came to work on the Armstrong farm as their servants, we had never before been treated as such, and the reality of it offended. While it may have been a lesson in assimilation into a new culture and integration into the mainstream society, where it concerned Willy, these considerations were never accepted. The memory of Mrs Armstrong's fragile temperament and vinegary disposition towards 'bloody New Australians' continued to rankle in her memory.

CHAPTER 14

Life in Naracoorte

No Bird Soars Too High
If He Soars With His Own Wings
William Blake, *Proverbs of Hell*

Disembarking our train in Naracoorte, we immediately went to see Mr Drouin in his shop to tell him what had happened. To his credit our new employer reacted rather philosophically, 'Well, the country Post Office store is still a week or two away from completion. You obviously can't start working there until the building is finished, but in the meantime we'll just have to deal with the situation. Give me a few minutes to speak with my wife.' While we sat and waited outside his office, Mr Drouin spent quite some time on the telephone. When he called us in again, he noticed our anxiety and a slight smile played across his face. 'Everything is fine,' he said, 'My wife agrees with me that while you are waiting to start work you can move in with us at home.' Turning to me he continued, 'I shall employ *you* as of today,' and looking at Willy, 'My wife is a nurse at the hospital, and she is doing a refresher course that takes up all of her working day. We have two primary-school aged children, a girl and a boy, and our youngest boy is still a toddler. We would be very happy if you agreed to look after the children until we both come home?' Willy's answer – that she would be happy to look after the children, and that she had had several years of babysitting experience in her school holidays in Holland – pleased Mr Drouin. Getting up from behind his desk our new employer said, 'That is splendid, then. I'll drive you two home now and introduce you to my wife.'

In many respects Mrs Drouin was the opposite of her somewhat doddering husband. Basically a very kindly person, she was forthright, with the no-nonsense manner characteristic of her occupation. When we apologised for the inconvenience that our stay in their home might cause them, Mrs Drouin replied that while our early commencement of working for them was a surprise, this would only be a temporary measure and since in her absence Willy would mind the children, the arrangement would actually suit her. After she had pointed out a few of their housekeeping routines, Willy and I settled ourselves in the spare room. In spite of the less-than-happy circumstances under which we had left the farm that day, with a fresh start in a new career we trusted that from now on fortune would again smile kindly upon us.

After we had unpacked a few small items, I went to the Council Chambers to report our change of address and occupation – as was required of immigrants at the time. The mayor reacted with evident disapproval. 'Humph,' he grunted, 'So, only a few months since your arrival in Australia you have already left your employers on the Armstrong farm. Well, this does not show much appreciation for how those good people have given you New Australians a start in life.' I suspected that he barely avoided adding Mrs Armstrong's favourite adjective 'bloody' to his 'New Australians'.

A new beginning

While Mrs Drouin was away during the day, Willy looked after the three children in the Drouin household and I began work in Mr Drouin's grocery store in town. Frank introduced me to his shop assistants, Cathy and Mervyn, and the two treated me courteously enough – but something about Cathy warned me that she was a person of whom I should beware. Thin, with nervously darting black, almost soulless eyes, her pale, worn-out face belied her relatively young age. My impression of her was that she seemed a hard-bitten, even an embittered, woman. I later learned that at least some of Cathy's sour disposition was due to her fiancé having been killed on a Second World War battlefield in Europe, and that she disliked the recent immigrants from the Northern Hemisphere, whether they were French, German, Yugoslav, Dutch, or any other foreigners for whom her fiancé had fought and died. Her barely veiled antagonism towards me was probably also due to envy. When Cathy thought that she could not be overheard I caught her mutter to Mervyn, 'Fancy, the boss giving the Post Office store job to bloody New Australians!' The venom with which she said this was disconcerting.

Learning the grocery business under Mr Drouin's tutelage was more difficult than I had imagined. The major problem for me was that I was unfamiliar with the Imperial currency system then in use in Australia. Used to the simple decimal system used throughout Europe, including Holland, I now had to learn that in Australia two ha'pennies make a penny, three pennies are a thruppence, two thruppences make a sixpence, twelve pennies are a shilling and twenty shillings a pound. Before the common use of electronic calculators, people mentally added and subtracted sums of this money in their head – a skill that I found difficult to master. Another aspect of the times was that shopkeepers such as Mr Drouin allowed approved customers considerable credit amounting to sometimes large sums of money being owed, to be periodically and sometimes annually honoured. For men on the land, clearing their outstanding debts often took from one wool cheque to the next. Keeping track of a customer's purchases in a personal accounts book put the onus of responsibility on the shop assistant for correctly calculating and entering expenditures, which often ran into many hundreds or sometimes thousands of pounds. When my employer noticed that I was inexperienced in this work, he urged me to quickly learn to overcome the deficiency. 'The client is always right,' he said, 'and the surest way to offend a customer is for you to make an accounting error. If you overcharge them, they will complain. On the other hand, if you charge too little, they are unlikely to tell you that you have made an error and the shop will have to bear the loss. If you have made a mistake and the amount involved is not in their favour, there is nothing surer than the client taking offence, and they may cease to be a customer.' Mr Drouin smiled but his eyes did not reflect merriment, 'So, if shoppers should not complain when you make an error in your accounting, and if I find that you have made anything but a small mistake, you will certainly hear about it from *me*!'

We had been in the Drouin household about two or three weeks when my twenty-fourth birthday approached. Mrs Drouin had learned my date of birth, and on the evening before my birthday she put on a lovely celebration dinner for me. Dressed in party hats, the family sat with

Willy and I at a table laid with festive silver and best chinaware, and when the birthday cake came to the table everyone sang me 'Happy Birthday'. At the end of the evening, Mr Drouin informed me in his quiet, almost self-effacing manner that tomorrow, on the actual date of my birthday, the family would leave for Adelaide 'on business'. Not wanting to hold the family up from going to bed for a good night's sleep before the long trip, I thanked Mrs Drouin for a lovely evening. Her reply was modest, but I should perhaps have detected a warning in her words when she said, 'It was a pleasure. Whatever the future holds for you in Australia, Frank and I hope that you and Willy will be very happy.'

An unhappy birthday

We awoke the next day to a bright, sunny, late spring morning. As expected, the family had left at an early hour and inside the house all was quiet. As it was a Sunday and I did not have to go to work, there was no need for us to get up in a hurry. In our bedroom I leisurely unwrapped Willy's birthday present of two handmade handkerchiefs with hand-rolled edges and my initials embroidered in a corner. Willy apologised to me, 'We can't afford a real present yet,' but I assured her that the handkerchiefs were better than any store-bought present could have been. My twenty-fourth birthday had started on a happy note.

When we came to the dining table, we found that before the family left, Mrs Drouin had already set two places for us at the breakfast table. On one of the plates lay an envelope addressed to me in Mr Drouin's elegant copperplate handwriting. Expecting a birthday card, while Willy prepared toast for us I opened the envelope. It contained a note from Mr Drouin:

> I am very sorry to inform you that I have changed my mind about employing you and your wife at my Post Office store. The reason for my business in Adelaide is that, I have decided to appoint a previous applicant for the position instead. With this letter I wish to advise you that, effective immediately, I hereby rescind any of our previous verbal understandings about appointing you to manage my store. Until we return from Adelaide you and your wife are welcome to stay in our home, but I expect that you will make arrangements for alternative accommodation. Yours very truly, Frank.

I was astonished by the message. *Truly?* I thought. *On my birthday?*

The day that had started on such a happy note had suddenly turned dark. Now that Mr Drouin had changed his mind about employing us, Willy and I agonised over what to do next. Where would we find work and where would we live? Another worry was that since I had been working for Mr Drouin for only a short while, the wages he had paid me had not much improved our critically small financial reserves. Realising in what real plight we were now in, Willy started crying. I comforted her as best I could. 'We can't let Mr Drouin sack us,' I said. 'I will fight him if I must.' But I had no idea how I should be able to honour my promise.

Something of a compromise

For the next few days before the Drouin family's return from Adelaide, I continued to work in the shop – not telling Cathy and Mervyn anything about the 'birthday surprise' from Frank. When the Drouins arrived back from Adelaide, Frank had evidently not expected us to still be staying in their home and he reacted with some annoyance, but I imagined also with guilt. 'Oh, you've not left then,' he muttered. 'Humph, yes, yes… I see… you probably needed more time,' and ostensibly to unload the car he scurried away. If her husband had been ill at ease with us, Mrs Drouin showed us no sign of animosity or awkwardness. She greeted us nicely and, after the long trip from Adelaide, she busied herself settling down her children. When Frank had unpacked their car, over a cup of tea in the kitchen he could no longer avoid discussing the issue with us, and he rather sheepishly asked, 'I assume that you have read the letter I left you?' Mrs Drouin watched and said nothing.

When I asked Frank why he had changed his mind about employing us at his store, I should perhaps have foreseen his answer. Nevertheless, his reply was as disconcerting as it was disappointing when he replied rather diplomatically, 'I am afraid that although you try well in your work, I have noticed that you lack vital experience in running a store – in particular that you are not very practiced in our currency system. In addition, I made a mistake to consider a youthful couple like you for the job. Operating a store that will be the focal point for people in the district, besides providing supplies of the usual store stock, the locals would probably expect its managers to have a wider, more mature grasp of social issues than can be expected from people of your age. Also, and I must say given that it is not your native tongue, at times I have detected somewhat of a problem with your command of the English language. I fear this will be a disadvantage with our local clientele, conservative people off the land, particularly for the Post Office side of business. The couple I have now appointed are English immigrants who have proven experience in store management. They are also older and I believe more socially adept. In short, these are reasons why I have decided to cancel previous verbal understandings and arrangements with you.'

Letting his comments sink in, I thought that none of this should undo the promise Frank made on the day that he had interviewed us, when he had got up from his chair, shaken our hands and said, 'The job is yours.' All I could now do was to make good my promise to Willy – that I would fight Mr Drouin on a point of honour, a deal sealed with a handshake.

When I reminded him of what I considered his gentleman's word, Frank's coldly legalistic reply startled me, 'It was a verbal offer, not a binding written contract,' said he. And then I remembered the careful wording of his note to me, '… I hereby rescind our previous verbal understandings…' The discussions had reached an impasse, when Mrs Drouin – who had been listening to us – acted with characteristic forthrightness. Turning to her husband, her words broached no denying. 'You may well be technically correct that these young people are inexperienced to run your store, and that without a written agreement you are legally free to change your mind about employing them, Frank,' she said firmly. 'I shall however remind you that you did make them the promise of appointment, which they accepted in good faith, and I agree with them that it makes your handshake on it a gentleman's point of honour. What our young friends do *not* know is that your decision to give them the job was considerably influenced by the fact that you knew you could pay them less wages than the English immigrants who had greater knowledge of Australian working conditions.' Mrs Drouin continued, 'Setting all this aside, let me tell you that I consider you to be morally wrong to break a verbal promise, and that what is at stake with them – but also with me, Frank – is your honour, nothing less.' Then Mrs Drouin looked at me and said, 'My husband will give you a job in the store here in town until you can find other work,' and, but not graciously, Frank capitulated, 'Yes, well, humph, alright.'

Thanks to Mrs Drouin and her sense of right and wrong, with which she stood up for us to her husband, Willy and I had gained breathing space in which to find alternative employment. In a foreign country we were at quite a loss as to where we should turn to even begin to look for work, and the reprieve was little better than a stopgap.

After our confrontation with Frank, and Mrs Drouin's fortunate intervention on our behalf, Willy and I did not stay with them for long. Mrs Drouin simply ignored any awkwardness, treating daily business as if nothing had happened to upset our relationship with the family. Not surprisingly however, the atmosphere in the household felt uncomfortable to us. The day after the discussions, before we started work in the store, Frank curtly announced to Cathy and Mervyn that he had appointed an English couple to run the Post Office store business and that from now on I would be working with them in Naracoorte. As our employer spoke, I noticed the furtive exchange of glances between Cathy and Mervyn, and it required little imagination that Cathy at least was decidedly not pleased with the new arrangements to have me in 'her' shop.

The caravan

Now that we would be staying indefinitely at Naracoorte, Willy and I needed to urgently find new accommodation. However, in the decade immediately after the war, housing and even rented accommodation was in very scarce supply in Australia, as elsewhere in the world. Although we tried very hard and diligently, we failed to find other quarters in Naracoorte. After a few days of fruitless searching, Frank Drouin – no doubt prompted by self-interest – came up with a novel solution. 'A friend of mine has a caravan that he will rent out to you at 6 pounds per week,' he said, adding, 'My friend also owns a vacant block of land on which he'll let you park the van free of charge.' With little hope to solve the accommodation problem in another way, we agreed that we would hire the van, which Frank collected for us and towed to his friend's vacant bush block on the outskirts of town. A rather exceptional answer to an immediate problem, Willy and I were pleased that we had somewhere to stay, but hoped to soon find something more suitable in which to live.

Before caravans became part of the national Australian institution, these vehicles bore little resemblance to today's modern and often luxurious mobile homes. The very small, humpback-shaped, rather neglected caravan that we hired at 6 pounds per week from Mr Drouin's friend could hardly be considered very liveable accommodation. Also, given my weekly wages of 10 pounds, it was not cheap rent. But, given the truism that beggars can't be choosers, we were glad to at least have our privacy back again.

The land on which the caravan stood had been mostly cleared of larger trees and shrubs, but waist-high bracken regrowth had completely covered the undeveloped building block. We had to always look out for snakes and other vermin among the vegetation. As the site lacked all the usual amenities of water, electricity, even sanitation, every day we each had to carry two buckets of water back with us from the town – thankfully only a 10 minute walk. This had to suffice for our drinking, cooking, and bathing needs. The unequipped caravan had nothing on which to cook. We solved this problem by purchasing a shiny, new, latest model, chrome-plated primus stove – it even boasted a heat reflector to warm the van against the gathering chill of late spring evenings. The lack of bathroom facilities was resolved by waiting until it had become dark enough in the evening to not be seen. We would carry a bucket of tepid water out into the bracken and shower under the stars in the Oriental way – splashing a quick dip from the bucket over us with a small saucepan, soaping, and rinsing with the rest. Although the caravan and the conditions of our accommodation were primitive, the little van was at least a home of sorts.

Our first home in Naracoorte – barely liveable but 'beggars can't be choosers'.

Willy finds work

While I continued working in Mr Drouin's grocery shop, Willy lost no time in trying to find suitable employment in town. Although she preferred a clerical occupation, if nothing was available in that line of business, Willy was determined that she would take on anything else – even cleaning, washing, and ironing, skills that she had, fortunately, *per force* acquired on the farm. In spite of her determination and although she made every effort to call on business premises, the reply she received everywhere was, 'Sorry, all our positions are filled.' In Australia, these were difficult times for anyone to find employment of any kind, and especially if one was a New Australian.

Although the rejections to her applications were disappointing, Willy did not give up and in a roundabout fashion her tenacity eventually paid off. At one of the local hotels where she inquired after a chance vacancy, the licensee once again told her, 'Sorry, the position is filled.' After a moment's reflection, he said, 'I'll keep you in mind if the present receptionist should leave,' and he added, 'Which she may.'

On her way from the hotel, Willy passed Naracoorte's rather grandly named Rose Café and Tearooms – where Mrs Armstrong had waited for us when we had gone to do our shopping and met with Mr Drouin about employment. Willy noticed a sign, 'Waitress wanted. Apply within.' Although she had no work experience as a waitress, she thought this was too good an opportunity to pass up and she resolutely walked in to apply for the vacancy.

As was suggested by its name, the Rose Café and Tearooms cleverly combined a dual function of business – the café section of it was somewhat like the Greasy Greek's, except more 'refined', and the other part of it was devoted to the stylish Tearoom, patronised by Naracoorte's gentry, where the tables were laid with starched linen, silver, and quality china. When Willy applied for the vacancy, she found the proprietors – a friendly, middle-aged couple – hard at work preparing for their morning teatime customers. Willy admitted that she had no previous experience as a waitress, and also did not hide from them that she had so far been looking for clerical work that suited her employment background. She also revealed that a little earlier in the day she had enquired at the Commercial Hotel, where the licensee had promised that he would keep her in mind 'if a vacancy should occur'. However, Willy promised, if she were given the chance to work at the Café and Tearooms, she would make every effort to quickly learn waitressing for them. Her luck turned when her earnest demeanour and promise persuaded the owners to give Willy the opportunity to prove herself. At my lunch break from work, when we met as usual for our sandwich lunch in the park, Willy jubilantly announced, 'I have a job!'

Our futures, which had seemed so precarious, had changed now that both Willy and I were employed, and hope returned to us. True to her promise, Willy quickly adapted herself to her job at the café and she quite enjoyed the novel experience of serving customers their teas or the meals that they had ordered in the café section. She got on very well with the clients and with her employers, who treated her well and kindly. On her first payday when Willy counted 5 pounds more in her wages than had been agreed upon, she reported the mistake. 'No, lass, it's not a mistake – you've well and truly earned it,' said her boss. This token of appreciation – but even more so the kind words that came with it – did a great deal to salve the wounds inflicted by Mrs Armstrong's unfair ravings.

Willy's employment at the Rose Café and Tearooms was unexpectedly brief. After some five or six weeks of happily working there, the licensee of the Commercial Hotel called in at the café to tell her that his receptionist had left. As promised, he had kept her in mind for the position – if she still wanted it? The prospect of working in a job for which she was qualified appealed to Willy, but although she had made no secret of her preference for clerical work when interviewed by the proprietors of the Rose Café, the offer from the Commercial Hotel now put her in a quandary. Deciding a straightforward approach would be best, Willy told her employers about the chance vacancy that had occurred at the hotel, and that she did not know whether or not to accept the position because she did not want to let them down. Their reply was generous. 'No, lass, don't fret about it,' the owner said to her, 'When you applied here you were honest with us and we know that you would prefer the clerical work. We'll miss you, but if it's what you want, then you must take the job at the hotel.' Willy's short career as a waitress ended on good terms and we remained friendly with her now past employers,

Australians who my father would have described as 'salt of the earth'. We never forgot the human kindness of the two hard-working proprietors of the Naracoorte Rose Café and Tearooms.

Working as a receptionist at the Commercial Hotel was an occupation that Willy had dreamed of, and she quickly proved her worth to the licensees. Mr Chandler, or Sandy, as he liked to be called, was a tall, loosely built man somewhat deliberate of speech like Mr Drouin, while Mrs Chandler was his exact opposite. Stout, short-legged and energetic almost to the point of volatility, she had a sharp but not unkindly tongue that, as she liked to say, helped her in directing and supervising the hotel's kitchen and cleaning staff. Although as the hotel receptionist Willy was immediately responsible only to Mr Chandler, his irrepressible wife at first attempted to appropriate Willy to her authority. Willy politely but firmly rejected her manoeuvrings. Taking to her employment like a duck to water, Willy's career at the Commercial Hotel blossomed.

A small incident occurred at the Commercial Hotel one day that gave Willy a small retaliation against her treatment by Mrs Armstrong on the farm. After the end of the Second World War, cigarettes were a scarce and highly prized commodity in Australia. Not readily obtainable except from a grocer or in a hotel, their distribution was fully within the discretion of the authorised vendor. Soon after she had begun working at the Commercial Hotel, Willy had a moment of triumph when Mr Armstrong, a regular patron, came to her desk to ask the receptionist to sell him cigarettes. His jaw dropped and his eyes nearly popped out of their sockets when he noticed that the hotel's receptionist was his former servant Willy, who he had only weeks ago unceremoniously dumped at the local train station. Recovering some of his composure he had no alternative but to politely ask for, 'A couple of packets of cigarettes, please?' Willy replied, 'Sorry, Mr Armstrong, we are quite out of cigarettes.' The little white lie was sweet vengeance for much that had been meted out to her on the farm. We never saw Mr and Mrs Armstrong again. Sandy had learned some of our early experiences in Australia on the grapevine, and if he noticed that these two patrons had ceased frequenting the Commercial Hotel, he did not comment on the matter to his receptionist.

Challenges and changes

While Willy was happy in her employment at the hotel, working in Mr Drouin's grocery store was a somewhat different story for me. Although it did not take me long to learn the basics of the business, including getting more proficient with Imperial measures and currency, my relationship with shop assistant Cathy was less than genial. As the longest-serving counter hand in Mr Drouin's store, sour-tempered and mean-spirited Cathy considered herself Mervyn's and my supervisor, and while she got on well with the former she seemed to almost enjoy nurturing an active dislike of me. It took little provocation for her to correct even small mistakes that I made in my work, and she did not pass up any chance to point these out to Mr Drouin. Or, when I had made an error in serving a customer, she almost literally jumped at the chance to loudly and patronisingly proclaim in front of the shopper, 'Sorry, but he's a New Australian and he still has to learn a lot about the grocery business, but let me be of assistance to you, shall I?' The words stung, but more so the thin smile of her contempt, the broad wink exchanged between she and the amused customer, and the venomous glare in her eyes when Cathy took delight in humiliating me.

The situation in was not greatly helped by Mr Drouin seemingly only continuing to employ me at his wife's insistence. Each and every week when Frank handed me my wages, he would ask me if I had found a new job yet. My apology, 'Sorry, but not yet,' was invariably met with a grunt and, 'Harrumph, well, keep trying.' I very well realised that not only was I working for him on sufferance, but certainly on borrowed time.

We had been in Naracoorte for almost a year, and not for lack of trying I had still not succeeded in changing my occupation. In the local newspaper we found many advertised vacancies for farmhands, 'married couples', shearers and similar rural jobs but, particularly where Willy was concerned, we had no intention of returning to such employment. Other advertised work – such as truck drivers, heavy machinery operators, cattle or sheep buyers, real estate clerks and several other occupations – was tempting, but because I lacked either the necessary experience or training, I knew that I could not apply for them. Another most enviable opportunity arose when a school tuck shop opposite the Commercial Hotel came up for sale. But without the necessary finances to purchase this business, it remained the stuff of dreams for us.

Life in Naracoorte

We were still staying in our hired caravan in the bush when late summer turned into autumn and the temperature became increasingly chilly. We knew that once the wet and cold winter should arrive we would have to consider finding accommodation elsewhere, or we would experience rather miserable living conditions. With Willy working at the hotel, we found at least a temporary solution when, in exchange for forfeiting some of her wages, we were allowed to occupy a spare room. However, Mr Chandler stipulated, this would be a strictly temporary measure. When we returned the caravan to Mr Drouin's friend, we saved ourselves the weekly rent of 6 pounds. Although we had the use of only one room in the hotel, it was dry and warm, and we had the luxury of a real bathroom again – saving us having to bathe out of a bucket in the open. Luck, or was it Providence, had changed our lives for the better, albeit temporarily.

At the start of winter, after many unsuccessful attempts to find accommodation other than the hotel, we were finally successful in renting two rooms in a house owned by a middle-aged widow. Ruby, as she wanted to be called – 'Never mind the Mrs!' – was a kind but garrulous person. When we returned from work, she would have long and animated discussions with us in her kitchen – indicating that she apparently needed company rather more than rent money. A compulsive talker, Ruby was adept at finding out people's life history and it took her little time to learn a deal of the backgrounds of our lives. Although she usually did most of the talking, when she found something interesting in our replies she would rather amusingly exclaim, 'Oh *yeah*, go *o-o-n*; you don't *s a-a-a-y*, go on with you, you don't *s a-a-a-a-y*?' The time that it took us to disengage ourselves from her prattling was a small price to pay for the comfort of two warm and dry rooms, which beat conditions in the poor little humpy-back van out among the bracken under the sky.

Mr Drouin's glowering weekly reminder to me, 'Have you found another job yet? No? Keep trying!' spurred me on to find an alternative job, *any* job. One day I spotted an advertised vacancy in the local newspaper for an assistant in a department store in the small town of Millicent, some 75 miles from Naracoorte. Against all previous odds, this time my written application received a favourable reply from the store's manager, and I was invited for an interview at Millicent. I successfully passed the interview and the manager offered me the job! The next day I informed Mr Drouin that I had found employment elsewhere. His reaction was a curt, 'Harrumph, good, that's done then.' I imagined that these few words did not fully reflect his relief that he had honoured his moral obligation to Willy and me, and no longer had to employ me. I took some pleasure in seeing the disbelief followed by envy in Cathy's face when I told her that I had been appointed trainee manager in the Eudunda Farmers Department Store at Millicent. Offering a career opportunity better than that of a counter hand in Mr Drouin's grocery store, this time I did not mind when I heard Cathy snarl under her breath, *'Bloody New Australian!'* Mervyn gave no indication of *his* feelings, but I would not forget how, always the sly one, he covertly sided with bellwether Cathy when she criticised and denigrated me.

Willy was of course a little sad when she had to give notice at the Commercial Hotel, where she had enjoyed working. Both Sandy and Mrs Chandler said that she would be very much missed, but they wished us luck for the future. In a round of farewells, we took leave of the owners of the Rose Café and Tearooms, my Dutch friend Hans, and a few other people at Naracoorte with whom we had become acquainted. On a cold day in early spring 1953, we left Naracoorte for the small township of Millicent, centre of south-eastern South Australia's pine forest industry. We had started on the path to yet more new directions and a future that still lay unfolded – the latter that we could not have imagined even in our dreams.

CHAPTER 15

Life in Millicent

A country town smaller than Naracoorte, the people of Millicent largely depended for their employment on the nearby paper mill and associated pine plantation industry. If there is some validity in thinking that every centre of human habitation has its own distinctive atmosphere, the Akubra-hatted menfolk of Naracoorte suggested that it was clearly a grazier's town. Conversely, on any working day, the many citizens of Millicent toting the famous working man's Gladstone carrying bag marked it the township of a blue-collar workforce employed in the paper mill and pine plantations. At Naracoorte, Willy and I, 'New Australians', stood out socially as 'Well, not quite… you know.' At Millicent, a more tolerant and egalitarian community received us more acceptingly.

Billygoat Corner
At my interview with the manager of the Eudunda Farmers Store I had inquired after accommodation, but my new employer, Mr Green, painted a picture of the shortage of rented private housing similar to the case at Naracoorte. He had made arrangements to temporarily accommodate us in a local boarding house, however, 'I may know of a small cottage that may shortly be vacated by its present occupants. I shall do my best to secure it for you,' Mr Green had promised.

Operated by a middle-aged couple, Mr and Mrs Maythers, the boarding house was named after a bend of the main road on the outskirts of the town. 'Billygoat Corner' was a rambling and in places a somewhat ramshackle building. In that respect the Millicent establishment little resembled the one at Naracoorte where we had memorably run into trouble with our hostess for innocently bringing a bottle of sherry onto the premises. It also differed in apparently taking in only single male boarders. When Mrs Maythers showed us to our room, she made quite a point of telling us that it was the only one furnished with a double bed. 'We usually take in single boarders only, but Mr Green asked us to make an exception for yous two,' she said. 'We is also pretty choosy about taking in New Australians because some of yous don't speak the language real well, see. And let's face it, yous have, like, foreign ways and manners, know what I mean? But Mr Green guarantees us that yous are good folk.' Our hostess, a lady of ample proportions, continued, 'We have several Yugosolav boys stay with us. We've grown quite fond of them, y'know, they're good lads. When Mr Green – he's a real gentleman, y'know – asked us to take yous in, he assured hubby and me that yous're alright. But isn't it funny, with the two of yous and our three Yugoslav boys, all our boarders are New Australians, not one Aussie among yous, what?' Although Willy and I failed to see anything comical in Mrs Maythers's mention about all her boarders being foreigners, there was no malice intended towards us. For politic's sake and also because we had no idea where else to stay at Millicent, we agreed with our hostess, 'Yes, that is indeed very funny.' Our stay at the Billygoat Corner boarding house turned out to be a happy time.

While she watched us unpack a few things in our room, our landlady – 'Call me "Ma", dear, our Yugoslav boys do' – continued to try to satisfy her curiosity about us. 'I know that hubby'll be working at Eudunda's, but what'll you be doing, then, dear?' she asked Willy. When my wife replied that she had no employment lined up so far, but that she had worked as a receptionist in a Naracoorte hotel and that she would be looking for similar work in Millicent, Mrs Maythers was evidently impressed, 'An important job, hey, you were doing well,' Ma commented. When she next asked what my work at Naracoorte had been, and I replied that I had served as a counter hand in a grocery store, Ma Mayther's, 'Oh well, any job is a good job, hey?' indicated that at the humble Billygoat Corner boarding house, egalitarianism evidently went only so far, and that social status did seem to count.

The distinction that Ma Maythers drew between Willy's and my social status reminds me of an attitude that in any community apparently borders on snobbery. I believe a classic example of this is what one may refer to as 'the Australian pub syndrome'. It is said that Australians like to believe that theirs is a country of equality for all. When in 1939 my family spent holidays in Australia, my father thought that this outlook could be crystallised in the saying, 'Jack is as good as his master.' Having picked up the slogan in an Australian pub, nominally the cathedral of Australian egalitarianism, my father thought that he could not detect differences between its patrons. He failed however to note how in the hotel's barroom customers congregated in groups where they drank, and with *whom* they drank. At least in an 'olden days' Australian hotel, those customers in blue shirts and grey twill pants, clutching their Gladstone bag, came in through the door marked Public Bar, while patrons wearing moleskin trousers and bedecked with Akubra hats entered through another door displaying the sign Private Bar. In Australia, much has been made – and continues to be made – of its lack of social class, with cries of 'such a friendly country, the people so genial, a "fair go" for all' echoing far and wide. But as Ma Maythers seemed to indicate when she approved of and admired my wife's recent work background and was less complimentary about mine, truth is often the victim of all slogans, and reality is often quite different from what people like to claim.

That first evening at the communal table in the dining room we met our fellow boarders, 'our Yugoslav boys' as Ma Maythers fondly called them. Mealtimes at the Billygoat Corner boarding house – and particularly 'tea', the evening meal – were jolly occasions presided over by our artless but good-hearted hosts Ma and Pa Maythers, and during the meals banter and laughter flowed to and fro. After tea, when the plates and dishes had been cleared away, Mrs Maythers often brought out a deck of cards. With a strictly enforced house rule allowing no greater denomination than pennies and ha'pennies, she and the Yugoslav boys liked to play a social game of 'penny poker'. The first few evenings Willy and I just sat and watched them play, but after initial shyness on both sides had worn off, one evening our fellow boarders invited us to join them. When we confessed that we did not know how to play the game, they laughed and offered to teach us, and, 'Go on, enjoy yerselves,' said Ma. Unpretentious as the Billygoat Corner boarding house was, it was less a place of rented rooms and rather a 'home away from home' for the Yugoslav boys and for us.

New jobs

The Eudunda Farmers Department Store occupied half a block in Millicent's commercial business district, and sold groceries, clothing, toiletries, manchester, hardware and a wide variety of other popular merchandise. Above every service counter hung a spring-tensioned tube attached to a flying fox-type conveyor system. When an assistant had completed a sale in their area, they placed cash or sales dockets inside the tube, which they then released to travel along the wires to a central point where the cashier dealt with them. Then, by the same means, the cashier returned change or paperwork to the counter from where it had originated. Used to the manual operations in the Naracoorte grocery store, I was impressed to find what was then considered a superior, 'modern' way of business at Eudunda Farmers, and I counted myself lucky to have made apparent occupational progress.

During the working day while I was occupied at the store, Willy did not sit still. As she had at Naracoorte, she began to canvass likely places of employment in the central business district of town. However, like at Naracoorte, the answer she received at Millicent was, 'Sorry, we are fully staffed,' or at best, 'If a vacancy occurs we'll keep you in mind.' After much fruitless job hunting, a married son of the Maythers – who worked at the nearby Forestry Research Station at Mount Burr, 5 miles outside Millicent – suggested she enquire at the station. Over dinner, when Willy told the company that she had been successful in finding employment as a clerical assistant at Mount Burr, Ma's praise, 'Good onya, love!' was genuine and warm-hearted.

The Triumph

One of our first major expenditures in Millicent was the purchase of a second-hand motorcycle. The boarding house was a fair distance out from the town's central business district, and a long way for us to walk back and forth twice a day. The twin carburettor 500cc Triumph Tiger motorcycle was advertised in the local paper at 120 pounds – a considerable sum of money for us. But such as we had once dreamed when we bought

Wally's Silver Anniversary Buick buckboard, our motorbike was our key to freedom. This time with experience in mind, 'The Buyer Beware', Willy and I took the precaution to ask for advice before we decided on the intended purchase. That evening at dinner when we mentioned our interest in the advertised motorcycle, Pa Maythers agreed that before we bought it, we should get someone with knowledge of these machines to inspect it for us. 'A cobber of mine knows all about motorbikes' he offered. 'I'll ask him to look at the one you have in mind.'

Pa Mayther's 'cobber' turned out to be a heavily tattooed younger man. His arms were covered with intricate patterns of blue, green and red rampant dragons, a skull and bones, a pair of cruelly taloned eagles descending on partly folded wings, and other phantasmagoria. For the times decidedly uncommon, he also wore his hair long in a luxurious ponytail. In all probability, he was a forerunner of the later 'bikies', members of the often notorious motorcycle gangs in Australia that were modelled on the infamous American Hells Angels. However, when we confessed that we knew little better than nothing about motorcycles and said we were interested in purchasing one that had been advertised, the cobber affably enough said, 'She'll be right, I'll have a gander at it fer yous, no worries.'

At the address where we were shown the Triumph motorcycle, my heart began to race. Standing perched on its parking stand, with racy lines, impressively large single headlight and gleaming chrome exhaust pipe, the silver machine looked magnificent. Our mechanically minded friend took less notice of the bike's appearance and instead asked the prospective seller to 'Start 'er up fer us, mate, willya?' When the machine burst into deep-throated growling life, memories of my father's Harley Davidson on the plantation on Java came flooding back and I could almost feel again the wind tearing at my clothes when I first rode it. At our friend's request, the owner of the Triumph produced a long screwdriver. Our cobber bent down with it, and holding the sharp end of the tool against the engine block and the handle of the screwdriver against his ear, somewhat like a doctor's stethoscope, he listened to the working parts. 'Bearings sound okay, can't hear a rattle in the engine block,' he said, and, 'I reckon the bike sh'ld be apples, probably pretty safe to buy if that's what ya want?' Unasked by us, our tattooed friend next began to bargain with the owner over the price, but the latter remained unmoved. 'I'm not skinnin' anyone by askin' a hundred 'n twenty quid fer it, mate,' he said, and our adviser agreed. 'Fair enough, but will ya throw in the saddle bags then?' When the man agreed to clinch the deal by including the handsome leather pouches all for the price of 120 pounds, we became the proud and very excited owners of a vehicle that – unlike Wally's ill-fated buckboard – actually worked beautifully. Later, when we toured all over South Australia and as far as Melbourne in Victoria, our beautiful Triumph Tiger gave us the freedom and independence that we had dreamed of. When we thanked Pa Maythers's friend and offered to pay him for his advice, he modestly replied, 'No worries, piece of cake, there's no charge,' and then he added, 'Worth a beer in the pub, but.' At the local hotel, where I shouted him not one but several beers, he contemptuously dismissed the publican's, 'A middy, mate?' with, 'Nah mate, make it a schooner.'

The cottage

Now with jobs and transport of our own, we were beginning to feel quite settled at Millicent. But we were still waiting for our promised house. When we had arrived at Millicent my boss, Mr Green, had taken us to the street and the house that he had in mind for us to rent, but as it was still tenanted we had been unable to inspect it inside. From where we stood, hidden behind a thick, thorny boxthorn hedge on a neglected block of land near the Millicent hospital, the perfectly square 30 x 30-foot house looked decidedly tired and neglected on the outside. Previously used as a hospital building, the roof and exterior walls of corrugated iron were unpainted and rusty. As with the cottage on the Armstrong farm, a covered, 4-foot-wide bare earthen veranda ran around all sides of the building. At one corner of the veranda stood a badly corroded 1000-gallon corrugated-iron water tank. We could not see it from the street, but we later discovered that because of several rusted-through holes in the sides of the tank, it could only hold half its capacity of water. Unprepossessing as it looked, we assured Mr Green that when it became available, we would have no hesitation to move into the little shack. Some weeks later we could finally move into the cottage, and Willy and I at last had a whole house to ourselves – our first real home since we were married!

Our home in Millicent, an abandoned hospital building, 1954.

If the little cottage had looked dilapidated on the outside, it was perhaps just as well that we had not earlier seen it inside. Thin plasterboard walls divided the 30-foot-square building into four rooms of exactly 15 square feet. One of these – the kitchen – had a wood stove installed, the dwelling's only fitting. Two other rooms Willy and I decided could be made into bedrooms, and the fourth – which had a door opening out onto the veranda – would make a sitting room. Rented unfurnished, we could afford to buy no more than a double bed mattress without a base. Everything else in the way of furniture would have to wait until we had built up enough capital; we could presently not afford tables, chairs and kitchen and lounge room furniture. For the time being we decided that we would just lay the mattress on the bedroom floor, our cabin trunk would make do for a kitchen table, and a couple of cheap seagrass mats on the floor would be our 'chairs'. These were complemented by a few pots and pans, four plates, cups and saucers and some cutlery that we had bought cheaply – other purchases would have to wait. 'The time will come,' we assured each other, 'when our home will be properly furnished.' As for the lack of running water, sanitation and drainage in the cottage, we had already grown used to dealing with this when we lived in our hump-back caravan on the bush block at Naracoorte. Now that we had our half-full rainwater tank on the veranda with plumbing to the taps inside, we would not have to carry buckets of water with us all the way from town. Though several of the usual amenities were lacking, when at the turn of a switch our rooms lit up with a warm glow we congratulated each other, 'At least we have the electricity laid on.'

Our original intention had been to make do without a bed base, but when we laid the mattress on the floor, the draught from under the doors in the cottage made us realise that we simply had to find a means to raise it off the floor. As we could not yet afford to buy a bed base, we decided that we could lay the mattress on the empty packing crates that had contained certain merchandise delivered at Mr Green's store. However, when we asked the Millicent greengrocer to sell us the banana crates – made of stronger timber than the flimsy boxes in which other goods usually came – he refused. 'Nah, can't help you,' he said. 'Too much trouble reconciling the deposit for empties.'

We tried everywhere else that we could think of, but without success. As a last resort I rationalised, 'When you take something that you don't need it is stealing, but when you "pinch" something, because you *really* need it and there is no other way to get it, that's different. That is not stealing. Tonight when it's dark, we'll just have to pinch a few banana crates on which to put our mattress.' Willy at first objected to doing such a dishonest thing. But in the end she agreed – what else could we do when no one would sell them to us?

After dark that evening, we made several trips on our motorcycle to the greengrocer's now deserted premises, each time returning with Willy clutching two empty banana crates and I balancing one in front of me. With the mattress now perched on nine banana crate 'empties' and out of the draught, Willy and I slept comfortably on our makeshift bed. As a sop to the conscience and so as to somewhat make up for our hopefully small sin of dishonesty, we never bought fruit and vegetables from anyone in town but the greengrocer from whom we had 'pinched' the crates.

Getting to know the neighbours

A day or two after we moved into the cottage we heard a voice at the kitchen door, '*Yoo-hoo!*' When we answered the call, we found a plump, middle-aged lady. She introduced herself, 'I am Mrs Max Hurley – your neighbour from across the road.' Our new acquaintance continued, 'We noticed that you are settling in, and I've just come to see if my husband and I can be of any help to you?'

We replied that, thank you, we were fine, and we asked her in for a cup of tea. Eyes darting around, Mrs Hurley surveyed the bare room. When she saw our temporary 'furniture' – the cabin trunk 'table' in the 'sitting room' and the mats instead of chairs – she remarked, 'You seem not quite settled in yet. Your things must still be on the way?' She did not comment when we told her that we could not yet afford proper furniture, that we had to save up for it, and that the present arrangement would have to suffice.

Chatting over her cup of tea, our neighbour explained that her husband was a teacher at the local primary school, that the elder of their two boys worked at the butter factory – which, together with the paper mill was one of the town's major employers – that their second son had just started his last year at primary school, and that – because he had nowhere else to live – they had a male friend boarding with them in their council house. Mrs Hurley gushed about the chooks she kept in the back yard and the many tomatoes and vegetables her husband grew. 'So don't buy veggies or eggs from the shops. You can have as much of them as you like from us for free,' she generously offered. Later, when we walked her to the road, Mrs Hurley cast a dubious eye over our motorcycle. 'Don't like them much,' she confessed disapprovingly. 'Max says that motorbikes are dangerous, and anyone who rides them is not a "New" but, a *Temporary* Australian, get it?'

'Yes,' we said, 'It's a joke.' And with it we had come just a little closer to becoming 'Australianised'. Satisfied that she had learned as much about us as could be politely gained for the time, our neighbour crossed the road back to her home. We knew her, 'See you again soon,' was not a parting comment, but a promise.

Late that afternoon a small old buckboard pulled up before the entrance to our cottage. At our door the unexpected visitor introduced himself. 'I'm Max Hurley. I understand that you met my wife earlier?' He continued, 'Look, my wife believes that you're presently a bit short of furniture in the house, so I've whipped around to some of our friends for any bits of old gear that they can spare. I have a few things on board my car that you may like to borrow until you get yourself new things.' The 'gear' in Max's utility consisted of an old kitchen cupboard, a kitchen table and four kitchen chairs, and a small sideboard. When we unloaded it, Max thought it necessary to almost apologise, 'It's old stuff but better than what you have now?' To this Willy and I answered that we were delighted and very grateful to Mrs Hurley for her thoughtfulness, he for his trouble, and his friends for their generosity. 'No worries,' Max replied. 'You needed a bit of looking after, right?'

From that time on we became good friends with Mrs and Max Hurley, who took an almost parental interest in us. On many Saturdays at what was then the end of the working week we received an invitation, almost an imperious demand, from the Hurleys to, 'Come over this evening for a chat, a few singsongs around the piano and a bit of supper after?' Max led us in song on these evenings and Mrs Hurley played the piano with grim determination, but alas not always faultlessly. We came to enjoy and appreciate their old-fashioned hospitality. When she judged her repertoire depleted, or when she had perhaps run out of energy, at around 9.30 our hostess would excuse herself to disappear into her kitchen. She would return with what she described as a 'light supper', laid out on a table that was almost groaning under the weight of plates of sandwiches, cake, trifle, and of course tea. 'In *Australia*,' Max and his wife thought to explain to us with foreign tastes, 'we don't much drink coffee – we prefer tea.' If, like most Europeans, Willy and I had been coffee drinkers, we soon learned to adapt to drinking tea in Australia. One reason for this change in our taste was that the local 'coffee' – manufactured by the Bushells Company and sold in a distinctive bottle that showed a Turkish boy with a red fez on his head – was an ill-tasting extract of chicory, a bitter brew that really did not deserve to be called 'coffee'. These evenings – often shared with other friends and acquaintances of the Hurleys – were the great Australian institution of the Saturday evening singalong. What better way of bonding between 'Old' and 'New' Australians?

Beginning to integrate
Willy and I found ourselves more readily accepted in the working-class Millicent community than we had been in conservative, stand-off, predominantly 'white collar' Naracoorte. In many respects our time at Millicent was a period of assimilation for us – of un-learning aspects of our upbringing in the Dutch culture, and, as my father had once encouraged,

of learning to adapt to the customs and ways of life in Australia. At Millicent more readily than at Naracoorte, Willy and I now mixed more freely with 'Old Australians'. We made acquaintances at work who would invite us to visit them or who took us on social outings – sightseeing, picnics, the local horse races, even to the local community hall where we learned contemporary favourite dance steps such as the 'Military Two-Step', 'Pride of Erin', the 'Slow Waltz' and other ballroom dances. This mixing in with the Millicent community – not forgetting Ma and Pa Maythers and the Yugoslav boys at the Billygoat Corner boarding house – was the dawn of our becoming an integrated part of Australian society.

The 1950s was the heyday of Australian immigration, mainly from England and Europe; hundreds of thousands of migrants came flooding into the country. At a time when the Australian national immigration policy aimed for the assimilation of foreigners into mainstream Australian society, many 'Old' Australians regarded it their national duty to impart on the foreigners, 'The way things are done in *Australia*, right?' With the example of the Hurleys and other well-meaning Millicent folk, there was little doubt that these 'Old' Australian people sincerely meant it when they told us, 'Feel welcome to join us.' In later years the philosophy of integration was surrendered for the utopian ideology of multiculturalism, which in practice reduces the significance of and eventually even inextricably alters the culture of the receiving country. In my view, sadly the warmth of the true Australian 'mateship' has been slowly eroded.

In practice, at the time Willy and I were still torn between two and possibly even three cultures, and were acutely aware of the need to find a place in the Australian society. Lest in our adopted homeland we remain on the outer of society, Willy and I could not envisage anything else but to become integrated Australians. The Millicent experience went a long way to make us feel welcome and accepted.

Willy learns to ride
Since we had acquired our own means of transport, one of our greatest pleasures was to explore Millicent's environs and beyond on our motorcycle. A great vehicle in many respects, the then current model Triumph was defective in one particular aspect – its pillion seat was no more than a small, hard, narrow squab behind the rider's comfortable

seat. Given that Willy and I unselfconsciously practiced gender equality as a matter of course, neither of us saw anything remarkable about me teaching my wife to ride our motorcycle. As the passenger, having to perch on a hard and narrow seat for an extended period of time would get quite uncomfortable, it seemed only sensible that we should take turns on the pillion seat. Willy learned fast, and she soon became a good and safe motorcycle rider.

Gender equity – Willy riding the Tiger Twin Triumph motorbike.

An amusing aspect of her newly acquired skill was that when we appeared in Millicent with Willy riding on the front seat and I on the pillion, we turned every head on the street. In a small and ultra-conservative Australian country town such as Millicent, it was unprecedented to see a woman riding a motorbike – particularly a heavy and powerful machine such as ours. In time, the novelty of seeing us share our driving wore off somewhat for the good citizens, but Willy's clinching victory over male conservatism came when she one day rode the bike by herself to the service station to fill up its petrol. As she pulled up at the pump – situated directly opposite the hotel – heads turned her way. Willy later said to me that she could almost *hear* the men think, 'How's she going to kick start that bike, hey?' It was not an unreasonable question given that she was slight of build and that kick-starting a 500cc motorcycle required quite some power from the rider. After she had filled the bike up with petrol, her moment of triumph over male chauvinism came when she started the machine with one powerful kick. As the bike roared into life, Willy rode off, leaving disbelieving blokes in the pub to ponder what had come of the times to see a woman, a *sheila*, encroach on what should be a man's business and prerogative.

A new door opens

Willy had been working at the Forest Research Station for nearly a year and over that time we had become socially acquainted with her colleague, scientist John George, and his wife, Wilma. In casual discourse, I had told them something of my background and training in tropical agriculture – qualifications that seemed of little value for a career in Australia's rural industry. Although no more than incidental chitchat, it appeared that Willy's colleague had remembered this conversation. One day he pointed out to her an advertised vacancy in the newspaper for an Agricultural Officer in the Australian Territory of Papua and New Guinea.

At the time, little was known in Australian society about New Guinea, other than that it was an island somewhere to the north of the mainland, and that during the war Australian troops had fought the Japanese there. Nor did Willy and I know a great deal more about New Guinea, except that I remembered from my pre-war geography lessons that half of the island was part of the Dutch East Indies colony. Oh, yes, and I even had an uncle serving in the Dutch administration there – my mother's younger brother, Victor de Bruyn, who during the war became famously known as the 'Jungle Pimpernel'. At the outbreak of the Pacific War my uncle had volunteered to stay on the island to relay information about Japanese troop and naval movements to General MacArthur's headquarters in Australia, for which service he was later decorated. When we mentioned the advertised position to our friends the Hurleys, and said that we were thinking about whether or not I should apply, Mrs Hurley bristled, 'New Guinea? What are you thinking of, young man, that you should want to drag your wife off to a country full of mosquitoes, snakes and cannibals?'

With even our intention to inquire after the job in New Guinea clearly disapproved of by Mrs Hurley – upon whom we looked as almost a surrogate parent – Willy and I spent many days discussing whether or not I should apply for the position at all. On the one hand, we both knew that if I answered the advertisement and my application should be successful, it would open up the way to a real career suited to my tropical agriculture qualifications. On the other hand, this overseas opportunity had come at a time when we had begun to make plans for a future in Australia. I had already embarked on somewhat of a career in merchandising, and we had lately been considering whether we should settle down in Millicent and perhaps begin to think of starting a family. In the end, Willy did not dissuade me from applying for the New Guinea position that, if successful, would change all that we had so far accomplished in Australia. 'The decision is yours,' said my loyal wife.

The responsibility lay heavily on my conscience and I struggled to conclude what to do for our future. I realised that my Dutch diploma lacked equivalence with an Australian agricultural qualification, which seemed to preclude me from ever entertaining a career in either an Australian state or national public service, or even in private enterprise. Reasoning that there was no harm in submitting an interest in the position in New Guinea, I applied for the position of Agricultural Extension Officer with the Papua and New Guinea Administration, asking for the relevant forms to be forwarded to me. How little did Willy and I realise that we almost failed to grasp the hand of Fate that held out a remarkable future to us, and that if we had ignored it we would have lost its remarkable opportunity.

After some time, I received documents from the Department of Territories in Canberra, which I completed and returned, hoping that I would be favourably considered. Many days and weeks went by without acknowledgement of my application and we had almost put the matter out of our mind when we received a large envelope embossed with the Commonwealth Crest. Inside was an invitation for me to attend an interview in Adelaide for selection to the position of Agricultural Extension Officer with the Department of Agriculture, Stock and Fisheries in the Australian Territory of Papua and New Guinea. Further advice was that a room had been booked for me in a city hotel, and that a return train ticket to Adelaide was enclosed. After a great deal more discussion with Willy, I kept the appointment in Adelaide – one of the most critically important decisions in our married life.

I returned from Adelaide and, although my interviewers had given me the impression that my application would receive favourable consideration, day after day no envelope appeared in our mailbox. We again put the matter in the back of our minds. 'The application cannot have been successful after all,' I rationalised. 'In Australia, my Dutch educational qualifications have probably not been recognised.' When we had almost given up hope, once again a large envelope embossed with the Commonwealth Crest appeared in our mailbox with news that I had been successful in my selection for appointment to the New Guinea Department of Agriculture. Dated the first week of October 1954, the letter advised:

> Validated 2nd November 1954, please find enclosed bookings and airline tickets for yourself, a single bus fare from Millicent to Mount Gambier, and airline tickets for travel by Trans Australian Airlines from Mount Gambier to Sydney, thence by Qantas Airways from Sydney to Port Moresby in the Australian Territory of Papua and New Guinea. On reporting to your Departmental Head, the Director of Agriculture, Stock and Fisheries in Port Moresby, suitable arrangements will be made for your spouse to follow you in due time.

The prospect of having to leave Willy behind in Millicent until 'suitable arrangements' could be made for her to follow me to New Guinea 'in due time', came like a thunderclap out of a clear blue sky. As did the realisation that we were embarking on a grand but also scary adventure that would once again upset whatever we had achieved since settling in Australia.

Much to the disapproval of Mrs Hurley – who kept fretting about, 'Fancy dragging your poor young wife off to a land of mosquitoes, snakes, and cannibals,' and her never voiced but implied reprehension for my thoughtlessness, lack of consideration, male chauvinistic selfishness and perhaps even a degree of unsoundness of mind – Willy and I decided to take the chance offered us by Fate, cutting through the Gordian Knot. When I gave notice at Eudunda Farmers Store, I felt very badly about letting the manager down – he had been a considerate and very supportive employer and teacher to me. In accepting my resignation, Mr Green kindly said that, while he understood my reason for wanting to establish a career for which my education and training had equipped me, I had done my work in the store well, and that he would miss me.

Next, a great deal of time and effort was spent getting together an outfit of clothes and other items suitable for the tropics. Among documents from the Department of Territories in Canberra came a long list of recommended articles for wear under tropical conditions, among which featured 'khaki or white linen shorts, short-sleeved shirts, stout footwear, eg. Army boots…' and a long list of other things including, '… importantly a mosquito net' and even the recommendation, 'In New Guinea, razor blades are in very short supply and males are strongly advised to lay in an adequate store of these before departure from Australia.' This advice apparently dated back to the war. In fact, I later found it was so outdated that I had at least a year's supply of shaving gear, even though razor blades were in plentiful supply even in small local trade stores in New Guinea. As for the recommended clothing, in a small country town such as Millicent – and even in the major nearby town of Mount Gambier – white linen shorts and short-sleeved shirts were unheard of, and it was only with difficulty that I obtained khaki shorts in a sports store. 'Getting in a bit early for camping, aren't you, mate?' the store's owner quipped, and he looked puzzled when I explained that I was not going camping, but that I would soon be leaving for New Guinea. 'New Guinea?' the man queried, and it was obvious that he only half knew what the name meant.

Flashforward

Before I departed for New Guinea, Willy and I had gratefully accepted the Hurleys' offer that, rather than being on her own in the cottage, Willy could stay with them in their guest room until either she should follow me, or I should return to Australia.

The generosity and the kindness of Mrs Hurley and Max, almost surrogate parents to us, left me feeling under an obligation to them. In this accounting of our lives, I am briefly jumping well ahead: two years later, on leave from New Guinea, we revisited Millicent. It was only then that Willy told me that, while staying with the Hurleys, when she had retired to the guest room one evening, Max had followed her and tried to accost her. He had only desisted when she had threatened to call out for Mrs Hurley. This betrayal by Max, who we had considered our trusted friend and almost a father figure, filled me with great bitterness and I refused to meet with the Hurleys. We never saw them again, and the letters they sent us I returned unopened. In spite of my anger with Max, I could not tell innocent, motherly Mrs Hurley the reason why we had broken contact with them.

CHAPTER 16

Millicent to New Guinea

On 2 November 1954 – incidentally my twenty-sixth birthday – a sad Willy and I made our way by bus from Millicent to Mount Gambier, from there taking a local bus to the airport. Neither of us had ever even set foot in an airport, and after checking in for the flight to Sydney, from an observation window the expanse of runway looked vast and very alien. Somewhat later we heard the drone of engines from an approaching aircraft and we watched the Trans Australian Airlines DC3 touch down on the runway, disembarking the passengers who made their way on foot over the tarmac to the terminal building. Behind us lay days of intense activity that almost equalled our preparations in Holland before our immigration to Australia. Giving careful consideration to the important letter from Canberra, we had decided that – although we were both loath for me to do so – I should travel alone to New Guinea. If for any reason the position or the conditions in New Guinea should prove unacceptable, then I could still return to Millicent and hopefully to my job at the Eudunda Farmers Store. Before fully committing ourselves to living and working in the Territory, I should assess the situation and, in particular, find apparently scarce married accommodation wherever I should be posted. Only then should we make the final decision on whether to remain in New Guinea, or return to Millicent and settle down.

Flight to Sydney

When the announcement came for passengers to board the TAA flight to Sydney, for a moment Willy and I stood irresolute; it was not yet too late for us to return to Millicent together. When Willy and I kissed, 'Till we meet again soon,' the die was cast, the Rubicon crossed, and the bridges behind us burnt. An unknowable new future had begun.

Strapped into my window seat when the aeroplane hurtled down the runway and lifted off the ground, just before we reached the terminal building, on the tarmac below I caught a glimpse of my wife's small, lonely figure and my heart ached.

When the DC3, the first aircraft that I had ever travelled in, gained height in the air over Mount Gambier, the lift of it climbing to its cruising altitude matched my mounting excitement at being actually on my way to New Guinea. A novice air traveller, I had for days been apprehensive about flying, and the night before my departure I had not slept at all well. It did not help a great deal that in gaining altitude our plane had to make a rather bumpy way through thick banks of cloud that totally enclosed the aircraft, so that I lost all sense of direction. Tossed around in my seat, I could only trust that all was well. When we broke through the cloud and the DC3 gained its cruising altitude and levelled out, the urgent roar of the engines became the reassuringly deep drone that is typical of this magnificent aircraft. The thought that only two hard-working engines kept us aloft made me apprehensive. However, when nothing untoward happened and my fellow travellers looked composed and some even slept, after a while I became better used to the sensation of being suspended in the air and my fears eased a little.

Looking out from the aircraft window, the town of Mount Gambier and its outskirts had disappeared and below us the Australian landscape looked quite different than at eye level. Heading in a roughly north-easterly direction, we were flying over the fertile belt that extends only a few hundred miles inland along the entire eastern seaboard, and as far north as the semi-tropics of Far North Queensland. It was astonishing to realise that this margin of rich agricultural country literally feeds Australia, and that the greatest part of the Australian continent is at best scarcely productive.

As we flew onwards towards Sydney, beneath the aeroplane wings I could make out tilled plots on the land that is Australia's natural larder, planted with what were probably wheat and other grain crops, paddocks with animals grazing on them, and here and there a lonely farm, or a vehicle trailing a plume of dust travelling to who knows where in the daunting vastness of the Australian Outback.

At some point our pilot changed course and we began to fly farther inland where the cultivated country began to make way for eucalyptus and other native forest vegetation. Below the DC3's wings the coastal plains became the rugged hills and the jagged escarpments of the Great Dividing Range, covered in primary forest practically undisturbed by human activity.

After we crested the Great Dividing Range, I felt the aircraft tilting slightly forward on a downward course, beginning to make a gradual descent presumably towards as yet distant Sydney. Reaching lower altitudes, the increased air pressure caused my ears to crackle, a discomfort that unfortunately remained even hours later. After about a two-hour flight we finally landed at Sydney, where I had to find my way from the domestic terminal to the international terminal. Although it was hours before the connecting flight to New Guinea, I was concerned that if I went sightseeing in Sydney I should not be able to find my way back.

Flight to Port Moresby

I had been waiting at Sydney's international airport terminal for the scheduled flight to New Guinea since noon. When at 7.45 pm the announcement came for passengers to board for Port Moresby, I was glad to make my way to the waiting aircraft. At the time, Australia's overseas airline, Qantas, operated two services from Sydney to Port Moresby – a daily DC6b Skymaster flight, and a twice-weekly connection by Catalina Flying Boat. As I *had* survived my earlier trip in a regular aircraft, I was perhaps illogically reassured that today I would be flying in the Skymaster – only somewhat different from the aircraft that flown me from Mount Gambier – instead of in an unknown Catalina Flying Boat. On the tarmac I was also relieved to note that the Skymaster was of a much larger size than the DC3 that had brought me to Sydney. Regardless, I felt quite nervous at the prospect of now facing a non-stop, eleven-hour, overnight flight with most of it travelling over the open sea.

At the top of the steep staircase that led to the door of the plane, a cheerful stewardess greeted me. Her confident manner somewhat reassured me – I would be flying with her, and if *she* did not seem disturbed, then I should also have nothing to worry about. In any case, there was no alternative but to board this plane to Port Moresby in the Australian Territory of Papua and New Guinea.

The airhostesses handed out orange drinks and chewy mint lollies to help passengers prevent their ears hurting on take-off. Settling back in my first-class seat – then an emolument for all Territory of Papua and New Guinea public servants – from my window I could see the aircraft's four engines come to life with a whine and splutter. When one after another they caught on with a powerful roar, the aircraft stood at a shuddering stop until the pilots in the cockpit released the brakes and we began to make our way over the tarmac. The aircraft came to a halt when it came to its assigned runway, waiting for permission from the control tower for take-off. As the cabin attendants went through routine procedures including demonstrating how to don and use lifejackets '… in the unlikely case that…', the flight crew in the cockpit carried out their pre take-off checks – revving the engines, releasing and applying air brakes and testing tail planes and ailerons. Finally, with the roar of all four engines working at maximum power, I watched the ribbon of runway passing underneath us at increasing speed until, with almost a jump, the Skymaster soared aloft into the domain that lent it its name.

When we reached cruising altitude, the stewardesses began to serve us a choice of beer, wines or spirits and appetisers, followed by a selection from a superb dinner menu that was part of the privilege of travelling in first class. Drinks and dinner over, when the cabin crew dimmed the cabin lights, most people reclined their seats for sleep. But in spite of the whirl of the day's experiences, or perhaps because of being too excited to feel fatigued, I was unable to follow the example of my more seasoned fellow air travellers. Instead I looked out of the porthole window, but in the inky black of the night sky, flying at some 30,000 feet, all that I could see were stars. When we occasionally flew through cloud banks that caused the Skymaster to bump and shudder, I, too, shook. On our north-bound course we still flew over land, and from time to time far below us tiny specks of lights indicated towns or settlements. Separated by empty distance, in the vastness of the Australian landmass, their names and geographic locations I could not tell. Eventually tiredness caught up with me, and I dozed off into restive sleep. But with my still vigilant mind not beyond hearing, I kept a pointless listening watch on the reassuring drone of our four aircraft engines.

I had no idea how long I had slept when a different pitch of the engines suddenly woke me with a start – was there something wrong? Then I felt the aeroplane dipping one wing and righting itself, and next dipping the other wing and re-righting itself again. Greatly alarmed I sat bolt upright in my seat, fearing that the aeroplane was about to crash. Were the engines failing? If so, why were the other passengers still asleep? Or did they not realise that something was amiss? From out of the semi darkness in the aisle, a stewardess came to my seat, 'Is there something the matter? Can I do or get anything for you, sir?' When I sheepishly explained to her what had woken me up, a little smile passed over her face as she assured me that everything was fine. 'At the half-way point, the "point of no return" between Sydney and Port Moresby,' she explained, 'the captain switches fuel tanks, which involves the slight dipping movements from side to side that woke you up.' Then she asked, 'Is this the first time you have flown with us to the Territory?' We chatted for some time, but while the hostess had somewhat reassured me, with hours of flying over the open sea remaining, sleep continued to elude me. I stayed awake, counting down the hours to our arrival back on firm New Guinea land.

Between catnaps, dozing off, and waking, I watched the passage of night until for a short while it took on the darkness of Indian ink, which heralds the new day. When the awakening sun began to draw thin, silver lines around drifting cloudbanks in the brightening firmament, uncountable billions of stars began to disappear and, paraphrasing Rudyard Kipling, when the sun rose magnificently above the horizon, 'dawn came up like thunder outer New Guinea crost the sea.'

PART 5:

New Guinea – Times Of Great Adventures

Australian Territories of Papua & New Guinea

Postings & Patrols

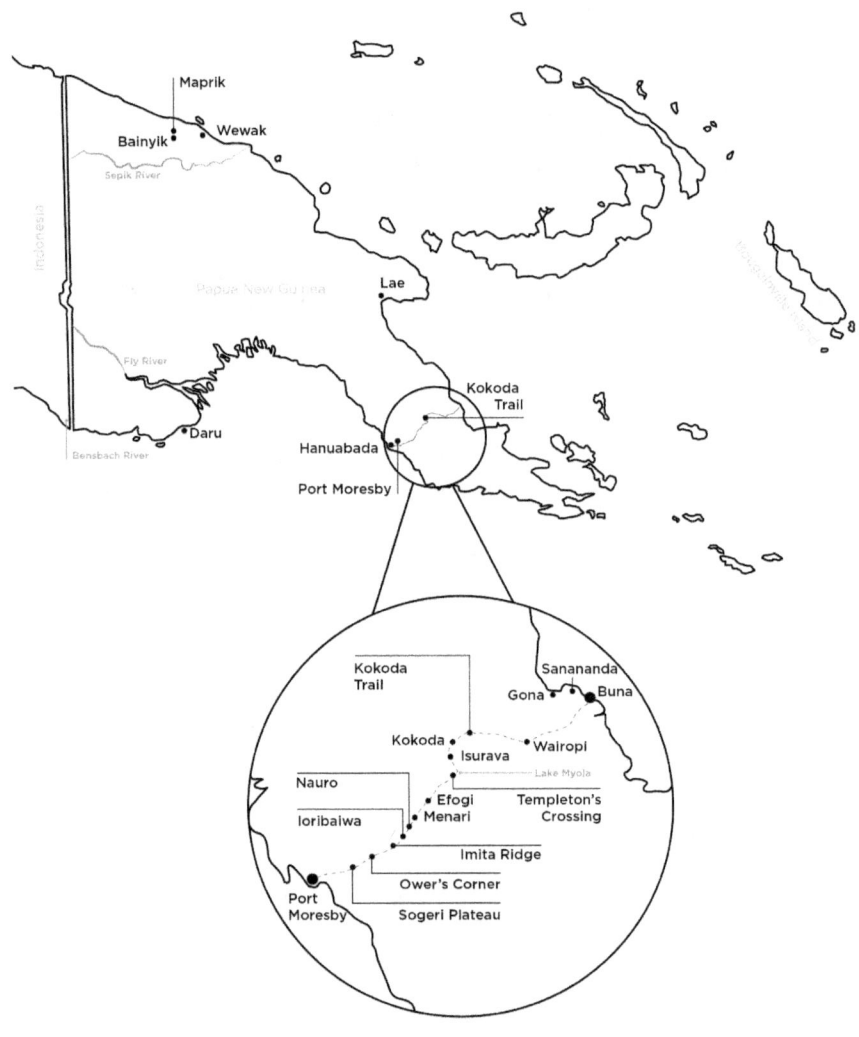

CHAPTER 17

A World Away

'Curiouser and curiouser,' said Alice ...
Lewis Carol, *Alice in Wonderland*

On its landing approach to Port Moresby, the aeroplane began to very gradually lose altitude. The magic moment came of my first glimpse of the Territory of Papua and New Guinea. The passengers were now wide awake, and the stewardesses bustled around in the aisles serving us breakfast. The plane continued its descent and as we came closer, I began to make out features of the sea below us – in the dawning morning it looked a dark grey-green, almost black. Under the Skymaster's wings, white sandy beaches fronted the sea, which lapped, wavelets frothing, at their margins. The sun had risen rapidly, and the colour of the water had changed to a clear emerald green. Below us lay coral reefs and patches of shallows in which I could see fish swimming and even a turtle, paddling a course to who knows where.

In the early hour of the day, the landmass towards which the aircraft was heading had been a featureless black, but as the rising sun began to pencil in details on the vast canvas of the green jungle-scape, splotches of multi-coloured flowers and leaves began to appear. A now familiar crackling in my ears and an uncomfortable air pressure warned me that we had descended to a height where we must be about to land, and as the cabin warning lights came on, I checked that my safety belt fitted snugly and securely, 'in the unlikely event that...'

The final landing stages went so fast that I could barely see the details of the sea and the land over which we were passing. Near the coastline I caught brief glimpses of small canoes with New Guinea villagers paddling or fishing in the lagoons. Next, we flew over thatch-covered huts built out over the water on platforms that were supported by crooked poles driven into the seabed. Then we were over land again – savannah grassland dotted with a series of small hills on which sparse eucalyptus trees grew. The dry, almost bare country did not at all resemble the lush, tropical landscape of my childhood Java. On its final approach, the plane made a wide circle overland before it straightened up to approach an airfield in a clearing directly ahead, embraced by parallel hills that extended to the sea. With its four engines now roaring at landing power, I watched the ground underneath the aircraft rearing up towards us at an alarming speed, until the Skymaster made its mercifully feather-light touchdown at Jacksons International Airport. Thus began, on 3 November 1954, the grand adventure that for the next twenty years would keep me and mine resident in the Australian Territory of Papua and New Guinea.

Arrival in the Territory

Our aircraft on the ground, passengers and crew had to wait for quarantine personnel of the Territory Administration to spray the cabin with over-the-counter cans of common fly spray, apparently against possible disease-carrying insects or other vermin from the Australian mainland. Their job done, the exit doors swung open wide and with a 'Thank you, and goodbye,' our smiling airhostesses saw their passengers off. It was 8 am as I walked down the staircase onto the already hot tarmac, and the oppressive tropical heat and humidity enveloped me like a wet blanket.

On the way to the airport reception hall, I noticed that a crowd of New Guineans had gathered behind a high safety fence to watch us disembark. With the memory of nut-brown Indonesians in my mind, the startlingly black appearance of the New Guineans surprised me, especially since none of the males wore clothing above the waist. On their bare upper torso or around the neck most wore items of personal adornment – a necklace of multi-coloured beads, a shell on a piece of string, a colourful handkerchief knotted around the neck, and some had plaited cane bands on their upper arms. Most of the men were dressed in crumpled and stained khaki shorts, but some wore a loincloth which I later learned was called a *lap-lap*.

The women sat or stood in small groups away from the men. Most wore copious grass skirts that left the upper body unclothed, and a few wore a Mother Hubbard type of garment that I later found out was here called a 'Mission' or 'Mary' dress. Men and women alike had their crinkly hair combed up in a high, exuberant bouffant style that some had adorned with a fresh flower or sometimes a leaf or a feather. To a newcomer like me, the dark-skinned, partly clothed and barefoot Papua and New Guineans looked exotic.

In a huge, corrugated-iron, wartime quonset hut – grandly called the Overseas Arrivals Hall – all passengers had to go through quarantine and entry formalities. In a daze of travel fatigue and the newness of everything, when I was asked if I had anything to declare, I replied truthfully that I had not brought any plant material or soil with me from Australia, and that I did not carry firearms or ammunition on my person or in my luggage: 'This is my passport, I am a person of Dutch nationality, and in Papua and New Guinea I will be working for the Department of Agriculture Stock and Fisheries in Port Moresby.'

The formalities completed, when I walked out into the public reception hall I noticed a person holding up a sign with my name on it. When I joined him, the young Australian man introduced himself as an Agriculture Department employee. He had come to drive me to where I would be staying in Port Moresby while in transit to my posting. My new acquaintance and I walked over to an old, probably salvaged wartime army truck parked behind the terminal building, where the Australian invited me to 'Hop in, mate.' After several attempts to start the dilapidated vehicle, its engine burst into spluttering life. The noisy exhaust evidently in need of replacement, with a muffled roar we turned out of the airport complex onto a winding bitumen road.

An introduction to the Territory

Instead of the tropical jungle growth that I had expected, the vegetation of the countryside we drove through resembled the semi-arid, inland Australian country-scape over which I had flown on the way from Mount Gambier to Sydney. In Port Moresby, tough, weedy plants and razor-sharp bladed *kunai* – blady grass – covered the 'grasslands'. The main tree species was eucalyptus, but the undergrowth consisted of scattered clumps of stunted bushes that I did not know the name of.

As we chugged along in the tired old truck, my companion chatted animatedly, evidently enjoying the chance to air his knowledge of the Territory to a newcomer. I learned that the airport, now referred to as Jacksons International Airport, had during the war been Jacksons Airstrip, and that in the bush around Port Moresby lay several other wartime airfields that had seen considerable action against the Japanese. 'On these abandoned strips you don't have to look far to find bits of aircraft parts, even guns and pistols, some of which are still in working order,' my informant said, adding that before long, the regrowth of bush vegetation would have totally reclaimed these scars on the landscape.

Chatting away, we had reached an area that was quite different in appearance from the dry grasslands. 'Before the war this used to be a huge swamp that the locals called Boroko. During the war the military referred to it as the Six Mile, indicating that it was a distance of 6 miles out from Port Moresby town – a practice that the Army applied to many of its local camps and installations during the New Guinea campaign.'

Driving through the Six Mile or Boroko area, my guide said that the army had begun to drain the swamp, building a satellite township of large tent camps for the troops and quonset huts in which to store supplies and war materiel. After the war, the Papua and New Guinea Administration undertook to further develop Boroko into Port Moresby's main suburb and primary expatriate residential area. 'Even today,' my informant continued, 'we often refer to certain landmarks by how the Army identified them. For instance the Australian General Blaimey's headquarters was called the Nine-and-a-half Mile. And at edge of the escarpment that rises 2000 feet above the lowland plains country, the Fifteen Mile marks the beginning of the Sogeri Plateau, with its expatriate rubber plantations. At the far end of the Plateau, the Twenty-two Mile, at Owers Corner, begins the Kokoda Trail, or Track.'

As we left the Boroko suburb, the road passed through a saddle in the hills and dipped about 200 feet down to where a cluster of buildings stood. Behind them I could see the sea. My self-appointed guide volunteered, 'This is Badili. It's a smaller suburb than Boroko, with a few expatriate houses, half a dozen Chinese trade stores and a Chinese tailor called Ping Sui. Badili also has a large compound that houses most of Port Moresby's itinerant labourers. A bit farther down the road at what we call the Three Mile, is Koki Market where fishermen sell the day's catch, and other vendors sell anything from yams, taro, betel nut, even smoked *magani*.' When he noticed that I did not comprehend the latter word he explained, 'Magani is the Papuan word for wallaby. The locals hunt them in the grasslands around town, to eat or to sell them smoked at the market.' Suddenly braking for a crowd of people crossing the road, he impatiently beeped the horn. He swore as they crossed, but his words sounded more like a sigh of annoyance than a curse.

After we had passed Koki Market, the bitumen road followed the contours of the hills. Blasted out of solid brown agate and dull-red ferrous conglomerate rock, the way was never more than 6 feet above the sea. The tide had gone out and local people, mostly women and children, fossicked in the rock pools left by the receding waters. 'The women and kids always do this when the tide's out,' said my companion when he noticed my interest. 'The men go fishing in the lagoon or out to sea – in the canoes you see moored or tethered to poles on the beach at Koki Market. The small outrigger canoes with the single crab-claw sail are called *motumotu*, but these days there aren't many of them left. There are also still some really large ones that in the Motu language are called *lagatoi* – *laga* meaning logs and *toi* the Papuan word for "three". These are olden times, blue water, outrigger trading canoes. Made from huge logs, the three hulls are sometimes 80 feet or more in length. They would support a platform on which the traders and sailors stored goods for barter. From this area, the goods were mostly highly prized clay pots baked mainly by the women of Hanuabada village. The lagatoi trading fleet, called *hiri*, used to set sail in November, travelling to partner villages as far as the Papuan Gulf country, where they exchanged the terracotta pots for sago and pigs from the people of the huge south-western swamplands. Outfitted with multiple enormous, claw-shaped sails made from pandanus palm matting, the outrigger canoes could not tack in the winds and so the Papuan sailors navigated south in the prevailing north-west monsoon. Six months later, when the south-east trade winds blew, they would return north, back home to Hanuabada and other Papuan coastal villages. Few lagatoi remain, as modern communications and commerce have made the traditional hiri trading voyages a thing of the past.'

Motumotu – small outrigger canoes with dual sails – at Daru.

When I finally got a chance to break into my informant's flow of words, I asked him if there was another language spoken in Papua and New Guinea than the Papuan to which he had referred. My new friend replied that the Territory of Papua and New Guinea is geographically divided by a cordillera – a mountain range that stretches east-west along the length of the island. The geographic northern half of the island is New Guinea where the lingua franca is Pidgin English, and the southern half of the island is Papua where the trade language is the so-called Police Motu, but where the classic Motuan language is still in use by the Papuans.

With an apparently encyclopaedic knowledge of the subject, my driver went on to tell me that until the war, Port Moresby was a typical Australian colonial town – a tropical outpost far from central government, in a territory administered by locally based Australian officers with wide powers. Though Port Moresby's beautiful natural setting is nowadays spectacular, before the Second World War the town was a poor and impermanent-looking place. At the time, neither government nor commerce had bothered to construct the substantial buildings with style and character that distinguished European settlement in the Indian subcontinent and in Asia. Instead, the government offices and addresses of private enterprise were generally of poor quality and worse appearance. The domestic housing – built after the North Queensland style of tropical bungalow with wide verandas – was of better quality, using imported timber cladding and zinc roofs. In essence, however, neither visitor nor colonial resident had much affection for this outpost of empire; it reminded an observer of a hastily built mining town, a collection of hot tin roofs, and utilitarianism writ large on everything.

The white population of Port Moresby was statistically very masculine, white males significantly outnumbering white females. The government employees, planters, merchants, traders, clerks, missionaries and miners formed the city's institutions on the basis of their own racial whiteness. Unlike the cities of Rabaul or Darwin, Port Moresby had no other foreign – often Chinese – community to act as a buffer between colonists and indigenous locals. A complication in race relationships – offensive by today's standards – was that the contemporary white population firmly subscribed to theories of biological evolution; notions of their own superiority easily translated into a belief in the inferiority of the Papuan and New Guinean 'child races' that the newly formed Australian nation was adopting. With generally scant knowledge of the people they were to govern, it was said that the 'natives' were in their babyhood, and 'savages, as far as civilisation and development were concerned'[xxiv].

As we drove on, I took in the surroundings. So much about the town was foreign, but here I would begin the career in agriculture that my parents had so much wished for me. I couldn't help reflecting how, but for a chance touch on the shoulder by the hand of Fate, none of this may have eventuated.

From Koki Market we had followed the road for a distance of two miles, and we had now reached an area called Ela Beach. A favourite recreational playground, Ela Beach had white sand on which casuarina trees provided welcome dappled shade. Until the late 1960s, a sign posted on several of the trees proclaimed it strictly reserved for 'Europeans only'. Past Ela Beach the road made a slight turn to the right, and as we came up a small rise, my companion chatted on, pointing as he drove. 'As you can see, at the end of the peninsula the terrain rises to a kind of bluff called Tuaguba Hill, a part of Port Moresby's town where mainly B4s live.' This time without my prompting he explained, 'That's the name or kind of title by which the old-timers here call themselves: B4 that stands for "Before the Second World War", see? They're very proud of this, and they regard anyone that came to PNG after the war as not a real Territorian.'

We drove through what my friend somewhat grandly called Port Moresby's central business district, which consisted of a couple of banks and two major department stores – Burns Philp and the Steamships Trading Company, the former which locals shortened to 'BPs' or 'Beeps', and the latter 'Steamies'. Among the other larger premises were the Papuan Hotel, the offices of Customs and the Police, and the courthouse. Port Moresby's CBD was completed with a number of business houses occupied by a variety of smaller private entrepreneurs, and several minor shops and Chinese trade stores.

In the middle of the town at a five-way intersection, on a covered rotunda raised about 6 feet above the carriageway, a traffic policeman directed the traffic. Barefoot, the man was dressed in a distinctive uniform – dark blue, short-sleeved serge shirt seamed in red bias around the neck and sleeves, and a uniform lap-lap of the same dark serge material held up by a broad leather belt with ammunition pouches on either side of the waist. 'Our Royal Papua New Guinea Constabulary is famous for their bravery and loyalty to their commanding European Patrol Officers,' my informant volunteered. 'To this day, the constabulary continues to play an integral part in the pacification of the Territory in areas not before contacted by the Administration. It can be dangerous work for both the Europeans and the local police – in fact, only a few months ago, in a semi-controlled area of the Sepik District, residents of Telefomin village killed two Patrol Officers and a number of the policemen with them.' Mention of the incident reminded me that a short time before I left Australia, the newspapers had been full of the murder of two Australians, Szarka and Harris of the Papua New Guinea Administration, in the Territory. This had been another occasion when Mrs Hurley had remonstrated with me about 'dragging your poor young wife off to a land of mosquitoes, crocodiles and cannibals!'

As we left the town centre we followed a narrow strip of road along the shore of Fairfax Harbour, carved out of the steep hill on which more European-type houses were built. A distance out in the water I noticed the wreck of a ship with only its funnel and a small section of the bow showing. 'That's the old Macdui, one of Burns Philps's overseas liners. It went down in the war when the Japs put a bomb right through its funnel,' my guide explained. 'Sometimes the tanks still ooze fuel oil, and diving or snorkelling around it you have to be careful not to become covered in the stuff.' In the distance out on the water I saw a settlement of huts built over the sea, 'That's Hanuabada, in the Motu language Big Village,' said my companion. 'Most Papuan staff members in the Administration live at Hanuabada. In the early days of contact with them, these Papuans were quite fierce warriors, but, pacified by the missionaries, they have long become devout Christians.'

At an intersection of the main road, about two miles from the centre of the town, we turned off onto a side street lined on both sides with mango trees. A little farther up, pointing to a large sign bearing the Australian Government Crest and the legend Department of Agriculture, Stock and Fisheries, my companion announced, 'This is DASF Head Office, where you'll have to report for duty tomorrow.' Some 50 feet farther, as he turned the truck into a dry, dusty compound, he advised, 'This is the Ranuguri European Officer's hostel of single men's quarters. They're commonly referred to as "dongas". I'll leave you now. Our working day starts at 7.50, when the offices at DASF will be open. You had best report early in the day before it gets too hot.' Pointing to a young New Guinean who had come out from the Ranugiri buildings, 'The boi will carry your suitcase inside for you.' This time I did not question the word by its English sound, but learned later that in Pidgin English it is written b-o-i. I shook hands with my driver, guide and informant, and he drove off. A bewildered new chum, I stood alone in hot, steamy, Port Moresby, capital of the Territory.

First impressions
Left with my few items of luggage, I stood baking in the fierce tropical sun. The servant or 'boi' picked up my suitcase and began to walk towards the hostel; 'Yu kam, masta,' the young chap beckoned me to follow him. Leading me across the yard and through the door into the building, the hostel manager, an Australian, looked up at me from behind the reception desk. After we had greeted each other he asked, 'How long will you be staying in Port?' I replied that I had no idea if, when, and to where my Department would send me. 'No worries,' the manager assured me, 'After your interview at DASF tomorrow let me know what your movements are. I'll book you in for a week, though, as it usually takes that long for the paperwork to be completed and for Head Office to let people at your posting know that you're on your way.'

Then the manager called out, '*BOI!*' and the same servant who had met me in the courtyard appeared. I followed him through the hostel's corridors until he put down my suitcase in a small, breathlessly hot single room. 'Room bilong yu, masta,' he announced in Pidgin English, then left. With my mind a-whirl with new impressions and travel fatigue, all I could think of was the next morning. It was crucial that I should find married accommodation for Willy and me, as this would determine whether or not there would be a future for us in the Territory.

By the time I unpacked some of my toilet articles and a few items of clothing, I was perspiring freely in the oven-like temperature of the small room. Although I had opened all the window louvers, the tropical heat and humidity enveloped me as if wrapping me in a wet blanket – the same sensation I had experienced when I emerged from the plane at Jacksons Airport. The discomfort I had then felt did not improve in the hostel. November is the period of the doldrums that precedes the wet season or north-west monsoon, which lasts from January to the end of April. In the dry season, from May to October, the south-east trade winds blow. These are especially strong in southern Papua, bringing welcome relief from the high temperatures and humidity. November was probably the climatically worst time of year, when the Territory experiences its greatest heat and humidity and when practically no winds blow. Although it was quite early in the morning, I was perspiring heavily and the blood racing through my veins was giving me a bad headache. At Millicent, well-meaning people had warned, 'Why would you want to stay in such a savage country...?' and I now began to wonder if I had been right in wanting to take Willy to live in this uncomfortably hot and steamy land.

Left with nothing else to do until lunch time, I took stock of the small, barely 8 x 8 foot room. It was furnished with a narrow iron bed – such as in the shearers' quarters on the Naracoorte farm – a rickety old clothes cupboard in a corner, a small mirror dulled by age and humidity on a wall, and a kitchen chair next to the bed. Thirsty from constantly perspiring I could have helped myself to a drink of water from a tap in the communal bathroom but – one of the most basic rules of hygiene on Java and after the war in Thailand – in the tropics one should never avail oneself of anything unboiled. I had forgotten to ask the hostel's manager if the local drinking supply was potable and, desperately hot and plagued with a migraine, I longed for a large drink of plain, common cold water.

Tired from the long flight, the emotion of all that was foreign and confusing drained me. Thinking of my poor wife left alone at Millicent, I could not make up my mind if we had done the right thing in applying for the position in New Guinea. Could it have been a bad mistake?

Lunchtime was at noon in the hostel dining room. I joined Administration officers who had recently arrived back from leave 'Down South' – as Australia was often referred to in the Territory – and who, like I, were waiting to be assigned a posting in the field by their Head Office. After lunch I gave in to my tiredness, and in spite of the oven-like temperature in the room I went to sleep until soon after 4 pm, when the donga began to fill up with permanent residents returning from their work. After dinner at 6 pm, when the heat but not the humidity had somewhat subsided, I took a walk to explore the immediate locality. A short stroll down from the hostel I came to where the waters of Fairfax Harbour lapped at a dirty, rubbish-strewn, dark grey sandy beach. The sun had sunk and its last rays briefly painted the horizon a faint pink. It faded so rapidly that a minute or two later it was pitch dark. Not a breath of wind stirred the air, the trying conditions of clammy humidity did not abate, and the suddenness with which the tropical night had arrived accentuated the sensation of having arrived in a different world. When I returned to my donga, whether because of my afternoon sleep, the turmoil of a confused mind, or travel tiredness, sleep eluded me for a long while. When I finally drifted off it was a restive slumber.

First posting

The following day started early, with the hostel residents rising before 6 am, for breakfast at 7 am. Remembering that the working day in Papua and New Guinea started at 7:50, after breakfast I walked the short distance to the Department of Agriculture, Stock and Fisheries Head Office where a junior clerk passed me on to the Administrative Officer, the Department's senior clerk.

I wore one of the pairs of khaki shorts and shirts that the information brochure on Papua and New Guinea from the Department of Territories in Canberra had suggested was 'suitable clothing for the tropics'. Noticing that everyone else in the hostel, on the street, and now in the DASF office was wearing only whites, I felt self-conscious about presenting myself at the Department's Head Office dressed in khakis. But there was nothing I could do, and I was soon ushered in to meet the Administrative Officer – a 'B4' such as my driver and guide had described PNG's long-term residents. I was impressed that, in spite of the hot and clammy weather, his outfit – immaculately starched and ironed long-sleeved white shirt, spotless white shorts and knee-high white walking socks – showed not a crinkle or a dot of perspiration. In comparison I could not but feel under-dressed.

After discussing details about conditions of pay, emoluments and other considerations of service with the Department, I received the most important piece of information: my posting would be at the District Agricultural Demonstration Station at Bainyik, in the Sepik District. The Administrative Officer then added, 'You have been allocated married officer's accommodation on the Station, where there is a native materials house available for you to move into.' These words raised the curtain on our family's future in the Territory: Willy and I had succeeded!

After my interview, before he dismissed me, the Administrative Officer said, 'Welcome to the Department.' Handing me a hard-cover, foolscap notebook titled 'Field Officers Journal', he added, 'Take my advice, young fella. Use your FOJ to daily record things of interest or importance. In the tropics you should not rely too much on memory.' Taking the officer's advice, my first entries in my brand new Journal were gleaned from literature and documents in the Department's library, where I worked for the next few days while waiting for my inaugural posting arrangements to be finalised. While I no longer have my Field Journals, my first entries framed a history of Papua and New Guinea which provided a valuable background which I would later reference on a regular basis to help me understand the attitudes and situations I encountered. What follows is a recollection of the summary notes I made in my first entries.

Field Notes: 5/11/1954

Broadly described as Melanesian, the people of Papua and New Guinea in prehistoric times were hunters. They neither grew crops nor kept animals for food. It remains unknown when agriculture, the purposeful growing of crops for items of the people's staple diet, became practiced in New Guinea. It could have happened on a number of different occasions by different groups of migrating people but, today, in modern times, all New Guinea peoples are gardeners. The most common traditional food crops grown are plants like taro, yam, banana, coconut and a few species of wild plants – sago, sugar cane – and certain kinds of banana and breadfruit. In Papua and New Guinea the villagers depend for their protein on the three domesticated animals of New Guinea – the pig, dog and chicken. They still also hunt wild fowl such as the cassowary and several species of pigeon, migratory wild geese, and wallabies, cascas marsupials and other small game for food, and the several species of birds of paradise for personal decoration and items of prestige, 'wealth'.

Before the coming of the Europeans, the people of New Guinea had developed a system of village subsistence farming, each village producing sufficient food for its needs. Barter and trading involved only a small quantity of specialised goods such as pottery and adze blades and spear points. Each year, at the onset of the north-west monsoon, lagatoi – great trimaran canoes from the Papuan coastal Motu villages – left on the traditional trading expedition, hiri, southwards to the Gulf District. The traders were often away for months, until the beginning of the south-east trade winds, when they could sail back.

Portuguese, Dutch, French, and English seafarers began exploring and charting the New Guinea island coast from as early as the fifteenth century. None established trading posts or colonies on what they considered the inhospitable and economically unsuitable island of New Guinea. In the seventeenth century, great rivalry existed between the French and English that extended to their colonies in North America, India and the Pacific. As a result of competition for new lands to conquer, for a brief period the British attempted to form a settlement in the north-west of the island of New Guinea, but it failed. The first extended contacts by Europeans with New Guinea and its people were European traders. They came for fishing, timber, sandalwood, for the plantation crop of copra from the coconut tree, and for black labour, New Guinean men, to work on the Queensland sugar plantations and in Fiji and Samoa.

The next main contacts between New Guineans and the Europeans came from the missionaries – by the twentieth century, missionaries were working in all the coastal areas of Papua and New Guinea. The pacification of the Papuan hinterland by Australian Administrators, and of New Guinea by German Administrators, extended from the 1800s well into the twentieth century. It often included missionaries whose activity sometimes preceded Administration contact.

In 1884, both Britain and Germany claimed sovereignty over New Guinea, respectively Britain obtained the southern half of the island – Papua – and Germany annexed northern or German New Guinea. In the Australian colonies, in respect of the German presence in New Guinea, fears were rising increasingly as, in the event of war, Australia might find herself threatened by Germany. The Australian colonies wanted Britain to annex New Guinea for several reasons:

If there were profits to be made in Papua they wanted them reserved for British interests, and to protect the steamship route through the Torres Strait;

In the event of war, they were concerned about a European power other than Britain obtaining strategic control of the area.

Representations in 1883 to Britain for it to cede control of the British Protectorate of Papua to Australia initially failed, until in 1884 the eastern Australian colonies agreed to contribute to the cost of administering Papua.

Until the outbreak of the First World War, comparatively little was achieved by either Britain or Germany in their Papua and New Guinea colonies. Both Germany and Britain set up systems of Native Administration, Labour Regulations, Land Sales, Health Services, Education and Economic Development, but neither in German nor British New Guinea did their administration extend far inland from the coasts, and large areas remained untouched until very recently.

The economic development of German New Guinea was slow, export income mainly coming from the production of copra on European-owned plantations but also collected from the villages. Attempts to grow other crops than coconuts mostly failed, but small quantities of cotton, kapok, cocoa, trepang, tortoise shell and pearl shell were exported, though copra always remained the mainstay of agricultural production. In the British Protectorate of Papua there was little plantation development, and the copra that was exported mostly did not come from expatriate plantations. For Papua, the main income came from gold, the first rush occurring in the late 1870s when gold was found inland from Port Moresby. Later rushes occurred in the Louisiade Archipelago, in Milne Bay, the Yodda goldfields up the Mambare River near the German border, and after the First World War at the famous Bulolo goldfields.

At the outbreak of war in July 1914, at the request of the British Government, an Australian Expeditionary Force of 1500 men, the Coconut Lancers, captured German New Guinea administrative headquarters at Rabaul. Having occupied German New Guinea, Australia placed that territory under military administration, but Papua remained under civilian administration. Under the auspices of the League of Nations, Australia took over the administration of the former German colony whereby, after the war, it became the Mandated Trust Territory of New Guinea. The next step was to decide if the mandated territory should be united with Papua but, under the New Guinea Act – passed by the Australian Parliament in 1920 – the mandated territory was organised as a separate unit. In 1921, a civilian government with separate public services replaced the wartime military administration – the Australian New Guinea Administrative Unit (ANGAU) – of what had become the Australian Mandated Territory of Papua and New Guinea.

Until the Japanese invasion in World War Two, the separate territories of Papua and of New Guinea might almost have been foreign countries. There was no free movement of white residents between the two, and it was an offence for a native person to cross the border between Papua and New Guinea without permission. There were even two different lingua franca, trade languages, Pidgin in New Guinea, and Police Motu in Papua.

After the Japanese occupation of New Guinea in 1945, the war brought changes in the region for both Australia and New Guinea. Before the war Australians knew almost nothing about the island to the north, almost on its doorstep. After more than three years of their men fighting in the jungles of New Guinea, Australians became more interested in the country. In 1941, Australia set up the Department of Territories, charged with the advancement of the people of Papua and New Guinea, of facilities in health, education, the economy, law and order, and the eventual greater participation in government.

Before World War Two, economic development in New Guinea and Papua meant mainly European enterprise, but after the war the Administration decided that more attention should be given to development in the villages. The Territory of Papua and New Guinea would develop a rural economy through primary industries, expanding existing agricultural produce mainly of copra, and planting imported cash crops – coffee, cocoa, and later tea and oil palm – thereby creating indigenous and expatriate wealth. The newly created Department of Agriculture, Stock and Fisheries was given the job of helping villagers by teaching them more about cash cropping, and agricultural extension work among the indigenous people became very important. By 1952, the Australian government had begun to vastly increase finance and staff, laying the foundations for the Territory of Papua and New Guinea's economic and political future [xxv].

Leaving Port Moresby

I had been in Port Moresby about a week when the Administrative Officer finalised the details of my posting and travel. At DASF Head Office I received airline tickets from Port Moresby to Wewak in the Sepik District to the north west, and from there on to the District Agricultural Station at Bainyik. Flying with Mandated Airlines – MAL – the Territory's internal airline service, I would stay overnight in Lae before flying on to Wewak the next day. The District Agricultural Officer at Lae had been informed of my arrival and would show me around the District Agricultural Station, where introduced foreign cash crops grew in demonstration plots and where the staff carried out agricultural extension work among indigenous farmers, similar to what my task would be at the Sepik District posting. At Wewak I had been booked in at the hotel, where I would wait for a connecting charter flight to Maprik with the light aircraft company Gibbes Sepik Airways. At Maprik I would be met by local subdistrict staff and taken by road to the Agricultural Demonstration Station near the small village of Bainyik. Looking at me over his desk the Administrative Officer asked, 'Is everything clear? Do you have any questions?' When I replied that I had nothing further to ask, he wished me good luck, and with these few words I was inducted into the twenty years of my service with the Administration of the Australian Territory of Papua and New Guinea.

After I left Head Office, back in my room at the hostel I packed my suitcase to be ready to leave the next day. I did not sleep well during the night – this time not just because of the heat, but also because of the excitement to finally be on my way to my posting. The next morning after breakfast I waited for my transport. It soon turned up, and I was on my way to Jacksons Airport and MAL's so-called 'domestic terminal'.

An unprepossessing building to say the least, MAL's domestic terminal was little better than a large, open tin shed without gates or entry and departure doors, let alone a passenger lounge. Inside the hall, small crowds of locals and a few white people – who, irrespective of their ethnic origin, in the Territory were universally called 'Europeans' – stood waiting to board a now familiar DC3 aircraft, which was parked on the tarmac. In spite of the poor appearance of its terminal, the importance of the airline company's Territory-wide services was unquestionable. As Papua and New Guinea's main internal carrier, Mandated Airlines linked major urban centres in Papua and in New Guinea with the capital Port Moresby. In the almost complete absence of vehicular roads – due to the incredibly mountainous terrain – MAL provided vital cargo and passenger transport services. Where its regional services terminated, local entrepreneurial light aircraft companies then flew passengers and cargo farther inland to Administration Patrol Posts, Agricultural Stations and Missions. These formed the backbone of Australia's pacification and modernisation efforts in yet sub-transitional Papua and New Guinea – poetically termed 'The Land of Past Yesterdays'.

At MAL's dilapidated, quonset 'terminal', preferring to stand out of the hot sun, I joined the 'white' passengers who stood, lounged or sat apart from the 'blacks'. The local travellers squatted or sat surrounded by heaps and stacks of their personal effects. In the crowd of indigenous people, men carried no more than a few personal items, usually only a lime gourd or a small string handbag with some betel nuts or native tobacco in it. But the women were invariably loaded down with often enormously heavy string bags that hung over the back by a strap around their foreheads. In these *billums* they carried a great variety of their personal possessions, including aluminium pots and pans, vegetables – such as taro, sweet potatoes, yams, a hand of bananas – and a host of other items for which I then had no names. Some bags contained a mongrel puppy or a squealing piglet, and in one instance I even saw a small baby fast asleep on top of the baggage. New chum that I was, I felt surrounded by, even immersed in, this exotic scene. Had it not been for the trepidation that I still felt about air travel, coupled with the oppressive heat and the unaccustomed smells in the MAL shed, I might have better enjoyed the experience.

I had been waiting for some time in the MAL building when, without apparent prior warning, people began to stream over to where the DC3 stood parked on the runway. I took the cue and followed the crowd to where a 'European' cabin attendant stood at the door of the plane, directing the passengers inside. Many of MAL's aircraft had been converted from previous wartime service, and people travelled 'side saddle' on benches that ran the length of both sides of the fuselage. Providing the most effective way of carrying both passengers and cargo, the latter was stacked in the middle section of the fuselage, secured from tail to cockpit door by stout, orange webbing that left a narrow isle on either side. Unquestioned by anyone at the time, it was a matter of course that the 'Europeans' occupied the benches up front, which allowed relatively more comfortable leg and headroom, while the locals sat in the less comfortable tail end of the plane. Such was then contemporary Territory air travel.

Flying 'the New Guinea way'

While the aircraft stood parked on the tarmac, doubled over in my seat so that I could look through a porthole, I waited as the flight crew in the cockpit of the DC3 went through the stages of the take-off – testing wing and tail flaps, revving first one and then the other engine, releasing and applying brakes. When all had apparently been found well and functioning, the aircraft began to taxi over the tarmac to the beginning of the take-off runway. Here it briefly halted, then both engines roared into urgent life and we began to move slowly, then faster and faster until the white marker ribbon on the tarmac became a hazy blur. Whether because of its enormous payload or the thin, simmering tropical air I did not know, but I imagined that it took our aircraft a worrying distance to get unstuck from the runway. Finally the nose of the DC3 slowly lifted, and by and by the rest of the aircraft became airborne – we were off into the tropical sky.

Our aeroplane gained altitude, and Port Moresby soon disappeared below us. We first flew in a roughly northerly direction over coastal savannah plains; minutes later the aeroplane banked due north towards Port Moresby's hinterland hills – the Owen Stanley mountain range, part of the Central Cordillera that extends from Milne Bay in the south west to the very opposite tip of the island, in what was then Dutch New Guinea.

The aircraft steadily climbed to higher altitudes until we were directly over the Owen Stanley Ranges with the tropical rainforest jungle below us. Even so soon after the end of the Second World War, little was known in Australia of how Australian soldiers in New Guinea fought and had turned back the then undefeated Japanese Army on the famous Kokoda Trail before they could reach Port Moresby. In the library at Head Office I had read a little of PNG's war-time history and military campaigns. Flying over the jungle-clad mountains, the thought of the breathless tropical heat, the impenetrable green growth, the mud and slush, and the impossibly difficult terrain in which Australian and Japanese soldiers had fought fiercely, a saying by an American general that 'War is hell', struck me as apt and abundantly true.

The DC3 that took us to Lae was not climate controlled, nor was the cabin pressurised. The higher we flew, the colder it became inside and my breathing also became laboured. 'I take it that you're newly from Down South, and I can see that you are not enjoying the flight much, but don't worry,' a fellow passenger reassured me, 'We are presently over the mountains of the Central Cordillera. It separates Papua from New Guinea, and in places reaches more than 14,000 feet above sea level.' He continued, 'We're now at probably 11,000 feet or a little over – that's why it's getting cold inside the old *balus* and, because it is not pressurised, the rarefied air makes breathing a little difficult.' When he noticed my puzzled look, the man laughed, 'Sorry, I used the Pidgin word "balus" which means "bird" – it also stands for "aeroplane".' As we continued our flight, at times we skimmed so close to the mountain crests that one could almost have touched the vegetation. As our balus noisily passed above them, from time to time it frightened flocks of sulphur-crested cockatoos in the trees below. The birds launched from their roost on clouds of white wings. I imagined I could almost hear their raucous, shrieking cries reverberate over the awesome, primeval jungle.

After a while my breathing became easier and when my ears began to crackle I knew that the aircraft was descending and that we must be approaching Lae. We now passed over small clearings where the green expanse of jungle had been disturbed by human habitation, and every now and again I spotted a dozen or so thatch-covered huts grouped around a bare-earthen, clean-swept village square. In and around the hamlets grew breadfruit and coconut trees, and in food gardens in nearby village plots I recognised a range of vegetables – the elephant-eared taro plant, sweet potato vines, cassava bushes, clumps of sugar cane and stands of banana trees. Ahead of the descending DC3 the corrugated jungle hills that rolled out under its wings became welded to a strip of white beach. The sapphire-blue sea lapped at land, where appeared the town of Lae, one of Papua and New Guinea's major urban centres.

Our touchdown was a quite unforgettable event for me. At airports situated in the lowlands of New Guinea, where coastal margins are generally narrow and towering hills reach almost into the sea, landing usually involves an approach from out to seaward. In this case, our DC3 also flew out from the land, making a wide sweep over the sea. When it headed back towards land, Lae's airstrip appeared hardly wide and long enough to me; surely little more than a few furrows-worth of cleared paddock was hardly a runway on which to put down an aircraft. I had learned that having engines at full throttle and the flaps down for air braking control was a normal landing procedure. However, for a new chum like me, the landing at Lae was a very unusual and daunting experience. At the edge of land and sea the tarmac-covered landing field of Lae airport began. Dead in line with our flight path, part of a sunken ship – a bombed relic of the war – towered out of the water. As the distance to the menace ahead of us rapidly closed, my heart was in my throat. My concern was not unreasonable, as it was by no means a fancy of imagination to fear that if the pilot should misjudge the height of the jagged remnants of the ship's bow, it would surely impale his aircraft. As we roared over the menacing obstacle, we successfully cleared the shipwreck – but with not much distance to spare. More breathtaking than romantic, this was my initiation to flying 'the New Guinea way'. When I commented on our daring deed to the cabin attendant he replied, I thought a little condescendingly, 'Piece of cake, no worries!'

Negrita

The bus that drove us to the Qantas hostel at Lae took us through country that this time I recognised as truly tropical and certainly different from the savannah grasslands around Port Moresby. The narrow strip of unsurfaced road on which we travelled through dense rainforest was edged by giant trees and barely disturbed, almost impenetrable, undergrowth. It was very hot, and in the coastal jungle the air smelt of a myriad of things growing, blossoming and flowering, withering and expiring, and originating new life; the cycle of existence in living organisms.

Lae was a much smaller settlement than Port Moresby. We entered via a part of town that was an untidy collection of shopfronts and neglected looking private homes. 'This is Chinatown,' the cabin attendant explained when I asked him about the area, 'Mainly Chinese merchants and tradesmen, and some people of mixed Chinese and PNG background live here. The European residential area and the large department stores such as Burns Philp, are in another part of the town.'

When we reached Lae's expatriate residential area, the streets were wider and the houses of Australian Administration Officers and business people were of noticeably better quality. They were set on large allotments amidst well-tended, colourful gardens where orchids, hibiscus, creamy flowered frangipani and colourful shrubs grew bountifully in the lush soil of the tropical climate. Most residences had screens to insect-proof them against mosquitoes and other tropical pests, and louvered-glass windows promoted maximum air circulation. In comparison with the dwellings in Chinatown, the European homes were statements of power, prestige and privilege – trappings of white colonial rule in New Guinea.

Like Port Moresby, at the Qantas hostel in Lae where MAL and Qantas passengers on international flights stayed in transit, the rooms were sparsely furnished and, in spite of the louvered widows, they were uncomfortably hot inside. Unlike the single men's dongas at Port Moresby where a strict ban was imposed on alcohol on the premises, the Qantas hostel featured a bar of which the residents took much, and evidently early advantage. Although it was well before noon, 'Come and join us, mate,' someone from the MAL flight called when he noticed that

I was on my own. 'My shout. What'll you have, beer, or a negrita?' While I understood the word beer, I had to ask what a negrita was. 'A negrita, my friend, is rum and water,' my new acquaintance explained. 'It's PNG's national drink. Here, let me introduce you to it.' He called out in Pidgin English, 'Boi, wanpella rum ekam long dispela masta,' and by and by the waiter carried my first negrita over to me. It was a concoction for which I would have to develop a taste. From my companion I learned that the beverage made more economical sense when compared with beer. 'Everything that is sent out to us in the bush,' my informant explained, 'has to be airfreighted to an outstation, which puts a considerable charge on top of the retail price. With an average of two dozen shots of rum in a bottle of negrita – compared with only three or four drinks of beer per bottle on which you have to pay the same amount of freight – it makes rum a much cheaper drink than beer. That's why we call beer, "New Guinea champagne". Negrita rum is what people normally drink, see?' We talked, we drank, and when it came my turn, I 'shouted' the PNG beverage of rum and water.

As I did not usually drink much alcohol and I was feeling terribly hot, consuming rum so early in the day did not appeal to me nearly as much as it apparently did to my companions. I was not sorry when my deliverance came. A stranger walked over to us and, mentioning me by name, introduced himself as the *Didiman* from the District Agriculture Station at Lae. 'Head Office advised us that you would be arriving here today, and I've come to show you over our demonstration and experimental plots,' he explained. Glad of an excuse to escape the increasing conviviality of my present company I happily agreed. As we walked away I asked my colleague, 'Sorry, what did you mean by the word "Didiman"?'

'Oh, sorry mate,' my colleague explained, 'You're new up from South. Agricultural Officer in Pidgin English is Didiman, that's what we're called.' He suggested that, since it was noon, before driving me to the Station we should stay at the hostel for *kai*. This time unasked, he explained that in Pidgin English 'kai' is the generic term for food, and that doubling the noun produces the verb – kai kai – which means eating. With these lessons in the lingua franca, I enlarged my Pidgin English vocabulary – which so far consisted of 'masta' and 'boi' – with two more words in the vernacular.

Over lunch in the Qantas mess, although my colleague was courteous and helpful in answering my questions about his work, his mind seemed to be weighed down. Explaining, he apologised, 'Look, I'm sorry, mate. I've asked one of my staff to show you around the Station, as I have to attend a funeral this afternoon. We'll plant two of our neighbours, private coffee planters who were killed by a runaway timber truck on a small mountain track.' This time I understood the local idiom and I silently contemplated the sadness of an expatriate having to witness the burial, the 'planting', of fellow foreigners in alien New Guinea jungle soil.

The District Agricultural Station

After lunch when I was shown over the Agricultural Station I recognised several familiar crops in the demonstration plots – coffee, cocoa, peanuts and dry-land rice. The latter two in particular, my colleague explained, were grown in the Sepik District as a cash crop, forming the basis for developing a local cash economy. The introduction of cash cropping into the local subsistence economy aimed to improve the standard of living and to give the people purchasing power to obtain goods and services that were presently beyond their economic capacity. A humanitarian reason for Australia attempting to introduce a Western cash-based economic system, it was also designed to augment – if not change altogether – the traditional barter dealings of the indigenous society. However, as a *political* objective, whereas the Australian government made large annual grants to the New Guinea Administration, the development of a Western capitalist economy through cash cropping would alleviate the Territory's present dependence on these grants. In addition, the development of a Western-style economy would allow for the introduction of an income tax, which was presently not levied on the public. The indigenous people of Papua and New Guinea could then begin to contribute to payments for and add to the services that the Administration provided, simultaneously becoming less dependent upon the Australian government. With the involvement of the Department of Agriculture field staff, good advancement was being made in implementing this modernisation policy Territory-wide, however, the introduction of cash cropping was proving to be problematic, particularly in regard to the traditional land tenure system. Within the framework of tribal custom, these changes had created legal and social difficulties in the indigenous society, some of which could probably not be solved. As a newcomer, and with no experience in promoting the Australian government's policies in New Guinea, I could not help but notice the almost missionary zeal with which my colleague spoke of his tasks and the objective of the Department. He complained, 'The damn kanakas sometimes don't understand the need for them to change their traditional ways of life. A good kick up the pants now and again helps to change their minds.' His comment reflected his eagerness, but the morality of it did not impress me favourably. In later years I came to question, the 'kick in the pants' approach, and other forms of 'persuasion' that were never officially condoned – and were not confined to Didimen. It seemed to me that this attitude and behaviour was contemporarily seen in the Territory as neither moral nor immoral, but as progress towards a better good; debatably, the end justified the means.

Another exciting flight

The next day, the airport bus took me back to Lae airport for the flight to Wewak – the headquarters of Administration Departments in the Sepik District. Our take off from Lae proved quite as spectacular as the previous day's landing. From out of the window of the DC3, the sunken ship just past the end of the runway clearly showed its bow standing many dozens of feet above the water. Doubts again arose in my mind if we should clear that unforgiving war relic's hurdle or be impaled by it. With brakes straining mightily to hold the aircraft in position, our DC3 pilots revved the engines until they reached full take-off power, and when the brakes were released, we began to charge down the runway towards the peril ahead. As the plane lifted off, I pulled up my legs in an involuntary reaction, and when we thundered over the wreck – the old enemy's handiwork menacingly laid in the way of post-war air traffic – I imagined that the wartime Japanese aviators were laughing gleefully.

Flying out over the sea, when the DC3 had gained sufficient altitude we turned on a course back inland, towards the hills around Lae that extend to the mountain ranges that fringe the vast Ramu River valley. Flying in a north-westerly direction towards the Sepik District and Wewak, I stared down upon the incredibly rugged, awesome New Guinean scenery. High escarpments with deep valleys between them; towering mountains that marched fold upon fold ever farther towards the horizon. In the jungle below us, silver traces of creeks and rivers snaked through an emerald green world of tropical vegetation and rainforest that had lain virginal for so many uncounted ages as to almost defy the notion of time itself. Yet, here and there appeared signs of human life; tiny, tiny patches, mere pinpricks of clearings in the primeval landscape in which human habitation – six, maybe ten huts – stood virtually drowned in a vacuum of undefined space.

After some three or four hours, the now familiar crackling and popping in my ears told me that we were descending on approach to Wewak. Over the mountains and valleys we had met with quite some air turbulence, and when I mentioned this to the cabin attendant he assured me that – especially at this time of year, in the wet season – this was nothing untoward or unexpected. However, whereas on previous landings at Port Moresby and Lae we had experienced excellent visibility, nearing Wewak today we were enveloped in dense cloud, and our aeroplane scudded through banks of driving rain with not a break on the now obscured horizon.

The flashes of lighting that forked out of the towering, black, monsoon rain clouds did nothing to reassure me, and my heart was palpitating even worse than it had done when we had to clear the shipwreck at Lae. Even without visibility, increased G-force pressure inside the cabin indicated that our aircraft must be in a flight pattern, possibly circling over Wewak below us?

Banking and dipping, the wings of the plane tipping angularly into cloud, we kept flying around for quite some time. Suddenly, so unexpectedly that I thought that this time we were in real trouble, our aircraft dived down into the cloud mass with both its engines screaming. In my consternation I involuntarily grabbed the arm of the man next to me on the bench seat. 'She'll be right, cobber,' he reassured me. 'Our pilot has found a hole in the clouds, the chance he's been waiting for to dive through this muck. See, there's the airstrip,' he pointed to where I could indeed now see land below. My informant continued, 'In the Territory this often happens. I take it that you're fresh from South, but you'll get used to it, no worries,' he said, as I somewhat shamefacedly let go of his arm. When shortly later we landed safely at Wewak, I had survived yet another experience of flying the New Guinea way.

Apart from a small shed on one edge of the runway, there was nothing at Wewak's Boram airstrip that looked like an airport terminal. On the grass with my suitcase beside me, I watched fellow passengers walk over to where vehicles stood parked with family or friends who had awaited their arrival. There was no one who had come to meet me, and there was not even an airport bus or other means of transport that could take me to Wewak. The man who had sat next to me in the plane had got into an old jeep parked on the side of the airstrip. I was glad when he offered, 'Hop in with me if you like. It looks that there's no one to pick you up, but I'll drive you to the pub where I guess you'll be staying?'

'Yes, thank you,' I said, relieved.

Wewak

Wewak township, Sepik District's regional centre, is built about 100 feet above sea level, on a coral island connected to the mainland by a man-made causeway. In the mid-1950s its 200-odd European residents all lived on the island, where there were fewer mosquitoes, and sea breezes somewhat alleviated the tropical heat and humidity of the mainland. Beyond the causeway of crushed coral dust, the road continued into the island's interior. On either side of the street stood houses, built on stumps some 6 feet above ground level to promote air circulation. Like at Port Moresby and Lae, the expatriate residences were mostly of timber construction and had wide verandas and louvered, insect-proofed windows. On the drive up from Boram airstrip to Wewak, I learned that my acquaintance worked for the Department of Native Affairs (DNA). When I volunteered that I was a 'Didiman' on my way to Bainyik he laughed with good humour and said, 'You're quickly picking up the Pidgin lingo.'

At the island's far edge, where the Pacific Ocean washes the sandy, black strip of beach some 100 feet below, the DNA officer stopped the old jeep. 'This is the Wewak Point pub, where you'll be staying,' he said, adding with a twinkle in his eye, 'I won't charge you a taxi fare, but if you insist you may shout me a beer.'

The Wewak Point Hotel, well named for its commanding position at the edge of the island, was a true olden-time Territory-style building. In contrast to most Territory housing, which was raised from the ground, the hotel stood on a concrete floor base. With *kwila* (hardwood) corner posts and framework, the external walls were of sawn timber planks and sheets of pleated bamboo, and the roof was covered not with corrugated iron, but with sago leaf thatch. The main premises – its lounges, bar, dining room and kitchens – were all of grand proportions and the guest rooms, 'dongas', stood separately in the grounds, a little distance from the main building. Situated on the highest elevation of Wewak Island there was always air movement – breezes came off the sea below and wafted around the premises, keeping the humidity and heat more tolerable. From the veranda on which I stood, no more than a dozen steps would take me to the very edge of the island, where the Pacific Ocean stretched out to a far horizon on the blue-black sea.

A few drinks later, when my benefactor left, the hotel was quiet and empty except for a handful of dedicated barflies, perhaps people in transit or beach-comber types with nothing better to do. After checking in at the desk I lay down for a rest in my room in one of the dongas until, soon after four o'clock in the afternoon – close of business in New Guinea – people began to arrive and a buzz of conversations sprang up in the lounges and on the terrace. Frequent shouts, '*Boi!*' rang out, and the Wewak Point Hotel began to fulfil its reason for being. In the Territory no early closing time was imposed, avoiding the notorious, frenetic between 5–6 pm 'swill' in Australian pubs. Down 'South', at 5.55 came the barman's warning, 'Last drinks, gents!' followed at six o'clock sharp by, 'Time! Everyone out please!' In the Territory, patrons could continue to pursue their favourite pastime, their dedicated imbibing of the Territory's national rum drink, 'Boi! Wanpela negrita ekam.'

The next morning, soon after breakfast, I went to present myself to the District Commissioner (DC), the senior administration official in the Sepik District – who, I discovered, was another typical B4 Territorian, resplendent in starched, immaculately ironed, white long-sleeved shirt worn without a tie, Bombay Bloomer type white shorts and long white walking socks. Still attired in my khaki shirt, shorts and socks,

I was again conscious of how the District Commissioner's appearance contrasted with mine, making me feel uncomfortable and somewhat inadequate. The visit to the District Commissioner brought me the welcome news that tomorrow I was booked to leave on a Gibbes Sepik Airways plane, as he termed it, 'on the milk run to Maprik'. There, the Assistant District Officer would arrange my further transport by road to the Bainyik Agriculture Station. At the conclusion of the interview the District Commissioner suggested, 'Before you leave Wewak, you may like to call at Tang Mow's store to buy a supply of foodstuff to last you for a couple of weeks. You should also make arrangements at Tang's for deliveries of bread, meat and vegetables on the Gibbes Sepik Airways milk run, which is how people on outstations such as Bainyik get their weekly supplies of fresh food.'

Tang Mow Trade Store

After I left the District Commissioner's office, I made my way to Wewak's Tang Mow Trade Store, located at a low point of the island where the sea almost lapped at the doorstep of a collection of huts and poorly constructed houses. In comparison, Tang Mow's Trade Store – owned by the remarkable Mr Tang Mow – was grand and apparently the local equivalent of Port Moresby's emporiums. Tang Mow's background and exploits had undoubtedly made him one of the Sepik District's identities and 'A Very Important Person' in his own right. The story of his life in the Territory began many decades earlier when he came to Papua and New Guinea from his native China to find employment and hopefully his fortune. He had first worked on the gold diggings at Wau and Bulolo, and when he had saved up enough money to start a business of his own, he began recruiting local labour for the goldfields and the plantation industry. After many years he left the goldfields, resettling at Wewak. Having become sufficiently well off to buy a small motorboat – which he called the *Susu*, Pidgin for milk – he began a 'milk run', trading with villages up and down the mighty Sepik River. His expeditions carried him past the upstream village of Ambunti where the vast swamplands of the Middle Sepik begin and where huge mosquitoes mercilessly torture man and beast day and night. Thanks to Tang Mow's iron will, determination and tireless industry, his business prospered until he eventually consolidated his life's work by setting up the local equivalent of a department store at Wewak, stocking everything from kerosene to caviar and – not to be overlooked – considerable supplies of the Territory staple, negrita.

When I called at Tang Mow's, it was his daughter-in-law – competent and charming Dorothy Tang – who came to my assistance. Welcoming me as a new arrival and customer, Dorothy helped me put together what seemed to me an enormous list of supplies to take to Bainyik the next day. In Australia, working in Mr Drouin's grocery store, I had known some farmers who had put in large orders, but those now paled in comparison with what Dorothy advised I should need for the next couple of months. Full cartons of bully beef (forty-six tins), tinned vegetables, mixed jams, peanut butter, honey, tea, Sunshine-brand milk powder (twelve tins), a 20-pound bag each of rice, flour and salt, several cartons of cigarettes, and of course a crateful of negrita rum (twelve bottles). The bill that came at the end of my shopping spree seemed a staggering amount, but when Dorothy noticed my apprehension she quickly reassured me, 'Don't worry about paying me right now. We'll send you the account and you can pay us when you're settled in at Bainyik.' With Mr Drouin's customers in mind, many who also paid their bills periodically, I agreed that the arrangement suited me under the circumstances. Back at the Wewak Point hotel I realised that, for the first time since I had been married, I had incurred a debt. However, I reflected, as a public servant, paying up my dues should not intimidate me quite as much as it would have done in less secure employment down South. In Papua and New Guinea, I had achieved a career path, my employment was safe, and my wife would soon join me – we had indeed 'made it'!

The milk run

Due to a combination of the sticky humidity and the heat, the excitement of the day's events and the anticipation of travelling the next morning to my posting, that night I stayed awake for a long time. After too few hours of restless sleep, I got up early and stood on the veranda with my gear packed ready to leave, watching the sun rise brilliantly out of the Pacific Ocean. Previously when I arrived at Wewak there had been no one waiting for me at the Boram airstrip, but today the District Commissioner had arranged for transport, in time for that morning's flight to Maprik, where I would be driven on to Bainyik.

When I arrived at Boram, instead of the DC3 that I had expected, a small aircraft – a venerable biplane that I later learned was a De Havilland Dragon – stood parked on the grass strip. Compared with the sturdy DC3 aircraft, the Dragon's size, fabric-covered fuselage and especially its two puny, dismally small engines suspended between its wings little impressed me. I could hardly believe that this contraption could actually fly and keep itself, passengers and cargo aloft. Adding to my disquiet, nonchalantly leaning against the Dragon I spotted 'Young Doug', to whom I had last evening been introduced. Almost a youth still, and less than an inspiring figure, Doug had spent his evening in the bar at the Wewak Point Hotel – the glass in his hand being one of who knows how many previous negritas. When I learned that Doug would be the pilot of the rickety contraption that really did not deserve the title of 'aeroplane', my apprehension was not eased in the slightest.

The aircraft was loaded and ready for take-off, and as I was the only passenger, Young Doug invited me to sit next to him in the seat normally occupied by a co-pilot. From my vantage point, I was able to watch the pilot going through his routine of checks before take-off – a list of procedures including moving the wing and tail flaps, pushing a number of switches and overhead toggles on the aircraft's dashboard, and, with the engines started, a variety of other safety checks. Take-off preparations apparently completed, Doug released the plane's brakes, and we began the run down the grass strip. In spite of my earlier misgivings, well before the end of Boram's runway our De Havilland Dragon came easily unstuck. As the old balus flew at its cruising speed of barely 90 knots, I had a grand aerial view of the Sepik District countryside.

Before we left Boram, Doug advised that heavy cloud was blanketing Maprik, preventing our landing. Instead, we would land at Hayfield, an alternate airstrip. The Assistant District Officer at Maprik had been advised of the changed flight plan, and arrangements had been made for me to be met at Hayfield and driven on to Bainyik. Ahead of us loomed the Torricelli Mountains that divide the Wewak coastal fringe from the Sepik Plains. When we crossed the mountains, beneath us unfolded vast wetlands dotted with small islands – mere elevations out of the surrounding swamp – mainly covered with sago palm. After a while the countryside changed and we flew over hundreds of square miles of vast, dry, rolling grasslands. Here and there I spied small creeks or billabongs, pockets of trees and vegetation and occasionally a small village. The terrain below us was gradually rising towards the distant hills of the Maprik subdistrict. We had been flying for about an hour when Doug pointed ahead to where the savannah abruptly ended and rainforest rose out of the grassland – as sharply as if someone had demarcated a line with compass and pencil. 'We're close to Hayfield,' Doug told me. 'Bainyik station lies just inside the bush – before I land I'll give the people there a buzz to let them know that they can send someone to pick you up at the strip.' I could see the airstrip in the grassland ahead, but instead of landing there we flew on above heavy rainforest, until we were over a large clearing in the jungle. Doug advanced the throttle, diving down so close above the trees that I was sure they would catch in the undercarriage Doug yelled 'Bainyik!' over the engine noise and pointed to a small cluster of buildings, where I saw a white-clad figure waving at us. The Dragon pulled out of its dive and regained altitude, and as we made our way back to Hayfield I added to my vocabulary the meaning of the word 'buzz' – a contemporarily common (if perhaps not legally approved) aeronautical way of alerting people on an Administration or Mission settlement that today, the aircraft had something on board for them.

Flying back over the grasslands, we made ready to land at Hayfield airstrip. As we approached, I noticed at the far end of the runway two small, forlorn, native materials houses and a cluster of sheds – an almost incongruous mark of human habitation in the vastness of the Sepik Plains country. Many Territory airstrips were often no longer than the minimum Short Take-Off and Landing (STOL) distance – regulation prescribed at least 1,500 feet of cleared runway for light aircraft. However, Hayfield strip was generously proportioned, wide and long enough to allow even a DC3 aeroplane to land on it. We put down with ease, and on the ground Doug piloted the Dragon towards the small settlement, cutting off the engines where several New Guineans and two men in Territory whites stood waiting. The New Guineans reached us first, and Doug put them to work unloading bags of rice, flour and salt, and cartons with tinned meats, fish, and other undefined cargo wrapped in hessian or other covering materials.

I noticed that one of the two 'Europeans' who approached us walked almost doubled over, with both hands clutching his right leg at the knee. The reason for this was a huge, red-raw, tertiary burn injury that extended from halfway down his inner thigh to his foot. His companion was a tall, thick-set, middle-aged man. 'G'day, Doug,' he said to the pilot, and turning to me, 'G'day, I'm Roy Lane, and my mate here is Freddy Strainey.' After a moment he added the rather obvious understatement 'Freddy has a bit of a problem with his leg.' I introduced myself to the men and we exchanged a few words about the flight and the weather, then Roy remarked, 'You must be the new fella they're expecting at Bainyik?'

At this point Doug announced that the labourers had completed unloading the cargo and it was time for him to be off. I thanked him for the ride, he hopped back into his cockpit, the engines spluttered into life, and this time from on the ground I watched the old Dragon take off from Hayfield. As the plane trundled down the runway she looked like a rheumatic old lady, her fuselage and double-decker wings swaying. The curious contraption slowly gathered speed, until after a seemingly long run it lifted from the ground and lumbered off into the Sepik District airspace, towards its next stop on the weekly 'milk run'.

Learning about local business

'Come and have a *muli* at our place while you wait for your transport from Bainyik to arrive,' Roy Lane suggested. Since there was nothing for it but to wait, I gladly accepted the invitation and, in deference to Freddy's terrible injury, we slowly made our way to Roy's place – one of the houses that I had spotted from the air. Seated in somewhat dilapidated and mould-stained wicker chairs on the small veranda, my host called out 'Hausboi, bringim tripela muli ekam!' A little later, a servant appeared with a tray holding three glasses of muli – cumquat lemonade. 'Sorry we can't offer you a rum,' Roy apologised, even at this early hour of the morning. 'We've run out of negrita until we unpack the gear that came on today's balus,' he explained.

Adopting the Australian idiom, I responded 'No worries'. Speaking for myself and not a fib, I added, 'It's a bit early for me.'

We talked as we sat and drank our muli. At only 10 am it was already even more stifling here than it had so far been in Port Moresby, Lae, or at Wewak. In the blazing sun the kunai grass plain radiated an intense shimmering heat, and without a breath of wind to bring relief, the country and everything in it baked. I perspired freely, but to my envy I noticed little if any discomfort from Roy and Freddy. 'You'll get used to the climate,' Roy promised, 'You're fresh from South and it will take a while.'

After Doug had 'buzzed' Bainyik Station, Roy said, it would take at least a half to three-quarters of an hour before I would be collected at Hayfield. 'The Station jeep is US, out of order, un-serviceable,' he explained. 'Instead, you'll be picked up by their tractor and trailer.' The talk returned to exchanging information about each other. Although I wondered what had caused Freddy's injury, I did not think it polite or appropriate to ask what had happened, and neither man volunteered the information. But otherwise Roy seemed to welcome the chance to talk to a stranger. 'Freddy and I are Traders. We do business with the locals in our trade store, selling tinned fish, bully beef, rice, flour, sugar, tea, kerosene, matches, the kind of European goods and things that the locals like and want to buy. Of course, we also stock lots of Native Twist trade tobacco and red lap-laps'. When I asked what Native Twist was, my genial host explained that it was coarse, low-grade tobacco soaked in sugar and rum, pressed and cut into roughly 12-inch lengths and twisted into double-pleated strands. The locals cut up small portions of this 'Twist', then pluck it out into thin threads that they roll in newspaper into long, sometimes foot-long, 'cigarettes'. 'It's poisonously pungent stuff that makes your eyes almost pop out of their sockets when you inhale the smoke, but they love it,' said Roy. When I asked him why they sold *red* lap-laps in their store, Roy explained, 'Khaki lap-laps are a standard issue to local staff employed by government Departments and in private enterprise. If a khaki lap-lap is stamped with a fat black arrow on it, those are prison outfits. So as you can imagine, khaki is not a very popular colour.' He continued, 'An important part of our business is that we recruit labourers from out in the bush, signing them up for two years indentured labour on copra and rubber plantations. From time to time we send out word to the villages, and when their young chaps sign on with us and we have filled an order from an employer, we fly the group to Wewak and from there they travel on by boat or by air to the plantation at which they have been contracted. Some of our colleagues, but not us, risk working in only recently pacified areas. The people there are generally keen to sign on for a chance to experience the world outside their traditional home grounds. With the people only recently contacted by Europeans, access to these areas is exclusively restricted to Administration *Kiaps* and police. Before people in private enterprise – such as we recruiters or even the missions – are allowed to enter these newly opened up parts of the country, official permission has to be first obtained.' When I asked him what he meant by the word kiap, Roy said that in Pidgin English it was the word for 'Patrol Officer', 'The same as how, in PNG, you and your colleagues are known as Didimen.' He went on to say that signing up for indentured labour was especially popular among the young men, as the village youths were generally keen to explore the exciting world outside their villages. 'For the young chaps, going to work on a plantation increases their eligibility to marry a village lass. When they return, they bring highly prized goods for the bride price – axes, knives, aluminium saucepans and other stuff that they've bought with the money they earned. After a couple of months in the bush, contacting and signing up villagers, a recruiter sometimes returns with a 'line' of a hundred or more 'bois'. When they have fulfilled their contract and they return home, you can easily pick the 'finishtaim bois' by the orange-painted wooden box that they carry on their heads. In these 'finishtaim boxes' they bring back to their village the things they have bought in the towns. That gives them the edge over other 'stay-at-home' hopefuls, being able to pay an eligible girl's parents the bride price for their daughter. The older men, the village leaders, sometimes resent the young fellows being away from the village, because they fear that they have lost some control over them. Also, these adventurers return with treasures and prestige that the traditional village elders cannot match, and their envy can then make things sticky for the young men – and occasionally also for the recruiters who next come to the village to look for labour.'

After a while longer of talking about their life and business in the area, Roy sat up a little straighter. 'That's your transport from Bainyik come to collect you,' he said, pointing to a tractor and a trailer that had emerged from the fringes of bush that bordered the airstrip.

CHAPTER 18

Bainyik

From where I sat on Roy's veranda, I watched as an old model W6 International tractor drew up on the airstrip beside the stack of cargo earlier unloaded from the plane. It was driven by a young New Guinean with a huge smile on his face and lips stained with the red of betel nut juice. When the tractor came to a halt, the four men who had come on the trailer began to load up the goods, which were evidently bound for Bainyik. They made sure to leave room around a forward-facing canvas chair, which was lashed to the deck of the trailer with ropes. When they had completed the job, the driver – who had remained grandly seated while his companions laboured – drove the tractor up to where we waited. My host exchanged a few words in Pidgin with the New Guinean, then said, 'You can hop on now, the bois are ready to take you to Bainyik.' I thanked both he and Freddy for their hospitality and, prompted by Roy, I sat myself in the canvas chair. After the driver had importantly, albeit unnecessarily, revved the tractor's engine several times, we drove off – with me feeling self-conscious in the seat, as yet unaccustomed to being treated as a *'masta'*, a colonial white man in New Guinea.

When we entered the dense rainforest that began only a few hundred feet from Roy and Freddy's trade store, the surface of the unmade roadway became slippery. But, somewhat to my dismay, the driver – who had set the tractor on a cracking pace – took no notice at all of the ruts and deep potholes, ploughing through them at undiminished speed. The young New Guineans who had loaded the cargo at Hayfield helped to hold my chair steady as I was bumped around, but I would have much preferred to sit less precariously on the deck of the trailer with them. Adding to my discomfort, and inadvisable for safety's sake, the tractor driver started an animated discussion with me in Pidgin, looking back at me over his shoulder as he spoke. Although I understood very little of the lingua franca, when he pointed at himself and repeated the word *Pogginangu*, I gathered that he was telling me his name – but as I did not know how to respond, I just smiled at him in recognition. Chatting away, and paying very little attention to his driving, Pogginangu kept up what I felt was an unsafe speed over the rough bush track, with the trailer frequently wagging like a happy puppy dog's tail behind the tractor as we slid from side to side in mud and slush.

Suddenly, and happily without feared mishap, our transport burst out of the semi-darkness of the jungle into tropical sunshine. As we passed plots that had been cultivated with several plant species, I recognised coffee and cacao trees, rice, peanuts and 'European' vegetables. New Guinean labourers working in the plots stopped and stared – at the tractor, at the cargo, or at the new 'masta', I could not tell. I also noticed tall kapok trees lining the track. In them hung ripened pods, the fluff from which people in Indonesia used to make stuffing for pillows and mattresses. Pogginangu became even more animated and he released a torrent of words, of which, as he pointed to a collection of native materials buildings, I picked out the repeated, 'Bainyik, Bainyik, Masta!'

First day at Bainyik

Later, on the veranda of his house, the Officer in Charge of the Bainyik District Agricultural Demonstration Station, Ron McCarthy, poured his wife Eileen a muli drink, and a glass of negrita and water for himself and me. I had expected him to be another old-timer, a B4 like my Director in Port Moresby or the District Commissioner at Wewak, but I judged that the man was only a year or two older than me. He and his wife, he told me, had also not long been married. 'We are glad to have you on Bainyik', Ron had said when I arrived on the tractor trailer. 'Eileen especially is looking forward to another woman on the Station, and we both hope that your good lady will soon join us. Your predecessor, a married man, left with his young family a few months ago and poor Eileen, the only white woman on the Station, has been feeling rather lonely.'

When Ron used the word 'lonely' I could not but agree with him about the isolation of the hundred-odd acres of cleared land in which the Station stood, a mere speck in the unending green expanse of the Territory's jungles. From the air, tenuous pinpricks of villages had occasionally appeared on the landscape, and that morning as I flew over Bainyik in the Dragon, it had seemed to me that the Station was no less isolated, truly a Territory outstation in the midst of New Guinea's tropical rainforest.

The Agricultural Demonstration Station was like nothing I had ever seen before. The houses were all beautiful, although made of 'native materials'. The Station was situated on a rise in the terrain, about fifty feet above a small mountain stream aptly called the Screw River – for the way that it twisted a snaking course through the forest, sometimes almost backing up on itself. In the low-lying areas on the Station grew pockets of sago swamp, which oddly enough provided the Station and its inhabitants with water for all purposes. Except, Eileen said, that drinking water in the tropics had to always be boiled. Her husband explained that the tannin released by the sago roots was thought to be a purifier, so the water out of the swamp was of a better quality than that from the river – which was possibly contaminated by upstream village life. 'It's a bit dark,' Ron said, holding up the carafe from which he had poured the boiled swamp water he added to my rum, 'but it's safer to drink than the river water.'

The conversation turned to our Maprik subdistrict Administration headquarters, and I mentioned that when we flew over the Agricultural Station, Doug the pilot had pointed a distance farther into the clouds and said that the settlement was only some 6 miles from Bainyik. Ron smiled. 'Yes, well, Maprik is indeed only a few miles distance from here as the crow flies,' he said, 'but wait till you hit the road to it. Even under favourable conditions it takes us close to an hour to get there in the jeep.' The unsurveyed jungle track ran through the narrow Screw River valley, up a steep mountain spur and down again into the next valley where Maprik lay. When it rained, Ron said, the muddy track sometimes became impassable. Occasionally, unpredictable flash flooding of the river made travelling by jeep to the subdistrict settlement impossible, as the ford became swollen with unstoppable run-off from its vast catchment area. The Station did not have radio contact with Maprik, and in an emergency the best that could be done was to send a messenger with a letter wrapped in oil-skin to keep it dry. Holding the missive by a cleft stick in his teeth, the messenger would climb hand-and-foot across a stout rope that spanned the banks to the opposite side of the Screw River, and would then proceed to Maprik on foot. Ron's words were undramatic, a bald statement of the facts of life of living on an outstation in the jungles of New Guinea.

The McCarthy's invited me to stay with them for lunch, and Eileen mentioned that tonight there would be a twenty-first birthday party for the wife of one of the Department of Native Affairs Patrol Officers at Maprik. 'You're coming with us, of course?' my hostess asked, in what was really a statement. 'It'll be a perfect chance for you to meet just about everybody in the subdistrict.' Then, as she looked me over, dressed as I was in my khakis – dead giveaways of a new chum – she asked, 'You do have your sharkskins, don't you?' When I confessed that I did not possess 'sharkskins' and did not know what they were, Eileen explained, 'Sharkskin is a kind of fabric, and it is also what people here call men's long trousers. They are hot to wear, rather sticky and slippery like silk, and difficult to wash and iron. But the men usually dress in them for parties or on official occasions. If you don't have a pair of your own yet, my husband will lend you one of his for tonight's celebration.' I did not think it diplomatic to say so, but I was tired from travelling and confused with all the new, surprising, intriguing impressions. As everything was so strange and unusual to me, I was not looking forward to meeting fellow expatriates so soon. However, I realised that my acceptance of Eileen's 'invitation' was a foregone conclusion – I would, 'of course', come with them, and my, 'Yes, thank you,' was merely a polite formality. I surrendered to what was inevitable, and 'the right thing to do'.

After lunch Ron showed me over the house where Willy and I would live on Bainyik. There was a huge housing shortage at the time, so we were very lucky. In Port Moresby, the Director had warned that it was constructed of 'native materials' – a term I had not understood until I saw the construction of the Wewak Point Hotel and the houses at Hayfield. The small, two-bedroom residence allocated to us was raised off the ground on stout kwila posts; the external and internal walls and ceilings were single sheets of pleated bamboo, and the roof was thatched with sago leaf fronds. Prevalent on outstations throughout Papua and New Guinea, the flooring was lengths of black palm harvested from the forest and split in half to be laid side-by-side with the rounded side up, making a corrugated surface to walk on. The house had no windows, only openings in the walls with hinged shutters made from the ubiquitous pleated bamboo material. These could be propped up with a stick, providing air circulation and letting in light, or in wet weather they could be lowered to keep out the rain.

Our residence had no doors, even for the two bedrooms, but when I remarked on this Ron laughed, 'We don't need them here. You can be sure that none of the workers will dare come inside a European's home. Our labour line is a quiet lot, and we have top *bosbois* to keep them that way. The locals at nearby Bainyik village are also quite alright, not a bad mob, and the Assistant District Officer at Maprik keeps an eye on them.' Inexperienced in the ways of New Guinea living, I did not debate the point, except to somewhat lamely argue, 'My wife would feel more comfortable *with* a door.' Before he left me to settle into my Bainyik home, Ron promised that our carpenter would make us a door for the main bedroom.

Before unpacking my suitcase, I made a closer inspection of the house in which Willy and I would live for the next two years. In the sitting room were six folding canvas so-called 'Manus' chairs. Separated from the sitting room by a low wall, the dining area was outfitted with a laminex table and six chrome chairs – standard government-issue furniture. In the main bedroom the furniture consisted of a double bed, a chest of drawers and a hanging wardrobe, and the second bedroom had only two single beds. Our 'bathroom', at the end of a passage between the bedrooms, had neither a bathtub nor plumbing, but a shower bucket that hung by a rope over a block and tackle. This contraption needed to be manually filled with lukewarm bathing water, prepared on the stove in the kitchen. In the kitchen, a kerosene refrigerator stood in one corner and a wood stove in the other, and along one wall stood a rough, homemade bench on which to prepare and serve the food. Completing the furnishings, fixed timber shelving on the kitchen walls provided space for storing pots, pans and cooking utensils, and beside the back steps – which led down from the kitchen to the outside – stood several 44-gallon drums. These held all of the household's daily water supply, drawn manually from the sago swamp. A few yards farther stood the 'smallest room in the house', a generously proportioned outside 'dunny'.

None of Bainyik's residences, married quarters, or the single men labour line dormitories were reticulated or had sewer laid on. So, from our 100-strong labour force, a number of men drew water for all the Station community's needs. Another permanent work party, the so-called *mumuts*, collected the nightsoil pans from each of the Station's toilet facilities, disposing of the contents in a large pit dug at the edge of the bush. Within the Station community at Bainyik, not merely by dint of their unenviable work, the nightsoil collectors were a distinctive group. The nature of this lay within the traditions of Papua and New Guinean society. In many pre-modern cultures, much credence is given to the assumed workings of the supernatural – and traditional New Guinea was no exception. People in the villages generally lived in fear of black magic – *poisin* in Pidgin – and of evil spirits – *massalai*. Reputedly *the* most powerful ingredient in working black magic against a person was any kind of body leavings from a potential victim – hair, nail clippings, crumbs of food, and the most powerful of all, excrement. Given these superstitions, it was not difficult to see why the mumuts on Bainyik were an elite group, and if they were not necessarily feared by their compatriots, they were at least looked upon askance. The mumuts were not only held in a measure of awe by their fellows, but they were also envied for the extra tobacco they received in their in-kind weekly wages.

A matter of interest for us 'Europeans' was that the Station lacked an electricity supply. Every house on Bainyik, including ours, depended on kerosene pressure lamps, supplemented by wick oil lamps, for lighting. Eileen had already offered to sell me two Tilley pressure lamps, several hurricane lamps, and two wick kerosene lights left behind by my predecessors. Having taken stock of my new home, I drew up a shopping list for Tang Mow's at Wewak. Given the need to provide light in our house, I told Ron that I had included a 44-gallon drum of kerosene in my shopping list, but that it would not be available to me until the next Wewak milk run. 'Don't worry, I'll lend you some of mine,' Ron generously promised. Further adding to my list, I decided to purchase a set of cane furniture that would be more comfortable seating than the Manus chairs, and – not to be forgotten – I made sure to also order several pairs of white shorts, shirts, walking socks, and a pair of 'sharkskins', which would make me look less of a Territory new chum than I presently did in my khaki gear.

Before we were due to leave for the birthday party at Maprik, and because I had no servant yet to heat my bathwater, I took a cold shower from the camping bucket. I was beginning to worry about how Willy would react to having to make her home in a small grass hut in the New Guinea jungle. Mrs Hurley at Millicent had called New Guinea 'a place of snakes and savages, cannibals and crocodiles'; to her derogatory opinion I now added a mental picture of our house without doors or windows, which could let mosquitoes, insects and other vermin enter practically unimpeded from the jungle around us.

Throughout the afternoon it had rained and thundered heavily. 'It always does at this time of the year,' said Ron, as he, Eileen and I boarded the wartime-salvaged jeep, ready to leave for tonight's birthday party. 'Fortunately the old Screw River is not flooding,' Ron continued, 'though the road will be very slippery and it'll take us more than an hour to get to Maprik.' When I expressed surprise that it would take us that long to travel the few miles to the Administration Centre, he responded wryly, 'You'll find out.' At Ron and Eileen's advice we were all dressed in working clothes, our good outfits packed in a canvas bag, 'so that our party gear won't get covered in grease and rust'. Piled onto the bare seats of the battered wartime jeep, without even a canopy to shelter us from the still falling drizzle, the tired old vehicle coughed into unconvincing life and we were off to Maprik. Eileen, who was evidently looking forward to the occasion, smiled, 'It's the big smoke for us!'

Driving to Maprik
Before we crossed the Screw River ford Ron briefly stopped the vehicle, putting it into four-wheel drive and asking Eileen, 'Put your foot between the gear sticks, dear?' To me he explained, 'The old jeep

has a habit of jumping out of gear, and we can't afford for it to stop in the middle of the river.' Then with the brief instruction to 'Hang on!' we were headed for the fast running but fortunately not too deep water, which came to just below the vehicle's rust pocked floor. With the engine turning over at low speed and the gears held in low ratio by Eileen's foot, we made steady progress through the mountain stream, though every now and then our transport sank into an undetected hole or swayed alarmingly between rocks on the riverbed. When we emerged from the water, Ron remarked, 'Piece of cake today, the old Screw's not running much,' as he steered the dripping old jeep onto the track to Maprik.

About half a mile past the river crossing, Ron said, 'This is Bainyik village.' The track ran past a dozen or so huts situated around a clean-swept village square; the small settlement had on one side a spectacular *Haus Tambaran*, one of the huge Sepik River ceremonial spirit houses. Built in a half-moon wedge-shape, the front of the Haus Tambaran was at least 30 feet tall and slanted at an angle inwards to the ground where the building measured about 15 feet wide. A single kwila timber pole dug deep into the ground was the main stay from which bush timber poles, sloping down like the ribs on an enormous dinosaur, formed the mainframe of the spirit house. The entire outside structure was covered with sago leaf thatch, but under the eaves of the inwards slanting front panel the cladding consisted of sheets of the peeled skin from the sago palm, a parchment-like material decorated with traditional designs painted in ochres and natural dyes. On one side at the front of the spirit house, an entrance 4 feet high and 3 feet wide – less than the average height of a person – seemed out of proportion in such an enormous building. 'A Haus Tambaran – a spirit house – is exclusively a men's kind of club that is out of bounds even to white women – and at pain of death forbidden to village females,' Ron explained. 'Inside, the tribe keeps spirit images, carved and painted figures, and from time to time the men hold secret initiation and other rites. I have been inside this one only once, but I'm not too keen to do it again – it feels quite eerie in there.' Before the jeep disappeared into the dense bush, I caught a glimpse of the village huts, miniatures of the Haus Tambaran, raised from the damp rainforest earth on stumps. In front of some of the huts, in the darkness of the early evening, people sat with the skin of their bare upper bodies glowing red in the shine of cooking fires. A troop of village dogs had appeared and came running after us, yowling and barking. Above the din of our vehicle's engine and the yapping of the bad-tempered mongrels, from somewhere inside the village I could hear the peculiar twanging nasal sound of a jew's harp played by an unseen person.

Haus Tambaran (spirit house) at Bainyik, Terry's first posting in PNG.

When we arrived at Maprik it was pitch dark. If the river crossing had been an unaccustomed experience for me, our drive on the steep and slippery track had been even more so. In the inky darkness the uncertainly functioning headlights of the old jeep had been barely able to light the way ahead. Every now and then Ron had yelled 'Gears!' and Eileen had responded by wedging a work-shoe-clad foot between the high and low ratio handles on the floor. Cleared of most of the larger stumps and rocks, the 'road' to Maprik – really no better than a track – snaked up and down smaller and larger hills. Whoever had built it had apparently simply followed an old footpath, or had paid less attention to surveying gradients than to connecting Bainyik and Maprik by the shortest route. In our tired old jeep, we sometimes barely made it to the top of a hill. In other places, in a heart-stopping, careering slide down what seemed an almost vertical incline, Ron sometimes only just managed to escape crashing into the bush or finishing up in one of the many small ravines alongside the track. As he had predicted, it took us something more than an hour to drive the 6 miles from Bainyik to the sub-district centre, and, as he had promised, I found out why. I suspected that after the 'do' at the sub-district centre, Ron would probably be the worse for uncounted glasses of negrita and water, and I did not look forward to our return trip to Bainyik. Getting back home in the middle of the night and with Ron in a post-partying mood, the drive would very likely post an even greater challenge.

Birthday party in Maprik

Situated on the side of a small hill, the Maprik subdistrict Administration Station consisted of about a dozen married Administration Officers' residences, a small complex of buildings housing several offices, a courthouse, a police lockup and gaol, and a fairly large hospital servicing the local indigenous community (the Europeans being treated at Wewak). The Maprik airstrip was built on a fold in the valley terrain – the narrow, flat piece of land along the banks of the Screw River only just met the Short Take Off and Landing (STOL) requirements. Alongside the strip stood a government administration bulk store and several private residences of local traders and recruiters. We arrived mud-spattered at the home of the Assistant District Officer, who was hosting tonight's party. When we climbed out of the jeep, he gave us the use of his bathroom, where we showered and changed into clean clothes. As Eileen had promised, when I met the two dozen or so guests at tonight's party, I became acquainted with nearly all of the subdistrict's expatriate residents.

By the time we had changed into our 'party gear', the festivities were already in full swing. For everyone present, this meant that more attention was being paid to the consumption of alcohol than to the plates of finger food on the table. I never lacked for a full glass of negrita in my hand. Unaccustomed as I was to drinking much liquor – let alone New Guinea's favourite, the potent rum drink – I wisely kept my glass sufficiently full to avoid too many invitations to, 'Here, have another one,' or, 'Go on, let me fill 'er up for you, you must be parched!'

By Territory definition 'European', the expatriate population of Maprik was a mixture of ethnicities. The majority of guests that evening were Australians, but the local Medical Officer – highly qualified and esteemed 'Doc' Aloysius Szymiczek – and his wife were both

Hungarian-born, and I was of Dutch origin. Somewhat precariously fitted in between the races at Maprik was an affable and much-liked mixed-race Chinese trader and recruiter, regarded more an 'honorary European' than a New Guinea 'kanaka'.

About the latter term, when I had earlier that day commented on the designation 'kanaka' and its unselfconscious use by expatriates when referring to indigenous Papua New Guineans, Ron had looked puzzled until he caught the meaning of my question. 'Oh, that,' he said, 'In Australia, the expression is often seen as derogatory, and a racist name-calling that has a history dating to the infamous blackbirding practice [the virtual abduction of Pacific islanders to labour in the Queensland sugarcane fields]. In the Territory it has no such connotations. Well, not really,' he qualified his explanation, 'The locals use the term kanaka on themselves – it literally means "free men", though they distinguish between it and "*buskanaka*" meaning kanakas living out in the bush – which is a vilification and almost a curse.'

The two things that struck me about my fellow party-goers that evening was how young the majority of them were, and their reasons for having come to work or find fortune in the Territory. With the exception of a very few, the men and women I met that evening were aged in their early twenties – in several instances, including the birthday girl and Eileen, in their very early twenties. The subdistrict's senior Administration official, the Assistant District Officer (ADO) was barely twenty-seven years old and, like Ron and I, his two Patrol Officers (POs) were about twenty-four years of age. The Cadet Patrol Officer (CPO), the most junior among our company, had not yet turned twenty years old. In the early 1950s, much of New Guinea was still underdeveloped, and some Districts were barely pacified or even un-contacted. Despite their relatively tender years, these young men held down jobs of real responsibility and not seldomly of danger. Charged with maintaining the Administration's law in the Territory, it was these young Department of Native Affairs officers that brought social and political change to the indigenous inhabitants of Papua and New Guinea. Medical officers – such as 'Doc' Szymiczek – improved health and welfare across the country. Department of Agriculture personnel – such as us at Bainyik – introduced economic improvement and innovation to an ancient system of subsistence agriculture. In socially fragmented, pre-industrial, immediate post-Second World War New Guinea – where there had been inter-tribal animosity and at times local warfare – Australian colonial Administration had brought about a degree of safety and co-existence. In the lingua franca *Rot bilong Gavman* – 'The government road' or the government way of doing things – was generally accepted by the local people. It had proven to them to be an acceptable alternative to former tribal isolation, social deprivation, and local warfare.

Maprik characters: Doc Szymiczek

Among the evening's guests, Hungarian 'Doc' Szymiczek intrigued me. As a displaced person, or 'DP', from post-war Europe, Doc had immigrated to Australia in the early 1950s. Although highly qualified with advanced degrees in medicine, he was denied permission to practise in Australia and he had fulfilled two years of then compulsory government labour on the railways. Released from his obligation but still not accepted for medical employment in Australia, he had learned that foreign-born doctors were sought to work in the Australian Territory, though they were generally restricted only to practising on indigenous people. When Doc had decided to take up the position of Medical Officer in the Papua and New Guinea Administration, he somewhat understandably still harboured a latent resentment about his two years of manual labour in Australia. In later months when I came to know him better, after many negritas he once confided to me, 'I didn't mind the labouring work on the railways, but I lived in constant fear of damaging my hands and losing the ability to perform surgery.' The eyes in the patrician face above the elegant gold cigarette holder in his mouth stayed coldly cynical as he concluded, 'In Hungary I am an expert surgeon, but in Australia they won't recognise my qualifications and experience. In the Territory I am allowed to practise on kanakas, but why? Perhaps because they are thought sub-human? I don't care being allowed to only work on them; they don't ask about my qualifications when they come to my hospital, and when I make them better they are happy with me. Also, I don't mind looking after them because they have many fascinating diseases. And even if they are "only kanakas", they are human beings. But the others, they are all bastards.'

His scorn of 'the others' was withering, and I wondered who exactly he meant – present company, Willy and me, hopefully excluded?

Maprik characters: Bill Royal

Another interesting member of Maprik's expatriate population that evening was an older couple, the 'B4s', Bill and Mrs Royal. Bill had come to Papua and New Guinea in the early 1930s to literally look for his fortune by goldmining in the Papuan Territory's hinterland. Whether by pure luck or hard work – or perhaps a combination of both – Bill and two of his mates were the three original discoverers of Edie Creek, the mother lode, the source, of the famed Bulolo gold fields. Becoming fabulously rich, after years out in the Territory bush Bill decided to take an extended holiday in Australia. Living the high life, young Bill bought himself a chauffeur-driven Rolls-Royce, and in Sydney he 'naturally' stayed in only the best hotels – where he did not merely occupy a suite, but hired an entire floor for himself and his inescapable sycophants and hangers-on. Often frequenting the racetrack, Bill seldom took home winnings from the large bets that he placed – not surprisingly, he was popular with bookmakers. The day inevitably came that Bill found himself stony broke, whereupon someone quipped, 'Slow horses and fast "fillies" were Bill's undoing.' Having lost his money in Australia, Bill used his last few pounds to book his passage back to New Guinea. The story goes that, having been driven to the wharf in his Rolls-Royce limousine, when his chauffeur asked what Sir would have him do with his motor, Bill handed the keys of his car back to the man and grandly replied, 'You may keep the bloody thing, mate.'

Back at Bulolo, fortune stubbornly evaded Bill. He got married, and he and his wife made a series of moves from one 'promising' location in the Territory to another, but all to no avail. Finally Bill and his wife had come to the Maprik subdistrict where, a few miles out in the hill country, Bill had discovered what he believed was a promising reef; but despite occasional small finds, the hoped-for significant commercial quantities of gold still eluded him. Too old to start searching for a fortune that but for a lucky break lay waiting to be unearthed, Bill now eked out a modest living, 'digging for gold' and trading at Maprik.

Maprik characters: Freddy Strainey

Although not a guest at the birthday party that evening, badly wounded Freddy Strainey, the Trader from the Hayfield airstrip, was also one of a rare breed in PNG. Freddy had come to the Territory working for Mandated Airlines (MAL) as a Second Officer on their fleet of DC3 aircraft. The gossip about him at the party that evening was about his alcohol consumption. Although by all accounts Freddy was an excellent aviator, he was young and apparently easily influenced by his peers. The social isolation of life in the Territory, coupled with the climate and the sometimes dangerous working conditions, had led Freddy to become habitually overindulgent in his consumption of alcohol. When, like many young and single men in the Territory, he fell prey to the 'demon grog', it eventually cost him his job with MAL. Next, Freddy had started flying for Bobby Gibbes's Sepik Airways. Although Bobby Gibbes was a tolerant employer, he could not indefinitely ignore a growing chorus of complaints about some of Freddy's unnerving habits when he was taking his hapless passengers up into the air. It was said that Freddy always carried a hip flask, not of under- but over-proof negrita in his back pocket, and that he had often been caught surreptitiously taking large sips from it as he went through his cockpit drill. An aircraft taking off from often rough, barely adequate and sometimes dangerous airstrips in New Guinea always created tension for pilot and passengers alike. When his drinking began to get out of hand, it was therefore little wonder that, as the old Dragon lumbered down a runway, people weren't happy to hear Freddy in a slurred voice urging the plane to, 'Get up, get up, you bitch!' Nor was their anxiety unreasonable when, after becoming airborne, they saw Freddy take several more slugs from his flask 'to steady the nerves' – or maybe to celebrate a not confidently expected successful take-off? Eventually, even Bobby Gibbes could no longer allow Freddy to continue flying the Dragon, and that was when Freddy teamed up with Roy Lane and became a Trader and Labour Recruiter at Hayfield.

Freddy loved flying, and never gave up hope that he would soon return to the industry. As such he was no different from many alcoholics, who often struggle to acknowledge their addiction. In the Territory, a disturbingly common phrase among many men – but also some women – was, 'I can give up the grog anytime I like, but not just now.' Only days before I arrived, it was Freddy's love affair with aircraft – and his other love, his addiction to rum – that had under bizarre circumstances caused the terrible burn on his leg.

One day, Freddy had had a falling out with his friend Roy Lane, causing him to temporarily seek solace with mates at Maprik. Single young men, like Freddy they were not uncommonly given to excessive use of alcohol, and that day the friends had embarked on serious, dedicated binge drinking. Later in the evening, when the company became inebriated to the stage that a great deal of common sense had left them, his drunken friends did not have the presence of mind to stop Freddy when he suddenly jumped out of his chair, rushed over to a motorbike parked nearby, and started up the machine. As his befuddled companions sat and watched dumbfounded, Freddy raced to the far end of the airstrip on his bike, from where he came tearing down the runway as if he was flying the old Dragon again. His friends heard him shouting his familiar take-off mantra, 'Get up, get up, you bitch!' Having consumed the full length of the airstrip, at the end of it the inevitable happened. With an almighty yell, Freddy fell down a small ravine, landing 20 feet below on the bank of the Screw River with the motorbike on top of him. When his friends reached him, Freddy was blissfully unconscious – whether because of his fall or the demon grog inside him, they did not know. The machine's hot exhaust was doing frightful damage to Freddy's leg. His friends extricated him, but when they could not revive him they decided they had best carry him to Doc Szymiczek's house. After Doc had surveyed the damage, the worthy medico reached into his medicine cupboard for a bottle and a small brush, whereupon he painted the third-degree burn from thigh to calf with iodine. The sting of the medication wakened Freddy, but when he saw what Doc had done to his leg he yelled and fainted again. Those at the party who related the story to me that evening predicted, 'Freddy won't be in a hurry to fly a motorbike again!' Although, and apparently with foresight of what rum addiction may do to a person, someone added 'Perhaps?'

Maprik characters: Hunter Kirk

On the evening of the birthday party, I met and heard of some local characters, but there were others at Maprik with even more extraordinary stories and backgrounds. One of these was Hunter Kirk, a local Trader and Recruiter who lived at the farthest end of the main settlement in his trade store beside the airstrip. Hunter had come to Papua and New Guinea in the early 1930s, the heyday of the major gold discoveries. Like Bill Royal he had been intent on trying his luck at prospecting. However, like most of his fellow diggers, he had been largely unsuccessful, and after many decades in the country his luck had run out and he had become flat broke. Hunter could not bear the thought of returning to Australia, and – colloquially expressed in the Territory idiom – he had 'gone native'. When at the party the conversation turned to Hunter Kirk in his trade store, someone warned me, 'When your wife arrives – as Hunter has gone native – if you should take her anywhere near his store, you had better leave her outside until you have warned the old boy, "Lady present!"' My informant elaborated, 'Hunter has lived among the villagers for so long that he considers himself to be one of their *lapun*, old men. Out here in the bush, old men and women walk around stark naked. So in his store, Hunter never wears anything but a singlet – except when a European woman visits. As a concession to her feelings, he wants time to slip into a pair of shorts.'

When the birthday party broke up in the early morning hours, it had started raining again and our hosts would not allow us to drive back to Bainyik. After the last of the stragglers had left for their Maprik homes, the birthday girl and Eileen went to sleep, but their husbands kept talking. Although I was frightfully tired, their manly example of how things were apparently done in the Territory made me feel constrained to also stay awake.

Later in the morning, when it had ceased raining and the weather had cleared to brilliant hot sunshine, Ron, Eileen and I climbed into the jeep for the return trip to Bainyik Agricultural Station. It went without incident, other than the occasional and by now familiar shout, 'Gears!' and the slipping and sliding of the vehicle over the slick mud of the track. These things no longer worried me quite as much as on the way into Maprik – I was on my way to becoming a 'Territorian'.

Hiring house staff

Following Territory practice, when I moved into my house on the Station, Eileen said that I needed servants – a house servant for cooking and cleaning, called *mankimasta* in Pidgin, and a laundryman, *wasboi*. This appeared to have been anticipated by the foreman, the head bosboi, who announced to me, '*Mi painim pinis mankimasta wantaim wanpela wasboi wok long haus bilong yu, Masta, Sah* (I have found a house servant and a laundryman to work for you, Sir).' When I agreed to conduct an 'interview', the bosboi returned with two men from the labour line; a youth of about eighteen years old to be my future house servant, and a somewhat older person who he declared was suited to be my laundryman. To be truthful, when the bosboi had presented me with his protégés I was rather taken aback by the appearance of the younger of the two. He was dressed in his work gear of a stained and crumpled lap-lap, his bare feet were muddy with the soil that he had been working in only minutes ago, and his hands were equally grimy. Being of a weedy and gangling build, possibly because of chronic under-nourishment, my *hausboi* Trenyan was not only of a somewhat unkempt appearance, he suffered a fearful squint and lazy eye.

Inexperienced as I was, and hampered by my lack of command of Pidgin English, the best I could do was to ask my prospective house servant in halting and imperfect lingua franca, 'Do you savvy cooking and cleaning?' and the would-be laundryman, 'Do you savvy washing clothes?' When both firmly affirmed that 'Yessah, Masta, Sah, mipela savvy planty (Yes Sir, we do, indeed),' I replied, 'Oh, alright then,' and thus acquired myself two servants for my little house in the New Guinea bush. Based on a naive trust in the bosboi's recommendation and the pair's assurances that they knew the requirements of their jobs, I thought that I had made the right decision.

The term 'mankimasta' – employed in the designation of an indigenous house servant – was assumed by even many long-term Territory residents to have been derived from the English root words 'monkey' and 'master', and that the reason for a person to be so called was that he was an 'ape-like' imitation of the European master. However, Pidgin English is a living language, and many of its words and expressions were – and continue to be – derived from languages as diverse as English, German, Malay and even Dutch. Pronounced by Pidgin English speakers, the archaic Dutch word '*manneke*', the diminutive of 'man', became 'manki'. Coupled with 'masta', this became 'mankimasta' – not altogether different from how an English butler is sometimes called 'a gentleman's gentleman'.

When I told Eileen that I had found home help, her reaction was rather less than encouraging. 'You've picked your mankimasta straight from the Station labour line?' she asked. 'Did you check if he has worked in a European household before, and have you asked him to describe what jobs he used to do for his former employer?' When I confessed that I had not checked these details with them she sighed, 'Oh, dear.'

Eileen also touched on another important matter that I had overlooked, namely my servants' personal hygiene. 'If you are going to keep these men you simply must clean them up,' she insisted. 'Give them each a cake of Sunlight soap and a scrubbing brush, and instruct them that every day – before they even come near your house – they must go down to the river for a thorough bath.' My friend continued, 'You must also make them throw away their present work gear and issue them with new lap-laps. Give the mankimasta two khaki and two white lap-laps, and every day after wearing these get him to wash them. During the day he must wear a khaki lap-lap for his work, cleaning, dusting and cooking, and change into a white one when he has to serve the food at the table. Oh, and make sure that he always washes and shows you clean hands before he handles food. The wasboi needs only two khaki lap-laps because his work is mainly outside.' My mentor in all things domestic in the Territory, Eileen concluded that she would lend me the necessary loincloths from her store. 'Next time you are at Maprik or at Hayfield you can buy lap-laps in the trade store and make good the loan from me,' she suggested. Then she called out for the servants in Pidgin English, 'Yutupela boi kam.' When the men appeared, she issued rapid instructions to them. They soon disappeared for a long bath in the river, after which they reappeared, gleaming, for Eileen's inspection. She ran a critical eye over them, then somewhat dubiously pronounced the pair acceptable for duty.

The first meal my mankimasta served me that evening was certainly a memorable one. I had given Trenyan one of those wedge-shaped tins of corned beef, a tin of potatoes and one of peas for my main meal, and a tin of sliced peaches for dessert. Handing him these, I instructed in my poor Pidgin English, 'Him for tonight, savvy?' To which he confidently replied, 'Yessah, Masta, me savvy.' Later that evening when he appeared from the kitchen to serve my dinner, Trenyan was dressed in his brand new white lap-lap. His face beamed with pride as he served me the meal he had prepared. Carefully arranged on the biggest 'plate' (actually a serving platter that he had found among the crockery), lay the whole contents of every one of the tins I had given him earlier that day – bully beef, potatoes, peas, and sliced peaches. I was hungry and I lacked language to tell him that the food would have tasted better if he had heated it up first, and that the peaches for dessert were generally served separate from the main meal. But so as not to discourage my new mankimasta, I ate what he had put in front of me. And for fear of invoking another disapproving 'Oh, dear,' I did not tell Eileen about that evening's unconventional dinner.

Cash cropping

In the next few weeks I began to learn the purpose and main work of the Agricultural Station – namely, the promotion of cash cropping of dry land rice and peanuts. The production of dry land rice is essentially no different from the gardening methods of traditional subsistence food crops in Papua and New Guinea. The cultivation of irrigated paddy rice, however, requires extensive use and knowledge of water reticulation and distribution – technologies that were unknown in New Guinea. Asian paddy rice is often grown on terraces built into the slopes and sides of hills, a technique that was equally foreign to New Guinean subsistence farmers and one that – given the island's often extremely mountainous terrain – is largely impractical. Furthermore, traditional Papua and New Guinean villages lacked beasts of burden – buffalo or oxen – to plough the ground, and the cost of farm machinery for the mechanical cultivation of the land was prohibitive. Australian policy makers and technologists thought cash cropping of peanuts and rice of the dry land variety suited local custom and practice, and with only the need for labour – provided by the villagers – it was also cost effective. Despite being actively promoted through the agency of the Agriculture Department, the introduction of these and other foreign crops into the subsistence economy of Papua and New Guinea had major and apparently unanticipated flaws.

Traditional Papuan and New Guinean swidden (slash and burn) agricultural practice involves clearing relatively small and temporary plots of gardens in the rich leaf mould of primary or secondary forest. In these plots the villagers grow staples of their traditional diet – taro, sweet potatoes, bananas, sugar cane and leaf vegetables. After two or three years without either natural or chemical fertilisers, and due also to the heavy tropical rainfall, the soil fertility leaches out and the land deteriorates to a degree where it is no longer sufficiently productive. As this stage is reached, the villagers abandon the old plots – which revert to secondary bush – and make new gardens elsewhere in the forest. This cycle of inherently shifting garden production suited the traditional small-scale communities of sparsely populated Papua and New Guinea.

In the post Second World War era, the Australian Government encouraged the introduction of permanent and annual cash crops, with apparently unforeseen consequences. The different land use and requirements of a foreign agrarian system, coupled with a vexatious and difficult-to-overcome system of indigenous land rights, upset the finely balanced indigenous technology. Especially in the case of coffee, cocoa, tea and oil palm, this meant that considerable portions of arable soils were now committed to permanently growing, large-scale plantations – putting pressure on land that would normally have been reserved for subsistence gardening. Even more critical had been the apparent oversight or lack of knowledge that traditional land rights in Papua and New Guinea are based on the notion of 'usufruct'. That is, land is owned by the community and it is allocated to individuals by common agreement, *not* covered by law. In the case of annual rice and peanut crops, land rights were less of an issue, but the necessarily increased exploitation of the forest exacerbated dwindling natural soil fertility, which further increased pressure on the resources of arable land when more and more of the forest had to be cleared to overcome the problem. In essence, the introduction and promotion of the foreign cash economy destroyed the self-sufficient basis of traditional village life.

The Australian policy of bringing *economic* change through cash cropping in Papua and New Guinea was further complicated by the fact that Territory Administration staff – but particularly officers of the Agriculture Department – were largely untrained in the social sciences and they had little knowledge or appreciation of indigenous custom and culture, the *social* basis of village life. From the Director of Agriculture down to the most junior Field Officer, Agriculture Department staff unquestioningly believed in the superiority of Western agricultural technology and the benefits that would flow from it for the people of Papua and New Guinea. This was a conviction they set out to implement in the Territory with a near missionary zeal. If it meant that more bushland must be cleared in which to grow village cash crops, to augment if not replace the 'primitive' subsistence gardening agricultural economy, then the 'natives' must be encouraged to do so, and if necessary by any means. This 'means to an end attitude' towards a presumed 'better good' for the indigenous peoples of Papua and New Guinea, was held by many if not most expatriates – and indeed it would seem the Australian policy makers in Canberra.

Reunited
The day after the birthday party, before we left to drive home to Bainyik, I sent a telegram to Willy via the Maprik subdistrict office's daily 'sched' – the scheduled two-way radio contact with Administration Headquarters at Wewak – advising her that I had found married accommodation for us and asking her '… as soon as practicable' to join me in New Guinea. Treating my request with speed and determination, Willy wired me back, giving me the date of her departure from Australia a fortnight hence, and her date of arrival at Wewak. I excitedly looked forward to our reunion, and replied that I would surely meet her at Wewak to accompany her to Bainyik. My intentions were of course sincere, but I had not reckoned on what the old poem says about, 'The best laid plans of mice and men…'[xxvi]

A fortnight after Willy and I had exchanged telegrams, I was waiting at Maprik for an aeroplane to pick me up to fly me to Wewak. However, being at the height of the rainy season in December, thick clouds over Maprik had prevented the Dragon from landing. To my dismay, when the pilot could not find a hole in the overcast sky, the aircraft flew on to another outstation. There was nothing for me to do but hope that the plane would return and to take me to Wewak – where poor Willy would surely be wondering if I had forgotten the date of her arrival. It was well into mid-morning when to my relief I heard the welcome stutter of the Dragon's engines. Now without a cloud in the sky, when it landed at Maprik I was soon on my way to Wewak. When we arrived at Boram, the MAL plane from Lae had of course long gone, but 'Young Doug' the Dragon pilot kindly dropped me off in his jeep at the hotel. There I found Willy, who had only just written the first words in a letter to 'Dear Mr District Commissioner…' Now that I had arrived, she had no need to ask the official for assistance to travel to Bainyik – wherever that was!

Recovered from the excitement of our reunion, we sat and talked under the whirring fans in the hotel, repairing gaps of absence and communication on both sides. Willy had travelled from Mount Gambier to Sydney's Kingsford Smith Airport where she was to board her connecting flight to Port Moresby. As her departure from Australia to New Guinea coincided with Christmas Day, when she had arrived in Sydney she had found practically all general businesses at the airport closed, and even the restaurants and cafés had shut down for the holiday. Knowing that her connecting flight to Port Moresby left at eight-thirty that evening, my wife had found a café that was still open for business and shortly before her departure she had a simple meal of spaghetti – all that was on offer. The great pity of it, Willy regretfully said, was that she and the other passengers on the Qantas flight to New Guinea were treated to an enormous Christmas dinner with all the trimmings, 'From champagne and appetisers to a traditional roast turkey and ham, and plum pudding after.' But she was so full of spaghetti she could manage to only to nibble at the lovely festive fare.

At Lae, Willy had stayed overnight at the same Qantas mess as I had. The next day, in travelling on to Wewak and arriving at Boram airstrip, she had not found me waiting as arranged. Finding no transport provided, Willy had been fortunate in meeting a good Samaritan, a Catholic priest and the only other person left on the strip, who asked her if anyone would be coming to collect her. When my wife told him about missing our meeting, and that no one else from Wewak was expecting her, he had offered to drop her off at the hotel in his jeep. At the Wewak hotel she had asked the publican for advice on what to do about travelling on to Bainyik... wherever that was. At his suggestion she had just begun to write a letter when I arrived. Tired, confused, but relieved that she had found me, Willy did not even ask why I had failed to meet her at the airstrip, 'You're here, and that's all that matters,' said my dear wife.

On the hotel veranda, in the late afternoon we watched the brilliant tropical sunset. Sometime later, just before it got dark, we applied sticky mosquito repellent to arms and legs, and took our antimalarial tablets. Soon after dinner in the hotel's dining room we retired to our room, giving in to mutual exhaustion. Before we fell asleep we assured each other, 'It is good to be together again.'

Next morning at Boram airstrip we did not find the De Havilland Dragon. Instead, one of Bobby Gibbes's more modern and larger Norseman aeroplanes would take us to Maprik. Noticing its ungainly, stubby airframe and single engine mounted directly ahead of the cockpit, Willy was not inspired with confidence and hesitantly asked, 'Is it *safe?*' Although I had neither real experience nor authority in the matter, I thought it wise to assure her, 'Yes, it's quite safe, no worries.' Without roads in New Guinea, there was no option but to believe – or perhaps hope – that it *was* safe.

As we stood waiting to board our flight to Maprik, a young man – really still a youth looking to celebrate his coming of age – appeared from inside the tin shed that constituted Boram's 'terminal' office and cargo store, where he had been sorting untidy heaps of cargo destined for the outstations. 'Be with yous in a tick,' he cheerfully called out. After a short while, making good his promise, he lead us across the strip to the waiting Norseman. 'I'm Dennis,' the young man introduced himself, and quipped, 'I can't imagine why, but everyone calls me Junior.' When we reached the aeroplane he said, 'I'll show you to yer seats in the old balus,' then went on, 'Yous're the only passengers today, so perhaps the lady would like to sit next to the pilot?'

Unlike the relatively low-slung De Havilland Dragon, the front end of a Norseman stands quite high from the ground and climbing into its cockpit required mounting a small step on the aircraft's side. In those days few women dressed in the nowadays common jeans and Willy was no exception, wearing a modish, full skirt that hampered her clambering up from the ground into the plane. I thought it very gallant of Junior to stand beside the aircraft to help her into the cockpit. Before I took my seat in the back I politely thanked him for the courtesy he had shown my wife. With a wicked twinkle in his eyes the young man answered, 'No worries cobber, it's always a pleasure helping sheilas into the Norseman's cockpit,' adding, 'It gives a bloke the best view in town.' I did not decipher the cryptic comment until we were well up in the air, and then it was too late to 'deck' Junior for sporting with my wife's honour. In any case, I could not help but be amused by his cheekiness – a youthful exuberance bereft of any really bad intent. Thirty years later, Dennis 'Junior' Buchanan – who had pioneered and established his own airline flying routes in the country's highlands – was knighted 'In recognition of exceptional services to the Papua New Guinea airline industry' by Her Majesty Queen Elizabeth II.

After an uneventful flight the pilot 'buzzed' Bainyik, and flew on to land at Maprik. From there, the Assistant District Commissioner made transport available to take us to the Agriculture Station. Arriving at Bainyik, we found the Station's entire indigenous population turned out, standing alongside the road to await the arrival of the new 'Missis bilong Nambatu Masta' – the wife of the second in charge at Bainyik. Ron and Eileen asked us to their home for drinks and lunch, after which I could finally take Willy to our little house in the jungle, our first home in the Territory. I led Willy to our dwelling, apprehensive as to how she might react when she saw that the only door was to the bedroom and made of flimsy bamboo, that we only had bamboo shutters instead of glass windows to keep out the weather, and that the rough, corrugated, split limbom palm tree flooring left gaps through which one could see the ground below. To my great relief Willy did not turn a hair; in fact, she declared the house quite cosy. When she added, 'As long as we are together again these small things don't matter,' our primitive bush house in the New Guinea jungle became home.

The tensions of two days travelling the long journey from 'South' alone; the flight from Wewak in an aircraft with only a single engine; the bumpy ride in the ADO's jeep from Maprik to Bainyik over the potholed and slippery track; the conditions of the tropical climate; the exotic environment; the foreign people of New Guinea – black and white alike – all would have been enough to test the pioneering spirit and mettle of anyone, but Willy took it in her stride.

Trenyan

Willy spent the next weeks discovering the ways in which living in New Guinea was so very different to 'Down South'. Early on we established the routine whereby, instead of having to get up early when I left the house at 6 am to allocate the men in the labour line their jobs, Willy would sleep in until just before 8 am, when we had breakfast prepared by our mankimasta. Although Trenyan had progressed in his duties to the point where he at least no longer served me all the ingredients of my meals on one plate, Willy decided that she would teach him to cook more varied and palatable fare than simply heating up food out of tins. She also wanted him to improve on the routine cleaning tasks that required working with soap and brush, rather than a perfunctory swishing of a few buckets of water over the corrugated limbom floors. We had decided that we could at least entrust Trenyan with preparing our breakfast, and that he could make us our tea and toast. One day, quite accidentally, Willy discovered just how remiss we were in this assumption.

When I had taken Trenyan on as a servant in our household, I had done so partly because I felt a little sorry for him with his lazy eye. In part I also admired what I saw in him as having a salutary initiative that set him apart from his fellows in the labour line. Ironically, that quality of enterprise almost cost our mankimasta his job. One of Trenyan's early accomplishments was that, lacking an electric power supply on the Station, he had become expert at preparing my breakfast without the aid of an electric toaster. Instead, holding a slice of bread on a long-handled wire fork above the embers in the cooking stove, by the time I returned from inspecting the labour line, he had produced nice golden toast for my breakfast. Since we lacked a toast rack, I had also taught him to prop the done slices on the kitchen bench, against the bamboo wall, to prevent them becoming soggy. Having mastered these intricate details of European food preparation – 'Fassion bilong Masta bilong Australia' – since Willy's arrival, Trenyan had continued to serve us our tea and perfectly prepared golden toast. Until one day Willy rose a little earlier than usual.

After her morning shower Willy came past the kitchen, where she spotted Trenyan squatted in front of the stove preparing that morning's breakfast. As I had taught him to do, he was toasting a slice of bread before the open fire. But to her consternation, Willy noticed that our mankimasta had solved the lack of a toast rack in his own way. Instead of standing the slices on the kitchen bench as I had shown him, Trenyan had apparently decided that there was an easier way of preventing them from becoming soggy, and which, incidentally, allowed him to remain comfortably squatting. This was to pop the slices of toast between his bare toes. He may not have fully understood the reason for Willy's wrath and her indignant insistence that he should *never* again dare to improvise on his cooking in this way. Our mankimasta certainly did not realise just how lucky he was that his mistress had also developed a soft spot for him. His clever but unwelcome toast rack nearly cost him his coveted job, which would have had him straight back in the labour line.

Initial problems of settling in soon resolved themselves, and – now under strict supervision – our hausboi made excellent progress learning 'Masta-type' cleaning and other household tasks. What he really enjoyed was cooking, frying, roasting or baking a variety of dishes, or making scones, biscuits and cakes. Since he was illiterate, he had to commit all the recipes to memory – no small feat!

Trenyan thrived in his job, his previous meek uncertainty replaced with a kind of dignified confidence in his exalted status compared with those in the labour line. His erstwhile sparse frame had also filled out with all the good leftover food from our kitchen, and notch-by-notch he had to let out the broad army belt that he wore to hold the lap-lap around his expanding waist.

Adjusting to a new life

Willy and I became gradually more used to the Territory climate. We no longer felt quite as affected by the 'soggy blanket' of high humidity that had quite bothered us in 'the wet', the monsoon season, when a tropical rainstorm would drench the Station nearly every afternoon. After the downpour ceased, less than a hundred feet away from our house the jungle's myriad occupants signalled their thanks for the life-giving water by bursting into chirping insect song, squawking or squealing tree dwelling-life, and throaty frog croaking; a cacophony of sound that reverberated in the steaming air. In the evening, our windowless and doorless house gave free access to the rich variety of rainforest life – especially the winged kind. It was quipped that we were in an environment from where all mosquitoes in the world originated, and Willy and I were always extra conscious of the danger of contracting malaria. Before sundown each evening, we applied the unpleasantly sticky mosquito repellent to every exposed area of our skin except the face, taking care not to get it in our eyes. Before every dinner we also made certain to take our anti-malarial tablets. As we had no means of keeping the amazing variety of jungle life at bay, as soon as we lit our lamps after dark, the light attracted moths, cicadas, beetles and all kinds of unidentified bugs and insects that would have been the envy of entomologists. Although we were always on the lookout for snakes – which were ever present in the bush, on the slippery jungle paths and in our demonstration plots – we fortunately never found one inside the house. The same could not be said for the large spiders that lurked in dark corners on a wall, on the ceiling, even on our mosquito net over the bed, waiting to pounce on the plentiful supply of their favourite prey, so readily attracted to the illumination in our house. Even if we sprayed the hairy crawlies with insecticide, from out of the deep forest around us their casualties were soon enough eaten and replaced by their fellows or other scavengers. Sometimes when it rained for days on end, crossing the flooded, swollen Screw River was impossible; at Bainyik we became even more isolated from Maprik and the European community. At such times the jungle in which we lived did take on an oppressive quality. The twanging of the jew's harp played in nearby Bainyik village only underlined our isolation.

Starting a family

For Willy and me, the move from Australia to Papua and New Guinea had been a watershed in our lives. As a public servant and now the Officer in Charge of Bainyik District Agricultural Demonstration Station, in a very real sense I was now working in employment with permanency and with an inbuilt career structure. At Millicent, though we had begun to consider the future in our married life, we had not then felt convinced that we were in a position to take the critical step of settling down and starting a family. But now, our doubts about that decision were no longer so well-founded.

It is probably well that many young married people lack the experience – or possibly even the imagination – to perceive what is involved when taking on parental responsibilities. For Willy and me, entertaining this wish in the jungles of New Guinea was an act of blessed ignorance, and if we had known the implications beforehand we may have approached it with greater prudence. But as it was, we threw caution and common-sense to the wind, and happily began to prepare for a long wished-for parenthood.

When a young couple plans to start a family, in most cases they can turn for advice to parents or members of their extended family. But as Mrs Hurley would have put it, 'In the wilds of New Guinea among cannibals, crocodiles and mosquitoes,' Willy and I had no one with whom to consult. Vexed by our ignorance and lack of advice, we thought that we had done well to purchase a copy of the book by the well-known American child specialist Doctor Spock. While we found that it is often true that *quasi*-medical reading is sometimes difficult for lay people to understand, living on an outstation in the jungle, any advice was better than none, and thus we had to put our trust in what we came to think of as 'The Book'.

We had assumed that parenthood would come quickly once we made up our minds, but for some disappointing time it remained elusive. However, Nature eventually won and we guessed that a baby was on its way. Willy was physically fit, but of slim build, and even a month or two after we suspected that a child must be on the way, there was no obvious visual indication of what people in bygone days called her 'happy condition'. After a little more time had passed and it seemed to us that 'we' were indeed pregnant, in deference to what we had read in The Book, we began taking what we thought was 'sensible' care of Willy – driving more slowly when she was in the station's Landrover, avoiding too-strenuous exercise and, as much as was possible on a New Guinea outstation, providing her with a nutritious and balanced diet. After three months, Willy proposed, 'Perhaps I should have a talk with Doc Szymiczek?' to which I agreed, 'Yes, let's go see Doc at Maprik.'

After what seemed to me an interminable time, Willy finally emerged from Doctor Szymiczek's surgery in the hospital at Maprik. When I eagerly asked, 'What did the Doctor say?' Willy looked slightly sheepish. She replied, 'I told him that I thought that I was pregnant. Doc shook my hand and said, "Congratulations, my dear!" Then he walked over to the medicine fridge and said, "Let's drink to it. Have a beer!" When I told him about The Book and what it said about pregnant women having to undergo regular medical check-ups, Doc asked, "You feel sick, no? You feel ill, no? You do not have any pains, no?" And when I said that I felt quite well, that I was not sick and that I suffered no pains anywhere at all, he confirmed his previous diagnosis, "Well, you must be pregnant; you are with child;

it is a perfectly natural condition of the female body. Congratulations, dear lady, have another beer!'"

In spite of Willy's somewhat disappointing consultation, Aloysius Szymiczek was undoubtedly a highly qualified medical doctor – in fact, he was a specialist medical researcher in his native country of Hungary. In Papua and New Guinea, Doctor Szymiczek rediscovered his specialist interests in medicine, and had developed a fascination with tropical diseases. No local patient was admitted to the Maprik hospital until Doc had photographed the person and his or her ailments – which ranged from unfortunates who had been mauled by a feral pig, to deformations caused by leprosy, framboesia, elephantiasis and other maladies. In essence, Doctor Szymiczek was so absorbed in the intellectually challenging field of exotic tropical health that a humdrum, every-day event such as childbearing was no more than, as he had put it to Willy, 'A natural condition of the female body.'

Despite The Book comprehensively covering the subject of an expectant mother needing regular medical check-ups, in our ignorance we perhaps put incautious trust in Doctor Szymiczek's blasé medical opinion. It was not until the fifth month of Willy's pregnancy that, if only for peace of mind, we felt that we needed more comprehensive attention for Willy than what she had so far received from our local medico. We suspected that, if she went for another pregnancy check-up with Doc at Maprik, he would probably only offer her renewed congratulations – and probably another beer. So we chartered a small plane at our own expense to fly Willy from Hayfield to Wewak, where she would attend the regional base hospital and stay overnight with acquaintances. The next day, when she returned to Bainyik, Willy told me that she had been seen not by one, but three doctors and that they had been incredulous, asking 'Is this truly your *first* pre-natal examination?' They had shaken their medical heads when she confirmed that this was indeed her first medical check-up. 'Anyway,' Willy exulted as she waved a piece of paper in the air, 'the doctors were so surprised with my story that not only did they arrange for us to be reimbursed for the plane charter, they now want to see me monthly until the baby is due! The Administration will pay for everything!' With due respects to Doc Szymiczek, it was comforting to know that Willy's pregnancy had been rather more professionally considered than finding it to be, 'a natural condition of the female body. Have a beer!'

When Willy's pregnancy became obvious, she became a person of great interest at Bainyik and a source of child-rearing advice for the women on the Station and in nearby villages. Every day a veritable 'mothers club' of pregnant women or mothers with babies would gather before the front steps of our house, waiting for *Missis bilong Masta* to listen to all sorts of problems that the women raised with her about their children. With the best will in the world, all that Willy could do was dispense common household medication to treat complaints ranging from headaches, minor fevers or stomach upsets, dealing out aspirins for mildly elevated temperatures, Epsom salts for improved bowel function, or charcoal tablets to treat diarrhoea. Naturally, if aspirins did not dampen a fever, Epsom salts failed to shift stolid sago porridge that had blocked natural plumbing systems, or charcoal tablets did not cure the opposite condition, Willy referred her 'patients' to Doc at Maprik. And every day a small crowd of women continued to come to our house to consult Willy, whose condition – *Bel bilong yu kariim pikanini* (Your belly carries a child) – bridged the cultural gap of the New Guinean women and their Western counterpart. When these black mothers called on their white fellow mother-to-be, they found a sympathetic listener to concerns that all parents share in matters of child welfare.

The months went by and early one morning, when I was fast asleep under the mosquito net, Willy shook me. 'Wake up, I think something is happening.' Startled into wide-awake awareness, it did not take me more than a second or two to realise that the 'something' my wife had mentioned must be to do with her now advanced pregnancy. After she had made her first visit to the Wewak base hospital, somewhat to Doc Szymiczek's disgruntlement, Willy had made several more trips to the town for medical attention. At her most recent examination the doctors had warned her that our baby's birth was drawing close, and they had made it clear that she should under no circumstances have the child in Doc Szymiczek's bush hospital at Maprik. Within a week of the date of her confinement, they instructed, Willy must go to Wewak to await the baby's delivery. When she woke me that morning, the possibility that events may have overtaken us sent a shiver of apprehension through me. Although the possibility that 'something was happening' alarmed me, I knew that I must not show my concern, and I reassured Willy, 'Don't worry; I'll look it up in The Book.'

By the light of a candle that I had lit in our sitting room, it did not take me long to find information in Doctor Spock's book about the symptoms of impending childbirth, and what I now read seriously alarmed me. Back in our bedroom, as casually as I could, I said, 'Look, I don't think we have anything to worry about, but I'll hop in the Landrover to have a chat with Doc at Maprik. Just go back to sleep and have a good rest until I'm back.' After I had tucked Willy in under the mosquito net, I forced myself to stroll out of the house then – unseen by my wife – I sprinted down the path to where the vehicle was garaged, praying that last night's rain should not have seriously flooded the Screw River.

After a rather hair-raising trip, driving much too fast on the track into Maprik, I pulled up at Doc Szymiczek's house – where at that early hour of the morning I found the family at breakfast. When I told him the details of what was 'happening' to Willy, Aloysius immediately sized up the situation and became quite as alarmed as I. 'No, no, she cannot have the baby in my hospital,' he said, rather illogically insisting, 'I will not allow it!' Agitated, he went on, 'Your wife must go to Wewak hospital to have the baby, the bush hospital in Maprik is not good enough for European womans.' While I agreed with him, the thought occurred to me: but what can we do about it?

'We get ADO to order plane from Wewak to pick up your wife and me,' Doc urged. After a moment of relief, we realised that today was Sunday, and that the Assistant District Officer would be attending Mass at the local Catholic Mission church. Undeterred, Doc dismissed this small detail, 'Never mind, we pull him out of church.' And thus began the saga of the birth of our first child.

To his great credit, when we burst in on his congregation the Dutch priest, Father Kruysberg, did not interrupt his service for a second. The local faithfuls sitting on logs, the Assistant District Officer in a privileged position in a Masta's deck chair right before the altar, Father continued to drone his incantations. When, after a hastily whispered explanation, Doc and I extricated the ADO from the church and he learned of our predicament, he promised, 'I'll try to reach Wewak on the blower, but we'll have to trust our luck as there is no regular sched on Sundays.' After an alarmed Doc explained Willy's condition and the probable implications if we should not succeed in making contact, the ADO did his level best with the transmitter. But he eventually announced regretfully, 'Wewak is off air.'

For several minutes the three of us stood downcast, not knowing what to do next. Then the ADO suddenly brightened up, 'I have an idea!' he exclaimed, 'I'll try the aircraft communication frequency to see if I can catch one in the air to Wewak'. The doctor and I stood behind his chair as the officer fiddled with the dials of the transmitter, until suddenly, 'Beauty, mate!' he exclaimed jubilantly. He was speaking with the captain of an aircraft on an MAL flight from Madang to Wewak. The captain agreed to relay a message to Wewak's control tower requesting that someone contact the hospital to arrange a medical emergency flight to Hayfield, to collect a pregnant European woman who was unexpectedly about to give birth in the bush.

Greatly relieved, I thanked the ADO for his help. I drove Doc Szymiczek to his house, where he hastily packed medical instruments and medications into his doctor's black bag, and a few personal items in a small suitcase to take with him, expecting that he would accompany Willy to Wewak. Back at Bainyik Station, Doc and I stepped out of the jeep to find an unsuspecting Willy at the dining table eating a lovely breakfast of chips and grilled sausages. When I explained that we had to fly her to Wewak, my poor wife lost her appetite, feebly protesting, 'It's gone away, I don't want to go to Wewak.' I was glad to have Doc explain to her that 'it' sometimes behaved in that way, and that there was no telling when 'it' might make up its mind and do what happens naturally. 'There is no doubt that you are having the baby – but not here in the bush, because is not good. You must go to Wewak,' the good doctor insisted.

We had not long packed Willy's and the baby's gear – that for many weeks had been ready for the occasion – when overhead the Station a small plane buzzed us, the sign for us to immediately leave for Hayfield where the aircraft would wait for us. Doc and I carefully packed Willy into the Landrover with pillows around her. And with Doc Szymiczek on the hard bench in the back keeping a medical eye on her, as carefully as I could, I drove off to Hayfield. When we got there, to Doc's disappointment, waiting for us beside the pilot stood a doctor from the Wewak hospital who had come to accompany Willy. With the small Piper Pacer aircraft operated by the Mission Aviation Fellowship too small to accommodate more than three persons, Doc Szymiczek and I would have to remain behind. My heart in my throat, I watched the Piper Pacer plane – by wags sometimes referred to as 'A Piece of Paper' – lift off from the strip. The emergency medi-flight with my wife and our unborn child on board disappeared into the haze over the mountains.

For the next two days I moved in with the Patrol Officer and his wife at Maprik so as to be near radio contact with Wewak. Everyone in the sub-district habitually listened in on the daily Maprik schedule radio frequency, and so the wider expatriate community was of course aware that Willy was awaiting the impending birth of our child at Wewak. I received much attention and well-meant advice from people, 'Don't worry, mate, your missus is in good hands with the docs at Wewak, no worries.' But of course I did worry.

The day after her medical emergency pickup Willy sent word over the radio sched that 'it' had apparently decided against the more immediate action suggested by the signs that had caused everyone at Bainyik and Maprik such consternation. The next day when she sent me the same message that our baby had still not made its move, I was beginning to doubt The Book, and I also wondered if Doc Szymiczek had correctly interpreted the signals that had caused my wife's emergency medical evacuation. I was sorry for having interrupted her lovely breakfast and for Willy's consternation when I had told her that she had to leave for Wewak immediately.

The third day after Willy had flown to Wewak the long-awaited news came – probably shared with every expatriate European in the sub-district on their blowers. A telegram, signed by our friend in Wewak read, 'Congratulations, you are a father. Mother and child well.' With this news, I was now keen to personally acquaint myself with my fatherhood and to thank my dear wife for her new motherhood.

Other than a once weekly 'milk run' it was not usual for Gibbes Sepik Airways to send an extra plane to Maprik. However, as I was keen to visit my wife and newborn child, the sympathetic ADO was able to divert an Administration charter flight on its way back from the small Ambunti outstation on the Sepik River to collect me at Maprik. When I told the pilot of the Norseman – who apparently knew little about the reason for his unscheduled stop – that my wife had given birth to our first child at Wewak, he understood. 'Congratulations mate. I did hear about a woman giving birth at the hospital yesterday,' he said jovially as he fiddled with the dials on the plane's dashboard. When he asked, 'Is it a boy or a girl?' and I confessed that I did not know, he said 'Well, let's not waste time then; I'll get you to your little family at Wewak to find out the answer yourself.' On landing at Boram strip the pilot offered me a ride to the hospital in his jeep. I gratefully accepted, and when he dropped me off at the hospital he farewelled me with, 'No worries, Dad – good luck to you all.'

In the hospital I explained to a New Guinean nursing aide my business, and, waiting for her to return with Matron, I looked around Wewak's base hospital. In 1956, the hospital's various wards looked rather more like barracks. They were constructed from the same bush materials as our house at Bainyik, but – as a concession to modern medicine and sterile medical practice – the hospital's operating theatre was built from 'European' materials – weatherboard walls, corrugated iron roof and linoleum-covered plank floors. While in most Australian towns Wewak hospital would have been considered a basic facility, it was a decided improvement when compared with Doc Szymiczek's bush hospital at Maprik. Thankfully, my wife would not have to share the ward with leprosy patients and sufferers of a variety of exotic tropical diseases and ailments. When Matron arrived to take me to see Willy in her ward she declared with an air of proprietorship, 'I'll first introduce you to our baby,' and opening a door to the hospital nursery she announced with a flourish, 'Meet your beautiful daughter.'

It is surely impossible for any parent to truly describe their emotions when they first see their newborn child. She was such a tiny little person; it was an overwhelming experience. Later, when I visited my dear Willy in her hospital bed, we reflected on how fortunate we were to have such a beautiful daughter, our Evalyn Ann. A dearly wished-for dream fulfilled; our lives would never be the same again.

A few days later when Willy and baby Evie were discharged from the hospital, we flew back home in a Cessna 172 that the Administration had chartered for us from the Sepik District's Sacred Heart Catholic Mission. At the aircraft's controls was 'the Flying Bishop' – American Monsignor Leo Arkfeld himself, who flew us to Maprik; as eminent and highly apposite an aviator as one could wish for. Safely on the ground at the Maprik subdistrict station we thanked His Excellency for the ride in his plane. He graciously shook our hand, replying with the Australian idiom, but with an American accent, 'No worries!'

The Flying Bishop's Cessna 172. Willy and Terry with newborn Evie after flying into Maprik.

At Bainyik we found the entire labour line, the bosbois, the Station women and their children lined up on both sides of the track. Somewhat resembling a royal procession, as we drove past the crowd waved, craning their necks to see us – but particularly the baby. The typically New Guinean, long-drawn yodelling cries with which they welcomed us – '*MastaMissispikanini bilong en ekam pini.i.i.i.s...* (The Master and Mistress and their child have arrived)' – sounded like a verbal applause. It was good to be home.

A Bainyik baby

In the little bush house at Bainyik, our baby daughter thrived. The women on the Station now came to ask Willy not only advice on child welfare, but especially to watch Evie grow up in physical good health. In comparison with the usually small village babies, our people called her *Lonpela* – the 'long' or 'tall' one.

Willy and Evie were a continuing source of fascination for the women on Bainyik, who took in every detail of the Missis's child rearing. When they took a rest from their routine chores of sweeping, weeding and minor maintenance of the Station grounds, from under our house on stilts Willy often saw dozens of pairs of coal-black eyes looking up through the cracks of the floor, watching intently. In the privacy of our bedroom, when Willy sat on the bed to feed our daughter at the breast, the village mothers could not see them, but they did notice the white woman bottle-feeding her thriving, bouncing, child supplementary substances that they thought was milk. This bottle feeding, they concluded, must therefore be the secret of Lonpela's size and health.

Other expatriates in the district had toddlers or young children, but as far as we knew, the local people in our area had never seen a European baby. When Willy told the indigenous mothers that she fed her child at the breast the same as they did, the women listened politely but obviously disagreed with her. '*Pikanini bilong mipela rabis lik lik, nogat kamap olsem Lonpela pikanini bilong yu* (Our children are inferior [smaller], not as healthy [long, tall] as your child),' they would say. '*Pikanini bilong yu e nogat drin susu bilong mama tasol, nogat, em e drin susu long bottel* (Your child is not fed only mother's breast milk, but it drinks milk from a bottle).' For these mothers from an ancient society, and for their fellow parent, Willy, whatever the differences in their respective child rearing practices, swapping information and stories worked in a positive sense for both parties. In the 'wilds of New Guinea' as Mrs Hurley had called it, Willy felt that with the company of New Guinean parents she was not alone as a mother. In later life we sometimes wondered where we found the courage – or was it blissful ignorance – to raise our infant daughter in a little leaf-thatched house in the jungle of New Guinea.

A promotion

After Willy and I had settled at Bainyik, the months flew by. Suddenly it was November 1956 and by year's end, Ron was due to take his recreation leave in Australia. Department staff had a two-year period of service, followed by three months of holidays. After leave, headquarters would decide a staff member's new placing. Unfortunately, when Ron and Eileen were on leave in Australia, Eileen fell ill and Ron had to resign.

When Ron left, I became the Officer in Charge (OIC), the *Nambawan Masta*, the boss at Bainyik. As such, 'Le Roi est mort, Vive le Roi (The King is dead, Long live the King),' my new status inevitably caused changes in the vested interests of our indigenous community. Being the mankimasta of the new Nambawan meant a surge for Trenyan's social prestige, and if any of his fellows had previously aligned themselves with Ron and Eileen's hausboi, they now quickly joined Trenyan's side. Another realignment of loyalties among our indigenous workforce concerned tractor driver Pogginangu. Together with the three bosbois on Bainyik, these four were the Station's indigenous influentials – with especial fidelity to the OIC Ron. Ron's favourite, Pogginangu in particular was wholeheartedly loyal to him, to the point that when his first child, a son, was born, he named the baby after his adored master 'Ron'. Where it concerned me, the Nambatu Masta, Pogginangu had always treated me with only just enough of the deference that we considered due from a black man to his white superior at the time. When I had instructed him in his work, he had frequently felt it necessary to tell me that his beloved Nambawan Masta would have him do it differently. Now that I had taken the OIC's place, Pogginangu could not find it in himself to switch his former loyalty and affection for his former boss to me. Also, somewhat inevitably, Pogginangu's former power base suffered, and in the game of Station back-stairs influence, when new players sprang into prominence, I gained my own band of sycophants. In the dynamics of our small community, when the former nambatu tractor driver, Nami, became the operator of our new Caterpillar D4 crawler tractor – a piece of machinery so supreme that it thoroughly outshone the old International W6 – Nami gained the top spot in prestige over Pogginangu. Regrettably a bad loser, Pogginangu barely hid his dislike – and even disdain – of me.

Another one of 'my men' was Takanambu, a worker in the labour line who had long badgered me to teach him to drive the Station jeep. Shortly after Ron left for 'South', Takanambu's persistence paid off. I let him practice driving the Station's brand-new, long wheelbase Landrover, which had replaced the tired old warhorse jeep, on Hayfield airstrip. Like Nami, Takanambu's prestige soared.

Before Ron left, my work mainly consisted of inspecting plots of land, supervising labourers and distributing seeds and plants to the local people. My work was more people-focussed; Ron's was more administrative, and he carried the overall responsibility for the station. Unfortunately, there was no replacement for my Numbatu Masta job. When Ron left, I had to take on both roles.

Taking leave in Australia

After I took over as the Officer in Charge at Bainyik, the remainder of my two-year term of duty went by quickly and it was suddenly our turn for the regulation three months recreation leave. When our holidays came due, we welcomed a respite in Australia. Two years of life in the Territory bush had sometimes challenged our physical and mental resources, which needed a break.

Our departure from Bainyik to begin leave in Australia was a carbon copy of how the previous OIC had left for his vacation. The entire Station workforce turned out, standing alongside the track all the way down to the Screw River, to see us be driven to Maprik, from where we would fly to Wewak on the first leg of our travel to Australia. In traditional New Guinea farewell fashion my 'men' – in particular our mankimasta Trenyan, tractor driver Nami and Landrover 'chauffeur' Takanambu – shed buckets of tears. In all honesty, Willy's eyes and mine also shed some of Nature's lubricant – sometimes it does the soul good to let it happen.

In the air to Wewak the Norseman flew us over Bainyik Agricultural Station, and on the ground below, now back at work or in front of their huts, we saw the people looking up at the plane. We could not hear them, but we imagined them calling out a last farewell to us, itinerant Territorians, *'Aiiiééé... MastaMissisLonpela igo pinis... aiiiééé... mipela sorri-iii!'* A lament that requires no translation.

In the three months of our holidays revisiting Naracoorte and Millicent, we became reacquainted with aspects of Australian society that we had almost forgotten about in the Territory. In the accent of our speech, remnants of which no amount of time will wholly erase, the familiar but almost forgotten ritual questions of the 'New Australians' mantra' recurred: 'Where are you from and how do you like Australia?' To our one-time equally ritual replies – that we came from Holland and that 'we *love* Australia, the people so genuine, so friendly,' – we now added that we worked in New Guinea. When people jumped to the conclusion that we must be missionaries, we purposely but deceitfully corrected them, 'No, we are mercenaries,' and we inwardly laughed at the confusion this answer caused. We also observed that the waves of immediate post Second World War immigrants from the Northern Hemisphere had not yet much changed the insular, xenophobic Australian society, nor the jealously held Anglo Australian culture. In the 'Old' Australian psyche we, and those like us from the early 1950s, remained 'New' and sometimes 'Bloody New' Australians.

But we also managed to have a lovely time, staying with old friends and showing Evie off to them, and spending time together. It was a pleasure to be able to go shopping and drive around. I even bought an old gramophone and some very popular rock music. But holidays must come to an end, and soon enough it was time for us to return north.

Local *singsings* were a part of life in the Sepik River District.

The visually arresting tribal dress of the singsings continue to feature today in the annual Goroka Show.

Bainyik

CHAPTER 19

Port Moresby

I had hoped that when we returned to the Territory from leave we would be sent back to Bainyik. Instead I was posted to the Department of Agriculture, Stock and Fisheries Head Office in Port Moresby to act in the capacity of the Territory's Plant Introduction and Quarantine Officer, who was on Long Leave. The role comprised uneventful and even boring work of a routine administrative and clerical nature – administering the importation of exotic plant materials from overseas for trial or distribution in the Territory. I was initially disappointed that I would not be returning to work 'in the field'. However, we had recently become aware that we were expecting our second child, and in this regard we could not have hoped for a better posting than Port Moresby. In 1956, 'Moresby' – as it was called – was a small, colonial town that many Australians did not realise was the capital of the Australian Territory of Papua and New Guinea. When compared with the steaming, dripping, jungle at Bainyik, Port Moresby's many social and particularly medical services were far superior. With a new baby on the way we had drawn the winning ticket for our next two years in the Territory.

Getting to know Moresby
When previously flying from Sydney to New Guinea, Willy and I had only briefly seen Port Moresby from the air, missing most of the landmarks that distinguished the Australian colonial outpost. Posted to our new backyard, so to speak, we began to explore Moresby's

environs. Fringed by the sea, in a very brief distance from the shore, the hills rise up to about 150 feet above sea level. On these hills the earth has everywhere leached to bedrock. In early times, residents of Port Moresby had to obtain soil from farther inland to form the beautiful gardens that give these once barren steeps their exceptionally tropical appearance. At the appropriate time of the year poinciana and coral trees burst into profuse flowering, painting the drab, dusty, corrugated promontories with dabs of vivid scarlet. Varieties of white, pink and yellow year-round flowering frangipani trees not only lend colour to the environment, but their heady perfume mingles with the salt-laden breezes that fan Port Moresby's tropical heat. Bougainvillea, crepe myrtle, bird of paradise, orchids, crotons and many other colourful plants and flowers make Port Moresby resemble a gaudy, Gaugin-painted landscape – a tropical paradise.

In the era immediately following the end of the Second World War, a major problem for Administration personnel posted to Port Moresby was the lack of accommodation for married couples. Critical shortages of building materials in Australia meant that the Administration's housing development scheme could not keep up with demand from the rapidly increasing expatriate population. This was an issue in the large urban centres such as Port Moresby, Lae, Madang, Rabaul and Goroka, and – to a lesser extent – in Finschafen, Wewak, Kavieng and similar smaller towns throughout Papua and New Guinea. As a result, when an officer returned from a spell in Australia it was common practice for them to temporarily move into a so-called 'leave house' – one whose permanent occupants were away on their periodic holiday entitlement. These temporary arrangements generally worked out reasonably well, as the home's owners were usually happy to have someone 'house sit' in their absence. When we returned from our holidays, my small family had no alternative but to accept temporary accommodation. Nor could we complain about the leave house allocated to us on prestigious Paga Hill, whose residents had gone on six months Long Leave in Australia.

In the years between the World Wars, Port Moresby's population had remained small. In 1935, inhabitants were estimated to number 2500 indigenous and 300 non-indigenous persons. In the post Second World War years, when the growth of the town's community was very rapid, by 1956 this estimate had risen to respectively 12,000 indigenous and 4000 expatriate residents. In subsequent years throughout the period up to national independence in 1975, the number of expatriate residents in Port Moresby continued to increase, and that of the indigenous community dramatically exploded into legions of tribespeople from all over the Territory who wished to participate in the bright, modern, Western city life.

Living in Port Moresby in the 1950s was to experience the active conditions of Australia's colonial history in Papua and New Guinea. Dating from the early days of the British Protectorate, the residents of Port Moresby lived in segregated areas of the settlement, causing a marked division between ethnic white and black groups. Before the Second World War, in a letter to the local newspaper written by a white 'B4' Territorian, the underlying assumptions of this racial division seemed clearly shown when he wrote, 'Although we are in a native country we have no desire to be amongst native-inhabited buildings... within the town limits, and desire less to be continually annoyed by coloured folk permitted within the town vicinity, unheard of in other native countries'[xxvii]. There is little doubt that this correspondent reflected the view of most white residents of Port Moresby. By 1956, when Willy and I came to live there, we felt that the town was definitely a white Australian settlement where white residents had little contact with the Papuans and New Guineans, except as servants or in other lowly employment in the town's essential services. In essence and in fact, where it concerned the colonialists but also the 'natives', Port Moresby was 'the white man's place', and white Europeans *were* the town.

Among other vestiges of colonialism was the segregation of races at Ela Beach, Port Moresby's favourite recreational swimming beach. As another early correspondent to the local newspaper had written, residents took exception to '... find themselves swamped in a sea (sic) of naked or ragged and dirty betel-nut chewing people who did not use lavatories. It is almost impossible for white people to walk along the Beach owing to cooking, etc., going on among the... natives'.[xxviii] Throughout our posting to Port Moresby, Ela Beach remained a proclaimed white reserve. Nailed to the beautiful casuarina trees that lined the shore were signs displaying the notice, 'For Europeans Only', ensuring that Ela Beach was the exclusive playground of the town's white residents.

Another example of ongoing colonial rule was the continued enactment of the Native Labour Regulations of 1914. These forbade any indigenous person other than a domestic servant, '… after the hour of seven o'clock in the evening to enter, remain, or to be within or upon the town limits of Port Moresby'. For the convenience of European householders, any exception to the curfew required the written consent of a Magistrate or an Inspector. In practice, this meant that employers needed to issue their employees with a 'pass', a written, signed and dated notice of the servant's *bona fides*, lest on his way back to the 'native compound' at night he should be detained by an authority. During our time in Port Moresby (1956–1958), we hired a domestic servant and so the Native Labour Regulations affected our household in general, but our mankimasta in particular. Such was our colonial life at the time.

Although my posting to Port Moresby had initially been somewhat of a disappointment, Willy, who was pregnant with our second child, now had access to proper medical facilities, regular pre-natal check-ups, and even courses in child care. These were a decided improvement to Doc Szymiczek's, 'Congratulations, you are pregnant, have a beer!'

Whereas at Bainyik there was neither electricity nor reticulated water laid on in our native materials house, all of Port Moresby's expatriate residences had both facilities as a matter of course. Also, instead of having to obtain supplies from Tang Mow Trade Store in Wewak by air on the weekly 'milk run' (or arrange for a twice-a-year bulk grocery order from the McIlwraith Company in Sydney, which then specialised in this service to Territory), we had the convenience of the Burns Philp and Steamships Trading Co department stores, where we could shop as we needed for our household. Burns Philp, however, retained a reminder of colonial times until the late 1950s. Overhead in the store, huge, manually operated punka fans provided cooling. The Papua New Guinean *punka boi* – counterpart of the British Indian *punka wallah* – performed his task sitting down with the punka rope tied to his foot, pulling the fans back and forth. The stirring of hot air in the shop did not do a great deal to relieve the oven-like conditions inside, but it at least gave customers the illusion of being cooled… a *little*…?

The Port Moresby posting was a pleasant change from life on a small outstation. Soon after we arrived back in the Territory, we bought an old but quite sound motorcar. This allowed us to explore the limited road network around the town – fewer than 95 kilometres in all. Some of these were surfaced, but most remained unmade clay tracks. They roughly followed the coastline north-west, terminating at Brown River, and passed through the lowland savannah grasslands south-east, finishing at Kemp Welsh River. Inland from Port Moresby, the road linked to the Sogeri Plateau. At 2000 feet above sea-level, the plateau was commercially important for rubber estates, and also provided Port Moresby residents with the opportunity to enjoy picnics, walks, swimming, and other recreational activities in the cooler Sogeri climate.

Willy and I celebrated a personal milestone in July 1957 when, having completed the then mandatory five years of residency, we became naturalised Australian citizens. Until then, I had been appointed in the Territory Administration in an Exempt Capacity, but having become a naturalised Australian I now gained Permanent Officer Status. This came with career advancement opportunities and full entitlement to superannuation provisions. Also, our Australian citizenship meant that although she was born at Wewak in the Mandated Trust Territory of New Guinea, our daughter was included in our Certificate of Naturalisation. Evie too had gained Australian citizenship.

Tapep

At the time we set up house in the Territory, few if any residents did not have a mankimasta, or hausboi, for the more menial domestic duties. In the big cities such as Port Moresby, Lae, Madang and Rabaul there was a more than ample supply of young men from the country looking for work. A daily stream of them presented at our door, eager to fill the position of home help. Keeping in mind the advice Eileen had given me at Bainyik, Willy and I carefully interviewed the local Papuan callers, and the New Guinean immigrants from the rural hinterlands who came to us saying, '*Masta, Missis, mi painim wok* (Sir, Madam, I am looking for work)'. From all the would-be servants, our selection of Tapep turned out to be a fortunate one.

When we initially interviewed Tapep, he revealed a detail of his background that nearly decided us against employing him. He came from an area of the Lae District hinterlands notorious for being home to the Kukukuku clan. Many of the tribe's older generation had been fierce warriors and some were thought to still practice cannibalism. When we questioned our would-be mankimasta about his background, he protested that he was a baptised Christian and a devout, practicing Roman Catholic, and that he had certainly forsaken the wicked ways of his forebears. Clinching his defence, he pulled from his billum (string pouch) a khaki shirt with insignia sewn on a sleeve, proclaiming '*Mi Boiskot* (I am a Boy Scout)' – meaning, by implication, 'Trust me'.

To our gratification, Tapep proved himself worthy of every assurance that he had given us about his previous training and experience in a European household, and, unlike with Trenyan, Willy did not find it necessary to train our new servant in his domestic duties. To our pleasure he and our little Evie took a mutual liking to one another, and Tapep often wheeled her around the yard in her pusher. On hot days, unconcerned how wet he got himself, he kept watch over her as he let her play under the sprinkler on the front lawn. Every Saturday, on his afternoon off, Tapep would don the khaki shirt and shorts and long khaki socks of his Scout uniform and squeeze his broad feet into an old pair of large black shoes. Thus dressed, he went out for his Scout Troop's weekly meeting. Despite the fearsome background of his Kukukuku *wantoks* (kinfolk), Tapep was a gentle person who had evidently come to terms with modern civilisation. We appreciated his devotion to our family. Settled into the routines of living in a major town, our everyday life passed by peacefully, and even somewhat idyllically, in the Territory's capital, Port Moresby.

A Moresby baby

In August 1957, the time approached for the birth of our second child. Willy and I arranged that, should I be needed when at my office, she would ring me to come home. The residents of our leave house had returned, so we had shifted to a suburb where Tapep did not have to commute to the native compound. Instead, he lived in the backyard of our residence in what was called the '*boihouse*', the servant quarters.

This time under proper medical care, Willy's pre-natal progress had been without incident and all signs pointed to an uneventful birth. When the time came near, 'it' did not as dramatically signal its intention to enter into the world as had done its sister, but, in its own way, it too caused somewhat of a stir. One morning when I was at work, Willy made the call, urging, 'You'd better come quickly – the baby is on the way!' The news made me jump into our car and push the poor old vehicle to speeds to which it had long been unused. By the time I reached our home, the same as had happened with its sister, the baby had changed its mind. My agitation and breaking of the speed limits had been unnecessary. Nevertheless, as there was no doubting that the baby was on the way, I drove Willy to Port Moresby's European hospital where late that afternoon our baby, Terrence John, was born. We were delighted with our healthy, vigorous son, a brother to Evie. My dear Willy and I counted ourselves blessed with 'a pigeon pair', to treasure then, and forever.

We delighted in our toddlers, Evie and Terrence – our 'pigeon pair'.

The impending birth of our son had caused some consternation in our household, leading to events that I did not become aware of until later. When I returned home after Terrence was born, I could not find Tapep anywhere; he had gone missing. When I mentioned his mysterious absence to Willy at the hospital, at first she looked embarrassed, then she explained what had happened. Just before she rang me at the office, Willy and Tapep had been busy in the kitchen when, without warning, her waters broke. Tapep had momentarily stood as if transfixed, his eyes bulging as he tried to accept the implication of the wetness on the floor. As realisation dawned on him, our faithful servant almost jumped out of his skin. He turned away from the scene and rushed to his quarters in the backyard. Emerging from the boihaus clutching his billum and a few other personal possessions, with legs pumping furiously he had disappeared out of our yard and down the street. Unless he had stopped somewhere to recover his breath, Willy speculated, he was probably still running. We never saw Tapep again, and could only guess that the reason for his hasty exit was that, witnessing the imminent arrival of our second child, he became terrified with an ancient dread or superstition. Or perhaps he had realised that an extra workload would soon be awaiting him with the arrival of a second *pikinini* (child), making him decide that he was not willing to live up to his Boiskot motto: Be Prepared!

A holiday in Scarborough

The time of our posting to Port Moresby passed otherwise quite uneventfully, and when my next leave became due, we decided to spend it at Scarborough Beach – where I had fond boyhood memories from my family vacation before the war. With four-year-old Evie and two-year-old Terrence, Willy and I flew from New Guinea to Melbourne then took ship's passage to Fremantle, from where we travelled by taxi to Scarborough. I barely recognised the countryside we passed through. Where in my memory kangaroos bounced in long fluid leaps over a sandy wasteland, we now drove through what had become an almost contiguous Perth suburbia. When the taxi pulled into what had been the sleepy little seaside village of Scarborough, I found that a major township had arisen and that ugly high-rise residential developments now cast long shadows over the golden beaches and once pristine dunes. The very centre of the old village had also changed, and I could find neither the Kool Korner Kafé on the esplanade, nor the small shop where, with deft strokes of flashing cleaver on the big wooden chopping block, we had watched Les Melon produce wondrous cuts of meat. When the taxi dropped us off at the rented holiday house, the driver remained seated behind the wheel and – like my father – I was left to unload our luggage from the vehicle's boot. In that sense Scarborough had remained unchanged.

Once settled into our rented accommodation, we began to explore Scarborough. I discovered that although the old village street names had been given more fanciful titles, by counting them back from the town centre I could locate where – in what used to be Fifth Street – Mrs Forster's Penteila Flats had stood. These too had disappeared, and the large block of land with the dunnies in the backyard had been subdivided to make place for three or so modern dwellings. Gone also were the brumbies that used to come down out of the dunes to steal the grass that grew on dispirited lawns.

But the beach remained unchanged. On windy days we could still hear the ocean waves rolling in and breaking, like echoes from the past. As we sat or walked on the beach in good weather, the wavelets that crept inshore still expired on the sands with a frothy sigh. Evie and Terrence loved the beach. Like my sister and I had done, they collected small treasures from the sands – bits of driftwood, colourful seashells. In the late afternoon, when the sun began to sink into the Indian Ocean, it painted the beach a golden sunset hue.

CHAPTER 20

Daru

Nature speaks in symbols and in signs
John Greenleaf Whittier, *To Charles Sumner*

As did all Territorians on holidays in Australia, Willy and I had speculated where we would spend the next two years in the Territory. Among many possible postings in the field there were some that Administration personnel looked upon with favour, but for one reason or another there were one or two that not only DASF staff but others in the Administration looked upon as a virtual banishment; 'punishment' for having somehow incurred their Department's displeasure. In the general opinion of Territory Administration staff, the least desirable posting in all of Papua and New Guinea was the small outstation of Green River in the Sepik District. Hot on its heels was the settlement of Daru in the Western District of Papua.

On our return from Australia, I reported to DASF Head Office and learned, somewhat to my chagrin, that I would next be posted to Daru. The news came as a somewhat unpleasant surprise – the Western District was considered the most underdeveloped district in the Territory, and an undesirable destination to spend a two-year term of duty. I felt that I had drawn the short straw, and the question that not unreasonably came to mind was, 'Why *me*?' It was therefore some relief when my Chief of Division told me that I was required to urgently take over from my predecessor who, for the sake of his dangerously ill wife, had been transferred to Port Moresby on compassionate medical grounds.

My superior officer also told me that I had received promotion to the rank of District Agricultural Officer, making me the Department's senior representative in the Western District. This somewhat took the sting out of a posting for which few – if any – of my colleagues envied me.

A Papuan 'water wonderland'

The Central Cordillera is the 'spine' of New Guinea, separating the Western District of Papua from its counterpart in the northwest: the Sepik District. In these western-most divisions of the Australian-administered territories of Papua and New Guinea, the aptly named Star Mountains extend from south to north. Containing some of the highest peaks on the entire island, they provide a formidable physical and geographical boundary between the Australian territories and what is now Indonesia. The towering Star Mountains and the Central Cordillera form the watershed for the Territory's great river systems. On the New Guinea side, the Sepik and May rivers drain the northern half of the island; almost directly opposite them, the mighty Fly and Strickland rivers drain the southern part.

In the Western District, the region's high mountain ranges slope south and west to the undulating hill country of the Oriomo Plateau, a somewhat inapt name, as the 'plateau' never reaches much more than 30 metres above sea level. In turn the plateau gives way to the Fly River lowlands, an enormous basin that extends to the Gulf of Papua and the Torres Strait. This far south-western part of the country – also known as the 'Trans-Fly' region – covers an area of more than 100,000 square kilometres, not including its mountainous hinterland.

The Western District is a country of extremes in climate. During the wet season (December to April) it rains almost incessantly and the combination of heat and humidity is enervating to man and beast. South of the Cordillera, from May till October is the dry season, and when the south-east trade winds blow a balmy sigh over all living things, the temperature is mild and the humidity almost disappears. The region has great variability in vegetation with vast mangrove, sago, and nipa palm stands growing in dank soil and often in incredibly deep mud. For miles inland the high tides completely submerge the coastal swamps, which at low tide are riddled with creeks. Farther inland, fringing the banks of the great rivers, oppressively dark, dense virgin forests seldom extend more than a few kilometres in width. Behind the heavily timbered area, the country changes into savannah; the open grass country becomes a second belt of vast, wide lagoons in an irregular chain approximately parallel with the rivers. The third distinctive belt is a region of low, undulating hills that form the watershed of smaller rivers flowing to the south. Here the soil is generally dry, hard underfoot and with frequent outcrops of ironstone. Several streams arise from this country, the largest of which are the Bensbach and the Morehead rivers. Among the lesser of the waters are the Mai Kussa, Binaturi and Oriomo rivers. These incredible bodies of water – the mightiest of which is the Fly River – far outshine the indubitable might of the Sepik and even the Markham rivers on the New Guinean side. Without question, the Papuan waterways and their surrounding country exert a particular fascination.[xxix]

About 5 kilometres from the mainland lies Daru Island, at the time home to a small Papuan population and the District's Administrative headquarters. Daru Island is separated from New Guinea by a dangerous channel, through which surges fast-flowing tides. These, and the shark and crocodile infested waters, make travel between Daru Island and the opposite coast hazardous for smaller vessels. On the mainland directly opposite Daru Island is the mouth of the fast-flowing but generally placid Oriomo River, reached by outboard-powered canoe. In 1958, farther inland on the bank of the river, nothing much grew but sago palm. There the Department had established the Oriomo Agriculture Station, where it conducted trials of cash crops that were thought suited to the soils and climate.

As rivers in the Western District drained the country, they often dislodged trees and sometimes even small islands of reeds and shrubs. These not infrequently carried on them small animals that could not escape before the ground on which they stood broke away. At times caught in a maelstrom along the river bank, the floating debris sometimes stayed endlessly circling, moving no farther until some day, somehow, something sent them onwards downriver and out to sea. Sometimes a huge submerged tree, a tangle of branches, the crown of a giant of the forest, would come bearing unseen downstream, making a hazard of its own, catching and entangling an unsuspecting canoe or even a larger vessel travelling on the river.

The world of these rivers has a character all of its own. Sometimes the rivers are placid, with lazy shallows along the riverbanks; at other times their fast-flowing centres make the same waters treacherous with tidal rips, undercurrents, and submerged debris. Early in the morning, when the ascending sun warms land and air, banks of fog form over the river. Swirling mists cover the surface with a white mantle of vapour for kilometres, until the increasing heat of the day makes the foggy dew gradually disappear. In the months of April to July, enormous clusters of exquisite, vividly red flowers as large as a man's hand appear on New Guinea Creeper vines that garland the tall trees along the river for miles. The beauty of the country is astounding and hard to convey.

The people of the Western District of Papua, in common with the rest of the country, occupied distinct tribal areas. Delimited by linguistic unity, a shared 'Police Motu' or trade language was the basis for the ethnic classification of people living within but also beyond the purely administrative boundaries between the Australian and the Dutch (later Indonesian) part of the island. Ethnic groups – tribes with their own language – exhibited a medley of linguistic variations and locally varying cultures. The groups of the Trans-Fly region included the Kiwai, Gambadi, Keraki, Mikud, Aram, Boigu, and Marind-Anim tribes.

Arriving at Daru

The DC3 in which we travelled from Port Moresby to the Western District took a lazy turn over the sea as the pilot prepared to land on Daru Island. Through the aircraft's window I could make out the margins of the island, fringed with thick mangrove and nipa palm stands. Behind this swampland extended relatively bare, sandy country covered with sparse grasses and clumps of struggling paperbark eucalyptus – the kind of vegetation that indicates poor soil fertility. As the plane took another turn over the approximately 5-kilometre-wide, long and generally flat Daru Island, I could make out the airstrip. Consisting of a red runway of pure clay and a small 'terminal' – in reality nothing more than a small tin shed – the airstrip occupied the highest point on the island. From the air we spotted an unsurfaced, red clay track that ran about a kilometre into the island to where a settlement of houses stood under mango and poinciana trees. The track terminated at the far western end of the island, where a cluster of what seemed to be office buildings stood within a few yards of where the sea lapped at a black sandy beach. On the water drifted a small fleet of traditional sailing canoes tied up to a long jetty that extended a couple of hundred feet out over the sea. Approximately 4 kilometres across the channel between Daru Island and the mainland, dense mangrove and nipa palm stood in swampland that stretched as far as the eye could see. The vegetation's drab, dark green colour contrasted with the hazy blue sea that girded Daru Island, which at that time of year was splendidly daubed with the vivid red flowers of poinciana growing along the road and in the gardens of residential homes. From the air, Daru looked picturesque – an almost tropical idyll – but we soon would be in for a surprise.

Completing its second wide, canted turn over the island, the aircraft levelled out and began its descent, finally touching down on the airstrip. But, instead of braking hard to control its landing speed, its two engines suddenly roared into urgent life. Willy and I were by now seasoned Territory air travellers. A DC3 does not have the reverse engine thrust that assists the braking in modern aircraft, so we knew that our pilot had undertaken an unusual manoeuvre. The plane had not travelled far over land when it became obvious even to less experienced passengers that it was struggling to maintain forward momentum. Indeed, not even halfway along the length of the airstrip, our DC3 came to a premature halt. The plane's engines switched off, and the captain and his co-pilot emerged from the cockpit. 'Sorry, people, the old balus got bogged,' the latter announced laconically as he opened the door, inviting the passengers to disembark. On the ground, the cause for our unusual landing was evident – the aircraft's tyres had sunk up to the axles in mud. We realised that but for the skill of our pilot, there could have been more serious consequences than getting bogged. As my little family walked away from the beleaguered DC3 towards the 'terminal' further down the strip, rain began to fall on us. It seemed an unprepossessing start for our next two years in the Western District of Papua, and our first impression of Daru was not very favourable. With every step, our town shoes became redder in colour and heavier with mud underfoot, reminding us of the decidedly more comfortable life in the comparative civilisation of Port Moresby that we had left behind.

Waiting to welcome Willy and me at the terminal was the District Officer – the second highest-ranking Administration official in the

Western District, after the District Commissioner. He invited the pilots and us to climb into the Landrover, the only vehicle on the island, and we were privileged to be driven down the 'road'. The other expatriate and indigenous passengers had to walk down the frightfully slippery and potholed clay track to the settlement. As we drove down the road, the District Officer remarked, 'As you will be aware, your predecessor's wife was seriously ill. Although your house is one of only three built of imported 'European' materials, due to the lady's medical condition, it has not been quite kept with the best of care.' As an afterthought the District Officer added, 'Your colleague and his wife were better naturalists and lovers of animals than they were fussy housekeepers.' We soon discovered that this was meant as a warning.

Be it ever so humble
The District Officer's veiled caution was not nearly sufficient to prepare us for what was to be our home on Daru. The District Officer left us *'to settle in'*, whereupon poor Willy – not usually given to emotional outbursts – sat on a suitcase and wept. Between her sobs, all that she could manage to say was, 'I want to go back to Moresby,' emphatically adding, 'Now!' And, really, who could blame her?

In our married life we had occasionally put up with what surely could be described as unusual accommodation: the leaky 'cottage' on the Armstrongs' farm, the humpy-back caravan in the Naracoorte bush, the little corrugated shack at Millicent, the bush house at Bainyik – even the leave houses in Port Moresby. But nothing compared with what we found waiting for us on Daru.

We were standing under an enormous mango tree in a neglected garden. All around us lay broken plant pots and boxes filled with soil in which even the weeds looked ready to give up their struggle for existence. The outdoor furniture consisted of a disjointed wooden bench, a few dilapidated, rain-soaked wicker chairs and a trestle table that barely hung together, repaired with bits of wire and rope. The dismal condition of these items did nothing to enhance the sorry sight of what would be our home. The District Officer had told us that only his home, the District Commissioner's residence, and ours were built with 'European' materials. Although our expectations had not been high, we were appalled our residence's truly indescribable state of neglect and disrepair.

An open veranda ran the length of the building on both sides. To our astonishment, there we spotted several mother hens followed by their broods of numerous chickens, all pecking and scratching around, busily looking for insects, moths and whatever else they found edible. Wide open doors hanging at crazy angles from their damaged hinges gave free access to the interior of the house, and these free-ranging birds had left ample and unmistakable evidence of their presence on the floors and furniture. The District Officer's diplomatic words that my colleague and his wife were 'better naturalists and animal lovers that they were fussy housekeepers' now rang as an understatement of the unmitigated disaster that was to be our accommodation on Daru.

I gingerly set foot inside the residence to discover the situation was worse than what we had seen from the garden outside. The filth left by the hens and their chickens indicated that they had probably been scavenging there for as long as our predecessors had occupied it. The floors could not have seen broom or mop and bucket – let alone polish – applied for years. If the living room covered with chicken manure was in bad condition, the kitchen was worse! Floors, benches and cupboards were filthy with fowl droppings and even the ceiling was sticky with grease from cooking fumes that had settled on everything. On further inspection, the three bedrooms, bathroom and indoor toilet were in no better repair. Willy had followed me inside, and on looking around she turned to me, and said simply, 'Please take me to the District Commissioner, immediately.' I knew that if the DC3 was not bogged on the airstrip unable to take off, she would have insisted on us returning to Port Moresby that same day. In fairness, I could not blame her.

Although Willy was normally of a placid nature, when occasion demanded it she could make her position and views known. The District Commissioner soon discovered that Willy could do so with a conviction that broached no denying. Furious that before we had arrived, no-one on Daru had checked to ensure that our residence was in a reasonably habitable condition, Willy confronted the District Commissioner with a terse description of the disgraceful state in which we had found the dwelling. Her ultimatum was, 'Either you have the house completely scrubbed out before sundown today, and from tomorrow begin to have it repaired and painted inside and out, or my family and I will be on the next plane back to Port Moresby.' Not even the District Commissioner doubted Willy's determination to make good her promise.

An epic clean-up

Daru's reputation as an undesirable posting destination wasn't helped by the island being home to one of Papua and New Guinea's major high-security gaols. The prison held some of the country's most intractable and notorious criminals – 'lifers' convicted of major crimes including multiple murder, rape, even cannibalism. Like the notorious Alcatraz prison, Daru was separated from the mainland by dangerous waters, which ensured that the prison island was virtually escape proof. With the DC3 bogged on the muddy airstrip, in a way our family was also held prisoner on Daru Island.

The island's incarcerated population provided a pool of free and freely available labour. When we left the District Office and returned to the wreckage that was our house, we had only to wait half an hour before a long line of prisoners arrived, accompanied by two local constables and armed with brooms, buckets, mops, soap, disinfectants and other cleaning paraphernalia. Some of those 'detained at Her Majesty's pleasure' went to work rounding up the offending livestock inside the house and in the grounds, another detail applied water, soap, scrubbing brushes and more water to all the floors, walls and ceilings, and a third party began to straighten out the garden, weeding and cutting the long grass and collecting the broken furniture and other useless rubbish left behind by the previous residents. When the first group returned from catching and chasing away the fowls and the odd curious dog that had wandered among them, they began to hose down and scrub the outside walls of the building. By the time night began to fall, the house smelt strongly of phenyl disinfectant and soap, and inside no traces remained of the neglect and filth that we had found. When the District Commissioner himself came to check on the progress, Willy grudgingly said that, 'for the present' she was satisfied that the house was marginally habitable. With a statement, not a request, she reminded the Commissioner, 'Tomorrow you will see to it that the house gets painted.'

Our first night on Daru we slept fitfully. The DC3 getting bogged on the airstrip; the sorry state of repair in which we had found the house; the lingering smell of the disinfectant that the prison gang had liberally applied everywhere to clean up our home – these were impressions that played on our minds. When I awoke the next morning the sun had barely risen above the horizon, sending a tentative ray into our bedroom. Keeping still in bed so as not to awaken my exhausted wife, it took me a few seconds to adjust my senses to the unfamiliar surroundings. I became aware of rattling and scraping sounds and the unmistakable smell of burning paper and wood coming from the direction of the kitchen. When I crept out of bed to investigate the noises, I found a man dressed in the government regulation-green prison lap-lap printed with black arrows. He was bent over the wood stove tending a lusty fire under the cooking plate. When I asked the man in Pidgin English, '*Yu mekim wonem*? (What are you doing?),' he replied, '*Masta, mi calaboose bilong yu* (Sir, I am your prisoner).' As I did not know what else to do under the circumstances, I accepted the man's answer to later have the matter cleared up in the District Office. Taking advantage of the lit stove, I began to prepare breakfast for my sleeping family. Outside in the backyard I could hear the *calaboose* (prisoner) hard at work chopping more firewood for the stove.

When I later enquired about the matter, the District Officer explained that all expatriate officers' homes on the island were allocated an inmate from the prison, providing free labour to help with chores in and around the house. As was common practice on Daru, one's 'calaboose' could be put to work to maintain the garden, sweep or wash down verandas, keep up a supply of firewood for the kitchen, and so on; in short, they would assist in a variety of menial household tasks. When I asked the District Officer if it was safe to have a convicted criminal in my house he smiled and said, 'Your chap is a trustee, a reliable prisoner.' It was not until days later that I discovered that my 'reliable prisoner' had been sentenced to twenty years imprisonment on Daru for a tribal double axe murder! Given his background, it seemed somewhat of an antithesis that our calaboose used a sharp axe to cut firewood for the kitchen.

There was no doubt that if it had not been for the bogged aeroplane, Willy would have made good her promise that we would have been on board its return flight to Port Moresby that same day. As it was, the day after our arrival, our two DC3 pilots were picked up at Daru by a Catalina flying boat that landed in the sea between the island and the mainland. It was not until three weeks later, when the airstrip had dried out, that they returned to Daru to supervise their aircraft being pulled out of the bog. By then, conditions on Daru had changed so much that even Willy had given up the idea of returning to Port Moresby.

True to his promise, the District Commissioner had spared neither manpower nor materials to clean up and completely renovate our house. Papuan tradesmen from the Public Works Department had straightened or replaced windows and doors that had hung skew-whiff or been damaged by animals – or perhaps even by my lackadaisical predecessors themselves. Torn and rusty mosquito wire had been renewed on all windows and doors, and broken louvres replaced. Scores of prisoners with pots of paint had redecorated the entire house inside and out. In the grounds, the garden had been cleaned up and the shrubs in it pruned and trimmed. Altogether these were considerable improvements from what we had found on the day that we arrived on Daru.

The Daru household

As was usual practice in the Territory, among first matters of importance was the search for suitable servants for our household. Contrary to elsewhere in Papua and New Guinea – where house servants are always male – Kiwai men in the Western District were too proud to perform such work. We learned that on Daru, in European households, only females worked as home helpers. Finding no shortage of applicants, we selected two local women – 'girls' as they were commonly referred to – of whom the elder, Anamia, was the equivalent of a mankimasta and the younger, E'eo, the alternative to a male wasboi. Both women had been taught at a local primary school conducted by the London Missionary Society on the island, and they understood and spoke English quite well. Anamia was tall, like most Kiwai people, slender, shy and gentle; she doted on the children and soon became our favourite. The plumpish and nervously energetic E'eo, named after the Kiwai word for the plover bird, seemed to live up to its habits of darting hither and thither. Like her namesake, she would often and somewhat disconcertingly burst into a loud cackling laughter – but this did nothing to detract from her good and honest nature.

Alongside the nameless prisoner, our *ex gratia* home help whom we simply addressed as 'Calaboose', our *hausgirl* Anamia and *wasgirl* E'Eo became part of our household – and indeed, part of our family.

Getting to know Daru

By the late 1950s, much of the coastal margins and the immediate hinterland of Western Papua had long been pacified and they were generally under firm Administration control. Nevertheless, the district's far mountain country and southern-most coastal part were exceptions, where the nature of the terrain made patrolling arduous and often dangerous. To the north and west, the remote high mountain region of the Central Cordillera presented exceptional problems of communication, being either not fully under Administration control, or even with still largely unknown Papuan tribes in the jungle-clad mountains. To the south, inland beyond the Bensbach River live the Marind-Anim, kinsfolk of the fierce Asmat tribe in (then) Dutch New Guinea, whose people at the time sometimes still engaged in cannibalism. Similarly, the central inland part of the Western District was so difficult to patrol that their small, scattered, communities were seldom contacted by the Administration.

High southern mountains descend to the central plain that forms the major catchment of the Fly River, the Western District's greatest waterway. The patrol post of Kiunga on the Upper Fly River was responsible for administering that part of the district, which was first explored in the 1930s by pioneering Patrol Officer Jack G Hides. In later memoirs, Hides wrote in terms of almost desperation about his passage through the extremely rugged area of the high mountain country:

> How am I to describe the difficulties it presents to men who try to cross it...? The rock is honeycombed and stands on end; it forms fissures and craters, large and small, and every step has to be watched, for the limestone edges are as sharp as broken glass. There are no running streams, no water, for the rain seeps immediately through the limestone. The fissures and cylindrical stone pits of this country sometimes appear bottomless to the eye... We found it impossible to cut a straight course... Finding a way northward we walked up narrow and silent corridors of rock, sometimes with the rumble of an underground river far below in our ears, or we cut past deep caves where we could hear the drip falling from stalactites.[xxx]

If Hides's memoirs recalled an earlier time of pioneering exploration, when I was posted to Daru in 1958, the Western District of Papua still truly remained an outpost of civilisation.

This high mountain country was far from an exception when it came to the problem of extending civil administration and economic development to the region. The Gogodara subdistrict – administered from the small Balimo Patrol Post – and the sparsely populated Lake Murray subdistrict on the Middle Fly River – controlled from the Lake Murray Patrol Post – were similarly remote, vast, inhospitable, mosquito-plagued wetlands, difficult to traverse by canoe, and almost impassable on foot. The small settlements in the lake lands area sat perched on low ridges that thrust up only a few feet above deceptively beautiful swamps. The water's surface was thickly covered in exquisite pink and white flowering water lilies, but was frightfully mosquito infested. The consequent high incidence of malaria in the region took a heavy toll on the Papuan population, and presented similar health problems for Australian Administration personnel posted in these areas. They faced risks to their physical health and inescapable loneliness and isolation. Few that lived and worked in the Western District found this easy to accept and deal with. Little wonder that many Administration staff regarded a posting to Papua's Western District a punishment.

If Patrol Officers experienced difficulties in bringing the Western District under civil administration, Field Officers of the Department of Agriculture also encountered problems in fostering the economic advancement of the indigenous people. My predecessor on Daru Island had been the Agricultural Department's first permanently posted extension officer to the District. He had found travel between Daru and the mainland villages difficult, even with an outboard-powered dinghy or an Administration-owned 45-foot workboat. Other than by casual observations made by patrolling Department of Native Affairs officers, the economic potential of the Western District had never been assessed. Little sound technical information had been gathered about the land, the soils and the influence of climate and terrain on plant and animal life. My predecessor had begun to explore the country for its economic potential, however, hampered by his wife's illness, he had made little progress. For the two years of my term of duty in the district, my work became essentially an evaluation of the economic conditions of the Trans-Fly region. At times it was arduous and sometimes dangerous work. By no means did it affect just me; it also shaped the lives of Willy and our children.

After two years of comparative social comforts in Port Moresby, Daru required us to reacquaint ourselves with life on a small outstation. Although it was the District's headquarters, even by Territory standards Daru was a place where many of the amenities of modern civilisation were lacking. Some of this had to do with the problematic, less-than-well-constructed airstrip on which our aeroplane had become bogged. In part due to the inclement weather conditions in the height of the wet season, the condition of the bare, clay-surfaced landing field reflected the low priority in terms of just about everything – including the allocation of personnel, materials and operating funds that the Western District received from Central Administration in Port Moresby. As we had already experienced, living on a penal island, to an extent Daru's European community also felt somewhat imprisoned. Daru Island in the 1950s was essentially a small, insignificant, poorly serviced Papua and New Guinea Administration Outpost: a 'Territory Cinderella'.

In many respects Daru was a-typical of other Territory centres. The island was home to a truly multi-racial population, made up of a majority of indigenous Papua New Guineans, a quite large number of persons of mixed ancestry, around thirty 'European' families of Administration personnel, three Australian missionary couples, two bachelor Australian trade store owners and an Australian crocodile hunter and his wife. Living in close proximity on a small island softened the social distinctions between its residents. At the time, Daru Island was a far more enlightened and racially tolerant community than anywhere else we had been in Papua and New Guinea.

The habitable part of Daru Island faces the mainland west. The eastern outline of the island remained undeveloped, subject as it is to the fiercely blowing monsoonal south-east trade winds and resultant high seas, which pound the shore and send up clouds of heavily salt-laden air. Residences of the expatriates and a few homes of persons of mixed ancestry occupied the high grounds on the island. Those of the indigenous people and the majority of those with mixed ancestry were built on the lower lying country, closer to the sea channel between the island and the mainland. With the exception of the missionaries and a few others in private enterprise, most expatriates were employed by the Administration, and many of the Papuans worked in various trades or unskilled labour for the Public Works Department. Most of the indigenous people on Daru hailed from the Kiwai tribal areas and lived together in customary groupings. Being traditional sailors, they used their large, seagoing outrigger canoes for fishing, selling their produce at the local market. Some dived for pearls and pearl shell, and the Administration employed others as skippers and crew for its four patrol boats.

Daru characters: Lenny Luff, Arthur Wyborn, the two Toms

Among the non-Administration personnel on Daru were several expatriates who, in the immediate post-war years, each for their own reasons, had come to live and work and sometimes to permanently settle on the island. Among these true Territorian identities were 'bachelor' Lenny Luff and his son-in-law Arthur Wyborn. Together, they operated Daru's local trade store – the modest counterpart of Tang Mow's Wewak emporium. The elder Lenny Luff, un-crowned king of Daru, reigned from behind the counter of his store and, like Hunter Kirk at Maprik, was often scantily clad. Like a minor monarch of yore, Lenny grandly laid claim to everything imaginable on the island, ranging from the numerous clutches of fowls, 'Help yourself to a chook for dinner, they're all mine,' to a virtual tribe of children he claimed to have sired. Rumour had it that patriarch Lenny had been known to make offers of marriage of 'his' nubile girls to lonely white bachelors who he considered eligible. It was said that when Lenny Luff offered one of his illegitimate daughters (or perhaps she was a granddaughter, he was not too sure) in marriage to Arthur Wyborn, he simultaneously made Arthur his son-in-law, a partner in business, and a shop assistant. Lenny gladly left most of the work to his new partner, while he pontificated from behind his shop counter. In turn and inevitably, Arthur himself became the patriarch of a cluster of mixed ancestry offspring.

Whereas it was not certain when Lenny Luff had come to live on Daru, knowing only that it was a long time ago, everyone was familiar with the histories of Arthur and the two other white expatriate bachelors, Tom Holland and Tom Pattle. Having served in the Australian Army in New Guinea, at the end of the war they each decided to forsake 'Down South', hoping to make a fortune in the Western District's copra plantation industry. While Arthur had begun to work for Lenny Luff in his store, Tom Holland bought a dilapidated coconut plantation at Madiri, on the mainland half a day's boat trip up the Fly River. Tom Pattle had done similarly with a plantation on Mibu Island in the Fly River delta. While Arthur 'married' one of Lenny Luff's daughters, both Toms elected to remain bachelors. Of course, there was no denying that over the years each had generously contributed to the expansion of Daru's society, siring illegitimate but comely offspring. As such, nearly every person of mixed ancestry on Daru was related to, or claimed to be inter-related with, one of the four pillars of the local society: Lenny Luff, Arthur Wyborn, and the two Toms.

Daru characters: Robert and George Tabua

Of the mixed ancestry community on Daru Island several clans had kinship connections to tribes of the Torres Straits Islands. One well-known family was the Maipu clan, related to Eddy Koiki Mabo who, in later years, would become famous in Australia for his work in relation to Indigenous land rights. The most prominent and respected Daru family was the Tabua clan. The spokesman for the local families, and by default their leader, in the late 1950s Robert Tabua worked as a postal services clerk in the Daru District Office. In later years, Robert was among the first indigenous representatives elected in the pre-Independent Papua New Guinea's House of Assembly. If Robert Tabua represented the stable, 'respectable', side of the Tabua family, his cousin George Tabua was the family's 'black sheep' – with alcohol the root cause of his notoriety.

George Tabua's reputation on Daru lay with his penchant for the demon grog, coupled with a violent temper. The island's social life revolved around the social club, built at the District Commissioner's personal initiative and completed just before our arrival. Throughout the 1950s and until immediately before self-government and eventually independence, Territory laws prohibited the supply of alcoholic liquor to indigenous people. The law did not apply to those of mixed heritage, such as members of the Tabua, Maipu and other clans, including the descendants of the Luff and Wyborn families. When the Daru Social

Club applied for a liquor licence, applications for membership by expatriate residents on Daru and also those made by individuals of mixed ancestry could be legally accepted. But while most members of the club behaved themselves, George Tabua unhappily established a reputation for being a 'bad drunk' and at times prey to anti-social behaviour. When George drank on the premises, management of the Daru Social Club was able to limit his consumption of liquor – but he could not be prevented from returning home with a private supply. When Willy and I joined the club it had become a kind of tradition on Daru that, especially on Friday evenings, George Tabua would get into trouble. He would spend many a weekend locked up in the island's prison, charged with having been 'D&D' – drunk and disorderly – or for violent behaviour while under the influence of liquor. 'Bloody George Tabua has chopped down his bloody dunny again,' was the Assistant District Officer's not uncommon charge laid in prosecuting George's civil misdemeanour. 'Throw the silly bugger in jail for a couple of days till he dries out,' was the almost stereotype sentence pronounced by the District Officer cum local magistrate.

Daru characters: Geita

Among the multi-faceted community on Daru Island the large number of criminals in the prison formed a community in its own right. As such, the prisoners had their leaders and followers, and among the former was a Papuan man called Geita. Soon after our rather eventful arrival on we came to know, and know of, a man called Geita. The island's only plumber, albeit unlicensed, Geita had come to repair and replace sections of the dilapidated plumbing in our bathroom and kitchen. Though other prisoners moved around freely in performing their tasks at our residence, an armed constable accompanied Geita wherever he went. When we asked the District Officer why that prisoner received such unusual attention, his chilling explanation lay in the man's exceptional criminal past.

In the community of prisoners on Daru, undisputed leader Geita was a quiet and courteous man with an air of natural dignity. Not only the prisoners but also the expatriate and the indigenous communities on the island recognised him as a person of consequence. Although we never felt threatened by him, Geita had been sentenced to life imprisonment without parole. Originally prosecuted for a double axe murder in his village near Hanuabada at Port Moresby, Geita had been sentenced to serve time in the medium security jail at Bomana near Port Moresby. There he had been a model prisoner until, for reasons that were not apparent and which remained unexplained, he had compounded his original crime by massacring two of his local warders and their wives and children, killing two entire families. It was fortunate for Geita that when he committed these horrendous acts the death penalty no longer applied in Papua and New Guinea. Instead, as the country's worst and most notorious indigenous criminal, he was sentenced to life imprisonment in the penal institution on Daru Island; his record marked, 'Never to be released'. Like everyone else on Daru, we became used to the sight of Geita going about his jobs, the armed police escort that accompanied him lending the plumber a surely unintended air of prominence and importance.

Daru characters: croc hunters and missionaries
Among the expatriate residents on Daru there were some with an interesting reason for being there, but without the somewhat dubious notoriety of Lenny Luff and his three amigos. One of these, a crocodile shooter and his wife, operated a potentially risky business with the husband hunting crocodiles in the great Fly River and its tributaries. His wife operated a small trade store at Daru, where she also bought crocodile skins from local hunters in villages along the other big rivers in the Western District for selling on to other traders. It was thought the pair earned good money from both activities. Their aim was to eventually move back 'Down South' to the Northern Territory and start a less risky way of life, setting up a crocodile farm of their own, which they achieved upon their eventual return to Australia.

Also interesting but in a different respect were the missionaries on Daru Island. The Western District was quite under-serviced in a number of areas and the medical missionary of the London Missionary Society, headquartered on Daru Island, was the only qualified physician in the entire Western District. With the Mission's goodwill their doctor serviced the outlying mission stations and also treated the people on Daru Island. Many of its residents, our family included, owe the doctor and Mission a debt of gratitude.

Missionaries in the Territory

Missionaries played significant roles in the development of Papua and New Guinea. Evangelists frequently preceded the administrators in making contact with indigenous people in unexplored parts of the country. Opinions may well vary between those who support the conversion of a heathen people to Christianity and those who would bemoan the inevitable corruption of an indigenous culture, but irrespective of the religious aspect of their work, the dedication, courage and selflessness of missionaries in Papua and New Guinea is unquestionable. On outstations in the Territory, where the conditions of living were sometimes trying for officers of the Territory Administration, the lives of missionaries of various religious denominations were demonstrably worse. For example, 'Dutch Father Kruysberg' of the Roman Catholic Sacred Heart Mission at Maprik had been stationed in the Territory for more than ten years without a leave break to his faraway homeland. As Father once confided, he was not expecting a vacation, 'Until perhaps in another ten years time?' Of the missionaries we knew, members of the Un-evangelised Field Mission (UFM), the Assemblies of God (AOG), and some smaller denominations often led precariously frugal lives. They went without even the few facilities that Administration personnel enjoyed, such as our weekly supplies of fresh foodstuff and a kerosene refrigerator in which to store perishables. Apart from such worldly considerations, experienced by many missionaries, there was the question of their faith – to them a compelling reason for bringing salvation to a heathen people. When I once asked him how successfully he had converted the local people to Christianity, it was again Father Kruysberg who threw some light on the subject when he replied, 'On Sundays my church is always full with my native congregation. They like the singing, they like to see me perform the liturgy of the Church, and they like to send their children to the small school I conduct for them. But when you ask me how many of them I have *truly* converted… oh, well…' the good Father held up fingers on one hand, 'Maybe three, maybe four, perhaps five?' With his stoicism after so many years in Maprik, a godforsaken pinprick in the New Guinea jungle, Father Kruysberg left me in wonder at a missionary's faith and fortitude, which one might conclude equally applied to the churches and ministers elsewhere in the Territory.

Hazards of Daru

My frequent absences on agricultural patrols of course affected my family. When I was away on patrol for two, three, or sometimes four weeks, Willy was left alone to look after Evie and Terrence, who were still only little. Given the relative isolation on Daru, this was always a matter of concern for us both. Fortunately, having the mission doctor on Daru Island meant that we had some access to medical services, but even this was only partially reassuring. Our children naturally experienced the usual juvenile illnesses of infections, colds and fevers, but they also suffered recurring bouts of tonsillitis, causing flaring temperatures that were debilitating to them, and a worry for their parents.

An especial problem for all Daru residents was malaria. Even with the greatest of care, taking preventative medication and using insect repellents, malaria was an ever-present health hazard on mosquito-infested Daru. The island also had a large population of snakes, the two most venomous being the Papuan Black and the Death Adder. Everyone on Daru lived in real fear of snakebites, and one always kept a careful lookout during the day, and especially at night, on the road or in the gardens around the house, even on verandas. Apart from the hazards of mosquitoes and snakes, the waters surrounding the island teemed with potentially dangerous marine life; sharks and exceptionally venomous sea snakes, poisonous stonefish in the thick mud, and saltwater crocodiles that lurked unseen in the shallows waiting for unsuspecting prey, including humans. These natural hazards were the less appealing side of life on Daru.

Apart from worries about my family's health when I was away on patrol for quite lengthy periods, another matter particularly bothered me. In our small 'European' community, our District Commissioner was known to be a 'ladies' man', with a roving eye for those of the opposite sex. When we first heard gossip about his alleged amorous exploits, Willy and I did not give the rumours much credence. However, on my very first patrol away from Daru – which took me a fortnight – Willy had first-hand experience of the District Commissioner's philandering ways.

One morning, Willy was awoken by the sound of the only vehicle on the island, unmistakably that belonging to the District

Commissioner. She heard the engine stop, then a knock on the front door. Willy went to answer, wondering why he had called at such an early time in the day, and asked if he brought bad news about me. The Commissioner answered, 'No, my dear, nothing of the sort. I have just come to see if you would let me in the house so that we might get on friendly terms with each other?' Willy was completely taken by surprise, and when the implications of his words became clear to her, she became enraged. 'Get out, NOW! Immediately!' she commanded. 'If you don't, I shall have no hesitation to tell your wife about you!' If Willy had been furious when she confronted the Commissioner on our first day on Daru about our home's state of disrepair, her rage at his imprudence now towered. And, she recalled with satisfaction, the would-be Casanova left in his Landrover, 'In quite a hurry.'

I was so angry about the incident that I did not allow the matter to gather moss and I let no time pass in confronting the District Commissioner in his office. I intended to made it crystal clear to him that if he ever again dared bother my wife, I would make sure that he would regret this in more ways than one. Having learnt of his dubious background, I planned to spell out another warning I had in store for him – a warning he could not possibly ignore and that, apart from quite probably ruining his marriage and social standing, would also have dire consequences for his career.

Back in 1941, as the Second World War pushed the Allies to their limit, the Japanese had captured most of the Southeast Asian and Pacific colonies controlled by Great Britain, Holland and France. Australia had made few preparations for war close to home and had sent only a small number of soldiers to defend its Territory of Papua and New Guinea. A few hundred troops guarded Port Moresby and Rabaul, and just twelve men and one officer 'protected' Manus Island. In their unstoppable drive south towards Australia the Japanese forces soon took control of the New Guinea islands and much of the mainland. With fierce fighting in progress, civil rule of the Territory was abandoned. For the duration of the war both Papua and New Guinea were governed by the Australian New Guinea Administrative Unit (ANGAU), forerunner to the post-war Territory of Papua and New Guinea Administration. With the Australian forces in New

Guinea inadequately prepared and outfitted, they were inevitably defeated by the Japanese, and many expatriate civilians, planters, miners and traders, together with most soldiers, were made prisoners of war. A small number of the men did not surrender, but hid with local sympathisers in the bush. From there, these volunteers – who became famously known as the New Guinea Coastwatchers – continued to observe Japanese troop movements, which they reported to the authorities in Australia.[xxxi]

One of these Coastwatchers was our District Commissioner. He had been serving on the island of New Britain at the outbreak of war in the Pacific and, seconded into the Army, had remained as a Coastwatcher to spy on the enemy invaders. It was claimed that, when the Japanese captured his unit, under torture he revealed vital information to the enemy, including details about operations and staff involved in the Coastwatchers. After the war he was court martialled, but the hearing ended inconclusively and the incident faded from memory – except perhaps for surviving Coastwatchers and the families of the dead. Most damaging to the District Commissioner, the story of the Coastwatchers and his role in it had been recorded in a book written about the period. Demobilised from active service, he rejoined ANGAU and subsequently the Territory of Papua and New Guinea Administration. There, in time, he reached his present rank of District Commissioner. Given his long service in the Administration, some people questioned why he had been appointed to a posting that was arguably the most neglected and least important of districts in New Guinea; he was little better than a warden on the penal island of Daru.

When I entered his office the District Commissioner well knew why I had come to see him. 'Your missus told you about my *faux pas* the other day?' he asked, looking decidedly uncomfortable when he saw the anger on my face. I did not immediately answer, but as I bent across his desk I looked the man straight in the eye before I very deliberately said, 'I shall give you fair warning that if you ever bother my wife again you will regret it. Let me remind you that you, too, have a family, and I am sure that you would not want your wife and children to know that you came to my house to proposition my wife when I was away from Daru. I assure you that if you ever try this again I shall do more than just warn you. If you should attempt to bother us I shall inform the media here and in Australia of the infamy that surrounded your war service. I shall let you imagine the scandal that it will cause if I remind the public of your alleged treason; it will give the media a field day.' I let my words sink in, then added, 'I am sure you get my point.' The muscles in his face slackened as he was revisited by the horror of a past he could not forget. The District Commissioner never again bothered my family. He was somewhat of a rogue, a would-be Casanova, a philanderer perhaps – but he was not a fool.

CHAPTER 21

First Patrol

In the absence of modern transportation and communications, the early exploration and pacification expeditions by officers of the Department of Native Affairs in New Guinea were undertaken on a grand scale. Involving one or two expatriate officers, from six to a dozen indigenous constables, and up to a hundred indigenous carriers, and sometimes staying in the field for six or more months, these foot patrols required complex planning and organisation. After the Second World War, modern air and road transport and radio contact changed the nature of patrolling in Papua and New Guinea. However, for a long time patrols were still quite elaborate affairs with a considerable number of indigenous porters to carry luggage, cooking gear, an often extensive stock of tinned foodstuff, kerosene pressure lamps and fuel, a small folding table at which to eat or write, a canvas sleeping stretcher, and similar creature comforts.

When I began my agricultural work in the Western District, my Department did not provide me with the finance or resources to match such elaborate explorations.

Learning the job
Before we left Port Moresby, my superior, the Chief of my Division of Extension, had given me the barest of briefings. 'In the archives there are copies of your predecessor's reports on his work in the Western District,' was practically the extent of the instructions with which I took up my duties. I should perhaps have not been surprised when I received such

little advice about the Department's policies and plans for the Western District. As I was to discover, in Port Moresby very little was known about the region, nor apparently had Head Office put much thought into the kinds of viable economic enterprise that could be introduced in such an inhospitable, sparsely populated area. With perhaps forgivable cynicism one might think that this outpost of civilisation did not do much to enhance the careers of our superiors, and that this was the reason they were somewhat lacking in issuing directions to their field staff.

At Daru I was my Department's sole representative, supported by a staff of three untrained Papuan Field Assistants. As the Chief of Division had suggested, I looked through copies of my predecessor's reports in the Head Office archives and also in my office at Daru, but these were few, incomplete, and not very informative. When I consulted colleagues in the Department of Native Affairs, they could add little to what I had garnered from my Department's files. Lacking sound data, I decided that I must start collecting technical information about the people, the land and the climate of the Western District of Papua, which I hoped would be my Department's agricultural Cinderella – emerging, beautiful, from obscurity.

In the Western District, except for the high mountain country, the terrain is dominated by rivers, nipa swamps and lagoons, and enormous savannah grasslands. Travelling through these areas is always problematic and weekly supplies of fresh food and other provisions were delivered to the few scattered patrol posts by Administration-chartered air transport. Another solution of sorts to the freight problem was the Administration's small fleet of 'workboats', two of which were 45-foot, keel-less craft drawing little depth in the water. Very suitable for work along the shallow coastline and in the rivers – the entrances to which were often peppered with continuously shifting sand banks – these workboats played an important role in the District Office's capacity to communicate with its outstation personnel. Two larger, keeled, 120-foot vessels – mainly used to ship bulk cargoes between Port Moresby and Daru – completed the local Administration fleet. In carrying out my duties in the field, apart from occasionally flying into a location that had a small airstrip and from there proceeding to patrol on foot, on my agricultural explorations I generally used one of the Administration's small workboats.

First Patrol

With technical agricultural information on the Western District sketchy or lacking, and the far inland mountain country thinly populated and difficult and dangerous to patrol, I set myself a priority task to begin exploring the small village communities on the coast and in the district's middle ranging hinterland of the Oriomo Plateau and the Fly River Basin. As I came to know the country, I was struck by the rawness of the environment but also its pristine beauty. Here, within their prehistoric traditions, the indigenous people lived what were to themselves whole and satisfactory lives, and 'civilisation' so far remained but a tentative concept. For me, an outsider looking into this ancient microcosm, the Western District of Papua will always remain a veritable water wonderworld.

Despite our not very promising initial acquaintance, the District Commissioner was aware of the difficulties I faced in establishing a technical basis on which future economic development of the district could be modelled. To my gratification, he gave me generous use of the district's small ships and I developed a special affection for the boat *Jade* and its indigenous sailors, headed by skipper Bardia. In addition and as required, I would often hire local motumotu (outrigger canoes), particularly when visiting Kiwai Island and other nearby coastal areas. These exploratory expeditions rate among the most memorable experiences of any of my postings in the Territory.

Jade

Driven by a powerful inboard Lister diesel engine, *Jade* was especially suitable for navigating the shoals and the treacherous sand banks. During the north-west monsoon the seas were usually fairly calm but when the south-east trade winds blew, travelling in the flat-bottomed vessel was not only uncomfortable but at times truly scary. With a maximum draught of only 5 feet and lacking a steadying keel, on the open sea *Jade* rocked and tossed fearfully between sometimes swamping waters.

In the open waters, flat bottomed *Jade* rode the waves well, but the vessel was designed to carry freight so it was not enclosed and had no cabin – passengers had to camp on the hatch covers of its cargo well. A full-length roof covered the boat from aft to stern, but it did little to shelter passengers and crew from the sun, the wind and the rain. However, the greatest personal inconvenience for me was the lack of a toilet. When required, people retired to a small platform aft of the vessel, built over the open sea. In good weather this was an unpleasant experience, but when the winds blew hard and whipped up the sea, and the vessel rolled and bucked and wallowed in the water, retiring to the 'facility' became such a hazardous undertaking that unless the need was urgent, one postponed it.

When *Jade* took me to an area I wanted to begin exploring on foot, if the sandbanks and reefs made approaching the coast hazardous, skipper Bardia would sometimes anchor out to sea and have me dropped off in *Jade*'s trailing dinghy. Or if we were travelling on one of the rivers, at a likely spot on the bank Bardia would tie *Jade* to a tree to let me disembark. Sometimes the workboat would wait for me, or sometimes it might motor on to unload its cargo at a small patrol post. On an agreed day *Jade* would return to collect me from my patrol to take me back to Daru. The explorations on which I used *Jade* became special experiences for me, and I developed a great affection for the sturdy little vessel, its Kiwai crew and their skipper to whom, with great respect, the Kiwais referred as 'Old Man Bardia'. These were men in the best of old-fashioned sailor traditions; true seamen, men of the waves, and they knew every inch and every sounding depth of the Gulf of Papua just as well as they did their tribal lands.

On patrol

For practical reasons, I decided to concentrate my patrols where the majority of the indigenous people in the Western District lived – in villages on the coastal margins of the mainland – and on the numerous islands, especially in the Fly River estuary. Beyond the narrow strip of reasonably arable land along the seaboard where the local settlements lay, vast mangrove, nipa palm, and sago tree swamps extended for up to 16 kilometres inland. Beyond this uninhabitable belt, extensive grassland country supported only small and scattered villages. Still farther inland, the even more sparsely populated hills of the Oriomo Plateau and the Gogodara hinterland rose fold upon fold ever higher towards the towering Star Mountains – a savage wilderness that I could not contemplate exploring, and which remained unknown to me.

As was my personal preference, I chose to travel light. Unlike the expeditions of yore, I made do with only one so-called 'patrol box', easily carried by two hired porters with a third man to spell one of the carriers in turn. Taking care to bring with me only a few essential items, I packed in my patrol box a change of clothing, the indispensable mosquito net, a waterproof groundsheet, a thin blanket on which to sleep and another to pull over me, a primus stove, two small saucepans, fork, knife and spoon, an enamel plate and mug, and a small kerosene lantern. The third 'spelling' porter carried a 2-gallon tin of kerosene, used to fuel the primus and lamp. I preferred to buy fresh local foodstuff in the villages. However, as emergency rations I brought with me six tins of bully beef, a couple of packets of SAO biscuits, 2 kilograms of onions, a packet of flour, a tin of margarine and some tea and sugar. Finally, not for our protection but to shoot game to eat, I also took along a shotgun and a small amount of ammunition.

Apart from the carriers, whom we recruited along the route, one or both of my Field Assistants usually accompanied me. James Suago and Annuo Mataio were Kiwai villagers who had learned the rudiments of agricultural extension work from my predecessor. I was fortunate to have these local men assist me to explore the country; from them I began to learn details of the land and the people of the District. Our combined efforts and their willingness to share with me some of their tribal knowledge led to mutual respect and regard for each other, and a degree of camaraderie between us.

Slightly in excess of 6 feet in height, James was taller than the average Papua New Guinean. Like most men from his tribe, he was deep chested with a lung capacity developed as a result of diving for pearl shell meat and spear fishing underwater without the aid of modern breathing apparatus. Resourceful, intelligent, and keen to acquire new knowledge, James was a valuable aide at work and a socially likeable companion. From him I learned some of the lore and the traditions of his culture.

First day aboard *Jade*

The first of my agricultural patrols was to visit the southern-most section of the Western District, an area where two major waterways, the Moorehead and Bensbach rivers, drain the Trans-Fly Basin. Accompanied by Field Assistant James Suago, we planned to travel on board *Jade* to the mainland, where we would proceed on foot. We stored our few items of patrol gear on the hatch cover that occupied the aft of the sunken engine room, and made living space for ourselves beside our belongings. Raised about 2 feet above the deck, the hatch cover was a dry and airy place on which to camp, and it also afforded us an all-round view of the scenery. The workboat was designed in such a way that passengers and crew could not escape the diesel engine fumes that streamed aft in the wind. Alongside the sailors and half a dozen locals travelling back to their villages, James and I had to simply endure the inconvenience.

Old Man Bardia's crew consisted of the engine operator, a helmsman, a spare deckhand, and a youth to take care of scrubbing, tidying up on board, coiling ropes and so forth. The day we departed, *Jade* left Daru early in the morning on a rising tide that lifted the vessel off the mud where it had lain tied up to the wharf. With a few turns of the wheel, Bardia pointed *Jade*'s bow due south, and when we had cleared the shallows of Daru Island the engineer increased the diesel engine's revolutions to the vessel's maximum speed of 8 knots.

Being the rainy season, the prevailing winds of the north-west monsoon were not blowing as strongly as the later trade winds, which tear up to New Guinea from the south-east. As we pulled away from Daru the channel became noticeably rougher, and when we left the lee of the island the flat-bottomed *Jade* began to pitch and roll rather too much for my liking. Chugging along on the blue-black waters of the open sea, I could hardly believe we had set out to sail on a boat as small as *Jade*. I vividly remember this first experience of travelling on a workboat, a mere speck on the vast expanse of water.

As we headed south-west down the coast away from Daru, Old Man Bardia noticed my interest in the land and the local seascape that we passed. When I asked him why we sailed quite a distance out to sea he began to instruct me in seamanship and his knowledge of the area. 'Not safe if we sail close to land, *Taubada* (Sir),' he explained. 'Too many sand bank near river mouth, also danger of big tree coming down river. He stay under the water, we can't see him.'

In the Motu trade language, 'Taubada' literally meant 'Big Man' and was the equivalent of 'Masta' in Pidgin English. It was a title of respect applied to the colonial whites, and it bothered me when the skipper so addressed me. A tribal Kiwai elder, on land Bardia exuded natural dignity, and on board *Jade* he was clearly the archetypal skipper and a figure of authority. As such, I felt that Old Man Bardia was, no less than I, a 'Taubada' – a 'Big Man'. However, for me to address him as such would have gone against custom, embarrassing him and the other Papuans on board. As a compromise, from then on I did not call him by his name, instead addressing him as 'Skipper'. It was a courtesy and level of respect that apparently did not go unnoticed by the indigenous community on Daru.

Jade's engine kept turning out a steady 8 knots on the reasonably calm seas. As we passed points of interest along the coast, Bardia called them out to me. 'That river, we call him Binaturi. Small village at mouth of Binaturi River, his name Masingara. Masingara people plenty clever fishermen. When barramundi come out from sea they swim up Binaturi for lay egg and Masingara men catch him.' I realised Bardia's polite comments to be of possible value in terms of the district's economic potential. The fact that wild barramundi spawn in the mainland rivers had not before been recorded by my department.

As the sun rose higher, so did the daytime temperature – even with wind freely blowing over us it became hot on board under the boat's full-length roof. We had nothing to do on our camp on the hatch cover, and the steady chugging of the boat's engine had a somnolent quality. After James and I had a light midday meal, we both curled up for a nap. I had not intended to rest for very long but when I awoke the sun was noticeably lower on the horizon and it felt much cooler on board, a pleasantly balmy temperature. Proceeding on the calmer waters of a channel between the Papuan coast and an island some miles out to sea, *Jade* no longer wallowed and tossed as badly as before. When Bardia noticed that I had awoken, he continued tutoring me on the topography of the area. 'That island is Australian Saibai Island, less than three miles from Papua mainland. Next island is a bit more far than Saibai, he also Australian island, his name Boigu.' Pointing to the Papuan mainland, Old Man Bardia offered further information, 'We now sail close to Pahoturi River. Near his mouth is small village called Mabaduan. Sometimes when *Jade* gets there late in day before sun goes down, we drop anchor in Mabaduan for night. But today is too early to stop, no good we waste time, better we keep going. Before sun goes down we find Mai Kussa River. We will anchor for night near small village named Bugi but cannot land there because of dangerous shallows and sandbanks. Better we stay out to sea.'

It was late afternoon when we reached the mouth of the Mai Kussa River, near which lay the Australian island of Boigu in the chain of Torres Strait Islands. The sun was about to dip into the ocean when we reached the lee of an islet near the coast where skipper Bardia had the engine cut and the anchor lowered.

Anchored in the calm and wind-protected waters of the small island, darkness came with tropical suddenness. Old Man Bardia had one of his crew light up a couple of kerosene pressure lamps, which shone their brilliant white illumination into the surroundings. James and I set about preparing our evening meal of sweet potato. In the bush we would have cooked over an open fire, but on board we used our primus stove to boil the potatoes. On land we would have also hunted for or bought our meat, but this evening we shared one of my tins of bully beef. We finished our meal with a mug of strong, very sweet, steaming hot tea, before stringing our mosquito nets over the bedding. When the pressure lamps were turned off with an audible '*plop*', darkness fell like a clap of unanticipated thunder. From under my mosquito net I looked up at the endless black firmament filled with incomprehensible numbers of stars.

The Morehead River

The sun had not yet risen when the rattling of the anchor chain awoke me. When I looked out from under the net, in the east the night sky was thinning with just a tentative tinge of morning's light. On our arrival last evening it had been ebb tide and we had gone to sleep facing away from the land. Now I noticed that, on the morning's incoming tide, Jade had turned 180 degrees and we now looked back on the mouth of the Mai Kussa River where it disgorged into the sea. The workboat's engine began its *phut phut phut*, the skipper turned the wheel over hard, and when the sea stretched out ahead of us, we resumed our way towards our first call on the mainland: the Rouku Patrol Post situated on the savannah of the Morehead River basin country.

At the wheel skippering his boat, Bardia obligingly continued to educate me in seamanship. 'We leave now, Taubada. When tide is coming in, it's a good time for spotting sand banks near the coast, dangerous for all ships, also for a small one like *Jade*. When tide comes in, we can see where white water breaks over the sand bank, we must steer *Jade* clear so she doesn't get stuck on him.' When he explained this to me, I began to notice curls of foamy white waves breaking in patches on the surface of the sea indicating, as Bardia had said, submerged sand banks. Thus I began to better appreciate Bardia's knowledge of the dangerously shallow Torres Strait waters.

The diesel engine continuing to reassuringly thump away below decks, *Jade* chugged out from behind the islet that had sheltered us. Staying quite a long distance out to sea to avoid grounding, Old Man Bardia began to describe to me the land we sailed past. 'That land we see is not the mainland but a large island named Strachan Island. No-one lives on Strachan Island, only some wild people from big bush sometimes come. They don't stay long, only to hunt and fish, then they run away again to the bush. On one side of the island is the river named Mai Kussa, on the other side of Strachan Island is another river named Wassi Kusa. Some people think Mai Kussa and Wassi Kusa are two rivers, but not so. Waters from Mai Kussa and Wassi Kussa run around Strachan but join together in the bush and make one big river. When Kiap from Daru or Morehead want to patrol here, I sometimes take *Jade* up Mai Kussa, come down Wassi Kussa, but I don't like this trip. Plenty dangerous for sand bank, and plenty big dead tree under water, they can ram boat if I am not careful.'

On our second day at sea, time, the land, and the seascape passed slowly. Little *Jade* kept up its steady pace towards the lonely one-man Rouku Patrol Post. As the day wore on my eyes began to hurt with the stinging reflection of sunlight on the water, a brilliance that intensified as the sun rose high in the sky. In spite of the stream of air fanned by our forward movement, it became hot again on the boat. However, unlike the Papuan men on board, I resisted the temptation to take off my shirt, knowing that I would get badly sunburnt.

We had been travelling a long time when all of a sudden one of the crew spotted a huge greenback turtle that lay, apparently asleep, on the surface of the water. Everyone on board suddenly became very excited. Old Man Bardia cut the engine down to low speed so as not to waken the creature, and we sneaked up alongside the still sleeping animal. I looked on with fascination as one of the crewmen took up position on the ship's bow. When we reached where the turtle drifted directly below him, he launched himself through the air, landing on top of the startled prey, which was now wide awake and eager to get away. A mighty struggle between man and beast ensued. The sailor managed to grab both the turtle's front flippers, preventing it from submerging, and with a huge effort he turned the animal over on its back, rendering it helpless in its own element. The passengers on *Jade*, myself included, hauled the hapless turtle aboard. 'Plenty good kai tonight, Taubada,' Bardia exulted as he pushed the throttle hard forward and *Jade* regained its deliberate 8 knots.

After two days sailing on open waters, I had become used to *Jade's* wallowing and pitching. The monotonous *thump thump thump* of the engine below decks and the pervading smell of diesel fumes continued to have a soporific effect on James and me, but the crew on duty, especially skipper Bardia, stayed wide awake, always on the lookout for sandbanks, reefs or underwater rocks that would endanger vessel and people. When I awoke later that morning, I found that we had reached the mouth of a very large river, before which we now cruised at reduced speed. Instead of making for the entrance, Bardia kept *Jade* out to sea, time and time again tacking back and forth past the river mouth. 'This one is Morehead River, Taubada,' he announced from where he had taken the wheel from the helmsman. 'Morehead very big river but plenty difficult to enter boat at his mouth.' When I asked him why, Bardia pointed ahead, 'You can see plenty white wave break over sand bank?' he asked, and indeed, where the river disgorged into the sea I noticed the tell-tale sign of white water. The skipper continued, 'It's low tide now. Water in sea and river mouth not deep enough for *Jade*. We wait for tide to turn high, and when we can see no more white water, we try to go inside easy, easy.'

Keeping well away from land, we waited until little by little the angry white breakwaters at the river mouth disappeared, and the incoming tide began to cover the treacherous sand banks. 'We go now,' Bardia announced, turning the wheel and launching *Jade* at full speed into the entrance of the Morehead River.

Old Man Bardia knew the sea like the back of his hand and he had made the trip to the Morehead River many times. His experience had taught him that at the mouths of any of the Western District's watercourses, even that of the mighty Fly River, one could never be certain where shifting sand banks lie. Before we approached the Morehead, the skipper had stationed one of his men at the very bow of the vessel with a sounding line in his hands. I cannot exactly remember the words with which the sounder relayed the depth of water under Jade's five-foot draught to his skipper. Every time the weighted line disappeared in the water, in a kind of singsong voice the crewman reported, 'Fathom four... fathom four... fathom three...' And, as Bardia adjusted the vessel's course responding to the information, 'fathom two... fathom two minus,' and so on. Thus, the skipper literally felt a gingerly way over whatever obstacle lay in our course. 'Fathom three... fathom three... fathom four... fathom four plus...' When *Jade* eventually cleared the river mouth and we entered deep water, I suspect that everyone on board breathed easier – including Old Man Bardia. No one knew better than he that running aground on a sandbank in the entrance to this river on a high tide would turn into a catastrophe – when the tide turned, stuck fast, the vessel should have to withstand the force of millions of tons of disgorging river water. An ebbing current would almost certainly tear little *Jade* to pieces, drowning the hapless people aboard who, in the middle of a huge, wild river, stood no chance of getting to safety.

Major waterways such as the Fly, Oriomo, Morehead and Bensbach rivers though fast-running are deep, and provided that ships can clear the shallows they are navigable for even quite large vessels. However, not until today did I realise how hazardous an undertaking it was for a boat as small as *Jade*. Even when we had successfully managed to enter the river, with a maximum 8 knots of forward momentum *Jade* had to continuously battle a current of at least 4 knots, and in places perhaps as much as 5 knots. With not much engine power to spare, navigating the vessel upstream was slow and at times problematic to say the least.

Once we were safely inside the Moorehead River, I had expected that we would travel in midstream. I was intrigued when Old Man Bardia elected to stay as close as possible to the river bank. When I commented on this the skipper explained, 'Water near the bank sometimes like to go upstream, helps make current little bit better for *Jade*, she travel more easy.' My tutor pointed to a section of the bank that we were passing, 'Look, Taubada. Rubbish goes upstream.' Indeed, I could see that grass, leaves, sticks and other debris drifting on the water's surface moved opposite to the current, flowing *up*, not downstream, and I understood Bardia sailing the workboat closer to the riverbank.

We slowly made our way up the river. Farther inland, we often saw clumps of reeds drift past us, and even small islands that had broken off a bank from somewhere up ahead. Sometimes still on them was a small animal, a goanna or once even a wallaby. At several places in the river Bardia pointed out to me how the current had formed maelstroms – usually small, but sometimes quite large, sucking vortexes slowly revolving in the water. About these the skipper remarked, 'No danger for *Jade*, but bad for people in small canoe on river. Sometimes it's alright when not in flood time, but when big rain makes water run very fast, when canoe get inside this place for *wada* (evil spirits) sometimes he sink, everyone inside die.' It seemed perhaps perverse when later that afternoon, Bardia chose a spot to make *Jade* fast to a large tree on the riverbank, not very far from a slowly revolving whirlpool.

On the way upriver the engine had worked at top speed, but judging by the interval of time that it took to pass landmarks on the bank, our progress was slow. I had nothing to do, and from my vantage point on the vessel's bulkhead I leisurely watched the passing countryside on both sides of the river.

When we entered the Morehead River we first travelled through miles of fetid, mosquito-infested mangrove, and later an extensive belt of nipa palm. Its foliage is used for thatching, mat and basketry weaving, and its fruit in producing liquor. A startlingly beautiful aspect of the vegetation that lined the river banks at that of time of the year were the garlands of the beautiful New Guinea Creeper vine, covered in large, scarlet flowers that wove in and out between large trees, truly making good my description of a 'water wonderland.' Behind this uninhabitable swampland, the country changed to a belt of coastal rainforest. It was too dank for *Jade* to make fast for the night, and we motored onwards until open grassland unfolded around us, where the skipper began to look for a convenient place for us to camp. The tree on which he made Jade fast stood on savannah country dotted with clumps of eucalyptus and, according to James, scattered stands of sandalwood trees. 'Sandalwood smells very good when he burn. Long time ago plenty of Chinese, also white men, come to chop down sandalwood and take them away,' James recalled. The lucrative sandalwood trade had been abandoned during the war. After the war, the traders had not returned, but geologists and oil exploration companies had moved in. Their mega businesses potentially would bring far more financial gain than could be expected by small-time fortune seekers chopping down trees for their romantically perfumed wood.

Turtle and shark

At Jade's anchor place we made preparations for the night, spreading sleeping mats, hanging mosquito nets and performing similar small chores. The crew then turned their attention to the turtle that they had captured earlier in the day. When the men started a fire and began making other preparations for tonight's meal, I assumed that they would slaughter the turtle, cut the flesh out of the shell, and then cook it – a welcome source of meat. However, I was about to discover an aspect of local custom that no flight of the imagination could have prepared me for.

Greenback turtles can grow to a very large size, and although the one captured today was not yet fully-grown, even for the eight persons in our company its flesh would be too much to finish in one sitting. Without means of refrigeration, Papuan and New Guinean villagers had no way of preserving perishable foodstuff, so they either ate anything they had hunted on the same day, or they smoke-cured it. When Bardia had promised us, 'Plenty good kai tonight,' I had assumed that what we did not consume of the turtle meat that evening, the sailors would preserve by cooking or smoking it. I soon found out that I was quite wrong.

As a youth, my father had taught me that it was alright to hunt, 'Provided you eat what you kill,' and I was not squeamish about shooting game or slaughtering an animal to put meat on the table. However, the way in which my companions butchered the turtle that afternoon constituted an unconscionable act of cruelty, certainly to my modern Western social mores. I had to remind myself that, in the context of indigenous Papua New Guinean tradition, it was morally neutral, neither right nor wrong, an age-old custom devoid of conscious brutality. Unlike my Papuan companions, the butchering of the turtle on the riverbank robbed me of an appetite for its flesh.

With Jade securely tied to a large tree and preparations for the night's camp completed, the crew set about gathering wood on the riverbank. When they had lit a blazing fire, one of the men – large knife in hand – turned his attention to the turtle, lying prostrate on its back. I expected that with a slash of honed steel he would quickly extinguish its life and then butcher it. To my horror, he plunged the blade into the living creature's belly just above one of the back flippers, from where he removed a hunk of raw flesh. Shifting to other body parts, he worked until he had harvested enough turtle meat for tonight's feast. When I asked James why the man had not killed the animal, speaking from the perspective of a culture so different from mine and without any idea of how his response affected me, my assistant explained, 'Turtle too big for us to eat all of him tonight, Taubada. If we kill him now, tomorrow the meat will stink, we cannot eat him. Better we keep him alive for fresh meat next day.'

The campfire burned bright, and the roasting flesh soon smelled delicious. Old Man Bardia himself came over to where I sat on the hatch and generously offered me a portion, saying, 'This part of turtle is very nice to eat, Taubada.' I of course thanked him for the courtesy, but I could not help observing that the morsel I accepted still twitched noticeably. When Bardia could not see me, I passed my share to James, explaining that I could not eat something that was still alive. James smiled when he assured me that the roasted meat was quite dead, but turtle flesh often continues to twitch with contracting sinews, stilled only after long cooking. Even so, my appetite had been extinguished even for tinned bully beef. That evening – knowing that safely stored on the aft deck, helpless on its back lay the poor, suffering, live turtle – I ate a purely vegetarian meal.

The incident with the turtle revealed another dimension of indigenous culture to me, an interesting insight into local Kiwai tribal lore. The Kiwai Islanders have an undoubted affinity with the sea, which made them much sought after as divers by European and Japanese pearlers at the height of the pearling industry. Old-timers recalled how the Kiwai were excellent sailors, superb divers and particularly that they lacked all fear of sharks. Later that evening, when James and I were talking about how the crewman had wrestled the turtle in its own element, I asked James if the man had not been afraid that the splashing might have brought sharks. With a slight smile on his face, James answered, 'He knows he's made no trouble in the village, he's not frighten of shark coming to eat him.' When he saw that I did not comprehend his response, he explained further, 'Shark not eat good man when he goes swimming to spearfish barramundi or other fish, or dives to get big pearl shell meat. When *Jade* crewman jumped in the sea today, he held the turtle's hands (flippers) so he could not run away, he was not afraid of sharks.' I still did not get the rationale of his reply, and when I asked James what he meant by 'good man', he answered with a slightly embarrassed look on his face. 'Oh, Taubada. Silly man in the village sometimes make trouble with woman, wife of other man.' He elaborated, 'Bad man make trouble, steal woman, he go inside bush with her to do man-woman things. If the woman is already married, this man makes no good trouble in the village. When he swims or dives in sea, all the sharks know they can eat him. But shark cannot eat man who makes no trouble, and that way good man is safe in the sea. When he swims to catch fish or turtle or he dives for shell, he's not afraid of sharks.'

APC camp

The morning after the turtle meat feast, the sun was well up before Old Man Bardia had *Jade* unfastened from the big tree on the riverbank. 'Today will be easy sailing on big river,' the skipper said, as I stood watching him navigate the boat away from the shore. 'Not a long way to Rouku Patrol Post, we get there maybe two, maybe three o'clock.' I sat on the hatch top of the hold and looked out over the countryside; time passed slowly as little *Jade* struggled upstream. Later that morning, I noticed what I thought to be an abandoned village. When I asked Bardia about it, he explained, 'That one not village but place for APC people. They come to work here for one year, maybe little bit more; then they go finish, leave camp in bush.' I understood that I was looking at a temporary and now deserted settlement for employees of the Australian Petroleum Company (APC) – an organisation that was actively involved in oil exploration here and in other parts of the Territory. Curious as to how the men had lived in this lonely savannah wilderness, I asked the skipper if we could break the journey for a short while so that I could have a look over the camp. 'All right, Taubada,' Bardia agreed. 'Plenty of time today. Rouku is not very far now, we'll get there plenty early.' He carefully steered *Jade* to a ramshackle jetty, where I disembarked to inspect the oil exploration complex.

Covering an estimated three or four acres of cleared bushland, the houses and storage facilities of the APC camp were all built of 'European' materials, raised off the ground. The skipper explained that in the rainy season the entire countryside in this region of the Trans-Fly was often flooded waist-deep. A feature of the site that particularly struck me was the network of planked boardwalks – hundreds of feet of them, raised about 4 feet off the ground, crossed from one end of the camp to the other. They were designed to connect the compound of houses, sheds and barns when the monsoonal rain turned drenched soils into pure, sometimes knee-deep mud.

To my surprise, some of the buildings I looked into had quite a few abandoned items in them – bunk beds, chests of drawers, other items of furniture, electrical fittings, light globes hanging down from the ceiling, and in what appeared a common room or recreation hall there were heavy benches, large armchairs and trestle tables. Later that day when I mentioned the APC exploration camp to the Patrol Officer at Rouku, he confirmed that about a year ago the company had ceased drilling for oil. 'They packed up personal gear and then they just walked away, leaving everything behind – and I mean *the lot*. Before the men left, their manager told me that I could help myself to anything I wanted that they had not taken with them,' the PO said, and then he showed me his pantry. 'Look – all these jars and tins of jam, honey, caviar, anchovies, baked beans, bags of flour, sugar, you name it. All from the APC camp. It's a pity though,' he only half humorously lamented, 'They left none of their beer and spirits.' When I said that it surprised me that the local Papuans had not taken away the items left in the abandoned camp, the Patrol Officer smiled. 'You probably don't realise how thinly populated the subdistrict is, and how far the distances between villages,' he said. 'The locals who went to help themselves to things in the exploration camp could not carry anything as heavy as bunk beds and trestle tables, and anyway, what use would they have for such gear in their huts? The people did remove anything that was of real value to them: foodstuff, curtains, clothing, and similar useable things.' When I later reflected on the Patrol Officer's explanations, it occurred to me how demanding the nature of Western culture is, and how excessive are its citizens' material expectations. In a remote part of Papua, when a party of oilmen established a rough, temporary oil exploration camp in which lived perhaps fifty or so whites, they had found it necessary to build an elaborate housing settlement using expensive imported construction materials. They even constructed an extensive network of boardwalks to keep their feet dry. In terms of material comforts they had reticulated electricity and water to all buildings, and their storehouse was stocked with an astonishing variety and quantity of food. A year or two later they had abandoned all of these comforts and goods, simply leaving all this affluence behind for anyone to help themselves– or to rot away in an abandoned camp site in the tropical bush.

When I re-boarded *Jade*, Old Man Bardia deprecatingly remarked, 'Before when I come on *Jade* this was a good place, Taubada, plenty of whiteman, also local workman. People in village close by would come to see good whiteman things, also to sell vegetables, bananas. When whiteman leave, his camp is rubbish again in bush.' I understood the skipper's idea of what to Papuans may have seemed evidence of enviable Western material wealth. But although I did not tell him so, I did not share his notion that the APC camp could be regarded a good example of 'European' prosperity and respect, in simply abandoning the camp to the bush.

Rouku Patrol Post

Late that afternoon when we reached the Rouku Patrol Post I was happy to accept the young Patrol Officer's invitation to stay the night. On board *Jade* I had enjoyed the company of James and Bardia. Talking with them I had gained a fascinating insight into a culture and a way of life so different from mine. Nevertheless, that evening in the Patrol Officer's lonely home, I enjoyed a fellow expatriate's company, and he apparently mine. 'Other than on the daily sched with Daru, I haven't spoken English for months,' he remarked. Although I appreciated the

Patrol Officer's company and conversation, and was very pleased with the 'European' cuisine and my first beer since leaving Daru, I especially enjoyed the conveniences of his bathroom – a luxury after the almost totally lacking facilities on little old *Jade*.

The Rouku Patrol Post was, at the time, the farthest and southern-most reach of Central Administration on the Australian part of the island of New Guinea. Mainly inhabited by the Keraki, Gambadi and Semariji people, a smaller and less contacted tribe were the Marind-Anim. They lived on the far western fringes of the sub-district, where the Australian Territory of Papua and New Guinea became the then Dutch-administered New Guinea – what is now the Indonesian province of Papua. Nominally controlled but largely unexplored on both sides of the border, that part of the region was hardly known, even to the Patrol Officer who described it to me. 'The country is mostly uninhabited, with only a few miserable little villages here and there, and even these are not permanently occupied,' he said. 'It is thought that the people on our side are closely related to the Marind-Anim of Dutch New Guinea, who in turn are affiliated with the Asmat tribe, which has barely been contacted by the Dutch authorities. By all accounts these are "wild" people, some of whom are thought to still practice cannibalism. The Netherlands and Australia recognise the international border, but you can bet the locals don't. I must therefore officially warn you that when you go "walkabout" in the area, you will be entering lands that have only recently been released from regulations that prohibit anyone other than authorised persons from accessing the area or contacting the indigenous people in it. Although the restrictions are no longer in force, when you come across any of these tribes, make sure that you avoid trouble of any kind. No one in the Administration knows for certain where the Marind-Anim tribal grounds finish, or how extensively and far the people move back and forth across the border in smaller or larger groups. Without radio contact you are on your own, and I shall not be able to help you in case of an accident or other trouble.'

Some years later, back in Port Moresby, the Patrol Officer's warning words revisited me when Michael Clark Rockefeller – son of New York Governor Nelson Rockefeller – vanished on the Dutch side of the border, never to be found. The cause of his disappearance remains a matter of speculation, and the incident attracted world-wide notoriety to the very area that I, too, had visited.

I had grown somewhat used to nights on patrol, rocking on *Jade* at anchor and listening to the wind singing through the boat's rigging, or tied up to a tree on the riverbank and hearing the occasional sounds of nocturnal animal life in the bush and the swish of the river current sweeping past the vessel. But as the Patrol Officer's guest, I slept soundly. The next morning, local calaboose prison labour emptied the *Jade*'s hold of a host of goods and materials needed to keep the Station operational: diesel fuel for the generator, assorted hardware, and bulk supplies of foodstuff for the Patrol Officer, the Native Constabulary and locally jailed villagers imprisoned for one or another offence. When the work was accomplished I took leave of the Patrol Officer and rejoined the ship's crew onboard *Jade*.

Old Man Bardia untied the cables from the bollards on shore, and the workboat took off for the Bensbach River, which drains the sedimentary basin of land on both sides of the international border. There I wanted to explore the vast grasslands of the western-most Trans-Fly area that bordered what was then Dutch New Guinea. This time, with a 4-knot current pushing us back downstream to the sea, we made much better speed than when we had battled upriver. It was well before sundown when we reached our previous camp on the edge of the coastal rainforest country, where we again tied up for the night. This time we fortunately did not feast on turtle meat, and James and I enjoyed our bully beef that evening.

Bensbach River

My purpose for visiting the Bensbach River was to investigate the veracity of stories I had heard in Daru about large herds of rusa deer rumoured to roam the plains country, and the possibility of their economic exploitation. The Bensbach River hinterland is mostly low-lying savannah grassland, subject to heavy flooding in the wet season, but parched in the dry. The deer had been introduced from Java by the Dutch to provide fresh meat supplies for expatriate and Indonesian settlers in Dutch New Guinea. Without natural predators in the trans-border region, the deer had flourished. Small numbers had begun migrating from south-western Papua as far as the west bank of the Fly River, where local Papuans reported seeing a few swimming to a small island in the estuary. At least one or two had even been spotted on the other side of the Fly River, having apparently negotiated their way from island to island across the massive estuary.

After camping overnight on the riverbank, we continued our journey downstream. This time we reached the mouth of the Moorehead River on a high tide and easily navigated our way out into the safety of the Torres Strait. Later that day, when we reached the Bensbach River, Old Man Bardia confidently pointed the vessel's bow to the shore. One of the crew kept plumbing the sounding line, but we had no difficulty avoiding the shallows that lay before the river's entrance. For quite a distance upstream, the Bensbach constituted the international border between the Dutch territory on the west bank, and the Australian Territory on the east bank. This foreign legality was acknowledged by neither the local people nor the deer that I hoped to find; I was truly on *terra incognita*.

Some of the big waterways in the Western District – especially the Fly, Oriomo, Binaturi and Pahoturi rivers – had long been explored by expatriate missionaries, government officials, planters, traders, timber cutters and others who either administered the local people or who engaged with them in commerce of one kind or another. However, in much of the sparsely populated southern Trans-Fly region neither the Administration nor private enterprise had had much contact with the local tribes. According to the Patrol Officer at Rouku, the local population generally lived in tiny villages, often in a section of the sparse savannah forest, where some trees had been cut down to make place for what were usually semi-permanent bush shelters and small, not very productive gardens. They were semi-nomadic hunters and gatherers, mainly still living off hunting, fishing and harvesting sago in the area's extensive marshlands. 'I can give you the names of a few of the villages along the Bensbach River, but don't expect that you'll necessarily find any one "at home" in them,' he had smiled.

As we continued up the Bensbach River we spotted an amazing variety of wildlife. Apparently unconcerned by *Jade*'s chugging noise in this seldom-visited jungle – the sound so foreign that it failed to alarm them – small colonies of lazy, slow-moving cuscus marsupials stared round-eyed down on us from their tree perches. On the river flocks of wild ducks and other water fowl flew up as we approached, splashing back onto the river as soon as we had passed, bobbing in the vessel's wake. On the riverbank we sometimes saw a perfectly camouflaged, jet black-feathered, shy and wily cassowary – *muruk* – that, except for the vividly blue feathers on their neck, melted in with the dark jungle. Now and then, head and chest high off the ground and ready to run for its life, a large goanna lay intently observing the boat and us, intruders into its domain. Elsewhere along the river James pointed out where the vegetation had been denuded into a kind of slippery slide some 3 feet wide. 'That's where crocodile sleeps,' he said, 'When he wakes up or he's frightened, he wants go back in the water. He slides on belly and makes a mark in mud like that.' Explaining the difference between salt and freshwater crocodiles, James continued, 'In this river we find only freshwater croc; he's a little bit dangerous. Saltwater croc lives in sea and in saltwater river. He's plenty too much dangerous, can kill men.' Continuing his tutoring, James also described physical differences between the species, 'Saltwater croc's mouth is more long, freshwater croc's mouth is more wide. Also, the colour of saltwater skin is more yellow, freshwater is more black.' On a commercial note James added, 'Croc shooter get more money for saltwater than for freshwater skin.' I stored this information away, not yet knowing for what purpose.

Steadily travelling up the river for hours on end, *Jade* took us through seemingly endless grass plains, land of the same type as where we had stopped at the abandoned oil exploration camp on the Morehead River. As we were now well into the rainy season, I realised how, without the planked boardwalks, the soil in the APC camp would have been a quagmire of deep mud. On this part of the trip it had rained every afternoon and often during the night. I would find the Moorehead Patrol Officer's warning, 'You'll have your work cut out to go walkabout on foot in the Bensbach area at this time of year' would soon be put to the test.

Farther up the Bensbach, yet still well before dusk, we came to a small village in a clearing on the west bank. Old Man Bardia said, 'This is where we stop. Water is getting not deep enough for boat to sail.

Better we stay here.' At the sound of *Jade*'s approach, which they would have heard long before we reached them, a small crowd had gathered on the riverbank near the hamlet. 'Lucky we find people in the village, Taubada,' Bardia commented. 'These people often go walkabout. Sometimes when I come here on a trip, there's no one in village; he's empty.' This, then, was one of the semi-permanent settlements about which the Patrol Officer had spoken. For my purpose it was indeed lucky that we happened to find it inhabited.

When the skipper shut the engine down, someone on the riverbank grabbed the ropes that one of the crew threw on shore, tying *Jade* fast to nearby trees. Lined up on the bank a visibly excited group of small children – ranging from toddlers to some in their pre-teens – stood pushing and shoving each other for a better look at us. Behind them, fewer than two dozen adult men and women and three or four elderly people stood silently observing the goings on.

When I set foot on shore the children became shy, and the larger ones stood indecisively on one foot, ready to flee. The very little ones took no such risk – they had crept behind their mothers, hiding, staring at me with round eyes. Bardia and James spoke with the men in the Motu *lingua franca*, and after a while when the excitement had died down, most of the villagers returned to their huts at the edge of the forest. Two elderly men, apparently the village leaders, stayed behind. They came aboard *Jade*, where I explained our business through James and Bardia. When we mentioned deer herds, the men confirmed that yes, there were deer about. Since the village people actively hunted them, there were fewer close to the village, but they could be found in large numbers in the grasslands farther away. When I told them that I wanted to see the large herds of deer for myself, the men responded with a kind of rolling extension of both arms, assuring me that 'a little bit far away,' one, two maybe three days walk from here I would find herds of deer, '*Bada heria, Taubada, momokani* (Very large, sir, truly).'

We next advised the elders that we needed three men as porters to carry my patrol box and the few items we needed to camp out in the bush, and asked if three men from the village could join us. They agreed that this should be possible, but… what to trade? Colleagues in the Native Affairs Department at Daru and the Patrol Officer at Rouku had advised me that this part of the country was too far from even a trade store for the people to be able to use money and that villagers engaged as porters wanted payment in kind. In the Territory, twist tobacco was nearly universally accepted as payment in exchange for local goods and services, and I had therefore brought a supply with me. The village elders agreed that the porters would accept twist tobacco, but…? It took James a great deal of talking and questioning to discover what the elders apparently hoped to gain that was even better than tobacco. After lengthy prodding and probing he worked out that when the men had come aboard they noticed that we carried a shotgun. One of them owned a shotgun, and it was cartridges for this that were even more desirable than tobacco. They would of course also accept tobacco as payment in advance for organising some of their younger village men as carriers. After haggling for so many sticks of tobacco per porter for such and such a length of time, and so many cartridges as a bonus for the village elder with the shotgun, we paid the deal makers some cartridges in advance. All this done to everyone's satisfaction, hands were shaken and it was decided that tomorrow we and the carriers would move off, in search of the elusive herds of rusa deer.

Rusa deer – east of the Bensbach
When day broke I was happy to leave the village early. *Jade* and its crew stayed behind, awaiting my return in about ten days time. With the porters shouldering my patrol box, James carrying the shotgun, and the relief porter carrying no more than my hurricane lamp, a 2-gallon tin of kerosene and a few small personal items for himself and his companions, we set off into the savannah. The previous day the village elders had vaguely indicated the direction where, they said, we should find some deer. Judging by the sun's position, our guides were taking a roughly northern course through the grassland. It had rained all night and in and around the village the soil had turned to slippery mud, so the narrow track that we followed was difficult going from the beginning. I was about to discover what it meant to travel on foot in this type of country at the height of the rainy season. Since we left Daru, the weather had been typical of the north-west monsoon, bringing the heavy and protracted tropical rains that in this part of the Territory sometimes fall for weeks on end. On *Jade*, the rain had been a nuisance, but not until today did I fully understand the Patrol Officer's warnings.

By noon that first day, heavy rain clouds were gathering on the western horizon. 'Big rain is soon coming,' James predicted, and indeed at around 2 pm the heavens opened. In the hot, steamy, lowland climate it is impossible to keep dry when exercising strenuously. In high humidity, walking through arduous terrain increases the body's temperature so much that it is impracticable to wear a waterproof garment, which traps the heat. When it began to rain, the porters simply stripped off their shirts, which they wrapped in a bit of oilskin sheet to keep dry. James kept his shirt on, because as a *gaviman taudia* (government man) he apparently considered it beneath his dignity to partly undress. Even with the sun now hidden by the rain clouds I knew better than to take my shirt off and risk serious sun burn. The only protection I had against the pouring rain was my old ex-army Australian diggers hat. Even if it gave only a little shelter, it had a strangely comforting effect. The worst discomfort for myself, however, came less from the incessant rainfall than from wearing my heavy ex-army boots. I noticed with envy how James walked much easier in lightweight, lace-up, calf-length canvas boots with rubber soles, bought in Lenny Luff's store. The longer I suffered my rain-soaked leather boots, heavy with the mud that packed under the soles, the more I began to detest them. I promised myself that I would visit Lenny Luff's store as soon as we got back.

That first day we steadily trekked roughly parallel with the course of the Bensbach River, but farther inland we could no longer see the water. From my elevated vantage point on the hatch cover of Jade the country had looked deceptively flat, but on foot this certainly proved not to be the case. In reality the terrain was quite heavily undulating, with deep depressions sometimes stretching several miles. At the end of such a hollow we would climb out onto reasonably flat land, then down into the next hollow, then out and down into the next, and the next. As the rain kept falling that day it added more and more runoff into these saucer-like hollows. Often we had to wade up to waist deep through stagnant pools of water that had been accumulating since the start of the wet season.

In spite of the discomfort caused by the rain, our small party kept up a good pace. Soaked to the skin because of the rain, the effort, and the clammy lowlands humidity, I felt no cold, but after hours of being drenched I began to look forward to somewhere dry to stay for the night. When James had earlier asked the guides where we would camp, they replied that we were quite a long way from the nearest shelter. Indeed, it was not until late afternoon that we reached a small hunting hut in a patch of stunted savannah bush. Constructed of bush materials, the inside walls and floor were bare, with only my patrol box for a seat. But despite the basic accommodation, tired and wet, I was very pleased to have found shelter for the night.

The porters soon lit a small fire with dry timber that previous users of the hut had thoughtfully left, and we all took off our wet clothes and footwear and put on spares. We hung our dripping gear before the flames to dry on an improvised clotheshorse made from saplings, and we soon felt warm and comfortable enough again. In one of my aluminium saucepans we boiled water for cups of hot, sweet, black tea, and for our evening meal we roasted sweet potatoes in the embers. Small creature comforts perhaps, but given the conditions it was sheer relief to be dry on the outside, with hot drink and food inside. The prospect of soon stretching out under the mosquito net to relieve the aches and pains in the body's yet unaccustomed muscles seemed a kind of bliss.

During the night when I sometimes awoke for a minute, I heard the rain falling, and the next morning when I looked outside the hut there was no sign of the weather abating. After a hasty breakfast of last evening's leftover sweet potato, we made ready to leave. The most uncomfortable thing was changing into yesterday's clammy, almost-but-not-quite-dried gear, the worst being the still-soggy boots. Stepping out of the primitive hut that had made us so cosy during the night, we walked back into rain that I suspected would be with us all day.

We had not trekked very far into the grassland when we came across the first signs of deer in the savanna. I had been walking behind the carriers through cane grass of twice a man's height – something I always did, partly because the local people knew their country like I never could, and partly because I trusted that their eyes would more easily spot any of the snakes that abounded in that type of country. Far from medical help, the consequences of that hidden peril I did not even want to contemplate. I had been walking with my eyes down to keep a sharp lookout myself for snakes and also because the overnight rain had made the ground underfoot a virtual mudslide. Suddenly, the carriers halted and the leading man pointed ahead, whispering in Police Motu, '*Edasina* (There).' We were downwind from them, so the animals had neither seen, heard nor smelt our approach. As they grazed peacefully, I counted about a dozen rusa deer. Suddenly one of the animals threw back its magnificent antlered head. With sharp eyesight, or a sixth sense, it must have spotted us. The stag alerted the others with a sharp bellow, and the deer immediately bounded away in long, panicky leaps. From my childhood days hunting with my friend Soekarno in Indonesia I recognised in the manner of their flight that these animals knew what it was to be pursued, and their experience had taught them to react with the fear that human presence dictates. Even as they made their escape, the sight of them confirmed what I had come for on this patrol – to establish if herds of deer really did exist in the Bensbach River country.

The next two days, until just before dark we walked along a route that our porters evidently knew well, and every evening we found the shelter of a small hut in which to stay the night. All the time the rain continued to fall, sometimes in a drizzle, but often with heavy downpours from out of dark, slow-moving clouds that saturated the entire countryside. On the first day the path underfoot had been slippery, but the track became increasingly difficult and we sometimes waded through water, mud and slush that reached our waists. I silently cursed whoever had invented army boots.

As if the prevailing wet conditions weren't uncomfortable enough, another trial – almost a hazard – were the leeches. 'Excuse, Taubada, leech sit on you,' James warned me, as he removed one of the creatures from where I had not seen it on my exposed arm. All of us suffered these pests of the jungle; hungry bloodsuckers that, often unseen, gorged themselves on us. Their bites left small trickles of blood running down the limb from which they eventually fell off, leaving small wounds that badly itched but that one did not scratch lest they develop into a festering tropical sore. As the pools of stagnant water deepened, the leech menace grew. 'Leech likes the water but he doesn't like to swim,' James explained, pointing out small colonies of them that had gathered onto leaves and tussocks above the waterline where, small and needle-like, they lay prostrate. When they sense a warm-blooded animal or human presence, leeches raise their upper body high, weaving and twisting, testing the air for the smell of blood. When their prey moves within striking distance, two, three, sometimes half a dozen of the pests launch themselves into the air, landing on skin, where their triangular sucking head immediately fastens and the leech begins its feasting.

People who are not used to leeches often react in horror, wanting to pull them off immediately, but this causes profuse bleeding and – under unhygienic conditions in the bush – if left untreated the broken skin may fester badly. James, the carriers and I knew better than to try to pull a leech off; instead we used a proven old bush trick to rid ourselves of them. We all smoked – the carriers their native twist, and James and I our fine cut tobacco – and when I found leeches on me I pulled out a small wad from my tobacco pouch. Wetted with clean rainwater off leaves or plants, I would squeeze the tobacco juice over the leech, which had become grossly distended, gorging itself on my blood. The bush medicine trick always worked and the offender soon let go, but the blood thinning agent that it injects into the wound makes the site itch badly, and especially at night I had to take care not to further damage myself by scratching.

Always aware of the leech menace, when we stopped for a short rest we inspected exposed limbs, neck and torso, but there were other parts of the body not so easily checked – ears, nose, corners of the eyes, even parts of the body below the waist, not readily scrutinised other than in private. It was there that I most feared leeches doing their damage, but on this patrol I fortunately escaped the indignity.

When we left our third camp, the porters turned away from the roughly northern route we had so far followed, this time taking an almost due-easterly direction. Although we occasionally came across small herds of deer, we had not seen them in the large numbers that reputedly roamed the plains. Our guides confirmed that this was a result of the animals being regularly hunted on their tribal lands, over which we had been travelling. The reason for our new course, the men said, was that it would take us to the upper reaches, almost to the origin of the Bensbach River – country infrequently visited by the tribe and where we would assuredly find considerable numbers of deer. If we crossed the river to the other side, we would see even greater herds of them –'*Bada, bada heria, momokani, Taubada* (Large, truly large, sir).' However, the leader of our porters said, that country belonged to another tribe of '*Tau tau namo las, momokani* (Truly bad people).' Though someone of their tribe might occasionally sneak across the river, he continued, they were always prepared to make a hasty exit if they should chance to come across these bad strangers. Although the porters did not say so, I had the distinct impression that these tribesmen would not, as they put it, have run away in bygone times, but that such a chance meeting would have resulted in a fight between the groups, or even in tribal warfare. When I asked James why they seemed to have few qualms about taking us across the river into this possibly hostile country, he translated the porters' reply, which did nothing to reassure me: 'They say, because bad peoples not make trouble for us when walkabout with white man.' I had the Rouku Patrol Officer's warning in mind that no-one knew for certain where the reputedly only semi-pacified Asmat tribe in Dutch New Guinea claimed tribal land ownership. Was it on that side of the border, or did their homelands extend somewhere into Australian Papua and New Guinea? I wondered whether I should be so bold as to ignore this warning.

Around noon on the fourth day of our patrol, the landscape of stunted clumps of savannah vegetation changed and far in the distance loomed tall river rainforest. The 'big bush from river,' as James called it, looked like a dark cloud on the horizon. When I asked how far away it was, James said that the porters thought it would take us all day to reach the forest on this side of the water, and if we crossed it, part of the next day would be spent clearing the river wetland forest on the other side for us to be back in savannah grasslands.

As the guides had predicted, it was indeed a long walk; not until about 4 pm did we reach the edge of the tall timbers where the wetlands to the river began. Where we halted, the forest rose quite abruptly out of the savannah and for the first time since we had set off from the village the guides had not found an overnight shelter. 'People say their village doesn't like to make place for sleep here, afraid maybe bad people come and make trouble,' James reported. The carriers put

First Patrol

down our luggage and disappeared into the jungle, from where they re-appeared with some bush timber that they had cut into poles with one sharpened end. Using a timber club, also cut from the bush, they drove these posts into the ground to form the frame of a small hut. They next dug four short, forked posts into the ground. Between these, two at each end, they placed saplings to form the structure of a bush platform. By laying more saplings across the main beams, they made a dry bed for us, raised off the saturated ground. They completed their work in less than an hour, and before darkness fell we were under shelter from the never-ending rain. Dried and warmed by the comforting heat of a fire, I marvelled at the bushmanship of my companions.

When we awoke the next morning, after a breakfast of last night's leftovers we entered the wetlands proper of the rainforest belt. If walking on the soggy plains had been difficult and tiring, it became an almost Herculean task to keep going in the waist-deep slush of swamp. Hard on me without anything to carry, I felt sorry for the carriers of my patrol box who not only had to keep themselves from falling, but must also bear the awkward shape and extra weight of the box hanging from the carrying pole over their shoulders. By now we each used a walking stick that we had cut from the bush. Prodding with it for the next step ahead, it helped us to find balance, holes in the track into which we might sink even farther in the mud, or worse, treacherous patches of quicksand hidden under forest debris and fallen leaves. Our progress was slow and it took more than two hours to cover the approximately 3 kilometres to the bank of the slow-flowing Bensbach River.

This far inland, the river had narrowed to about 6 metres, but it was still too deep to wade to the opposite bank. The carriers said that we would have to build a small raft to float my patrol box, the shotgun and our other gear across the river, as we swam and pushed it along. It did not take the men long to cut down lengths of bamboo and tie them together with vine from the bush. When the work was finished, we placed everything on the raft to float it to the opposite bank. Before we entered the river, I asked James if it was safe and whether there were crocodiles in the water. His reply was neither wholly convincing nor very reassuring. 'Carrier say not many crocodiles are here and they are not saltwater but only fresh water croc.' It was with some trepidation that I entered the water.

On this and later patrols it often amazed me how seemingly unconcerned the local people were about the crocodile menace, inescapable when their village lies alongside a river or at the beach. From the coast to far inland, villagers can recall how, two years, one year, a month ago a crocodile had taken a person – often a child, sometimes an adult – standing with others from their community on the bank or bathing in the stream. Even when this had happened only a short while ago, the equanimity with which indigenous people seemed to accept such a terrible thing puzzled me. Women continued to wash clothes in the river, men and children bathed, splashing and diving often at the very spot where a crocodile had taken someone. Was it fatalism, or was it simply that this was a normal part of their lives? Like all of humanity, New Guineans know that death is inescapable and that it comes to every person at some time, but in their understanding, death in the jaws of a crocodile is a random event, a chance happening that may or may not apply to *me*. And so, fear of a chance of dying must not restrict my living.

Swimming behind the raft we reached the western bank of the Bensbach River without mishap. After unloading our gear, the porters tied the bamboo structure to a tree for our return. When we set off through the wetlands the going on this side of the river was as bad as it had been on the other side – we again had to battle the ooze and avoid the deeper potholes and quicksands. When we finally struggled out onto the relatively dry western savannah – the land of the 'bad people' – everyone was so tired that, although it was well before sundown, we decided that we would strike camp early.

Rusa deer – west of the Bensbach
During our walk, James carried the shotgun and used it to hunt the evening's meal – fresh meat to vary and conserve my tinned bully beef. One day he had bagged a couple of Torres Strait pigeons, and on another a spoonbill. While I had no trouble eating the pigeon meat, I was at first not keen to try the spoonbill. As large as a good-sized chicken, I suspected that it's diet of mainly fish would make it taste oily. When James had plucked the bird, I noticed that its flesh was a strangely saffron yellow colour quite unlike that of chicken. Contrary to my expectations, when the men had roasted the bird over the fire, it

First Patrol

proved quite tender and tasty – even better than the pigeons. Although James had managed to catch us various fare on the east bank of the Bensbach River – the traditional hunting grounds of our guides – we had been unsuccessful in getting close enough to take a shot at any deer. After we arrived on the west bank and had rested a while, James suggested he should take the shotgun to hunt. I decided to go along with him to try our luck in bagging deer for the night's kai.

We walked some way through the grasslands without seeing game other than some wallabies, which spotted us first and bounded away before James could take a shot. In any case, I was not keen to eat their meat. Although for Papuans and New Guineans it is a valued food, I knew that wallabies were often infested with parasites. Unless their meat is thoroughly boiled, or – as preferred by the villagers – cured and dried over smoky embers, it is not safe for consumption. We had not travelled far from our camp when, having found no sign of deer, we decided to turn back towards the river, thinking that we would have a better chance of finding bird life in the marshlands. Suddenly James froze in his stride and pointed, whispering, 'Taubada, there.' Following the direction of his outstretched arm, I spotted the head of a single deer. Although it could not have failed to see us, it did not flee.

Desperately struggling, the deer was unable to extricate itself from a deep hole of quicksand, into which it had sunk up to its neck – the same hazard we had ourselves all day sought to avoid. On previous occasions when we had spotted deer, James would have had to act fast to have any chance of taking a shot at the nearest animal. This time he simply loaded the shotgun with a cartridge from his pocket, walked to the animal and with a single shot at close range put the unfortunate creature out of its misery.

It was a major task for the two of us to heave the dead deer out of the quagmire. Finally we got it onto higher and drier ground, where we hauled it over a forked branch in a nearby tree. Like I had learned to do on the Armstrong farm in South Australia, before we started butchering it I slit the animal's belly and punched the still-warm skin off the carcass. The animal was too large and heavy for us to carry it whole back to camp, so we decided to butcher only its best parts – two eye fillets and two hind legs, which James wrapped in some large leaves plucked from the bush. When the porters saw the bounty with which we returned, they cut some saplings for a spit on which to roast the meat over the embers. I looked forward to tonight's feast far more than I had the turtle meat, but when I had my first taste of roast venison I found it gamy and tough. In spite of the spoonbill's strangely coloured meat, I would have definitely preferred it with our sweet potato.

After the evening meal I asked James why the animal had come so close to the river only to become caught and bogged in the quicksand. He explained, 'Deer from this side try to get to the other side of the river to get better food, or to find deer brother, sister or friend already there. Before they cross the river, they send one man deer to find a good place to walk in swamp and cross to the other side. Sometimes the deer drowns, sometimes crocodile eat him, sometimes like today he falls in a big mud hole and dies. When other deer see this kind of trouble, they know this is not a good place for walkabout, and go find other place.' I understood that, sad as it was for our deer today, this was the Law of the Jungle. Having immovably fallen into deep mud, if we had not come along and shot it, the injudicious stag would still have paid with death for its mistake. From us it had met a quick fate, preferable to slowly perishing from exhaustion and starvation.

Our guides had indicated that the western grasslands were vast, covering several days walking distance, and I guessed that they extended well beyond the international boundary between Dutch and Australian New Guinea. Totally unaware of the imaginary line drawn across a piece of paper, I knew that neither the porters nor the so-called 'bad people' from the Dutch New Guinean tribe would give any credence to the artificial demarcation. I had every reason to worry about what might happen if we ran into a group of the semi-nomadic Marind-Anim. James and I kept a wary eye out for any signs of them, but in the next three days we thankfully saw none.

After nearly a week of incessant rain, the weather finally cleared up and the sun came out from behind rapidly thinning clouds. If at first I welcomed the dry conditions, it did not take long for me to wonder if it would have been preferable for the rain to return. When the sun broke through the clouds and the earth began to dry out, it caused a suffocating dampness nearly as hot as steam in a sauna. Travelling light with only one guide accompanying us while the others stayed in the base camp, James and I set out to explore the savannah country farther away from the river. As the porters had promised, we now found ample evidence of rusa deer, one herd of which I estimated at over a hundred animals. It was evidence that on this side of the Bensbach River the herds were larger because they were hunted by villagers less than on the eastern bank. Having confirmed the existence of an unexploited natural resource, we returned to the camp to join up with the other porters. It was time to board the waiting *Jade* and sail back to Daru and my family.

Rafting downriver

Talking over the return journey with our porters we decided that, instead of walking back to their village – which would have taken us days in the same difficult conditions – the easier option was to enlarge the raft big enough to hold us and our gear and float on it downriver to the hamlet. Evidently happy with the plan, the men set to work cutting new lengths of bamboo, with which they began to build a stronger and larger pontoon. After several hours, the raft was of sufficient size and freeboard to take us and our gear. Next, the porters cut down a small tree and from it fashioned a kind of long-handled paddle. They constructed a steering device, operated by inserting the paddle into a kind of slot formed by two thick bamboo poles placed 9 inches apart at the aft end of the raft. A helmsman could steer the craft by pushing the paddle to the left or the right, higher or lower in the water. Ingeniously conceived, it was an effective rudder and I again admired the men's bushmanship.

A raft is not the most comfortable way to travel on water, especially when it is loaded down with five adult men and their equipment. We had taken care to distribute the weight of our gear as equitably as possible, placing the patrol box in the middle, which James and I used as a backrest. One of the porters acted as helmsman at the stern, one stood in the middle ready to act on the left and right sides, and the third stood at the front, poised with a long bamboo pole to ward off any snags or obstructions that we might come across on our course down the river. Ready to leave, we climbed aboard and the men pushed the raft into midstream where the river ran fastest and there was less floating debris to entangle the raft. From my vantage point, mile after leisurely mile, I watched the countryside pass by at a comfortable 3-knot current.

The journey by raft was a memorable, almost magical experience. Knowing that I was on my way home put me in a genial mood and, instead of being physically challenged on saturated land all day long, I blissfully enjoyed sitting down and doing absolutely nothing strenuous. As the sun rose higher in the sky, the early morning mists that had hung low over the water cleared away and the river ran ahead of us like a band of liquid silver through the jungle greenery. A slight breeze kept the temperature pleasantly mild and as we drifted downstream I could observe the large flocks of ducks, magpie geese and other waterfowl. They swam or ducked everywhere and foraged on the riverbank. With a quick peck in the air at a flying prey, a flashing dip of beak into the water for a tadpole or small fish, they pursued a never-ending quest after food for themselves or their unseen offspring in a nest somewhere in the reeds. On the wing were parrots, hawks, eagles and others I did not know. From a long way off in the jungle sometimes came the peculiar, unmistakable 'sawing' sound of hornbills in flight, a low-pitched vibration of air passing through the feathers of their wings. As they passed overhead, their spectacular deep blue and vividly red-coloured head and ivory-white curved bill momentarily slashed through the air over the unrelieved green of the forest. With its astonishingly rich bird life on the water and in the trees, the Bensbach River jungle was surely an ornithologist's delight.

Drifting slowly downstream, I noticed that we were approaching a bower of leafy branches overhanging the water on both banks, fashioning a kind of tunnel of greenery. Several feet across, in its centre high above the river hung the largest, most amazing bunch of faultlessly white orchids I have ever seen. Highlighted by a perfectly aimed ray of the sun, the blooms shone dazzlingly white against the black-green foliage, an exhibit of exquisite natural beauty. The sight has remained with me as something extraordinary, a sensation that has perhaps touched few people.

Continuing down the river we saw many crocodile mud slides and once or twice we startled one of these reptiles from its basking sleep on the bank. When a slumbering saurian became aware of our presence its deceptively lifeless body would startle into immediate and violent action. With a flying run it slithered down its mudslide, disappearing into the water. Barely a ripple stirred the surface where it hid, biding its time to burst out from the menacing darkness of the pristine, tropical waterway.

Morning passed into afternoon and it soon become necessary to find shelter for the night. Our oarsman steered the raft to a spot on the bank and when we disembarked, I was surprised to see that previous river travellers or hunters had built a small hut up in the branches of a large tree. I enquired if we would stay here for the night, and James confirmed with a logical and comforting reassurance: 'Carriers say we sleep here tonight. Safe from croc, he can't climb tree.'

As we had to ascend to the tree hut by means of a hanging vine ladder, we unpacked only what was essential for our overnight stay, leaving everything else on board our securely tied pontoon. The hut was small but comfortable enough, and – more importantly – we were out of reach of any crocodiles in the water or on the ground. We could not light a fire, so that evening I ate a vegetarian meal of cold roasted sweet potato. James and the carriers ate cold left-over venison, the taste and texture of which I found even less appealing than when it had come straight off the fire. Without light, we went to sleep early. Even though I had done very little work during the day, the rest I took was welcome.

It took all of the next day drifting and paddling farther downstream before we reached the village where we had left skipper Bardia and his crew on the workboat. Back at the village, I paid our three carriers the agreed wages of tobacco. As they had worked well for me and helped me so much, I also gave each what I could spare of sugar and salt, and as I had noticed that they had enjoyed eating my onions, I added those as well, keeping only a few for James and myself – small tokens of my appreciation, but which they truly deserved. Other than in the Kiwai language of the Western District of Papua there was no indigenous word in the Territory for 'thank you,' so when the carriers received their due wages they did not comment. But when I added my 'presents' their faces lit up and, accepting the gifts, they said the Kiwai word '*Essoh* (Thank you).' I returned their thanks, repeating 'Essoh; essoh.'

Return to Daru

Three days and nights after *Jade* left the Bensbach River hamlet, in the early evening we arrived back on Daru Island. The trip had been uneventful and, with nothing to take my mind off soon being home, even with skipper Bardia keeping the little workboat travelling at its maximum 8 knots, I was frustrated by how slowly the time to reach Daru seemed to pass. Back on the island, in driving rain, darkness had fallen and before we parted James warned, 'Look out for snakes on the road, Taubada. When rain falls, snakes like come out of wet bush to find a warm place on the road. Better you make plenty of noise when walking, warn snake you come so he can run away.' I thanked him for his advice and concern, and in the pitch-black evening, with only the feeble light of my hurricane lamp to light the road ahead, I trod cautiously, making as much noise as possible. When I came near our house, its lights shone out into the dark like a beacon and I could hear the voices of Willy and our children inside. Calling out to them, they poured out onto the veranda. My family had not known that I was returning today – their excitement made me glad and thankful to be home. Even Anamia slipped out of the kitchen to join in the happy atmosphere. We all laughed and talked, until Willy suddenly exclaimed, 'Phew, but how badly you smell of smoke and perspiration! Be off to the bathroom!' Anamia confirmed her opinion with a cheeky giggle, 'Taubada smell like bush village man.' On patrol I had only been able to perfunctorily bathe in the sea or the river, and there had of course been no way to wash my clothes. The scented soap and fresh water in our bathroom felt kind to my skin, the food that Anamia cooked while I was bathing tasted delicious and, when Willy and I retired for the night, the sheets felt crisp and smelt clean, and the bed was warm and soft. It was good to be home.

Reporting back to the Department

Following my first extensive exploration of the economic potential of the south-western part of the Western District of Papua, I wrote up a detailed Patrol Report including recommendations that I forwarded to Head Office in Port Moresby. I described the countryside, the vast grass plains, and how in the wet season the 'saucers' of land filled up with rainwater to form virtual lakes. I wrote about the treacherous marshlands that fringed the river and of the teeming birdlife in their uncounted hundreds on the waters and in the trees. I mentioned how we had come across a large greenback turtle and that Bardia and local people in the area spoke of considerable numbers of them coming ashore to lay their eggs. I did not forget to report hearing of large shoals of barramundi that at certain times of the year made their spawning run up the great rivers. I went to some pains describing in detail and at length what I had seen of large herds of rusa deer in the grasslands of the Bensbach River region. I made it a point to spell out my thoughts on any observations that I had gathered in the exploration of the area, and the natural resources that I considered of possible relevance to the local people for their as-yet untapped economic significance. Having sent my Patrol Report off to Head Office, I waited in vain for a reply from my superiors – who evidently were not disposed to acknowledge the unprecedented technical evaluation and information in it. Other than gathering data that had not been available until I investigated local resources with possible economic potential, I did not claim that I was competent to draw up policies that were the prerogative of the Department's expert branches: Animal Industry Division with respect to the deer herds; Fisheries Division regarding the existence of seemingly limitless resources from the sea; Agriculture Division to largely disengage from introducing imported tropical cash crops to be raised in a wilderness of swamps and leached soils. Neither in my time nor, I believe, since did the Department of Agriculture Stock and Fisheries see fit to even investigate my observations for any value that they may have had. If the decision makers had thought it fit to consider the suggested possibilities in my report, the economic future for the people in that most neglected area of the Territory, the Cinderella Western District of Papua, may have been very different indeed.

Even with the wisdom of hindsight I could find no real explanation for the thundering silence that met my report in Port Moresby. But the Western District's low priority may have had a quite simple political explanation. Crudely put, it was a matter of numbers. The Australian government's post war policies for administering the Territory of Papua and New Guinea aimed at improving village welfare through social, economic and political development and greater self-sufficiency. More to the point, installing a cash economy in Papua and New Guinea would lead to taxes being levied on Papua New Guineans, who would then contribute to the costs – then borne by Australia alone – of providing social and other services. In the far south-west of Papua the indigenous population was small and scattered, the terrain and climate posed considerable difficulties, and – other than a few prospectors, timber gatherers and struggling copra planters – there was nothing much to entice modern industry to invest in the District. This may explain why there was little more than token support from Central Administration for the Western District. I came to believe that even if the kind of economic development that I had suggested could be devised, the policy makers and their Heads of Administration in the Territory considered that the number of people in the region was too small to contribute to the government coffers, and that the cost of any improvements would be too great. If that was the case, then hardcore economics, political realism and career-driven aspirations may have prevented our Agricultural Department's Director and Chiefs from taking a humanitarian interest in attempting to change the future of the peoples of the Western District of Papua.

CHAPTER 22

Adventures up the Fly River

The lack of interest that my first exploratory patrol in the district had received from Port Moresby Head Office was professionally disappointing to me, but on a personal level I had enjoyed the opportunity that 'patrolling' gave me to do something adventurous and exciting. I made several more of these discovery visits to areas up and down the coast and bordering the district's waterways. If the patrols that I carried out in the Western District have become a singular adventure to me, in particular a visit to the Fly River – and the scatter of islands in its huge delta – stands out as exceptional.

Planning for the trip

When I planned a trip to the mighty Fly River to investigate what local resources could be identified in the area, I had three objectives in mind: visiting Tom Pattle, the owner of a coconut plantation on Mibu Island in the Fly River delta; paying a call on Tom Holland, who owned the fairly large Madiri coconut plantation on the south bank about 130 kilometres from the Fly River estuary; and satisfying a private curiosity about crocodiles and crocodile shooting, which had arisen from conversations with my Field Assistant, James, on our trip to the Bensbach River. The reason for the first task was that Port Moresby Head Office wanted me to purchase a supply of seed coconuts. An uncommon variety grew on Tom Pattle's plantation and the Department's botanist needed a sample for experimental cross breeding. My next stop, visiting Madiri coconut plantation, was to study a mixed agricultural husbandry practice employed by Tom Holland. In addition to producing copra, he also ran a semi-commercial herd of goats, which he sold as meat – or occasionally live animals – to local villagers. I also wanted to investigate if there was a possibility that coastal villagers could commercially exploit the abundant local resource of seafood – particularly barramundi, prawns, crayfish and crabs. To accommodate visiting small villages along the coast and the many scattered islands in the Fly River delta, I decided to take the Department's 12-foot, outboard-motor powered dinghy with me on *Jade*. This would allow me to travel from island to island, and from village to village, before skipper Bardia would later pick me up at an agreed-upon time and place, and take me back to Daru.

The private matter I had in mind for this patrol had been unwittingly suggested by James when he accompanied me on the Bensbach River visit. He had explained the mudslides on the riverbank where crocodiles basked in the sun, and we had also talked about professional crocodile hunters and villagers involved in the trade of hunting and selling crocodile skins – a very lucrative business. At the time, villagers were prohibited from owning rifles with which to hunt, but James had told me that, besides trapping or spearing crocodiles, the villagers often used shotguns – which Territory laws and regulations allowed authorised indigenous persons to legally own. When I protested that, surely, shooting crocodiles with a shotgun was very dangerous, he smiled and said, 'Not dangerous, Taubada, when you know what do.' Unbeknown to him, with these words James had sown a seed for yet another adventure while on patrol.

Making preparations for the expedition to the Fly River, when I told James of wanting to hunt crocodiles, he enthusiastically assured me that he was only too willing to teach me. This time the shotgun that we took along as part of our patrol gear would not only serve to shoot our meat. Although I wanted to experience shooting crocodiles partly out of curiosity and partly for the thrill of the hunt, there was also a pecuniary motivation. Although I was well aware that government officers were not permitted to have sources of income other than their official employment, I reasoned – a little self-servingly and deviously – that I would hunt for sport in my own time. And if I happened to come home with valuable croc skins, there was no reason why I should not give these to Willy as trophies, a present with which she could do as she liked.

To Mibu Island

When the day for the Fly River patrol came, I left our house before sunrise and made my way down to the jetty where skipper Bardia and his crew were waiting. The day before, Old Man Bardia had forecast that high tide would come about nine o'clock. 'Better we leave Daru early, by five o'clock, to give plenty of time. It takes three, maybe more, hours to get to the river mouth,' he said. I understood the skipper's concern about wanting to make the Fly River on a rising high tide. On a previous visit to the large Parama Island I had travelled in a single-hull motumotu outrigger canoe, which drew only a few inches in the water. The canoe had easily cleared the inevitable and hard to spot obstacles, but the telltale white breakers marked sandbanks or submerged rocks. Although *Jade* drew only medium depth in the water, negotiating the vessel into and around the Fly River estuary would not be without problems – even on a high tide.

In many respects, the Fly River is an even more incredible waterway than its counterpart in the north, the mighty Sepik River. From the western to the eastern banks, the mouth of the Fly is close to 100 kilometres wide, disgorging up to 6000 m^3 per second into the Gulf of Papua. In places it is deep, in others so shallow that on an ebb tide mud and sandbanks are exposed, sometimes for considerable distances. Within the estuary lie several large, inhabited islands, and many smaller islands and islets. Any ship larger than a canoe that enters the Fly must navigate the deeper waters, but the ever-shifting locations of sand banks mean that a navigator must always exercise considerable caution. Not uncommonly in the past, overconfident skippers have run fast aground in the Fly River, in a place that only a week ago had been clear of obstacles. Upriver from the estuary, the river begins to narrow quite abruptly until it is only 1.5 kilometres wide. The shape of the river causes it to resemble a huge funnel, which can cause a tidal bore wherein the incoming tide turns the river's current back on itself, forming a huge wave that moves inland, swamping all before it. Not only is the river's topography a matter of casual interest, it is of real and practical importance for anyone who wishes to navigate this astonishing, majestic waterway.

As Bardia had predicted, it took a good three hours to reach the estuary. It was the start of the south-east monsoon, when high winds from the south blew over the seas and the island of New Guinea, and Old Man Bardia kept the mainland well out on *Jade*'s lee, following a course about 4 kilometres out to sea. 'Papuan people call this wind "Laurabada"; it will make danger for *Jade* when we sail close to land,' the skipper volunteered as I stood watching him navigate. 'Close to land, the waves get very big and sometimes come from everywhere. It makes it difficult for *Jade* to walkabout on the sea,' Bardia explained. Today, the keel-less *Jade* pitched and rolled, heaved and wallowed as Laurabada blew a virtual gale that whistled around the ship's awning. I could do no more than trust that the skipper's seamanship would bring the little workboat to comparative safety in the lee of the chain of islands in the estuary.

When we came to the entrance of the Fly River, once again Old Man Bardia reduced speed and placed one of his crew at the bow. Sounding the depth, we 'felt' our way into the river, 'Fathom four… fathom two minus… fathom two… fathom three… fathom four…' Satisfied that *Jade* had safely cleared the sandbanks and we were in deep water, Bardia advanced the throttle and we continued at full speed towards Mibu Island.

Mibu Island's coconut plantation was owned by expatriate Australian bachelor Tom Pattle. His lifestyle and reputation somewhat matched that of other Territorian eccentrics like Hunter Kirk at Maprik and Lenny Luff at Daru. It was said that Tom hadn't been to Daru for eleven years because he thought it was too crowded. But when pressed, most people agreed that Tom avoided Daru company because of his great thirst for rum. Not for underproof (UP) but for overproof (OP) – 'a real man's drink.' Although no one voiced it openly, it was also said that he disliked the company of whites and that, in the parlance of the day, he had 'gone kanaka'.

The sun had just passed its zenith when Bardia turned *Jade* into Mibu Creek. The crew had barely finished securely tying the vessel to a stout hardwood bollard at the end of a rickety jetty when a European man, who I took to be the plantation owner, emerged out of a grove of coconuts. He walked along a dirt path that led to the water and as he approached I had the chance to observe him. He was about fifty years old, five foot five tall, stocky of build, and dressed in a pair of khaki shorts and a blue singlet; his face was sunburnt red and topped with a great mane of white hair. Seeing me, his demeanour indicated suspicion and reserve. Coming closer, his 'G'day,' was no more welcoming than the cold eyes with which he observed me. I introduced myself and told him that I worked for the Agriculture Department. When I explained the reason I called on him today, Tom visibly relaxed. 'Thought you were a nosy bloody Kiap (Patrol Officer),' he said. 'Come to the house, we can discuss your business there.'

Before we walked up the dirt track I pointed to some crates and cardboard boxes that *Jade*'s crew had unloaded onto the jetty. 'Lenny Luff asked me to bring these along for you,' I told him. Tom's mood changed markedly and he became almost friendly. Thanking me, he explained the goods as 'emergency rations', which I knew for a fib. Lenny Luff had packed up a few tins of meat, fish, and powdered milk and a bag each of flour and sugar, but he had also packed several cartons, each with a dozen bottles of OP rum. 'Tom doesn't muck around with the underproof stuff,' Lenny had warned me. 'Better remember that when he offers you a drink.' I soon found that Lenny had given me good advice.

Everywhere on the coastal fringes of the Western District, the land beyond the black, sandy beaches is pervasive, inescapably deep mud – a fact of life that even dictates where people live. Like every village in the region, Tom Pattle's house stood on the highest available point on the island, a small hill only about 10 feet above the sea. As was Territory-wide practice, the home stood in an area of cleared and levelled bare earth where the soil was reasonably dry, and was built on stilts off the ground. No different than many Territory outstation residences, Tom's house was entirely constructed from locally harvested building supplies. The load-bearing posts were of hardwood, the walls and floorboards of roughly sawn coconut palm timber, and the roof covered with coconut leaf thatch. On the veranda of his house, Tom waved me to a chair also made from coconut timber and though the sun had only just passed the yardarm he said, 'Sit down, let's have a rum.'

When we had discussed business and Tom had agreed to sell me the seed coconuts, he began to actually enjoy the novelty of my company.

As his mood mellowed he said, 'Drink up, drink up; Lenny has sent me a couple of bottles of negrita with the grocery stuff you brought.' Forewarned by Lenny Luff, I knew that Tom had received rather more than 'a couple of bottles' of OP rum. I suspected that once he was 'in the grip of the grog' he would not stop drinking until he passed out or the bottles were empty – whichever came first. I had not yet eaten lunch and I drank my rum and water slowly. Tom – who had probably also not yet eaten – kept refilling his tumbler with 'a touch' of water. 'It's important in the tropics to keep the fluids up,' he said, 'A good slug of OP rum disinfects the water and kills off any bugs in the glass.' – impossible for 'sissy-weak' UP rum!

With the alcohol lubricating his words, Tom began to feel he could speak freely. He confided that when he had heard us approach on *Jade* he had expected a 'nosy bloody Kiap' – an officer from the Department of Native Affairs – on periodic inspection, coming to check that he was observing regulations and conditions pertinent to his plantation work force. 'The bastards always prod and poke, and if they can't find anything wrong they'll invent something,' he said, voicing the dislike of authority shared by many Australians.

We talked, we drank, and the time passed. With darkness an hour or so away, I said that I should return to *Jade* for the night, but my host protested, 'Why bother? Have kai with me, and stay the night – saves you having to walk down to the boat.' I knew that refusing the dinner invitation would offend Tom, but I had no intention of sleeping at his house. In the roof of the house without ceilings, thick cobwebs hung down from the rafters in virtual curtains. Large spiders ran busily to and fro on these silken paths, some of them feasting on an injudicious victim caught in the net. Years of bare, muddy feet walking over the coconut timber floor had left caked mud and dust, and damp footprints showed where new soil had been walked in on unclad feet. Dead insects, crumbs of food, other indescribable rubbish – a veritable smorgasbord for the inevitable rats and cockroaches – covered the trestle table and dining chairs. Although I could not see into his bedroom, I was fairly certain that it would be in an equally sorry state. Accepting Tom's offer of dinner, I said that I might as well sleep on board *Jade* where I had my mosquito net, clothes and toilet articles. Tom did not insist and I had the feeling that he was glad I did not take him up on that aspect of his invitation, possibly due to a young Papuan lass I had seen busying herself in the kitchen. I thought it likely she had been banned by Tom from the living areas of the house when I arrived so he could keep up the pretence that she was just a servant.

From where we sat on the open veranda, I looked out over the swept, bare earth yard where some scraggy fowls pecked around for seeds or insects in the dust. Tom Pattle's other livestock included a cassowary chick and one or two dogs, the usual village curs that kept incessantly scratching, trying to rid themselves of fleas.

Without a word of warning, Tom suddenly ducked behind his chair, coming up with a shotgun at his shoulder – which for a spine-tingling moment I feared was levelled at me. **BOOM!!** Before I had time to jump out of my chair, the gun went off – it's report so close to me that I smelt the burning cordite and felt the percussion ringing in my ears. 'Chook for dinner,' Tom announced laconically, and I followed his gaze to where a dead fowl lay out in the yard. Its mates had scattered in cackling alarm and the dogs had taken to their heels, howling with fright. Tom turned around to place the reloaded gun back behind his chair then called out and presently the girl emerged from the kitchen. She collected the dead bird, squatted down on her haunches, and in full view of us she plucked the chook, a heap of feathers growing beside her. To Tom's concern, at dinner that evening I ate very little of the boiled chicken, helping myself rather more to the vegetables and sweet potato. 'You're not only slow drinking your rum, you're not much good on the tooth either,' my host chided me. How could I tell him that there was a very good reason *why* I ate as little of the chicken as I could decently get away with? After the girl had arisen from where she had plucked it, I saw her lower the unwashed, naked bird into a large pot of water on the kitchen's wood stove. First its head, then its body with a few forgotten feathers still attached, and finally its unwashed feet, which only moments before had scratched in the soil for seeds and insects. The sight and thought of it made me squeamish about Tom's 'Chook for dinner.'

After the meal – washed down with more OP – I returned to *Jade* to sleep. The next morning I found myself plagued with a terrible headache and could not recall much of how I had made it back from Tom's house. As I did not see evidence of snakebite on me, I thought

I must have just been lucky or I had perhaps remembered to be sufficiently noisy to scare them away on the track down to the jetty. While I may have exercised as much caution as possible last evening, I knew that not snakebite, but the OP rum had 'bitten' me.

I had agreed with Tom Pattle that, to save time, I would not wait at Mibu for his labourers to collect and sort suitable seed coconuts for me to take back to Daru. Since I wanted to call on the owner of Madiri plantation farther upriver, I would go there first and in a few days on my return trip, I would call again at Mibu Island to take delivery of the nuts.

Madiri Plantation

With due reverence for my stomach, I abstained from breakfast. After Old Man Bardia and the crew had finished eating, the skipper had the workboat untied from the jetty and we headed northward up the Fly River.

At Madiri, I wanted to observe how Tom Holland combined the cultivation of coconuts with running a sizable herd of livestock on his plantation. In addition, the District Commissioner had asked me to deliver Tom a consignment of spare parts for Madiri's diesel generator and had said, 'Since you're there, let me know how you think old Tom Holland is faring. We've had to put Tom on the Dog Act for a year, you see. I just want you to find out if there's any illicit grog on Madiri that some of his mates from here may have sent him, or that he has bought or begged from someone. Don't tell him, though. People like him tend to be a bit touchy on the subject, and he won't take it kindly if he thinks that you're spying on him.'

The 'Dog Act' was the colloquial name for an element of Territory law that prohibited the supply of alcoholic liquor to, or its consumption by 'any person otherwise legally entitled to the consumption of liquor but deemed to be suffering acute alcoholism and a risk to society and self'. The Act was only enforceable by an authorised Officer of the Administration such as a Patrol or Police Officer, and so I had no authority to enforce the prohibition. However, the District Commissioner's request that I check on whether or not he was complying with the law was in line with the Act's underlying purpose, being for the person's 'own good'.

The sound of Jade's diesel engine was audible a very long distance over the waters of the river, and when we reached Madiri plantation its owner stood waiting for us at the jetty. In his mid-forties, Tom Holland's sparse frame and slightly trembling hands, but especially his watery and wandering eyes, marked him as a habitual drinker, one of the many acute alcoholics in the Territory.

When Tom found that we had come to his plantation to deliver spare parts for his generator he responded warmly, 'Thanks, mate; the damn power plant has been on the blink for months, now I can begin to repair it.' He then invited me to stay the night. It was late in the afternoon and would take some time to unload the gear, so it made sense that I should accept the invitation. Unbeknown to Tom, it would give me the opportunity to find out if he was complying with the 'Dog Act' or not. To my relief, Tom Holland's house on Madiri plantation showed a better standard of housekeeping than I had found in Tom Pattle's, and I gladly accepted my host's invitation to stay the night. Tom asked me if I wanted a drink, saying, 'It'll have to be a muli juice, I can't offer you any grog.' In the Territory, other than for abstaining missionaries, offering anything other than alcohol for a drink was so unusual that many would have regarded it an insult. But I of course knew Tom Holland's reason for this break in custom, and I also knew that he knew that I knew... but neither of us commented on why his was a 'dry' household.

After Tom and I had watched the crew unload the cargo for Madiri from *Jade* and store it in the plantation's machinery shed, we retired to the house where I showered and changed clothes. I was resting in my room when, in the nearby kitchen, I heard my host pump up a primus stove and caught the smell of the methylated spirits that pre-heat it. Next, I heard the telltale 'sssshhhhssss' as the kerosene fuel ignited under pressure. A little while later I suddenly heard a great 'whoosh' and fearing that something had gone amiss, I darted over to see. I found Tom bent over a large saucepan in which a foul-smelling liquid was ablaze with a light blue flame. The truth of the situation dawned on me as we looked at one another. Guiltily Tom admitted, 'I get very bad rheumatism and the pain just about sends me mad. The only thing to relieve it is to rub the joints with alcohol but, well, you see, I'm not allowed to buy it. So, from time to time I just make some toddy for myself; purely medicinal, but.' He suddenly begged, 'Look, you won't tell on me, will you? You won't tell the bloody Kiaps back at Daru that I've been cooking up some coconut toddy for me arthritis?' Indeed, I could not find it in my heart to condemn the man, and I promised that I would not tell the authorities on Daru.

Apparently trusting that I would keep my word, Tom readily answered my questions about how coconut toddy is made. 'Coconuts flower on a long stem in the crown of the coconut tree,' he told me. 'I sometimes send a man to cut through it with a sharp knife, which of course means you sacrifice the coconuts, but on a plantation full of coconut trees, one or two bunches make little difference. For a week or ten days, the severed end of the stem continues to drip a sticky, sweet liquid into a bamboo tube tied to it, and every day I send a man back up the tree to collect it. When you drink the unfermented stuff fresh, it makes quite a pleasant non-alcoholic drink, but when it is left to stand in a terracotta pot, after some time it becomes "jungle juice".' When I asked him about the whooshing sound that had come from his kitchen and the blue flame that I had seen in the pot on the stove, Tom said, 'Some people will drink the stuff without first burning off methyl alcohol that might also have formed during fermenting. Methyl alcohol has a lower point of ignition than pure 80 to 90 per cent strength alcohol – which is safe to drink when the 'metho' has been burnt off. If you don't first burn off the metho, drinking it can send you blind.' Suddenly Tom realised what he was telling me, and he hastily added, 'I don't often drink the stuff though, only a nip or two when the pain in me joints gets too bad. I use it for purely medicinal purposes, you know, to kill the pain of me arthritis.' Next he offered, 'Have a sip?' I judiciously declined, partly because of the bad smell emanating from the product, but more so because of Tom's comment about methyl alcohol sending one blind. Who could really guarantee that he *had* burnt off all the methyl alcohol in his 'medicinal' toddy?

That evening, before, during and after dinner, Tom kept popping into the kitchen to 'Rub some of the stuff on me joints, the arthritis is killing me.' The smell that came from the pot on the cooking stove – and of Tom himself – grew increasingly worse, and I could not help noticing that his eyes became ever tearier and his gait increasingly unsteady. Later in the evening he gave up the pretence and came out of the kitchen with a tumbler-full of alcohol, which he downed in a few gulps before mumbling through numb lips, 'Me arthritis is real bad, it's killin' me tonight.'

The next day neither Tom nor I mentioned the previous evening or the state of his 'arthritis'. If I had expected my host to be hungover or perhaps still drunk, I had obviously underestimated his capacity for recovering from his jungle juice. He did not partake of breakfast that morning, being perhaps not *quite* 'sober as a judge', but, I thought, why should I judge him for treating his malady – real or imagined – with illicit homebrew alcohol?

After breakfast Tom Holland showed me over his property, explaining how he had trained several of his workers to look after the commercial herd of goats. The animals foraged under the coconut trees, keeping the area they grazed clear of low bushes, weeds and grass, which made it easier for the labourers to collect the fallen coconuts and also saved on the plantation's maintenance. Next I inspected the cattle yards, in which the goats were periodically rounded up to be treated for intestinal parasites, and where individual animals were selected for live sale or for slaughter. With these observations, including my 'undercover' assignment, my job on Madiri plantation was completed. On my return to Daru, when the District Commissioner asked me if I had seen Tom taking any negrita rum on Madiri, I kept my promise when I truthfully told him that I had seen no bottles of rum there.

Hunting crocodiles

Later in the day we left Madiri on the cusp of the rising tide, heading upriver to an island in the Fly estuary. Accompanied by James, I intended to use the dinghy and outboard motor to call at several small villages in the chain of estuary islands, to investigate the possibility of developing economically viable coastal village fishing ventures by harvesting the reputedly plentiful local crab and crayfish. But first, starting where *Jade* dropped us off at a small, uninhabited island, James and I awaited nightfall to 'in our own time' begin some harvesting of our own.

As James had explained to me on the Bensbach River patrol, the first step in hunting crocodiles with a shotgun was to carefully peel open the crimping of a cartridge and replace its content of seven lead BB pellets with chopped up nails, bits of old battery lead, or similar shrapnel. The result was much more deadly than the original, producing a killing load of shot. Hunting, James told me, always took place at night and always when there was little or no moonlight. 'White hunters shoot with a rifle and can be far from where croc sits in water or land. Village man hunts croc in canoe. With torch for light, he finds the eye of a croc in water or on bank, so canoe can come very close. All the time, hunting man keeps shining light in croc's eye, so croc thinks torch is star or moon. He doesn't see the man, that way he doesn't get mad, no worries'. My Field Assistant then explained that hunting crocodiles with a shotgun necessarily involved paddling or drifting the hunter's canoe as close as possible to the reptile lying in the water or on the riverbank. Any farther away from it than four or at most five feet, the blast of shrapnel would spread too much to ensure that the animal was killed outright – and a wounded croc would not only quickly submerge into the river before it could be retrieved and hauled aboard, but it might attack canoe and hunter. As for substituting shrapnel for the standard BB shot, James explained it helped to ensure the crocodile was killed quickly. His lesson continued, 'When hunting crocodile, man can shoot him in only three places. Number one, hit small place on back of head where his body start. This makes croc die plenty quick. Next good place to shoot croc is in the eye, kill his brain dead. Next, can shoot croc's jaw, but that one is little bit not good; won't make him die, but when croc dive in water he can't close mouth. This way makes crocodile know he will drown if he doesn't stay on top of the water. Then he'll climb bank river, try to get away in bush. On land I can shoot him again, but I look out plenty careful, because croc is now very mad, very dangerous.' I asked James how he would know that a shot crocodile was actually dead and incapable of causing untold havoc when it was hauled aboard. 'No worry, Taubada,' my Field Assistant assured me, 'When we pull croc inside canoe, we chop his neck with tomahawk to make sure he's proper dead and can't bite us.'

James knew that I owned a .22 calibre rifle, and before we left Daru had suggested, 'Maybe Taubada should bring his .22 rifle too? That one is very good for shooting shy crocodiles.' I did not understand what he meant by a 'shy' crocodile, and I also doubted the use of such a low-powered peashooter rifle would be very wise, no matter how 'shy' was such dangerous game. James explained that, when on the lookout for prey, a swimming or drifting crocodile normally has its head fully exposed above the water. When it becomes 'shy' – or suspicious of anything unusual – it sometimes submerges to where only its nose is exposed above the surface, allowing it to breathe while continuing to observe any sign of danger from under water. Even a small rifle can come in handy, my Field Assistant said, because it gives the hunter a chance to shoot a bullet through the animal's nose. This prevents it from closing its nostrils to keep the water from filling its lungs and, like a shot to the jaw, makes it impossible for the wounded crocodile to fully submerge. Lest it drowns, it has no option but to surface, and would then make for the riverbank to escape into the bush. 'When croc climbs on bank, we shoot him dead with gun.'

Making camp for our night on the island, James and I started a small fire over which we cooked our evening meal, then we waited for darkness and the tide to turn. Then, with the outboard motor only barely turning over so as not to frighten away any crocodiles, we would let the dinghy drift downriver. The hours crept by. We could not see farther than a few feet ahead to detect if the tide had turned, so every so often James would throw some leaves into the water to test the direction of the current. For a long time it remained unchanged. The mosquitoes were voracious and I was keen to start the hunt, so it was a relief when after another test of the river James finally announced, 'We can go now.'

I had never hunted crocodiles, let alone tried to do so with nothing more lethal than a single barrel shotgun. Under the circumstances I was quite content to let experienced hunter James have the gun and for me to be his apprentice in the indigenous way of crocodile hunting. James sat in the bow with the loaded shotgun and my .22 rifle next to him, while I took charge of steering our dinghy. With a five-cell battery torch in his hands my companion scanned the waters ahead and on the bank, tutoring me as we went. 'Taubada please work engine slow, slow, so I can easily find croc's eye in water with torch. When we see red colour, that one is from croc eye, if he white, is not croc,' James explained. 'When we see eye from croc, we run engine little bit faster to where croc stays in the water. All the time I keep light from torch in croc's eye, he can't see us. When we come close-up, maybe four feet away, I shoot, Taubada stop motor, we grab croc, pull him inside, cut croc's neck *kwiktaim* (very quickly) with tomahawk. We make him proper dead, then he can't make big trouble for us.' I found to my surprise that the strong current made steering the small dinghy a difficult task, and I had yet to learn to 'feel' the combined effects of the current, the dinghy's drift, and the correcting force of our outboard motor turning over at just enough slow revolutions to steer the craft. As we drifted downstream, James continued sweeping the river with the torch for the telltale red of a crocodile's eyes on the water or on the banks. Sweep after sweep produced nothing for a time, when he suddenly hissed, 'A croc!' With my companion steadfastly training the beam of light on the target I increased the engine's revolutions just enough to allow me to steer the dinghy towards the two specks of red just above the water, where the unsuspecting crocodile continued to look directly into the beam of light. Twenty feet, ten feet, nine, six, four… with a report that shredded the still of the night, James fired. I immediately cut the engine and before the crocodile could sink into the deep of the river – with no option but to completely trust in the hunter to have actually killed and not just stunned – James and I grabbed the beast. Up came first its head, then its shoulders, then the body and the tail, and when we had hauled the approximately 6-foot reptile aboard, James cut its spinal cord, making certain it was no longer alive.

Throughout the night we continued our hunting, finishing up with four crocodiles, each of between 6 and 9 feet in length – the *only* sizes a shotgun could feasibly kill, even with shrapnel shot from its single barrel. Each time we picked up the telltale red of a crocodile eye on the water I was just as excited as when we had spotted the first one. As James discharged the gun and we grabbed to pull each croc into the dinghy, I gave little or no thought to how much we gambled on only a relatively ineffective shotgun to kill these formidable and dangerous beasts. During the night we saw more pairs of glowing red eyes turned towards us than we took, with James rejecting a number of them, judging by the width between their eyes. 'That one is too big for shotgun, maybe 12, 15 feet long.' With this somewhat imperfect selection method he avoided any that might measure longer than 9 feet. Happy to accept his judgement, I was not tempted to dispute him in the matter.

Crocodile hunting in the Fly River – not for the faint hearted!

At the break of dawn, when the torch could no longer compete with the light of the rising sun, our hunt was over. We had reached the small village where I had planned to investigate where the people caught crabs or crayfish, and to estimate the extent of this natural resource for a possible future cash income for the villagers. As we pulled ashore, men from the village came to meet us. Seeing the crocodiles we had shot they began to help James skin them, happily accepting our offer for them to keep the meat in return. The crocodiles were young specimens, providing the best quality of commercially valued 'belly' skin used for the manufacture of luxury purses, handbags and leather shoes. As I watched the men at work, James showed me how to begin the skinning by making the first cut along the length of the spine with a razor-sharp knife. Somewhat in the same way that I had learned to do with a slaughtered sheep on the South Australian farm, he carefully flayed the skin all the way off, from the back of the crocodile to the last careful knife stroke that fully separated the skin from the animal's body. The men worked steadily, trying to get the job done before the heat of the sun spoilt the hides. When completed, we 'pickled' the skins with a thick layer of coarse salt that we had brought with us. We liberally applied the salt over the cut surface, then rolled the skins as tightly as possible into bundles to prevent air reaching inside, which would cause the skins to ferment and spoil them for tanning. 'Ready for Taubada to sell to Lenny Luff at Daru,' James announced. At first I did not quite comprehend what he meant – then it dawned on me that he took it for granted that I would claim the skins for myself. 'No, James – you and I hunt together, and we will share the skins,' I said. At first my assistant's eyes showed some disbelief, but then he broke into smiles of pleasure, '*Essoh, Taubada, tank you bada heria* (Thank you, sir, thank you very much).' As far as I was concerned, it was no more than a fair apportioning of booty between partners.

We made our way back to Mibu and reached Tom Pattle's plantation without mishap. Since *Jade*'s crew had already loaded the seed coconuts on board, I took leave from Tom. This time I resolutely rejected his invitation to 'have a rum with me', and let Old Man Bardia take us back to Daru.

Crab fishing

On another expedition patrolling the Fly River chain of islands we explored the opportunity for commercial crab fishing. With James explaining to the villagers that we wanted to look for crabs to send to Port Moresby, and that this might provide them with a future source of income, they were eager to show us where they collected crabs in the mangroves. As it would be difficult to manoeuvre the dinghy through the narrow channels that ran through the mangrove swamp, James and I, along with four men from the village, boarded a single hull dugout. Taking care not to upset the vessel's precarious balance, James and I sat in the middle while two men at the bow and two at the stern of the canoe paddled us to where a small creek drained the large mangrove swamp into the sea. The tide was still too high to go looking for crabs so instead, barely inside the mouth of the creek, two of the younger villagers jumped into the water with homemade spear guns, goggles and snorkels. Floating on the surface, one of them suddenly submerged before coming up with a good-sized fish at the end of his spear. Later that evening, I wrote in my Field Officers Journal that about two hours of spear fishing yielded more than a dozen large fish and a number of excellent sized crayfish. It seemed the village enjoyed an apparently inexhaustible variety and supply of seafood of highest quality.

As the tide turned and the ebb exposed the mud flats in the mangrove swamp, the men paddled us farther up the creek. Reaching a certain spot, we all got out of the canoe and the villagers walked barefoot around the tangled roots of the mangroves looking for telltale bubbles in the mud – these betrayed where the crabs had dug in, waiting for the tide to return. When a man found such a vent, he poked around in the mire with a stick until, with a quick flip, up came a blue swimmer crab or, from time to time, a larger mud crab. The men bound the snapping claws with vines so they were immobilised, and stored the crabs away in the bottom of the canoe. Both crab varieties were of excellent size and quality, which I confirmed that evening by taste test when the villagers generously shared an excellent meal of the fish, crayfish and crabs with us. In my report to Head Office about fishing activity and likely numbers of crabs and crayfish in the swamps, I suggested that there seemed to be potential for establishing a commercial village fishing industry – arguably a more viable economic proposition than planting coffee or another introduced plant species, which would struggle in the marginal soils and salt-laden air of the area. As had happened with my Bensbach River Patrol Report, this communication was never acknowledged by DASF Head Office in Port Moresby, giving me reason to think that it had been filed in what some wags called the 'TBH File' – 'Too Bl**dy Hard'.

A close call

After an overnight sleep and a day's work, James and I planned to again spotlight for crocodiles on the east bank of the Fly, and we left the village a good two hours before dusk. With the assistance of an outgoing tide and the outboard motor working at full speed, the dinghy took us across the vast expanse of the estuary. Traveling in our small craft was like braving the open sea. We landed on the east bank, we lit a small fire and had a quick meal and a mug of tea. We then slept briefly, to enable us to stay awake and hunt during the night. When we awoke, dusk had fallen; the moon was still in its fourth quarter, and it would soon be pitch dark. The wind had picked up and turned quite cool, so we relit the embers of our fire for warmth. The smoke also served to keep at bay at least some of the myriad mosquitoes and gnats that rose off the muddy river margins.

All the while James kept an eye on the river to gauge the right time to leave. The outgoing tide finally ran its course and we boarded the dinghy, this time I was in the bow with the shotgun and rifle while James did the steering. It was my turn to sweep the torch beam back and forth, up the riverbank, back to the mud flats and onto the water, hoping for the telltale red eyes. Suddenly, so unexpected that it startled me, just above the water near the river's bank I picked up two shining red orbs. I had spotted my first crocodile.

James, who had also seen the glowing eyes, prepared to navigate the dinghy to where I could shoot from close range, and in a soft whisper he tutored me, 'This one is maybe a 9-foot croc, head nice on top of water; we don't need small rifle to shoot nose – okay for Taubada to shoot him with gun.' As we approached the unsuspecting animal I concentrated hard on keeping the beam of light shining directly in the crocodile's eyes. The distance narrowed, thirty feet, twenty feet, ten, five, four... when I discharged the gun, the report deafened me for a second or two, but then I remembered it was my turn to be first to bend overboard and drag the body into the dinghy. There was no time to wonder if I had killed the croc outright or if it might come alive under my hands. James and I hauled the crocodile on board and executed the *coup de grace* with the tomahawk, making sure that it was indeed slain.

Throughout the evening, before approaching any prospective crocodile, James estimated the distance between its eyes taking care that it measured no more than a maximum 9 or 10 feet in length. As he rejected one – 'That one's too big, maybe 15 foot, we leave him' – and accepted another – 'This one is okay to shoot' – I discovered that even an experienced hunter can make mistakes.

At one point during the night, my spotlight again picked up crocodile eyes on the riverbank. Both James and I judged them to be two baby crocs lying a little way apart from each other. Although these would be too small for tanning and thus worthless in the skin trade they would be suitable as stuffed crocodiles for the tourist trade. As James had taught me, to shoot such small animals I exchanged the shotgun with my single shot .22 rifle. I waited as James steered the dinghy close enough to the riverbank for me to take a shot at one of the baby crocs, then quickly reload before the other one got away. The dinghy drew closer, closer, very close… when suddenly I realised our mistake. Instead of two baby crocodiles, we were actually approaching one fully mature, enormous beast. Measuring over 20 feet long, it was the largest crocodile I have ever feared to see. At that heart stopping moment it was too late for me to exchange the .22 rifle for the shotgun, not that it could have killed a monster of such size. It would have been more than foolhardy to even try using a puny shotgun on such an enormous and dangerous animal. James urgently whispered, 'Stay still, Taubada. Keep the torch in croc's eye all the time, do not let go. No good if he finds out we're people. If he gets very angry and jumps on top of us from bank, he'll kill us dead.' I needed no reminding. Never letting the torchlight out of the crocodile's eyes, we held our breath and waited until the giant made up its mind and – excruciatingly slowly – crawled away from us down the riverbank. When it reached the edge, it disappeared into the water without as much as a ripple. It took some time for us to recover from the fright and breathe easily again, and only much later did I reflect that James had been right – crocodile hunting is, 'Not dangerous, Taubada, if a man knows what to do.'

More Fly River adventures
On another expedition to the Fly River, James and I again set out to shoot crocodiles – this time with James standing at the dinghy's bow with the shotgun and my .22 rifle. Having spotted a crocodile, he judged it to be no more than 9 feet and safe to shoot with the shotgun but, as it had only the very tip of its head above the water, he shot the animal through the nose with the rifle. I had steered the dinghy very close to the riverbank when the submerged croc quickly surfaced lest it should drown. With no time to pick up the shotgun, James leapt into the river and grabbed the croc by the tail, determined not to let it escape. The reptile began quickly climbing up the steep river-bank with James clinging on desperately. Knowing the very real danger if it turned on him, James yelled, 'Get the bloody gun, Taubada, get the bloody gun!' Realising the danger, I jumped out of the dinghy and into the river, holding the shotgun above my head. But I had forgotten about our differences in height – James stood at six-feet-something and

I only five-foot-nothing. While his head had stayed above the water, mine went under as I plunged into the deep river mud. Emerging from the mud and slush, I threw the dry shotgun to James, who finished off one very angry croc. We had bagged another valuable skin. It was the only time James ever used such vigorous language on me, but under the circumstances it was most amusing.

On another patrol, on a moonless evening James and I again went on the hunt. As usual we had to wait for the tide to turn and we made fast on an uninhabited island in the middle of the Fly estuary, planning to move from one small island to the next. Having built a small shelter, we slept, waiting for the high tide. Before going to sleep, James had scanned the sky, forecasting, 'Rain's coming, maybe proper big wind, Laurabada, come this way.' In the south, dark cumulus clouds had gathered on the horizon, rapidly expanding across the sky. We were at the end of the wet season and the milder winds of Lahara, the north-west monsoon, were about to give way to Laurabada, the strong south-east trade winds of the dry season, which blow from the waters of Australia all the way over the New Guinea islands. Between these seasonal air movements is a short period of uncertain wind direction, with unpredictable, savage rain and vicious electrical storms.

When we awoke in the late afternoon I could see that the weather had now built up all over the sky. Although we should have known better, we went ahead with our plan to hunt crocs on the islands. On my part it was an act of foolishness but also one of ignorance, as I had no idea what it meant to be in a small dinghy at the mercy of the elements on the mighty Fly River. On his part, James had made a very unusual error of judgement.

Our camp was quite sheltered by tall vegetation and Laurabada bent only the tops of the trees. Massive, dark clouds scudded through the dimming evening sky, with spectacular displays of forked lighting splitting the heavens. Inexplicably, both James and I ignored these warnings and before daylight disappeared we loaded our gear into the dinghy. The wind now blew in occasional gusts that stirred up the waters of the river, but against common sense we pushed off for the evening's hunt.

This time it was James's turn at the bow, and at the stern I had the job of running the outboard motor and steering the dinghy. The sun had gone down and it was pitch dark, though occasional lightning whipped overhead, followed by rolling thunder drumming in our ears. However, the strong wind that had blown all day had died down, lulling me into complacency. I thought that Laurabada had run out of breath; how wrong I was.

Looking for a likely place to hunt, we set off on a course between two islands. Without warning the fury of a gale-force south-east trade wind struck. Miserably unprepared, we were in real trouble – if the small dinghy should be overturned in the tempest that howled over the vast open waters we would be drowned. The storm had caught us so quickly that there was no time to turn back. In any case, being somewhere between two islands, we had reached 'a point of no return' and were in real danger. The gale had whipped the shallow waters into short, vicious waves that came unpredictably at us from everywhere. It was so dark that, at peril of getting swamped, I dared not risk changing course towards either bank. 'Keep bow into the waves, Taubada; no good if dinghy capsize,' James shouted over the howling wind. 'Better to find deeper water, then turn and make for bank.' I knew that James was right; all I could do was keep running with – not broadside to – the short, choppy waves. Our best hope was in deep water, where the heavy and unpredictable swells would abate enough for me to alter course and make it back to land.

Except for sudden flashes of forked lightning, we were enveloped in an almost liquid, inky-black darkness. Desperately searching the waters, I could neither see ahead nor behind. The dinghy pitched and yawed alarmingly, and I feared we would be caught broadside and capsized. Over the howling wind, which nearly blew my words away, I yelled for James to shine the torchlight behind me so I could see where the waves were coming from and so correct my steering to keep our small vessel from overturning. Tying a rope to a bollard, James wrapped a coil around one hand and stood at full height, shining the torchlight above my head. Holding onto his makeshift bridle he 'rode' the plunging and wallowing dinghy like a rodeo buck jumper on a mad bull. The torch in his other hand feebly lit the water behind us, giving me a chance to steer our tiny craft to run with the waves.

The electrical storm was now right over us, and not even the howling of wind and the sandpaper sound of troubled water rushing against the dinghy's skin could block out the ceaseless *SWISHHH-BOOM* – the sound of bolts of lightning tearing up the clouds overhead, immediately followed by deafening claps of thunder. It seemed the elements of wind, water and sky were punishing us, those who had so arrogantly underestimated primordial power.

In an eternity of helplessness I couldn't tell how long we struggled in this precarious position. Caught in such a wild, 'year-one-since-the-world-was-made' experience, a kind of vicarious sensation gripped me, producing an almost other-worldly dimension of consciousness. Of course, had the worst happened, this strange exultation would not have served me, and even more importantly it would have been no consolation for my poor wife and children. Later when I thought about it, I realised how foolish it was that we lacked lifesaving gear, even inflatable vests. If the dinghy had overturned on an outgoing tide we would doubtless have drowned in the forces of the river current, too great and formidable to battle for even the strongest of swimmers. As it was, all that stood between us and this terrible fate was our cheap, government-issue, 10 horsepower outboard motor. If it had died in those stormy seas, our families at Daru would have been in mourning for us.

Although I had no time to look at my watch, I guessed that it took more or less an hour before we reached deep water, where the waves were still enormous but more predictable. 'Taubada like to turn dinghy around now, we go back to land?' James suggested. 'Maybe we can find a good place to stay till Laurabada stop.' I agreed, and James kept shining the torchlight behind the vessel for me to judge the oncoming waves. Turning successfully, I tried to keep the swell behind us so as not to be caught broadside by a rogue wave, and steered the dinghy back to where we guessed we would find the island from where we had started that evening. Tossed around by the seas in the pitch black of the night, with no landmarks by which to navigate we had no clear idea of our position. All we could hope for was that we were actually heading towards land: either an island or the riverbank. Suddenly James exclaimed, 'Taubada, there!' and pointed to a dark smudge in the water ahead of us. Our hope was rekindled – if we could reach it, no matter whether it was an island or the mainland, it promised safety.

After what seemed like hours we reached the safety of an islet. Protected from the worst of the winds, we made fast in a small creek and were finally out of danger. Around our swampy sanctuary the fierce storm was still raging, but tied up to our tree in the mangrove vegetation, even if the ground around us was pure marshland, it was almost heaven. Nature at its most unforgiving had taught us a severe lesson in humility.

The next morning I marvelled at how high and wild the waves in the river still were, and I realised just how sorely we had tempted fate. I silently thanked whatever guardian angels or benevolent force had taken care of us. The red raw blisters inside James's hand, with which he had gripped the rope to steady himself in the bow, attested that I had not been alone in stark fear. As he scanned the water, James quietly admitted, 'Last night we nearly died in the river, Taubada.'

The creek in which we had found shelter was so narrow and shallow that we could not get inland farther than a few yards from where it emptied into the sea. The landmass was so low that there was no dry land on which to make camp so for the next two days – until Laurabada stopped blowing – we lived in the dinghy. Uncomfortably cramped as we were, we counted ourselves fortunate. We were at least on land, and all we had to do was wait for the weather to turn before venturing back to Mibu Plantation where *Jade* lay waiting to take us home to Daru.

Daily life on Daru

Adventurous expeditions such as those to the Bensbach and the Fly rivers were of course not the extent of my work in the Western District of Papua. Between these and other patrols, I carried out my administrative duties and also resumed the normal life of a married man with two young infants. The children adored Anamia and she in turn was devoted to them, giving Willy plenty of spare time. In the colonial homes of tropical countries, where servants carried out practically all the housework and the menfolk were often away from their families for long periods, sometimes bored housewives sought stimulation in gossip, mischief-making, and other questionable activities. Unlike some of the women on Daru, Willy decided that she would return to the workforce, taking up a position in the Department of District Administration. This was the beginning of an administrative career that lasted the remainder of our time in the Territory.

In the absence of a hotel on Daru, Willy was also often kept busy playing host to visitors of one kind or another: administration personnel on posting to an outstation waiting to be picked up by a small plane; overnighting pilots of our monthly air service; even crocodile skin buyers that came to haggle with Lenny Luff or our local croc hunter. This was not an entirely voluntary job; rather, as the District Commissioner had pointed out, 'None of the other ladies will do it.' When the District Commissioner went on to explain that the Territory provided personnel on duty with a travelling allowance for their board and lodging, including in private homes, Willy saw an opportunity. There was no reason that our visitors should not be charged board and lodging, and my astute wife saw the extra income that this brought in as a chance to bolster our meagre finances.

One evening, as Willy once again accommodated our regular two DC3 pilots, at dinner the pair appeared somewhat disappointed. Willy asked, 'Is there anything wrong with the food this evening?' Our family made very good use of the local market where fish, crayfish and prawns were in abundant and cheap supply. So far, every time the pilots had stayed with us they had eaten selections of this seafood. However, on this occasion Willy had decided that, since she got well paid catering for the visitors, it seemed unfair to charge them good money for cheap food. So she had replaced the seafood with a leg of roast lamb. The First Officer looked uneasily at Willy and replied, 'No, no, there is nothing wrong with the lamb, but... well... you see... we always look forward to our trip to Daru because you have beautiful crayfish or other delicious seafood on the table for us; something that we seldom have in Moresby.' While Willy's intention was good and honourable, where it concerned the pilots, the change in dinner menu was a little disappointing.

During business hours when Willy worked in her office, Anamia and E'eo capably ran most routine household matters. Our double axe-murderer, Calaboose, still turned up every morning, wielding his axe to cut firewood for our kitchen. He was a favourite of our children, often playing games or picking ripe mangoes for them. The relationship that had developed between them reminded me of my own childhood with my almost-uncle, Jongos Pak Kasim, on our Java plantation.

Our social life on Daru centred on occasional meetings with others in the Daru Social Club, and – common in the Territory – we made our own entertainment with parties, barbecues or dinners at each other's homes. On the multi-racial island, people of all backgrounds mingled amiably, and from time to time all took part in attending ecumenical church services or sporting activities – basketball, soccer, tennis and others. 'All is for the best in the best of all possible worlds,' according to Enlightenment philosopher Voltaire's satire *Candide* [xxxii], which is often misquoted as, 'The best of both worlds'. Whether applied in one sense or the other, in the Western District of Papua where the indigenous Papua and New Guinea merged amicably with the Western world, I have often felt that I have quite *literally* experienced 'the best of all possible worlds'. Others may have regarded a posting to Daru as a kind of punishment, but my family and I look back fondly on our time in the Territory's Cinderella Western District.

Farewelling Daru

When I again came due for leave, the Western District's reputation as an undesirable backwater made it difficult for Head Office in Port Moresby to find a replacement for me, and the usual two years of service stretched into two and a half years. With our children needing medical attention in Australia, the Department eventually send a relief Agricultural Officer. In failing to find someone to willingly take up duty in the Western District, the Department's solution was to post a more or less 'shanghaied' bachelor colleague to take over from me. Of course, I couldn't be sure that my replacement would find his posting as fascinating as our family had done, but I certainly wished him well.

The expatriate community on Daru bid us bon voyage with rounds of parties in the Social Club and in private homes. Although the indigenous community did not usually farewell Officers of the Administration, to my surprise, my Field Assistants James Suago and Anuo Mataio invited me to a *mumu* (feast) that they had organised for me in their village. Seated on a wooden stool in the place of honour, I would have preferred to be seated less conspicuously on mats on the ground like my hosts, but I could not offend their well-meant courtesy. The farewell for me was a very elaborate affair; a feast of sago sausages filled with fish, turtle or dugong meat alongside whole mud crabs, crayfish, barramundi and an assortment of plantain bananas, taro, sweet potato and other delicacies. After the feast came lengthy speeches by James, Anuo, and a number of Kiwai notables, and to each address I had to reply with a speech of thanks.

In indigenous New Guinea when people depart for work elsewhere in the country or away from the village, relatives and friends act in a display of anguish, including wailing and tears. As the evening drew to a close, I shook hands and thanked each person in turn. The tears that many shed may have been a traditional farewell gesture, but I fancied that those of my friends James and Anuo were tokens of real affection. And I, too, was affected when in final farewell to all I said, '*Essoh Kiwai taudia* (Thank you, people of the Kiwai).' Old Man Bardia, skipper of *Jade*, took my hand, and I like to imagine that he spoke for those present when he replied, '*Oi be.*' In the colloquial Australian idiom it roughly translated to, 'You'll do.' I felt honoured that, with these two simple words, my Papuan friends acknowledged that I had mattered to them. This thought has remained a treasured memory for me.

For their part, Willy and our children had their own farewells to make. Anamia had agreed to follow us to our next posting in Port Moresby, so wishing her goodbye was not too wrenching, but E'eo would stay behind on Daru. Her farewell was uninhibitedly tearful, and – like her namesake, the plover – she was loud in her lament. On the morning of our departure from Daru, our double axe murderer Calaboose turned up as usual to light the stove and chop the next load of firewood. Before we left for the airstrip he handed Evie and Terrence each a small basket made of plaited coconut leaf; within each nestled a perfectly ripe mango that he had especially picked for them from the huge tree in our garden. It was the best he could do to show that he, too, was sorry to see us leave. Flying over Daru Island for the last time I felt sad. But the memory of the Western District of Papua, a posting that many considered to be a punishment of sorts, in our minds remains summed up in the shibboleth, 'a Papuan Water Wonderworld.'

Postscript: reflections on the real impact of 'civilisation'
When we left Daru and the Western District of Papua we carried with us our memories of the people, the sea, and the majestic waterways: the incredible beauty of the riverscape with its garlands of scarlet flowers draped over the green jungle trees; the abundant fauna – deer and cassowary, the round-eyed cuscus staring down at us from the trees, the astonishing birdlife, the crocodiles, the sea snakes, the turtles and a wealth of other wildlife. I cannot now help but fear for the future

of all that made our posting to the Territory's 'Cinderella District' an unforgettable experience. In the years after we left, Willy and I and our children heard of economic development in the District utterly different from what I had suggested in my Patrol Reports to Head Office in Port Moresby. It is no secret that the exploration and exploitation of the copper and gold mines in the Star Mountains about which Patrol Officer Haines wrote has had major consequences for the Papuan peoples that live along the great rivers, especially the incredible Fly River. The carelessness of the mining company involved in tearing up the land, the greed, the callousness, the indifference that marks major Western commerce in the pursuit of serving Mammon, has polluted the once pristine wilderness. The green jungle has withered and died from the poison in the cheaply built containment dams that have overflowed into the waterways that drain the high mountains. No longer unsullied is the sea that borders the Western District, and no longer can the people harvest the barramundi, crayfish, crabs, and other riches of the ocean. Their land and waters have been poisoned by tailings from the gold and copper mines of white men, who they once held up as the paragon of Western civilisation. A sad thought that troubles me today – our Water Wonderworld is ailing, if not dead.

Sic transit gloria mundi
Thus passes the world's glory

CHAPTER 23

A Time for Consolidation

The secret to success is constancy of purpose
Benjamin Disraeli, *Speech* (24 June 1870)

In 1960, after six months Long Leave in Australia, we returned to Port Moresby where I took up my next posting as the District Agricultural Officer of the Central District of Papua. To my disappointment – and with some chagrin – I found that DASF Head Office had ignored all my Patrol Reports about the Western District, steadfastly disregarding the suggestions and recommendations concerning possible viable economic activities for the Papuans of the Trans Fly. However, I consoled myself, I had at least tried to elucidate my discoveries and opinions to my superiors.

We remained in the Territory's capital, Port Moresby, for the remainder of our time in Papua New Guinea – from 1960 until we repatriated to Australia in August 1974 (immediately before Papua New Guinea National Independence in 1975). In many respects this unusually long posting for an Officer of the Administration was beneficial to our family, particularly as our children reached school age. They were able to attend educational facilities superior to those available in most Territory districts.

Getting reacquainted with the capital
In 1960, we found the Moresby township much as we had known it on previous postings. Although it was the Territory's capital and major city, Port Moresby was still little better than an insignificant colonial outpost.

The capital's playground, Ela Beach, was still a 'Europeans Only' reserve; at counters and checkouts in the two main department stores, Burns Philp and Steamships Trading Company, expatriate shoppers still lined up ahead of indigenous customers; on the city streets it remained quite common to see young women from nearby Hanuabada village clad in traditional grass skirts with nothing to cover the upper part of their bodies; and every day local fishermen sailed a small flotilla of motumotu, with their distinctive crab-claw sail, to the nearby reefs, later in the day selling their produce at the Koki Market. On the city footpaths, Papuan men and women still sat with their children – and occasionally a dog – patiently waiting for a customer. Their goods included betel nut, beautiful necklaces, armbands and purses made of tiny seeds or a variety of small shells – each drilled through by hand and strung singly or in multiple strands. They also sold the ever-present billums (string bags) on which multi-coloured beads were sewn or tribal designs embroidered, and wood carvings from precious Pacific ebony. An indigenous policeman still directed the thin stream of motor traffic with hand signals from the rotunda in the town centre, and the Mastas and Taubadas, their wives and children still lived and behaved with the same taken-for-granted confidence borne of their privilege.

Occasionally a tourist vessel would arrive in Fairfax Harbour, its passengers visibly agog at the strange sights, sounds and smells that confronted them in this exotic, 'primitive', frontier town. Conspicuously dressed – the men in expensive, loud Hawaiian shirts and the women in brightly coloured skirts not dissimilar to those popular with Papua and New Guineans – these foreign visitors walked around the Port Moresby shopping centre on the lookout for bargains, or boarded buses to Koki Market. The more adventurous explored the 'wilds of New Guinea' as far as the rubber plantations on the Sogeri Plateau a few kilometres up the road. As tourists do, they usually finished up buying souvenirs from the patient street vendors, who at least that day did a brisk trade in clumsy models of miniature outrigger canoes, a bundle of spears, a bow and arrows, a billum string bag. But I fear they missed out on the real New Guinea, with its incredible beauty, wilds and wonder.

Literally and figuratively speaking, living in Port Moresby was a colourful experience. In their traditional attire and decoration as also in their choice of modern dress, many indigenous people of Papua and New Guinea were partial to strong colours. We saw many extravagant tropical designs of palm trees, hibiscus, frangipani and other bright flowers, or beach scenes with bright yellow sand, scarlet sun, and improbably blue sea. The colours of the rainbow were also evident in the hues applied as body decorations at ceremonies and the big singsings (festivals) that from time to time took place in the country. On these occasions natural colourations of yellow, red and brown ochres, pitch black charcoal soot, bone white clay and sometimes synthetic paints were applied to face and body. Participants wore arm and head bands of creamy cuscus skin, cowrie and pearl shell, and dog-tooth necklaces. Wild boar tusks were worn through large gaps in pierced ears, and ceremonial head-dresses were fashioned from the brilliant feathers and even the whole preserved bodies of the bird of paradise. On the streets of Port Moresby it was no novelty for us to move among vividly dyed lap-laps and multicoloured Hawaiian shirts worn by local men and brightly coloured Mother Hubbard or so-called 'Mission' or 'Mary' dresses favoured by local women. Also common were men and women alike adorned with strings of multicoloured beads, an ostentatious kerchief over the head or fastened around the neck, or hibiscus or frangipani flowers perched in hair or tucked behind an ear. Christmas tinsel was even woven into the tall hairstyle especially favoured by Papuans. And once, in the air above a man's head there even flew a madly flapping, brightly coloured butterfly, tethered on a string of cotton fastened to his ear.

Although in the early 1960s Port Moresby very much remained an outpost of the Commonwealth of Australia, signs of changes in the Territory began to increasingly appear. On returning from a 1958 meeting of Commonwealth leaders in London, Australia's prime minister Robert Menzies had famously warned of 'the winds of change' that would 'sooner, rather than later blow in the colonial countries'. In the mid-1960s, these 'winds of change' did indeed begin to blow in the Territory, heralding a new era of global decolonialisation. But in

1960 when we returned from Long Leave in Australia to begin our fourth term – no longer 'newcomers' but 'Territorians' – we as yet barely felt their breath.

A new home

We were allocated a brand new house in Port Moresby: Section 5, Lot 55, Lokua Avenue, Boroko. Constructed in the then popular L-shape floor plan, the building was raised on 6-feet-tall concrete posts. The master bedroom, two smaller rooms and the toilet and bathroom were reached off a passage that ran the length of the 'L'. On the short part of the 'L' there was a large living and dining area and an enclosed kitchen. As was usual in the Territory, instead of windows, moveable glass louvers opened out to provide cross ventilation. These could be shut when it rained or when the south-east trade winds blew too boisterously. This type of residence at Boroko sat in a large garden, at the end of which stood the so-called boihouse, the servant's quarters. Built on a concrete slab, the boihouse provided a fairly large combined bed and living room, a shower and toilet, and a covered outdoor living and cooking area.

We arranged through the District Office at Daru for Anamia to join us, travelling on the Catalina flying boat service that terminated on Fairfax Harbour. Willy had driven to meet her, and as the seaplane drew up alongside the quay, among the disembarking passengers was a frightened and bewildered Anamia, understandably shivering with first time flying nerves. '*Sinabada* (Ma'am), I never flew in a plane before. I got very scared,' the poor woman said through chattering teeth. Willy loaded Anamia's few belongings into the car, and they drove off through Port Moresby with Willy behind the wheel. Hailing from a small settlement that had only one motor vehicle, if Anamia had been scared of flying that day, when she encountered what to her was teeming road traffic in Port Moresby, it absolutely terrified her. She ducked her head into her lap, 'Sinabada, I'm very frightened! Too many cars are coming very fast, they'll kill us,' she wailed. Willy shushed her, promising, 'Don't worry, I'll get you home safely.' But until they reached our house, following the adage of 'what you don't see can't hurt you', Anamia kept her head firmly in her lap.

Anamia quickly adapted, and soon she was very efficiently performing the day-to-day household duties in our Port Moresby home. Willy had restarted her administrative career in the Staff Section of the Department of Public Works and, as she had been doing on Daru, Anamia collected our now four- and five-year-old Terrence and Evie from the nearby pre-school, minding them until we returned home from work. Willy and I regarded Anamia as a member of our family, and the children adored her. She stayed with us until we repatriated to Australia, when she returned to her home on Daru Island.

Willy's career

With Anamia efficiently running our household and taking our children to and from school, Willy had time to devote herself to a career with the Public Works Department in Port Moresby. Starting as a clerical officer in the Staff Section – nowadays Human Resource Department – it did not take her very long to make a number of promotions that, within a couple of years, saw her head the Section. As shown by a number of testimonials, Willy's industry and capabilities were very well recognised by the senior Public Works leadership:

> Department of Public Works, Boroko, Papua New Guinea
> Subject: Wilhelmina Josephina Elisabeth Brockhall
> '... Mrs Brockhall has been... responsible for the administration of some 2100 officers, the total staff employed by the department... Her intellect and integrity are of the highest standard...'
> (Signed E.P.Scott, Construction Manager, 7 January 1966)
> '... [Mrs Brockhall] has proven to be an officer of well above average diligence and efficiency. She is extremely competent and possesses a breadth of knowledge and experience with this department...'
> (Signed C.J.McD Best, Acting Director, 26 August 1974)
> '... Mrs Brockhall performs her duties with real zeal and determination... she is a good team member and displays a keen interest in improving her subordinates whilst at the same time she displays outstanding loyalty to top management...'
> (Signed W.A. Roberts, Assistant Director Planning, 3 September 1974)

The highest point in Willy's career came when she was appointed Chief Finance Officer of the Department, with responsibility for a budget that exceeded millions of dollars[xxxiii] and her own staff team of fourteen. It was a remarkable achievement for one with such humble beginnings as an Australian immigrant – a so-called 'New Australian'. As attested by the following letters, her favourable reputation did not change in later years:

> MEDICAL BOARD OF VICTORIA
> '... I am writing on behalf of the Board to convey to you our special thanks for the great assistance you gave to the Board... The spirit... and the efficiency with which you carried out your... tasks is greatly appreciated by the Board.
> (Signed President Medical Board of Victoria, 29 November 1990).
> '... On behalf of the Medical Board, I am writing to thank you most sincerely for your years of excellent service to the Board. You have developed a very extensive understanding of all of the functions of the Board...'
> (Signed Kerry L Breen, Acting President, 5 February 1992).

The Kokoda Trail

My career with the Department of Agriculture, Stock and Fisheries proceeded as expected. As the District Agricultural Officer of the Central District of Papua, I was responsible for the supervision of European Agricultural Officers and Papuan Field Staff posted to several outstations in the district. Since an indigenous agriculture-based economy had long been well established in the area and a variety of cash crops – rice, coffee, coconuts, peanuts and more recently rubber – had been imported and were growing in villages throughout the district, the work was of a fairly routine nature. However, the Department of Agriculture had conspicuously left the people of the Owen Stanley Ranges out of the loop of its agricultural extension work. Among my most vivid recollections of the time were visits that I paid to villages in the Mountain Koiari tribal lands in the mountainous hinterlands immediately behind Port Moresby. My association with these people began when I received a visit in my office from an extraordinary man, *Hanua Polis* Ubui (Village Constable Ubui) from the village of Efogi on the Kokoda Trail.[xxxiv]

A Time for Consolidation

When prior to the First World War both the British in Papua and the Germans in New Guinea attempted to establish a colonial administration, they found an indigenous ruling class lacking. To overcome this, both metropolitan powers appointed village officials, who served the central administrations, to control their territories and subjects. At the outbreak of the First World War Australia captured New Guinea from the Germans and retained the German-appointed village headmen, 'Luluais'. In Papua, the British installation of village constables – 'Hanua Polis' – remained an administrative arrangement until Papua and New Guinean Independence in 1975. During my time as the District Agricultural Officer, it was Village Constable Ubui who initiated my contact with the Mountain Koiari tribal people in the Owen Stanley Ranges, an area largely overlooked by the Territory Administration in general, and by the Department of Agriculture, Stock and Fisheries in particular.

The hinterland of Port Moresby is famously known in Australia for the wartime battles fought on the Kokoda Trail. Turning out to be of vital military importance, this small, slippery, incredibly difficult jungle path was where largely unprepared Australian troops pitted themselves against the Imperial Japanese Army.

> The Japanese invasion took New Guinea by surprise… The first bombs were dropped on Rabaul, on 4 January 1942. On 21 January there were air raids on a number of towns… Port Moresby had its first raid on 3 February, Samarai four days later, in March, Japanese forces landed at Salamaua, Lae and Finschafen… A thrust by sea at Port Moresby was repulsed by Allied aircraft in the Battle of the Coral Sea on 8 May. The enemy then decided to attack Port Moresby overland from Buna, where they landed on 22 July… The major contribution of the New Guinea natives (to Australia, not Japan) to the prosecution of the war was manpower… During the few months breathing space before the Buna landings, an effort was made (by Australia)… on the construction of a road to Kokoda… A road suitable for motor transport and pack animals from Port Moresby was completed, which ended at Owers Corner on the northern-most end of the Sogeri Plateau, from where began the now famous wartime Kokoda Track… The Track allowed war materiel and supplies for the Australian soldiers to be carried as far as Efogi; from there to Kokoda it was only barely a jungle path…

an eight day journey... for the troops opposing the Japanese advance... There were parts where, as the soldiers put it, 'Three miles a day, up on your hands and knees, down on your backside', was regarded as good going. 'How stretcher-cases got through,' an eyewitness wrote, 'passes my imagination, as walking files (of native stretcher-bearers) had to swing from branches and cling to the side of precipices like flies.' A high medical authority referred to this achievement, the super human efforts by the so-called 'Fuzzy-Wuzzy Angels', as 'an object lesson in stretcher-bearing'... The Japanese – who were in military control on the northern side of the Cordillera that divides the territories of New Guinea and Papua – began to penetrate south from Buna in New Guinea to the village of Kokoda in Papua. From there, vital to their ultimate plan to invade Australia, they aimed to attack and capture Port Moresby. In Australia, Allied army command realised that should the Japanese Army succeed in capturing Port Moresby, they would then be within striking distance of Darwin on the Australian mainland. Now part of Australian wartime legend, in response to that dire possibility the Kokoda campaign began, seeing fierce fighting between Australian and Japanese soldiers on the Trail between Port Moresby on the coast, and inland Kokoda[xxxv].

The Kokoda Trail begins at Owers Corner on the Sogeri Plateau and finishes at the inland village of Kokoda, after which it is named. Along it lay a number of the villages of the Mountain Koiari people – Uberi, Ioribaiwa, Naoro, Menari, Efogi and the wartime famous village of Isurava. Known for the 'Golden Stairway', the almost perpendicular climb from the bottom of a ravine up to the village, Isurava sits directly below the pass over the Owen Stanley Range to Kokoda. In spite of the military notoriety that the Kokoda Trail earned during the war, up until the 1960s there had not been much Administration contact with the Mountain Koiari people, other than sporadic visits to the area by Department of Native Affairs Officers. When in the mid-1960s I began visiting the area on foot, in spite of the hardships that the people had undergone as a result of the fighting during the war, the Koiari villages had received practically nothing in return from Administration services. The extraordinary service to the nation by the incomparable stretcher bearers (the so-called 'Fuzzy Wuzzy Angels') and the carriers (the lines of porters who bore goods from bullets to bread to the fighting men of the Australian Army) had apparently been forgotten by Australia until a visit to my office by Hanua Polis Ubui of Efogi.

The visitor who entered my office was dressed in the Native Constabulary uniform of black serge lap-lap and short-sleeved serge shirt, both items banded with red bias at the seams, and a red-banded, peaked cap. Ubui executed a perfect salute, coming stiffly to attention with hard stamp of his unclad right foot on the concrete floor, snapping his right hand to the rim of his cap, then coming to military 'at ease' and introducing himself in the Motu lingua franca. When I told him my Motu vocabulary was restricted and asked him if he spoke Pidgin English, he answered that he did, and for the length of our association we communicated in Pidgin. The reason for his visit, said Ubui, was to ask me for help in assisting his fellow Mountain Koiari tribespeople to grow coffee as a means of cash income. The villages on the Kokoda Trail were poor, and the Koiari people led impoverished lives; they wanted clothes and blankets to keep off the bitter cold of the high-altitude nights. They also badly wanted kerosene, so that instead of having only the shine of outside fires in the evenings, they could light their huts with hurricane lamps. The villagers also craved for the luxuries of sugar, tinned fish, rice and, most precious of all, salt. People never had enough salt because the bags were too heavy to bear all the way from Sogeri. The tribe knew that the villagers in the coastal lowland grew cash crops such as rice, coffee and peanuts, which gave them money to buy many useful and desirable things. But, the village constable said, no one from the *gavman* – the government – had come to show them how to begin growing a cash crop.

I promised the enterprising constable that I would see what could be done about his request, and after thanking me, Ubui departed with another outstanding military salute, saying in Pidgin English, '*Tenk you tumas, Masta* (Thank you very much, Sir).'

When I began to make inquiries of the Department of Native Affairs Office at Sogeri – responsible for the local administration in the area – the Patrol Officer there admitted that, as it was such a physically hard job to patrol the Mountain Koiari region, he only sporadically visited the villages along the Kokoda Trail to gather census figures or perform routine tasks of administration. No-one from Health, Public Works, or any other Administration departments – including the

Department of Agriculture in Port Moresby – had attempted to extend their services to the hinterland area, as the crow flies a distance of only 30 miles. From Hanua Polis Ubui's visit in 1961 until 1974, I became very familiar with the Mountain Koiari people on the Kokoda Trail.

First trek up the Kokoda Trail

When I was planning my first visit to the Mountain Koiari, I asked Ubui how I should pay the four porters who would carry my patrol gear. His succinct answer was, 'Salt.' This common and cheap household item was, in the 1960s, a precious commodity that the Mountain Koiari people greatly valued. Bagged salt, Ubui pointed out, is heavy and awkward to transport. Carried on a porter's back, the small granules – which penetrate even the best of hessian bags – grate the skin like sandpaper. In the tropical heat and humidity, the salt mingles with the inevitable sweat of physical exertion, and the sting of it on raw skin is hard to bear. A cupful of salt a day, Ubui proposed, would serve to pay the carriers of my patrol box, and I could also exchange it for fresh produce from people's gardens.

On a hot day in 1961 I set off from Owers Corner to visit the Mountain Koiari tribe. It was the real beginning of my friendship with Hanua Polis Ubui – a humble village man, but one of extraordinary personal capacities. Not until Ubui took me to his country did I appreciate the rigours of patrolling the area. I imagine the experience of my first visit was quite as physically distressing to me as that of the Australian soldiers during the Kokoda campaign, albeit without the fighting. Neither my agricultural extension visits to the Bensbach River – through mud and slush in unceasing rain – nor my other foot patrols in the Western District had prepared me for the weather and terrain on the Kokoda Trail.

My patrol party included Ubui, two carriers with my patrol box shouldered on a bamboo carrying pole, and a relief man with no more to bear than my hurricane lamp and a tin of kerosene in my water bucket. Two other men portered a half-full bag of coarse salt that would serve as payment for any and all services on this visit. A quarter of an hour easy walking from Owers Corner to where the Trail proper begins, Uberi – the first village on the mountainside – was clearly visible across a ravine on the Trail and seemed to be within only minutes walking distance from where we started. The narrow but fairly well-cleared footpath that we had been following cut through tall grass and low bush vegetation, running along a ridge to where it suddenly plunged steeply down into a ravine, at the bottom of which – a long way below – I could hear the gurgle of a small stream. On the footpath we were so far making good progress and I was glad that I was wearing the same kind of lightweight, calf-length, lace-up canvas jungle boots that my Field Assistant James Suago had worn in the Western District, and which were so much more practical than the heavy, Australian Army issue leather boots.

As we made our way from the ridge down into the ravine, the heat and humidity increased, and by the time we reached the small river at the bottom it was uncomfortably hot. On the other side of the stream began a steep climb up the side of the precipice, and it took nearly an hour of hard work before we reached Uberi, a hamlet of half a dozen or so huts which, other than by a couple of elderly men and women, were deserted at this time of the day. The other villagers were working in their gardens or gathering produce in the bush.

From Uberi it took another hour of steep climbing before we crested the ridge of the mountain – only to find that we had once again to descend down, down, down to where another creek ran, and then to climb up, up, up to the top of another steep foothill of the Owen Stanley Range. I was sweating freely and, unused to this kind of exertion, I was tiring. With nothing to carry myself, I felt sorry for the men carrying my patrol gear and salt, who in spite of the heavy load on their shoulders kept up a steady pace in the stifling heat of the Trail.

It was late in the afternoon when we reached Ioribaiwa. Being 35 miles out from the centre of Port Moresby, during the war it was also known as 'Camp 35'. Ioribaiwa sat only 13 kilometres from Owers Corner where we had left that morning, but it had taken us all day to reach it. A hamlet not much larger than Uberi, Ioribaiwa was situated on the narrow spine of a very steep fold in the Owen Stanley foothills. The huts were built on a reasonably level area of ground where the ridge is perhaps 5 metres at its widest. Most villages on the Kokoda Trail are built on the high ridges in the terrain, probably because it is too hot and humid in the valleys, and the gradients are too steep to construct houses. A disadvantage for the villagers is that their homes are often located a considerable distance uphill from a water source. All of the community's water has to be carried up from the stream or creek at the bottom of the ravine to the settlement above. As we made camp at Ioribaiwa that afternoon, Ubui asked for water for our party. Three women, each with a bucket, walked downhill to the small creek that we had waded through on approaching Ioribaiwa, returning half an hour later with our water buckets filled. Although I had perspired heavily on the day's walk and I could well have done with a good bucket shower, it would require the villagers to fetch me yet another bucket of water for drinking and to cook my meal, and I could not indulge myself. I made do with a wet towel wipe instead. As the sun went down, except for the light of cooking fires, the village got very dark. As we were at an altitude of about 3000 feet above sea level, it also got quite chilly. I began to appreciate Ubui's plaint of how most of his people lacked warm clothing, blankets and lamps. I retired early but, as every muscle in my body ached with the unaccustomed exercise of the day's walking, my sleep was troubled.

The following morning we broke camp early. The sun had only just risen above the treetops when we set off for the village of Naoro, a full day's walk of eight to ten hours from Ioribaiwa. Only a few yards from where Ioribaiwa village lies on the spine of the mountain spur, the track rises steeply for many miles. It traces the side of a bare hill, denuded of all vegetation other than the tough, sharp-bladed kunai grass, which in the villages is commonly used for roof thatch. The daytime temperature was rapidly rising. As we climbed ever higher into the mountains up this punishing gradient, the grassland through which we walked absorbed the heat of the sun and it became even hotter here than in the ravines and valleys of the previous day. A good two hours later, I was glad when we reached rain forest. Although the dense vegetation prevented wind circulation, the foliage at least kept the direct sun off us. As the day wore on, it grew increasingly damp and hot, and every step I took up the unforgiving mountainside compounded my heat stress and exhaustion.

The unusual exercise of the previous day's walking had made me stiff and sore, and I soon discovered that I was less fit than I had thought. The pain in many parts of my body, especially my calf muscles, became acutely uncomfortable. Although unburdened with any gear, I could not keep up with the porters who, despite the heavy load they carried, were well ahead of me. I could not match their stamina. The day grew even hotter. I did not carry a water bottle, instead relying on the streams for water, and I began to suffer dehydration. On the seemingly unending climb up the steep mountainside, my thirst got steadily worse until I was so exhausted and in need of a drink that determination deserted me and I could walk no further.

Sitting down on a slightly levelled section, my despairing eyes could see where only a short few yards ahead the track ascended up yet another steep, steep, fold in the cruel terrain. I was sure that it would be the same further on. Utterly exhausted, I simply could not will myself to continue. I was suffering a debilitating thirst and the symptoms of dangerous dehydration and heat stroke.

At this altitude on the mountainside, well away from the small creeks and runnels coursing the valleys and ravines, there was no water to be found. I felt dizzy and I utterly despaired that I should be able to continue on to Naoro. The carriers had long disappeared ahead of us, but Ubui had stayed with me. When he vanished into the bush without a word, I thought that he had surely abandoned me. Unable to stand up and move from where I sat, some way off in the vegetation I heard sounds of chopping and the rustling of small shrubs falling. Although reassured that it must be Ubui, I had no idea why he had left me or what he was doing. The noises went on for a while, and when they stopped I began to wonder if the village constable had abandoned me after all. To my great relief Ubui was suddenly back, carrying in his hands his chipped enamel mug filled with clean, clear water. 'Drink, Masta,' Ubui invited me. As I slowly savoured the liquid to the last precious drop, energy returned to my deprived body. I fear to think what should have happened to me that day if Ubui had not rescued me from my predicament. After the life-giving drink, I found I could face continuing on to Naoro – which, according to Ubui, was still another three hours walk away.

Reaching Naoro, the first thing I did was light a fire and boil a large billycan of hot water for tea. As I thirstily sipped it I remembered the few times that my father had mentioned how, as a Prisoner of War in the jungles of Burma, his greatest deprivation had been thirst. In his despairing mind he had conjured up images of ice cream sodas, but especially of pots full of steaming hot, aromatic plantation tea. So many years later on the Kokoda Trail I came to truly comprehend that the hunger I had suffered in the prison camp could not compare with my father's wartime experience of debilitating physical torture, all for want of a drink of common water.

Later that evening, after a good meal and several cups of tea had restored my vitality, I reflected on the day's incident. I realised that when utter physical exhaustion and acute dehydration set in, it befuddles the mind as if electrical circuits are shorting, strangely affecting thought and action. Although I knew that it is dangerous for anyone to be without a supply of drinking water, I had not expected this to be the case in tropical rainforest and I had not taken the precaution of carrying a water bottle with me – a bad mistake, the consequences of which I now realised could have been serious. When I later asked Ubui where on the mountainside he had found the cupful of water, he replied that he had chopped down stalks of young bamboo growing in the bush. Some of these contain water in the hollows between nodes, a few drops in some, a spoonful or two in others. He had cut down and split many bamboo stalks to gather the water that he had brought me. Without it, as Ubui said, I would have become very sick.

Terry on the Kokoda Trail – thirty-five years old and in the prime of life.

The Efogi airstrip – a miracle in the making

The Mountain Koiari tribe is only small, and their deeds helping in the Allied victory over the Japanese had apparently been forgotten after the war. Had it not been for one of those former 'Fuzzy Wuzzy Angels' – that extraordinary man, my friend Hanua Polis Ubui, from the small village of Efogi – the Mountain Koiari people would perhaps still be living in poverty and sub-human conditions.

In the four years of my association with the Koiari people, many subsequent foot patrols into the mountains enabled me to reach a stage of physical fitness that began to equal that of the villagers, and the memory faded of that first dreadful experience of utter exhaustion and incapacitating thirst. At thirty-five years old, I was in the prime of my life and I revelled in my healthy condition, which now allowed me to take the rigours of walking the Trail and surrounding countryside as easily as the locals. On a succession of agricultural extension patrols in the Owen Stanley hinterlands, I encountered village people living in conditions that I sometimes found difficult to understand or bear. Even on my first visit, I discovered how true Ubui had been when he told me that his people were impoverished and that they lacked many of the comforts that those in Port Moresby took for granted. As he had said, when the sun went down in the evenings, except for the light of the cooking fires the villages were enveloped in darkness without even a small kerosene lamp to light inside the huts. Most people had neither adequate warm clothing nor a blanket with which to ward off the chill of night. In these high altitude villages, families slept around a fire that they kept burning inside their huts, but which often gave little relief from the cold. When deeply asleep they, especially infants, sometimes rolled over into the fireplace, getting terribly injured in the red-hot embers. In addition to these discomforts and risks was the craving for salt.

In what was a very sad experience, on my very first visit to Efogi I discovered the plight of the Koiari people, who, after their extraordinary wartime contribution, had been simply abandoned by Australia and particularly the Territory Administration.

Arriving at Efogi for the night, women came to my hut selling bags of sweet potato, baskets of tomatoes, and even English potatoes, beans, and cabbages. For payment they wanted salt, only salt. I saw one mother give her child a lump of the coarse trade store salt, and the youngster sucked it like a lolly. Living within eyesight of affluent Port Moresby, I was particularly shocked at just how neglected these people were when a woman brought me her sick one-year-old baby, pleading for a cure. Even with only the basic knowledge of infant health care and medicine that most Western parents have, when I noticed the baby's shallow and irregular breathing and glazed, unfocused eyes, I knew that it was very seriously ill. With Ubui interpreting for me I explained to the anxious mother that I was not a trained doctor and that I did not really know what ailed her child or how to cure it. The best I could do was to give her an aspirin tablet, the only medicine that I carried with me. I also gave the mother a few spoonfuls of my milk powder, explaining to her how to make it into a drink that I hoped would strengthen her sick baby. In spite of being able to do so little for her, I was touched by the gratitude of the poor woman and her unfounded faith in me to help her desperately ill child.

A few hours later, after sun-down on the high ridges of the Owen Stanley Range, the village lay in darkness. I sat alone in my hut, cooking my evening meal – a pot of rice and some of the vegetables that Ubui's people had brought me. An eerie quiet had fallen over Efogi and even the dogs had stopped yapping. Suddenly the stillness was broken by a woman's high-pitched wail. The hair-raising, long-drawn keen was followed by a loud chorus of women and men, wailing with phrases and words in their language that I could not understand. My skin prickled all over and I was shocked to realise I was hearing the lament of a despairing mother and villagers for the poor little baby who had just died.

The people kept up the dirge all night and at dawn the entire population of Efogi left the hamlet. By the sound of their wailing I could audibly follow their procession as it passed deep into the bush. Sometime later came a long, loud, final wailing cry – the community's last farewell to one of its own. As the people returned to the village in small groups, fires sprang up in front of huts, dogs scratched themselves and took up their barking again, and the business of everyday life returned to recently bereaved Efogi. I later visited the tiny grave, which lay at the foot of a large tree.

Its branches were covered in profusely growing Spanish moss, with long strands hanging down over the baby's grave, waving in the wind like mobiles in a nursery.

Missionary influence
On repeated visits to Mountain Koiari country, one thing that I found difficult to understand was aspects of Western missionary influence in the area. Without prejudice, what I specifically struggled with were certain religious principles held by the evangelising Seventh Day Adventist denomination. Before I undertook my first patrol, I enquired of Ubui if I should also bring along Native Twist tobacco as an item of exchange and barter. He answered that his religion forbade smoking. While I could find no reason against the Koiari people deciding to totally abstain from using tobacco, I found it difficult to understand another of the Church's injunctions, namely on the consumption of meat. With few exceptions, in the immediate post war period, the indigenous people of the Territory of Papua and New Guinea lived on the borderline of an adequate, balanced diet. Much of their food intake consisted of carbohydrates – sago, plantain banana, sweet potato, taro, yams and other root crops – and their diet included little or no animal or even organic proteins. Although practically everywhere in the Territory villagers kept pigs, these represented traditional currency, which was only sometimes expended on major ceremonial occasions. When at these events Papuans and New Guineans feasted on pork, they were expending social wealth. Their pig husbandry was not aimed at providing the people with a balanced diet. While Papuans and New Guineans traditionally hunt game – wallabies, cassowaries, feral pigs, birds and other wildlife – to supplement their starchy diet, the local Seventh Day Adventist beliefs forbade their consumption. In my opinion, the indigenous diet in Papua and New Guinea was so deprived of sufficient protein that the Western missionaries' religious injunction on consuming meat amounted to a misplaced theological prohibition. In His mercy, would a loving God deny the less fortunate on earth a possible better life and health through a more balanced, more protein rich diet? And if not, what would be His judgement upon a religious belief that would deny them this succour?

However, some Mountain Koiari Adventist converts were able to imaginatively re-interpret the taboo to their advantage. When Ubui noticed tins of bully beef in my emergency food supplies, he pointed to one of them and said that the church forbade his people to eat *this* meat. Indicating another tin of bully, however, he declared, 'But this food is all right to eat.' When I asked him why he could not eat the bully beef in one tin but that he could eat the other one, he pointed to the labels of the evidently different brands that I had bought. 'This tin has the head of an animal on it, which is the meat that the church says we must not eat,' he said. Holding up the other tin he argued, 'The food in this tin is all right because it is made from a coconut tree, and it is therefore not meat.' Looking more closely, I realised that according to Ubui the tin branded with the head of a Hereford bull contained forbidden meat, but the tin with a coconut tree on its label must be vegetarian. When Ubui asked me if I would let him have a tin of the 'coconut food', I did not have it in my heart to tell him that, whether illustrated with a coconut palm or with a bull's head, both these tins contained the same forbidden meat. I agreed that, of course, he could have one of my tins with the coconut food; and to be truthful, I had no qualms in telling my friend a beautiful lie.

A harebrained scheme

After a number of exploratory patrols, when I analysed my observations of the mountain country, it became apparent that the most vexing problem with Ubui's plan to grow coffee in the Owen Stanley Ranges was the difficult access into and out of the area. Although not of immediate concern, within five years of planting the coffee seedlings into the fields, the villagers would be faced with having to porter heavy bags of processed coffee down to Sogeri by way of the Kokoda Trail – the region's only access to the lowlands and its markets. When I mentioned the problem to colleagues at DASF Head Office, no one had a workable answer. One day a solution came to me in a flash of pure inspiration – borne out of sheer ignorant optimism. In retrospect, had I given it sober thought, I should never have gone ahead with what really was an improbable plan.

A Time for Consolidation

On one of my periodic visits to Efogi, the women had brought vegetables to trade. Standing next to a veritable mound of fresh beans, tomatoes, cabbages, potatoes, watermelons, mandarins and other locally grown vegetables, I pondered the beautifully fresh produce – which I had bought for only a few cups of salt. Its quality was as high as the fresh produce presently flown in from Australia to supply Port Moresby. The thought suddenly hit me that if only we could find a practical and effective means to transport this produce to Port Moresby, the Koiari could immediately start earning a cash income. People would not have to wait years before the coffee trees that they were now planting in village nurseries came into production. The solution to the transport problem came to me in a flash.

On foot patrols, as I battled heat, humidity and mud on the Kokoda Trail, I often heard aeroplanes passing overhead. I sometimes wished to be a passenger in one that could land in the villages – but of course the exceptionally rugged terrain of the Owen Stanley Ranges made such an idea preposterous – or did it? Standing beside my vegetables and idly looking out over the landscape, my eyes focused on a large gap of cleared jungle vegetation that terminated at the edge of a sheer cliff face, dropping hundreds of feet down into a ravine. I had noticed this feature in the mountain terrain before and not thought much of it, but today I asked Ubui how it got there and why it remained apparently unused for their gardens. He explained that during the war, white men – Kiap Patrol Officers, or perhaps missionaries – had instructed his people to cut down the bush there to make a place on which *balus* could land. When the villagers had completed this work the white men had left, but no planes had come – perhaps confirmation that, even in those desperate days, the strip was far too risky. As the Taubadas, the Mastas, had said they must not make gardens there, the Koiari had left the clearing unused. It still seemed little more than preposterous when I mentioned to my friend that, if we completed the wartime landing strip, we could bring the benefits of modern civilisation to the Mountain Koiari people. In his excitement Ubui reverted to Police Motu, '*Namo, bada, bada heria, momokani!*' Loosely translated, 'Fantastic!'

Quite frankly, the 'fantastic' idea would have scared any reasonably qualified engineer. Constructing a landing strip for light aircraft on merely a gash in the jungle on an almost sheer mountainside with only local labour – impossible! However, perhaps precisely because I lacked any engineering skills or training whatsoever, I could not let go of the idea.

At about 5500 feet above sea level, Efogi lies just below a saddle in the Owen Stanley Range that encircles the village in a horseshoe shape. It is situated between Mt Obree (10,264 feet) in the south, and Mt Victoria (13,363 feet) to the west. Sighting down from Efogi one can almost see the coast, but deep valleys and razorback ridges descend all the way down to the Sogeri Plateau, where the motorway to Port Moresby begins. Even if a qualified engineer could be found who would be prepared to construct an airstrip on the side of a mountain, the topography of the land on which Efogi village lies is such that it should discourage even the boldest aviator to land an aircraft on such hazardous terrain. But still, I could not let go of the idea.

Ubui was ecstatic at the idea of starting a commercial venture growing fresh fruit and vegetables for Port Moresby, and at my suggestion of reconstructing the abandoned wartime airstrip. In the next few days he gathered the Mountain Koiari elders and influential leaders of Efogi and the surrounding villages, to whom he and I outlined our plans. The Koiari people enthusiastically embraced the idea, but if they had known the ignorance with which I had proposed the project, they would not have taken me seriously.

I knew nothing about airfield construction and took the precaution of first discussing the project with a Port Moresby businessman, the owner and operator of the small airline company STOLAIR. The company's name was inspired by the acronym of the aviation technical term 'Short Take Off and Landing'. It's owner, Ron Ferns, specialised in providing freight and passenger services to outstations in the District, flying single-engine model 178 and 182 Cessna aeroplanes. Before he set up in private business, Ron had been a well-known and very experienced Department of Civil Aviation inspector and flight instructor. Famously reputed to, 'Fly anything, any time, anywhere' in Papua, Ron agreed that if I were to build an airstrip at Efogi he would also service this village, putting my plan into action and forever changing the future and fortunes of the Koiari people.

A Time for Consolidation

Armed with vital information from Ron Ferns that STOL aircraft need a minimum 1500 feet of runway, I returned to Efogi. Over a period of several weeks of backbreaking work – using only axes, bush knives, spades and women's digging sticks – the villagers began to remove the timber and tropical vegetation on the 'gash' that had regrown so rapidly in the jungle, and to extend the length of the strip by clearing more trees and undergrowth. Starting from the edge of the precipice, the people cleared away rotting logs and, using nothing more than spades, they dug out the stumps of the large, freshly-felled trees. With a clearer view of the terrain, somewhat to my concern I found that the space was reasonably level for a distance of roughly 500 feet, but then it ran for 1000 feet up the mountainside at an angle of at least 12º before the gradient again levelled out to a more comfortable 5º. In effect, an aircraft landing on the strip would have to negotiate three distinct inclines. Despite my optimism when we began the work, when I stood on the newly cleared land and noticed how awkwardly canted the site was and how acute was the gradient of its longest leg, I began to doubt if any kind of aircraft – even one flown by the adventurous Ron Ferns – could touch down. Realising how devastating it would be for the keen-as-mustard Koiari tribe, and how disappointed my friend Ubui would be if I voiced these doubts, I bit my tongue – but I did not sleep well. Over the next three weeks we continued the work until we had cleared the mountainside for a space of 1500 feet long and about 100 feet wide – stipulated by Ron to be the minimum required measurements for a bush runway for light aircraft. After weeks of hard physical labour the job was done and with the best will in the world I could do no more. I returned to Port Moresby and with my heart in my mouth told Ron Ferns, 'The airstrip at Efogi is ready… I think?'

That same day Ron took me out in one of his Cessna's. In only twenty minutes flying time we passed over Efogi and I couldn't help but remember the four days of exceptionally hard slog on foot over the Kokoda Trail to reach the village. From the air I could clearly make out the configuration of the land below us – the encircling horseshoe of the Owen Stanley Range behind the village formed the vessel, and the valleys and ridges extending all the way down to the coast resembled the tail of a funnel. As we entered the airspace directly above the village Ron steeply banked the plane. With one wing pointing downwards and the other into the sky, we made a wide turn following the high ridge of the mountain range that runs towards towering Mt Victoria in the distance. Straightening up, we approached the village head on. As we reached the edge of the precipice, to my horror Ron put the plane into a steep dive. But instead of landing he pulled the aircraft up sharply, following the varied gradients of the strip to the end, where we had built a small shed – the Efogi 'terminal'. As the plane climbed out of its run over the clearing and roared into the open air at full power, the Owen Stanley's loomed too closely ahead for my liking. High above the village we could see its people coming from everywhere, out of their homes, their gardens, the nearby bush. Men, women and children stood waving their arms in the air, running down the track to their new airstrip. Sitting next to Ron in the cockpit I could almost *feel* the villagers' excitement. The brand new Efogi landing strip lay bright and clean in the green jungle below, inviting the first ever aircraft to land in the Mountain Koiari homeland. After a last run over Efogi, Ron flew back to Port Moresby. I could imagine the disappointment of the people that we left behind, but I knew it would not be for long.

Before we left Port Moresby that day, Ron had advised me that Department of Civil Aviation Regulations prohibited passengers to be on board an aircraft making an inaugural landing on a newly constructed airfield. Although this was disappointing to me, I was secretly glad and also relieved that I should not have to make what was surely a hazardous landing. Back at Port Moresby's Jacksons Airport, I asked Ron what he thought of my bush airstrip and whether he thought that he could land his Cessna on it. 'Piece of cake,' he declared.

Efogi landing and impact of the airstrip

As prescribed by the Department of Aviation, Ron Ferns made the initial landing at the Efogi airstrip solo – and without mishap. The next day he flew me to set foot on the new airstrip myself. It was an exciting experience, and quite as hazardous as I had imagined. Flying over Efogi, from inside the cockpit of the Cessna the 12° gradient of the first 1000 feet loomed alarmingly up ahead. I thought that we must surely crash straight into the side of the mountain, but at the last moment Ron pulled up the nose of his plane and we 'pancaked' on the bumpy surface. As soon as we touched down he increased the Cessna's engine to full throttle, preventing us rolling backwards off the edge of the precipice into the ravine – not an unlikely scenario given the acute slope on which we landed. Climbing out of the cockpit at the end of the strip we found all the villagers lined up before the 'terminal' to give me a welcome that I shall never forget. Before the entire village my friend Ubui embraced me and we shook hands, sealing our partnership and friendship. As a representative of the white men who owed the Mountain Koiari people so much for their wartime service, it is my hope that by undertaking the project, I may have redeemed a nearly forgotten debt.

The completion of the small bush airstrip at Efogi changed the lives and the fortunes of the villagers along the Kokoda Trail forever. As I had hoped, being able to regularly airfreight fresh garden produce to Port Moresby began to earn the people an immediate cash income. At night after sundown, when hurricane and even kerosene pressure lamps lit up the village, the houses were no longer enveloped in darkness. Instead of being clothed in little better than thin rags, the villagers were now better outfitted, especially in the evenings when everyone was able to don warm jackets – which soon became commonplace. It was also not long before I noticed that salt had lost its value as currency, and I now had to buy vegetables and food with cash. Even more telling were the youngsters, who no longer sucked lumps as if they were lollies. At night when the villagers slept, they could wrap themselves in nice thick blankets; no longer needing to keep a fire burning inside the hut, preventing terrible burn injuries. In time, the produce from village coffee trees would also be airfreighted to the city, and the resulting cash income further improved living conditions for the people along the Kokoda Trail. An improbable airstrip had given this forgotten people a rightful share in the benefits of a rapidly modernising society.

My last, most gratifying and comforting thought on these remarkable improvements was of the poor little baby who had died so pitifully on my first visit to Efogi. With the airstrip, the villagers could now travel to Port Moresby to be saved by stronger medicine than an aspirin and powdered milk.

Terry returned to Efogi in 2019 to place a plaque honouring his friend Ubui. The whole village turned out on the airstrip to welcome him back.

Legendary bush pilots of the Territory

Bush pilots were vital contributors to the development of the Territory of Papua and New Guinea, but their deeds remain little known, and were perhaps not sufficiently appreciated by even the Territorians themselves. In the vast continent of Australia, where the saying 'the tyranny of distance' is not a mere figure of speech, pioneering aviators helped build the nation by providing remote areas with access to communication and services. Their deeds are part of the national record, legends and ethos. In the Territory of Papua and New Guinea the terrain often meant that people in small-scale traditional communities lived in such isolation that they were the only human beings in their known world. Here, some of the more prominent Territory aviation pioneers played *their* role in opening up the country, and they have become part of New Guinea's history. Bobby Gibbes, founder of Gibbes Sepik Airways at Wewak, was one such legend. Ranald Dennis Buchanan – who everyone knew better as 'Junior' and in his youth as 'the gofer' – was clerk and baggage handler at Gibbes Sepik Airways. He became the pioneer owner of Territory Airlines (TAL), a light aircraft company in the New Guinea Highlands, and was later knighted Sir Dennis for his services to aviation. And then there was Roman Catholic Bishop Monsignor Leo Arkfeld in the Sepik District, who had flown Willy, our newborn Evie and me from Wewak to our little house in the jungle at Bainyik. There were other such remarkable men and women, but not all achieved the same reputation. Ron Ferns of STOLAIR at Port Moresby was another intrepid bush aviator I encountered. He deserves to be mentioned and remembered – without a doubt, Ron's 'piece of cake' attitude and willingness to extend his air services to little Efogi contributed greatly to the development of the region and the country. Ron and other Territory bush pilots helped open creaky doors to modernity and eventually Papua New Guinea's nationhood.

Leave in Holland

Although it was unusual for officers in the Territory Administration to stay in a field posting for longer than one, or sometimes two Terms, I remained District Agricultural Officer of the Central District for a total of three Terms. My lengthy posting had the advantage of enabling me to consolidate much of my work with the Koiari and other indigenous communities in the District. In a number of ways our long-term residency in Port Moresby was also beneficial for my family. Willy's career with the Public Works Department blossomed; as its Chief Finance Controller she advanced to high office. In addition, our children began attending primary school in our suburb of Boroko with their education uninterrupted – usually not the case when parents received postings to less socially serviced districts in the Territory.

In remembering the 1960s, I now believe that Willy and I had increasingly assimilated into the Australian way of life, becoming less 'foreign Dutch' and more Australian. The process of our assimilation into Australian society was so gradual that we did not become conscious of it until 1966, when we paid our first visit to Holland and discovered our former Dutch countrymen now regarded and treated us as foreigners. Recalling my father's saying of years ago, 'When in Australia, we must adapt,' Willy and I had apparently followed his direction, subconsciously assimilating the culture of the land that we now called home.

It had been fifteen years since we immigrated to Australia. Returning to Holland, it was good to be reunited with the families we had left behind – and especially to see the three generations together. My and Willy's parents were excited to meet Evie and Terrence, although Willy's parents were less demonstrative and the children weren't used to her mother's mannerisms. My father in particular doted on the children, buying little books for them and making them special dinners and snacks.

Evie celebrated her tenth birthday in Amsterdam. She and Terrence were quite interested in this new place, so different from the tropical environment they were used to. There was no shared language between them and the neighbourhood children, but that didn't stop them from being included. Our overseas holiday went by too quickly but this time when we once again waved our families goodbye, we knew that despite the distance our farewells would not be forever.

Lake Myola – a hidden jewel

Following my successful introduction of vegetable and coffee cash cropping into the Mountain Koiari region, my visits to Efogi were more often by aeroplane rather than by walking the Kokoda Trail. Ron Ferns kept his word, and a weekly scheduled flight carried freight and passengers from the village to Port Moresby. To provide the villagers with technical assistance around their cash cropping projects, I had stationed one of my senior indigenous staff, Field Assistant Iana Guguia, and two junior assistants at Efogi. The people of the Mountain Koiari tribe prospered, and Ubui and I remained friends. Whenever I stayed in his village, he always looked after me, bringing presents of fresh vegetables. I reciprocated with return presents, not of the forbidden Hereford-brand bully beef, but with tins of 'coconut food'. With the main objective of economic development in the area reasonably achieved, on one of my occasional visits to the area I quite self-indulgently decided to satisfy my curiosity about a natural feature of the area – Lake Myola. Seldom visited by white people, Lake Myola was named after the daughter of the Patrol Officer who explored the high alpine reaches of the Owen Stanley Range.

As Lake Myola is within a day's walk from Efogi, Ubui, Iana and I decided that we would not need porters. We would ourselves carry a few days rations and our basic camping gear of a couple of saucepans, blankets and our mosquito nets. The 'lake' is reached from Efogi through the next small village on the Trail, Isurava, also made famous in wartime. At the time I barely knew its history, though to me the village had a brooding, as expressed in German *unheimisch,* air about it and I never felt quite at ease there. At times when I patrolled the area, even if I was very tired I did not like to stay the night at Isurava, but preferred to walk two hours past it to reach Efogi. It took Australia more than fifty years after the war, but at Isurava there now stands a monument dedicated to the many Diggers who so heroically fought and died there.

My companions and I left the main Trail at Isurava, following a narrow and badly overgrown path that led uphill towards a crest 7000 feet above sea level. At about 5500 feet, the rainforest made way for alpine scrub and dense stands of pit pit cane grass. As pit pit often grows in clusters to a height of 8 or 10 feet it is difficult and potentially hazardous to walk through. On the seldom-traversed footpath that we followed, where stands of cane became near impossible to penetrate, Ubui negotiated a way through the growth following tracks made by wild pigs, which abound in the area. Because their religious beliefs did not allow the villagers to hunt the animals for meat, they were powerless to prevent these wily and sometimes dangerous animals from ravaging food gardens, and the numbers of wild pigs had grown to almost plague proportions. When cornered, when a sow is with piglets, or for some other unpredictable reason, they will attack and maul a human intruder, leading the Koiari to regard them as very dangerous. It was a relief for me when, higher up the mountain, we reached the zone where the pit pit cane grass peters out, making way for alpine meadow grassland where we had a better chance to spot and avoid any roaming feral menace.

The alpine country was quite beautiful. In the grassland grew exotic shrubs and plants not found at lower altitudes. Testimony to the pure highland air, mosses trailed long beards from height-stunted trees, the soft purple, white, and pink flowers of erica plants grew on the turf, and to my surprise I noticed scattered stands of rhododendron bushes. Although the landscape was very attractive, soggy peat sometimes had us sinking above the ankles, making it no less difficult to traverse than the cane grass – but we at least did not have to worry about being surprised by wild pigs. The sun had passed its zenith when we reached solid, gravelly ground again. After another hour of climbing we reached the crest of the range, where below us I looked out over the truly fabulous sight of Lake Myola.

In the literal sense of the word, Lake Myola is a misnomer. It is not a body of water but the caldera of a long dead volcano, the bottom of which is dry land. An estimated 8 kilometres across and 150 metres deep, several small streams meander through it, draining the grass- and shrub-covered sump. From where we stood on the lip of the caldera, to the north I spotted the wreckage of a large aircraft, an Allied bomber that on its return from an air raid over Japanese positions had crash-landed in the 'lake'. From afar, in the bright afternoon sunlight I could clearly make out its distinctive corrugated metal fuselage with half its wings intact. At that time of day the eastern crater wall was brilliantly lit by the descending sun, while the western side was already in half darkness. The gathering shadows warned us that before the area was in total darkness we must reach the wreck, where we intended to make camp under the remainder of one of its wings.

Ubui lead us down into the apparently seldom traversed caldera. No path ran through the alpine vegetation, but as it was sparse and low growing we had no trouble descending the crater wall in time to make camp. Looking up at the wing of the wrecked aircraft from ground level, the stub of wing was surprisingly large and it served us well, keeping off the drizzle and mist that at this height often envelopes the mountains. Ubui and Iana busied themselves cutting down small trees and using the branches to form a platform on which to camp and spread our bedding. My comrades also built a fireplace for our cooking, where we kept a fire going to light up the darkness and fend off the night's numbing cold.

For the next two days I explored Lake Myola, discovering a chasm in the old crater walls where small, freezing cold streams run towards a low point, draining into a tributary of the Brown River, which eventually disgorges into the sea 60 kilometres west of Port Moresby. Except for a few minor hillocks, the surface of Lake Myola is surprisingly level. Stunted alpine trees, shrubs, mosses, grasses and flowering plants grew, but except for the abundantly growing rhododendron I could not identify them.

At dawn on my final morning at Lake Myola, with the bottom of the crater still in semi darkness, I received a vivid impression of the flora. We watched the lip of the western wall being lit up by the sun as it struggled through the clouds in the east. Inside the crater an icy blanket of mist enveloped us, making us shiver and sit closer to the fire.

As the sun's blazing orb rose higher in the sky, its warmth tore the veils of fog apart, suddenly revealing an amazing display on the crater wall – hundreds of rhododendron bushes covered with multicoloured blooms. Sunbeams cast spotlights on brilliantly illuminated blossoms, resembling a display of colourful, glittering gems in a jewellery shop. This wildflower dawn at Lake Myola, alongside my memory of the huge bunch of perfect orchids suspended over the Bensbach River, remain highlights of the times I 'patrolled' the incredible beauty of the Territory.

Night trek from Efogi

One last adventure crowned the experiences of my years of agricultural extension work in the Territory of Papua and New Guinea. On a Monday or Tuesday I had flown to Efogi for a short visit to check how the coffee planting was progressing in the Koiari villages. Before leaving I made a promise to my family: I would *definitely* be home in time to attend our children's first school fancy dress party on Saturday. However, on the day that I should have flown back to Port Moresby, I looked up at the sky and my heart sank. Heavy cloud covered the mountains, and drizzling rain was falling that did not abate. At about noon, in the heavily overcast sky above Efogi, I could hear the unmistakable sound of a Cessna aircraft engine – I knew it was the STOLAIR plane, come to collect me. It circled Efogi for half an hour, but when the clouds refused to part for even a minute, the pilot eventually gave up trying to land and I heard the plane disappear back to Port Moresby. Lest I should be guilty of breaking my promise to my family, I made a snap decision – to walk out overnight along the Kokoda Trail. Usually a three and a half day walk, if I left Efogi on foot and kept going, I could perhaps still reach the Sogeri Patrol Post to be in time for my children's school party the next day.

When I told Ubui and Iana that I planned to walk to Sogeri during the night, they were incredulous. They pointed out that, while I knew the way well, walking by myself in the pitch dark jungle was something that should not be undertaken lightly. If anything should happen to me – if I should fall down a ravine or otherwise injure myself – no-one would be there to help; it could be days before anyone found me. When they realised that nothing they said would stop me, Iana said that he would walk back to Sogeri with me, and Ubui insisted that we take a small kerosene lamp along with a few bananas and some nuts from the okari tree in his garden to eat on the way. I was thirty-seven years old, superbly fit, and – perhaps foolishly – determined not to break my promise to my family. At 2 pm that Friday, Iana and I set out to complete the three-and-a-half day journey to the Sogeri Patrol Post in under twenty-four hours.

Iana's offer, his insistence, that he accompany me on the overnight trek was an extraordinary act of gallantry, and one of considerable personal courage. My time in the Territory had shown me that the Western world regards superstition in a different manner to the indigenous peoples of Papua and New Guinea. What we call 'superstition' is an integral part of their system of religious beliefs, and something that is interwoven in all aspects of their daily living. The inhabitants of Papua and New Guinea had mostly been converted to, and actively and devoutly practiced, the Christian religion. But in their interpretation of Christianity, they incorporated some former supernational beliefs that many in the Western world reject, or at least claim to repudiate. For many Papuan and New Guinean people, the supernatural forms a connection – a bridge between the known, everyday world in which we live, and the unknowable realm in which dwell those who have departed life. Awesome and frightening to the Papuans and New Guineans is the belief that these spirit beings are neither truly dead nor properly alive. For Iana to want to accompany me at night on the Kokoda Trail – where innumerable sad and perhaps wrathful ghosts of slain Australian and Japanese soldiers might bemoan their cruel fate – was an act of extraordinary loyalty.

When we left Efogi, Iana and I set a cracking pace from the start. Carrying nothing heavier than the kerosene lamp and the small hessian bag of rations, we made exceptional progress. We reached Manari village – normally an eight-hour walk from Efogi – in just on four hours, in the early evening. There were still a few people about in the open and, hardly slowing our steps as we passed through the village, Iana explained to them what we planned to do. Though the villagers said nothing, their faces spoke their thoughts – surely it was foolishness, if not madness, for us to tempt the natural hazards on the Trail… not to mention the possible unearthly perils?

We continued down the Trail from Manari. As it got dark we lit the kerosene lamp – its feeble light providing more moral reassurance

A Time for Consolidation

than effective illumination on the jungle path. Reaching Naoro, the next village, at around 11 pm, we had completed almost two days of normal walking time on the Trail. If we succeeded in keeping up this pace – brisk walking, sometimes half running – I calculated that we stood a chance to reach Sogeri sometime in the early afternoon of the next day. That thought buoyed my resolve and kept up my spirits that, in the feeble light of our small lamp, badly needed bolstering in the pitch-dark jungle.

The heavy cloud continued to cover the sky, releasing drizzle over us from time to time and preventing the moon from shining. Even so, we had surprisingly little trouble finding our way. Preserving energy, Iana and I walked in silence. I could not help remembering that during the war the area had seen terrible violence and suffering, and of course many deaths. I knew that for my companion to be where such carnage had taken place was a frightful ordeal, but I also realised that the brooding dark of the primeval forest aroused an involuntary dread in me. As we plodded on through the near stygian darkness I was thankful for the feeble glow of our little lamp. It helped keep at bay my fear of whatever unholy agencies were about – which my Western upbringing should have dismissed as humbug and an unreasonable flight of fancy, but which felt very real in my overwrought mind and overworked body.

At night the forest had a beauty very different from in daylight. In the tangled mass of the undergrowth around us colonies of fireflies sometimes winked their green phosphorescent light. On the ground lay decaying logs of fallen trees ablaze with a lambent luminescence, the product of vegetative decomposition. We discovered other surprises in the night time jungle. As we forded one of the countless rivulets or creeks that everywhere intersect the Trail, our lamp sometimes showed up freshwater crayfish and small fry in the shallows, and frogs and unidentified nocturnal insects on the banks. As Iana and I waded through yet another of these creeks, we got a fright when, almost underfoot, we startled an enormous eel. At least 5 feet long and almost a hand-span thick, it thrashed away in sinuous twists. As it disappeared I readily agreed when Iana said, 'That one is very big, he has plenty of sharp teeth. We were lucky not to step on him!'

With the new day on the point of dawn, we passed through the sleeping village of Ioribaiwa. We had eaten nothing more than a couple of bananas and a few okari nuts since we left Efogi and we were both getting very hungry. We spotted a bunch of bananas hanging off a rafter in front of one of the houses and stopped briefly to help ourselves to a hand of the fruit. Leaving some money behind in payment, we kept walking as we ate the sweet banana flesh, reviving our flagging energy. We knew that if we kept up our present rate of progress we should reach the last village on the Trail, Uberi, in perhaps six hours. Two hours after that we would arrive at the Sogeri Patrol Post. Although Iana and I were getting very tired, we were almost at the end of the longest continuous walk either of us had ever undertaken, and the thought lifted our spirits. I was buoyed by the knowledge that I was almost at the place where I could ring my wife to collect me, and I would still be in time for the children's school party that afternoon.

Sometime around 8 am Iana and I were standing at the bottom of a deep, deep valley, facing the last major hurdle of the terrain back to Port Moresby. Iana and I had now walked for almost eighteen hours without resting. The energy from the bananas at Ioribaiwa had quite burnt itself out and we had few physical and mental resources left with which to face the punishing climb out of the valley. At the foot of the mountain we sat down for a short rest, trying to work up the willpower to keep going. Iana pulled out a handful of okari nuts from his pocket and said, 'This is the last food we have. We eat him now, to make us strong for the climb to Uberi.' In my turn, I felt in the back pocket of my trousers for the small flask of negrita rum that I had brought with me. Although I was well aware that at the time it was a criminal offence to supply an indigenous Papua New Guinean with alcoholic liquor, without hesitation I replied, 'We'll eat your okari nuts and drink my rum.' In the exercise of common sense one may sometimes be excused for ignoring man-made laws – so we rested, ate the nuts, and shared the small flask of neat rum. On the night-time Kokoda Trail trek, through the jungle of the Owen Stanley Ranges, my friend Iana and I were equals.

Experience had taught me that it would take a full hour to climb to the top of the ravine, but in spite of the rest and sustenance I was suffering dead-tired muscles and, in a dispirited state of mind, I dreaded the long, torturous climb on clumsy footholds hacked into the clay. I was so tired that I almost despaired and was on the verge of capitulating to an all-consuming exhaustion when I remembered Mr Miles from the Japanese prison camp, who had taught me the meaning of Rudyard Kipling's verse *If*:

> If you can force your heart and nerve and sinew
> To serve your turn long after they are gone,
> And so hold on when there is nothing in you
> Except the Will which says to them: "Hold on!"
> … Yours is the Earth and everything that's in it,
> And – which is more – you'll be a Man, my son!

The climb up the mountain was indeed an ordeal, and when we reached the top we were both exhausted. However, knowing that Sogeri was now only a few hours away, after a short halt we got up and continued.

With no major rises in the terrain we reached Uberi in good time. There we descended down to the last small waterway near the village before climbing up the last hill to the edge of the Sogeri Plateau. Iana and I split up at Owers Corner, he taking a shortcut to his village and I continuing on to the Sogeri Patrol Post. Before we parted I thanked Iana for having volunteered to accompany me, knowing the dread he held of the old battlegrounds. When we shook hands, I thanked him, '*Thank you bada heria, Iana* (Thank you very much, Iana).' I was deeply touched when he responded with a simple, '*Namo, Taubada* (That's okay, sir)' – I knew that we understood and respected each other well, and that no more needed to be said.

It was just on one o'clock in the afternoon when I walked up to the Patrol Officer's house at Sogeri. Answering my knock on the door, he looked at me as if seeing something peculiar, and I realised that in my mud and sweat stained clothes I must look and probably smell quite disreputable. When I told him I had come from Efogi overnight, he questioned me, I thought a little disbelievingly. 'Did you say that you left at two o'clock yesterday afternoon?' He looked at the clock on the wall, 'It's 1 pm now… do you mean to tell me that you covered the normal three day walk from Efogi in 23 hours?' When I confirmed this, he responded with a shake of his head, 'I'll be damned, how's that?' Then he looked again at my dishevelled self. 'Have a shower,' he offered. 'I'll lend you some of my clothes – you can't stay in that gear – and I'll make you something to eat.' I thanked him for his kindness, but before I took him up on the offer of a badly needed shower, I asked if I could ring Port Moresby to let my wife know that I had arrived, and ask if she could pick me up at the Patrol Post in our car.

Showered and dressed in my host's shorts and shirt – which felt marvellously comfortable and clean – when I sat down at the table for the bachelor meal he had prepared for me – packet mushroom soup and risotto – my stomach felt as if twisted in a knot. Now that I had reached my destination I could give in to all-pervading tiredness in every fibre and sinew of my body, and I suddenly felt that I could not eat a bite. I knew that after such long and strenuous exercise on a virtually empty stomach I must not give in to my present queasiness, so I willed myself to eat the bowl of steaming hot mushroom soup, but I could not eat my host's risotto. As I waited for Willy to arrive to take us home to Port Moresby, too tired to sleep, the Patrol Officer and I talked, and I rested in the comfort of an armchair. I let my body recuperate somewhat from the exertion of the longest walk of my life – which I would never *ever* want to repeat, ever!

About an hour-and-a-half after I rang, our car drew up before the Patrol Officer's house. I had kept my promise to my family that I would be home for the children's school party. But to my surprise, when Willy opened the car door for me, on the back seat I found two sick, unhappy children huddled under blankets. Of course it was not their fault, but there could be no party for my poor ailing infants – chickenpox had made the longest and most arduous walk of my life unnecessary.

The night-time trek over the Kokoda Trail was the last adventure in my Papua New Guinea career. In 1974, a year prior to National Independence, Willy and I would take voluntary retirement from our respective positions with the soon to be defunct Australian Territory Administration.

CHAPTER 24

The Times They are a Changing

Follow your own bent no matter what people say
Karl Marx, *Das Capital*

The 1960s was a time when the world – including Australia – seemed to be taking a collective deep breath, adjusting from the recent upheaval of a catastrophic war and associated social change. The emerging global ethos aimed to discourage isolationism, encouraging an emerging consciousness of the world as a single place. However, little seemed to have changed in the way lives had been lived for generations in Australia. In spite of massive immigration in the post-war period, much of the 'Island Australia' ethos remained stubbornly adhered to by those of Anglo-Saxon descent; the thin line of social distinctions between 'Them' and 'Us', 'Old' and 'New' Australians, was still very much evident.

For us, the 1960s was not only an era of assimilating the Australian way of life, it also became a time of considerable personal adjustments to the realities of the times. The world's colonial powers were rapidly decolonising and even in the backwaters of the Australian Territory of Papua and New Guinea the 'winds of change' – which Australian Prime Minister Robert Menzies had predicted in the 1950s – began to be felt. In the epilogue to the second edition of her book *Australia in New Guinea*, Lucy Philip Mair[xxxvi] wrote:

... In a sense independence has come to every colonial territory both too soon and too late. Too soon for development of the resources in personnel that are needed to solve the problems of a twentieth century state, too late for the end of paternal rule to be attained without creating resentment and suspicion among its subjects. There is no particular reason to hope for a brighter future for New Guinea than the rest of the Third World is experiencing (but)... One can at least say that Australia is seeking to prepare the Territory for what lies ahead.

In the decade immediately before Papua New Guinean independence, the need began to arise for expatriates in the Territory of Papua and New Guinea to 'sooner, rather than later' take stock of the building momentum for the indigenous society to attain economic and political independence from Australia.

Stirrings of change

For those in the Australian Territory of Papua and New Guinea with eyes to see and ears to hear, the 1960s was a watershed in the country's modernisation, but even more pertinently, the politicisation of the indigenous people. Echoing the perspective of the Dutch in Java before the war, with the exception of a handful of visionaries, the majority of expatriates remained dismissive to signs that, for colonialism in the Australian Territory, the times were *actually* changing. For many, in the immediate post war period the people of New Guinea had appeared socially, economically and politically underdeveloped – they could be more or less justifiably described as 'primitive' or at best as belonging to 'one of the child races while the Europeans were adults in civilisation'[xxxvii]. Most expatriates seemed to think it impossible that the country should ever be anything but an Australian-administered Territory, or at best a part of the Commonwealth of Australia. Yet, for those with foresight, evidence of a sea change in indigenous Papua New Guineans' aspirations towards a new future was gathering. Much of this movement was actively fostered and promoted in Australia, in particular by then Prime Minister Gough Whitlam, and a scant few Territory expatriates. Among the indigenous Papua New Guineans, wrote Lady Rachel Cleland – wife of the then Administrator of Papua and New Guinea Sir Donald Cleland – was Michael Somare, respected and loved by both whites and blacks.[xxxviii] He would become Papua New

Guinea's inaugural Prime Minister, a man with great foresight and a vision for a time when Papua and New Guinea would shed its past shackles of benevolent colonialist overlordship in favour of taking charge of its own destiny.

In small, banal, everyday ways, in the latter years of the 1960s life in the Territory was changing – giving rise to old-timers, the 'B4s', bewailing the disappearance of 'the good old days'. In the late 1960s and early 1970s, white patrons in the shops no longer took preference in the queues at checkout counters; buses no longer had front rows of seats 'reserved' for white commuters, leaving the back seats for the black people. One day, very quietly and unannounced, the sign 'Europeans Only' disappeared from Ela Beach.

The gradual re-definition of the racial *desideratum* throughout the Territory went fairly unremarked by the expatriate public. One exception that polarised opinions on the interrelationships between the white and black races in Territory society was a bond that developed between a certain black man and a white woman. The former an upcoming name in the list of influential indigenous New Guineans and the latter a young Australian schoolteacher, they chose to publicly display an apparent intimate relationship for all to observe on Ela Beach. In today's times the incident would probably go quite unnoticed. However, even the most fair-minded in white *and* black Territory society at the time could not construe it other than as deliberately provocative behaviour. Most importantly, it had the effect of polarising public opinion 'for' or 'against', or 'whether or not', the Territory of Papua and New Guinea should ever aspire to join Australia as its seventh state, or if it should achieve self-government or eventually independence.

> … when people first began to talk seriously about the Territory's future, they often assumed that Papua and New Guinea would join Australia as a seventh state… When the educated (indigenous) people of the towns began to speak out, they mostly seemed to favour self-government… but they did not always know what was involved… Few people in Australia gave the matter much thought; they still did not think that the future of the Territory had to be decided urgently; most waited and hoped for the best…[xxxix]

'Waiting and hoping for the best', for black and white alike there were many in the Territory for whom this example thrust the racial question to the fore, raising pertinent questions about the efficacy of a 'marriage' between the different races and cultures of Australia and Papua New Guinea, and doubts that this union could ever be achieved.

The surge towards modernity that gripped the Papua and New Guinean population in the late 1960s triggered other social problems. A population of young men from rural Papua and New Guinea had begun to drift into Port Moresby and other large Territory centres. Poorly if at all educated, untrained and unqualified, there was very little chance of these men finding employment in the cities and towns. As the numbers of these rural immigrants swelled, so too did urban crime, often outpacing the Territory authorities' capacity to maintain law and order. Burglary and home invasions, bag snatching in the street and similar petty offences began to occur ever more frequently. Major crimes of violence also began to plague the previously safe and peaceful suburbs, on the edges of which sprang up shanty towns filled with desperate, out-of-work people. In the city and its suburbs, it quite suddenly became commonplace for shops and expatriate residences to have windows reinforced with so-called pig-wire fencing material, in the Territory dubbed *boiwire*. Whereas not many years previously people's homes had 'of course' stayed wide open, the home's doors were now carefully shut during the day and locked after dark. Little better than a dubious deterrent, in practice the boiwire around a home's windows hardly prevented a determined miscreant from breaking and entering. Where it concerned my family, these signs reminded me of post-war Indonesia – times that I did not wish to revisit in Papua and New Guinea. For Willy and me the thought increasingly occupied our minds: what should we do, and whither should we go?

A hard decision
Another concern was our children's education. By the end of the 1960s both had commenced high school and, given the changing social situation in the Territory, their future became an issue that

we could not afford to ignore. Evie and Terrence had received excellent primary schooling following the so-called Territory 'A' – the Australian primary school curriculum stream for white children. In the Territory 'T' curriculum stream, indigenous school children were taught English as a foreign language. Some expatriate parents – among them Willy and I – argued that the different language-based teaching would inevitably cause a lowering in academic standards, placing white children at a disadvantage in terms of their academic future as they would generally finish their schooling in Australia. At the end of a Recreation Leave in 1968 spent in Australia, Willy and I had to make one of the most difficult and heartbreaking decisions of our lives, opting for our children to continue their education in Australia. We entered them as boarders in the rural city of Armidale in New South Wales; fourteen-year-old Evie at the New England Girls School and twelve-year-old Terrence at The Armidale School. Evie felt the separation very much and suffered rather badly, but Terrence simply said 'Bye!' and walked off, leaving us in tears! He thought it was a great adventure. It was a hard decision for us, but both children really benefitted. They did well at school, met some very nice people, and the discipline stood them in good stead.

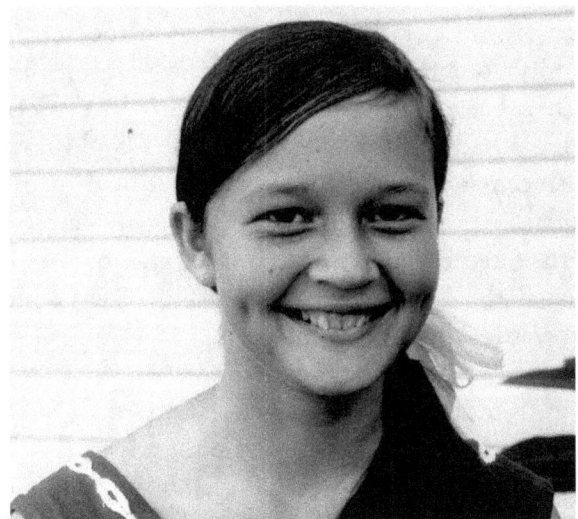

Thirteen-year-old Evie prior to attending New England Girls School.
Evie felt the separation keenly in her first year.

Twelve-year-old Terrence revelled in the many opportunities of The Armidale School.

Changing direction

For Willy and me, accelerating social change in the Territory began to increasingly affect our thinking about our own future. By the end of the 1960s I had been serving for sixteen years in the Department of Agriculture and I had come to a point where I could no longer aspire to career advancement. With no better educational qualification than diploma standard, the inevitable truncation of my career path had for many years frustrated my ambitions. This led me to enrol in a Bachelor of Arts degree at the University of Papua and New Guinea – the first crucial step towards our new future.

As a young institution, the University of Papua and New Guinea was staffed with highly qualified and motivated academics, full of zeal and purpose, eager to play their part in producing the educated indigenous leaders the emerging country, on the brink of its national independence, urgently needed. In its infancy, the university exuded an atmosphere of optimism, a contagious enthusiasm and a thirst for teaching and learning that diffused from the Vice Chancellor down to undergraduate students – among whom I proudly took my place, graduating in 1974.

My university studies, majoring in social anthropology and Melanesian history, were a further cause of my growing disaffection with certain aspects of the Australian Government's policies and practices aimed at promoting economic change in indigenous Papua and New Guinea. Increasingly I felt that I could not support the Department of Agriculture's, in my view, questionable practices in disseminating Canberra's political aim of promoting economic independence. With a lengthy background of personal experience living with the people and witnessing their cultures, I felt such policies came at a very real and damaging cost to the culture and mores of indigenous Papua and New Guinea. In 1970, eager to distance myself from the Department, I applied for the position of Registrar of the Administrative College of Papua and New Guinea. It was a chance for promotion that would lead to a new academic focus and would potentially change not only my career, but my whole life.

The college's inception in November 1963 was part of the Australian Government's post Second World War approach to modernising the Territory. For the first time, the Territory Administration was taking a direct role in expanding educational facilities for indigenous Public Servants. Its Commission on Higher Education (1963–4) envisaged expending intensive effort in improving the educational standards of indigenous people in a range of skilled occupations such as teachers, health workers and public servants in middle management positions. The required tertiary training was to be carried out by establishing a number of colleges, with the Administrative College focusing on administration and management. The Commission felt it to be of great importance that the Administrative College should be closely related to the University of Papua and New Guinea, and eventually become an institute of administration within the university[xl].

The principal function of the Administrative College was to specifically further what was called the 'localisation' of the Public Service, partly by courses for new recruits, but mainly by enabling already serving locals to qualify for posts at higher levels. This 'localisation' of the indigenous public servants had begun in 1957, when an Auxiliary Division was created. Divided into three grades open only to indigenous people, the lowest grade required three years of primary education, the highest two years post-primary. In raising the educational standards of recruited or serving indigenous people in the Administration, it was expected that opportunities for higher-level career advancement would then open up for those in the public service. One of the students who had qualified and was set for rapid career advancement was my former Field Assistant, William (Bill) Lawrence. He was the immediate Principle Elect of the Administrative College, and would subsequently become the Public Service Commissioner of the Papua New Guinea Administration – its highest official. To him I owe a debt of gratitude for a new career and a new direction in my life.

My appointment as Registrar came from an incident several years earlier when, stationed at an agricultural outpost, Bill attended an agricultural conference in Port Moresby. At the conclusion of the conference, the Agriculture Department's Human Services Section had denied him a travel warrant, which would have recompensed his sister for his board and lodging. The refusal smacked of racial bias, so I had Bill accompany me to personally request the Director to rescind the decision. Gratifyingly, the Director agreed that an injustice had been done.

When I applied for my appointment to the Administrative College, unbeknown to me, Bill was understudying the College's expatriate Principal as the latter's indigenous replacement on National Independence. When making the choice of most suitable candidate for the College's Registrar, Bill saw my submission and said, 'It is he who we want.' Fate had stepped in and my past Field Assistant was to be my immediate superior. The position of Registrar of the Administrative College of Papua New Guinea would be the prelude for our repatriation to Australia, and the conclusion of twenty years in the Territory.

In the early 1970s, during the final four years of our service, Willy and I had to make many personal, career, and forward-planning decisions. Our belief was that, in the words of past Prime Minister Menzies, it was better for us to leave the Territory 'sooner, rather than later', a view reinforced by my experience of the freedom struggles in Indonesia. Studying for the Bachelor of Arts Degree at the University of Papua and New Guinea, I had already taken a major step towards our resettlement. However, after twenty years of absence from Australia, it was fair to say that we had no real idea of how to put that higher qualification to proper use. The government had been promoting the voluntary resignation of expatriate Public Servants in Papua and New Guinea to make way for indigenous nationals. Canberra devised a monetary inducement as compensation for loss of career, colloquially referred to as 'A Golden Handshake'. It was accompanied by a career advisory service for officers affected by the accelerated pace of the 'localisation' of the Public Service. My advisor urged me to complement my Bachelor of Arts with a post-graduate Diploma in Education at an Australian university – which he termed 'a bread-and-butter qualification'. This proved sound advice, very considerably assisting us in remaking our lives in Australia.

Before leaving Papua and New Guinea, I successfully applied for a Commonwealth of Australia Government study grant. This gave me a year's Commonwealth studies scholarship and enabled me to enrol in the post-graduate Diploma in Education at the University of New England in Armidale, New South Wales – the rural city where our children attended their boarding schools.

Farewelling the Territory

After twenty years of living and working in the Territory of Papua and New Guinea, on 24 August 1974 Willy and I boarded our aircraft at Jacksons International Airport for repatriation to Australia. The Boeing 707 jet had long since replaced the old DC6b Skymaster that had brought us to the Territory at the beginning of our New Guinea adventure. In the air over Port Moresby, on our way to Australia, the pilot followed the same flight path as the pilots of twenty years earlier. As the plane banked a wide turn over the city, we could make out our street, and even our house – Section 55, Lot 5 at Boroko. Straightening out, below the left-hand wing tip lay Ela Beach, and on the right was Hanuabada village with its dwellings elevated on stout posts driven into the sea bed. Engines at full thrust, the 707 continued its climb, breaking through a light cover of scattered clouds that dappled the turquoise waters of the reef shallows with weird shadows. Heading south over the sea, I took one last look at the Owen Stanley Ranges rising behind Port Moresby. With a heavy heart I said a silent good-bye to my friend Hanua Polis Ubui and his Mountain Koiari people, and the now less used Kokoda Trail where we had built our life-changing Efogi airstrip. I silently remembered the Western District, our Papuan Water Wonderworld, and my Kiwai friends: Old Man Bardia, James Suago, Anuo Mataio and our home help, the triple axe murderer known only as Calaboose. Nor did I forget to salute 'my men' at the Bainyik Agricultural Station in the Sepik District: Trenyan, Takanambu and Nami. In her turn I knew that Willy, too, said an unvoiced farewell to Anamia, who had returned to her people, to E'eo, our good-hearted, laughing washerwoman, and to the Papuan 'girls' and their spirited games of basketball on Daru Island. No doubt she also reflected on our little bush house in the jungle at Bainyik, with the near birth of Evie, fortunately delayed until a few days later at Wewak, and the very different birth of Terrence in a 'real' hospital in Port Moresby.

We didn't speak of our feelings; words would have only released the tears both of us were trying so hard to control. From the aircraft window, the coastline of Papua and New Guinea grew smaller, faded, and finally disappeared. Thus ended twenty years of our great adventure in the Territory of Papua and New Guinea, which had meant so much to us in so many ways. Bound for 'Down South', a new future lay ahead in Australia.

PART 6:

In Retrospect

CHAPTER 25

Starting Over

*The thing we long for, that we are
For one transcendent moment*
James Russell Lowell, *Longing*

At the time of writing, sixty-nine years have passed since, in 1952, Willy and I arrived in Australia as immigrants – a young married couple, often baffled by the social customs and conventions of a foreign country. Two years later we first set foot in the Territory of Papua and New Guinea at the start of a grand adventure. In time, our life in the Territory helped our social integration into Australian society and repaired our precarious financial position.

Settling back into Australia

No less than people from other nations, Australians tend to judge those who enter their society from the outside by their background, education, occupation and – perhaps more so than in Europe – by their apparent wealth. When in 1974 we repatriated to Australia from New Guinea, both Willy and I did so with a history of successful careers, and, for me, with the advanced qualification of a Bachelor of Arts from the University of Papua New Guinea.

This meant our re-absorption into Australian society occurred reasonably seamlessly. If my post-graduate Diploma in Education set me on a new course towards the future, Willy devised her own important path – taking care of our financial and investment matters, for which her long experience with the Territory Public Works Department stood her in excellent stead. At the core of this was avoiding investing our 'Golden Handshake' unwisely – unlike some of our former compatriots who were talked into dubious ventures by unscrupulous operators. After extensive consultations with bank managers and others with sound financial credentials, we decided to embark on real estate investment. Willy made it her new career to oversee and manage these activities, which she did with great success.

By the time we resettled in the city of Armidale, Evie had completed high school and was successfully employed in one of the local banks. Terrence was still in his final year of high school, Year 12, and intended to apply for training in a military career with the Australian Army. All things considered, back in Australia with the nervous energy of the preceding few months somewhat dissipated, I was looking forward to resuming my academic studies.

Terrence graduated from Portsea Officer Training as a First Lieutenant in the Australian Army.

I soon became absorbed in the academic world, just as I had during my undergraduate studies in Port Moresby, this time in the discipline of education at the University of New England. Attending my new alma mater fascinated and challenged me, and the lectures and tutorials I attended expanded my horizons. When in 1975 I graduated with a post-graduate Diploma in Education, I had been fortunate to attract favourable attention from the Head of the Centre for Educational Studies, who not only encouraged me to continue studying, but also offered me a position tutoring undergraduate students in the Centre. For the next eight years I continued tutoring while completing a Master of Education and attempting candidature for a Doctor of Philosophy in the field of the social sciences.

Mirrabooka

Life goes on and, as quoted from Heraclitus, 'There is nothing permanent except change' – our successful resettlement in the city of Armidale turned out not to be as permanent as we had planned. After eight years, when my employment contract with the university came up for renewal, I made the decision to abandon my two years of PhD research so that Willy and I could embark on one last great adventure.

My long-held dream – a combination of my childhood memories of our plantation on Java and our experience on the Naracoorte farm – was realised when we purchased beautiful Mirrabooka: our own property in South Gippsland, Victoria.

Acquiring the farm involved a very elaborate process of visiting rural properties, starting from Cairns at the top of Australia, and working all the way down the country. We eventually selected Mirrabooka, literally one neighbouring farm away from Bass Strait: next stop Tasmania!

It had always been somewhat curious to us that, though there appears to be a degree of negative sentiment towards Aboriginality in Australia, it is quite common to find, often proudly worn, a wide range of Aboriginal names given to landmarks, places, and similar. It was therefore little surprise that the property we were purchasing was called 'Mirraboo', the Aboriginal name for an astronomical constellation. As new owners, we replaced this with 'Mirrabooka', which more specifically denotes a body in the cosmos and reflected our immigration journey and resettlement in our new home.

Willy was delighted in the Mirrabooka homestead, the kind of 'proper' house that we had not found elsewhere. While other properties featured many functional benefits, their houses were almost primitive dwellings – doors hanging skew-whiff and windows that needed a packet of sturdy screws to refasten them to the frames; not to mention the timber cladding that begged for not one but many tins of paint. For many farmers, hard-pressed to pay their bills, the promise of 'We'll get around to it someday' seldom eventuated.

On Mirrabooka the stately brick homestead and the magnificent home paddock with its beds of flowers and shrubs bordering the picturesque trout-stocked lake fulfilled all Willy's dreams. For me, the South Gippsland hills covered with lush green paddocks offered the hope of new dimensions in our lives. But we still had much to learn about 'living on the land'.

Flower gardens and a trout-stocked lake in front of the homestead fulfilled all Willy's dreams.

While it is often said, 'We are all Australians', our 'cousins from the bush' often consider themselves a world away from their city counterparts. In addition, with us being immediate-past 'New Australians', how would we be received by our traditionally conservative rural neighbours? Although I had extensive experience in tropical agriculture, apart from our early stint at Naracoorte, we lacked experience of Australian 'life on the land'. Over time we gained that experience, but it was hard-won.

'Mirraboo' was operating as a dairy farm when we first acquired it, providing us with an immediate income. While grazing sheep or cattle would have been an easier lifestyle, it would have left us without a cashflow until we were more adequately established. However, while this was a salient point in deciding on the property, ultimately the dairying venture proved unsuccessful.

Dairy farming, by its very nature, is unceasing, mean and back breaking work. Cows need to be milked twice a day, every day, 365 days of the year – and that doesn't including the tilling and other farm operations. Although Willy and I liked the cattle and were prepared for hard work, we did not have the skills and experience needed for dairying. The solution appeared to lie in appointing sharefarmers to work the dairy – experienced operators in a working partnership, acting on behalf of the owners, and sharing the income and certain expenses. Ultimately the dairying did not prove to be profitable, but it certainly served to build up my experience of Australian farming.

A fortunate change in direction came with the resignation of our sharefarmer. When I asked him if he knew of a replacement, he replied, 'Sorry, no, but why don't you change to grazing cattle. It's less work; you and your wife could operate the farm together.' With a twinkle in his eye, he added, 'Save you having to pay another bloke like me. Just buy the missus a box of chocolates now and then.' These chance few jesting words entirely changed the direction of our farming on Mirrabooka. Beef cattle grazing became a lifestyle involving our whole extended family, from Willy and me, to my mother and sister Conny, right down to our grandchildren.

Looking back, alongside disappointments and setbacks, Willy and I have also enjoyed success and highlights for which we are deeply thankful. In our married life we never forgot our modest beginnings, and nor did we fail to claim credits where these were earned. In this respect, Mirrabooka and its cattle grazing was the crowning period of our lives. Through Mirrabooka on the rolling green Gippsland hills I was reminded of the terraces that wound around the mountains of our tea plantation on Java, of the emerald-green tea bushes of my childhood. It took me back to the jungle wildlife, fleeting, scurrying shapes from out of the wilderness; the noisy chatter from monkeys in their arboreal shelter; triumphant cries from outstretched necks of meandering bush fowls and other birds; the near silent cacophony of 'white noises' from insects and small jungle animals. Mirrabooka was also full of meaningful sounds, the hoarse bellow of a bull and the softer '*Moo*-oo' of cows in their paddocks, and kangaroos, foxes and wombats adding a silent feral presence. My grandchildren often laughed that I did not like the wombats; the wretched things dug large holes in paddocks and dam banks overnight, risking injury when riding motorbikes, or damage to farming equipment.

Located on the hillside, our house overlooked an incredible view of huge, wide open spaces; paddocks that in the far distance were marked off by the Strzelecki Mountain range that reaches the edge of Bass Strait. Taking afternoon tea in the lounge room, Willy and I often watched how, on its passage to the far horizon, the setting sun painted a kaleidoscope of colours as it settled on the sky-line; a beautiful, beautiful country.

Family visits were a great delight. Coming from the city, Mirrabooka provided the opportunity for our grandchildren to ride motorbikes, drive around paddocks and fish in the small trout lake near the house. They learned about life on the land, throwing hay to the cows, watching calves being born, and digging up potatoes for dinner.

The grandchildren learnt to ride early at Mirrabooka.

We all grew to love Mirrabooka, creating many precious memories that are treasured by our children and grandchildren, which they in turn will pass on to the next generation of our Australian Brockhall family. I thought often of my father during those years, and how he loved both countries – Java and Australia; how he would have loved to see his family in the second homeland expanding through the generations.

For the first time since childhood, at Mirrabooka I felt free – free from the strictures of confinement, free from dancing to the tune of others, free at last to work my land on my own terms. Hearing the laughter of our grandchildren, they could have been my Indonesian friend Soekarno, and the small Javanese children in the kampongs. The bellow of a cow could have been the drawl of a buffalo; the sunset calls of currawong and magpie the echo of the rich birdlife of Java.

For the first time since childhood, at Mirrabooka I felt free.

After a joyful fourteen years, Willy and I retired. Closing the main gate behind us for the last time, life on our beautiful Mirrabooka became another of our treasured memories. It was our last great adventure together in such fortunate lives. Looking back, I am never sad when my mind returns to Mirrabooka, because as always, Willy is there to share my feelings. Although departed, she remains my wife, my partner, my friend, my confidant, my companion in our long married life. Willy will never be any other than truly and forever the love of my life.

Closing the main gate behind us for the last time, life on our beautiful Mirrabooka became another of our treasured memories.

Retirement

Retiring to Melbourne, I started writing this book. Often a confession of the heart, the memories came flooding back. Four years later Willy and I moved nearer to family in Brisbane where we lived for ten years, before relocating to Armidale, close to our daughter Evie's family. Sadly, by that time, Willy had been diagnosed with dementia; she passed away quietly in 2017.

Starting Over

Retirement is often a time of rest and leisure, but I've never really stopped working since I left Java in my teens – I just can't imagine I ever will. Work has different meanings. Gone are the days when I would pick up a spade or an axe for the task at hand. But there are other kinds of work.

I have always tried to continue learning – awarded a Degree of Doctor of Philosophy in Social Sciences, focusing on trans-nationalism and trans-migration, at eighty-one years of age (Tim Marsden/Newspix).

I have always tried to continue learning. In 2007 I embarked on advanced studies, renewing my candidature for a doctorate. On 16 October 2009, aged eighty-one, I was awarded the Degree of Doctor of Philosophy in the Field of the Social Sciences, my thesis focusing on trans-nationalism and trans-migration. This last great academic endeavour owed its inspiration to my mother's sagacious primary teaching, enlarged with the kind of inspiration that fired my imagination and gave me a thirst for knowledge that has never left me.

On Reflection

> Was there aught that I did not share
> In vigil or toil or ease,
> One joy or woe that I did not know,
> Dear hearts across the seas?
> I have written the tale of our life
> For a sheltered people's mirth,
> In jesting guise – but ye are wise,
> And ye know what the jest is worth.
>
> Kipling, *Departmental Ditties*

CHAPTER 26

Finis

Beneath the rule of men entirely great,
The pen is mightier than the sword
Bulwer-Lytton, *Richelieu* **Act ii, sc 2**

This is the story of our lives that I dedicate to my dearly beloved wife, Wilhelmina Josephina Elisabeth, your mother, grandmother and great-grandmother. I have attempted to tell it bearing in mind what humble Mr Miles of the Tjimahi concentration camp taught me: that in a poem or a work of prose the writer paints pictures with his words. If I have been somewhat successful in this, then I hope it may be remembered that my writing is a legacy which I pass on to you, whom I love beyond all boundaries of substance, space and time. I am your father, grandfather and great-grandfather Ferdinand Jacobus Brockhall, and I bid you, 'Till we meet again'.

Valere[xli]

Brief were the days among you, and
briefer still the words I have spoken.
But should my voice fade in your ears,
and my love vanish in your memory,
then I will come again,
And with a richer heart and lips more
yielding to the spirit will I speak. Yea,
I shall return with the tide,

And though death may hide me, and the greater
silence enfold me, yet again will I seek
your understanding.
And not in vain will I seek.
If aught I have said is truth, that truth
shall reveal itself in a clearer voice, and
in words more kin to your thoughts
I go with the wind, people of (mine Kin)
but not down into emptiness; And if
this day is not a fulfilment of your
needs and my love, then let it be a
promise till another day …

Gibran, *The Prophet*

AUTHOR'S NOTE AND ACKNOWLEDGEMENTS

My original intention in writing these memoirs was not to arrive at a publication, but simply to share my life's story with my family, who are most precious to me. Blessed by a loving childhood, my life has been a journey – some steps were not of my choice, but nonetheless they form a rich part of the tapestry, woven through many lands and circumstances, that has shaped me and my views. This journey is littered with the joys and sorrows, delights and sufferings, hopes and adversities of life; but it always moves forward towards new beginnings. To share this with my family, with the hope that it might be of help and encouragement in their own journeys, is my greatest wish.

My son-in-law, Graham Truscott, saw a broader interest in my writings and encouraged their publication. He has played a critical role in planning and arranging for the publication of my manuscript, *Tea, War & Crocodiles: tales from an extraordinary life*, into book form. Therefore I must say 'Without Graham Truscott the publication of the draft would never have been achieved.' The shaping of it into a literary piece has taken him very considerable time and work. I gratefully acknowledge that Graham has given his attention to reading and evaluating the raw material, and has most helpfully offered me positive suggestions for improving on it.

With my love of family, it has also been a joy to have the remarkable assistance and enthusiasm of three generations of our combined families offering their assistance as a publishing team. I am very grateful to my daughter, Evalyn Truscott, and granddaughters Rachael Giblett and Paula Riley, for their meticulous reading and checking of the draft material for correct spelling, punctuation and other grammatical accuracies. My appreciation must also go to my granddaughter, Meaghan Smith, and to Paula and Graham for the hours spent in discussion and taped recording of interviews – these have developed a clearer and deeper understanding of my experiences.

My editor, Kathryn Tafra, has gently remoulded this body of work, adding a fluency that I hope readers will enjoy while always taking great care to retain my style and 'voice' in every sentence. Being a close friend of my granddaughters has also enabled Kathryn to be a vital part of our close-knit family team.

I gratefully thank all for having been part of what has surely been an unprecedented and joyful adventure in the process of publishing my book.

Finally, I salute Graham, husband to my beloved daughter, and grandfather of the steadily growing number of souls in our succeeding generations, for the critical role that he has played in the publication of my book. But above all I want Graham to know that I regard him truly as my friend.

ENDNOTES

INTRODUCTION
i. Mitchener, J. A. (1980). *The Covenant*, London: Secker & Warburg Ltd. *The Macquarie World Atlas.* (1984). Sydney: Macquarie Library Pty Ltd.
ii. Brockhall, Ferdinand J (Jnr). (2010). *Uit de oude doos: Recollections from the past*, unpublished.
iii. Cinchona is the name of a tree with anti-malarial properties, introduced from Brazil. At the time, before chemical anti-malarial drugs had been invented, the bark and roots of the cinchona tree were manufactured to produce quinine pills. The city of Bandung on Java was the only factory in the entire Southern Hemisphere that fabricated the medication, and the Djolotigo-grown cinchona bark was therefore a lucrative crop.

CHAPTER 1
iv. Kipling, R. (pg 406) *Rudyard Kipling's Verse, Definitive Edition.* London: Hodder and Stoughton Limited.
v. Spencer, H. (1886). *Beyond Good and Evil: Synthetic Philosophy.* Leipzig.
vi. Hollingworth, R. (1965, rev. 1999, 72-73). *Nietzche: The Man and His Philosophy.* Cambridge.
vii. The sawo is a much-loved, dark-brown skinned Indonesian fruit, the botanical name for which I do not know.
viii. Pronounced 'Mēēnem'. Note the spelling of titles here and elsewhere is in the former Dutch grammatical use; in current Bahasa Indonesia e.g. *'Babu tjutji'* should read *'Babu çuçi'*.
ix. Pronounced 'Sēētjas'.

CHAPTER 2
x. Voltaire. (1759). *Candide, ou l'Óptimism.* Penguin Classics.
xi. The Spice Islands (Maluku Islands, or the Moluccas) are a small group of islands to the north-east of Indonesia, between Celebes and

New Guinea. They were known for being the largest producers of mace, nutmeg, cloves and pepper in the world.
xii. Carroll, L. (1865). *Alice in Wonderland*.
xiii. Dickens, C. (1838). *Oliver Twist*.

CHAPTER 4
xiv. In passing through three Japanese internment camps, although her luggage was searched each time they moved to a different one, my mother managed to keep my father's shaving kit and my grandfather's gold fob watch and gold chain in her possession. I am ahead of the narrative when I write that on his twenty-first birthday, our dear son received these sentimental items – with their history attached – into his care.

CHAPTER 6
xv. This is the Dutch spelling. Bahasa Indonesia spelling is *Çimahi*.
xvi. Kipling, R. (pg 406). *Rudyard Kipling's Verse, Definitive Edition*. London: Hodder and Stoughton Limited.
xvii. Donne, J. (1624). *For Whom the Bell Tolls*.
xviii. Cattle.
xix. Kipling, R. (1859). *A Tale of Two Cities*.
xx. *Centuries* (1503–1560)
xxi. Paraphrased from *Encarta* encyclopaedia.

CHAPTER 7
xxii. In contemporary Dutch spelling *Tjideng*, in Bahasa Indonesia *Çideng*.

CHAPTER 11
xxiii. Kipling, R. (1919) 'Departmental Ditties' in *Rudyard Kipling's Verse, Definitive Edition*. London, Hodder and Stoughton Limited.

CHAPTER 18
xxiv. Extracted from Inglis, A. (1974). *Not a White Woman Safe: sexual anxiety and politics in Port Moresby, 1920-1934* Canberra: ANU Press.
xxv. Biskup P., Jinks B., Nelson H. (1968). *A Short History of New Guinea*. Angus and Robertson Ltd.

CHAPTER 19
xxvi. Burns, R. (1785). *To a mouse.*

CHAPTER 20
xxvii. Ingliss, A. (1974). *Not a white woman safe...* Canberra: ANU Press.
xxviii. Ingliss, ibid.

CHAPTER 21
xxix. Williams, F. (1936). *Papuans of the Trans-Fly.* Clarendon Press.
xxx. Lea, D.A.M. and Irwin, P.G. (1971). *New Guinea: the Territory and its People.* Melbourne: Oxford University Press.
xxxi. Paraphrased from Biskup P., Jinks B., Nelson H. (1968) *A Short History of New Guinea.* Angus and Robertson Ltd.

CHAPTER 23
xxxii. Voltaire. *Candide, ou l'Optimism.* (1759). Penguin Classics.

CHAPTER 24
xxxiii. In today's currency, approximately equivalent to a billion dollars or more.
xxxiv. In the time that I spent in Papua and New Guinea, the track from Kokoda to Popondetta was never referred to other than as the 'Kokoda Trail'. The American word 'trail' has more recently been replaced by the Australian 'track', but both are still in use.
xxxv. Paraphrased from Mair, L.P. (1970). *Australia in New Guinea.* MUP.

CHAPTER 25
xxxvi. Mair, L.P. (1970). *Australia in New Guinea.* MUP.
xxxvii. Ingliss, A. (1974). *Not a white woman safe...* Canberra: ANU Press.
xxxviii. Cleland, Lady Rachel, 1985, *Pathways to Independence,* copyright 1981.
xxxix. Biskup, P., Jinks B., Nelson H. (1968). *A Short History of New Guinea.* Angus and Robertson Ltd.
xl. Fisk, E.K. (Ed). (1966). *New Guinea on the Threshold.* ANU Press.

FINIS
xli. Meaning, 'Be Strong'.

BIBLIOGRAPHY

Biskup, P., Jinks, B., & Nelson, H. (1968). *A Short History of New Guinea.* Angus and Robertson.
Brockhall Jnr, F. J. (2010). *UIT DE OUDE DOOS: Recollections from the Past.* Unpublished.
Burns, R. (1785). *To a mouse.*
Caroll, L. (1865). *Alice in Wonderland.*
Cleland, R. (1985. c1981). *Pathways to Independence: story of official and family life in Papua New Guinea, from 1951 to 1975.* Cottesloe.
Dickens, C. (1838). *Oliver Twist.*
Donne, J. (1624). *For Whom the Bell Tolls.*
Fisk, E. K. (Ed.). (1966). *New Guinea on the Threshold.* ANU Press.
Gibran, K. (1977). *The Prophet.* New York: Alfred Knopp, Sid Harta.
Gunn, Æ. (1907 (p 7)). *We of the Never-Never.* London; New York; Melbourne: Hutchinson & Co. (Publishers) Ltd.
Hollingworth, R. (1965, rev. 1999, pg 72-73). *Nietzche: The Man and His Philosophy.* Cambridge.
Inglis, A. (1974). *'Not a white woman safe': sexual anxiety and politics in Port Moresby, 1920-1934.* Canberra: ANU Press.
Irwin, P., & Lea, D. (1971). *New Guinea: the Territory and its People.* Melbourne: Oxford University Press.
Kipling, R. (1859). *A Tale of Two Cities.*
Kipling, R. (1919, pg 406). *Rudyard Kipling's Verse, Definitive Edition.* London: Hodder and Stoughton Limited.
Mair, L. (1970). *Australia in New Guinea.* MUP.
Mitchener, J. A. (1980). *The Covenant.* London: Secker & Warburg Ltd.
Nostradamus. (1503–1560). *Centuries.*
Spencer, H. (1886). *Beyond Good and Evil: Synthetic Philosophy.* Leipzig.

The Macquarie World Atlas. (1984). Sydney: Macquarie Library Pty Ltd.

Voltaire aka Arouet, F.-M. (1759). *Candide, ou l'Óptimism.* Paris: Penguin Classics.

Williams, F. (1936). *Papuans of the Trans-Fly.* Clarendon Press.

www.ingramcontent.com/pod-product-compliance
Lightning Source LLC
Chambersburg PA
CBHW070713020526
44107CB00078B/2359